NAAFI
BY LAND & SEA

NAAFI

BY LAND & SEA

Compiled by Sue A Lowe

Written by those who 'Served the Services'

First published in Great Britain in 2020

Typeset in AdodeGaramond
Editing, design, typesetting and publishing by UK Book Publishing
www.ukbookpublishing.com

ISBN: 978-1-913179-96-0

CONTENTS

PREFACE

My NAAFI journey started 15 years ago, joined the Board as Operations Director in 2009 and became Managing Director in 2016. During this time our Armed Forces has been through significant change, from major conflicts in Iraq and Afghanistan to the overall reduction in strength and withdrawal from Germany. When the Armed Forces change, so does NAAFI! When I joined, we had over 6,000 employees delivering primarily retail and leisure services in the UK and across all overseas locations. Within a few years the UK operation had been handed over to MOD outsourced contractors and the international business was beginning to shrink. Today we are a much smaller efficient operation, with just over 250 employees who not only continue to run retail and leisure facilities for our service personnel and their families, but also deliver full soft facilities managed services including catering, cleaning services, wholesale and support to major exercises. We still operate in Germany, Falkland Islands, Ascension Island, Gibraltar, Brunei and on-board HM Ships. We support exercises in the UK and continental Europe for both HM Forces and NATO and we remain on 30 days' notice to deploy as EFI, our uniformed service, alongside any worldwide operation.

These last few years have been incredibly busy as it was thought that NAAFI would close its doors for good after the Germany drawdown in 2020; however, we were always working very hard in the background to secure NAAFI's long-term future. This began with the NAAFI Board and Pension Trustees securing a Government guarantee for the NAAFI pension and its 5,500 members. These discussions with the Government took almost a decade before it was finally awarded in 2019. NAAFI remains the fund's sponsoring employer; however, this guarantee secured our going concern. This allowed us at NAAFI to deliver a vision for the future to the MOD and with the support of the NAAFI Board, we worked with key MOD stakeholders to design a future model that ensures NAAFI will remain providing services in all our existing locations and deliver any surpluses back to the Armed Forces as either central and local welfare grants and investment in our facilities. To formalise this new future, in 2019 we signed a 10-year Overarching Service Arrangement confirming our status as the MOD's in-house provider and in 2020 we signed 10-year Service Level Agreements with each of the locations.

So, what's next? We are now making up for time lost due to the last few years' uncertainty and investing heavily in our facilities and services in our sites all over the world to the benefit of our customers. We have also just launched the NAAFI Welfare Fund. This Fund will run for 10 years and will provide a minimum of £7.5m for welfare projects on and around Armed Forces bases to enhance the welfare of serving personnel and their families. This will be administered through the Armed Forces Covenant Trust and immediately from launch, the bids have begun to arrive as we look to award £750,000 by March 2021 before the process will start again! Through this funding and the enhancement of our facilities we will continue to deliver our commitment to enhancing the lives of those that we serve.

I could not provide an update without talking about our Centenary. In December we reach the milestone of our 100th Birthday (and on 1st January, the anniversary of when trading began). We are excited and fortunate to have reached this milestone as we believed for many years we may not get to this point. We have some special commemoration merchandise and events planned for 2021 and we dearly hope that we will be able to proceed throughout the uncertainty of the current COVID-19 pandemic. You will read later in the book, in Tim's update, we are very proud and honoured to be funding the new memorial at the National Memorial Arboretum which will be unveiled at some point early/mid 2021.

Finally, I wanted to say a big thank you to all NAAFI employees past and present. It is you that have delivered the face to face service to our Service personnel and their families in many locations and conditions, some very challenging, some quite dangerous and some hilarious! You are the beating heart of NAAFI and without your determination, courage, good humour and willingness to 'keep calm and carry on', our business and the critical service it provides to the best customers in the world, we may have never reached our 100th Birthday.

Steve Marshall
NAAFI Managing Director

INTRODUCTION

SERVITOR SERVIENTIUM

The idea for the book started in 2017 while on Whitehall for the Remembrance parade at the Cenotaph. It was a conversation about the history of NAAFI, NCS and EFI and few seemed to know the origins or how they were started but everybody knew they had served. The discussion continued to the foundation of NCS EFI Association, which had been going for years, but exactly how many years? That was where it started, the history, the people, the origins and why for so many years with changes here and there, NAAFI was still going.

Looking into over 100 years of history was not going to be easy. The recent years would be mostly reliant on personal testimony. For the earlier years, the hunt was on to find the archives, the remains of the museum and as much factual information as possible. It was not about rewriting history but telling it as it was written.

The idea developed into a compilation of stories, either written about the people or written by the people, who saw the company through war and peace, as it expanded and contracted to meet the needs of the Armed Services through the years.

Then the work started, to develop the timeline from the birth of the canteen movement, all the way through to present day. Ensuring that besides major events, it highlighted the people who served the services.

I do hope that the hundreds of stories create a picture of the diversities of NAAFI, NCS and EFI, along with the sheer scale of operations undertaken by them. It was important for me to represent as much of every aspect of the company and the dedication to the Armed forces. There was so much I was unable to include due to the scale of the research undertaken. Picking out a few stories was not an option and making sure that every aspect possible and endeavours covered was so important. Very few realise the magnitude of this wonderful organisation and its lasting impact for its 100 years, established on the 6th December 1920 and the organisations which laid the way for its conception.

The profit from the sale of the book will go to the NCS EFI Association funds, to support the service personnel from the Naval Canteen Service and the Expeditionary Force Institute (RAOC/RLC).

Sue A Lowe

Copyright Rachel Fox

VIP SECTION

ADMIRAL OF THE FLEET SIR BEN BATHURST GCB, DL

There are many components of shipboard life which go towards winning that ultimate accolade of being known as a "Happy Ship". The leadership and character of the Commanding Officer is perhaps top of the list but close behind is a well-run ship's Canteen and this is dependent on the Manager. It is the NAAFI Canteen which provides those essential "extras" whether they be razor blades or "Nutty", soap or shampoo, cigarettes, or beer. Sailors are a demanding lot so the load on the loyal and hardworking NAAFI Manager is heavy, especially as he has to anticipate demand and restocking, no easy task on a long overseas deployment. But a successful and well-run Canteen has the added bonus of generating a substantial NAAFI rebate which is the bedrock of the Ship's Welfare fund.

ADMIRAL THE RT HON LORD ALAN WEST OF SPITHEAD GCB DSC PC

Like generations of those in the Navy I have fond memories of NAAFI and in particular Canteen managers on small ships. Indeed in 1965 when I joined up until the very early 70s when naval food dramatically improved, the Canteen "nutty" kept body and soul together.

I could tell many a tale of the Canteen managers I have served with in some 14 ships but one stands out.

In 1982 I was Captain of HMS ARDENT, one of the task group that took part in the recapture of the Falklands. She was sunk on 21 May after many heavy air attacks. On the way down south, Canteen managers were given the opportunity join the RN so as not to break the Geneva Convention as they were taking part in armed conflict. John Leake, my Canteen manager, opted to join the Navy rather than leave the ship. He had been a soldier in the Devonshire and Dorset regiment before joining NAAFI in a heavy weapons platoon and so he became one of my machine gunners.

On 21 May the day of the landings he won the Distinguished Service Medal – one of just 12 awarded for action in the war.

A citation in the London Gazette recorded that 'throughout the air attacks he remained cool and calm and even though the ship was being hit by bombs and canon fire. He fired large quantities of accurate tracer at the attackers and inflicted damage on a Skyhawk. His courage, steadfastness and total disregard for his own safety undoubtedly saved the ship from many further attacks and was an inspiration to all those in the vicinity'.

The UK papers loved the thought of a Canteen manager confronting Argentinian aircraft and a famous cartoon appeared of him throwing NAAFI buns at the attacking aircraft. During the raids one 1000lb bomb went through the Canteen without exploding but totally wrecking it.

I wish NAAFI well on its centenary and may it continue caring for the Forces.

VICE-ADMIRAL SIR ADRIAN JOHNS KCB CBE DL

NAAFI was an ever-present part of my naval career from my being a customer as a young Sub-Lieutenant to my membership of the NAAFI Council as Second Sea Lord. I would highlight just a couple of particular memories.

As First Lieutenant of a frigate, I gathered around me a small band of key players who I knew would always have a feel for what was happening and the mood in the ship. The Canteen Manager was one of those key players and his contribution to the morale of the ship's company was hugely important.

Later, in command of HMS OCEAN, I had a much larger NAAFI team. When we went on a war footing for combat operations in Iraq, we had to sign them on to the books and put them under the Naval Discipline Act. In the true tradition of the press gang, a tot of Pusser's rum helped the process no end!

LT GEN SIR SCOTT GRANT KCB, QUARTERMASTER GENERAL AND CHIEF ROYAL ENGINEER

Looking back on a long military career, much of which was spent abroad, I realise that every NAAFI facility was very different. Some, like the large store that was located in Rheindahlen in the 1990s, resembled a high-quality UK supermarket, whilst others, like the family shop at Dodesheide in Osnabruck in the 1980s or the very basic facility in RAF Masirah in the early 1970s, were geared to the specific needs of the well-defined local Service community. Yet, each of these facilities, although very different in size and product range, made a very similar contribution to the welfare of Service families living far from their homes in the UK.

First, the NAAFI provided a meeting place – a comfortable British meeting place – where Servicemen and their families could come together to shop, to have coffee, to exchange news and to make new friends. The importance of such meeting places to the wellbeing of Service families cannot be overstated. For a young wife, with a new baby, who might never have lived abroad before and who found herself accommodated in a hiring in a small Germany village some distance from the nearest Army garrison – as was sometimes the case in the early 1970s – a trip to the NAAFI was a very important social event. For the single soldier, who might yearn for the friendly atmosphere of the British pub, the NAAFI provided a meeting place to drink with friends, play darts and listen to music – a meeting place where one could be in barracks but relaxed and off duty.

The second contribution that NAAFI facilities made to Service families was that they gave them ready access to British products – products like Branston Pickle, digestive biscuits, and Boddingtons beer that Service families enjoyed but which were not readily available on the local market. The fact that Service families would drive from Belgium to Holland for the sole purpose of shopping in a NAAFI facility is a measure of the importance to them of having access to such products.

And the final contribution that NAAFI made to Service life was that it was always there: whether in the UK or abroad, in peacetime or on operations, the NAAFI was always there to provide support to the Services. In 1970 there were only about 250 all-ranks serving on Masirah, a harsh desert island off the coast of Oman, with few local inhabitants and virtually no civilian facilities. Nevertheless, there was a small NAAFI shop, built in 1964 to ensure that the Servicemen on Masirah, who were generally on 13-month unaccompanied tours, could buy the basic necessities of life, the little luxuries that raised morale, and presents to send home to their loved ones in the UK. It was a very small shop, but it was vital to the morale of everyone serving with RAF Masirah. It was because I knew, from personal experience when serving abroad, of the key role that NAAFI played in sustaining the morale and wellbeing of Servicemen that I was very proud indeed to serve on the NAAFI Board when I retired from the Army.

COMMANDANT ANTHEA LARKEN CBE

Having joined the Women's Royal Naval Service (WRNS) in 1956, I was the last Commandant in 1993, when the WRNS was merged into the Royal Navy. My first memories of the NAAFI were, when on Officer Training Course on HMS Excellent in Portsmouth, of enjoyable evenings dancing and meeting interesting young men! I was then drafted to RNAR Eglinton in Northern Ireland where in addition to very good coffee, the NAAFI was the place to socialise and have fun with service friends. When at NATO HQ in Belgium we used to travel to the NAAFI shop in Antwerp several times a year for those items from home not in the local Belgium shops. However, I really remember the NAAFI Clubs as friendly fun places to socialise – an important part of service life.

TONY HALES, CBE, PRESIDENT OF THE NCS EFI ASSOCIATION

My involvement with NAAFI spans about 20 years in different roles as Chair of the Corporation, Chair of the Pension Fund and President of the NCS EFI Association. Everywhere the forces went, NAAFI was there just behind with those little essentials such as toiletries, confectionery, drinks and entertainment. The supply chain to a supermarket in the UK is something we take for granted. The supply chain a thousand miles away sometimes through dangerous hostile territory as we saw on the "Jingly" trucks arriving in Kabul from the port of Karachi or through the smoke-filled air from the burning oil wells in Iraq is something quite different.

A supermarket storeroom is one thing, another is the storage space on a Royal Navy ship, invariably the afterthought, after the propulsion and weapon systems have been accommodated. But the greatest memories are of people from Eddie Blanchard, who served on the Arctic Convoys in WWII to the young NAAFI women, risking their lives to work on camp in Belfast during the troubles. Their dedication, humour and commitment brought a real touch of humanity to those serving over and above the supply of products. It may not sound much to run a little shop or club albeit thousands of miles from home but add in the regular threat of attack night after night in particularly hostile territory, then it took some remarkable people to keep volunteering to serve those who serve on the front line.

Over 500 NAAFI people lost their lives serving, and they and their thousands of colleagues, who quietly just did their jobs deserve our thanks for 100 years of service to our Armed Forces and their families.

MARY PITTUCK

My career with NAAFI has been varied to say the least! I began as 'live-in' NAAFI staff in Montgomery Lines in Aldershot many years ago. In those days most locations had a kitchen where we made all the sandwiches, pizzas and the famous NAAFI Toasty. These were then sold in the shop, diner or bar which were all under the same roof and all staff would work across all these areas. It was here I was introduced to my very first NAAFI day-time uniform – an orange A-line dress with checked tabard. I was very soon to learn that this melted incredibly quickly when exposed to an iron for too long, much to my manager's annoyance! The evening uniform was much nicer, a brown skirt along with a white blouse with orange and brown stripes. It was also here that I took my Bronze, Silver and Gold and was awarded my sheriff badges.

Finally, it was there I met and married my husband and where we started our family – not an uncommon NAAFI story!

Following this, we moved to Minden where I rejoined NAAFI. This time, I had the added complication of having two small children with only 14 months between them and a husband, who was continually on one deployment after another, also not an uncommon NAAFI story (albeit, I'm pretty sure my husband volunteered for most of his deployments!).

At this point noting the kind of jobs available, I didn't think a career would be possible for me and gave up any hope on having a long-term career due to the constant relocation – a typical Army wife story!

Fast forward to mid-1990s when we moved to Gütersloh and I went to work at Princess Royal Bks (PRB) in the NAAFI on camp. This included a kitchen operation, a diner, a shop, the Pigs Bar and of course, Club 47 (the Bop). I loved working here, it was a vibrant, dynamic workplace and the staff were from all over and all very different! When retail split from leisure, I moved to work in the old Families Store, where I ran the small cafe in the foyer.

Once we moved back to Bulford in the UK, I went for a job with NAAFI in 'Wagon Lines' at Alanbrook Bks, Larkhill. This was a very large multi-site consisting of Wagon Lines bar, a leisure offer in Roberts Bks (the Bks next door), a very busy sub bar (run off-site from a freezing cold Nissen Hut) and a large vending and gaming operation. It was here my career began. I was promoted to Supervisor and was then successful in getting a manager post in Ward Bks, Bulford. After a few short months I also got the Wagon Lines multi-site back after the manager left. Following this I took on the vending and gaming area as well as the NAAFI Leisure operation in Middle Wallop. In addition, I became a union H&S representative and an NVQ Assessor. Needless to say, with two children under 10 and a husband (who was still often away), life was incredibly busy.

After a few years doing this, I saw a job advertised as a Training Advisor, so I went for that and got it. I can write a whole book about my experiences doing that, but none of them burn brighter in my memory more than losing my footing and falling off the back of the stage in front of a packed audience of my peers at the National Training Awards, where we were being presented with an award for the Managers programme. I couldn't forget it if I wanted to, as too many of my former training team colleagues (now my friends) who were there won't let me!

NAAFI then went through many years of transition, where I had various posts – Training Team Leader, UK; HR Project Manager, where I implemented a new payroll system; HR Advisor (Transition), where I developed the NAAFI Toolkit; HR Advisor (Overseas); where I was responsible for Brunei, Falklands and Ascension Islands, Gibraltar NCS; HR Business Partner (EFI & NCS); Senior HR Business Partner (All overseas); HR Manager (Corporate); HR Manager (General); HR & Risk Manager (current).

Much of my time recently has been dedicated to managing the NAAFI Welfare Fund, administered by the Armed Forces Covenant Fund Trust. We have received over 400 grant applications to a value in excess of £5,000,000 for projects to improve the welfare of our Armed Forces and their families, and I am very much looking forward to being involved in and seeing some of the projects we have funded next year. In addition, I have been working on developing the NAAFI 100 logos, merchandise and celebrations. Beyond all of this, I remain committed to my day job, as the NAAFI HR & Risk Manager and in continuing to work with the rest of the Senior management team on what the future might bring.

These roles have given me vast exposure to all elements of NAAFI as well as significant career experience and have allowed me to move all over with my husband, whilst retaining a career of my own.

More than that though, NAAFI has given me the opportunity to meet a huge amount of loyal, hardworking (for the most part), fabulous people full of character (good and bad) that I would have never met in any other walk of life. Many of whom, whilst I don't see them very often, I will consider true friends for the rest of my life and I will be forever grateful to NAAFI for this.

Mary Pittuck
HR & Risk Manager
November 2020

STEPHANIE ABEL, CHAIRPERSON OF THE NCS EFI ASSOCIATION

NAAFI has always been part of my life – growing up, my mother worked for NAAFI and at the age of 18 I started my NAAFI career in Northern Ireland. After a couple of years in Northern Ireland I moved back to the mainland and worked in Larkhill, Arborfield and Gosport. I always thought about joining the armed forces but decided EFI was the best route for me, so I took the plunge and went for it. I served in Iraq and on exercise Aurora (joint training exercise on board ship with the US Navy) and then took up a role in EFI HQ Bulford.

After 10 years I decided to leave NAAFI but having the opportunity to join the NEA committee was an offer I couldn't refuse. Then in 2018 becoming the Chair of the NEA committee was a huge privilege and one that I'm proud of.

When I think about NAAFI my fondest memories are those of friendship and camaraderie. I always have a huge smile when I think about the people I have met and the friendships I have made. I have so many happy memories and so many stories of good times and hard times. NAAFI gave me the gift of some lifelong friendships that I will cherish forever and be forever thankful for.

The NEA is like a golden thread that keeps many of us together. Having a place where people can come and share their stories and/or reconnect with old friends is great. There's also a serious side to the association and when things aren't going well for someone knowing that we can provide support means a lot and hopefully provides people with reassurance that we're there for them.

2021 will be the association's 75th anniversary and I hope that myself and the committee will continue to connect people and see old comrades each year at the AGM for many more years to come.

Stephanie Abel, Chairperson, NEA

1894–1919

The first NAAFI Canteen Girl

With every good story it always starts with its origins. Now I would like to start from the beginning of the Navy Army Air Force Institutes, but its history is rooted far further back than you might think. The very first Canteen girl was Kit Ross, she became somewhat of a legend in the late 1600s / early 1700s.

After she married and had their third child her husband disappeared. She tracked him down and followed him to the Army and joined up as a man! After many campaigns and being seriously wounded, it was while being treated in hospital that army surgeons discovered her sex; soon the whole story was known, and Kit became as famous as Marlborough himself. The officers of the regiment contributed to her female attire and Lord John Hayes who commanded the Scots Greys insisted that she and Richard be married again.

Wondering how to remain with Richard as his now acknowledged wife, Kit became the cook for the regiment but so missed the excitement and the profits of her marauding days that she decided to turn into civilian trader and so began as the first of the 'Naafi canteen girls'.

During the fighting at Malplaquet, she lost sight of him; she searched the woods while shots splintered the trees around her, but after searching among the corpses she found his body. She picked up the corpse and carried it to a quiet spot where she buried him. Eleven weeks later Kit married Hugh Jones of the Royal Grenadiers. He was mortally wounded at St Venant a year later.

In England in 1712 Kit, now better known as Mother Ross, was received by Marlborough, and presented to Queen Anne. She awarded her a pension of a shilling a day for the rest of her life. With the money she had saved from her campaigning days she took a small inn and another husband; he was a Welsh Fusilier, Pte Davis.

In 1739 her husband came down with mysterious fever and was admitted to Chelsea Hospital. Kit herself suffered from scurvy, rheumatisms and oedema. She nursed him until the end and died herself four weeks later, on the 7th of July. She was buried in RHC cemetery with full military honours. Kit Ross was a strange mixture of the good and the bad qualities of both sexes: she fought savagely, nursed gently and despite the afflictions which followed her, she kept her charm and good humour to the last. She was the first NAAFI Girl.

Kit Ross was rumoured to have a gravestone at the Chelsea hospital but after some research the RHC tell me that this unfortunately is not the case; however, she is commemorated with a memorial in the grounds.

The regimental Institutes 1894

The regimental Institutes, got going, in the late 1800s. It was now that developments which would forge the foundations of the NAAFI we have today. But before that, they had to learn many lessons and understand the best way to operate to benefit both the institutes and the services it served.

The canteens – wherever the King's soldiers served the canteens were right beside them and although honesty boxes where the norm, a locked till was proven to be more profitable. The first-time canteens used administrative systems was in 1894 – Maj Harry James Craufurd, of the Grenadier guards and president of the Canteen Depot at Caterham. The Major wasn't happy with the supply chain, so he consulted his colleagues, Captain Lionel Fortescue and Surgeon Captain Herbert Murray Ramsey, who was a medical officer of the Scots Guards; they discussed the best structure to supply the canteens. The plan was to form a cooperative society, which they registered under the Industrial and Provident Societies Act and affiliated to the cooperative union. As officers of the British Army they did not have the funds, so they managed to collect £400 and founded the Canteen and Mess Cooperative Society. They agreed under these rules no one could hold more than £200 worth of shares, the interest was limited to 5% and anything over was rebated to the regiment.

Mr Charles Haygate, a friend of Maj Craufurd, was consulted as to starting the business and in 1895 took on the duties of secretary. They found a small unit in the East End of London and after the first year they realised the advantages it offered, and this was discovered by other regiments. In 1896 the society moved to Regency St, Westminster. Capt Fortescue started to develop Maj Craufurd's original idea. He laid out plans to make the society much stronger by buying individual shares and slowly take the society as their own. Eventually this would mean the whole of the army, making it the Army's Cooperative Society and its own business for officers and men. Both wholesale and retail, without official interference, which Capt Fortescue never lost hope in.

A few years later, in 1899, during the South African war, the Canteen Society had two systems; the first with the regimental tenant system, where they would supply both liquor and grocery and was given out by the commanding officer. The tender of the firm which offered the highest rebate to the customer/regiment being the rule, accepted the contracting firm. They would furnish not only the supplies but the workers for the canteen. The second, the district contract system, they contracted on behalf of all the units under the command; this had the advantage of purchasing in bulk, but they must supply their own staff, diverting soldiers from their duties.

The Canteen & Mess Cooperative Society secured three district contracts and in 1900 its trade rose. Lord Roberts, the commander of the Cape Town side, noted the benefits that were being enjoyed at the units serviced by the Canteen & Mess Cooperative Society (C&MCS) and he set out to take some of the action. They agreed terms, the new depot opened. They continued to service Lord Roberts, his armies as well as Sir Redveres Buller, on the Durban side. While all of this was happening, it was discovered Sir Buller had formed a military organization called 'The Natal Field Force Canteen'; it was swiftly renamed 'South African Garrison Institutes' and took over the African side of the C&MCS.

When trade stopped in South Africa, they found themselves in trouble; they lost 90% of their trade and Maj Fortescue (Capt) had been killed in action in June 1900. Maj Crawford was in very poor health and Capt Ramsey was occupied with his military duties. They were three poor men who needed funding to continue the success of the system they had set up and was proven to work. Being not for profit, although good for the troops, was not good for their pockets. What would become of the Canteen and Mess Society now?

Mr JF Herring, a philanthropist and financier, checked over the bookwork, did the maths and decided to support the C&MCS. After the death of Maj L Fortescue, his brother Lord Fortescue had taken a keen interest in the society, its goings on and he now became quite active. He became the first chairman of the committee, then remained with the Coop and Mr Herring, and the society began to overcome the difficulties. Within two years they had repaid all their debt and liabilities and started to grow.

The 1903 report

In 1903 a report was issued from Lord Grey's committee, which read that commanding officers of regiments should be permitted to either use the old regimentals system which was used before the South African war or to utilise the new styled 'Soldiers' Central Cooperative Society' model. We know that the C&MCS was based on cooperative ideals and this worked and also gave back to the army, although still open to an amount of dishonesty on occasion. The commander in chief was to be the chairman of the committee of the 'Soldiers' Central Cooperative Society', an auditor would be appointed by the War Office and must be a chartered accountant. Out of the eight members of the committee, only two disagreed with this recommendation of using the cooperative model, on a report written by Lord Cheylesmore an officer of a senior age from the Grenadier guards, although he had seen much change in his career and service to King and country, there was still mistrust of any new systems for the welfare of the troops. The 'Soldiers' Central Cooperative Society' was not a choice they wanted to make as they knew little, if anything, about the cooperative model and where any profits should be invested and how this would be controlled.

The tenant system issues still continued, mainly with where the rebate went. The larger units became quite profitable and small units could not get contractors to operate their business; the corruption had not gone away. The only canteens where bribery corruption were not commonplace was in the coop system. There goods were of low quality, were substandard and choice for the soldier was poor. This led the authorities to issue a list of firms to use. Unfortunately, those that did not use the model set by the C&MCS on the cooperative values, could raise retail prices and they could choose not to declare their profits and keep them for themselves. The evolution under the guidance of Mr Heygate continued to modify the system under the C&MCS and to automatically return profits as agreed to the regiment.

Before the outset of war in 1914, the military authorities opened what was known as the accounting scandal. Not much survives today of the full goings on, but we can only touch upon small areas to report. Early in 1914 there were allegations of bribes offered to employees of the War Office, which were duly accepted by some of the military customers and the matter ended up in court. The allegations were conclusive and consequently certain officers and non-commissioned officers were prosecuted and dismissed from service in the Army.

The scandal hit the headlines and the press were all over it, but they did not mention Lord Grey's Committee from years before, which did urge an investigation into the subject of campaigns ran by the government. This meant a new committee with a strong resolve, to sort this issue of dishonesty and corruption once and for all, although we know now that, what would happen in this committee would form a nucleus for things to come. Some of the members of this committee were Lord Rotherham, the chairman, Lord Leverhulme and Sir Burbidge.

Royal Navy 1899

March 11th, 1899, the Navy and the army already reported In the Navy and army illustrated magazine. In this edition it showcases The Royal naval canteen in Malta with a plush theatre, billiard room, reading room and canteen. It's hosted personnel from harbouring ships and those stationed in Malta. It tells us that the sailors, all the soldiers working it themselves and limited supervision of the canteen committee comprised officers with limitations, but they who had disposal of the funds from the canteen. This social centre with strictly moderated prices, regulated to provide a reasonable profit. The surplus funds was used at the discretion of the committee to fund entertainment, sing songs, theatrical shows, or outings for the men. Some of the rules of this canteen in Malta strictly prohibited gambling where they took certain measures to prevent it. Billiards was the game of choice to entertain themselves when they had free time. This particular establishment seated 1000 men. Back in 1899 they state an increase of £16 net profit over the returns for the preceding month, but they do also say that there had been an expenditure for furniture and tools. You cannot help but think that this establishment was well fitted out and provided the top end facilities.

While all this was going on, the Royal Navy already had to abide by The King's regulations and Admiralty instructions 1913, in relation to messing, cabins and canteens. The establishment of canteens as a rule would be dry in each of his Majesty's ships and naval establishments; this would include accommodation. If the captain considered it not advisable to establish a canteen, he must make a full report to the commander in chief or the OC of the squadron who would then report back to the Admiralty with their opinion to the reasons, for and against.

The interesting part would be that this did not apply to small vessels such as torpedo boat destroyers and torpedo boats where the space was not available to place a canteen. Not without relaying all of the information, as the Navy relied on the tenant contract system (855) and then some other variations which I will go into. The system maps out the selection of the tenant, contract, administration, termination of contract and the adherence to the contract. The document goes on to refer to the revised tenant system (856).

The revised tenant system used the power of the committee, whereby the affairs could be scrutinised under the watchful eyes of the executive officer of the ship (as ex-officio president), a senior Lieutenant as vice president, the accounting officer as honorary secretary and treasurer, the medical or another commissioned officer together with some of the representatives of the ship's company. This committee would decide upon the administration of the ship's fund, inspect canteen goods and prices, test weights and measures, and generally supervise the working of the canteen. The committee would also purchase local goods at foreign ports and ensure these were at fair market prices.

Any complaints would be made to the Petty Officer and then forwarded to the committee. Payment of bills would go to the accounting officer and credit to personnel was not permitted. Everything down to the accommodation for canteen stores was negotiated, including the amount of stowage allotted in the actual contract. On saying that, the captain may grant additional accommodation if reasonably required and available.

For the tenant running the canteen some articles were forbidden; these would include items that were in the official supply of the stores and available for purchase by officers and men under article 1700. The dress code of canteen staff on board ship would be: dress neatly and suitably with any instructions on the subject laid down by the commander in chief or officer commanding the squadron.

The third system, ordinary service system (857), where it would be impossible to conduct a canteen under the tenant system (revised). The canteen could be established on the ordinary service system and goods could be obtained from tradesmen and the general administration of the canteen is undertaken by a committee and the captain is to direct the accounting officer, to act as business manager. The business manager would be responsible for purchases, sale prices, custody of cash, and cash transactions for the canteen.

Shore establishments and his Majesty's yachts would use the canteen system at present in existence in the Royal naval barracks, training establishments and other shore establishments were at the option of the captain to continue enforcement, subject to modifications to the system. Unfortunately, the regulations laid before them did not specify any dishonesty or where any of the profit goes to.

WW1 1914

Let's not forget the scandal and the exposure of the malpractice at the War Office who were responsible for giving canteens the contracts. This gave the C&MCS a massive boost, as all regimentals institutes desperately turned to them for their expertise. August 1914, war broke out with Germany – this was going to be one of the biggest challenges ever been set before them.

As war started, the C&MCS became overwhelmed like South Africa in 1899, so as in France in 1914 they had no idea how they were going to deal with the enormity of canteens needed. In Flanders the locals started to monopolise the business to be had. The War Office had a meeting with the head of the C&MCS, who was the most experienced of all canteen contractors, and sought their expertise. To deal with the decision they also involved the managing director of

Richard Dickeson and Co (who also supplied the Navy); this contracting firm would now join forces with the society.

The society took the lead with the same constitution as before, under cooperative principles. This saw the formation of what was lovingly known as the EFC, The Expeditionary Force Canteens. Naturally the matter of funding had to be dealt with, as profits will always be given back, but the South African Garrison institutes stumped up funds to get them on their way. It will always be remembered that the 'Natal Field Force Canteen' assisted in funding the massive undertaking in providing canteens for the men of World War One. The funds did not belong to the state; all loans were paid back in full with interest.

At home now the C&MCS and Richard Dickeson and Co did not have the manpower to service all of the needs of the soldiers whilst training in the UK. Thousands daily needed canteens and as in previous years contractors sprung up looking for a piece of the pie, at the soldier's expense. This needed to be regulated to protect the military personnel. Lord Rotherham's committee suggested a board to supervise the contractors, in January 1915, just a few months after the declaration of war. Three areas were outlined.

The first, to allow no one to supply the troops except approved firms or contractors.

The second, to fix the retail prices which work to govern the supplies of all contractors.

And the third, to secure a flat rate of rebate of 10%, from every contractor, or, if the contractor had put up his own premises an agreed percentage on the takings.

With the board that had just been formed, a body of officers who acted as canteen inspectors, were responsible for supervising canteens to ensure they maintained the quality of goods and services supplied. It became apparent that these inspectors for the board worked independently, but within a short time they were amalgamated and renamed to the Army Canteen Committee, ACC. The ACC did their best to protect the soldiers from poor products and high prices.

The Army Canteen Committee 1917

With the newly formed ACC they needed supporting and this once again fell to the C&MCS. On the setup of the Expeditionary Force Canteens, the cooperative principles were what had been relied upon so far. In October 1916 the ACC recommended the tenancy system should be abolished and it should be conducted as a central organisation and controlled by the army itself. On the 1st of January 1917, the ACC was registered at the board of trade as a 'company not for profit' and limited by guarantee.

The ACC took over all businesses from all other contractors and became a central organisation providing all the services needed. Within the first few months it is said to have absorbed many of the contracting firms including Richard Dickeson and Co, and benefited from the experience of loyal employees from Mr J W Liddell in the merchants account branch,

Mr Austin Bailey, inspector of canteens. It was from this date the canteen and mess society were no more, all except the EFC who were needed overseas; all of the coop ideals, traditions and ways were now all under one roof.

Sir Alexander Prince, on behalf of Richard Dickeson and Co, sacrificed all his business interests for the good of the union of all the other canteens.

To me this seems all these years of hard work recognising where the issues lay, finding ways of looking to resolve decades old corruption came to a head, with the principles of honesty and working towards the good of the British army. Their needs were more important than profit.

The marker of success by April 1917, was shown by 2000 canteens opened by the ACC; these stretched in this short amount of time to Gibraltar, Malta, and Egypt.

The next step in the development of the canteens that served the army was in June 1917. This was the turn of events that saw the Royal Navy, our senior service, ask that they may share the same benefits and service of that of the British soldier. The Royal Navy were welcomed with open arms, but this meant a name change again, and they would be known as the Navy and Army Canteen Board, the NACB. This also saw the development of a cap badge in the shape of a ship with the King's Crown which would be worn by personnel serving the NACB and they were dressed in uniform. Although now there are very few pictures of this being worn, there are still cap badges over 100 years old around. This also includes the Expeditionary Force Canteens, the only difference being the cap badge.

Copyright Sue A Lowe

Copyright Sue A Lowe

The picture shows Miss Dorothy Izzard who joined the NACB previously The ACC at Kempton barracks, Bedford, in 1916, where she later became the manageress. She later served at Kettering, Henlow, and Weedon, where she met the Prince of Wales when he visited the camp.

Nearly a year later, in April 1918, when the Royal Air Force was formed into a separate service, it was passed by the agreement of the Air Ministry and the NACB that they would also join the fold. At this point reminding ourselves that in 1895 Capt Fortescue had dreamed up the cooperative system for canteens, that would not only be the property of the officers and men of the army but now including every officer and man of the fighting services benefiting from the ideals he had wished for, but unfortunately he was no longer here to see, as he had been killed in action. The good thing was that his brother, with the help of the others, had fulfilled his wishes. The Treasury guaranteed a substantial overdraft to grow the business, which also maintained the EFC. But as in previous years this was paid back very quickly and, in the year of 1918, the turnover exceeded £40 million.

It would be unfair at this point not to go into more detail about the Expeditionary Force Canteens on the Western Front. In 1915 it was created from small beginnings at Le Havre in France; it started out with a single second-hand Ford car. Months later there were half a million troops on the Western Front, and it became clearer that they needed to increase and expand quickly. In the first six months they amounted to 3 million francs and by the end of the year 18 million and this time it increased until the last year of the war – in 1918 the turnover was 223 million francs.

The EFC, the providers for the army and its auxiliary services on the Western Front, more depos established with a final total of 17 for as many areas, these pushed out onto the frontline until 577 branches were in France They supplied a range from buttons to bottles of champagne, a package of pins, to a full set of equipment to an officer.

On the 2nd of January 1916 the EFC issued a general price list. Their head office was number 10 Regency St, Westminster, London, SW. The honourable director AW Prince and the general manager and secretary Mr F Benson compiled the price list for use at home and abroad. The overseas manager was Capt EC Wright; he looked after the headquarters in France in Boulogne.

To start with there were 5 depos:

Boulougne,36b Rue Victor Hugo,
Calais, 25 Rue St Denis,
Dieppe, 17 Rue Desmarquets,
Le Havre, 93 Boulevard De Strasbourg
Rouen, 64 Rue Jeanne D'Arc

The price list included the constitution of the Expeditionary Force Canteens 1916

The following statement respecting the constitution, organisation, and objects of the Expeditionary Force Canteens is made for general information:

(a) the Expeditionary Force Canteens are established under the authority of the army council and War Office institutions under the control of the army council. To certain officials of the organisation, temporary commissions in his Majesty's army have been granted, while subordinates are all in uniform with varying ranks. The entire staff are recognised as being engaged in the performance of duties under military authority, and our, for the time being, therefore, the military law.

(b) The honorary director of the Expeditionary Force Canteens is Mr A W Prince, chairman and managing director of Messrs Richard Dickeson and Co. Limited. The honorary general manager and secretary of the organisation is Mr F Benson, general manager of the canteen and mess cooperative society limited. The overseas manager is Capt E C Wright.

(c) Neither of the 2 firms to which the above mentioned gentlemen belong take any share whatsoever of the profits made by the Expeditionary Force Canteens, the whole of which will be passed to the War Office, after special audit, and devoted to the good of the soldier and his dependants under the orders of the army council.

SS long, Brigadier General (director of supplies and transport).
War Office 26th of March 1915.

The EFC list details the special arrangements for dealing with orders which are to be sent by rail or post; all orders have to be sent to Havre, and must be accompanied by a remittance, or drawn against a Depot account which can only be opened at Havre. Credit accounts can only be opened here. If this was not adhered to the orders would be delayed. At this time checks could only be accepted if authorised by army agents and converted at a rate of 26.50 francs to the pound. Any items that were not on the list could be procured with as minimal delay as possible or substituted at the discretion of the organisation. The goods were delivered to the railhead and would reach units via the divisional supply column and brigade supply officer by way of AMFO. It would be worth noting that any items shipped by AMFO could not exceed 56 pounds in weight, any shipped by MFO could not exceed 11 pounds. It was requested that all items be ordered with a weight as often cases would have to be split and repackaged to not exceed the maximum weight of item. Discounts on purchased goods for resale in officers and sergeants' messes, regimental canteens and other institutions run for the benefit of the British soldier will get 5% discount, but the units' identity need to be clearly established.

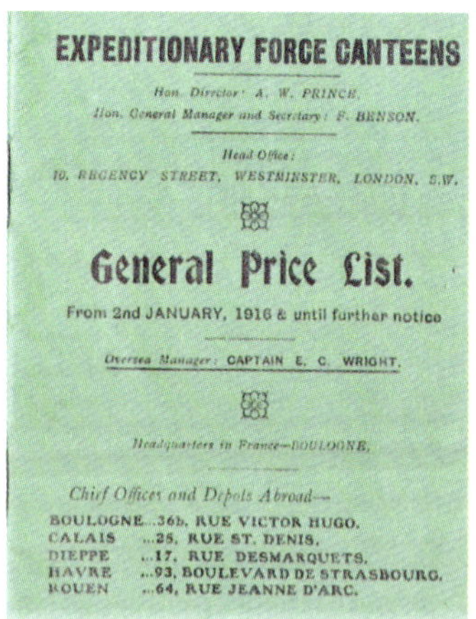

EXPEDITIONARY FORCE CANTEENS

Hon. Director: A. W. PRINCE.
Hon. General Manager and Secretary: F. BENSON.

Head Office:
10, REGENCY STREET, WESTMINSTER, LONDON, S.W.

General Price List.

From 2nd JANUARY, 1916 & until further notice

Oversea Manager: CAPTAIN E. C. WRIGHT.

Headquarters in France—BOULOGNE.

Chief Offices and Depots Abroad—

BOULOGNE ...36b, RUE VICTOR HUGO.
CALAIS ...25, RUE ST. DENIS.
DIEPPE ...17, RUE DESMARQUETS.
HAVRE ...93, BOULEVARD DE STRASBOURG.
ROUEN ...64, RUE JEANNE D'ARC.

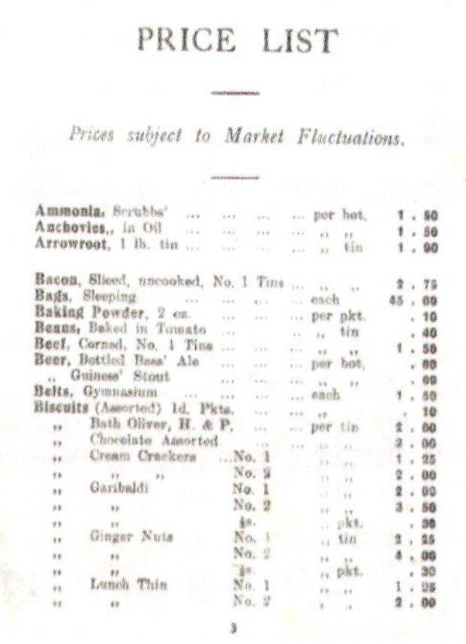

PRICE LIST

Prices subject to Market Fluctuations.

Ammonia, Scrubbs'		per bot.	1 . 50
Anchovies, in Oil		,, ,,	1 . 50
Arrowroot, 1 lb. tin		,, tin	1 . 90
Bacon, Sliced, uncooked, No. 1 Tins		,, ,,	2 . 75
Bags, Sleeping		each	45 . 00
Baking Powder, 2 oz.		per pkt.	. 10
Beans, Baked in Tomato		,, tin	. 40
Beef, Corned, No. 1 Tins		,, ,,	1 . 50
Beer, Bottled Bass' Ale		per bot.	. 80
,, Guiness' Stout		,, ,,	. 90
Belts, Gymnasium		each	1 . 50
Biscuits (Assorted) 1d. Pkts.		,,	. 10
,, Bath Oliver, H. & P.		per tin	2 . 00
,, Chocolate Assorted		,, ,,	3 . 00
,, Cream Crackers	No. 1	,, ,,	1 . 25
,, ,, ,,	No. 2	,, ,,	2 . 00
,, Garibaldi	No. 1	,, ,,	2 . 00
,, ,,	No. 2	,, ,,	3 . 50
,, ,,	¼s.	,, pkt.	. 30
,, Ginger Nuts	No. 1	,, tin	2 . 25
,, ,,	No. 2	,, ,,	4 . 00
,, ,,	¼s.	,, pkt.	. 30
,, Lunch Thin	No. 1	,, ,,	1 . 25
,, ,,	No. 2	,, ,,	2 . 00

3

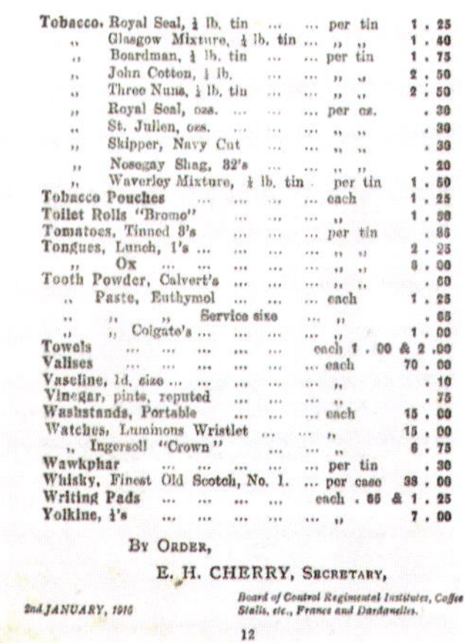

Tobacco. Royal Seal, ½ lb. tin	per tin	1 . 25
,, Glasgow Mixture, ¼ lb. tin	,, ,,	1 . 40
,, Boardman, ¼ lb. tin	per tin	1 . 75
,, John Cotton, ¼ lb.	,, ,,	2 . 50
,, Three Nuns, ¼ lb. tin	,, ,,	2 . 50
,, Royal Seal, ozs.	per oz.	. 30
,, St. Julien, ozs.	,, ,,	. 30
,, Skipper, Navy Cut	,, ,,	. 30
,, Nosegay Shag, 32's	,, ,,	. 20
,, Waverley Mixture, ¼ lb. tin	per tin	1 . 50
Tobacco Pouches	each	1 . 25
Toilet Rolls "Bromo"	,,	1 . 50
Tomatoes, Tinned 8's	per tin	. 85
Tongues, Lunch, 1's	,, ,,	2 . 25
,, Ox	,, ,,	8 . 00
Tooth Powder, Calvert's	,, ,,	. 60
,, Paste, Euthymol	each	1 . 25
,, ,, ,, Service size	,,	. 65
,, ,, Colgate's	,,	1 . 00
Towels	each	1 . 00 & 2 .00
Valises	each	70 . 00
Vaseline, 1d. size	,,	. 10
Vinegar, pints, reputed	,,	. 75
Washstands, Portable	each	15 . 00
Watches, Luminous Wristlet	,,	15 . 00
,, Ingersoll "Crown"	,,	6 . 75
Wawkphar	per tin	. 30
Whisky, Finest Old Scotch, No. 1.	per case	38 . 00
Writing Pads	each . 65 & 1 . 25	
Yolkine, ½'s	,,	7 . 00

By Order,
E. H. CHERRY, Secretary,
Board of Control Regimental Institutes, Coffee Stalls, etc., France and Dardanelles.

2nd JANUARY, 1916

12

As for the Ford car, albeit second hand, the fleet was now 249 lorries and vans, 151 cars, 42 motorcycles and 14 trailers. Without the EFC the First World War would have been even more difficult to win. At this point it's important to mention that the members served alongside the fighting men and they were not exempt by any means from the devastation of war. During the German advance in spring 1918, 60 to 70 canteens were fully wiped out. They served the troops often under heavy fire, and canteens were never abandoned, unless for military reasons and evacuation made it so. Numerous occasions the canteens were used as field dressing stations and they were highly disciplined, as were the serving soldiers around them. For those that survived the canteens being destroyed, they either managed to get back and reopen another, or volunteered as a stretcher bearer, or picked up a rifle and joined the fighting troops. Many were killed or wounded but no more than a few awarded a medal for their service.

Behind the line's rest houses, officers' clubs, and recuperation for those who returned exhausted from the trenches, they added leave billets and other comforts for both British and the Americans that needed them. The important thing was that this added respite for a brief moment to forget the horrors of war.

It took a huge team to ensure the chain of supply; the departments were as follows: Butcheries, bakeries, upholstery Department, equipment Department, printing Department and also for entertainment they had a cinema, 170 in total which provided a brief but needed distraction. With the final German offensive of 1918 most of the theatres were closed so they organised six mobile cinemas and did this free of charge and as the war came to an end they opened cinemas in demobilization camps, imports of embarkation, and as for their reason for being, they were that the troops needed them.

Honourable Maj Lionel H Fortescue (17th Lancers)

In Filleigh churchyard an octagonal cross stands in memory of the honourable Maj Lionel H Fortescue (17th Lancers) and others who had fallen in the South African war. The memorial is 13 feet high and made of Devonshire granite; Sir Redvers Buller contributed amongst others to the memorial. The inscription reads: 'To the memory of one who never wearied in helping others, Lionel H D Fortescue, third son of Hugh 3rd Earl Fortescue, Maj, second in command, 17th Lancers. He was born on the 19th of November 1857 at Castle Hill. He fell in action at Diamond Hill in South Africa on the 11th of June 1900'. He was buried in the field of battle. The memorial of which erected by his friends and neighbours shall long pay tribute to the legacy left behind him and continued by his brother John.

I feel that at this point in the prehistory I should quote Lord John Fortescue and his tribute to what they did do in the time of the great war:

> 'In fact, wherever the King's soldiers went, the canteens followed them, whether to the Arctic Circle or to the Equator. The question is often asked, "Who won the war?" and it must be admitted that the EFC did its share towards the Great War by helping to keep

> the British soldier in good morale as well as in good physical condition. I am familiar with the past campaigns of the British Army — the campaigns which won the British Empire — has too often had before him the picture of British soldiers dying like flies from yellow fever, cholera, scurvy, enteric fever, dysentery (the two last frequently the result of bad food), heat, cold, starvation and, sometimes, sheer despair. He can, therefore, form some idea of the tens of thousands of lives that must have been saved by the labours of the EFC.'

The bravery of all who served will always be remembered, the sacrifices of the military personnel and the supporting forces that made it possible.

"Success is seen to be won by those who are in front, but without those who are behind them, it is seldom possible to achieve"

S.A Lowe 2020 copyright

Navy and Army Canteen Board aboard HMS Queen Elizabeth by William Humm (as he recalled in 1971)

William served with the Navy and army canteen board as canteen manager at sea during the service of the first HMS Queen Elizabeth. During the First World War, he was on board the 27,000-ton battleship. The QE was one of many formidable ships of the grand fleet, with a complement of 1400 officers and men. A number of famous people served on her including Admiral Earl Beatty, who was commander in chief of the grand fleet and captain EE Chatfield, Commander G Blake and first Lt H Balgrove, all of whom later became Admirals.

William recalls: 'Among my customers was midshipman Louis Mountbatten, who is in charge of the picket boat and later became the captain's writer. I well remember how, when I went to shore for stores, he would ask me to buy him a box of chocolates or sweets for his crew, he always bought Blue Bell metal polish and Blanco from the canteen for the boat.

'During the visit of King George V and Queen Mary, in June 1918, the Queen visited the canteen with Captain Chatfield. Admiring the display, she spoke of her delight to see such nice kippers and lovely chocolates for sale. She told the captain that she would like some chocolates, I was told to make up half a pound. But we had no paper bags! In those days, most goods were served loose to sailors' hats or mess utensils. So, I made her paper cornet and served the Queen with her chocolates.

'I also remember the surrender of the German fleet. We steamed out of Scapa for a rendezvous with the rest of the fleet in the North Sea. We then went on to Scapa Flow, the German fleet and the Allied fleet formed two lines and steamed past us in the QE, each ship saluting as she passed. All crews were action stations in case of treachery, but Admiral Beatty allowed as many men as possible on the upper deck to view the surrender. All the canteen staff were able to have a magnificent view from the boat deck.

'Working hours were even longer in those days. We got out of our hammocks to open up at 0700 hrs and it was often 2200-2300 hrs before we turned in. Of course, we had to attend action stations by day or night, and we had to open up the canteen again when the disperse sounded. The QE was on canteen messing, so the canteen in the six-inch battery, a space about 14 feet square, served over 1000 men. For staff, there was a manager and for assistance, and we sold everything from a pin to a pig.'

Many of the items sold in the canteen would seem strange to a canteen manager today and so with some of the prices. One of the more popular lines with clay pipes, 5d each. Cigarettes could be bought at 2.5d for 20. Three castles and Abdalla's were the most popular with the men going on leave. Some packs contained small silk flags, and the men made fire screens and other articles by pasting them onto a backing.

They sold all kinds of fresh and dried vegetables, which were hard work to carry. Cheese was carried in 160 lb crates, while dates were in 28 lb blocks, and safety matches were packed into wooden cases of 30 gross just to be awkward for the staff!

There were hundreds of small items, including medicines, pins and needles, collar studs, stationery, and Royal Marine canes and cap grummets. For tea and supper, the men bought jars of jam, tins of meat or fish paste (known because of the shape of the tins as 'depth charges'), and jars of chutney, or bottles of sauce, each which cost 1d. A common supper used to be 1d worth of cheese, 1d worth of chutney, 2d worth of ham, cut from gammon cooked in the galley, sardines or herrings in tomato sauce. Bacon was cut by hand, sometimes as many as six sides in a day. We even had whole pigs or lambs to cut up, while sausages were taken on board two tons at a time.

There is a big difference between 1971 and 50 years ago. In those days we had no ice cream, soda fountains or bookstalls.

One thing could be for sure, having this sort of insight of a first-hand account 50 years after it happened is invaluable to the history of the company.

Post-war EFC 1919

At this point it would be good to review how the EFC coped during World War One. At the top of the organisation were men with some of the best business minds in England. It did not make a difference whether they were fit and able for military service or not. They had a monumental task when they only came from backgrounds like hotel managers, restaurant managers and the like. They had to run rest houses or leave camps, and often with four meals a day, 200 beds, millions of meals for both British and American servicemen. You could only hazard a guess at the gigantic task of following the British soldier amid all the complexities and surprises of military operations and making sure they had supplies and luxuries at their feet, that without them they would not have had. They had to source goods from America, Australia, Japan, and India and also distribute these to the fighting men at a time when even the sea was as unsafe as the land.

The people at the lower ends of the organisation were often a small staff at some of the busiest stations. They would accomplish great feats of supplying the troops in the most adverse conditions. The staff themselves came from trades like billiard cushion repairers, butchers, builders, carpenters, cinema operators, engravers, fireman, hairdressers, amongst a few of a long list and even today some of the professions that have served with the lower ranks of the EFC don't even exist anymore.

The history mostly refers to the men but it might be appropriate to mention the valuable assistance from the women's auxiliary army corps, WAAC, women drivers, cooks, waitresses, saleswomen and even maids took risks, also in bombing raids where on many occasions they saw a number of them killed by a single shell. They never failed to do their duty and they worked alongside the EFC, maintaining the supply to the troops but also assisting with uniform and the like.

The EFC, which operated without any direct cost to the National Treasury and the government, indeed made no change to the services performed by staff or labour accommodation or any expense on public funds. They were self-sufficient, the original loan paid off in full and the facilities for the soldier at home enjoyed at a very small expense.

The only people that would benefit on the whole were the King's soldiers and sailors.

There are two ways that this all happened, firstly by the persistence of the officers who 20 years before had insisted the Co-op principles were the best method to stop the corruption and benefit the troops. Secondly by conversion of the principal contracting firm Richard Dickeson and Co, under the guidance of Sir Alexander Prince to the coop system and support which it gave after. That is the first point the officers admitted that it worked better than they had expected, they succeeded not only in what they set out to do but also in benefiting all branches of the King's fighting forces and all at no cost to the National Treasury.

You may have heard of the canteen millions; this money was given this name at the time. It would be easy to tell you what happened. When the EFC had been wound up its funds were amalgamated with those of the NACB, and it was found that there was a sum of about £8 million between them. So, who did this money rightfully belong to?

There was no doubt whatsoever about this in the minds of those who had all along been working with the idea of the C&MCS. In their minds, the money had come out of the soldiers' pocket and must go back there, all of it. So, the whole of the £8 million was handed over to the various service charities.

Copyright Sue A Lowe

Somaliland 1919 by VRS White written in 1931

Little did I think in November 1919, when I walked into the headquarters of the NACB at Alexandria and requested that arrangements be made for an Institute service to accompany my unit to Somaliland, that 12 years afterwards would find me a member of the successes of that canteen board. Because the story of this expedition may be of interest to the unique history, I'm attempting a short description of it. Immediately after the Great War, a small RAF independent force was selected to proceed to Somaliland, pick up our machines and stores in Egypt, and to arrange for the canteen service to accompany us. HMS Ark Royal put in at Alexandria and in this old seaplane carrier are personal machines, work conveyed to Berbera, the port of British Somaliland directly across the mouth of the Red Sea from Aden. As adjutant, one of my duties was to make the canteen arrangements, and after an interview at the headquarters at Alexandria sufficient supplies were arranged for and the manager was given local rank for the expedition.

Upon arriving at Berbera an advanced party preceded upcountry immediately to open an advanced base and took with them the comforts from the canteen stocks. The main body followed as soon as our machines were erected, and a strange cavalcade we were. Our airmen were mounted, some on the small Somali ponies, others on donkeys, and our RAF stores and canteen stores were conveyed on camels to the number of about 1200.

At the end of the first day's trek a request was made for canteen supplies to be sold to the airman and after consultation with the canteen manager this was arranged. Cases of beer, cigarettes, biscuits were opened, and sitting in the African moonlight one thought that war was really becoming quite a good sport after the dreary months of endless mud in France.

Thus, on our four day trek our airmen were looked after, and each halt we were able to add real home comforts to their meagre rations. On arrival at the advanced base it was not long before a really good canteen was in working order. An EP tent served for the shop and mother earth for tables and chairs.

We were of course on active service and liable to attack at any moment, but when one considers how the service man is looked after today and how, without up to date camping equipment, he would fare in later years, one appreciates the strides that have been made in making at least the domestic side of warfare more comfortable for the present day soldier and airman. Whether the canteen manager had the number of returns to do then that are necessary nowadays I know not or nor do I know whether he was his own stock taker, or whether he trusted to the good old standby of destroyed by shellfire, but this I do know, that our men appreciated his work.

Some 12 months afterwards the African general service medal was granted for the expedition, the expedition that was sent to quell the tyrant known as mad Mullah. The expedition having been kept secret would also remember that success was achieved, and that mad Mullah driven from Somaliland.

(Sections of the pre 1920 chapter were "Reproduced, with permission, from John Fortescue A Short Account of Canteens in the British Army, originally published 1928, reissued 2015, Cambridge University Press" (originally commissioned by Sir Frank Benson, CVO, CBE, then published))

1920–1929

1920-1921

NAAFI the beginnings 1920

In 1919 the EFC was dissolved into the NACB. The big question was what should be done next?

In March 1920 the Secretary of State for war, Sir Winston Churchill, appointed an interdepartmental committee. The chairman was Sir Archibald Williamson who was an adviser on what would be done with the present system of the Navy and army canteen board and if it should continue as it was. Some of the questions to be answered were, should it be brought under the War Office administration? Should a different system be used? Based upon the findings and the evidence of the past decades and the unyielding determination of the founders of the canteen and mess cooperative society, which led to the organisations which were either developed or failed or slipped back into the old ways of corruption, the decision was in their hands.

The committee unanimously decided that the cooperative canteens, or as previously known regimental institutes, for all three services of the armed forces should be a joint organisation and given the name the Navy, Army and Air Force Institutes or as we lovingly know it "The NAAFI".

This decision was made after months of hard work on the 9th of December 1920. It was without question that a lot of work was to be done to bring this new Institute into being and on this day the new institute was established. On the 1st of January 1921 the Navy Army and Air Force Institutes started trading; even so, there was still hesitation with some of the authorities and yet another committee, this time of the House of Commons, with Sir Samuel Roberts at the chair. He outlined the principle involved for NAAFI: "from the evidence that we have heard, we are convinced that the maintenance of a permanent organisation of the kind is most desirable as a matter of policy, both because the amenities which it affords to members of the forces and more particularly because it provides the nucleus of a service capable of immediate expansion on mobilisation'.

Maj Lionel Fortescue did not live to see his greatest ambition become something which he could only dream of, but his brother Lord John Fortescue had continued his work to great success. The canteen and mess cooperative society with its constitution, originally for the army, now serviced The British Forces as a whole. If they knew that it would be for 100 years and beyond, they would have been overwhelmed.

1922

The story of the Institute furnishing 1922 to 1933

During and immediately following the Great War, the furnishings consisted mainly of unattractive folding tables and uncomfortable chairs of the Windsor type. The only means of displaying articles for sale was by use of shelves fastened to the walls. Floor coverings were a luxury and existed in only a few of the establishments. Pictures consisted of advertisements, usually unframed, and odd prints pinned to the walls by the troops such as haphazard material.

Following the general reduction of HM Forces from a war to a peace footing, the necessity of providing comfortable types of furniture was appreciated, and as negotiations with the War Office had, in 1922, reached a satisfactory position, one Institute was completely furnished with new materials for the inspection of the authorities with the view to arriving at a suitable scheme which could be applied to all establishments.

The establishment selected for this purpose was the St Lucia barracks, Bordon, as it was unoccupied for some months. At that time, it was hoped to include the scheme, recreation rooms. Unfortunately, however, it was found that the total sum involved was far more than the amount available, therefore it was necessary to confine the scheme to those rooms for which NAAFI provided a service. In addition, the original proposals were somewhat elaborate and were amended accordingly. The photographs you can see of the restaurant at St Lucia barracks, Bordon and which was a vast improvement on what they had.

During 1923 a number of establishments for the RAF, commencing with Shotwick / Sealand, were refurbished. It should be noted from the photograph, this would be a classic example of the characteristics of the scheme, which was generally adopted from 1924.

The next development was the furnishings of a model establishment in each command, and in early 1924 significant funds had been obtained to warrant the adoption of a general scheme which was to apply to all establishments. The general refurnishing scheme commenced in June of 1924, and at the end of that year 25% of all establishments in the home commands had been completed. The work continued through 1925 and 1926, and by the end of that year the greater proportion of the establishments in home and overseas commands had been refurbished.

The establishments in the overseas commands presented a much greater problem than was experienced with the establishments in home commands – the climatic conditions necessitated the manufacture of special materials and construction to suit various districts in the command. Articles which were found necessarily in one country were useless in others, therefore overseas command had received individual treatment.

An idea of the work that was involved below gives you an idea of what was required to refurbish. 11,500 tables, 31,350 small chairs, 16,600 armchairs, 3400 easy chairs, 670 settles and wall seats, 700 billiard seats, 1600 noticeboards, 1300 menu frames, 14,100 electric light shades, 30 acres of floor covering, and 59 and 1/2 miles of material for curtains.

Since the completion of the scheme, the quantities of the easy chairs, and wall seats had been greatly increased. It was not, of course, to be expected that such a huge task like this could be undertaken and completed without a fair amount of criticism arriving, but on this score all that needed to be said was that some of the criticisms were constructive. Even important questions of the colours of the lino and the curtains was overcome, although many harmonious incidents arose.

With the completion of the refurbishing scheme the necessity for effect and maintenance became very apparent and therefore a maintenance staff was engaged. This policy had proved to be a real economy as in consequence of the furnishings being kept in a fit state of repair, the lifetime of the various articles had been extended much beyond the period which was estimated to be. Replacements were made when necessary to do so and in addition new types of materials were introduced from time to time. And so, the NAAFI Furnishings Department had begun.

1923

Sir Frank Benson, CVO, CBE – a look back at his time 1923

The summer of 1914 I was on holiday in Cornwall, away from the world and freed from all newspapers, until that evening at a pub at Rock, when I awoke to the startling fact that we were on the verge of war. There followed a memorable dash to London, with the price of petrol soaring at each refill and then a frenzied month of action, where all you could do was snatch some sleep under the office table. Here came a fork in the road. Down one highway went the normal, yet abnormal home business, and down the other the demands of the Expeditionary force, and it was our job to traverse both routes. I could write a volume on each, but a brief note must suffice.

On the home road I met the Rotherham Commission, which recommended a simplified system under which the contractors and the society alike were to conduct canteens at home. Per capita rebates and the society's method of monthly balance sheets applicable to each canteen were abolished, in favour of a fixed percentage of return on turnover. Even so the situation got completely out of hand and led to more representations to the Rotherham Commission, and to direct intervention by the War Office. So, we merged the Board of Control of regimental institutes in hands of that intelligent official Mr EH Cherry.

At that moment the long, loan struggle of the Canteen and Mess Cooperative Society stopped. Struggles and difficulties remained, but the lone hand had passed to a border and wider control without the change of any final advance in the original conception of a single service for the services was hopeless. In turn came the Army Canteen Committee, which brought out the contractors and took over the society, followed by the Navy and Army Canteen Board, and finally by the Navy army and Air Force institutes. At last all three services were combined in the running of their own organisation, financed by themselves and free of state control. Thus, the dream of the society came true.

Down the other road I went as general manager of the Expeditionary Force Canteens, formed as a branch of the Society but run the same as the Naval Canteen Service. With the distinction that it was run in collaboration with Sir Alexander Prince, chairman and managing director of Richard Dickeson and Co, it was the largest of the army contractors. At last the long feud between the societies and the contractors was ended.

I suppose I must be a cantankerous individual bound up in the original ideals to which I devoted my younger days and as ever thinking more of the structure and the human side of the show and its progress. That brought me to when I was sacked from the NACB, and in due course was demobilised from the army after the EFC had been finally wound up into the NACB. Heaven only knows how glad I was to come back in 1923.

All the rest is modern history. Which reminds me that the history of canteens has already been written by an old friend, the honourable Sir John Fortescue, army historian, and incidentally, a charming member of a charming family, which like the Lyttelton Family has been from the very outset a foundation stone of the Service canteen movement. The influence on the Fortescues and the Lytteltons on all that we have striven to achieve. Some say that Sir John's history makes dry reading, that may be because when I commissioned him to write it, I insisted that it should not be an advertisement for personalities in 1923. I merely told him that I had returned to NAAFI to find the machinery sound, threw in some need of oil, but in greater need of finding its soul, a point he touched upon in the last two pages of his book. Years later, in the last letter I was to receive from him, he asked me how we fared, and I was happy indeed to be able to reassure him.

THE MISSING YEARS 1924-1926

It would be great to have the information to cover all the years in which NAAFI found its feet converting all the Canteens into NAAFI establishments. Taking over each establishment with the remaining staff and products, renewing the signage and paperwork.

The enormity of the task would have been daunting, with canteens all over the world and onboard ships. Using the skills from ACC, EFC and NACB working to the guidelines set before them, under the rules and regulations.

1927

Miss Gertrude M Phillips 1927

Miss Phillips was born in Yorkshire and was educated in southern Ireland. Later she qualified in domestic science as a teacher of that subject at an Irish training school of domestic economy, in Dublin. She taught everything including cookery, laundry, dress making, housewifery, home hygiene, science and the theory and practice of the education. Miss Phillips finished her training and volunteered for war service with the St John's Ambulance Association, and while waiting for work with the Association she taught in a Belfast technical Institute. April of 1917 she went as VAD to Naas military hospital.

In January 1918 she joined the NACB and was in Ireland until 1921; this was when Ireland became a Free State and most of the troops left the country. Her work was much more diverse and interesting from that in England, as the country was in such disturbed state owing to the political feelings. Bomb throwing was common and she had several narrow escapes. The military lorries carrying troops were especially favoured and although she had many friends it was very wise not to go too near them just in case a bomb was thrown by the rebels.

In 1922 Miss Phillips was in the lowland district of Scotland and from there, after the reduction of troops, she was transferred to the southern area and in charge of the first OTC camp. October 1923, she had the distinction of being the first restaurant Superintendent to assist Miss Crichton at headquarters training centre where her work was much appreciated.

A year later Miss Phillips returned to the southern area and from 1925 to 1927 she was stationed at York. The following two years from this she was in charge of a restaurant in the old London and eastern area and then moved to the Tidworth district. She became stationed on the HSE and OTC camps and Salisbury plains. She was an expert walker and had a unique love of plants and gardening. She continued working for the Company for many years. Some of her final moments were playing pranks on other staff as she watched Barbara, one of the counter hands, dress up in a boiler suit, a brightly coloured muffler in a large check cap, carrying a suitcase which indicated that he'd come to stay, with really thick glasses on; he demanded to see the district manager or one of the managers, the character in front of her was claiming he had been sent by head office to fix the boiler and it took some time and for a crowd to gather before they realised that it was Miss Phillips and her staff playing a prank which provided much amusement for most of the camp.

Unfortunately I cannot find a record for when she retired but I think it is just wonderful to see the women celebrated in such a way. Even the customers loved to write verses about the staff. This was written by an airman at W camp in Hendon:

The Canteen Girl

Airmen dark, or fair and tall,
shy and bold, she knows them all.
She sells all things, this girl in blue,
from razor blades to Irish Stew!

Behind the counter every day
So much to do in every way
To cheer us up many a joke she makes.

When in the midst of dirty dishes
She knows that every airman wishes
That she may have the best of luck,
For keeping all our spirits up

A poem about the staff:

The manageress was an overall Brown,
and she is a lady of local renown;
to the boys she's known as 'the little Brown girl'
but they treasure her, all of them, just like a Pearl.

Then there is Kathleen, The Queen of cooks;
no need has she for your old recipe books!
All that she makes she must make by the score,
yet her customers are always craving for more.

Next, Doris is one of numerous band;
she carries the high-sounding title, "charge hand"!
So dainty, so trim, so invariably neat,
a pleasure to everybody to meet.

So, to the one who has plenty of work to get through,
yet always cheerful whatever's to do,
are made of the Kitchen and how much she means,
although all her work is done back o the scenes.

Here there must follow 3 Noble names,
are stalwart night guardians, Jock, Thomas and James.
Still others contributes to make up the crowd
of which we, and NAAFI, must surely feel proud.

1928

Servitor Servientium

Servitor Servientium: in 1928 this was the new addition to the NAAFI crest and the new motto for the company. Although this was Latin, it was intended to provoke the question, exactly what does this mean? The new company motto translated as servant of those serving; this was to state that the service in which it offered was to those serving, and really did outline the values for moving forward.

In years to come the translation would change to 'Service to the Services' or 'Service to those who Serve' – this was to remove the servant aspect as NAAFI was here to serve the services and not be their servants.

The Services Canteen Dinner – how the EFC dinner club was started

Immediately after the Great War an annual EFC celebration was inaugurated, taking on the form of a regimental dinner confined to the officers and QMAAC officials, at which orders and decorations were worn and ranks strictly observed, the chairman and the vice president being two senior officers or officials present. This was continued for a second year on the same lines, but then it was agreed, after a very full discussion amongst the leaders of the EFC, that there were reasons why the official character of this meeting should be abandoned, and henceforth rank should be completely ignored, and that the chair should be filled by special nomination each year, each chairman nominating his successor, and the dinner should be open to all ranks, but exclusively for men, and that dress worn should be the option of those attending. The idea of an EFC Corps Dinner was abandoned in favour of an EFC dinner club.

This constitution lasted for two years, but from the outset difficulties had been arising. Some personnel whose services were more intimately associated with the EFC than with the NACB, were officially attached to the latter organisation, but more to attend as dinner guests. Moreover, certain officers of the canteen and mess cooperative society which had started the EFC, and of which the society had no organisation, was originally a subsection and had no status at the gathering but that of a guest. Hence, the further meeting for discussion, it was decided that the dinner should be open to all who had served, whether in the C&MCS, the EFC, or the NACB.

After the dinner held in 1925, further difficulty became apparent. Many of the former personnel of the C&MCS and the EFC and the NACB were now in service of the NAAFI and whereas these could attend the dinner, the remainder of the NAAFI staff could only do so as guests. It was decided, therefore, after further discussion that the dinner should be opened to the personnel of all organisations which had been or were engaged in the creation and the development of the modern services canteen.

Colonel Benson, formerly general manager and deputy Comptroller of the EFC and the present general manager, was proposed to chairman for the dinner to be held in 1926, and at the dinner it fell to him to explain the decisions which had been reached, as it had similarly fallen to him on previous occasions to explain the changes in prospect.

In connection with this last phrase, the leaders' representative or various organisations concerned had met several times and it had been agreed that the arrangement for forthcoming dinners, and a selection of the chairmen year by year should be placed in the hands of the committee of which the personnel had been formed.

The EFC Dinner had become the Services Canteen Dinner, still conducted by the EFC club but now not merely an annual meeting of old friends who work together in common cause, old friends who, as the years go by must become fewer and fewer, but a meeting of all those who had been, on now, or maybe in the future representative of the canteen movement, which for all time will continue the tradition of the EFC and honour each year, the toast of the wartime organisation.

What made an in-house Journal? 1928

Written by the Editor of the Imperial Club Magazine 1931.

Perhaps it would be good to explain how an in-house Journal could be conceived. The editor of the Imperial club magazine gave us an insight into how this happened.

In volume 2, 'If you decide that six numbers make a volume, and this then would naturally be the beginning, what would there be to get excited about.' It was not such a long time ago that we sent downstairs one day, to ask for a large, blue pencil and when we had got it, made a careful point at one end and bit down hard on the other, saying over to ourselves several times in an auto suggestive tone of voice; "we are the editor of a new magazine to be called the Imperial club magazine and we go to press on such a date! We are the editor."

When we had said this over and over what we judged to be a significant number of times we wrote down the words to the same effect on a number of bits of paper, some of which were then stuck up here and there about the building, while some others we put into envelopes and posted off far and wide. Then, in our painstaking conscientious way, we checked our office dictionary to make quite sure that we knew exactly what was meant by a magazine.

We found that a magazine meant, 'a periodical publication containing articles, by various authors.' This encouraged us a good deal because it was more or less exactly what we had thought out for ourselves. If anybody came to see us about the matter, we repeated this in an impressive tone taking care to have the blue pencil in evidence, sticking it negligently behind our ear, and they always went away thinking things over very seriously indeed. As for us, we sat firmly in our chair waiting for the articles to arrive by various authors.

Lo and behold they did arrive! A perfectly adequate number of various authors took us at our word and believed it when we said, we are the editor of a new magazine, to be called the Imperial club magazine and to go to press on such and such date, and in simple faith of these first contributors, all honour and thanks to them, created and brought into being such a magazine as we said in 1928, No1 Vol 1.

1929

The canteen outlook in the Royal Navy and the Army

The honourable Sir John Fortescue's interesting and illuminating book on the history of the canteens in the Army brings into prominence the essential difference in the growth of the canteens in the Army and the canteens of the Navy, and in the outlook of the services on canteen matters. Put shortly, the difference in this: the Army canteen system has been built up by, and is largely controlled by, the officers, but in the Navy almost entirely run by ratings. Sir John Fortescue had outlined in his book, that the NCS originated in the bumboat system, and then developed along two different lines which, until 1917, existed side by side. These two systems were the ship or cooperative canteen, and the tenant canteen. In the former case, the canteen was conducted entirely by the ship's company, the resulting profits forming the ship's or canteen fund; in the latter by the canteen tenants who paid rent on the fund based on numbers served. On the formation of the NACB the canteen tenant ceased to exist, except on the China section. In a few instances the ship's canteens continued, but the last of these were to be taken over by the NAAFI on the 1st of July 1929. Although a piece of the canteen of each ship had been, and is controlled by, the canteen committee, which is a body elected by the lower decks, the officers for the most part acting in the advisory capability only. As in the other services, the formation of duties and powers of the canteen committee were strictly laid down by the King's regulations, but their duties were taken far more seriously in the Navy.

This system of representation had been extended with the result that they were now fleet and port canteen committees, the headquarters canteen committee, and three lower deck representatives appointed whole time, two stationed in Imperial court and one at Malta.

1930–1939

1931

Mr Gerald Alexander Prince 1931

It was in this year that they reported the death of Mr Gerald Alexander Prince, son of Sir Alexander Prince, who, together with our present general manager, brought the Expeditionary Force Canteens of the Great War into being. This was a very sad blow to the business and there was little doubt that Mr Prince, had he not passed, would have gone far. He was born on the 30th of July 1898 and educated at Clifton College, which represented at boxing in the lightweight, public school class in 1916. In Christmas 1916 he left Clifton and joined the RASC and served in France until the end of the war, eventually transferring to the Royal Air Force, in which service he was training for his pilot certificate at the time of the Armistice. On demobilisation he joined Messer Travers and Co Ltd. Cannon Street, and from then in January 1928, he entered the service of NAAFI. He died on the 19th of June 1931, after a long and painful illness, the result of an infection during his war service. He left behind a wife and three children.

The Late Mr. Gerald Prince.

Mr William Jago on his retirement 1931

At the close of business on the evening of the 31st of December 1931, a large gathering assembled at the restaurant at headquarters, Imperial court, Kennington, to witness a presentation to Mr William Jago, naval staff Superintendent, upon his retirement from the service of the company.

Born in the year 1864 in County Cork, Ireland, William was educated at either national or church school, whichever happened to be the nearest to the Coast Guard station in which his father was serving at the time. A young man, he entered the grocery and provision trade, and he did not rest until he became his own master at the age of 26 and was controlling his own shop; he was prepared to supply anything from an elephant to a shirt button. His activities were not confined to meeting the needs of the civilian population, for, with the love of the sea in his very veins, he bought his own boat and made deliveries from his shop, of groceries and provisions for HM ships stationed at Bantry Bay.

Those were the days of the cutter fly, and the coastguard gunboats, Argus, and Amelia, whilst among the big ships on the station were the old 'Aurora', 'Valiant' and 'Dreadnought'.

With keen insight and enthusiasm, he worked hard, his cheery optimism and ingrained wit helped him always to get there. His business developed and prospered, and in the year 1902 he came under the notice of William Miller Limited, the well-known naval contractors, for whom he acted as an agent in Ireland until 1912, when he was persuaded to leave Ireland. He entered the head office of William Miller Limited at Portsmouth. His long experience in supplying those who supplied the ships provided invaluable to his principals, and William was soon appointed director of William Miller Limited.

The appointment he continued to hold with ever increasing satisfaction to his firm until May 1917, when they were transferred into the NACB, at Knightsbridge. A month later all the other naval contractors were similarly absorbed; the naval section of the NACB was reorganised and began to feel its feet. William took under his wing the organisation and control of the naval canteen staff, both ashore and afloat. Up to December 1931, the date of his retirement, he toiled relentlessly in the effort to make the staff worthy of the great company.

It was safe to say that he knew the history of every member of naval canteen staff and he would admit that as he considered it necessary.

1932

Entertaining the forces 1932

Long before the Entertainment National Service Association (ENSA), the 'Imperial players', entertained the forces. Nine companies of the Imperial players, each consisting of six artists – it was anticipated that before Easter of 1932 over 900 performances would have been given. Reference had been made to previous articles, to the nine months of preparation necessary before a concert party sets out from Imperial court – the actual rehearsals occupy less than a fortnight, but an endeavour had been made to strike an entirely new note in concert party production in 1933.

An extract from the '79th news', which was typical of many notes about the Imperial players and the entertainments organised by the managers, which appear from time to time in the service journals, and which indicate in no uncertain tone not only how popular our own entertainers were but how these entertainers inspire regimental talent.

Extract from Journal '79th news', October 1932. Entertainments.

'There is plenty of scope for the soldier to amuse himself in the entertainment line in Aldershot, but it had been thought that mention should be made of that provided regimentally. Band concerts are well patronised and so are the visiting concert parties found by the NAAFI during the winter months. In camp at Thursley, we had the entertainment run by Mr Trevor Jones, of the NAAFI each night, and practically all their concert parties came down. We appended the detail of an excellent concert which he organised from the Gordon's and Cameroon's in camp, ably assisted by L/Cpl Leesmith. These artists who took part were numerous junior ranks with talents lending themselves to NAAFI entertainment's 'Imperial players.'

The soldiers' own stamp 1932

A postage seal designed by the Navy Army and Air Force Institutes, had been brought into use for the British forces in Egypt. When, this spring, the Egyptian Postal charges were increased, it was felt that the troops would not be called upon to pay the higher rates, and now the special postage seal had been approved.

The stamp was being used on correspondence emanating from the British forces in Egypt. All this, though this was not a stamp, this was a Postal seal. It was noted that the Egyptian post office prepaid postmark was being used in the customer place for the postage stamp and the seal in the appropriate place for a seal. These seals, it is understood, did not evidently come into use until the 1st of November 1932, the first one being used on the 2nd of November 1932.

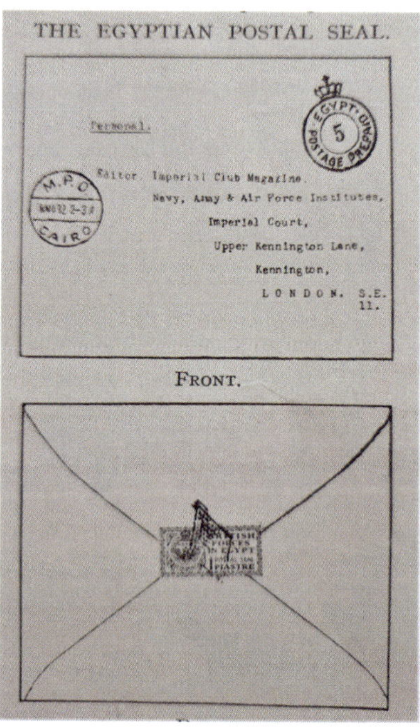

1933

The late Sir Alexander Prince 1933

The death of Sir Alexander William Prince, KBE, which occurred at Claridge's hotel on the 25th of March 1933, meant that the canteen movement had lost one of its great figures, a good friend, and a keen supporter. Sir Alexander was 63 years of age and his death followed that of his son Gerald. The son of Mr William Prince of Canterbury, Sir Alexander was educated in Dover and abroad, and at the early age of 26 became a partner of the late Sir Richard Dickeson in the great firm bearing his name which did so much good work in the canteen world in the days of the 'tenant contract' method of running campaigns.

In 1907 his marketability carried him to the post of managing director of the firm, and in 1909 he became chairman. He had much to do with both the canteen and victualling reforms in the Royal Navy, and in 1914 it was he who went to the War Office and offered to join hands with the C&MCS and he also joined with the general manager in forming the Expeditionary Force Canteens. He was the first appointed honorary director in 1917 controller (war office) of the EFC, and on the home front a great deal of success of that very successful organisation; the final inspiration for the formation of NAAFI was due to his untiring and devoted work for the services.

Sir Alexander was also deputy chairman of the War Office, Expeditionary Force Canteen's committee and a member of the War Office Advisory Council on army contracts, service for which he was knighted in 1917 as he resigned from Messrs Dickeson, an appointment as managing director of NACB. This latter appointment he relinquished in 1919, and in 1921, on the formation of the NAAFI he accepted the invitation of the army council to become honorary advisor to the quartermaster general and to the chairman of the NAAFI on matters connected with the army side of the NAAFI. In 1922 he was on it with the title KBE.

Sir Alexander Prince was not a light of canteen affairs alone, for he was director of the commercial union assurance cutter company, president of the British control oil fields, chairman of the Trinidad petroleum development company, of the Anglo Venezuelan oil trust, and of the Palmerston investment trust. He was also a director of the central area exploration company in Venezuela. In freemasonry, Sir Alexander held past provincial rank. In 1897 he married Edith, daughter of Mr Isaac Jonas of Edgbaston, and they had three sons. The funeral took place at the liberal Jewish Cemetery.

EFC memorial lamps, Imperial court, Kennington 1933

Outside of the Imperial Court, Kennington, two lamp standards had been erected on each side of the main entrance as a memorial to those who fell while serving the EFC in the Great War. The standard would take the form of plaster pylons, each bearing two bronze lamps on bronze brackets. Bronze tablets on the base would bear the inscription, "to the memory of the officers and other ranks of the Expeditionary Force Canteens who fell during the Great War, 1914 to 1918".

The lamps and standards were designed in conjunction with, and were being erected by, the Plasterer Decoration Company Limited, in Stannary St, London SE11, whose managing director, Mr EG Payne, had been responsible for the many examples of plaster decorative work, including the preliminary modelling in plaster, of the detail of the cavalry memorial in Hyde Park and preliminary scale model of the Sydney Harbour bridge.

In addition to the lamps, an illuminated and framed Roll of names who fell was hung in the main entrance Hall.

The lamps had been completed by Christmas of 1933. They had successfully replaced two rather large lions which had been removed in 1930. Amongst those that had lost their lives because of the Great War were 5 officers and 88 other ranks.

The Roll of honour was removed to make way for the WWII memorial but was said to have been kept with the Museum archive.

When NAAFI moved to Amesbury the EFC bronze plaques were removed and placed either side of the stand holding the WWII Role of honour. This meant that both the WWI and WWII memorials would be kept together and placed at Bulford Church where wreaths are laid each year by, members of the NEA.

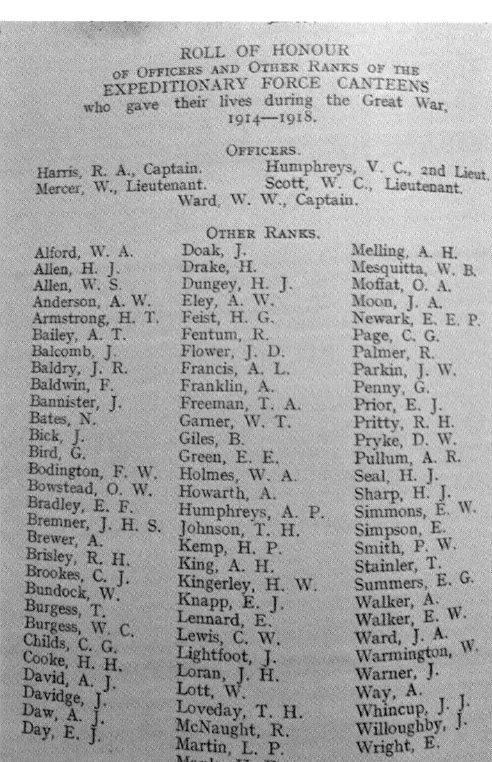

ROLL OF HONOUR
OF OFFICERS AND OTHER RANKS OF THE
EXPEDITIONARY FORCE CANTEENS
who gave their lives during the Great War,
1914—1918.

OFFICERS.

Harris, R. A., Captain.
Mercer, W., Lieutenant.
Humphreys, V. C., 2nd Lieut.
Scott, W. C., Lieutenant.
Ward, W. W., Captain.

OTHER RANKS.

Alford, W. A.
Allen, H. J.
Allen, W. S.
Anderson, A. W.
Armstrong, H. T.
Bailey, A. T.
Balcomb, J.
Baldry, J. R.
Baldwin, F.
Bannister, J.
Bates, N.
Bick, J.
Bird, G.
Bodington, F. W.
Bowstead, O. W.
Bradley, E. F.
Bremner, J. H. S.
Brewer, A.
Brisley, R. H.
Brookes, C. J.
Bundock, W.
Burgess, T.
Burgess, W. C.
Childs, C. G.
Cooke, H. H.
David, A. J.
Davidge, J.
Daw, A. J.
Day, E. J.
Doak, J.
Drake, H.
Dungey, H. J.
Eley, A. W.
Feist, H. G.
Fentum, R.
Flower, J. D.
Francis, A. L.
Franklin, A.
Freeman, T. A.
Garner, W. T.
Giles, B.
Green, E. E.
Holmes, W. A.
Howarth, A.
Humphreys, A. P.
Johnson, T. H.
Kemp, H. P.
King, A. H.
Kingerley, H. W.
Knapp, E. J.
Lennard, E.
Lewis, C. W.
Lightfoot, J.
Loran, J. H.
Lott, W.
Loveday, T. H.
McNaught, R.
Martin, L. P.
Mayle, H. E.
Melling, A. H.
Mesquitta, W. B.
Moffat, O. A.
Moon, J. A.
Newark, E. E. P.
Page, C. G.
Palmer, R.
Parkin, J. W.
Penny, G.
Prior, E. J.
Pritty, R. H.
Pryke, D. W.
Pullum, A. R.
Seal, H. J.
Sharp, H. J.
Simmons, E. W.
Simpson, E.
Smith, P. W.
Stainler, T.
Summers, E. G.
Walker, A.
Walker, E. W.
Ward, J. A.
Warmington, W.
Warner, J.
Way, A.
Whincup, J. J.
Willoughby, J.
Wright, E.

Naval canteen service motor launch refurbishment 1933

An insulated lighter for Malta. Being stationed at Malta meant you had difficulties with getting refrigerated goods on board HM ships, in satisfactory condition. It was difficult at the best of times. Getting them from the cold store onshore until they reached the ship's refrigerator often meant there was a serious risk of having the goods being affected by heat. With a view to facilitating and improving the stocking up of the ships, especially for cruises, it was decided to augment the naval canteen motor launch service for Malta, by an insulated lighter craft. For this purpose, the motor launch Shamrock at Devonport was completely overhauled and specifically fitted out. Originally it was intended to send out by freight steamer early in May of 1933. Just as she was due to proceed to Southampton, the winds sprang up, and although the attempt was made, the storms became so violent that she had to return to port and the opportunity was missed. The next vessel available was proceeding directly from London, so consequently the Shamrock had to work a way around under her own power from Davenport by easy stages, to Portland, Portsmouth, Chatham and eventually up the Thames to the King George V dock.

This presented no issues to her crew, and she was delivered on time and shipped on board the P&O company's SS Bangalore, on the 2nd of June, under the supervision of Mr Pottinger, the engineer in charge of the motor launches, and eventually reached Malta on the 10th of June.

Her first big try out came in connection with the sea stocking of HM ships, the Mediterranean fleet for the first part of the summer cruise, and this was a great success, the report being that she proved of immense assistance in the delivery of perishable goods in both harbours; both were sea stocks, an ordinary routine.

The following in connection with the fitting out of the vessel for her special purpose may prove interesting.

Originally built for the NACB, by the Medway slipway company in Rochester, she was 42 feet long, with a 12-foot beam, her draft aft, 3 foot 6 inches. Fitted with a 26 horsepower Kelvin petrol paraffin motor and Kelvin reverse gear. Cargo built, she carried an auxiliary mast and sail, equipped with lifebuoys and lifebelts and fire extinguishers. The installation was carried out throughout with slab cork and bitumen. The sides, platform, bulkhead, underdecks, coamings and under-hatches had been a standard thickness of 6 inches of slab cork throughout. Behind the cork the boat's ribs had been tarred, also the wood lining. Between the lining in the cork on the sides and under the decks and bulk heads there was a sheath of light gauge galvanised sheet iron, to prevent insects getting at the cork. The face of the cork had been covered with a wood lining, and the platform and halfway up the sides was covered with a heavier gauge sheet iron. In the platform for the full length of the insulated hold, there were two insulated hatches, slightly tapered, so that when in position they fitted tightly. These could be lifted at any time to run off any water or moisture into the bilge. All bilge water runs aft and is pumped out by a semi rotary pump situated in the engine room. On each side of the hold there had been two insulated wing doors, tapered, and when in position these were secured with batons and wedges.

On top of the hatchway was fitted an insulated hatch, but this was not for loading or unloading cargo, but only for airing the hold.

When the boat was not carrying refrigerated goods, the two insulated platform hatches, four wing doors and the insulated top hatch were unhooked and stowed at one end of the hold. When the hold was in use for refrigerated goods, they were placed in position, and cargo was loaded only through the hatch in the foredeck and passed into the hold through the insulated swing door in the foremost bulkhead.

Regarding the cooling of the hold, it should be appreciated that normally the temperature of the hold was at least atmospheric temperature. So, although the cargo would be protected from the sun, defrosting would be bound to take place, so to bring the whole temperature down, ice was placed in the hold for a day before loading the refrigerator cargo and then renewed as necessary. For light when they were working in the hold, two portable electric battery-operated hurricane lamps had been provided. For ordinary duties and delivering daily supplies at Malta, cargo could be carried on the decks and on top of the hatchway, the decks had been specially strengthened; there was also a main beam right across the hold.

The hull had been copper sheathed, as a preventative against the ravages of the wood of the hull by the many small destructive creatures which thrived in the warm waters of the Mediterranean. Altogether the fitting out of the Shamrock as an insulated lighter was well justified and she would form a welcome and useful addition to the naval canteen motor launch service for the Mediterranean fleet at Malta.

1934

Mediterranean fleet 1934

A signal from the commander in chief to Cyclops: request you arrange with fleet canteen Superintendent for NAAFI motorboats to be alongside Queen Elizabeth at 1115 Wednesday.

'Flap? I should say so! The whole Mediterranean fleet at Navarin, and all our boats cruise, piped down, after a heavy day's work. The Admiral's inspection tomorrow!

However, the OOW of Cyclops sent the FCS ashore in the picket boat who warned of the coxswains of our boats: and then there was scrubbing and polishing. Not only that our boats never needed much of that, but just to get that little something extra.

The next day's delivery started at 0500 as usual and after that our five boats assembled alongside the Cyclops, where final clean-up was made, and the awnings unshipped. At 1100hrs the squadron proceeded at 5 knots to the fleet flagship in line ahead FCS flying his Pennant in the Saint Bernard and himself standing alongside the coxswain.'

'It seemed a style all the staff were mustered on the quarter deck of the Queen Elizabeth, to watch the evolution. The squadron in line ahead, made for a point just abaft the flagship's gang way and as Saint Bernard put her helm over to go alongside, all our boats turned together and went to stern taking time from Saint Bernard, which of course, brought them into line abreast with the Saint Bernard. The fleet canteen Superintendent went on board and reported to the captain of the fleet, who congratulated him on the Seaman like manner in which our squadron had been brought alongside. Each boat was called alongside in turn and the captain of the fleet went on board and carried out through the inspection of the crew, hold and engine room, asking searching questions of our men as to their service and their knowledge of their boats.'

'The horror of it! In one boat he found a real live cockroach, an awful silence as he pointed out to it. The coxswains were not to be defeated, and dealt with the offending article.' At the end of it all they were congratulated on the condition of the motorboat service and in due course the following letter reached his area manager in Malta:

> From the captain of the fleet, Mediterranean. Date 14th of August 1934. The area manager NAAFI, Malta. While at Navarin took the opportunity of inspecting the NAAFI boats embarked in the fleet and their crews. I have the pleasure of informing you that the appearance of the crews and cleanliness and upkeep of the boats was satisfactory in all respects.
>
> WJ Whitworth, captain of the fleet.

The Blue Nile cinema at Khartoum 1934

Amidst the lights, glamour and music, decorations and Paris creations, the cinema was officially opened by Maj General SS Butler, CMG, DSO, on April 30th, 1934; the quote directly from the Sudan Daily Herald:

> 'The result of four years' endeavour was seen when brigadier SS Butler CMG, DSO, opened the Blue Nile cinema at Khartoum, South barracks in the presence of a large number of distinguished guests, including the governor of the province, and a big audience.
>
> The open-air cinema, spreading fanwise from the screen, had seating for 800 spectators, including 72 seats in 12 raised boxes. Seating for all classes is alike in the form of wicker armchairs. On the terrace behind the box rise is a row of buildings with three well-appointed bars and other services. The entrance to the cinema is on the Blue Nile embankment facing North, with a frontage of lawns, flowers, shrubs, and beautiful trees. A clever scheme of diffused light produced a delightful effect.
>
> The Kaid el 'Amm in a short speech before the programme opened with a news bulletin and the famous film, 'Cavalcade', said that the Blue Nile cinema for British troops was the outcome of four years' hard work, and that everyone should be proud of the magnificent result obtained. He expressed deep gratitude to the officials of the NAAFI in London, especially Mr Cherry and Maj Wilberforce, who sympathetically considered this plea for a cinema for the troops and eventually supplied the necessary funds.
>
> The opening performance was complete success, not only for the night's entertainment but also for the lavish hospitality, in the form of refreshments and sandwiches extended to the guests. The Blue Nile cinema was firmly on the map.

1935

The EFC 'B' mess dinner guest night 1935

The EFC 'B' Mess, guest night dinner at the Connaught rooms, on Friday, November 30th at which the general manager, Col Benson presided. Messers Baker and Westerndarp were the guests' representative of the NAAFI, which, as Col Benson stated in his speech from the chair, was stirred by the EFC. The occasion was quite obviously an intimate and happy link between the modern canteen movement and the 'B' mess with all its traditions of the canteen service in the Great War of 1914 to 1918. At this point Mr Baker did not miss when replying for the guests. Here indeed was a family party, here the atmosphere could be and was that of the past rather than the present in the future.

To say that evening was a cheery one is to put things mildly. Songs and shanties reminiscent of the camaraderie of wartime days when all were pulling together so well in a common cause interspersed both at the dinner and the speeches, the latter not being allowed to go without humorous and friendly interruption, which is only possible at an informal gathering where all are understanding each other. There was no doubt at the time thats the EFC 'B' mess still stood together, the effort made by Mr Brightman to attend, with a heavily bandaged eye.

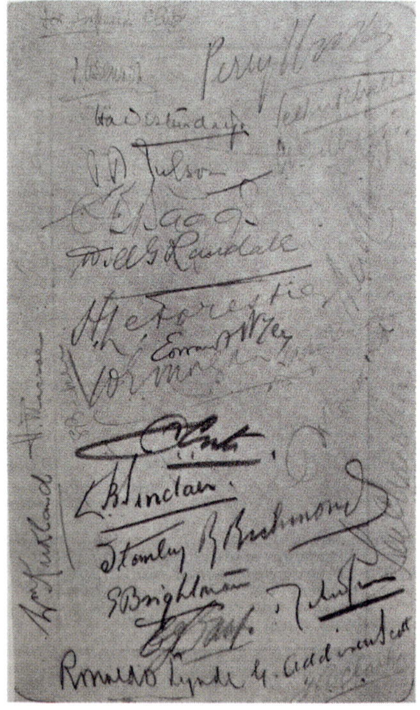

The annual dinner was held at the Connaught rooms for the services canteen. Although we don't know if this was an official Association or it was just an annual get together for old comrades of the Great War, it was safe to say that they did their best to support each other years later.

They even went ahead and signed the menu.

1936

Then new canteen motor launches, Silver King, Silver Queen, and Silver Prince 1936

To complete the 1936 programme of replacements, 3 launches had been built to the order of the company by Mr F Curtis, West Looe, Cornwall. In view of the prospects that canteen boats may have to be carried in smaller ships in the near future, it has been necessary to modify the standard design for building boats. The smaller dimensions and lighter displacement without sacrificing efficiency. These three boats were each 30ft-long with a 9ft beam, the dead weight of each of them with full equipment on board was just under 5 tonnes. Their machinery, comprising of 13 horsepower Kelvin paraffin motor with AP freshwater drip, is situated right forward. Cargo space is amidships, and cabin aft provides accommodation for a crew of three. The coxswain's shelter is situated forward, and the engine controls are conveniently arranged so that when necessary the boat can be manoeuvred by one man. By getting the builders to put on extra spurt we were able to make the launch date Wednesday June 10th, 1936 which coincided with the visit of Commander Jolly, and Commander Anderson. On the evening of the ninth, Captain Boulter arrived in connection with these states, and we took the opportunity of inviting him to join the early risers at the launching ceremony.

At 0630 the next morning, we sailed for Tolu by Road and on arrival there we found that Mr Curtis and his merry men had the Silver King and the Silver Queen, already on split yarns.

Commander Jolly cracked a bottle of wine on the stem of Silver King, in full ceremonial style, she quietly slid into the water. Commander Anderson having chosen the lady and christened her, and set her going after her consort. The party then adjourned to the ship hotel where full justice was done to a very welcome Cornish breakfast. It was unfortunate that Silver Prince could not be finished in time to complete the trio, but a few days later she was sent on her journey in a fitting style by Mrs Curtis, the wife of the builder.

The three boats subsequently proceeded into Davenport to be equipped for their duties with the fleets. Silver Prince was first away and was attached to HMS Rodney for the home fleet autumn cruise. Silver King had proceeded to Portsmouth under her own power and would join HMS Hood, for the passage to Malta. Silver Queen was ready for sea but was standing and awaiting her orders.

1937

Hong Kong typhoon 1937

In Hong Kong district on the night of the 1st and 2nd of September a terrific typhoon ravaged Hong Kong; it was chronicled as the worst catastrophe in the history of the colony. The wind force reached 164 mph and the barometer dropped to a low record of 28.20. Hundreds of boats and vessels broke their moorings and they were tossed on the rocks and many would never be floated again, others were floated some months later. The wreckage of some ships on the rocks were a grim reminder of the tragedy for all ships at the time. In the harbour the huge waves surged in the pitch black of night with torrential rains and gusts of wind and lightning that lit up the sky, while passengers were stranded on these boats with others drifting nearby.

Chinese boat people were the worst sufferers and it is estimated that 10,000 in and around Hong Kong were lost that night, some 1200 junks and sampans were totally lost. It gave a harrowing detail of crews being engulfed into the mountainous waves which tossed the craft around like toys. On land the damage was more superficial, but a tour of the island revealed thousands of trees that had been stripped bare or uprooted at crossroads, houses on roofs and generally a trail of wreck and ruin. Firemen pumped water out of buildings and tended a fire on the sea front that was being fanned by wind, while a boat sat on the Main Street stranded after being washed ashore.

Many of the NAAFI's buildings were damaged; the roof of the Lyemun grocery shop had been torn off and the building had been flooded; many of the other buildings suffered broken glass but were mostly undamaged. The most serious incident was involved with the loss of the SS Kwang Chow, which was wrecked completely and piled high on the rocks of an island near Hong Kong; this ship contained 91 packages of urgent stores for the Shanghai district.

After the typhoon had caused such damage, there were further scares to be dealt with, as well as the lack of sanitization and freshwater. There was a bad epidemic of Cholera as a result where all staff of NAAFI had to undergo the necessary ordeal of inoculation. This was short lived as they had to deal with the Japanese conflict in North China and become a supply base and accept all Shanghai and Tientsin consignments for forwarding when this was possible, and because of this Hong Kong was flooded with refugees from all nationalities, which meant that accommodation was scarce and food prices increased.

From Pacific to Atlantic in 8 hours through the Panama Canal, An account from staff in the Mediterranean 1937

Passing through the Panama Canal for the first time, you must be prepared for the strenuous day. There were so many things to look at and so much strange rising and lowering of our large ship, that we could hardly bear to leave the scene of action, even for meals, and hours of standing over the ship's side, combined with the tropical heat, made you rather exhausted by the end of the day.

The canal was, of course, one of the greatest engineering feats in the world and the Americans are justly proud of it. It was when they eventually excavated the canal after an unsuccessful attempt had been made by de Lesseps, the creator of the Suez Canal in 1880. When the Panama Canal was first opened in August 1914 it was roughly 50 miles in its entire length. There are 6 parallel pairs of locks, each 1000 feet long and 70 feet deep – an average time in filling and emptying the lock is 15 minutes.

Approaching from the Pacific, we call at Balboa, and then proceed a few miles in land to the first two locks at Miraflores. It is most interesting to watch the ship being attached by steel ropes to the little trolleys that run on rails either side of the lock. These trolleys they call mules, and they draw the ship slowly into position between the dock walls with no effort at all. Once inside the lock, the gates are closed, while this operation goes like clockwork and with little delay or fuss. Where you can watch over the water rising foot by foot up the stone walls until you are high enough to pass on to the next lock. The gates are opened, our mules come to life and draw us into position once more. We rose 58 feet altogether at the first lock and 2 miles further on the Pedro Miguel locks, take you up another 27 feet. The most breath-taking views were before then, the channel is cut through 9 miles of hills, a remarkable feet of excavation and they come out onto a lovely lake where there are numerous small islands covered in banana plantations. Before the lake was formed by constructing a dam and flooding the Chagres River, these islands were actually mountain peaks.

Where in this water there are plenty of alligators and you can see one or 2 basking in the mud at the edge of the lake. The scenery is made up of vegetation and everywhere is very green and fertile. Going through the 1st lock it's all green lawns on either side, as it belonged to the golf course at Panama. The artificial lake is 24 miles long; after crossing it you come to the Gatun lock, where you are lowered through 3 locks down to sea level again. A few miles further on is Cristobal, the port for the eastern side named after Christopher Columbus, and on leaving being carried to the Atlantic with only 550 miles to go to Kingston.

Imperial Club Magazine sent by request of their Royal Highnesses 1937

In 1937 The Christmas publication there was great joy that the magazine itself had been running for 10 years but also joy that with everything going so well, the pride in the fact that their Majesties Queen Elizabeth and Queen Mary were some of their most interested readers. A copy was sent on every publication to the Palace for their enjoyment which also gave them a broad interest in the Corporation. Mrs FP Robinson in a letter from Buckingham Palace dated the 4th of August 1937 says "both her majesties were glad to receive copies and asked me to say that they would be interested to receive copies on further numbers". As you can imagine the editor was overjoyed and they felt hopeful that it would inspire people to contribute and send in articles to be published for the Royal readers. The magazine started to get a role of being important for the HM forces.

Mr Arthur Edward Carlton, recollections of Bloody Sunday and retirement 1937

Mr Arthur Edward Carlton retired in this year, but his career was an interesting one for the Corporation. From the quiet beginnings of a grocery business in Hastings in 1891 his career extends over 43 years of varied and arduous distinguished service. He was long remembered in the canteen movement in association with such men as Colonel Ramsey, Captain Barry, and Captain Harman, with all of whom he worked with at one time or another. He joined the firm Richard Dickeson and Co in 1894 and by 1900 Mr Carlton was held in such esteem as to be made joint manager in Cape Town, joining the Boar War. On returning to England in 1902 he occupied various positions and then in 1908 he went on as manager in Ireland which was then to be seen as possibly the most important, and certainly the most exciting activities of his life.

This was the first of the long and bitter battles of the Irish troubles. Mr Carlton, who was described like a hero of Mr HG Wells' war time novel "saw it through", coming under fire and witnessing many great events, finally becoming ill in health. He was very surprised to hear in 1918 that he had been mentioned for his service to the Secretary of State for war. As in previous chapters, by this time accounting control had been unified as he had become the first area manager of the Irish command under the Army Catering Corps. After a spot of ill health, he took up the position as an area manager and then headquarters supervisor from that time until the year of his retirement.

Mr Carlton was in Ireland from 1908 to 1922, although he did take a short break between 1918 and 1920. He recollects his relationship between The British forces and the changes politically within this period. He enthusiastically gave a reception to King George and Queen Mary on the Coronation visit and it is worth mentioning this because of the feelings of the population at the time. About this time the Irish citizen Army was formed – it was commonplace at this time to see the army on the streets surrounding Dublin. It was on the fateful Easter Monday morning they saw large numbers of volunteers making their way to the city.

Later in the afternoon he writes that Sinn Féin had blocked off then occupied many important buildings including the general post office and a well-known Stephen's Green. He tried daily and desperate efforts were made, but he was unable to reach his warehouse and office till towards the end of the week, when he was fortunate enough in meeting a senior British officer whom he knew well and was responsible for guarding one of the many canal bridges, which he then explained to the officer through the dedication of his work "the troops must be fed "and he was given permission to cross the bridge at his own risk on all fours but later obtained an armed escort, from HQ Dublin Castle, arriving after at the Navy Army Canteen Board warehouse.

He managed to later deliver groceries to the troops in an improvised armoured lorry with a military escort; it was the first occasion of being under fire, for sniping was rampant at this time. Days later he was fortunate enough to be in Dublin HQ when the truce was called, and gradually the political situation in Ireland started to quieten down. He was possibly one of the first to obtain a military pass, allowing him all over the streets of the County of Dublin, and later another pass was issued by the Dublin Metropolitan Police which enabled him to pass through the streets of the city and all over Ireland by either motor or rail. He made use of this to pass through the streets of the city and this time a lot of fires had been extinguished.

Most of the shops were unrecognisable and buildings burnt out, vehicles were overturned and had been used as barricades and possibly one of the most disgusting sights were the dead horses. His experiences of the week of the rebellion may be interesting but there were no letters or papers and perishable foodstuffs were very difficult to obtain, and the greatest drawback was not being able to get bread – this difficulty was solved by an early morning tram into the country, where a baker had supplied each person with one loaf and that was at normal prices.

He left Ireland in April of 1918. He was then surprised to read in the Times paper published September 7th, 1918, which a friend had given to him, that he had been mentioned. He could not have gained that distinction had it not been for the loyal support of the wholehearted cooperation that he had received from all the great staff. Again, in 1920, he was ordered to return to Ireland where the position was becoming desperate. British troops in large numbers had been and were being continually drafted to all parts, detachments of various regiments occupying warehouses, prisons and uninhabited mansions. In all cases the NAAFI was called upon to provide a canteen service.

Bloody Sunday horrified everybody. His story, however, more closely concerns the NAAFI activities and difficulties which were from time to time accentuated by the labour troubles. On more than one occasion it was suggested that they were employing other than loyalists. He knew he could only dispute the suggestion and warehouses in common with other trading concerns were searched for firearms. Nothing was discovered although at the end of the war a few of the employees were found to hold positions in the Free State Army.

More than once the lorries were held up by armed men and the driver and the loader taken away and swiftly locked up, often in outhouses, the lorries then driven away and later returned empty to the place where they had been seized; the men were then released and instructed to return with the empty lorry quickly and quietly to the NAAFI. Staff arriving from England were warned off keeping their own opinions to themselves, but despite that 2 or 3 received anonymous letters and telegrams ordering them to leave the country in the interest of all concerned. They did; in one case a person in question was escorted by armed car to Kingston, the port of Dublin.

The duty of the NAAFI was to supply the British Army only, a duty faithfully carried out, and he did this successfully, although this was without protection to life, property, or goods. The only loss of life of the staff was the death by burning of the wife and child of the storekeeper at Newbridge, the base for supplies to the Curragh. On that occasion some of the goods in the store were evidently soaked with petrol and set alight before the storekeeper and his family – they occupied the quarters over the store and were unaware of fire when the floor collapsed. The two inspectors living in the premises adjoining narrowly escaped the fire.

It was forbidden to import such items manufactured in England like biscuits, candles, and cigarettes. It created a difficult proposition and careful consideration was needed as all these goods had to be purchased in Ireland. He was summoned to command HQ and interviewed and then immediately ushered into the Chief's room. He had written a circular, which was in the Chief's hand. He was then told that this had been discussed in 'the house'. From then on in any goods that were imported not only couldn't be handled by any Irish Labour but needed a military escort to protect the personnel and also the warehouses in Dublin and Cork.

Late in 1921 brought a feeling of relief and by February 1922 a large number of British troops had left the country, and the barracks were handed over to the new Irish Free State army. There were negotiations for them to take over some of the warehouses and stock, but this did not mature. He recalls how he was a sick man now and was granted leave to go home to England. He did not return to his old position and was sick for some 8 months. Something which shows the camaraderie and dedication of the staff was that he did not have the opportunity to go back to Ireland and thank his staff for their dedication and service, the faithful resolve in difficult circumstances.

Arthur Carlton held the late Col the honourable CM Ramsey in great esteem and it's claimed that he was an inspiration. Arthur did, however, years later realise that's why he was in Ireland – he had pulled over to help a gentleman who had broken down some miles outside of Dublin. After assisting him and the man had thanked him, he gave him a business card and he put this in his pocket; it was only after he realised that Sir Roger Casement was the gentleman he had helped prior to the rebellion.

Mr Austin Bailey Retires 1937

Mr Austin Bailey was known first and foremost for his signature and in this year 1937 retired from service after 22 years of work within the canteen movement. Mr Bailey had been a member of the London Stock Exchange prior to the 1914-1918 war. He became a special constable and a civilian clerk within the 15th Durham Light Infantry. On the 9th of April 1915 saw him appointed the quartermaster to the battalion and he held that responsible position when his unit went out to France on the 11th of September 1915; it was said that quartermasters are born not made!

He didn't remain long in his regiment – just before Christmas he was invalided home and remained on light duty until the 23rd May 1916; he was then appointed as a Lieutenant, an inspector of canteens under the ACC. This was covering the London district under Maj Astor who became Lord Astor later. He was transferred to Chester in December in 1917 until June 1919 where he served as a captain on the western command staff as an assistant inspector of the quartermaster's general service. Then on the 24th of June 1919 Capt Bailey as he was then known was appointed as an officer in charge of the NACB. Between June 1919 and 1920 he travelled all over France for duties in Flanders, Boulogne and Wimereux.

Late in 1920 he was promoted to major and took charge of the Egyptian branch of the NACB where its headquarters was in Alexandria where post-war reconstruction was taking place, but although this was a peaceful posting the upheaval came when the organisation changed on the 9th of December 1920 from the Navy Army Canteen Board to the Navy Army Air Force Institutes.

In 1923 Maj Bailey was transferred to Chester as an area manager. He was responsible for the conduct of the Institute service for the whole of the western command including the South Irish coast defences. He became assistant secretary to the overseas Institute service and in 1931 assistant secretary to the home Institute service until he retired in 1937.

Royal visit to Edinburgh July 1937

Their majesties the King and Queen visited the Scottish capital on the 8th of July. In the past the city had seen many Royal visits but on this occasion it was something quite special; there was much admiration and affection for King George the 6th, and the warmth and the attachment that the Scots feel towards Queen Elizabeth, as Her Royal Highness is one of their own people.

Their Royal highnesses were greeted with such enthusiasm and masses of people assembled, representing not only the people of Edinburgh but also Scotland. The visit was a week long, which had a historic and powerful appeal for the children. Princess Elizabeth and Princess Margaret were magnificent representations of their generation. The little ladies contributed equally to the Royal visit to Edinburgh, which lived long in the memories of those who were there.

It is recorded that one humorous incident was as follows: ex Sergeant George Alexander, 84, doffed his cap at the Queen as she paused before the parade of "wet" review veterans outside Holyrood House. Alexander leaned over the shoulders of his companions and he looked at the Queen frankly and, in the eye, and addressed her in a rich Scottish accent:- 'Aye, but you're a Bonnie lassie. I should have liked to hae the courtin' o' ye masel'. The Queen apparently smiled broadly, looked at the King, and both broke into laughter.

I think it would be important at this point to note what a wet review was because if you don't come from Scotland you possibly would never have heard of this event.

On the 25th of Aug 1881, 40,624 of all ranks of Scottish volunteers paraded in Queens Park (now called Kings Park) for review by Queen Victoria. Approximately 2 hours before the appointed time there was a cloudburst and no ordinary words can describe the conditions under which the troops paraded. It was considered a crucial test of discipline and not a single accident occurred, nor was there any trouble or disorder. Although over 200 deaths were said to have been directly attributed to this review, there was not much evidence of this.

The Queen herself had to start for the parade half an hour earlier than originally planned. The weather was so bad that at the garden party the rain was that heavy guests were soaked in seconds, and some cars were marooned in flood water, and some of the finery was not so fine after.

The company's connection with the Royal visit was to supply breakfast for 910 regular army and territorial troops and teas for almost 240 in the Waverley market, a barn of a building absolutely devoid of anything in the way of a kitchen, scullery or even a store room – every item of equipment had to be hired including the services of 4 men to lay out the tables and forms and do all the work attendant upon the handling of the equipment. Boilers, hot plates and all the heated items very quickly generated heat.

The Waverley market had 4 service points installed, one for each of the men. All tables were lettered with all the cooperation of the units in lining up their men, and in true style every single one of them was served a hot breakfast within 7 minutes. On their return a cold lunch was laid out by 1330 hrs. Each man's plate had been covered with waxed paper to keep food fresh. On their return there was 20 minutes of silence which showed how much the troops were enjoying their food. Many complimentary remarks were made and an official letter of appreciation from the Scottish command arrived sometime later. Miss JB Miller, the restaurant's Superintendent found this message gratifying, along with the rest of the staff who had worked 12 hours to achieve this success.

1938

The NAAFI entertainment branch and Entertainments National Service Association ENSA 1938

The Entertainments National Service Association, or as we know it, ENSA, began to take shape shortly after the September crisis of 1938 when it was indicated to Mr Basel Dean, that in the event of war, the official work of entertaining the troops both at home and abroad would be entrusted to the Navy Army Air Force Institutes. Accordingly, Mr Dean, who had run the entertainments branch of the Navy and army canteen board during the latter half of the Great War, held preliminary conversations with various professional friends, notably Mr Leslie Henson, Mr Owen Nares, and Mr Godfrey Tearle, with a view to drawing up a report and a plan of organisation for the authorities in the light of the past experience and the conditions of the day. This report was submitted to the NAAFI on the 18th of April 1939. The main principle was that the entertainment world should be left free to carry out the work at which it was expert and for the entertainments branch of the Company to deal with the control of the administration of entertainments. This report was eventually approved by the War Office. In accordance with the plan laid down there and the Entertainments National Service Association came into being as a voluntary mobilisation of all sections of the entertainment world for the purpose of providing all types of entertainment for the troops that might be required from time to time by NAAFI. Sir Seymour Hicks was invited to become the 1st president.

The entertainment branch of the Company was mobilised on the 5th of September 1939 under Mr Dean; he was appointed director of entertainments. Meanwhile, many leading personalities in the entertainment world had accepted either the chairmanship or membership of sections of ENSA. On the 11th of September, Drury Lane Theatre was taken over by NAAFI as the headquarters of the entertainments branch and for the use of ENSA. The list of ENSA sections with then rapidly extended and their membership completed. It was stated that ENSA is fully representative of the entertainment's world.

The first NAAFI concert organised by ENSA was given at Pirbright camp, on the 9th of September, Miss Francis Day and Mr Thorpe Bates being amongst artists who appeared.

On the 25th of September the regular supply of entertainments began, when 12 concert parties were sent out, two of each to the home commands. One-week later cinema and entertainment began, being provided by means of a mobile cinema unit. From that date up to and including the 2nd of March, the total number of admissions to NAAFI shows at home organised by ENSA reached the remarkable total of 2,141,600.

General distribution of both living and cinema entertainment for the British Expeditionary force began on the 22nd of November, although cinema entertainments were provided for a certain section of the RAF in France some weeks prior to that date, certain concerts were given in advance of the general scheme by Miss Gracie Fields. Disregarding the number of attendances at these preliminary entertainments, of which no record has been kept from the 15th of November up to and including the 2nd of March, the total number of admissions to entertainments in France was 1,024,949.

The principle of leaving the entertainment side of the work to professional people was an unqualified success. In no other way could such a huge volume of entertainment have been provided in so short a space of time.

ENSA sections and regional committees – the following is a list of the sections of ENSA that were formed at this time and were in operation in the early days.

In the concert party, Mr Greatrex Newman
Concert: Mr Thorpe Bates,
Dance bands: Mr Jack Hylton,
Hospital concerts: Dame Sybil Thorndike and Miss Lillian Braithwaite,
Musical: Mr Earnest Irving,

Musical plays: Mr Leslie Hanson,
Overseas: Miss Lina Ashwell OBE,
Plays: Mr Godfrey Tearle,
Review: Mr Jack Buchanan,
Variety: Mr Will Hay,
Variety Theatres: Mr George Black.

Later they were added to this list, a Singsong section and a Lecture section, under the chairmanship of Miss Lena Ashwell. They then added a military concert party section under the direction of Mr Cyril Phillips of the Birmingham Repertory Theatre and Mr Herbert Bryan who was responsible for the material.

Influential regional committees were formed in each of the military commands. Included in the membership of these committees were not only the prominent citizens in the districts concerned, but also leading theatrical managers in the provinces and distinguished amateurs, some of whom had been suggested by the British drama League.

With ENSA being such a large part of the organisation in such short amount of time being able to give a brief overview of each of these sections would help understand the magnitude and the difference that it made to every serviceman's life whilst fighting for their country.

Concert parties: 30 different concert parties could be engaged from time to time and the total number of artists engaged in this work was some 250. This also included the service provided by the Scottish committee.

Concert sections: 490 concerts had been given by the spring of 1940 providing work for approximately 3000 artists. This section had given a certain number of classical concerts at the request of commanding officers as well. In each of the cases artists prominent in the concert world, gave plebiscite programmes, chosen by the officers and the men. The classical concerts were at the time an unexpected success.

Players section: The work of the players section did not begin until the November, largely because there wasn't at the outset any buildings available to receive ordinary stage productions. Very shortly the entertainments branch of the NAAFI would be able to arrange a circuit of camp theatres that would enable companies to tour consecutively for 3 or 4 months. Despite the restrictive conditions 243 performances of stage plays had already been given by the spring of 1940. The work of this section had been rapidly extended, not only in the home commands, but also with the BEF, where facilities for the presentation of players had already been provided.

Variety section: Over 720 variety performances by this time had been given in the country. Several musical hall units had been sent to the BEF consisting in all of about 70 different acts. In the home units, 293 acts had already been engaged and in all 480 artists appearing in those acts. Since this section began work, over 1000 acts by this time had been interviewed and auditions had been given to 300.

Dance bands: 40 different dance bands, including nearly all the famous dance bandleaders, had given concerts. Total number given in this country alone was 209, employing 702 musicians.

Many famous dance band leaders had already gone to BEF where they had been outstandingly successful.

Hospital concerts: This section was under the joint chairmanship of Dame Sybil Thorndike and Miss Lillian Braithwaite; by this time they had done notable work. It had already given 69 concerts and prepared for a wide extension of the work. The type of concert given was a specially selected with a view to cater for the particular needs of the patients.

Overseas section: They were mainly concerned with the organising and the selection of the companies for work with the BEF. Although at the time this work did not begin until towards the end of November, 31 companies had already gone overseas employing over 480 artists. A large number of the stars had also gone overseas, including Sir Seymore Hicks, Gracie Fields, Lesley Hanson, Jack Buchanan, Claire Luce, Mai Bacon, Binnie Hale, Violet Lorraine, Lupino Lane, Ralph Reader, Will Fyffe, George Formby, Joe Loss, Billy Cotton, Victoria Hopper, Dennis Noble, etc.

Singsongs: The work began in the middle of November 1939; it provided parties of 3 or 4 who toured the smaller camps in a small van, equipped with a piano and supplied with sheet music. This type of entertainment requires no stage appointments and it is designed to supply the entertainment needs of isolated units. During the month of February, it had 17 parties working in England and Wales. By the beginning of April there had also been 8 singsong parties at work with the BEF. The section also provided a very large number of accordion players who gave a one-man concert to 'Searchlight' units and other very small formations. Within the 'Searchlight' units they also had small EFI establishments providing for their canteen needs. The total number of artists engaged by this section since its beginning and up until the April was 126. The average number of shows given in England per week up to this date was approximately 100 singsongs, whilst accordion players averaged between one hundred and 125 shows per week.

The lecture section: It began operations with the BEF, in November 1940. A large number of well-known and distinguished lecturers would visit the BEF at regular intervals. Mr Will Hay lectured on astronomy and also on the wireless. Although the provision of cinema entertainments did not come within the scope of ENSA's work, the Company had been given the cinema division. The film renters had at all times desired to be cooperative in the work. And from there in addition to ENSA there was also FENSA. This committee operated within NAAFI in the provision of the films for the BEF. FENSA was also congratulated on the men in France seeing the very latest films, many of which have not been generally released in the country at that time. Their Majesties the King and Queen, on the 24th of November 1939, honoured Drury Lane with a visit, which forms the subject of a separate account.

Copyright Sue A Lowe

The ENSA, rationing of entertainments 1938

To cope with the enormous number of requests for entertainment it then became apparent that the system would have to be devised in controlling the allocation and distribution of what was available. This was not only for the home commands but also the units of the BEF. Each command HQ at home was notified within a month of the amount of entertainment they were to receive in the following month. They were allocated by the area entertainment officers and managers of parties that report for detailed instructions. A similar system was set up in France with BEF. The professional entertainment to an army in war in its scale was without precedent in our entire history or in the history of any other nation. When the work began it was intended that the entertainment should be one of the additional amenities provided for his majesty's forces by NAAFI, when taking into account the amount of people at each one it becomes a bit of a national issue. It had proved very fortunate for the troops that the original scheme was made so flexible and proved capable of such rapid expansion. They wanted to make sure that very few mistakes would be made but with such a new entity issues were bound to arise. The criticism was only to be expected, much of it was misdirected, and the rest of it was ill informed, not to mention some of it was quite spiteful. After a visit to Drury Lane Theatre, the quartermaster general expressed himself as quite satisfied that the work was proceeding on the right guidelines. Criticism, though, had fallen under the same 4 headings:

#1 After the 11 weeks of totally free entertainment, the War Office and the air ministry decided that there should be small charges for admission to all NAAFI entertainments. It had not been fully realised that the entertainment on this huge scale would have proved a serious drain upon the resources of NAAFI. After they grew accustomed to the free shows the troops had difficulty and realised that without any reduction in the total cost a charge made for admission would assist NAAFI to provide more entertainments. They had to take into account the high cost of transport and the necessity of giving shows to very small audiences; these service entertainments could never be expected to pay their way. Certain classes of entertainment remained free such as Singsongs, which were popular everywhere. Whereas in France a certain amount of the entertainment was charged for, a purely nominal price, but by far the larger part was provided free.

#2 Sometimes they had complaints of vulgarity. In cases where the complaints had been proved firm disciplinary action was taken. On the whole entertainments had been remarkably free from this time. They had to take due regard of the fact that in a citizen army, all tastes and opinions must be represented, which meant that some people did get offended. Then there was the other end of the scope, some complained that the entertainment was too high brow and light, while others seemed to take the entertaining the troops as the opportunity for undue licence. The taste of the officers is not always the same as the taste of the men and the appreciation varies from unit to unit. Finding a reasonable middle course was difficult but necessary.

#3 There had been criticisms of the chaotic arrangements in France. There were obvious reasons for this as the provision for entertainments in BEF had to be made under strict conditions. Any entertainments for the distribution had to be secret under the most careful nature; this meant that they were liable to cancellation or alteration at any time. And as you can imagine, when this happened a certain amount of disorganisation was inevitable. But when you think about it, everybody was quite new to this and they stayed behind the lines of an army in war.

The spirit that had been displayed by the majority of the artists in such harsh conditions that nobody was used to was not only had the parties which been taken over by Mr Henson, Mr Buchanan and Mr Fyffe and the other leaders in the theatre and variety worlds, including Mr Joe Las and Mr Billy Cotton of the dance band section, and they all displayed notable spirit and cheerfulness in the face of major mishaps and also a vast majority of lesser known artists had conducted themselves in a manner which brings great credit to not only the company but also to the profession. It would be fair to mention that where there had been poor leadership it was obviously magnified, and people sought publicity for complaints in the popular press. Generally, the discipline under which EFI was liable to was also imposed upon the entertainment parties as well. There were many that thought that this took away from the artists, but it was necessary. Everyone in this war had to go through and endure discomfort and even hardship for the national interest. There were only one or two drama queens who were not happy with the conditions.

Unfortunately, the tendency of some artists to voice their complaints meant that a crop of them were published in the press. These stories were immediately examined and in most cases proved to be exaggerated or untrue, and often gave rise to the circumstances to almost be found duly necessary to the restrictions of the war time environment and the abnormal weather conditions, although mostly from the failure to observe the simple regulations that were laid down by the military.

When you think about it, as in the press today, there was no doubt that if there had been more news imported from France the majority of the stories about ENSA would never have been printed at all. Then returning prosperity of the entertainment world had become necessary to impress the national importance after work that NAAFI and ENSA were doing, not only on the public stage but also the artists themselves. This work could never be carried out without the guidance and financial support of NAAFI who provided a great deal of the much-needed employment for artists. The corporation's financial arrangements for the payment of artists were made in close cooperation with various professional bodies. Some embarrassment had been caused by artists and musicians of standing offering to give their services for free for the entertainments, whilst ENSA artists in need of employment had been paid. This suggested that the standard of rates of pay by the Corporation were unnecessary and not appreciated, but actually of course this was contrary to the case.

Arrangements had been made with the BBC for the broadcasting of what was known as the ENSA half hour; it did so much more to publicise the work of ENSA, in highlighting the first-class entertainment provided now on the wireless for BEF. The ENSA half hour, which started off as a trial, was contributed to by all sections of ENSA; this included parties, who at the time had just been to BEF or were just coming back. The broadcasts were made as part of a scheme for service entertainments and they aimed to give both the public and the troops an amount of general information. Through the Theatre it had been inadequately represented during the first six months of ENSA, this was not due to reluctance on the part of the Theatre to join in its national work; it was due to the fact that there were practically no suitable buildings available for theatrical performances. This was swiftly remedied on both sides of the channel and theatres did not want to lag behind and surely after a short period were leading the many sections of ENSA. Many leading actors and actresses were included in performances for the BEF moving forward. On the completion of the first six months of the entertainment service provided for the troops by ENSA and the NAAFI, a tribute to all those who worked hard at Drury Lane and elsewhere for the success of the scheme. They paid tribute to not only the sectional and regional committees, but also the staff at Drury Lane and the director and all the members of the Institute and the entertainments branch. The value of what had been done in this short time is inestimable and no doubt it was realised by the War Office and the air ministry with no support and the Corporation's continued success of the ENSA, FENSA and the NAAFI entertainment branch was assured.

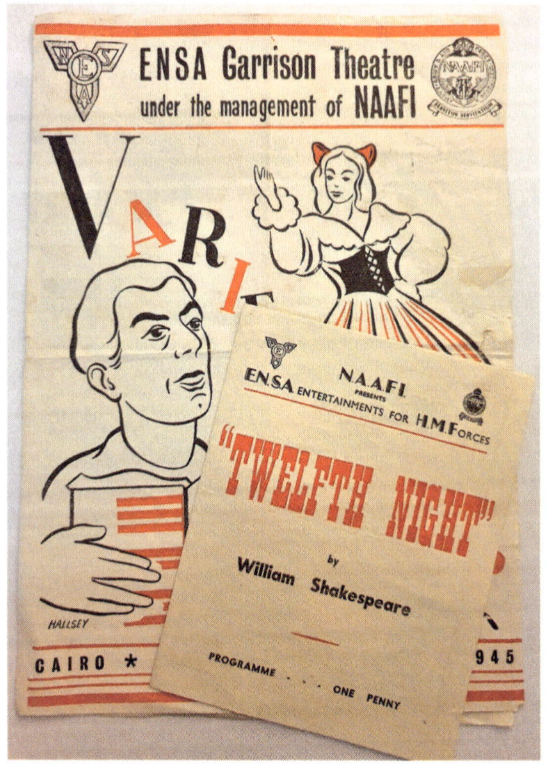

1939

Plans for headquarter evacuation 1939

On the 29th of April 1939 the government issued a circular in which it was recommended that arrangements should be made in advance by large businesses and organisations in congested areas, particularly in London, to move to a neutral area in anticipation of hostilities to come.

Considering this advice, the search began over an area within a radius of about 20 miles of South West and West of London for buildings into which the nucleus of the headquarter administrative and clerical staff could be moved at short notice. After a series of disappointments, a suitable building had been found near Claygate in Surrey. At this point in time plans were firmly underway to make the move to Claygate.

As part of the scheme for evacuation it was intended to begin to de-centralise the work at the home accounts branch, the personnel of which would be divided into 5 sections; the home accounts central office to be accommodated at HQ, home accounts sub offices at Liverpool, York, Aldershot and Salisbury. The decentralization would not have normally been done if it hadn't been for the impending war to come.

The new uniform 1939

This uniform was quite something, as it has now become an iconic representation of NAAFI. The new blue uniform had been selected for the female staff. This would replace the white overalls and cook hats that had been worn since the conception of the company.

It is written "it is one of an attractive type which is becoming to the brunette and blonde alike", it would be simple, it comprised a smartly cut blue overall with short sleeves and a double breasted effect formed by 2 rows of white buttons. The overall fastens on the shoulder, and on the right breast is the corporation's badge embroidered in white. The collar is upright with two effective points in front at the neckline. At the back at the waistline there is a small belt like the belt on the guard's great man's coat. No ties are worn with this uniform. The hat has a small pointed effect, it is slotted with white adjustable ties, and finished by a white bow at the back of the head. The overall is short and is completed with black stockings and shoes. These uniforms were gradually issued to all staff concerned.

The cook's uniforms had also changed, the specially selected low necked overall of white, bound with blue, with the badge in blue on the right breast. There is no belt in front at the waist, but the one at the back. The cook's cap is the same as the tam-o-shanter type and was appreciated by all that wore it.

This new uniform was one of many to happen as the country entered WWII. The Institute had some great challenges ahead.

The Auxiliary Territorial Service 1939

The ATS had recently been inaugurated from the women's corps and The Institute decided that this new body of women would be to interest staff, in this time of war or emergency that they would be working so closely with each other. The Auxiliary territorial service had been formed as part of the Territorial Army. It had its own officers, NCOs and the troops were divided into cooks, clerks, store women and orderlies. There were also some women motor driving companies mainly recruited from the women's transport service known for so long as F.A.N.Y.s (first aid nursing yeomanry). The women of the Institute already knew parts of the job the ATS would do, for example cooking and clerking for the men of the services.

The controllers of the ATS so far appointed for the various areas were HRH The Princess Royal, Lady Violet Astor and the Duchess of Devonshire. They were the chief commandants and senior commanders in charge of the districts, in charge of the district's company commanders and deputy company commanders in charge of the companies, with company assistance to help them in the large companies. The NCOs consisted of senior leaders, section leaders and assistant section leaders. There were local service companies who, when mobilised, worked in their own neighbourhood and there were general service companies who were attached to a unit and were mobile in time of war. Some companies were for general duties and consisted of cooks, clerks, store women and orderlies, others were clerical companies only, and others again were composed of only motor drivers.

Enrolment in the corps was 4 years' voluntary service in peacetime, but in the event of mobilisation they would automatically become part of the army for the duration and going into nearly all areas. The volunteers in the companies were very keen, although were only needed to attend 10 drills a year, once a week to be the general rule nearly everywhere. Almost all of the members of the ATS worked during the day, and meetings took place generally in the evening. Some of the lessons they learned: army organisation, messing, hygiene, first aid, and other activities including physical training and drill. There was at this time some questions as to why bother to train women in drill. But they had overlooked the sense of discipline that it gives the body, the mind and the real sense of worth, and they realised in asking this question and understanding the answers was that the ATS ladies were not to be playing at soldiers and it was really useful for steady discipline and training.

Still at this stage many of the companies had not got their uniforms which were provided free by the state for volunteers and the officers were given an allowance for ordering their own. Measuring all the women was going on and before long they all were equipped with the uniform which was very much like the WAACs – this consisted in the last war, as a khaki coat and skirt with collar and tie with a peaked cap but the coat was made on the same pattern as the Royal Air Force coat, without a leather belt.

When mobilised they would use the same facilities as the men, being the canteens of the EFC. At this point they knew that it would be very likely that on mobilisation of the Institute staff that the NAAFI would come into very close contact with the members of the ATS.

Something to be noted about the women of our armed forces was the varying nicknames that were given to them. The ATS was already being referred to as the WATS. The WAAC, WRNS and the FANYs, were nicknamed, "The Wacks, The Wrens and the Fannys" during the war. Nicknames during that time were usually a term of affection and the members of the Institute called the Naffys but after a time they ended up calling it themselves.

Dover by Maj EW Shepherd

Dead on time the boys walk through,
We stand ready we girls in blue,
Whether goods, you bet your dollars,
For we've got NAAFI on our collars,

We know well what the boys all need,
A cheery smile and a good old feed!
On they come like a living River,
Burbling onions, chips and liver!
(Superior boys say "Horlicks milk"
No cotton for them, they are used to silk.
Not for them the Nelson cake,
That's not what their mothers bake)

It's a life of fun, full of downs and ups,
Teas and dances, plates, and cups,
Camps, inspections, sunshine, storm,
And always the good old HQ form.

We wonder when we get to heaven
Shall we still be known as 527?
Shall we be serving Angels then
As now we serve our serving men

"527" R (Dover Castle)

The Expeditionary Force Institutes B E F by the officer commanding EFI N V P 1939

On the 4th of December 1939 a visit was paid to the BEF zone in France by His Majesty the King. The Royal party, who were met at the port of disembarkations by the commander in chief and the Adjutant general, included the Duke of Gloucester, Sir Alexander Hardinge and Col Piers Legh. A strenuous inspection of the BEF followed. Something like 100 miles a day being covered by road. On the 7th of December President Lebrun and Mr M Daladier lunched with the King, who had earlier in the day inspected half the GHQ area under battalion of guards drawn up in their billeted areas. On the 12th of December, General Lord Gort issued an order of today in which he published the following message from the King: "It has given me the greatest pleasure to visit the troops under your command in France, and the days which I have been able to spend among them have been full of interest, for I have been able to see for myself something of the conditions in which they are living and of the work on which they are engaged. I am satisfied from all points of view that the British soldier is at least the equal of his predecessor, both in efficiency and spirit. I send my best wishes to all of the BEF and assure them of the complete and unfailing confidence placed in them by their fellow countrymen."

Looking back at the first six months of the war and their own activities during that time, tribute must be paid to those had prepared the ground for sending a canteen organisation abroad. The immense amount of work which is studied in detail of the various branches of our organisation was designed to meet every possible contingency in an undertaking in which, from a tactical and operational point of view, little could be foreseen.

If that work fell short of the mark in matters of minor detail, it undoubtedly laid a firm foundation upon which the first five hundred men were sent overseas in a very short time. Those of them who were called upon to assume positions of administrative responsibility abroad have good reason to remember with considerable appreciation the work of those who had so admirably paved our way.

I shall also retain my earliest impression of the splendid way in which our own NAAFI staff responded to the first summons to serve with the EFI and one could only regard with extreme satisfaction and pride, the way in which they pulled into Kennington from every district in the area, cheerful and eager to do their bit, a characteristic attribute of our regular fellows if my experience of their service in emergencies in any condition.

The main bodies of the original Expeditionary force proceeded overseas in two parties, each to a separate destination. The officers who were charged with the command of these parties had no small task before them. They were going to an unknown destination where no NAAFI organisation existed, and with but a hazy idea of what they would find when they got there. They arrived with their parties intact despite such difficulties and anxieties as entraining, embarking, and disembarking, rationing, train, and ship duties on route, and finally billeting their men at the bases which they would eventually arrive.

In the meantime, the supply officers who were in charge of the transport, were competing with similar problems and difficulties in bringing their motor vehicles over by a different route, and they too, soon joined up with the main bodies.

The officers in charge of these 2 parties lost no time in making the necessary arrangements for the reception and warehousing of their first shipments of stores and equipment. In spite of the fact that the first shipment of stores for one party was dispatched by the military to a port at which we least expected its arrival, a situation which necessitated the urgent organization of a transit staff, it was not too long before the service of the troops was established at the bases while, in addition, supplies of essential comforts such as cigarettes, chocolate biscuits, toilet requisites, etc. Some 20 lines in all, was sent forward in large quantities to the bulk issue stores (BIS), which had been set up by those officers who had been sent forward in advance. From these various units they were able to obtain supplies in bulk for the troops.

The other parties had, in the meantime, established itself and in a comparatively short space of time the officer in charge, after completing his preliminary arrangements, pushed forward to make sure contact with the Royal Air Force, where with the able assistance of his subordinate officers, he laid the foundations of what was a large and flourishing area. In addition to warehouses and offices, this includes some 150 establishments.

Since the early and somewhat hectic days, the business started to gradually settle down to a more normal routine. Everyone profited from the experience and all learnt to fit themselves into the intricacies of the military methods and to learn a good deal of the army routine which was so essential to any organisation which was working with and for the troops on active service.

Conditions were always improving and as is the standard of the service to the forces. Furnishings manufactured in France, indoor games from home, the purchases of the innumerable pianos and wireless sets will, when completed. The free issue of sports gear and the daily issue of newspapers by the EFI, to the units, which provided both outdoor recreation and in constant touch with home news and the world outside. Cinemas, live entertainment undoubtedly played a large part in keeping the troops cheerful. A separate article has been devoted to this branch of our organisation in France, although I doubt whether it will include all of the details of the effort and energy of those who are responsible for the extraordinary number of performances which already entertained thousands of troops which the entertainment branch was justly proud. There was a great deal of work done. With the reorganization of the areas an extension of the supplies Depot, a good deal of improvement was affected. The installation of mineral water factories and bakeries went far to improve the service to BEF. In conclusion the sterling work done by all officers, non-commissioned officers and men in the initial stages of setting up the Expeditionary Force Institute in France was second to none and was greatly valued by the British Expeditionary Force.

GHQ EFI and a good game of darts by SSM F Wilson 1939

Camaraderie is something which keeps all personnel going in time of war whereon this account definitely outlines this was in abundance even during the start of the war.

Some fellows here are members of that most noble order of darters, the qualifications being the ability to throw a 'pretty one', and to fall in with all the good things that go with this game, which is very popular here and if the ability to throw a pretty one is a sign of a misspent youth, then all I can say is that it has never interfered with the normal growth of our life, at least amongst the members here.

The officers were "given" a dart board and the other ranks "found" one and you know how it is, sooner or later with the game of darts, one or other gets the idea that he can take on the world, and so one day the other ranks thought it would be a good thing to take the officers on. Sit back and imagine a cosy little room in a quiet little town in wherever, good company, and the stage is set. Well the O.R.s who thought it was easy meat, won the first, the officers the second, and in the decider, our adjutant's got away with a double Top in his 1st start, his 2nd went for the double 5, and the 3rd the treble 12 which, of course, gave the officers a great deal of encouragement; needless to say that in the second round, the officers get pegging away, and all returned on average over 50 throughout the game!

Some going but the other ranks could not get off and were behind 400. They, however, struggled on and had about 120 to go, when the Col brought one "out the bag" (let's say 2) and got one and 11 to win the game for the officers. This as you may well imagine put "down the house". But one of the lads who evidently suspected hidden talent from an unknown quantity, previously reminded him that he was wanted by Q maintenance, but the plea fell on deaf ears with disastrous results.

Our second in command, Maj Tanner, who kept helping to keep the party alive by insinuating that wicked game called 'cricket' you know the game 'that's not cricket' unless you happen to be on the winning side, and it's believed that this is where the other ranks found their feet a bit.

However, so much for our game of darts and thanks all round for a very enjoyable evening. Still the OR (other ranks) are getting in some practice and live to fight another day.

Naturally, on active service, the opportunities for sport and other club activities must give way to the agencies of the service but although lacking in action, the sporting spirit is there and we will survive as, to use a nautical term, 'we are in a good ship'.

Quite a number of us have spent quite a while travelling around and seeing things, but we are now settling down, and arrangements are well in hand to make our staff billet for the ranks a home from home, as we have managed to convert a spare room into a reading and writing room with something borrowed here and something granted there, and we still have our doubts for use in the room with such games as chess and draughts etc. This will be a real boost to us, as there is little to do in the few spare hours at our disposal, except to visit our local cafe or go to bed. One must mention, however, that the very fine shows put on in this locality by the NAAFI entertainments branch and ENSA, where we have all been privileged at some time or other to see "our Gracie" and such shows as Leslie Hanson's party, Harold Halt's party, Ralph Reader with 8 lads from the gang show and Jack Bracken's show. After this match they had also started fixing up a chess match with a local unit as well as a darts match with an RAF component.

Entertainment organised for the British Expeditionary Force 1939

The very first entertainment organised by the EFI took place on the 15th of November, under the personal supervision of Mr Basil Dean, director of entertainments, for the Institutes. Miss Grace Fields, the star attraction, was supported by Sir Seymour Hicks and many well-known English artists. Two performances were given. From this state the performances were hurried forward, and several officers arrived in the country on the 17th of November to organise both cinema and living entertainment. Four small mobile cinema vans, with films 16mm proceeded to the forward areas and commenced operations. These light 10 cwt, Ford vans, equipped with projecting apparatus and screens, were able to find the outlying stations and give performances to the troops in barns, old garages, and any convenient hall.

Five standard mobile units (35 mm) arrived in the L of C area at the beginning of December and gave 10 performances per night for the first few weeks. Two mobile units (35mm) visited the striking force and gave 4 performances nightly. By the middle of December, with the arrival of a further four small vans, some 17 units were operating, giving 34 performances per night. Organised living entertainment commenced on the 28th of November.

Lesley Hanson, Sir Seymour Hicks, and Ralph Reader Parties toured the forward areas AASF and L of C, giving 2 performances per night. By the 3rd week in December some 12 parties were distributed throughout the country, giving nightly entertainment. Figures available show that during the month of December there were 532 cinema shows with an attendance of 118,266 personnel, 274 living entertainment shows were attended by 230,989 personnel. During January the numbers were 384 shows at the cinema with attendance of 90,837, 243 living entertainment shows attended by 241,199 personnel. The only occasions on which any performance had been cancelled would have been during periods of bad weather or through military restrictions.

Even in the midst of all the doom and gloom for this year, it goes to show the boys and girls never left home without a sense of humour; it would be fair to say that even in today's language back in the 1940s it wasn't that dissimilar when trying to communicate in French:

> Two soldiers went into a village to get some bread. One said to the other, "Leave it to me, chum, I can do the lingo." They went into a shop and he of the lingo said to the lady at the counter, "La pain?" The lady at the counter replied, "lapin, monsieur," and then went behind and brought him a live rabbit!

The women and how they fitted in, 1939

Where it would be fair to say that the European war brought anxiety to not only us but to every human being in the land, it also brought a phenomenal unity and friendly way to everyone, even the casual passer-by. They passed through a very cold winter the coldest it had ever been since 1881 and the darkness of the streets had also made it quite depressing for most people in the country. They welcomed the longer days again despite all the misgivings as to the use our enemies may make of them. The ladies of NAAFI had to work hard, and they joined in their hundreds as they said at the time: 3 Cheers to the unlimited number of old employees who returned to work, they loved. They came offering their loyal and welcome service to the Company from the bottom of their heart. Many of them came with a heavy heart knowing that their soldier, sailor or airmen husbands and friends had gone to the front; they and others who had been parted from their children all to help the nation's calls. The one aim and one aim only was to give the best possible service to the men who were fighting in the war which had been thrust upon them.

It would be safe to say that NAAFI was in every place and on every ship alongside all those serving for our country and His Majesty the King.

1940–1949

1940

Vincent O'Brien and EFI men watched as 300 NAAFI men died when SS Lancastria was Bombed 17th June1940

There about 1200hrs NAAFI men in our compound in the forest of Blain in the West of France when, on Saturday the 16th of June, our siesta was rudely interrupted. We were told to get our things together and be ready to move out.

Canteen stocks were thrown open to the troops except for the bottles of wines and spirits which was smashed with crowbars, the liquor being allowed to mingle with the dust of the French Orchard. Some fellows grabbed boot polish, writing pads and such, but the wise men took razor blades, tobacco, cigarettes and less valuable but very welcome later, chocolate. We travelled by truck through the night seeing the glow of several large fires here and there. These are rumoured to be fuel dumps. As we approached St Nazaire, we had to march some considerable distance.

During the fallout, we lay down in a group on the floor of a factory and slept for a few hours. We were up and about with the sun and there was Khaki as far as the eye could see. The highlight of the morning was the mail distribution. I was amazed to find there were two or three letters for me as I thought, all was not lost yet.

We were kept moving in short marches through the environs of St Nazaire. About midday there was a big steel barrel at a wide road junction with a roaring fire under it. Soon there was tea brewing. We didn't know then but that was the last team we would drink for two or three days. We were amongst the last of the British army to reach the quayside and there were 300 of us on the last tender to leave shore.

We had to leave our kit bags and luggage on the quay as there was no room for them. We headed for a big liner away out in the Bay. Were about halfway there when we heard the aircraft and the guns firing. We crouched down on the bottom of the boat. Soon the surface of the water turned white with stunned or dead fish floating belly up.

As we drew nearer the ship, we saw start it was the Oronsay. Suddenly we heard the noise of a dive bomber and looking up, we saw it diving out of the sun straight down at the Oronsay. When it seemed to be about 10 feet from the deck it looped upwards and the bombs released. They said that two of the bombs dropped over the side and bounced off the superstructure. There was one hell of a bang and the ship disappeared in a cloud of smoke and splinters. But as the smoke cleared, we saw the ship sitting there serenely as before.

We were stopped in our tracks but soon on the go again and circled the ship to the Leeward side. As soon as we boarded we were instructed to drop our overcoats and equipment to make our way up to one of the top decks where we were lined up in rows of three with clothing loose and boots undone ready to swim for it. We were warned not to move around as the ship was top heavy, so we stayed put.

Our range of vision was limited but I noticed that where the Lancastria had been there was only some patches of burning oil and small boats moving around. We remained at anchor until dusk and then we were moving at last and so ended the most eventful day in my life. When we arrived in Plymouth all the healthy lads had to stay put until the wounded had been taken ashore.

I think it was a Tuesday when we finally disembarked and marched through Plymouth. I was deeply touched by the cigarettes, sandwiches, fruit and confectionery which the crowd had held out as we marched along. Have I earned it I remarked, my thoughts were similar that, apart from the last 48 hours we had been living it up in full and plenty for six to eight weeks, while these good people would be denying themselves to support us?

One of the boys brought us an evening paper which reported that there had been an evacuation of the western French port, without a single casualty. My faith in press honesty crumbled at that moment. As the truth of it around 300 NAAFI men had died when the Lancastria was bombed and it was not being reported.

Later that night we boarded a train for London and arrived at EFI HQ in Bishopsford Road, Mitcham the next day.

NAAFI blackest day 17th of June 1940 by Michael Walker

In March 1914, Anchor Line of Glasgow ordered a new ship from a Clyde shipyard. The ship was to be named the Tyrrhenia. The First World War intervened and the Tyrrhenia was not launched until May 1920. Before she was completed, she had been bought from Anchor Line by the Cunard steamship company. Due to the delay in completion, to her design being different to any other Cunard and to the fact that she changed hands before completion, she was always looked upon as the odd ship of the Cunard line. Built to sail at 17 knots, the 16,700-tonne ship had six passenger decks to carry nearly 2000 passages in comfort, as well as having extensive cargo capacity. The name proved to be a stumbling block with the travelling public, who could neither pronounce it nor spell it correctly, so in 1924 her name was changed to the Lancastria. Since the 14th century, sailors have believed that changing a ship's name spelt disaster. The story of the disaster which overtook the Lancastria, as related by NAAFI survivors, was now told by Michael Walker.

In 1940 a 16,700-tonne luxury liner taking troops of the British Expeditionary force from the French beaches was sunk by bombers of the Luftwaffe's Kampfgeschwader 30. The ship was the SS Lancastria, lying at anchor in Quiberon Bay, off St Nazaire, with about 6000 troops on board. The Lancastria received a direct hit and sank within half an hour. Some 4000 or more men died in what may have been the worst disaster in maritime history and is certainly the worst single human tragedy in NAAFI for 50 years.

Over 300 of those on board the Lancastria were NAAFI men in the uniform of the RASC EFI. Many had trekked hundreds of miles, bringing with them millions of francs from the canteens they had to abandon to the advancing Germans. All of them considered themselves lucky to have got a place on the Lancastria – England and safety could only have seemed a few hours away when the bombers struck.

Two of the EFI survivors still worked for NAAFI at headquarters in 1970 when this account was first written. On the 17th of June they recall the nightmare of Saint Nazaire as they remember lost comrades. Geoff Singleton in years to come would work in the wages branch and Bunny Burrows in the prices branch, but in 1940 they were both swimming for their lives in oil waters where the Lancastria sank. They had both been working in Rheims with the advanced air striking force when the German advance forced the BEF back to the beaches. They were pulled back to Nantes and from there went to Saint Nazaire to be ferried back to the UK.

From Nantes they had army trucks to take them just outside Saint Nazaire, then they marched on to the port. Mr Burroughs recalled, 'we got there at about dawn on the 17th of June, the day France accepted the German surrender terms. The Lancastria could not get into the port because the water was too shallow, so she anchored out in the sea roads. They took us out on small lighters.'

Nearby the liner SS Oronsay was also loaded with troops to take them back to England, there were seven other passenger ships, six destroyers, and two armed trawlers. Two of the other liners had already been bombed, the Franconia had been put completely out of action, and the Teiresias sunk. During that morning the German pilots attacked Oronsay. 'Around about midday, they sent home Heinkels and bombed out the Oronsay,' said Mr Burrows. 'Then they came back later for us.'

The Oronsay was hit on the bridge, and although much of the steering gear was put out of action, she was able to get underway and steam about the harbour, making a difficult target for the German bombers. The 550-foot-long Lancastria still at anchor, was a more tempting target.

The bombers returned at 1550 hrs in the afternoon. 'I was in the dining room, having a late lunch. There was a great explosion, and then all sorts of chaos. People were jumping over the side of the ship. It began to sink very soon after it was hit. The dining room was only one deck down, so it was easy to get up to the main deck from her, everybody ran upstairs.

Mr Singleton had finished his meal and was on the deck when the Lancastria was hit. 'The deck was where I was, was one of those with the glass around the side, and we smashed the glass panel with a rifle butt to get out. We had to be careful not to push the glass down on people already in the sea, which was covered in oil. We then had broken the glass, they climbed up and slid down the inside of the listing ship. It was a lovely sunny day and the water was not cold,' continued Mr Singleton. 'I was a fairly good swimmer, I don't remember being afraid that I would not get picked up. There were lots of other ships about. I swam away from the ship because I thought it would suck us down when it sank. I looked back and I could see that it had turned over and there were people on the keel.'

In fact, a number of men stayed on the ship until it finally sank. They were singing, 'there will always be in England' and 'roll out the barrel'.

'I found myself with Bunny Burrows. We took most of our clothes off to make it easier for us to swim. With them was a sailor who could not swim. None of them had lifebelts. The two NAAFI men took him with them and tried to keep him afloat, but they lost him as the swirling tide began to disperse the swimmers. Mr Singleton was in the water for about half an hour before he was picked up by a French trawler. He was taken to the SS John Holt which, with five other ships escorted by the armed trawlers HMS Agate and HMS Cambridgeshire, had arrived in Quiberon Bay at seven that morning after a voyage from Newport.'

Mr Burrows was also in the water for about half an hour before he too was picked up by a French trawler and taken to the Oronsay. Major CV Petit was second in command of the RASC EFI saving the advanced air striking force. 'Major Heart was another officer commanding,' he explained, 'and we were operating about 120 canteens in northern France right up to the Maginot line. As the EFI man pulled back they destroyed any stores they could not carry. Receipts from the canteens had been deposited in a French bank. Heart went to the bank with an armed party and seized the NAAFI credits, which amounted to about 7 million francs, and took them to Saint Nazaire, then arranged for the money to be taken to England. The money arrived safely in Falmouth at just about the same time as the Lancastria was sunk.'

Major Petit boarded the Lancastria at about 1100 hrs and after a visit to his cabin, had a meal. Then he returned to his cabin to sleep. He was awakened by the explosion when the Lancastria was hit at 1550 hrs. He rushed up on the deck, where the confusion was, and gave his life jacket to two of his men who could not swim. He later heard that he had been picked up and landed safely in England. He himself slid down the side of the ship and found a clear line of water through the massive floating oil. He struck out vigorously and was soon clear of the ship.

Planes then started machine gunning the figures in the water, dropping incendiary bombs. Some 160 tons of fuel oil was seeping from the Lancastria's tanks, but the flashpoint of the oil was high; although one incendiary burned for some time, it failed to set fire to the fuel. The Lancastria sank at 1618 hrs, just 20 minutes after the attack. Major Petit was still swimming at 1800 hrs. It was then he found a floating deck chair. It was built of teak, very buoyant and gave him considerable confidence. As daylight vanished, he saw the destroyer HMS Highlander and leaving the deck chair, swam for the ship. He was spotted by the assistant paymaster and with the help of two sailors, climbed the Jacob's ladder onto the deck. A sub lieutenant handed him a tot of rum. The following day, the survivors on board the Highlander were transferred to the Oronsay. Due to the bomb damage sustained by the liner, all the charts had been lost, and the captain brought the Oronsay back on the 23-hour journey to Plymouth with a strained motoring map of France and a compass as his sole discretional equipment.

In 1945, Major Petit formed the Lancastria Survivors Association which met for a parade, a service of Remembrance, and a reunion each June. Due to the major's poor health from 1969 to 1971, the reunions had not been held; it was from a hospital bed he spoke to NAAFI news of his memories of June 1940. Mr Burrows and Mr Singleton and other survivors then met informally on the 17th of June to raise a glass in Remembrance of lost colleagues. In June of 1971 Major CV Petit had unfortunately passed away, and one of the other survivors said it seemed likely and perhaps fitting, that the Lancastria Survivors Association would die with the major as he was not only its founder but also its life force.

A fourteen-day miracle 1940

The central Institute for the AASF was requisitioned Somewhere in France on the 2nd of March 1940 and then officially opened on the 16th of March 1940. The canteen offered a full restaurant service, breakfast, dinner, tea and supper, for all ranks; it was open for 12 hours a day. A full range of indoor games was available and there was also a piano and a wireless radio. The first menu was arranged for a football match, between the two service teams, which comprised a full roast dinner followed by apple tart and cream with cheese and biscuits and all the trimmings.

The photographs that accompany this article, to a large extent tell their own story as they show what the premises looked like when it was taken over, and how it appeared when it was officially opened by the Air Commodore, only 14 days later. The official opening was followed by a game of darts between the Air Commodore and the officer in charge of EFI. The Air Commodore insisted on throwing the first dart and he was also the winner at 101 up.

The premises as requisitioned 2/3/40.

Facilities for Darts.

Also, in March of that year, somewhere in France on the 30th of March, a premises was opened in the first hutted Institute. This comprised a restaurant, a small corporal's room, and was built in the spare time, by a company of Royal Engineers. The photographs show what can be done in a wartime situation to bring comfort and a piece of home to service personnel; it was preferable to the tented option that the EFI was running until it was finished and then they moved in.

NAAFI khaki outdoor uniform 1940

With the change to the new blue, mock double-breasted, iconic uniforms also came a change to the civilian women's uniform. The management decided that they should wear a uniform of Khaki which they were all proud of. It was one of the smartest in the country and many outside the service were very curious to know who they were and what they were. Every service man and woman knew, but when it came to the time, they used to be mistaken for the Canadian Air Force or the Australian ATS one, which amused them as the onlooker thought this but didn't think to ask.

The uniform for general staff comprised a tunic and skirt, 2 khaki blouses, 2 ties, khaki felt hat with bronze badge in front on the hat band and a good Mackintosh, provided free by the Company. On the strap of the tunic or shoulder titles.

NAAFI on a Navy-blue background (for the Navy),

Red letters (for the army),

Pale blue edges (for the Air Force).

These titles are also shown on the Macintosh straps and look very attractive.

As the voided cap badge was issued about a year later with the 2 collar badges only the RAF style shoulder titles were issued.

Khaki stockings and Brown Lotus make shoes were purchased from the Company; this was a cost to the member of staff. The manageress' uniform was similar in cut and type to the general staff, but the manageresses were supplied with 2 tussore shirt blouses and 2 khaki ties. The felt hat with bronze badge and Macintosh were as for general staff and were supplied free of charge. If the manageresses cared to, they might purchase a greatcoat in khaki at their own expense.

Restaurant and welfare superintendents and Staff were supplied with the uniform of similar cut but differing from others in having navy blue, red and pale blue stripes on the shoulder straps instead of the initials. The uniforms were worn at all times and enabled them to pass the sentry on camps and barracks easily without being cross examined.

The bronze badge was originally issued as a non-voided NAAFI Crest with Lug and pin fixing to the back firstly without a serial number (1940) then with a stamped number on the back (1941). In late 1941 this changed to a voided cap badge of the same but the addition of 2 smaller badges for the shoulder or the collar. The voided badge was lighter and slightly thinner, which meant it used less metal to produce and in turn helped with the war effort.

Barbra Hawker HMS Collingwood 1940

In 1940 at HMS Collingwood, Barbara Hawker, known by her friends as Babs, joined NAAFI NCS at the age of 18 as a canteen assistant. It wasn't until 15 years later when she had worked hard and worked her way up to chief chef that she would leave. During the war years, those who worked on a naval base would be members of the Naval Canteen Service whether they were to go to sea or not but not be attested into the Navy.

Babs would marry and become Mrs Patmore. Her new husband was a great friend of the bride's brother, who was lost with his ship whilst in convoy with the Navy in 1942. Her brother had served with him during Dunkirk.

Some of the memories she held, were shows put on by John Penrose and the ENSA group; one of her favourite pastimes was to collect autographs from the performers. It would not be till November 1953 that Babs would return to NAAFI on a part-time basis as a cook.

It was very kind of her son Alfred to let me use some of the photographs of his mother. She wore various overalls depending on her position, with the Khaki uniform under the overalls serving the services with NAAFI NCS.

1941

Adrift by WH Loxton NCS 1941

Our little cargo ship slipped quietly down the Mersey bound for West Africa. I was one of the 12 passengers who lined the rails as blitzed docks were left behind. It was 1941. We cast a last, lingering look at the 'Liver building' as our ship crept out into the open sea. Darkness fell. We turned and went below and when the introductions were over, settled down for the evening.

The next morning, we discovered that we had joined other ships and that our convoy was assembling somewhere off Northern Ireland. By the evening some 40 odd ships were in line and the convoy was on the move. We must have picked up our escort during the darkness because the following morning we saw two very peculiar looking destroyers of American origin. 50 of them I was told, had been exchanged for a 99-year lease as part of our West Indies possessions. It was not comforting to see such a small escort, especially as we proved to be a slow convoy. As the days went by, we amused ourselves by watching the messages being flashed from ship to ship and the escort vessels fussing around the convoy to keep it together. Then, one morning, we awoke to find our ship completely on its own! Not another vessel in sight. During the night the order had been given to disperse. At breakfast the Capt. had told us the reason; the German battleship Bismarck was loose somewhere in our part of the Atlantic.

The knowledge that our ship was on her own, liable at any time to submarine attack, could be blown out of the water by the Bismarck, was startling and I do not think breakfast was enjoyed by anyone. The small piece of the artillery the ship carried at her stern presented a rather pathetic sight. We now have to wear lifebelts day and night, besides taking our turns at the submarine watches. At night the strictest blackout regulations were imposed and after days went by, the strain began to tell on all of us. We were now in the tropical waters of the flying fish and the occasional shark's fins was seen. The weather was hotting up.

One Sunday morning during one of the spells on a submarine watch, I saw a small white streak in the water rapidly approaching our ship. There was hardly time to shout a warning before there was a violent explosion as the torpedo caught us amidships. A terrible, acrid smell enveloped us and splinters were flying everywhere. Then the second explosion, another torpedo had almost blown our stern away. Crew and passengers began using axes and attempted to release the lifeboats and rafts; the order was given to abandon ship and it was everyman for himself. The ship had taken a very nasty list, there was no hope of getting down below for any personal belongings. I was only lightly clad in shorts and T shirt, but without hesitation I jumped over the side, hoping to miss the wreckage, and hit the water. I was not too lucky and suffered a knock or 2, and after flopping around for some time, managed to cling on to some wreckage. After a few minutes debris floated by and with difficulty, I scrambled aboard it. From this vantage point I saw the ship take its final plunge, her stern, or what was left of it high in the air, before she slid into the depths with a terrific hissing and the waves closed over her. A high sea was running and one minute I was on top of the waves and the next deep troughs of water.

While I was on top, I caught a glimpse of the U boat, which I later learned had surfaced, had a good look around and then moved off, apparently satisfied with its sinister work.

In the late afternoon a lifeboat with about 30 survivors aboard spotted me and took me off. The raft was tied onto the boat in case it was required. And thus began what was to prove an awful 6-day spell in open boat in tropical shark-infested waters. Some 60 survivors in 2 lifeboats were all that remained of the passengers and crew. We were approximately 200 miles from West Africa and if we all rode steadily, we stood a reasonable chance of survival. The first mate took charge of the boat and under his guidance, we organised ourselves into some assemblance of a team, a team prepared to survive if possible. We looked a sad and somewhat gruesome spectacle as some of the wounds suffered were rather frightening. One of the engineers pulled out of the water with half his face and arm blown off but was still alive. He was given all the help that was possible but died the next morning. It was grim, when he was thrown overboard, to see the shark thrashing the water in the fight for his body. When we took stock of our provisions, they were proved to be very poor, a small keg of water, few tins of milk and some chocolate and some biscuits. Strict rationing was enforced but by the 3rd day we were down to a tablespoon of water a day which was rolled around our mouths and then swallowed. There was also a few cigarettes, I think lasted 2 days.

It was pathetic to see one cigarette being passed amongst 30 men, each taking a puff. The chap who had the end came to be envied. It is rather difficult now to remember which events happened on which day and some events are best forgotten, especially after the hot sun got to work and the craving for water started to take hold. It was a blessing that there were no women on board although, perhaps, they might have had a sobering effect on some of the savagery which at times was displayed. It seemed that we rowed and slept, rowed, and slept in the same spot for years. Eventually we had to restrict our rowing to the night-time as all we could do in the heat of the sun was lie in the boat and try and forget our hunger and thirst.

One night, through the darkness some way ahead we saw a long black shape which we all took to be a U boat on the surface charging its batteries. We all kept still and quiet; suddenly the shape began to move, and we realised, with relief, it was a whale. The creature dived and we were thankful – a flick of its tail could have cracked our boat. The following morning a violent storm blew up and our small craft was buffeted badly. Our condition became worse due to sickness and fatigue, but the storm proved to be our Salvation as it brought a heavy downpour. A small piece of sail was spread to catch the rain and we soon had enough to fill one keg and then drink to our hearts' content.

By afternoon the storm had subsided, the sun was as pitiless as ever. That night we experienced thunder and lightning as have never heard or seen it before. A tropical thunderstorm can be a grand spectacle when viewed from the safety of a bungalow, but in an open boat miles out in the Atlantic, it somehow loses its appeal.

Our existence dragged into the 4th day, in the late afternoon, we heard the sound of an aircraft. It caused great excitement and raised our hopes tremendously, we prayed it would be "one of ours". Then we spotted it away in the distance, a Sunderland flying boat presumably carrying out its normal submarine patrol. Clothing was stripped off and we waved frantically and shouted in vain in an attempt to attract the attention of the aircraft. As the flying boat disappeared into the distance a gloom descended on all of us. The next day, at about the same time, we again heard the noise of an aeroplane and again we saw the Sunderland far away in the distance. Excitement was intense as we felt sure she must be searching for us and in our efforts to be seen we nearly capsized the boat. Again, we were disappointed, or so we thought, as the aircraft continued on its flight until it disappeared. But early the next day an engine was heard yet again. This time we were spotted, and the aircraft circled around us. It was a walrus amphibian more affectionately known as a steam pigeon, and it landed on the water about 40 yards away. It could not get closer as the rough sea was running, but the pilot shouted across to us through a megaphone that he had radioed our position and help could be expected in the next 24 hours. He also threw over to us a bag of oranges, which fell into the water. One of the men in the boat went over after it and that was the last we saw of him. Whether the sharks got him, or the effort was too much we shall never know.

With a wave from the cockpit the pilot took his plane off and with everybody tremendously bucked, we lay back in the boat. About midday the next day the walrus she reappeared, circled us, then dropped what appeared to be a bomb. We were amazed, threw ourselves to the bottom of the boat and waited for the explosion.

Nothing happened and raising our heads we saw a column of smoke rising in the sky; it was a smoke signal to indicate our position. An hour or 2 later the sight of a whisper smoke appeared on the horizon and shortly afterwards a ship took shape. It proved to be a small Royal naval vessel named Winston but when it came alongside or as near as it could it appeared to be a large ship the size of the Queen Mary. The Royal Navy lads were grand as they tenderly lifted us from our boat and on to the Winston. In no time at all it seemed that we were entering Freetown Harbour, where we were transferred to HMS Vindictive where I found an old NCS associate, Mr Blackler. With his help and guidance, for which I am forever indebted, I soon comfortably bettered down on deck and medical attention, food and drink was soon forthcoming. After I had been fed and bathed the Navy shaved me. In those days I sported a moustache, but in the Navy it is either all on or all off and so I lost my beautiful moustache and I have never had one since.

The Imperial club 1941

The Imperial club was formed in 1921 with the objective to create good feeling and fellowship among the staff ensuring indoor and outdoor recreation and to provide its members with opportunities of entertaining their friends at club functions.

The first chairman of the Imperial club was Mr EH Cherry, CBE, who was in office until he retired in 1944; he was succeeded by Mr AL Trundle OBE.

The club itself was divided into various branches, headquarters being the main branch; the chairman would then appoint chairmen of each of the subsidiary branches. The members were made up of any employee of the NAAFI, or any member of the services attached to NAAFI. Each member had to be nominated by an existing member and a small subscription was charged for this membership.

Each of the clubs were suitably accommodated and the management made the necessary alterations, decorations and fixtures and fittings. This was all done by the company's own works, building and supplies branch. In some areas the accommodation for the club was difficult and this meant that even though there was the need for a club the clubhouse, or lack of it, meant that it had to be closed in this area. During the war years some branches were closed which was due to the need of war activities.

In 1939 there were 23 branches of the Imperial club in the UK with a total membership of 2000. During the war the number of branches swelled to 40, including 2 clubs' full staff of the NAAFI offices in New York and Montreal. Some of the wartime clubs had to be closed, in particular those in Norwich and Southend, then Crossford and Peckham but the overseas branches increased.

During these times of hardship, the activities of most of the clubs were reduced, particularly the outdoor sports as football and cricket, as there was a shortage of young men and this made it difficult to assemble teams. At the Imperial club sports ground at Mitcham, the London branch which controlled all the games, they managed to maintain the cricket and football including tennis and netball sections. Outside visitors were invited to play whenever this was necessary to increase the numbers of men available.

The indoor entertainments including dances which had proven to be popular. But again, the shortage of young men was overcome in some branches by regular invitations to the servicemen stationed locally. Table tennis and darts were still firm favourites, and several branches had their own dramatic and musical sections.

Headquarter branch, Claygate.

Following the movement of the headquarters to its wartime establishment in Surrey the club was opened in a local village Hall.

London branch, Imperial court, Kennington.

This branch was temporarily closed down in 1939, it was reopened in the October of 1941 with the membership drawdown from the staff of the Imperial court and Kennings Way. It had a concert and review section; other sections comprised cricket, football, tennis, table tennis, darts and netball.

Aldershot

This branch was formed pre-war, their activities were holding dances and the usual club amenities.

Ballymena, Northern Ireland.

Opened in 1941 the club moved to Belfast with the home accounts branch office. The main activities were dances and they had an active table tennis section.

Bournemouth

In May 1942 the club had an active cricket section but mainly concentrated on indoor recreational activities of billiards, dancing, darts and table tennis.

Bovington

This was another pre-war club which later moved to a more spacious premises in the camp.

Bristol

Opened in 1943, the club had to close down the following year.

Burton Manor

The opening of this club was 1941 and it only operated for the staff of the western command headquarters.

Catterick

When this was a fantastically active club before the war and it also managed to hold regular dances and whist drives.

Cardington

In 1943 this club was also comparatively small in number but held a number of activities; this included dances held by the permission of the Royal Air Force in the station gymnasium.

Davenport

The club relinquished the premises during the war to the NCS and only got them back in 1945.

Edinburgh

The branch was opened in 1941 and had been active throughout the war.

Folkestone

Opened in 1943 the club changed its premises in its early years.

Liverpool

Also opened in 1941, due to the decentralization in 1939 when they were pleased to be located above the accounts' office.

Preston

Formed in the spring of 1943, it had an enterprising theatrical section which regularly presented its own review entitled "Servitor Servientium".

Redhill and Reigate

This small club opened in 1944 with its premises adjoining the Redhill warehouse; it was also used during the day as staff restaurant.

Salisbury

After a few changes of premises, they arranged an opening function in December of 1945. All through the disruption the club maintained a number of activities including tennis, cricket, dancing and also various outings.

York

The club was opened in 1940 and its original lacking premises were subsequently replaced by others in Castlegate House; this was redecorated for the sole purpose of being an Imperial club.

Overseas

Branches where located in Cairo, Baghdad, Gibraltar, Alexandria, Jerusalem, Bermuda, Ismailia, Haifa, Mombasa, and in Western Europe, Brussels, and New York and Montreal. For a short period, a branch was operating in the Suez Canal zone also.

Chairman Sir William F Beale OBE, board of management 1941

1941 to 1953: Sir William F Beale

Sir William gave an interview in 1961 to reflect on the 20 years he'd spent with the company. He said in an interview: "I may have been privileged to make the company, NAAFI owes me absolutely nothing. On the contrary, it is I who owe NAAFI so much, so many good friends, so many adventures, such a host of contacts in commercial and ministerial circles, such a valuable broadening of my personal and business horizons. I can never repay NAAFI for all of those blessings."

That modest remark was fairly typical of a modest and essentially genuine person that for those people who knew him called him Billy. His NAAFI story began at the end of 1940. He was a member of the University OTC and mounted troop in which he acquired some military training which was to stand him in good stead later on in life. In 1929 he came from Cambridge and joined the family business of Greens store in Ilford, a small but growing chain of family grocers. By 1940 at the age of 32 he was a junior director of the firm with 10 years' experience in the food business behind him.

A family friend and business associate at the time was Capt Lancelot C Royle. One of the recommendations from a report issued by Macharg/ Royle was that a number of young men with practical knowledge of the food and retail and distribution business should be brought into the company to strengthen its team in the face of daily expansion of the company's wartime commitments.

On the 20th of December 1940 Billy Beale was telephoned by Mr Royle asking him to meet him at Liverpool Street station at 0830hrs; they met, and the conversation was brief and brisk. Mr Royle said you've got to come to work for the company, and Mr Beale replied when do I start. So, Christmas Eve 1940 was the day that began a 20-year career. He attended an interview with RJ Wallace, who was at the time the manager of the Home Institute service at Ruxley Towers. He was also seen by Mr Frank Benson who was then the general manager.

Benson regarded him coolly: "what makes you think you can help us?" he asked. Billy Beale proceeded to tell him in no uncertain terms, whereupon Benson, who liked straight speaking, visibly thought and thereafter gave him a complete support. New Year's Eve saw him installed at the Station Hotel, in York where under WD Haysey, he was to serve as a trainee group supervisor. Day-to-day he was attached to 'Big Bill' Tompkins who later became command supervisor; he was a large man with a large smile and a calm and reassuring manner. In January 1941 he spent touring around Yorkshire trying to pick up the way the company worked, grasping every aspect of the business that he could. Mr Beale was later transferred to Imperial Court where he and Mr Wake served as joint assistant command supervisors to the late Norman Peters until eastern command was moved. Wherever the job moved you moved with the job at the time and at this time he had to find a suitable headquarters for NAAFI in the new eastern command. He found premises in Langley Rd, Watford, which became the eastern command HQ for the rest of the war.

He was now responsible to Reggie Alltoft, command supervisor. His first meeting with him was in a hotel. Reggie mysteriously produced a tin box from which he extracted a bottle of gin, where he stated, "now this is how we will run eastern command", 2 hours later the plan was complete, and the bottle was empty!

He opened the first NAAFI shop in Watford High Street, following an order that NAAFI should site some of its wartime shops in main thoroughfares. In January 1942 he was told that he was to be posted to West Africa in just two weeks' time, he had a brief training at Norwood and was made 2Lt. On the day he left, Colonel Merry took off his pip and made it into a Crown – he was now Maj Beale. Although his training was brief, he could recall his OTC training because if he hadn't have had it, he wouldn't have survived the following months. On the troop ship he was put in charge of 75 unattached officers, all regulars. Wisely, he paraded them and called forward the four senior captains. To his relief two of them had been at school with him. He took them aside and requested that they helped see him through this and they did. A case of 'it's not what you know, but who you know'.

As they reached Freetown they boarded the Highland Monarch, a very fast craft which made an unaccompanied dash to Takoradi, and this is where he met Peggy Welsh, a district manager, and the others returned to Freetown to greet district manager Mr Loxton, who had survived a torpedo ship.

In Bathurst he spent some time with George Rawlinson – he was now command supervisor for the NCS. It was on his flight back to Freetown that he had an adventure which hit the headlines and a full account in the picture post. The small aircraft ran out of fuel and the pilot made a dicey landing on a narrow strip of palm fringed beach in French territory. Things were not too happy with the French at that time and there was every prospect that, if discovered, they might have been out of the war for good. However, their radio was in good order and after a time a British plane appeared and dropped a rubber dinghy with instruction to paddle a certain course and rendezvous with a British frigate. They paddled for almost 3 hours and there was no Navy in sight, then the aircraft appeared again and informed them that they were paddling in precisely the opposite direction. They managed to get back on track with enough time to meet the Navy ship. When they reached Freetown, the word had got around about the incident and of course there was a certain amount of leg pulling.

They stayed in West Africa until August 1943 when he handed over to Jimmy Nuttall. For six weeks he was lost in a transit camp until Sir Lancelot raised merry hell at the War Office, whereupon he was promptly found and rushed home. After a spell of leave he insisted on a proper training period at Norwood, which by now was one of the best training depots in the country. He was next sent on a Mission to the Azores with the promise that if he completed it in time, he could have Christmas at home. He was cutting it fine but on Christmas Eve he found himself in the bomb rack of a Lancaster bomber bound for Prestwick and was home for Christmas with just two hours to spare.

It was now 1944, the year of destiny. He was attached to Brigadier Hamilton, EFI, at Norwood for the task of writing EFI order of battle for "Overlord", the invasion of Europe. Each day he attended St Paul's School, Montgomery's planning headquarters, and received a daily briefing from the Brigadier RG Feildon!

During this time, he met among others Col Prideaux, Col Hardy, Brigadier Matthews who at the time was the chairman and managing director of Crosse and Blackwell, all the boys together in 21 army group. Then came the day. Brigadier Peters went over with EFI advance party and Billy Beale, now Col Beale, joined him in Normandy in August 1944. As the campaign progressed, he moved to Brussels, to Bad Salzuflen, and finally to Hamburg 11 HQ EFI this was a far cry from being a messing store clerk.

Col Billy Beale had 275 EFI officers through his headquarters at a time. After the war he gave a dinner at London restaurant for all his EFI officers and from that function originates the Gulf match which today, as the annual NAAFI EFI day, has a permanent place on the company's calendar.

1942

North Africa, The Star 7th of December 1942

Soon after the recent landings in North Africa a small party of NAAFI officers had arrived at the North African port to establish an extensive canteen service. They were the advanced guard of a considerable NAAFI force who would operate static and mobile canteens and bulk issue stores to serve the British allied forces.

The canteen millions 1942

Keeping account of the canteen pennies had always been a hot topic. On the 1st of September 1942 as the chief accountant, Mr EF de Latter OBE opened his newspaper, he read an impassioned demand, the NAAFI should tell the whole world what it proposed to do with all of its hoarded millions after 3 years of war. Whereas when he reached the office that day he was called to submit a statement of the NAAFI accounts from the Westminster bank.

Now as the story goes as far back to the 1920s and before the millions were there for all to see, but this time unfortunately, they were on the wrong side of the Ledger. The account that morning showed that they were overdrawn at the bank to the tune of £12 million. Neither the bank nor the company viewed this condition without undue alarm, so obviously this was one calling for care and vigilance. The bank had allowed the company to go overdrawn at significant extent solely because, like themselves, they were a prudent organisation. They had first assured themselves that the overdraft was covered by NAAFI's material resources – this was mainly by the way of stocks and equipment stored in thousands of centres in various parts of the world which, after all, are cash in another form. On the other hand, they were satisfied with the trading position and at that time justified with an overdraft that in due course should be in a position to reduce when the stocks were sold and resumed their original form as cash.

It also proved indeed that the following year in 1943 and again in 1945 there came brief periods when, given the various fluctuations, the overdraft was wiped out, and were actually in credit. This happy condition did not last, however, as it was generally taken that NAAFI wartime operations had been run on more or less a permanent overdraft at the bank. The company had to pay for enormous stocks, long before they turned it into money, over the counter. The complexities of NAAFI's accounting rose mainly because of the volume and the geographic spread of the trading and the numerous local factors being customs duties concessions and currency fluctuations and other influences which have to be taken into account and out of all of this 6% dividend had to be distributed monthly to units on their canteen trade.

To give an idea of some of the costs, throughout the war they were spending at least £2,000,000 a week on purchases. There were times when they paid £3,000,000 a month for cigarettes. Tons of potatoes a day costing up to £8000 and this was another item that was essential to the operation and the premiums for war damage insurance cost the company £1000 a day at one time during the height of the fighting. The complexities were endless, so the Canteen millions were real, just not in hard cash for all to see.

NCS benefits 1942

Many of the men of the NCS were put into uniform at the outbreak of the war and served in HM ships. The decision to actually enrol them into the Royal Navy did not come into effect until the August of 1942.

Their position meant they would take up action stations as a civilian during a battle; many lost their lives at sea. This created somewhat of an anomaly, according to the Admiralty regulations, the period served as civilian could not be counted as service the same as Naval personnel.

Later representations were made to the Admiralty and this brought a reversal of the ruling. The period served overseas or afloat as a civilian now counted both for the purpose of arriving at age and service release group and in assessing the gratuities, in the case of those who lost their lives, will benefit their dependants.

HMS Petard Tommy Brown and the code books 1942 by Tony Hales CBE Chairman 2001-2008

My first external engagement as NAAFI Chairman was to speak at a ceremony in North Shields to dedicate a window to the memory of Tommy Brown.

Tommy was a truly remarkable young man. He was a canteen assistant aboard the destroyer HMS Petard, when it cornered German U Boat U-559 in the Eastern Mediterranean on the 30th October 1942. Lieutenant Fasson and Seamen Grazier and Lacroix stripped and boarded the sub from a whaler launched from the destroyer. Tommy Brown followed them. At the subsequent enquiry Tommy described what happened. "I got on board just forward of the whaler on the port side when the deck was level with the conning tower. Inside the U boat, the lights were out. The First Lieutenant had a torch. The water was not very high but rising gradually all the time. First Lieutenant was down there with a machine gun, which he was using to smash open cabinets in the Commanding Officer's cabins. He then tried some keys, which were hanging behind the door and opened a drawer, taking out some confidential books, which he gave me. I placed them at the bottom of the hatch. After finding more books in cabinets and drawers I took another lot up and climbed down again. There was a hole just forward of the conning tower through which the water was pouring. As one went down through the conning tower compartment, one felt it pour down one's back – I went down below to the bottom of the ladder. . . . First Lieutenant was trying to break some apparatus from the bulkhead in the control room. . . We could not get it free, so we gave up. The water was getting deeper and I told the First Lieutenant they were all shouting on deck. He gave me some more books from the cabin. I took these up on deck. This was my third trip."

Tommy shouted information to one of the officers on the whaler, Connell, and said he was going down again. Connell had seen that the U Boat appeared to be sinking and shouted that no-one should go down and the others should come out. Lacroix made it out through a wall of water as he forced himself up the ladder. Tommy was at the top and could see Fasson and Grazier at the bottom of the hatch. He shouted to them as the submarine slid under the water. There were cries from the drowning crew members as the British sailors shouted for their shipmates. Suddenly Tommy's head bobbed up out of the sea. He and Lacroix survived, Fasson and Grazier went down with the submarine. The code books they had recovered from U-559 were sent to the code breakers at Bletchley Park and were critical in helping to break the German Navy Enigma code. The breaking of that code saved countless lives, ships and supplies on the British North Atlantic convoys from the German Sea Wolves.

Tommy was a hero, who had made his own very vital contribution to the war effort, but his action led to his real age being discovered – only 16. He had actually joined up at the age of fifteen. He was sent home and awarded the George Medal in great secrecy. The Germans were not to know the magnitude of their loss. Before Tommy could collect his medal, he too died tragically in a fire in his home together with his younger sister Maureen. By this time, he had returned to the NAAFI as the can man on HMS Belfast, which was in port close to his home. His mother collected the medal from George VI but the reason for the award was never revealed to her or anyone outside the hidden few for fifty years. It was deemed to be classified under the Official Secrets Act. Once the enormity of his achievement was known, NAAFI was contacted by his family to help mark his life in some special way; hence the stained-glass window, to which we contributed, in Saville Hall, in his hometown.

It was very moving to meet Tommy's sister and extended family and both Charles Hill (the NCS Manager) and I felt very proud to be able to represent NAAFI at the Veterans' Parade and to speak at the dedication ceremony. There is a wonderful dignity in the parade of veterans, and we treasure Tommy's medals in our Amesbury office today. The courageous exploits of these men also provided the basis for a box office hit film U-571 but the heroes were portrayed as Americans to sell more tickets!

NAAFI man died at Dieppe gun Evening Standard 10th of September 1942

NAAFI revealed that one of the several men on their staff who took part in the Dieppe raid was killed by a Manning machine gun. He was canteen manager R Laybourne, of Newcastle upon Tyne, who was posted to a destroyer. During the action he took a station in an ammunition supply party. The machine gunner near him was shot and killed, leaving the weapon unmanned. The canteen manager took over without hesitation, but he had only fired a few shots before he was killed too. This is a sad loss to the NCS.

The battle of Alamein October 1942 Major J Prentis

In October 1942, the battle of Alamein heralded the triumphant advance of the 8th army, and by the end of November it was obvious that it was no flash in the pan, the Afrika Korps and Italian army were definitely on the run.

The supply of Christmas fare, the responsibility of NAAFI, and always a big job, looked like being tricky business. As Middle East chief supply officer, the arrangements were a headache, and early in December I set out by road from Cairo to find the 8th army headquarters, somewhere in the western desert. The idea of getting all possible information of the anticipated position of Christmas. The headquarters were eventually located outside Benghazi, and after getting all available information I thumbed a lift and a plane back to Cairo. In view of the details obtained, it was decided to establish three distributing points: Tobruk, for troops on the line of communication, Benghazi, 250 miles further west, for the main body of the troops, and a third point, somewhere further forward, depending on the progress of the advance for the actual fighting forces.

This Third Point eventually turned out to be Marble Arch, on the boundary between Cyrenaica and Tripolitania, about 100 miles west of Benghazi. Orders are then accepted from the hundreds of individual units comprising the 8th army and western desert air force, each unit indicating the point from which it would collect it supplies. The next problem was to get the necessary goods consisting of some 23 tonnes of turkey and other poultry, 14 tonnes of pork, 18 tonnes of Christmas puddings, 11 tonnes of Christmas cake, 8 tonnes of nuts, to the distributing points. Tobruk was comparatively easy, as the single railway line had just been extended from Mersa Matruh, and refrigerated trucks were available to carry the poultry and pork.

In case of the other two points, it was decided to ship the poultry and pork to Benghazi by a small refrigerator ship, the SS Darien II and to forward the remaining supplies by road transport. Having set everything moving, I crossed my fingers and took the plane from Cairo to Benghazi on the morning of the 21st of December.

To everyone's relief, on the morning of the 22nd December, the SS Darien II had sailed into Benghazi Harbour, having escaped the mines, submarines and enemy aircraft which still infested the Mediterranean.

The first convoy of lorries from Cairo had also arrived. We immediately started loading lorries to go to Marble Arch, with goods for the advanced troops, and at dusk a convoy of 10 lorries started on its way to take the 100 mile journey with eight tonnes of poultry, 5 tonnes of pork, 8 tonnes of puddings, 5 tonnes of cake, and 2 tonnes of nuts.

On the 23rd we had plans to begin issuing from Benghazi, but our troubles now started. We were very short of puddings, cake and nuts, owing to the non-arrival of further road convoy from Cairo. Heavy rain had turned part of our issuing yard into a quagmire. And owing to the continuing advance of our troops, our plans were thrown completely out of gear by numerous units, who were supposed to draw from Tobruk, coming to Benghazi for their supplies. After a great deal of trouble, we eventually got through on the phone to Tobruk and, as anticipated, found they had the supplies available.

The RAF was approached and promised to provide a transport plane the next morning to bring any spare goods to Benghazi.

Christmas Eve dawned, and we anxiously awaited the arrival of further supplies. First of all, a road convoy from Cairo, with puddings, cakes and nuts pulled in. They had told the tale of breakdowns, punctures and other mishaps, which was not surprising; a third set off on a 1000-miles race against time over a road which was, in places, no more than a desert track with instructions to deliver the goods at all costs. They eventually arrived with half of the lorries being towed by the remainder, but they had made it.

Mid-morning found me at Benina airfield, anxiously awaiting the promised reinforcements from Tobruk. Planes of all descriptions were landing and taking off every few minutes, and eventually about midday, a Bombay troop transport dropped down and turned out to be our plane, with turkeys, puddings and other fare.

Issues were continued throughout the afternoon until darkness put an end to our activities – a strict blackout was being enforced, as Benghazi was a nightly objective for enemy bombers. Christmas Day found us at it again, but by noon there was not even a turkey leg or nut left. Every unit had received Christmas fare, and in the afternoon, we concentrated on a last-minute issues to troops in the facility.

At 1800hrs all the staff officers, NCO and men sat down together to a belated Christmas dinner of all the things of which we had seen so much during the past few days. No one's appetite seemed to have suffered, but we were not left in peace for long. The meal was hardly finished when the message arrives that a steamer had just commenced discharging NAAFI stores, so everyone had to set to unloading the lorries as they arrived from the docks. The last load arrived at 0300hrs on Boxing morning, when everyone called it a day, and retired to a well-earned sleep.

It's no mean task to supply Christmas dinner including a bottle of beer per head, for over 2000 men spread out over a distance of some 400 miles, especially when everything had to be weighed, checked, invoiced and paid for at the time of delivery. However, we all thought it worthwhile, especially when we later heard that messages of congratulations had been received at NAAFI Middle East headquarters from, among others, the commander of the 7th armoured division (desert rats), General Leese, commander of 30 corps (who later succeeded 'Monty' as 8th army commander) and General Freyburg, VC, commander of the New Zealand division.

A tale to tell, December 1942 written by RD McBurnie.

Those of us who served overseas with the EFI during WWII have been with a sure house of memories upon which we shall be able to draw for many years. I remember particularly the Franco Belgian frontier at 0200hrs a morning in May 1940 on the eve of battle. I had been trying to locate the bulk issue store to evacuate the men, I stopped to take in that graphic scene, a ready, glowing sky, the thunder of guns and the rumbling of tanks in their harbours.

Many other incidents leap to mind from out of those crowded years – the evacuation in 1940, the landings in Norton in North Africa in 1942, the storm during the Normandy landings which caused the Liberty ship I was on to drag her anchor, the liberation of Paris, watching from a distance the tragic parachute drop on Arnhem. My first crossing of the Rhine by Jeep over a pontoon bridge, seeing, from the air tier upon tier of aircraft heading for Essen in 1000 bomber raids and hosts of other incidents. But the event which stands out above the rest for me was the time I tried to buy some oranges in North Africa, which is not surprising because that was the first time I thought I'd really "had it".

It was late December 1942 and I was stationed in Algiers as the HQ supply officer EFI/1st Army. I had made arrangements for a certain influential Frenchman to accompany me to the Philippeville and Constantine areas where I hoped, with his help, to arrange the purchase of a considerable quantity of fruit. It was just at this time that Darlan was assassinated, and the French political scene was quite chaotic. When, a day or 2 before the project trip, my French friend had not phoned to confirm the arrangements, I went around to his office. It was occupied by 2 French police officials who informed me that the owner had been arrested on political charges and was imprisoned. After questioning me they asked me to accompany them to the headquarters of the Algiers police where I had a long interview with a senior police officer who made the Frenchman's case sound very grave indeed.

In the few weeks since I had met the man, I had come to know him extremely well. Since the landings he had proved very helpful to the allies and I was convinced that the whole affair was a mistake, so I set about seeing what could be done to secure his release.

Eventually Lieutenant Colonel WN Hamilton, who was then OC EFI 1st army, obtained permission for the Frenchman to accompany me on a trip as planned. One morning in early January, the prisoner was brought to my office in handcuffs by a French officer and 2 gendarmes. I shall never forget his impatient plea, "my God! What have they done to me? Tell them to take these b. . . . . . things off". I did as he asked, and they released him. I had to sign have for "the body" and guaranteed to return him to Algiers. In addition, I was obliged to take an officer of the French security police on the trip as an added precaution. Completing the party was a very wealthy Arab who had extensive interests in the North African farmlands we would be passing through; it was in his Buick coupe that we were to make the journey.

The outward trip of some 300 miles was almost without incident. We were delayed here and there by tank convoys and at Constantine we were invited to the home of a very rich and well educated Arab to be present at the wedding of his son. The bridegroom's father, I remember, made much of the fact I was the father of twins, a boy and a girl at that. I think perhaps I was being held up as a good example to the bridegroom! Champagne and honey cakes followed.

The next day we went on to Philippeville. By 1800 hours we had successfully completed our business and set out on the return journey. We slept for about 4 hours at a farmhouse outside Constantine – there were no beds but some very luxurious Turkish rugs – and then set off for Algiers about 0700hrs.

The Arab gentleman was driving; I sat next to him with the French frontman on my right while the security officer sat on a tip up seat in the back. We took the coast road through the mountain range. It was wild, desolate, it was ape country with sheer drops from the road of between one and 2000 feet. But neither dizzy drops nor treacherous bends seemed to worry our driver as we sped along at times touching almost 80 mph. Twice he was stopped by tank convoys and one officer threatened to put us off the road for driving at such speed. It seemed to have some effect on the driver for a while – he kept down to more moderate speed but eventually, as we drove along the ridge of escarpment, I saw the needle shoot up to 75. I remonstrated with the driver, but he smiled, shrugged and remarked, "Allah will look after us". Then suddenly an awkward bend was rushing towards us at sickening speed. I knew we weren't going to make it full stop; with brakes screeching we swept round on the very brink of a giddy drop, the car miraculously hanging on to the road. Completely out of control, we careered across the road, shot over the further edge and out into space, tearing up a huge milestone in passing. I was sure the end had come. I remember thinking this is it. Fancy dying like this. Things that had happened in my past life rushed before me I could see quite clearly my wife and 2 children, then the crash.

Fortunately, on the side of the road, after the initial drop of about 30 feet, there was a small plateau. We plunged down onto this and began turning over. I counted 3 complete somersaults before I blacked out. Even as I began to come around, I remained convinced I was dead. I became more rational and I generally felt myself all over expecting to find at least a few broken bones but as far as I could tell I seemed to be unhurt. I looked around; the car had miraculously finished the right way up. The windscreen was shattered and there was no sign of the driver. The prisoner was slumped in his seat covered in blood from 2 ugly gashes to his head. I was sure he was dead. I looked behind me. The security officer lay motionless on the floor of the car amongst a heap of baggage. I climbed out to look for the driver and found him a good 30 yards away, conscious, but in great pain from his dreadful wounds.

From nowhere it seemed crowds of Arab suddenly appeared. One of them who spoke very little English told me that the British army was just down the road and offered to take me in his mule cart. I climbed shakily on the back of the cart and we set off. The fates were with us that day and we came across the army ambulance engaged in duties connected with typhus prevention. The Copeland charge was loath to leave his post and I had to write a requisition for the ambulance. With that he was happy, and I drove back with him to the wreck. As we approached the car, I saw that the Frenchman had regained consciousness and had struggled out. He tried to come around the car towards us. He gasped "my God, am I dead", and collapsed by the side of the car. Inside the car the security officer had also come to. "Don't move me," he barked, "I've broken my back." As a matter of fact, he had. The Frenchman had also broken his back but still somehow had climbed out of the car.

There were only 2 stretchers in the ambulance and the 3rd had to be improvised before all three injured men could be put aboard. However, by this time, the mare of the nearby town of Akbou, sent word to our wealthy Arab friend (the driver) offering the hospitality of his house for the injured man. The two gendarmes from the same town had also arrived and they began to question me and then took me off in their Citroen to police headquarters; they kept up their questioning until my head was spinning. Eventually an elderly English lady came into the room having heard the British officer was there – she was a missionary teaching in the local school. She spoke very sharply to the police in fluent French, had me conducted to her house where I must have been placed in bed. And I knew no more until late the next morning. I awoke to find Maj Lamb, HQ works officer, and Major Pritchard, the deputy OC at my bedside. They had been driving by the scene of the accident and recognised the car, he had inquired where I was, only to be told that the occupants had been killed. Luckily, they decided to investigate and found me. They arranged for the car to come out and pick me up and take me to Algiers.

My prisoner made quite a good recovery, went back to hospital and was eventually released. Although a great and patriotic Frenchman, he was re-arrested at a later date and detained. His release was eventually negotiated at the end of the war by the British officer of worldwide fame. The security officer lived and was incited by the Arab who also recovered. That was more or less the end of the incident but in case you are thinking of asking me next time you bump into me, "no I don't want to buy any oranges!".

1943

633 NAAFI casualties Evening Standard 16th of October 1943

NAAFI announced that the War cost the NCS and EFI, 633 casualties. This figure was thought to be proportionally as high as any of the Armed Services, comprising 288 killed, 53 died later, 41 were missing and 251 had been made prisoners of war. The only plus side to this was the prisoners would enjoy a windfall, when they returned home. From the day of their capture NAAFI had set aside their wages which would be paid to them in full, less their family allotments.

1944

NAAFI at ANZIO Manchester Guardian March the 2nd 1944

NAAFI had been busy at Anzio beach head. An advance party landed only six days after the assault troops. Two days later Mr Launcelot C Royle, chairman of NAAFI, stepped off a destroyer to inspect the preliminary arrangements for the supply of goods to the fighting man. Mr Royle reported that one officer and 12 other ranks landed on the beach head on January the 28th, and canteen goods began to arrive the following day.

NAAFI captures brewery Daily Herald 15th of May 1944

NAAFI, which landed in Normandy on D day plus 17, had captured its first brewery. The news appeared in the report issued yesterday by the board of management of NAAFI. The first brewery to be occupied is at Foeury-sur-Orne, South West of Caen. As soon as possible NAAFI would begin brewing and then, an official said, we shall be able to reduce the price considerably below the present pill bottle of one and 1/5 pints for imported beer. Reporter R Gordon Cummings.

The invasion sports pack Evening Standard, 1st of July 1944

Many hundreds of special invasion sports packs, specially devised by NAAFI, have already arrived in Normandy. Measuring 18 inches by 18 inches by 16 inches and weighing 36 pounds, one of these packs contained 2 football cases, four bladders, one rounders stick, two rounders balls, one lace tightener, one lace awl, one repair outfit, one adapter, 12 football laces, one tin of dubbin, 3 tennikoit rings, one dart board, four sets of darts, one set of draughts, one draughtboard, one set of dominoes, one cribbage board and pegs, one set of Lotto, 12 packs of cards and 50 books.

The whole outfit was portable with handles for easy carrying.

Remembering D-Day 6th of June 1944

When 2 NCS veterans of the D-Day landings made a sentimental journey to HMS Dryad, where General Eisenhower and his staff planned the historic invasion of Normandy. For Mr HOJ Holness, senior district manager, Portsmouth command, Mr Arthur Jackman, regional accountant, Portsmouth region, the visit stirred some vivid personal recollections of June landings and after. In May 1944 Mr Holness recalled, 'I was commissioned and attached to the Naval staff for the great invasion. Just before D-Day I was joined by Arthur Jackman and together we boarded the SS Ascania. two days before the day the ship's canteens were opened and from then on, they never closed night or day for two months.

'Apart from the normal duties NAAFI staff carried out first aid tasks during action stations. The Naval surgeons were amazed and grateful at the abilities of our lads. On one occasion when the staff on SS Thysville were showing the strain of their double tasks, I asked the principal medical officer to excuse them medical duties. He immediately offered me his sick bay attendants to assist with NAAFI work if he could retain the first aid services of the NAAFI boys. It was a proud moment for me. It wasn't long before we could see the necessity for the NAAFI boats, which had now made their appearance. What a wonderful job they did, supplying those hundreds of ships with their own canteens.

'Ashore at Arromanches, our headquarters, we only had one Jerry can of freshwater for drinking and bathing, but it seemed bottomless. It was amazing how many baths we managed from this meagre supply. I remember well the night when I was called out to soothe one of our staff who was running the Arromanches canteen. Heavy and continuous duties had proved too much for him and he finally cracked under the strain. At midnight he was found standing in the middle of the Main Street holding up the entire forces at gunpoint. He looked as impressive as Gary Cooper in 'High Noon'. After a hesitant start I encouraged him to let me have the gun. I am pleased to say that after a long overdue rest he recovered completely and remained with me right through to Germany.

'Mr A Jackson remembered the awful feeling boarding SS Ascania and being told that, once on board there would be no more shore leave this side of the channel. Then I saw what appeared to be the millions of troops packed on board. Actually, there were only about 6000. During the ship's trips across the channel we were under continual bombardment, a Naval officer gave me a running commentary of those of us packed below. The chaotic sounds of continuous gunfire gave me an empty feeling in the pit of my stomach.

'The memories of which remained freshest were the humorous ones. I particularly remember the American crew of a small personal craft who attached themselves to us. The Coxswain's name was Benson. I cannot recall the name of the comical Bowman, but I can still hear his 'hey Benson, the bottom shore looks pretty here' when we got stuck fast in shallow water. Then we were under fire from German guns at Sword beach, his yell, 'hey Benson, it's a bit warm here, let's go home'. Commodore England later called the Americans over and gave them an order, only to be told by Benson, 'not me, I'm working for these guys here'.

'Then there was the day when an army officer came for a bottle of Scotch. I told him it was impossible, but he pleaded that he was on forward patrol at nights and we finally let him have a bottle. A few days later a dispatch rider turned up with a barrel of oysters – the officer's patrol included a local oysters' beds.

'The day the war almost stopped because of the shortage of spirits. Landing craft were everywhere queuing up for their spirit ration. I was standing on deck with a portable loudspeaker trying to tell them that we had sold out, as ordered by my CO. Eventually we had to display a large notice over the side of the ship saying, 'sorry no booze!'. Sometimes the receipt of supplies was anything but smooth. Once skipper brought over our supplies but was unable to find us so, he put it, he dished it out amongst the ships. It took hours of hard work to trace the goods but eventually we managed to get most of it back. I could add 1000 more memories.

'There was the staff on the 'Thysville', one of our store carriers who found themselves carrying out first aid duties and giving blood transfusions after a very heavy attack. The day the Pegasus was sunk, and the surviving assistant apologised because he had not recovered the cash from the safe. The thousands of others where the real heroes of Normandy.'

June 1944 Written by Norma Windsor, Kettering, Northamptonshire.

I did not witness or take part in any adventure but, like many staff I was involved in the preparations for D-Day. I was 19 years old and I had been with NAAFI for about a year when volunteers were called to work in camps in strategic places around the country.

We were only needed for two or three months, so my friend Joyce and I decided to go. Nothing was mentioned about an invasion, but the thought was on everyone's mind. One day in April we found ourselves at Bradford station travelling to an unknown destination. We transferred to a bus and ended up in Aveley in Essex. The camp was under canvas in a large park and we were one of the first arrivals. We quickly organised and opened our canteen. This was housed in a large marquee and because the weather was bad, we stood on duckboards behind the counter. To begin with life was normal. We used our free time as we pleased and as London was only a train journey away, I saw my first West End show.

Eventually the camp filled up. Troops and equipment arrived, and guns and tanks surrounded us. The men to whom we served endless cups of tea showed the determination associated with British servicemen. Our days were hard. We were up early scrubbing and polishing before breakfast. As soon as we opened it was all systems go before a break in the afternoon followed by a full evening's work. The camaraderie with colleagues made up for any difficulties.

The first time I heard the guns I froze with fear. The noise was unbearable, but I quickly adapted. Now we could not leave the camp, all outings were barred, letters censored, and I cannot remember any radio bulletins. The 6th of June 1944 dawned, we were up as usual but there was a strange atmosphere in the camp; it was silent. Going into NAAFI there was just one lonely soldier leaning against the counter.

'They are gone,' he said simply. On looking outside, it was if all the men and machinery had been wiped off the face of the earth. After all the hurly-burly of the last few weeks the quiet was uncanny. I thought of all those lads with whom we have laughed and how we had gathered around the piano in the evening for a singsong. I then realised that many of them would never return to their homes. In those seconds I grew up and saw the futility of men fighting each other. Life went on. More tanks and equipment started to appear in the field around us before crashing and grinding on to Tilbury. We tried to carry on as usual, but this became impossible once the flying bombs and rockets started to come over.

The first night this occurred, a voice came over the tannoy and announced quietly: 'pilotless planes are heading this way, take cover.' I gathered my tin hat and blanket, and with several other girls spent the night in a slit trench. The guns boomed but no one had any idea what these weapons were.

More and more troops arrived. The word invasion was now on everyone's lips and the question was when would it happen? The invasion proceeded, bombs flew in the day and at night we got used to the sound. Once the engine cut out, we would dive for cover and two or three minutes later we would hear an explosion. Fortunately, none landed on the camp itself.

Some weeks later we made our way back to our original camps. My last memory of this time is of standing at St Pancras station when a siren went off. Then came the unmistakable buzzing of a flying bomb. The engine went silent and everyone threw themselves to the ground, except for one solitary old lady who was left sitting on a railway bench sobbing her heart out.

NAAFI 1944-1946 Written by Joyce Rigg age 19 years

Wrexham, At Cefn Mawr had been less well spent as we were kitted out with hats and weekend leave, in readiness to go to Normandy.

On one wet and windy midnight, we were awakened and told to pack up and depart on the boat train, to Tilbury docks in London. Arriving in daylight, we were sent into the large and open-ended hangar, and given tea. It was very cold, and although we were heavily clothed, we were wired with excitement!

We had envisaged a troop ship! But none were in sight. After a long wait, we were shepherded along a quayside and halted alongside a massive grey hulk of a cargo boat – the St Helier, towering above us; we scrambled on board. The crew were most helpful but spoke little English. The sea was so rough, that we seemed to be already sailing. We girls were helped down into the hold of the ship. This was not an easy task with the movement.

Hammocks had been slung down the centre of the concrete floored room. The crew members helped us get in and fall out of the swaying rope beds. Marie and I found there were some bunks alongside the wall, so we opted for them. The smell of the oil fire was choking. The sway of everything and the noise was deafening. But NAAFI was packed into a small area, where we were met with smiling crew members, who had set out a lovely buffet. Despite the swaying of everything, I believe we forgot to be seasick. Accordions played as we sang "Bluebirds over the white cliffs of Dover".

Sent below, to get some sleep, took some time as some of the girls didn't make the hammocks at all and opted to sleep on the floor. Marie and I hadn't been so clever and the nightmare, can only describe how things were after eating – of course the sickness took over. The sea was so rough, we thought we were sailing. But after a while, there was a lot of activity on deck. Clanking of chains and shouting orders then a shuddering of everything and the anchor was raised. We were at sea.

Toilets we had to find? Instinct took us up on midships. Where the only two toilets were! Outside them were piles of life rafts, would just be sat upon to wait your turn. Crew members just swab the decks around our feet.

Never was daylight more welcomed. Breakfast? No thank you. The five manageresses must have done a really good job at looking after us because by the time we reached Normandy we were whole again, in readiness for landing in London, crafts onto the Mulberry Harbour, full packs on our backs, to climb down rope ladders, in pouring rain.

We scrambled ashore at the Arromanches and at a nearby cafe, we were given tea, and a great welcome. In transit we were taken to the Lang rune, a small hamlet. Where we slept on pallets, in a barn. All nice, cosy and dry amid the hay in the loft. We were so exhausted, that the happy end of duty chats were non-existent.

In the morning, our manageresses chose the staff thoughtfully and friends made were taken together – Marie and I were to go to a nearby company at Juno beach. I remember most of the staff, Mrs Blanksby from the Midlands and a cook, Maude Bowker, and her sister Marry, the chargehand May Dobson. Along with Anne Elkington, Joyce Rigg from Lancashire and G.A. Marie Nichols and an Australian girl, along with three French girls and a Chinese lady.

The star canteen, which had been a brothel – all the trappings were still there, red curtains and all, it made for a nicer area than the tea bar which was on a concrete floored barn. No electricity except for an old generator, that was always on the blink. We carried candles or Tilley lamps, the soldiers found for us. Up the concrete staircase, no boudoirs just windowless huts with mesh and cardboard to keep out the rain. One toilet with no water to flush, we carried buckets of water for ablutions.

We were a happy NAAFI family.

D-Day memories 1944, written by Meta Joyce, Ashington, West Sussex.

D-Day was a memorable time for Valerie Elliott and me, two shorthand typists from Northern Ireland command office at Dunmurry, just outside Belfast. After volunteering to serve overseas we were posted to headquarters at Ruxley Towers, Claygate, in December 1943 and then onto auxiliary territorial service (ATS) training camp in Scotland in March of 1944. We returned to Ruxley Towers in May.

On the 17th of May we reported to the RASC EFI HQ where we became the first 2 girls to join the 'O' force EFI. It was there we typed much top-secret correspondence and copied sketches of landing beaches, Juno, Sword and Gold. We didn't know the location, but we always assumed that they were in France.

We also typed letters for the distribution of compo rations (NAAFI put together items for the early days of the landings before NAAFI service could be established). As the actual dates were unknown, we referred to the events as D plus 1 and so on up to 30. As we became aware D-Day had come and allied troops had invaded the North Coast of France. We listened to his speech from the Supreme allied headquarters in the officers' mess.

Valerie and I were very excited. We went about our work that day in high spirits, listening to the news reports as often as we could, and wondering when we would be on our way to France.

On the 3rd of August 1944 we joined a draught of canteen staff posted to Normandy and sailed out of Southampton in a convoy. Were even asked to do some typing for the Navy whilst onboard!

The troop ships anchored off Mulberry Harbour in rough seas, which posed a problem: how to get the girls on board ashore? About 1200 men climbed down rope ladders into landing ship tanks (LST) alongside, it soon became obvious that we had no option but to follow them! And this we did wearing battle dress blouses and skirts. One by one we went over the rails to much cheering from the men below who had been ordered to look towards the shores of France but didn't!

Just 10 feet from the LST the rope ladder ran out. This meant we had to wait until the LST rose on a wave and then jump into the arms of a waiting sailor. And they never missed a catch!

The next day reported to 11 HQ NAAFI BLA at Sully to resume our duties with EFI 'O' force.

Behind the lines June 1944

'Allied naval forces, supported by strong air forces, began landing allied armies this morning on northern coast of France.' This short statement, made from General Eisenhower's HQ on the 6th of June 1944, was the first the British public knew about the historic D-Day landings that were to signal the beginning of the end of the World War II.

Just five months earlier a similarly low-key announcement was made by NAAFI chairman Sir Lancelot Royle as he faced the board of management. Having just returned from a meeting at the War Office he came straight to the point. 'Gentlemen, this is it, from now on we work for D-Day.' That was the company's first glimpse of the support role it would be asked to play during the build-up and landing of thousands of troops along the French coast on the 6th of June 1944.

The task was enormous. Thousands of men and women had to be specially trained and equipped for the job, huge quantities of goods had to be assembled to be in the right place at the right time, and road, rail and shipping freight had to be planned to the last detail. NAAFI had to book its space in the invasion queue. Somewhere amongst the line-up of troops, equipment, ammunition, transporting supplies, a slot had to be found for EFI personnel, NAAFI mobiles and huge stocks of goods.

NAAFI's place was finally settled. The phrase 'D-Day plus 30', was on everyone's lips. It meant that 30 days after the landings NAAFI was to be in action in France. It finally transpired that the first EFI personnel landed in Normandy on the 23rd of June, D plus-17.

The problem was how to supply frontline troops during the first hard and bloody 30 days. It was then that NAAFI had a brain wave. To cover the period between landing and establishing canteens on the beach head, special NAAFI canteen packs, containing cigarettes, soap, razor blades, writing paper, boot laces and other items were prepared in their thousands and delivered to units as part of their invasion equipment. NAAFI also had to follow the ebb and flow of waves of troops in the build up to D-Day. Hundreds of camps from which troops had departed had to close, and hundreds more open up in new areas.

In one typical month 300 canteens were closed and another 350 opened in new locations. Almost overnight these establishments had to be furnished, equipped, stocked and staffed in readiness for incoming troops. 3000 NAAFI girls volunteered to look after these men. Confined to their camps, staff willingly cut themselves off from the outside world to serve customers in their last tense weeks before the invasion.

Elsewhere, plans for EFI landing were in hand. The brief contained three stages which would develop into full canteen service. Firstly, and as soon as the general staff would permit, EFI staff would go ashore and dump the canteen goods on the beaches. If they came under fire the staff would requisition the nearest warehouse and make the supplies ready to issue in bulk.

Other buildings would also be taken over as headquarters and billets, and camps, stores and depots quickly constructed. Next, as the fighting moved inland, NAAFI set up base canteens to supply troops with tea, beer, snacks pancakes. To support these activities a fleet of mobile canteens carrying the same type of stock would serve as near to the frontline as allowed.

Finally, all EFI services would move forward to make up an elaborate system of canteens, restaurants, leave clubs and shops in more settled areas. It was there that NAAFI girls, members of the ATS /EFI would arrive and relieve men of their duties further forward.

Although D-Day had been planned for the 4th of June, a gale in the channel postponed the offensive. The order which sent 4000 ships sailing from base ports eventually came on the evening of the 5th of June. It was the largest amphibian operation in history which was designed to see 40,549 allied casualties in the first 15 days of battle. As the morning on the 6th dawned,

NAAFI contributions to the operations were visible. The men of the NCS were either at action stations or serving ratings during lulls on board warships that protected the convoy.

As the 150,000 troops approached the beaches in landing crafts, each carried their portable NAAFI canteen packs – the first time in history this had happened. With only one exception at Omaha beach the landings were a success with the allies achieving surprise in both the place and timing of the assault. It was then that NAAFI turned to step into the line of fire. On D-Day plus 6, 12th of June, four officers and nine other ranks of the EFI left their Norwood Depot. A few days later they were on board ship anchored within sight of the French coast.

They sat there for five days in worsening weather. Frustrated with wasting time at sea, Colonel N.V. Peters MC, who led the reconnaissance party, thumbed a lift ashore in a motorboat. The following day the rest of the party joined in. Within 46 days Colonel Peters, as an officer commanding EFI, was in command of a force over 1300 made up of 51 officers, 952 other ranks RASC /EFI, two officers and 54 ATS /EFI, and 259 locally engaged French staff.

NAAFI's army operated two base canteen depos, temporary issue stores, six institutes, 8 advance canteen posts, 55 mobile canteens, a bakery, a Carpenter shop and for ENSA camps and hostels. NAAFI, alongside its customers, the services, was on the road to Berlin.

Normandy by Maj General G Surtees 1944

In June of 1944 the allied armies landed on the beaches of northern France to open up the long awaited second front. In this article the author who was commander, lines of communication, 21st army from the end of 1944 pays tribute to the men and women of EFI and to the planning of the organization which help them provide creature comforts to the invading armies during a long and arduous campaign.

A real look at the Normandy landings in June 1944 showing soldiers smoking cigarettes as freely as usual. But how they came by them was far from usual, through NAAFI of course, but free, to a total of over 17 million cigarettes and more than £3000 of tobacco. Welcome to the troops were these special packs designed to provide cigarettes, matches, razor blades, soap, stationery, for 430 men for 21 days. Their simplified system of supply plan for the first month of the campaign, proved so successful that it continued, improvements being made to the contents and suggestions from the units.

D-Day plus 17 saw the landings of the first EFI personnel, NAAFI in uniform serving to the fighting troops. The advance party lost no time, setting the pattern for getting things done quickly regardless of difficulties. Within 24 hours a base canteen depot was set up at Sully under canvas. Within one week it was being supplied direct from Mulberry Harbour, the RASC handling the EFI stores. On the 13th of July 8 bulk issue stores opened and two mobile canteens started operating. A week later 18 more were on the road and a 'Nobby Bar' appeared in Caen.

It was as well that NAAFI had got off the mark so smartly, for now came the Swiss advance of the armies, far more rapid than anybody anticipated, so stretching administrative resources, especially transport, to the limit.

There was not enough to meet essential operational needs – petrol was the biggest issue, leaving little or nothing for NAAFI but somehow and anyhow they managed, relying on the railway from Caen, where the depot had been established in a barrack hastily patched up close to the line. A trickle of stores through to Dieppe was helpful. NAAFI supply to the fast-moving fighting formations, covering 40 miles a day, approached the impossible. But the mobile canteens did their damnedest. Postage to corps and carefully routed to serve as many units as possible, by hook or crook the vans kept pace with the pursuit. Their crews needed no urging. The further forward the better they liked it. It was not for them to get mixed up in battles, but they did, and many had adventures enough. They drew supplies from the nearest mobile canteen depot or BIS store, sometimes stocking up for seven days to cover longer advances. The items carried comprised tea, milk, sugar, biscuits, cigarettes, lemonade powder, soap, toothpaste, boot laces and stationery.

Behind the mobile was the NAAFI company steadily built up. Reinforcements of personnel included, late in July, the first draft of ATS EFI. By the end of August imports amounted to the value of over £3 million. On the 11th of September headquarters EFI moved from Sully to Brussels only a week after liberation. In October the home service took over NAAFI supply work in the rear areas. By the end of November, the value of goods handled reached £10 million despite restriction on many commodities due to the world shortage.

The plans for Christmas fare was set back a bit by the enemy offensive in the Ardennes, resulting in unforeseen switching of formations. The difficulties were dealt with and the normal army issues supplemented with tinned turkey, pork, Christmas puddings and oranges. In addition, large quantities of slab cake, sweets, apples, pears and cigars were made or brought in Belgium and France, while captured enemy wines went down better than beer brewed locally from ingredients supplied by NAAFI. EFI next had to concentrate on preparation for the crossing of the Rhine. In the forward area, premises for use as depots had to be found, repaired where necessary by EFI workshops' branch and stocked. Before long came an emergency call to cater for freed prisoners of war, our own and allied, on the first stage of their journey home. Previously the numbers had been small, and the need met by mobile vans on airstrips. Now provision had to be made for up to 250,000 including gifts such as necessities of shaving soap, toothpaste and toothbrushes, as well as the complete range and scale of other NAAFI items.

These demands were fully met so were those of 200 mobile and 180 static canteens by then distributed throughout the Theatre of operations. NAAFI's extensive effort to provide for the troops of the 21st army group, about a million strong, were mostly on the move and who ended the campaign spread out from Normandy to the Baltic. Over this 600 mile stretch NAAFI establishments numbered nearly 400, ranging from small, advanced canteen posts in front of the Brussels Montgomery club, capable of coping with 10,000 daily. Figures fascinate few, but nothing else can illustrate the scope of this successful service. Here are some selected examples of the imports from the UK and USA over the period of June 1944 to April 1945 in round figures: 400 million cigarettes, chocolate, 2 ounce bars 83 million, confectionery 1lb bars 3 million, razor blades 80 million, toilet soap tablets 28 million, whiskey bottles 2million, gin bottles 1 million, bottle beer 25 million.

The NAAFI job took a bit of doing and a lot of people to do it: 155 officers, 1950 men, 13 officers and 727 other ranks ATS EFI and 6000 locally employed civilians. VS, ladies who ran the amenities in clubs, organised sightseeing tours, concepts, libraries, games, and other entertainment where possible, and operated canteen supplying released prisoners of war.

But that let that last word in aiming to serve lie with the mobile canteens crew who by misreading their map and taking a wrong turn entered the Belgian town of Saint Vincent ahead of our forces to have their van mistaken for a resistance armed car and to liberate six allied airmen hiding in a cellar.

1945

The end of WW2

NAAFI lost over 500 staff in World War 2, with 250 taken prisoner. The names of those who fell in combat are recorded in the Book of Remembrance, which was firstly kept on display at Imperial Court London Kennington, then was moved to the headquarters in Amesbury. The book now resides at the church in Bulford.

Some of the many stories of bravery of staff serving with NAAFI either at home or with EFI, or the NCS. Some of the greatest examples of sacrifice were Tommy Brown's story, our young 16 year old junior canteen assistant who sailed for port set aboard HMS Petard, his first trip to sea and a 19 year old canteen assistant, EC Smith, on board HMS Kandahar, who went overboard in the dark, in rough sea to rescue 19 sailors from HMS Fiji, sinking off Crete.

When the invasion of Europe was a few weeks old, a manager stood in a Normandy cornfield talking to a group of NAAFI girls. From beyond the ruins of Caen came a grumble of artillery, and now and then the earth shook with heavy bombs striking the enemy lines, a dozen miles away, while the air throbbed with the noise of aircraft. Yes, in the cornfield, all was amazingly peaceful and ordinary. The sun shone serenely, and the NAAFI girls were making the most of it. One was washing her hair in a tin basin and balanced on a stack of corn.

The normality of the scene was impressive. Back home thousands of other NAAFI girls were no doubt similarly employed in their afternoon leisure, reading books, writing letters and washing their hair or smalls. But here, within miles of the frontline, it was refreshing to see English girls carrying on so unconcerned. In familiar blue overalls, posed against the familiar NAAFI tenting common to every summer camp at home, it was as though they had carried with them a corner of the English scene and recreated it in whatever foreign field the fortunes of war might find them.

When Goering launched his assault on British airfields in 1940, the NAAFI girls found themselves overnight on the frontline of war. And they did not flinch. At one RAF station in Oxford, during the daylight raid, the canteen wall collapsed. The girls retired to their living quarters to tidy up. The Raiders came again, and this time the living quarters received direct hit. Several of the girls were wounded, some seriously. Yet by the evening those who could do so were back in the canteen, putting on a makeshift service in the debris.

NAAFI girls were killed and wounded, alongside the fighting men and ground staff they served. More than 50,000 NAAFI girls who, in good times and bad, faithfully served the troops in camps, barracks and air stations at home and overseas. They were a gallant army whose victories were seldom publicised, victories over prejudice and unfair criticism, victories over boredom and isolation, victories over eternal washing up. Their service was of a kind which lacked glamour and the limelight, yet they stepped up to the task and gradually won respect and admiration of the troops everywhere during and after World War Two.

NAAFI News Staff Edition Christmas in 1945

The NAAFI News staff edition was born Christmas 1945. Unfortunately in the spring of 1940 the beloved Imperial club magazine stopped being published as there was an acute paper shortage due to the war. The Imperial club magazine was designed to record the activities in history from the Company at home and overseas. It was also proved to be an invaluable sauce of factual and historical data recording the lives, careers and deaths of so many employees who worked for the Company even before its conception some 30 years before.

With the Company missing this vital publication it left a void which nothing had filled for the 5 years that it was out of production. Despite the Company approaching paper control in a bid to save the Imperial club magazine they finally abandoned the idea, the paper shortage was desperate. In the spring of 1941, it does seem that the very first issue of NAAFI news appeared. This publication was but a few pages, which was for the first five years a bulletin, as a single sheet, it was published weekly and sent to some 200 home and overseas newspapers. The function of which was to keep the press informed of the activities of the Company and serve as a corrective to the ill-informed who wished to criticise the good that they were doing. Even though it was very limited in information it proved at the time to be quite successful and over the war years thousands of excerpts from the British press quoted stories from the bulletin bear testimony to how useful this was. The publication was made from desperately thin paper which very few expected for it to continue; unfortunately there is no surviving copies of this. The 1945 Christmas edition marked the 5th birthday of NAAFI News. Although just a few, 100 does not seem an awful lot for the newly formed NAAFI news but its predecessor the Imperial club only had several hundred published at a time.

In 1944 the brand new publication was drastically reduced but the press still received a copy. It was hoped by conserving paper, that it would be possible to produce the occasional circulation of a publication, to reach the majority of the staff at home and abroad. Then in 1944 the paper control relaxed the regulations to ease the situation and so produce the NAAFI news staff edition magazine, and report on the activities and goings on, and also to include contributions from staff. The editor was Claude F Luke, assistant editors Herbert Harris and Hilary T Wills, all of whom resided at Ruxley Towers.

Some iconic pictures that were taken during the war were one of an EFI girl and a cheerful young soldier shaking hands. This happy snap was used for an iconic poster encouraging people to join; it symbolised the comradeship and the partnership between Miss Naffy and the fighting men. The picture in fact was just a happy coincidence, a snap taken while the girl, Corporal Lily Brooks, of Oldham and the soldier, Driver W Garrett, also from Oldham, met while stood in front of the sphinx at the pyramids, with the right light and the right shadows, with the right smile, as this Lancashire girl and lad met for the first time, since they had danced together previously in Oldham just days before the war started. They do say a picture paints 1000 words but in this one there is such a huge story behind this iconic snap.

It was only now that the realization started to set in, the Company had to look to its post-war plans and start the speeding up of the démobilization. Sir Launcelot C Royale, who was the chairman of the board of management, writes: 'I propose to tell you what I can, but I must stress that our whole scope depends almost entirely on the size of the post-war Navy army and Air Force, matters of which have yet to be settled by the cabinet. In these circumstances therefore some of my statements will have to be made in the nature of the intelligent anticipation or at the worst plain guesswork. As soon as we know what the future sizes and dispositions of the NAAFI were to be, we shall be able to plan, with considerable precision the staff requirements of NAAFI, in the post-war years. But it is already certain that NAAFI will be much larger than it was before the war'.

Before the war in 1938 the Company had a staff of some 5000 personnel and about 700 establishments in total. After the war staff numbers swelled to 120,000 which operated over 7000 establishments. It was obvious now that this could not be maintained and within a few years pending the British military and their strength reductions, the Company would follow suit. Whichever way they would rank amongst the largest distributive organisations in the country.

Even at this point in time, everybody wanted to know what the future of EFI would be and gradually, overtime as it is the policy, overseas personnel would eventually serve as civilians, as this was the case before the war. The process for this would be carried out gradually and the personnel of RASC /EFI and ATS /EFI where repatriated or released from their positions. At this point in time the Company could offer first rate employment with first rate prospects, whether it be overseas or at home. During the war, training schemes were carried out in a limited way but in the post-war years this was extended, to educating young employees with the fundamentals of the way the Company was run and eradicating any 'blind alley' jobs. A permanent training centre, for the cooks and senior canteen staff, as well as for certain officials and clerical staff, was already under construction.

At this point in time the announcement was made, no outdoor uniform would be issued to new staff, engaged for home canteens, after the 1st of January 1946; existing staff though were still allowed to wear the uniform until the 1st of January 1947 – they had already started arranging replacements. Up until this point staff were issued with free shoes but this then stopped on the 31st of December 1946. Staff could also buy the shoes but for those that didn't wear uniform they had to surrender 7 coupons for every pair.

Recognition for staff after the war saw the announcement that a defence medal for all NAAFI staff would be issued under the army council instructions, all civilian staff who had worn the authorised khaki uniform for 3 years in the UK or overseas were eligible for this medal. The NCS staff enrolled in the Royal Navy and all ranks of the RASC/EFI and ATS / EFI were entitled to the award as members of the services if they had fulfilled the necessary conditions. The medal itself had a ribbon with three colours, the centre being Flame with green edges (symbolising the attacks on our green and pleasant land)and black stripes to represent the blackouts.

It was unfortunate that not all staff would be entitled to this, the War Office insisted. That the issue of this medal was only for wearers of the khaki uniform. However uniform civilians and 'service members' of NAAFI staff may also qualify for the 1939-45 star called Atlantic star,

Africa star, Pacific star, Burma star, Italy star and the France and Germany star, if they had a necessary service in the respective areas. At this time the general eligibility before the 1939 to 45 star was based on 6 months' service in various overseas operational areas. Once the 1939-45 star had been awarded, the recipient was eligible to apply for any one of the area campaign stars if he or she had served in the area.

The little ships 1945

Not all NAAFI staff were aware that in all larger HM ships, our NCS provided canteens, libraries, bookstores and soda fountains, all of which required regular replenishment from warehouses ashore. For this task a small fleet of canteen motor launches, in home in foreign waters, had been employed for many years. Sailors everywhere were familiar with these perky delivery boats, going from shore to ship, bringing fresh supplies and returning home with the empties and with indents and messages for the next day's requirements.

From Scapa Flow and the Firth of Forth down to Weymouth Bay and Plymouth Sound, the sturdy little craft of the NCS are known and welcomed by the big ships they serve. They chugged along the Medway, they flit in and out of Malta Harbour, they are found on various parts of the Italian and Grecian coasts, as far off as Africa, the burgee of the canteen launches is a welcome sight for a British sailor, heralding the arrival of fresh items for the canteens, new books for the library, fresh eggs, vegetables and fruit.

Normally most of the launches have fixed homeports at Chatham, Portsmouth, Devonport and Malta. Some more lifts to board the decks of warships and remain with them for protracted cruises. But when the occasion demands, the tough little boats are capable of long journeys on the open sea such as that of the 'Elfirda' and 'Cisiter', which, in the early days of the war, went under their own power from Davenport to Greenock, and the Orkneys. In 1944, in Scapa Flow, the 'Cisiter' was run down by a drifter and thankfully stopped; within eight weeks her 70 tonnes dead weight had been raised, beached, repaired and re-floated ready for the next job.

In the worst weather of the winter of 1939, one coxswain delivered a new launch from Cornwall to Scotland, braving violent storms, icy conditions, enemy submarines, aircraft and mines. His small boat, 48 feet long with a 12-foot beam, survived all hazards. When he started, he was warned, 'that boat won't drown you, but she might starve you'. And indeed, she was stormbound and icebound for several days, and any cooking on board was impossible. And at one point on the 700-mile journey, the local naval authorities refused to permit the craft to proceed through a minefield.

In 1945 it was not so many years since a canteen aboard or warship was an unheard-of luxury. Any additions to the ship rations had to be purchased from the old-time bumboats that flocked around the vessel as soon as she neared port. Then came the first canteen boats, dependent on sale or oars. Old sailors may still recall the Bumboatmen at Portsmouth, who sailed the 'Sultan 'and the 'Sultana', and the 'Turkish delight', and at the last of the contracted sailing boats, 'Wave' and the 'Maggie'. In the late 1890s, steam began to oust the same craft, and steam canteen boats like the 'Favourite' 'Minnie', the 'Egret' and the 'Puffin', appeared at Portsmouth and elsewhere, and rapidly earned a reputation for delivering goods on time in the face of headwinds and tides and natural enemies of the sailing boats.

Steamboats in turn made their way for motorboats. Some of the earlier of these internal combustion engines were both experimental and explosive. They stopped at the most awkward moments, and passing sailors of HM Navy did not improve matters by offering a tow, or suggesting another penny in the slot. Mr Potinger informed us that the first canteen motor launch was built in 1903, 24 feet long, with a 6 feet beam, with a 6 hp engine, and a fine boat they thought her in those days. But in 1944 the 'planet', which joined the NCS fleet was a launch of 54 feet long with a 16-foot beam and had a 54hp engine.

By the outbreak of war in 1914, the fleet's canteens were being served by a fair sized fleet of efficient motor launches, some used as water vans, carrying goods to the ships, and a few fitted floating shops, to which sailors came and made their own purchases. At that time, the motor boats were controlled by a group of private contractors, but with the oncoming of the NACB, and later NAAFI, the NCS was born and for the past quarter of a century HM ships' canteens had been run by the service's own organisation.

In 1939, the NCS could muster 26 launches with a total carrying capacity of some 400 tonnes, varying in size from 30 feet to 70 feet in length and 9 feet to 19 feet beams. This fleet, already prepared for instant war operations, was promptly expanded by the purchase of three Looe Luggers, while 25 tonners laid down the previous year, came into service. Another, the 'Ruxley', was launched in 1940 and the keels of four more the 'Claygate', 'Brompton', 'Catterick' and the 'Kenning', were laid down at once. The new craft for small, powerful boats, 48 feet long with 12-foot beam, and equipped with a 30 hp Kelvin engine.

The present strength of the launch fleet comprised 44 craft and a total personnel of 170 men. The staff worked on their entire fleet from 10 tonners to 60 tonners – this was done by the chief engineer and two girls, with two mechanics and two apprentices to effect repairs. They boasted that not a single boat had a major breakdown at sea. Each small boat had a crew of three, with four or five for the bigger craft. They recruited mostly from the sons of naval men, though during the war all kinds were taken on and did well, fitters, plumbers and bus drivers among them. First class navigators, tough and courageous, these stalwarts well deserved the respect which, despite the leg pulling, they were regarded by HM ships. Their work was arduous as any trawler's hand. Somehow, despite the secrecy demanded by war conditions, they had to keep in touch with fighting ships. They would sail in all weathers in temperatures often below zero, and in the northern waters they had only a few hours of daylight in which to operate. After dark, during the war, no riding lights were shown; on the canteen launch at sea after sunset was as liable to be fired at by our own guns as by an enemy submarine.

As a wartime measure, all launches making the South or South East passage had their wheelhouses fitted with armoured protection and carried a Lewis gun against air attack. One launch, 'Ruxley', engaged an enemy plane off the South West coast and claimed to have brought it down. A sturdy independent craft, the coxswains were all characters, when Captain Duke, former naval manager, made a three-day trip in one of the launches in Scotland.

Resourcefulness in all manner of crises had earned the canteen launches high praise on many occasions. Shipwrecks and other emergencies of the sea always find the boat crews eager to give assistance. Before the War one of the launches rendered invaluable aid for 10 months, in all weathers during the abortive attempts to raise a sunken submarine 'M2'.

During the war, perhaps the most dramatic exploit was the work of the launches, at Scapa Flow throughout the fateful night when the 'Royal Oak' was torpedoed. News of the disaster reached the store's depot at about 0200hrs and, shortly afterwards, in the blackness, and the cold and dreadful silence of the small hours, the launches 'Muriel' and 'Chaucer', soon followed by others, put out to search for survivors. Among the many dead picked up, was the body of a canteen manager aboard 'The Royal Oak'.

Ashore a search party was formed to comb the cliffs for any survivors who may have swam to shore. The 'Royal Oak' sank barely a mile from the cliffs. After hours of climbing and stumbling in the darkness, they heard a cry, and eventually came upon, an 18-year-old lad clad

only in a shirt and covered in thick brown oil. He was the only survivor picked up from the shore. Long after the sun had risen, the canteen launches continued to search The Flow, but at last, when only a huge patch of oil marked the spot where the ship had gone down, the little boats came home, to carry on their normal task of serving those who serve.

On the 13th of February 1940 Mr R W Bailey, driver of MB 'Star', received a letter, from the board of management from NAAFI Ruxley Towers in Claygate. The letter read: "I am directed by the board of management to refer to the excellent work done by employees of the NCS Scapa when the HMS Royal Oak was sunk, and express to you personally the appreciation of the board of your efforts and connection with the rescue work and assisting others in distress." This was signed 'yours faithfully Mr Crosier, Secretary of the Navy Army Air Force Institute'.

It's quite rare to find a personal account of men who served in the early years of the NCS. Dick (Reginald) Bailey was one of generations of the Bailey family men to serve.

Andrew Bailey, the son of Dick (Reginald W) Bailey and grandson of George Walter Bailey, submitted these stories after looking for more information on his family's history with the little ships of the NCS. His father had been with NAAFI NCS from around 1934, and his father before him since before World War One. Below is the story of Dick Bailey in his own words.

My life on the boats, Memories by Dick Bailey.

My earliest memory relating to the river and boats comes from about 1927 when I was 10 years old, and we were living in Pier Road. I used to go with Grandad onto the NAAFI boats early in the morning. If Grandad went off early without me, I used to cry, and sometimes I would gallop down to the wharf by myself. We used to go from Gillingham Pier to the battleships, taking supplies. One boat had a shop in the hold. We used to take it to small ships and the sailors would come aboard and purchase goods, such as toothpaste and soap, eggs and bacon etc. The call was 'Canteen boat, alongside!'.

The boats were old fishing boats or sailing trawlers. The boats I remember at Gillingham were called 'Onward', 'Grace' and 'Leila'. 'Grace' was a mobile brush which used to go round the water lines of vessels in dock. Grandad had this vessel later. I liked the 'Onward' best; it was long with iron bulwarks, and I could snuggle down in the sacks of the cabbages on deck. We used to go to ships in Stangate Creek and to Burntwick Island in the Medway, where there was a naval base. We would deliver beer to the canteen there. There was a very long pier and lots of mud. I used to go with another boy called Archie Hutley. We used to go into the base, and we would be given lemonade by the men. We also used to visit the wreck of the ship that blew up, called the 'Bulwark', and we would service the salvage ship. We used to visit various battleships in Sheerness Harbour to supply their canteens. I would help carry the stores onto the battleships and to the canteen in the foc'sle. This was an open space; during the daytime there were long tables with forms fixed to the hull, but the men's hammocks were stowed there and hung up for the night. It didn't smell of bodies but there was a strong smell of fuel oil.

Grandad used to let me steer the boat coming up the river. The ship had a steering wheel, and a telegraph bell. You would ring twice to go ahead, once to stop, and three times to go astern, and to finish the engine you would go ding a ling. The engineer would respond to your signals, by controlling the engine. I remember one engineer, Mr Barlow. I used to go to his workshop. I learned how to dismantle the Kelvin engine, do the valves, and put them back etc.

When I left school aged 14, I was a co-op van boy earning ten shillings a week. This lasted two years, then they put you off to avoid paying you more. However, I left before that happened and went to Cooper's bakers in Pier Road, again for 10 shillings a week. I had been hankering for this job as it was closer to home and handy for the top of the pier. I couldn't get on the boats until I was 18. Grandad wangled it when I was 17½. I started in the NAAFI as a trainee boatman. I hankered after going away on the small boats which were hoisted onto battleships, because you got extra money for that. The small boats that we used for delivering the goods were hoisted onto the battleships and we travelled with our boats stowed on their decks. We slept in the hold of our own boat and ate in the battleship mess. The food was bloody awful compared to Granny's food, things like soup with vegetables in. On smaller ships like the canteen messing ship, it was better because the sailors bought and cooked their own food in the ship's galley. However, most of the modern cruisers just before the war, like the 'Sheffield', were quite good. Ships like this weighed about 10,000 tonnes and had about 1200 men on them. Battleships were about 27,000 tonnes, such as the 'Resolution', the 'Ramillies' and the 'Revenge'. We travelled from Invergordon to Scapa on the 'Sheffield'. This was the last one we travelled on because the war had started.

The sailors were lovely – as I was young, they would come and talk to me. They would be working, especially on the guns, and painting and scraping, brushing up the decks. The sea men would be on deck, but there were also stewards, cooks, signalmen, radio operators. The captain used to come on his rounds. He would inspect our boat, make sure it was clean and tidy, and check that there was no loafing about, and that people were wearing clean overalls. He would congratulate you on your boat's tidiness, and if everything was stowed, cleaned and put away, and the engine polished. We had our own lifting gear to hoist us on board the battleships; it was stowed inside our boat and lashed up under the deck. This was quite a hair-raising process if it was a bit rough, with a strong wind or a flood tide. It was as much as I could do to lift up the ring of the sling, and put it onto the crane hook, with the boat rolling and pitching about.

Once the war started you had to be in uniform, so I joined the Navy in Scapa Flow. The senior officer in charge on the pier enjoined us as naval auxiliaries. I was a Petty Officer to start with because of my years' experience as Cox'n on boats. I started in Gibraltar, landing from a troopship. I had to go and see my launch lifted out of a merchant ship which had been transporting coal. The boat was new, but it was in a pickle, very mucky with coal dust. It was a 'Star' class boat, a new NAAFI boat, the Silver Queen – 36 feet long.

I stayed in Gibraltar for a while. Then I had to hoist aboard a big merchant ship which sailed from Gibraltar, the 'Ocean Faith', but after about half a day the ship got engine trouble and had to return to port. I joined another ship outside the harbour called the 'Empire Viceroy'.

This was a big ship with heavy lift derricks. Our ship was only eight tons, not heavy enough to make the new gear lower us down. I used to stay on the boat being hoisted. Now I was stuck on this small boat up in the air. They threw me up a line, and I made it fast to the crane hook. They then put it onto a winch and then were able to heave the launch down.

The 'Empire Viceroy' took us to Malta. It was a big ship and didn't enter the harbour, so our boat was hoisted out and we motored into Malta, to the Imperial quay. We had to report to the St Angelo naval base. We worked around the harbour for a while servicing warships. I remember one of the Customs officials in Malta called Joe. It was his job to take a note of the duty-free stores. His family was starving after the siege. We used to give them our rations and food, because they were living on swedes.

There were three crew on our boat. We didn't know where we were going next – they gave us the number of a ship, we were hoisted onto it, and sailed to Alexandria. We were hoisted out there and given the base ship to report to. Then we were directed to the shoreside where we stayed for a while. Then we were hoisted by a floating crane at Alexandria. We were then put on to a goods train with a long truck known as an 'alligator', so we went across the desert on a boat on a train! When we got to Suez we were hoisted off and given the number of a ship across a vast bay. The ship was hiding under trees, and we were hoisted aboard that by another floating crane. We joined a convoy for a while, and then the ship we were on was on its own. I was lookout on the bridge and kept watch, looking for torpedoes.

This was an old Greek ship – and so was the skipper. We used to take our meals in the galley and one day I complained about the food. There were live animals on deck – goats, ducks, chickens. There was a Lascar crew, and the meat had to be killed every morning fresh before sunrise, ready for lunch. It was a huge galley, and the cook would chuck a handful of ghee onto the cooking plate. Blue smoke would rise up and then he would whack whole chops it on for a few minutes and then onto the plate. The meat wasn't cooked, and you couldn't chew it. I went up to the bridge to complain to the officer. The captain came out and rattled on in Greek. I asked the CO what the captain had said. The reply was, 'If anybody comes up complaining about the food, I will chuck you and the food overboard. Don't you know there's a war on?' I replied, 'Of course I b. . . . . know there's a war on!' We had come through the English and Mediterranean war to get to that place. And he said that to me!

The First Officer was a nice man, and he patted me on the back. After that we kept our own stores in the bilge to keep them cool and used those. The bread on the ship wasn't too bad, twisted rolls.

In Columbo we worked servicing warships. We used to go up the canal at the back of St Joseph's College which was a naval barracks. There was a big lake behind the College which we used to motor up. We were supposed to sleep in the barracks, but we slept in the boat. We used to get hold of rations, scrounge and help ourselves. For example, we might go to a ship and get 500 cases of Baxter's sausages as part of the job, then we would prise open the case and take some out and nail it up again! The first trip of the day used to be at six o'clock in the morning to get frozen meat. We would get sides of bacon, whole lambs and mutton, or slabs of beef, and shift it quickly to two or three ships, together with dry goods. For example, a destroyer would come in and would get two sides of bacon. We mostly serviced small ships, as big ships had their own stores. We used to supply fresh fruit, cases of ham from the store ship, as much as you could lift, tinned fruit, peas. A lot of it came from Canada, and South Africa.

We stayed in a big house in Columbo, which was a lovely place in those days. We would tie the boat up of a night-time and stay there with NAAFI people. We explored the town wearing our uniforms. We got to know some of the locals. One man who worked in the NAAFI store invited us to his daughter's wedding. We went to the house afterwards, away from the town, and had very nice spicy food. There was also a lovely local boy called Peter aged about 17, who was our daily labourer.

One of my crew was John Smith, known as Joe. He was a big boy, very homesick and about to get married. He was pining desperately for his girlfriend. He went somewhere else in the end.

We started getting people joining us who were looking for passage to Australia. We had to hand the boat over to two or three of them who took it to Australia. We did nothing much towards the end of that period, we just had to wait for a troopship. When it came, I was separated from my crewmates who went into different parts of the ship, but we could meet up.

It was quite a good life when you weigh it up. Where we were, you could walk from the bungalow to the beach and the Indian Ocean in 10 minutes. There was a canteen in the Navy place. But Edna didn't know where I was for six to eight weeks at a time, although she did start getting airmail letters once we were in Ceylon.

Pte W Arnold tells story of time spent in Celebes 1945

On the 25th of November 1945 a small draft was assembled in the SEAC for dispatch to an unknown destination, it was later to materialise as the Celebes, situated in the heart of the East Indies between Borneo and New Guinea. The next day they would wait on another new EFI venture, in the Moreton Bay, just a small BIS draft under the leadership of captain DR Levett, bound for Balik Papan with its first stop. Within 4 days they were there but had to put up with the three day wait before they could get across to Madagascar, this was the capital of the Celebes group of islands. The stay was a pleasant one and they were made very much at home by the Australians who were then in residence. The sea was quite near, and there was a good-sized beach. The final stage was completed in the 'Circassia', and Madagascar was eventually reached after an excellent trip with, rather strangely in those days, ample accommodation on board.

A grand welcome awaited them from the Aussies who arrived in advance of the British brigade which was eventually to take over the territory and they soon settled into making the most of their 3 weeks' before they took over the BIS. Although the town was small it was quite attractive. The Aussies proved the very existence of hospitality and there was plenty of sightseeing, with the excellent swimming to be had. Christmas of 1945 lived up to the usual expectations and by midnight they were all well-oiled, so much though that they decided to celebrate by firing off some Japanese rifles, which in view of their unbalanced condition was accompanied with their backs to the wall. The police were not long in making enquiries but by that time everybody just sat there and were blatantly drinking. New year passed much the same boisterous spirit as some had the bright idea, which they decided not to do, by firing of a Japanese mortar to make a heavier barrage.

Soon afterwards they were at work, some stayed to get on with the job and others went back to Balik Papan to obtain more supplies. There was much opposition in the matter of obtaining supplies, but they beat the Dutch to it. A week later the WVS and the FANYS arrived and a canteen was opened in Madagascar in no time. In addition, a rest centre was opened up and everything was then ready for when the British troops arrived a week later. Once the boys had got back from Balik Papan they had a further shipload of stores that had arrived from Singapore so there BIS was in a very good position. The most gratifying things were that the Australians now had access to the canteens, something which was entirely new to them and they were not used to the support afforded by the British.

All of the staff soon had their particular civilian friends and many pleasant hours were spent on picnics and sport outings. Dancing was very popular but there were several clashes between our boys and the Dutch! Although there was plenty of work, they had plenty of time for relaxation in Madagascar; as far as the EFI was concerned it was short lived.

At the end of April 1946, the brigade pulled out and took a month to clear up. The cook house, Chris and Eddie's corner house, worked overtime during that period. At the end of June, the job was done and the day before their departure saw the whole of the staff gathered together for a farewell party. A grand finale to the Madagascan escapes! The next day they were on their way to Singapore which they had left some 7 months earlier, so they had many misgivings about what lay before them. Despite the bleak nature of the territory they found that life would bring the same happiness as they found before.

Of the people who had accompanied this small party it can be said they were just pals together Captain DR Levett, Sgt Stead Pitman who later became a Warrant Officer of the BIS at Singapore, Cpl Lofty Livesey, William Burford, a cashier, Wilf Obadiah, a clerk, Nick Nichols and Norman Primmer as a storeman, Gordon Haslam, a driver, Edward Wootton, a cook and the writer who they christened Louie by his friends. Although a short deployment, a good one and stuck in their memories ever since.

His dream came true: Mr George Cocks. 1945

An English autumn with the smell of burning leaves lingering in the soft warm air was the dream that kept Frederick George Cocks alive when he was a prisoner of war in Japan. The colour of an English garden contrasted cruelly with the wartime surroundings when he was a Stoker at the large furnace in an industrial plant at Magaki, near Osaki. All captains and uniformed personnel were considered part of the Japanese force, whether the man in uniform was a Guardsman or a sanitary engineer.

His own uniform was that of the RASC EFI, in which he held the rank of staff Sergeant. The Japanese appointed him as group leader of a section of 50 men. They lived in huts, with just rice and beans with a small allowance of meat once a month. One day in 1945 the prisoners were told that they were to have the following three days off in mourning for the Japanese who had died in the war. There was a growing excitement among the prisoners. The war was over in Europe and rumours circulated that the far eastern war was over. The rumours were strengthened by the arrival of American aircraft flying over. The first stage of freedom for Mr Cocks found himself aboard a hospital ship which sailed for Yokohama, and home via Manila. He eventually arrived home on Guy Fawke's Day 1945. He picked up the threads of his interrupted career with NAAFI as a district account at Ruxley Towers in July 1946. He joined NAAFI in October 1921 as a canteen assistant at Aldershot grocery shop and for a short time was an assistant manager.

In 1934 he joined overseas service and after a training course in London he made his first trip abroad, just Singapore, in April 1934 where he managed grocery shops and restaurants in a new cantonment at Changi for three years. It was a small area but there was a gradual build of business and a staff of 10 was eventually needed to run a restaurant for the troops of the Royal engineers, Royal Artillery and over 60 families. There was also a shop and restaurant on the offshore island of Tanglin to run. He returned home on leave in July 1937, married and returned with his bride to Singapore, then a peaceful cosmopolitan city marred only by the closing of the naval base, but still unaffected by the impending threat of the approaching war. The new couple's free time passed in a pleasant social round with a lot of time spent in the local swimming pool or in playing mah-jong.

In 1938, he and his wife left for Hong Kong, where he took up the position of canteen Manager and warehouse manager until the capitalization of Hong Kong. His wife was evacuated to Australia and stayed in Melbourne until 1943, before returning to the United Kingdom. He was taken prisoner and was held nearly a year in Hong Kong, before moving with other NAAFI personnel – this included Mr DW Joyce – to Japan. They were transported in the hold of a ship with 300 other Europeans. He returned to the Far East in 1954, to a modern and rebuilt Singapore. He met many people he had known before the war, including a man he had been a junior assistant with in Hong Kong in 1938. Many years later he returned home and moved to Aldershot at the end of his 20 years' service with the company.

1946

Reputation 1946

Start of 1946, this saw a swarm of criticism whether it be bored soldiers, barrack room lawyers, the lack of cigarettes for a few days or the NAAFI tea made the wrong way, it led to letters to the press, cartoons and even questions in the House on the front bench. But in true style it miraculously blew over, although the service could have improved the study day-to-day education of the services and the public in the principles and practice of how the company was run and how it yielded the best results. Although probably it was the consequences of the millions of fighting men, drafted from overseas, and discovering NAAFI at their side wherever they went from Iceland to Singapore. They saw the company in Crete and Greece where the NAAFI men, and later on the NAAFI girls, sharing the hazards and discomforts of the northern African campaign. The staff swarmed after them into the Scilly Isles and Italy and even following them hard on their heels to the Normandy beaches and into the heart of Berlin. Even in the Italian mountains the supplies were brought to them on the back of mules and in the desert the camels were laden with stock; where they had to get the stock across African rivers, they loaded canoes. The NAAFI men and girls were killed and wounded and captured in their duty and loyal service to their comrades in arms. They had finally won the respect and gratitude of the vast majority of the serving men by this point.

The clubs were opened and the newspapers began to compliment the sterling work done by the company and the staff; the post bag at headquarters groaned with letters of thanks and compliments from the serving men and women, paying tributes to the work of the staff in all parts of the world. A key event which is more than worthwhile remarking on, but also to make sure that this event be recorded as it was in 1946.

A Royal visit to Portsmouth 31st January 1946

HRH Princess Elizabeth arrived on the 31st January 1946 to open the 1st NAAFI since the end of the war. Mr Wynne-Tyson escorted the Princess on a tour of the club. She saw the light and airy games room which was well equipped the cloakrooms with baths, shampoo room and facilities for washing, drying, and ironing clothes. She was also shown the sales kiosk in the main hall and WVS information Bureau at the Tavern which she admired. There was some question about the amount of beer which would be consumed; the Princess gasped amusingly at the quantity revealed! She was incredibly interested in the new soda fountain and chatted to one of the attendants as to how many flavours were supplied. In the restaurant it was explained what its function was, and the Princess remarked on how much she liked the colour of the room. There were various gadgets in the kitchen which appealed; this included the washing up machine, the potato peeler and chipping machine, and the apparatus for turning out 60 slices of buttered bread a minute.

Before the tour came to an end the Princess was guided to the table with a portrait of His Majesty the King, above as she signed her name on the vellum, when a small hiccup meant the gold fountain pen that had been placed on the table for the signing would not work. She was quickly passed a pen and the Princess also signed the visitor's book on the same page that the Queen had signed it on her visit. When they made their way into the ballroom where the opening ceremony took place and the moment the Royal party came down the centre of the room the band of the Royal Marines played the national anthem.

The Princess gave a speech:

> *My Lord Mayor, my Lords, ladies and gentlemen, I have just completed a tour of this club, and I'm glad to know that the men and women still in the forces, and those who come after them, are to enjoy the endless amenities, comfort and recreation available in the splendid surroundings. It is a club of which every member may well be proud, and in a traditional service centre such as Portsmouth it is assured a long, busy, and useful life. I am delighted to know that there is already a chain of similar NAAFI clubs stretched from Aberdeen to Singapore, by the way of France, Belgium, Germany, Austria, Italy, the Middle East, Ceylon, Burma and Malaya; in fact, in almost all those far flung areas where British troops are still serving. If they compare with this Portsmouth club, then the relatives and friends of men serving overseas may feel reassured that their menfolk are so well served.*
>
> *Most of these clubs will eventually close down as the need for them disappears; but the Portsmouth club will remain a permanent feature of this great city. This is the first post-war club which NAAFI established as a permanent social centre for other ranks of 3 services. I understand that other similar permanent clubs are planned for various naval and military centres in this country; undoubtedly, they will make no small contribution to the welfare of the men and women of our peacetime Navy, Army, and Air Force.*
>
> *The work of NAAFI during the war is well known to all who have served. NAAFI has done great things in the face of immense difficulties; And although much credit is due to those who have planned and directed the vast flow of NAAFI stores, equipment and personnel, to all war fronts and to the majority of the fighting ships, I think a special word may be said for the hard working staff who have spent long, hard years in direct service of their brothers and sisters in arms.*
>
> *The men and women of the NAAFI, by the nature of their jobs, have shared the hazards and sacrifices of war. Hundreds of NAAFI men serving on battlefronts and in ships at sea have been killed, wounded, and taken prisoner; many NAAFI girls have gallantly endured shelling and bombing for long periods. I recall among others, the NAAFI girls at Dover who flatly refused to be moved from their posts throughout the long ordeal of that gallant town. And I think of the girls who, during the Battle of Britain, continued their work on southern airfields in the days when dive bombing and frequent casualties were accepted with a fine spirit of fortitude and loyalty to the men they served.*
>
> *That same spirit is the keynote of this Club, and will I am sure find a ready response in the hearts of all the men and women who now and in the years to come, find rest, refreshment, and recreation within these walls. I wish good fortune to you all who serve in this club and all who are served by it, and I now have the great pleasure of declaring this club open.*

The Princess so rightly received a standing ovation at the end of her speech. The commander in chief gave an amusing address and a vote of thanks from Sir Launcelot-Royal, by way of the entertainment; this included Geraldo and his orchestra, Miss Phyllis Robins and Miss Gillie Porter.

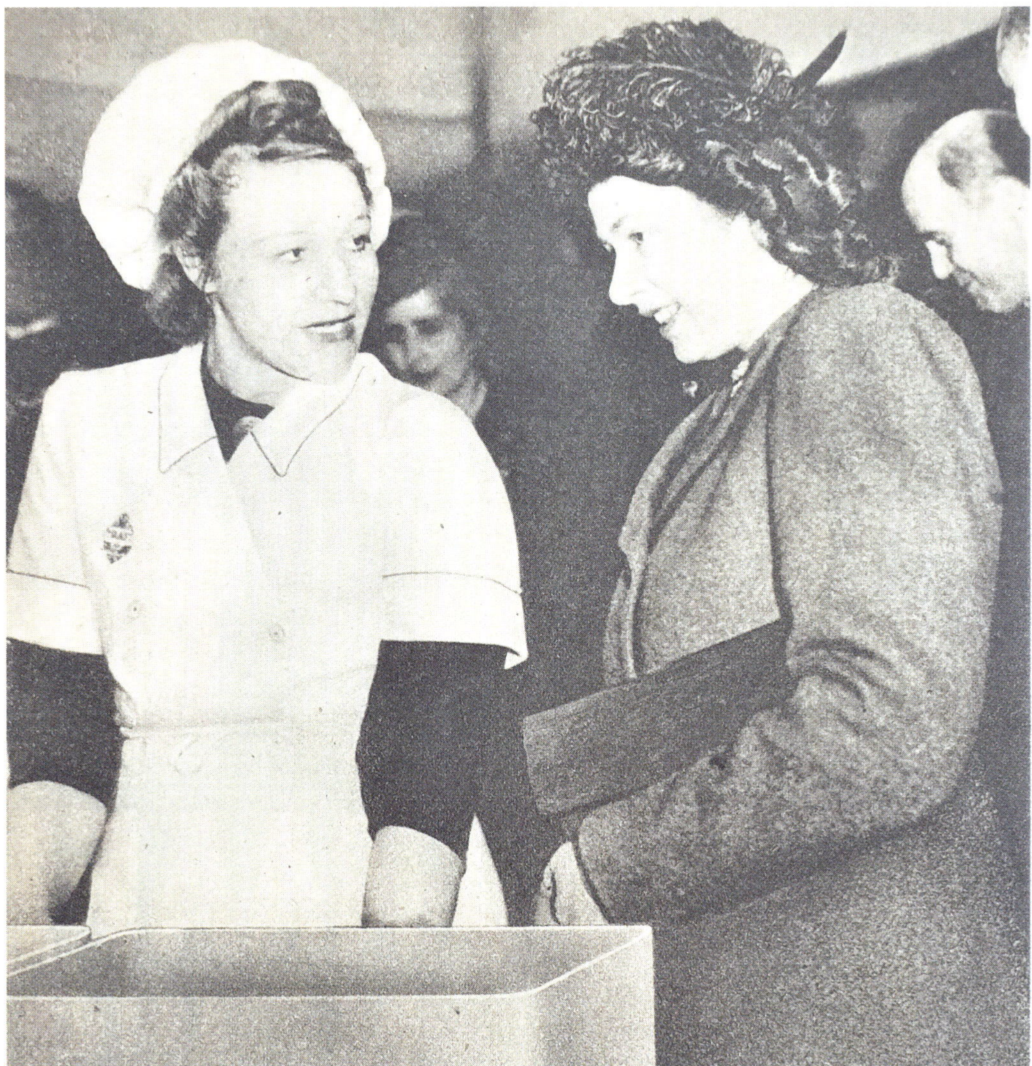

Identity Crisis 1946

In the summer of 1946 NAAFI still had an identity crisis. The discontent felt from the very people it served was quite pronounced and unfortunately joining an important conference that was attended by the government and NAAFI officials the chairman of the meeting blatantly opened the business with the remark: before we start what exactly is NAAFI?

Six years of hard labour growing to meet the needs of the armed forces expanding so quickly and understanding that new departments were opened and closed during this time, the recognition was still not quite there yet. But yes, it was recognised that with the challenge confronting them in 1939 the company recognised this as an opportunity. Scores of thousands of young men were drafted into the peacetime services each year and when their period of conscription was over, they would return to civilian life full of tales of their experiences in the NAAFI.

The way was clear, this was their chance to ensure that by ever improving the amenities and the efficiency, courteous and cheerful service, start this course of education of each of every one of these short term sailors, soldiers and airmen will carry back to civvy street the memories and the sound of the knowledge of the canteen organization and its ideals, methods and its usefulness. The goal was, with its reputation and the aim was for 10 years following, 2 million men would have completed their military service and must give the same verdict, "NAAFI treated us well". Only hard work at this point would build their reputation and cast them firmly in the hearts and minds of all service personnel that came through every establishment the company opened.

Votes of confidence came from all 3 areas of the armed forces and 1st up from the senior service, Fourth Sea Lord, Vice Admiral Sir Douglas Fisher KBE, CB. Wherever the Navy went, we found that we could rely on NAAFI to supply us with some of those small luxuries of life, which helped turn a grim day into a happy one, into a friendly base. After action stations, and during the daily routine, the canteen was a place of popular resort, contributing much to the life of the ship and the contentment of the ship's company. Life on board without NAAFI would certainly be hard to contemplate. The canteen's float provided an especially close link between the Royal Navy and the NAAFI, the staff sharing to the full and dangers of discomforts inherent in service at sea and in war. Thank you for all your cheerful efficient service. The Royal Navy is confident that she will continue it in peace as in war.

This was closely followed by the quartermaster general to the forces Lt Gen Sir Daril G Watson, KCB, CBE, MC. In the army we know and appreciate the longer loyal service at home and overseas of the NAAFI men and girls, the men of the RASC/ EFI, the girls of the ATS /EFI, the civilian workers, the mobile drivers, the canteen assistance, the staff of NAAFI shops and NAAFI clubs, and all those backroom personnel, the officials, clerks, typists, warehousemen, drivers, and many others who have done so much to ease the lot of the British soldier. On his behalf may I make a request to you all? Do not relax your efforts now that the war is over. The army of today and the new army of tomorrow look to NAAFI to maintain and even surpass the high standards of service it's achieved during the war years. I know you will not fail them.

And finally, from the air member for supply and organisation, Air Chief Marshal Sir Leslie N Hollinghurst, KBE, CB, DFC. We of the Royal Air Force, are only too conscious of the service given to us by the in NAAFI throughout the war. Wherever we have been, the Battle of Britain, from the beaches of Normandy to Berlin, from Gibraltar to the Cocos islands, NAAFI have been. Our battle honours are shared but your work is not finished. The Royal Air Force look forward confidently to an ever-improving standard of that service which has already made you justly famous. The establishment of well-appointed clubs in many of the large towns in this country and abroad, the thought which has been devoted to improving the appointments of existing institutes are welcome signposts to the future. Keep it up, we need you no less today than we did yesterday.

Reginald Stagg MVO OBE 1946

Reginald Stagg MVO OBE, who retired in this year and handed over the reins to Mr Stanley Barker OBE, left a short write up of his years with the company as he looked back at 52 years' hard work and over 30 years including two wars. He can look back at the conditions of the canteens and happenings of the war in 1914 and look at the conditions after the Second World War in 1946; they should congratulate themselves on the results that they achieved. He started canteen work at Bovington camp in 1914, when Lord Howick asked the War Office for permission for R Stagg &co, to be put on the list of civilian contractors to conduct a regimental Institute for the 9th Northumberland Fusiliers. Permission was obtained and soon he was giving his wholehearted personal attention to the job, he had requests from other units at Bovington to take over their institutes including the Berkshire regiment, and the Ox and Bucks Light Infantry and others.

He did not see that his time at Bovington was about to make history in the canteen business by being the first contractor to employ women in canteens. The improvement was instantaneous; it raised the standard of canteens and the cleanliness, and the customers were delighted with the innovation. The turnover increase and the consequence the profits increased to a satisfactory level. Reginald had no hesitation in saying that had it not been for the introduction of women in the canteens they would not be as popular with our customers as they are today.

B J Sayer MBE, the NCS 1946

Born in Chatham, he had the early ambition to become a dockyard apprentice, but his parents moved to London and at the age of 14 he entered the service of Messers Kearley & Tonge Limited at their Aldgate office. He was paid no more than £20 a year, paid in monthly. His first job was extending the order sheets and receiving from the branches, his arithmetic was a strong point and he was soon anticipating an increase in wage. Unfortunately, this was deferred for 6 months.

In 1917 he joined the Navy army canteen board was engaged by the first naval manager, the late Mr James Yates, whom he had known through his business dealings with the Messers K&T limited. He was sent to Kirkwall to take charge of the warehouse and sort out the stock issues. He soon found that he had a tough job in seeing that the canteen managers did not try to hoodwink him. But after some restructuring, they were now no longer to purchase goods on their own account, and they had to adhere to the new rules. He fondly remembers one morning arriving at the warehouse to find all of the staff lined up with slips of paper in their hand posing as musicians, with the canteen manager of HMS Barham acting as bandmaster. They greeted him to a song to the tune of 'a long, long trail':

There are miles of red tape winding,
Round the NACB
It reaches right from Knightsbridge
To Scapa by the sea
There are miles and miles of forms
To be filled in by me
Then you wonder why I moan and groan
At the NACB.

Now some of the later requests from the Depot manager in this period had quite a few strange commissions to execute for the commanding officer. He tells tales of how he was requested to produce a dozen baby bottles – this was to fit a wooden replica of a sow that had died giving birth and in a bid to save the litter they needed bottles in which to feed the piglets, which on another occasion he was asked to obtain a dozen live rats to test the dog. In 1924 he went to Invergordon as Atlantic fleet Superintendent. He found it was the practice of the local fishermen to hawk their catch round the ships each day, gradually lowering their prices until they are disposed of it. This naturally decreased his own sales, so he made a bargain with them to purchase their catch first thing every morning. One morning they had over caught on live crabs, they begged him to take the lot for a pound. This he did and when the canteen manager came aboard, he told them to club together and give him a pound and they could share the crabs and do what they liked with them. The next day he was aboard ship and passing the galley, when the chief cook shouted, 'oi are you the canteen bloke' he said yes – 'look at those pans'. His range was smothered with small saucepans each man had taken his live crab to be cooked. At this point he didn't buy any more live crabs.

One of his oddest requests was when he was building up stocks for Overlord, bars of chocolate were not available and he had to accept all Mars bars. He was very amused, when Depot managers telephoned headquarters, asking when the chocolate would arrive. 'Have you had any Mars bars?' the reply would come back 'I'm chock a block with them', 'that's your chocolate'! These are happy days that he recalls from the many years he spent with the NCS.

Capt. J A Carr RASC EFI 1st March 1946

John Carr, who was born in Leyton, East London in August of 1914 enlisted in the RASC in March 1940. Commissioned 2nd Lieutenant in December 1942 he served in North Africa and subsequently for three years in Ceylon and later transferred to NAAFI/ EFI then promoted to Captain.

Posted to Palestine in March 1946, during the hostilities he was killed in a terrorist attack in the Goldsmiths officers club, in Jerusalem, on the 1st of March 1947. Some sources state that he died of wounds at the local British military hospital on the same day.

The incident occurred after a reprisal, for the incidents that happened when the SS Ulna, carrying illegal immigrants, ran aground at Haifa on the 28th of February 1947. IRGUN and STERN carried out a series of terrorist attacks throughout Palestine on the 1st and 2nd of March 1947. The most serious of these was the attack on the Goldsmiths officers club in Jerusalem.

The attack itself took part at 1542hrs on the 1st of March, when light automatic fire was directed at the gardens of the officers' club. After an exchange of fire one of the terrorists placed a phosphorus bomb alongside the guard tent then another threw a suitcase through a side window of the club. Some other unidentified objects also placed against the side of the building, then they ran off. What came next was a large explosion destroying the south end of the building, which collapsed burying several occupants. Alongside Capt Carr, a number of other fatalities and casualties occurred. After this a 1900hrs curfew was imposed on the Jewish area of Jerusalem and on the 2nd of March 1947 martial law was imposed on part of the Jewish area of the North of the city.

The birth of the NCS and EFI, Old Comrades Association 1946

At the end of the war, so many of our own personnel were coming back, to be demobilised, and in the early part of 1946 it was suggested on the 25th March 1946 that the formation of an Association to assist those coming back from the front and the far corners wherever our armed forces served.

The old Comrades Association started to take shape, NCS/EFI OCA.

Sir Launcelot C Royle, the chairman of the board of management was elected as the 1st president of the Association at the first general meeting held at Ruxley Towers on the Monday of October the 21st 1946. S Baker, FH Crosier, TE Pegg, R Stagg and AL Trundle were elected as vice presidents.

At this point the committee had no funds and an announcement was made subject to certain conditions that the management were willing to assist the Association by making grants to its funds; they would also pay for their secretarial costs of the general committee at the headquarters. The biggest statements that could have been made which sits with the Association even today was made by the very first chairman Lt Col R Merry – he said that he felt everything should be done to foster the feeling of comradeship which had grown out of the war.

If possible, the Association should endeavour to assist those who had served and their dependants, referring to the question of the Association Journal the Colonel did not think it practical for anything of this kind to be attempted at the present time. Arrangements had been made at this time that any of the Association's activities should appear in their NAAFI news. This was to make sure that people who were not members should find out about the Association and those who were already members could see that although their service was over, they would be part of something bigger.

After discussions following the agreements regarding the objects and rules of the Association were reached.

1. to foster a feeling of comradeship amongst all ranks and commissioned, enrolled or attested, who have served, or are serving, in the NCS, RASC/EFI, ATS /EFI, and to assist members who through no fault of their own, are in difficulty or distress;
2. to assist families' independence of members.

Copyright Sue A Lowe

The NCS RASC/ATS as part of the EFI, are eligible for membership, except personnel discharged for misconduct. The annual subscription at this time was 10 shillings a year for officers, 4 shillings for CPOs, POs, WOs, and sergeants, and 2 shillings and sixpence per year for ratings and other ranks. Subscriptions were paid directly to the secretary, who would return 3/5 of each of the member's subscription to the branch to which the member belonged. The general committee had the power to expel members for non-payment of annual subscription or for conduct prejudicial to the good name of the Association. They designed an attractive badge which would then be forwarded to members, together with a membership card embodying the rules when they joined the Association; this happened in early 1947.

All the funds were to be invested in the general committee who would administer them for the objectives of the Association. Branches of the Association were then be formed throughout the country and also overseas. It was only then after the 1st general meeting, that a special meeting was held to determine the areas in which to have branch committees, and potential chairmen of these committees would be approached by letter. It was decided that the branch committee should consist of at least 5 members. Some indication at this stage for the association's benevolent aims and this was gained from the committee's decision that, in urgent cases, the chairman of the branches could authorise an amount up to £3 for members of the Association in need of financial aid. Relief grants were only up to £10 and could be given, provided at least 2 members of the general committee approved the grant. Larger grants could only be authorised by approval of the general committee at a meeting. It would be worth mentioning here as there were EFI ladies to be part of this Association; the decision was made that the OC of the ATS of the EFI Depot be Co-opted as a member of the general committee.

NAAFI EFI South East Asia and Far East, Singapore. The EFI SEArchlight Publication.

SEArchlight publication was first edited by Leo (F Walmsley), who from January 1946 worked tirelessly on getting the EFI SEArchlight out to so many troops with his final number being 72.

Whilst EFI troops were serving overseas, they still suffered the same pitfalls as every other serving soldier. In Singapore on a boat bound for home and then they were taken off, having their leave cancelled or that time extended. This could also happen in reverse – in 1944 in

Norwood a batch of some 20 members of the 'O' force had their embarkation leave cancelled, after they'd had their leave pay, ration cards and passes, and they ended up staying at Norwood for a further 3 months, and then they got no leave. But this was back in 1944 when the war was still on and travelling was just the luck of the game. But after the war any hiccups in transportation, the blame was laid completely on their superiors for mishaps and even they were in the same boat as staff. In all honesty, as it was then as it is today, it's always depended on a higher authority, who would have to consider the pros and cons before taking any decisive step, to move or not to move.

Some of the members of EFI were veterans of the First World War and unfortunately, the SEArchlight publication was the only place where people would find out when they'd lost one of their beloved members. Sgt Walter McGuire, on the 22nd of April 1946, who was only 47 years old, passed away in Singapore due to cancer. He was a bit of a character, a somewhat of a big personality with the other staff. He had teamed up with the Normandy force at Norwood in March 1944. He was a Lancashire lad, with bright red hair, and a physical training instructor, he instilled personnel with confidence, and his pleasant personality endeared him to all. Everybody knew him as Mac, and he would think nothing of spending half a day, touring the London canteens, to build up a stock of cigarettes; this was the time when they were scarce, but the need of his comrades was more important and he was often giving somebody a cigarette or a sub until they got their own.

He served right through the North-western European campaign as a bulk issue stores and restaurant manager; he volunteered to do a little more in SEAC. He went to Sumatra from Madras in the October and took over the bulk issue store at Palembang and this was where in the March he was evacuated to Singapore before he passed. His final resting place was under the tropical palms in Wing Loon Military Cemetery at Changi.

On the 22nd of April a new draft arrived, the ATS /EFI ladies arrived; these were 16 manageresses. A few of them had already gone to Hong Kong to prepare the way for the auxiliary staff who would be posted. In the June EFI personnel in A &S groups were released from BAOR. Personnel were being moved to SEAC from Paris, others were coming back from the Middle East.

In Java the NAAFI activities were coming to a close and these were handed over to the Dutch army who were now taking over Sourabaya and its three establishments.

Although they were handing over, their final farewell was a party in the officers' club. The farewell party was made up of a small naval force dressed as glamour girls and pirates. In the middle of a dance session half a dozen naval officers suddenly appeared, dressed in a chef's cap and a white apron; they produced a stove and a 20 inch frying pan which they set up in the middle of the dance floor and they proceeded to fry eggs; the omelettes were then served to the GOC and his party. They sang He's a Jolly Good Fellow, Auld Lang Syne and generally had a raucous time whilst it was being played out on the radio where the listeners must have thought it was V day in Sourabaya. The comments were fed back from Captain Gordon who was somewhat shocked at the goings on but he commented: "When we first arrived in Sourabaya, the going was very rough and 5 Ind Div. were not particularly interested in there NAAFI /EFI but now on leaving all the ranks vote it would have been a poor show without you."

The GOC's visit to the district office before he left for Batavia, stopped to say: "The party was a very fine show indeed, it may be a long time before they get to, amongst other things, dance to music, orchestral concerts, free cinema shows, and beer at 3d a glass, all under 1 roof." He conveyed his personal thanks to the NCOs and the rest of the staff for all the good work and most importantly for maintaining harmony amongst the allied troops.

Gallantry award 1946

The Expeditionary Force driver R.W. Chesworth had a dramatic story to tell after an incident on the road in Italy with an armed soldier who attempted to steal his NAAFI car when the driver of the car, Chesworth, part of the EFI, reported to Ruxley Towers to receive his gallantry award. The story goes that one morning in April of 1946 he was driving a saloon car near Conegliano, when a soldier thumbed a lift and the driver obliged. During the journey the soldier said very little except to ask a few questions about the dashboard instruments. Five miles beyond Bassagliopente, when the car came to a crossroads and pulled up, the soldiers said to him, "carry on driving around this corner and no harm will come to you". Chesworth felt a revolver thrust into his ribs. He says, "I stopped in the middle of the road so that I could attract the attention of passing vehicles, I then hit him in the face with my fist and grabbed the pistol. I heard a shot and saw smoke from the barrel, but I didn't know what had been hit. I unlocked the door with one hand and kept hold of the pistol with the other. I then kicked him through the door, and he fell onto the ground. We then began fighting in the road. He kept grabbing for the pistol, and I kept on trying to hit him with it.

"While we were fighting, I realised I had been shot, I felt a pain above my left thigh, and I was weak from the loss of blood which was now all over my battle dress." He got up and ran away to the car which was now 20 yards away. "As it was starting off, I jumped onto the running board and pointed the pistol at him, the soldier cried, 'don't shoot', he said 'it's loaded'. His voice was high pitched as though he was screaming. I tried to fire the pistol, but it was jammed, I then tried to hit him with it but caught my hand on the roof of the car. As he swung the car sharply, I lost my balance and fell onto the road. He increased his speed and got away."

Luckily his wound was not serious, and he was able to resume duty after a short spell in hospital. As well as the gallantry award and inscribed clock, he also received a cheque for £25 – this was provided by the company's underwriters. Before leaving Ruxley Towers he remarked to an official of the OCS: "I served right through the Italian campaign in the anti-tank regiment and didn't get a scratch. I had to join NAAFI to get shot!"

It just goes to show the company staff, although serving the services, were also putting their lives on the line like every other soldier.

Remembrance Day 11th November 1946

On the 8th of November 1946, Leo writes in his editor's section in the SEArchlight just before Remembrance Sunday. One of the most touching parts of this particular issue, was faded photograph of white crosses, in a portion of Kranji Military Cemetery in Singapore, one which clearly can be seen to say 'unknown empire soldier', with a small section underneath which reads 'the monuments of man are dust, and rust soon clogs the memory; but nature knows no human lust, and guards the shrine eternally'.

> *'November the 11th at 1100 hours! There is not one among us that has not stood in silence to pay tribute to those who died in two world wars in order that our kith and kin might be spared the tyranny of a ruthless foe. Whether it be at a cathedral with all the splendour of ecclesiastical ceremony, or on a grassy lawn before a simple village memorial or even in the public highway, at that solemn moment when even the pulse of modern Commerce ceases to beat, or just alone indoors, each one of us will think back to the days that were, when, in dire adversity, we banded together and sacrificed all for the common cause.*
>
> *But after November the 11th will it be? Are we to be unmindful of the Supreme sacrifice of so many until next November? Or are we to reform in serried ranks and endeavour, each in his different sphere, to give of our best to the greater glory of those who died?*
>
> *Peace is now with us. Nuremberg is passed and Tokyo war trials will conclude the final act in the most memorable and terrible phase of our history. Yet, civil reconstruction lies ahead if anything a greater task than the one which we have already accomplished.*
>
> *Self-aggrandisement, prejudice, suspicion are creeping back on exerting an overpowering influence on our daily actions. Unless we can halt our steps, disruption will replace the coordination which formally resigned Supreme in our midst.*

Copyright Sue A Lowe

Take by all means that which fortune offers, but give also, and as generously as you will give for your poppy in the next few days. Is so and so worth another chance? Can I pull my own weight or a little more? Compile your own personal balance sheet now and prove, by your own actions, that they did not die in vain.'

To the bombed mothers of all nations.

No flags proudly flying,
Nor sadly drooping in the breeze,
Panoplied the climax of your dying:
Only the voice of the whispering trees
Went with you on that slow, cold road,
None of the pomp of state was there:
Not for you was the last abode
Of heroes great, great ones, poets fair.
No national hymns for you were sung,
Nor your praises chanted in church and choir.
Only tearless sobs, from the heart harsh wrung,
Were the songs that wafted your spirits higher.
Was it for this that you, shuddering, bore us?
Plunged in the earth, that earth might be free?
We shall come back to you, O proud dead mothers,
Bearing not honours, but lilies in sheaves.

There shall you lie
Neath the soft waving Flowers
And the sun climbing high
In the quiet noonday hours.
The star splattered sky shall kiss you at night
And the cold light of dawn not break your sleep
The Flowers will smile tenderly in the new light
Far wiser than mortals who made but weep.
We shall come back to you, O dead proud mothers,
Bearing not honours, but grief in our hearts.

So, rest then, so rest,
In earth gentle bosom lying:
No more by the cares of man be oppressed.
Silence forever the world's harsh crying
So, rest, and let us remember the glory

Of all that you gave from an over-full heart.
This is not the end but the start of the story:
Give us the strength to play our part.
We shall come back to you, O proud dead mothers,
Bearing not honours but hope in our hearts.
– SQMS W A Noakes RASC/EFI

Copyright Sue A Lowe

I cannot help but be personally touched by this part, whilst reading it really did give you a sense of what these men were going through. But this was not all doom and gloom, it's a support network, where not only serving members of EFI had their say but also, those who had already gone home who were getting sent a copy to keep them in the loop in the name of comradeship.

Deputy chairman, board of management setting up in America 1946

Mr R G Erskine CBE joined the company in 1941. Before joining NAAFI, he spent most of his time in Scotland and London as a banker. He knew of the Expeditionary Force canteens in the First World War, but his knowledge of the canteen service was very limited until he joined the company. His duties on the board concerned with the company's financial commitments so he was right at home.

His initial task was to get to know who the NAAFI were and his 1st impressions where chaotic, they were getting on with the job in the midst of the war. He was incredibly impressed with the loyalty of the staff and the constant cheerfulness of the canteen girls.

Everything around him seemed to be makeshift especially in the field – when one canteen closed another would open.

In the September of 1941 he accompanied Mr Pilcher to America to make preliminary surveys of the possibilities of NAAFI securing essential supplies from the United States and Canada. They had already made contact with the Canadian Pacific Railway from London, but in America the main task was to discover how the company's requirements could be met under that lease lend operations. They went on to Washington and nobody had ever heard of the company at all.

So, at this time they approached the government departments and officials, and they had to explain who they were and what they did for the British armed forces. In the 1st few months they made progress and they crossed the Atlantic again the following year; this meant that their Montreal office was a hive of industry. They had secured permission to start operations in the USA and had opened their first office in New York. Although their first office only comprised himself, Mr Thorne and his wife, a typist, over time the Montreal office and the New York purchasing office was in full swing and within months they had started employing more staff. Within no time they had made themselves fully known and understood by the majority of the government departments and leading manufacturers in both the United States and Canada.

This is where he had vivid memories of the 3 Atlantic crossings during the war, two by Clipper and the other by Queen Mary which sailed soon after D-Dday, taking back wounded soldiers and returning aircrews. The connections with the government in Washington during wartime would forever stick in his memory. One quite unique memory, he writes, Mr Neil and Mr Roberts of the CPR paid a visit to the UK and it was thought appropriate to take them to see the Clyde, where they had a memorable weekend including a visit to John Browns with one of the largest aircraft carriers being commissioned and Vanguard – although this was very hush hush in those days.

Even during the darkest days of the war, he always looked forward to Tuesdays. Tuesdays were board meeting days when he would go from Imperial court to Ruxley Towers to get out of the city for a day, even knowing Ruxley Towers was not out of the war by any means and it had its fair share of bombing, particularly the flying ones which gave several near misses.

NAAFI club at Salisbury 1946

A brand new NAAFI club at Salisbury was opened on the 1st of November. The opening of this new club was in a former American Red Cross club and this would serve members of the armed forces in Salisbury until a new establishment where a permanent club along the lines of the one in Portsmouth could actually be built. It was officially opened by Maj J Morrison who was a member of parliament for Salisbury and it was dedicated by the Dean of Salisbury. The entertainment was provided by Billy Ternent and the orchestra, Peter Kavanagh, Marjorie Holmes, and Edgar Sawyer.

The Mayor exclaimed, 'This was a red-letter day for the men and women of the British armed forces', which was keeping in the spirit of the times. On the ground floor the amenities included a ballroom with a stage, lounge, a Tavern furnished in a Tudor style with Oak settles, tables, chairs, red and green leather stools, and sporting prints. This also had a quiet room with cream and green furnishings with a leaf pattern carpet, a Barber shop, a shower and baths, telephone kiosk, gift shop and an information bureau. The first floor had a restaurant, in red and green, to seat 200 personnel and there were also 2 cafeteria counters for hot and cold service, with chromium trails. There was also a games room with billiard tables and a reading and writing room in brown and green. The modern kitchen could supply 600 hot meals in an hour. The club accommodation was suitable for one thousand, and staff, mostly recruited locally, now numbered 100. The manager at the time was Mr JM Gibson and the assistant manager was Miss D Johnson.

Big changes in the workplace 1946

It was in the Christmas of this year that saw a shakeup of the job roles within the company. There was a distinct difference between male and female pay of up to a 25% shortfall for women, but this at this time was the norm in any company. They also reviewed the job roles which meant that specific grading wasn't accepted procedure. This included:

Group A: no responsibility, every task allotted, supervised, and scrutinised.

Group B: operations requiring a limited number of well-defined rules, a measure of responsibility with small tasks, mostly checked or supervised, with daily routines covered by a timetable and a short period of control.

Group C: responsibility must have been greater than Group B, but the tasks are still of a routine character, this would mean checking group B's work.

Group D: this was an independent role with the arrangement of work calling for exercising initiative and also the daily routine varying.

Group E: this role is more important, it was clerical work with measured control of sequence of jobs and overwork of small groups of staff. No routine queries and requiring technical knowledge or responsibility without supervision.

Group F: the duties involved supervision of sections and responsibility for execution of complete divisional off work, regular contact with management and administration, special knowledge of legal accounting and statistical and other matters. This required a high level of experience and discretion.

The clerical job grouping schedule was implemented and confirmed by branch heads that all jobs were covered and respectfully grouped. Where the necessary rates of pay were required, they were appropriated.

During this time members of the RASC /EFI would have the qualifying period for promotion from second Lieutenant to Lieutenant shortened for those commissioned on or after the 1st of July 1947 to just 2 years; for those commissioned between January the 1st and June 30th in 1947 this would be 18 months and for those commissioned between July 1st and December 31st of 1946 would be 12 months.

There was also a new training scheme for cooks. Under this new programme, trainee cooks would spend a month under the guidance of a qualified cook in a specifically selected canteen. During this period, they would receive a thorough instruction in NAAFI cookery methods and recipe books, in addition to obtaining knowledge of the day-to-day cooking requirements in a typical canteen.

On completion of their month training, a report would be rendered by the management and welfare Superintendent and the trainees, if suitable, would complete their training by taking a fortnight's finishing course at the HQ training centre. At this point there was also a similar training scheme for male cooks. All instructors for cooks in all cases would be of the same sex as the trainees. And anybody who volunteered to train the learners would receive a special bonus in addition to their standard pay on completion of a satisfactory period of training.

From the August of 1946 the railways had issued cheap day return tickets for journeys on suburban lines from London and big towns. The cheap day returns were only available on Tuesdays, Wednesdays and Thursdays after 0930 hours and returning journeys had to be made at any time on the date of issue between 1630 hours and 1830 hours. Any member of staff travelling on the company's business hours were only allowed to obtain a cheap day return ticket whenever available, but they were not allowed to use their vouchers and must claim this back on a 'form 43'. The wartime privilege whereby rail warrants were issued every 12 months were only granted to mobile male and female employees in restaurant establishments; this was then withdrawn on the 31st of December 1946. From the 1st of January '47 a maximum of two return rail warrants in each 12-month period were allowed for the purpose of proceeding on annual leave in accordance with conditions of this concession, thus meaning the benefit was cut drastically.

All of these changes came at a time when the company had to be very savvy about the way that it operated and where its money was spent. Being able to expand and contract its staff but also make a profit to send back to the units was always at the forefront of their minds and ensuring everybody had what they were entitled to where possible.

1947

Paper shortage 1947

As 1947 started, NAAFI again fell foul of the paper shortage. This was the same story across Britain. In early spring just as the spring issue was taking shape the weather turned very cool, so cool in fact that the pulse of the country grew weak. The paper mills stopped milling, the printers stopped printing and many popular publications across the country ground to a halt.

Although the summer was warmer, the paper shortage was still in full swing and the availability of the paper so popularly used by the company for its publications was unavailable. NAAFI only managed to get a Christmas edition of the NAAFI news out to staff.

This was the 26th year the company had been running and what a big year this was – the honour of the patronage of His Majesty the King was given in February. This really was a showstopper and the work done at all levels was being recognised and the Royal family particularly benefited during the war years and now showed their recognition with this great honour.

Over the war years Her Majesty the Queen in 1943 spent time at the training centre in Woking and in 1945 during a visit to Manchester the King and Queen inspected the club and more recently were accompanied by the two princesses who paid an informal visit to the club in Aberdeen. HM the Queen made a tour of inspection of a large NAAFI warehouse in Bristol and in the early days of the war. The connection at that point couldn't be any stronger and the patronage from His Majesty meant so much to everybody within the company.

OCA General secretary 1947

Now the OCA had been formed it needed a general secretary to be permanently appointed.

The first OCA general secretary was SSM HW Bowen, the chairman Lt Col R Merry OBE of the general committee of the newly formed Association. They had worked hard during the past 11 months on the preliminary organization of the Association, making sure people knew about them.

The newly formed association, NCS & EFI personnel, had been scrutinised and a leaflet explaining the aims and objects of the Association together with a membership form and personal letter from the chairman was sent to all NAAFI ex-servicemen and women.

Mr CE Latter, legal adviser to the company, informed the committee that the Association would be considered by the charity commissioners as a charitable organisation under the War Charities Act of 1940. It would be possible to apply for exemption from registration and after discussion it was proposed that the application should be made to register the Association as a charitable organisation.

After discussion, a subcommittee was appointed to deal with the question of unified system administration and finance in various branches. Col Merry proposed Wilson HT Bird as the secretary. The chairman said that he had found it impossible to obtain a fully enamel brooch but he had ordered 5000 part enamel, part gilt badges which would be issued to all members; 3000 of the badges would be the stud type and 2000 would have a brooch pin. He did not expect they would be ready for distribution for another 3 or 4 months.

A column in EFI SEArchlight, NAAFI SEAC magazine was read to a meeting of the general committee. The magazine proposed that a local branch of the OCA be formed in SEAC immediately. It was felt that it would be better if overseas areas waited until they received official direction from Norwood before forming local branches and Brigadier Hamilton SEAC was cabled to this effect.

The association's address was agreed that the HQ of NAAFI should be the permanent address of the Association, but that temporarily both the addresses and location of the HQ would be at the RASC/EFI depot, Westow Street, Upper Norwood, London SE 19.

The OCA, NCS and Expeditionary Force Institute would have 12 branches within the UK, which would be adjusted as the OCA developed. By the end of the first year, November 1947, of the NCS and EFI OCA they had gained 4360 members. This was not including any of the members enrolled in BAOR and CMF – as an estimate at the time it brought the membership to 5000. With the calculation of nearly 19,000 potential members who had already received a personal letter from the chairman of the general committee, together with a circular that detailed extracts from the rules of the OCA with a detachable enrolment form to send back.

There was very much a buzz from the general committee who had already received some excellent feedback about the future success of the OCA, many letters of appreciation and offers of help had already been received from members who would have just joined. The NCS and EFI had no idea of the immediate success of the Association and that it was so needed amongst comrades. Within the first year the general committee had held 10 meetings since the inauguration of the Association. The main body of the business at these meetings had been concerned with the preliminary organization of the branches and defining the policy of the Association for the administration of the Benevolent Fund. The rules of the Association had to be printed in a handy form and a copy to be sent to every member together with their membership badge.

The general committee had already started to receive applications for assistance for the Benevolent Fund and the help that had already been given in grants. The general committee had already gratefully received the donations to the Benevolent Fund for this very purpose.

They were also able to name all of the Areas and their chairpersons:

AREA 1: London, Essex, Hertfordshire, Middlesex, Bedfordshire, Surrey, Sussex and Kent. Chairman, Lt Col JA Hallett,

AREA 2: Dorset, Oxfordshire, Berks, Wiltshire, Hampshire, Bucks and Channel Islands. Chairman, Maj HC Stamp MBE.

AREA 3: Cornwall, Devon, Somerset and Scilly Isles. Chairman, Lt ES Clifton.

AREA 4: Gloucestershire, Hereford, Monmouth, Glamorgan, Brecknock, Carmarthen, Pembroke, Cardigan and Radnor. Chairman, Cmdr T Nicholas.

AREA 5: Staffordshire, Cheshire, Shropshire, Montgomery, Caernarvonshire and Anglesey. Chairman, Lt Col GW Banks MBE.

The first general meeting was held as a reunion dinner on the 29th of November 1947 at the Stafford hotel in Chester.

AREA 6: Lancashire, Westmorland, Cumberland and Isle of Man. Chairman, Capt BH Hare.

AREA 7: Yorkshire, Durham and Northumberland. Chairman, Maj DGA Smith.

AREA 8: Cambridgeshire, Norfolk, Suffolk and Lincs. Chairman, Lt WM Pashley.

The first general meeting was held on the 12th of June 1947 at the Cross Swords hotel in Grantham. The second meeting was held on the 23rd of August 1947 in Lincoln at the Thornbridge hotel where this was a less formal affair as members were invited to bring a plus one.

AREA 9: Derby, Notts, Leics, Warwick, Worcestershire, Northants, Rutland. Chairman, Maj D Salberg.

The first general meeting of this branch was held on the 8th of June 1947 at the Alexandria theatre in Birmingham; the chairman had pointed out that the area was very large and therefore suggested that committee members should be elected from each county.

AREA 10: North Scotland, Orkneys and Shetland. Chairman, Capt R Clubb.

The first general meeting was held on the 2nd of July 1947 at the Imperial hotel in Aberdeen. The second meeting was held at the Princess cafe on the 6th of July 1947; the major point of discussion was how to increase the membership due to the extreme nature of the distance members would need to travel to get to meetings.

AREA 11: South Scotland. Chairman, Capt AS Warren.

The first general meeting was held at the Central Halls, Bath Street, Glasgow on the 25th of June 1947; 80 members attended

AREA 12: Northern Ireland. Chairman, Lt Col BHC Clark MC.

The first general meeting was held on the 30th of July at the Grand Central hotel in Belfast, further meetings and social occasions were organised.

AREA 13: BAOR. Chairman, E Faraday Esq.

The first general meeting was on the 16th of May 1947 where members were invited to bring one British/allied guest.

AREA 14, AREA 15: undesignated

AREA 16: CMF. Chairman, Maj WH Loxton

AREA 17: Gibraltar. Chairman, AJ Bond Esq.

The first branch general meeting was held on the 24th of June 1947 when they entertained the CPOs and POs of the Royal Navy barracks, Gibraltar. This was less of a formal affair and was largely made up of a short meeting with billiards, snooker and darts matches, and refreshments were supplied by the branch.

AREA 18, AREA 19: undesignated.

AREA 20: Middle East. Chairman, Col S Richard

On the 23rd of October 1947 in El Alamein, members attended the anniversary celebrations.

AREA 21: SEAC. Chairman, W Carr Esq.

The first Association branch committee meeting was held in the form of a dance cabaret. The warrant officers and sergeants mess in Singapore hosted the occasion on the 3rd of May 1947.

AREA 22: West Africa. Chairman, Capt JB Fair

While of the chairpersons listed for each of the areas all had a wide experience of the company. During the association's infancy in May of 1946 Lt Col Merry OBE, the chairman of the general committee, and SSM Bowen, the general secretary, went on a tour to each of the areas, interviewing the chairman with the necessary documentation for the functioning of the Association and the branches.

From this we can conclude that the first full year of the Association was very successful, providing not only a much needed break for serving personnel, a platform for many who had already left to retain the comradeship from their time served and the much needed benevolences and assistance where needed.

The Duchess of Kent opened the second permanent club in Colchester 29th of April 1947

The previous year HRH Princess Elizabeth had opened the very first permanent club in Portsmouth, and on the 29th of April 1947 the Duchess of Kent opened the second permanent club in Colchester. Her Royal Highness the Duchess of Kent gave this speech:

> *"Having just seen what this club can offer, I feel that the soldier will be hard to please who cannot find some pastime to suit his taste, whether it be in reading, study, writing, or music, dancing, cards and billiards, or merely for a rest and a conversation. All the experience which NAAFI obtained during the war years in conducting service clubs at home and overseas had gone into this new venture and they seem to have thought of everything. I would like to congratulate the NAAFI on providing a club which every soldier in the Colchester Garrison may well be proud."*

This was a gracious tribute from Her Royal Highness as she opened the club at Colchester. The club itself was 30,000 square feet which had parquet floor throughout, a large lounge, a wide well-lit concourse, restaurant, tavern, ballroom and concert hall, sales kiosk, reading and writing rooms, billiards room, barber shop, shower baths and a valeting service. The Duchess was greeted as she arrived by the president of the NAAFI, Admiral Sir Harold Borrough, and after a short procession the senior officers of the services of the NAAFI officials was conducted round the club by LC Wynne-Tyson, Deputy General Manager. Other distinguished guests also included the quartermaster general to the forces and the AOC in C Bomber Command, the Lord Lieutenant of Essex, the bishop of Chelmsford and the commander of the East Anglian district. They were some of the clubs which would stand the test of time and still be open in 2020, albeit in different hands.

Maj EJD Edwards visited Hong Kong in 1947

Maj Edwards gives a fantastic overview of his time in Hong Kong:

> The island of Hong Kong – its name suggests everything that is far eastern. The island itself with an unbelievably rugged coastline with the centre of the island rising abruptly to the famous central peak of which was almost entirely hidden during our stay. Hong Kong itself was built compactly on the lower slopes of the peak facing the mainland of China with a very busy town called Kowloon.
>
> Beyond Kowloon, stretching into the mainland of China, are the new territories which come under the British Crown. The social activities and amenities for the service personnel would be distributed over the island of Hong Kong and Kowloon on the mainland. As an EFI Major, his life was spent constantly using the ferry service and the time that took to

travel around ensuring the right amount of service to the services. NAAFI's achievements in regard to the clubs and the restaurants for both officers and other ranks were in his opinion exemplary and the quality and the variety of the food surpassed anything he had experienced in the Far East. At this time with the numbers decreasing in the Far East naturally, they began to drawdown the facilities available, and one of the first establishments to go was the Gloucester hotel; it was being run as a successful officers' club under the capable management of Sgt AD Thompson.

Sgt Thompson then went on to manage the Lido, the officers' club at Repulse Bay. This was built shortly before the war and was exclusively a bathing club. It was a well-designed building standing at the water's edge with hundreds of bathing cubicles and a number of small dressing rooms attached and furnished with chairs and tables. The main officers' club on the mainland of Kowloon was part of the famous Peninsula hotel; this was the largest building in the area. The NAAFI portion was beautifully decorated and the whole club was run by a Chinese manager, Mr Wong. Mr Wong had been with the company ever since it had introduced itself to the services in Hong Kong many years before.

The other ranks' club was adjacent to the Peninsula hotel and originally was a YMCA, a very fine building with ample facilities. This club had the usual restaurant, bars, restrooms, sports rooms, tailoring and Barber shops and a really excellent indoor swimming pool. The management was in the hands of ATS S/Sgt E Wakefield.

On the island of Hong Kong, they found the well-known Union Jack club, conveniently situated and run by ATS Sgt JW Norman. On the small ancient Portuguese island colony, where the company had established the famous Bella Vista ORs' residential club as well as a small officers' club. At the time it was a strange mixture of European and Far East, but the Bella Vista was a success, plus because it was run by Sgt G Wiley, who spent the whole of the war in uniform. During the drawdown on his exit from Hong Kong he took a photograph from before the war of a NAAFI staff dance with Mr Pegg as the central figure. This photograph was carefully hidden away during the Japanese occupation. Deep in the bleak new territories where the military outposts nestling at the foot of the grim and colourless mountains. He saw them on a wet and depressing day, passed a small grey Chinese village where the barefooted women were carrying water across the mud. Within the parameter of such an outpost inside a shabby looking Nissen Hut, was revealed. This was a very comfortable little NAAFI canteen and the kitchen beyond, over the welcome fire stood a Chinese cook frying juicy wings of chicken for awaiting customers.

On the frontier there were small detachments of troops, whilst over the frontier into Hong Kong streamed hundreds of Chinese traders with their wares. Due to the troubles in China, Hong Kong became a refuge for merchants and the disadvantaged.

The reason why.

Of times when on pleasure bent
I wander to the mess;
is there I find a sweet content,
A certain happiness
the happiness that comes to men
whom not a soul will spurn;
a laugh, a song, a drink again,
"good luck till you return!"'
To meet the pals I've travelled with;
Aye, and roughed it too;
why, bless my soul, this old Smith,
"I don't mind if I do"'
"do you remember so and so,
and that little bit of trouble?
Jack and Jim; Alice, flo?
-Thanks! I'll have a double"
Till finally, when time has gone,
you find that in addition
to reminiscing, yarning on,
you're in a bad condition.
But man is fickle, well you know,
so when he's had enough,
shake your head and sigh with Sorrow –
tomorrow he'll be rough.

AA Green

SEArchlight 14th of March 1947

One of the largest contingents to leave for home was the majority of the draft of EFI who went out to SEAC in 1945. These comrades who joined when there was a shortage of manpower in EFI and these bodies that were attached, will be representative of hundreds who had laboured with EFI in SEAC. Some made their first acquaintance with the Norwood Depot and flew straight out. Some had been with the company for some time, others were very new, but now would be the time to mention some of these comrades.

The author of one of the most poignant poems written in November 1946 called 'To the bombed mothers of all nations', SQMS WA Noakes, or better known in the SEArchlight publication as WAN. He left HQ accounts Department on completion of his tour of duty in SEAC. He went out in the September of 1945 after having served for a long spell in the Middle

East. He was a classically trained pianist and provided hours of constant entertainments to music lovers in Singapore, and when he departed, he was sorely missed.

Sgt Tommy Gamble, he joined from ENSA on disbandment in September 1946; he had been employed since that time with EFI as their QM stores, in Singapore. While with ENSA he was a stage manager in Calcutta, Bombay, Japan and Singapore. He served with the Royal Artillery from February 1944 until August 1945 and for 8 years before that he had somewhat a hazardous occupation supervising the filling of the Royal Ordnance factory. He returned home to Welling in Kent.

Cpl WH Green, who was the driver before he transferred to EFI in the March 1946 after he was attached for 6 months. Originally from the Royal Artillery, he went out to SEAC in early 1945 and he joined movements and transport at Madras in October 1944, he then served in Singapore and Burma. He went home to Rishton, in Lancashire.

Sgt EH Bryant, who was one of the first SEAC pioneers who arrived in Madras in April of 1945, he served in Malaya from September 1945 until he left with the others but went home to Wandsworth.

Corporal AJH Tilling was a bulk issue store charge hand and better known to his comrades as Tilley. He joined NAAFI at the end of 1942 and became something of a globetrotter; he served in the Shetlands, the British West Indies and the United States. He arrived in Singapore with the AF draft in April of 1946 and he served throughout his stay in Singapore at the BIS before he returned home to Bristol.

Cpl RJ Duggan of the port detachment, Singapore, originally came from the Welsh regiment and first became attached to EFI in Ceylon in August 1945. When he moved to the India base he joined the warehouse staff and when he arrived in Singapore, at the end of January 1946 he was posted to the port detachment, but at that time it was just shed number 40. He went home to South Wales.

Gnr W Kickman, originally from the Royal Artillery, joined EFI in Ceylon in September 1945 and was later posted to Madras where he was deployed as a driver. Soon after he left for Sumatra and turned up in Singapore in December 1946, he was employed at the heavy goods transport garage. He returned home to Derby.

SEArchlight 11th of April 1947 NAAFI and the Indian soldier by Maj EJD Edwards

In 1941 the Indian soldier didn't have service like the NAAFI canteens have in the Middle East. Up until now there is only one reference to the adventure, but I think importantly adding this to the history of the company is essential to understand the influence worldwide. NAAFI had affected the South East Asia and Far East with their endeavours to provide a Top-class service for our serving military; this was a modest but a valuable service the EFI arm of the company provided. A valuable member of the team was Subedar Maj Kidar Nath, who was from northern India. The Major was well known to hundreds of the SEAC, he was consistently on the move and his labours – he singly directed the welfare of the Indian troops. He was directed to NAAFI as a civilian by the defence Department of India to assist in the provision of the canteen facilities for the Indian soldier. He was made a viceroy commissioned officer in 1943. He got down to the job promptly and the first Indian canteen was opened in Trincomalee in 1942. This type of canteen was entirely new to the troops and provided instant access to the facilities, very similar to the British soldier.

This format was extended in Ceylon and a large IORs' club was opened at the Fort Railway station, Columbo, whilst many of the other establishments were soon functioning in the interior including Kandy. The service was soon rolled out to the Malay Peninsula, Netherlands East Indies and northwards to Hong Kong. When the war ended, this altered the planning for the canteens, but the welfare of hundreds and thousands of men still had to be considered. The Indian canteens were opened in Kuala Lumpur and other parts of Malaya, Pen Yang, Singapore, Hong Kong, Java, Sumatra, and the Cocos and Maldives islands. Burma was the most important ground for Indian canteens as well as several clubs were amongst the establishments in the country.

One notable establishment was the India leave centre called Sandycroft; it was on the beautiful island of Penang which accommodated 150 men. Their canteens where very different from the European counterparts as Indian soldiers at this time only ate 2 meals per day against the four, five or six meals of the westerners, who in all probability ate far too much. At the Sandycroft, tea and biscuits were served early in the morning, but their first real meal was lunchtime served from 10:30 to 11:30. NAAFI provided an extensive menu of curries with the usual chapattis, rice, Dal, curd, hot chutneys and fresh fruit. Dinner was then served at 1800 hours although sweetmeats were taken in the afternoon. And dinner was much the same as lunch apart from the addition of fish and eggs to the curries.

The layout was very similar to the British canteens, but their activities were slightly different where the European troops played games such as darts, table tennis and draughts, the Indian troops played Carrom. Indian chess was played by the rich and Pachesee, which is the poor man's chess, were played in the NAAFI canteen. The music was drastically different and singing filled a great part of the Indians leisure and they were seen to listen for hours to never ending love songs, with the Indian harmonium, tablas and dholak hand drums, Indian bells and flutes providing the enchanting accompaniment.

The Indian soldiers drank very little in the way of alcohol, although Indian rum is a favourite drink. Tea is the first favourite, but for the Indian it must be very sweet and very milky, without exception –to one gallon of tea is used 12 ounces of sugar and 6 ounces of milk. The food comprised almost entirely of sweetmeats, the sweetest kinds of balushai, jalaibi, shakar, para and laddo. These were made almost entirely from sugar and flour in jalaibi, 3 pounds of sugar were used to one pound of flour, which will give you some idea. The hot varieties on offer consisted of pakora, samosa, and mathi. The pakora was made with a yellow flour, any vegetables available at the time and lots of chillies and salt. Pakora you can eat more when hot and if you want to eat it as the Indian soldiers do you have it with rum.

NAAFI supplied every commodity in demand by the Indian troops, this in turn showed the Indian soldier something that they would never turn back on. They demanded a higher order of welfare and amenities which far exceeded, and I think that the former contractors could ever have dreamed of initiating.

The prayer.

Those prison walls were dark and grey,
Where men did cry, yet some did pray;
For in their hearts they did know
That someday soon they'd see that foe
Driven from this island small
Where many comrades had to fall.
In those grim fights to beat the jap,
We lost many a fine young chap,
But those who live this very day
Remember always when they pray
The relatives of the varied race
Of those whom they will never trace.
God will keep those dear ones near,
The man who did not have a fear!
They were the men we owe so much to,
The men who were so good and true.
Remember, when you pray again,
They died for us, but not in vain.
written by Bob 1947

SEArchlight 18th of April 1947

Members of the EFI issued a notice from the War Office instructing all overseas commands in September of 1946 that the army leave regulations did not apply to EFI personnel. Personnel were not denied leave but based on their military status and the company's leave scheme they had at times a less favourable leave facilities than other branches of the army and in some cases leave had been granted via military channels, which unfortunately shouldn't have happened. NAAFI had to fulfil its commitments whatever the conditions and it was unreasonable at the time.

The Company issued instructions in October 1946 to the effect that they would not be granted equal leave that personnel serving in SEAC after the 31st of December would have an entitlement, which would be similar. Any EFI requiring leave had to submit an F/458 in duplicate and forwarded to the supervisor in respect of everyone to see if they were entitled to the same leave under their army regulations. This all depended on the type of service and the time spent in Theatre.

On the 16th of May 1947 the much-loved editor of the SEArchlight publication for SEAC had papers and was ready to leave, this was issue 72. He records affectionately, as so many of us even do now, our feelings of apprehension about leaving a place that had been called home for so long. So many of us have shed a tear as the train pulled away for one last time en route to our other homes. And although he produced this publication for 18 months, he recorded such revealing and poignant moments in time.

He writes:

> *Pleasant associations of my stay will not pass into oblivion. They are permanently impressed on my memory, a tribute to the hospitality, courtesy and generosity of our eastern friends which have at times been beyond the comprehension of the average westerner. Unpleasant thoughts had been put aside, it was way better, or even a few as they were. For my many friends in uniform this parting is but temporary. We shall meet again, I have no doubt, somewhere, maybe still in the harness or in Mufti, or as a last resort in the ranks of the OCA of which I have been proud to be not only a member but your representative on the SEAC branch committee.*

F. Walmsley, affectionately known as Leo, had no idea that by issue 88 the SEArchlight would be no more. It was on the 5th of September 1947. Thousands of NAAFI staff in South-eastern Asia and the Far East relied on this small 4-page paper published in Singapore. The production of it was a labour of love by Maj EJD Edwards, Capt. DG Wright and the undisputed editor, SQMS F. Walmsley.

Thank you GHQ in the canal zone Egypt 1947

The question from many at the SEAC was what was it like at Fayid? But it was true to say that they all lived either under canvas or in huts and not wanting to give a false impression of life in the desert. Even though in May of 1947 they believed that in 6 months' time the area would be totally unrecognisable. At this point many gardens and trees had already been planted to keep the dust down and give everything a more homely appearance. They had already built churches, cinemas, canteens, shops, bathing beaches on the great bit of lake, sports grounds and bus services. The climate was definitely a lot hotter in the summer but in the evenings the north-westerly breeze of Egypt brought a welcome coolness.

Living on the canal of course meant a big change in the lifestyle of many thousands of servicemen and women after the urban pleasures of Cairo and Alexandria; this was a more relaxed affair. There was a new routine for everybody to get used to on and off duty. The new setup meant the service folk and their families relied more on NAAFI for the essentials and the welfare and NAAFI could offer to brighten their leisure hours.

Club and canteen amenities in the new Township of GHQ at Fayid, and the subsidiary headquarters and installations at Suez, Geneifa, Fanara, Abou Soueir, Port Said and Port Fuad were almost entirely the NAAFI responsibility. This was one of their biggest undertakings, but the company was no stranger to the canal. At this point in time there were not many places where they were not the oldest inhabitants, so the new responsibilities were based on a long tradition of service in this area. The company covered catering in 5 of the family villages already in operation, more villages were being built but generally speaking the families appreciated the service and Taste of Home. NAAFI had already built a shopping centre near the villages and a huge department store, one of the biggest of its kind the company had ever run. Service people and their families could buy most things from cosmetics, flowers and groceries to sports equipment and bicycles. They already had a separate lido club on the edge of the lake for the officers, warrant officers and sergeants and also for the junior ranks, each with a restaurant service available. They already had an all-night canteen for late workers and numerous unit canteens with a bulk issue store and mineral water factory. When they had already started to build NAAFI holiday camp at Port Fouad which could hold families and another close by which could hold 750 junior ranks.

1948

Capt Pitt and the Sniper 1948

1948 Capt M.J. Pitt became one of the luckiest men alive. He was the district officer in Sarafand. On the 5th January he decided to drive home alone to a neighbouring camp to collect canteen takings. He was passing through an Arab village when an Arab sniper appeared from behind a wall and took a shot at him, the bullet entered the back of his neck and then swerving sideways and passing out of the side of his neck, nicking the lobe of his ear. He got out streaming with blood and badly stricken, he glanced at the Arab who was sighting for another shot, sent him back to the car with what might have easily been a mortal wound. He drove 4 miles to the camp where he collapsed and was packed off to hospital.

Ten days later he was out and about, and he agreed to act as a support escort to a party of ATS EFI girls on a Sunday day trip to Jericho. This was the first pleasure trip the girls had had for weeks. On their return, on entering Jerusalem their truck became caught up with a Jewish convoy and at that precise moment when the Arabs opened fire with rifles and machine guns, the Captain called the girls to throw themselves to the bottom of the truck. The next moment the bullet hit him near the spine fracturing 3 ribs and came out through his arm, nicking his elbow. As he fell, he was heard to shout that **** have got me again, and in the next breath apologise to the ladies for his involuntary lapse of language. He returned home as fit as a fiddle on leave and awaited the next posting with a fantastic story to tell.

The defence minister opened the third permanent club in Oswestry 1948

The 3rd permanent home club was opened in Oswestry on the 6th of April 1948 by the Rt Hon A.V. Alexander, CH MP Minister of Defence. The mayor of Oswestry, Miss E.G. Rogers,

J.P. presided and other distinguished guests included the Bishop of Shrewsbury, who dedicated the club, Lt General Sir Frank E Simpson, KBE, CBE, DSO, GOC in C Western command and Air vice marshal T.C. Traill, CBE, OBE, DFC. In the speech, Mr Alexander said that the rate of intake into the services in the next few years would be about 150,000 a year under the national service scheme, and he was anxious to see the development alongside the ordered programme laid down by the NAAFI or further clubs because if the abundant need for relaxation in decent conditions to keep the men and women away, so far as possible, from temptations on which they rarely came across at home. The new club, on which work had continued for the past 18 months, in a converted house with several fine features, including a large Oriel window in front and a magnificent Bay window in the lounge overlooking the gardens. Wide lawns, flowered gardens and many fine old trees added to the charm of the surroundings. In its 15,000 square feet of floor space the club included a restaurant, fine up to date kitchen, writing room and lounge. The tavern, ballroom concert hall, quiet room, games room under sales kiosk which also included WVS information Bureau. Mobile cinema shows would also provide part of the entertainment, which also included billiards, table tennis, darts, chess, whist drives and dances each evening. Boot repairs, dry cleaning services, and the hairdressing salon, were many of the amenities available to the service personnel and their families. The club had a staff of 85 and in charge of these was Mr B.G.B Reeve, the manager. With that WVS services organised by the WVS liaison officer Mrs Beard.

The victory club in Hamburg was visited by the Right Honourable Arthur Henderson, the Secretary of State for Air, who declared himself extremely satisfied with the NAAFI and WVS collaboration in serving the troops. He was surprised to learn that on an average 5000 men and women were still passing through the club every day.

Rear-guard in Palestine Reported by Maj George Turnbull 1948

The last 12 of the 300 ATS EFI girls to serve in Palestine were evacuated by air to Egypt on the 14th of April to Fayid. Col H.G. Swithenbank, who was officer commanding EFI Levant paid a fitting tribute to the 12 lost and the many other girls who had stuck it out in a terrorised Palestine since the early part of 1947.

The ATS EFI girls had been magnificent and ever since the troubles began, he could not praise them enough for their unfailing loyalty and excellent behaviour all the way through. The EFI would have been quite lost without their help, not only in the offices and clubs but in the canteens. None of them had ever asked for a posting, despite life being behind the wire and never once heard them complain. There is no doubt at the time that, quite apart from their jobs, the presence of these girls in Palestine did a great deal to help them and all the units who were lucky enough to have them on their camps. One notable instance occurred in February when for the first time in months a staff outing was arranged to Jerusalem that day. After a few hours of relaxation on the beach the party started back for Jerusalem. On a twisty piece of the steep mountain road, 3 trucks caught up and began to pass the Jewish convoy. At that very moment the Arabs in the hills opened fire on the Jews, and the NAAFI party found themselves up to their neck in the fighting. Drivers tried to get clear of the civilian vehicles, but in the chaos of the movement were unable to pass on the narrow roadway.

During these awful minutes the girls remained quite calm and collected. Not one of them panicked. They just sat still and gave their RASC EFI drivers the full opportunity to get the vehicles out of the mess. One girl spent a few minutes bandaging up a soldier, who had been wounded by a bullet. All the ATS EFI who had been in Palestine during the recent months now had either gone home for release or had been posted to other parts of the Middle East. Notably the girl with the longest continuous service in Palestine was a Cpl J Thorpe who had completed 17-months' service.

OCA Summer 1948

In the summer of 1948, the OCA was really taking off and after just over a year this Association was now firmly established in its activities both at home and abroad. It had become a source of pleasure and enjoyment for many of its members who had taken part in social reunions arranged by the various branches. The general committee realised the difficulties of travel and accommodation between branch meetings and started to make every effort to implement the policy that the general committee would promote local social gatherings as near as possible to the members' homes. It hoped that members would then show the appreciation of the efforts of their branch committees by giving these gatherings their support in every way possible. These local get togethers were to do much towards keeping our Association thriving with larger reunions. The members of the Association at this time had grown to 4724 and the new members were being enrolled daily. Members overseas had not been completed but they had received 587 memberships to date which makes the total now known of 5311. In just three months it was growing by one hundred members. The Benevolent Fund had now made 61 grants for Support. Each case was carefully considered and almost every case, and a detailed report had been received from SSAFA as to the needs of the merits of the case. The reports had been of the greatest assistance to the committee in deciding on relief upon evidence was necessary.

Each of the branches at this time started to report back what was going on and how they were helping to foster the comradeship between members new and old. Branch number one held its first big reunion at Seymour Hall, Seymour Place in London on the 29th of November 1947 to which members invited their wives and friends. The Royal Artillery Ballroom Orchestra was engaged with this dance at which 750 people were present and it was agreed by all that the occasion was an immense social success. Their 1st annual general meeting of that branch was held at Imperial Court on the 7th of February 1948, at which 250 members were present to hear of the year's work, and to elect a secondary branch committee for 1948. Many useful suggestions were made for members' future activities, all of which would be carefully considered by the new secondary committee. Maj C.V. Petit was elected by the branch committee to be their chairman for the coming year, with Lt Col J.A. Hallett as vice chairman. A reunion of members was then held at the Norwood Depot on the 3rd of April 1948 whereby the commanding officer Lt Col R Merry OBE hoped that this would be the start of a continual series of social events.

Branch #2 in Portsmouth organised a dance held at the Clifton Ballroom, Osborne Road in Southsea on the 4th of December 1947 and over 500 members and their friends were present, having travelled long distances to support an excellent function. The chairman and the general committee and also the general secretary were present with Portsmouth subcommittee outdoing themselves. This social function on the back of their success, Bournemouth and Dorset subdistricts took up the challenge and organised an equally successful dance which was held at the Garrison Hall, Bovington camp, on the 18th of February 1948 where some 250 members and their friends spent the most enjoyable evening drinking and dancing.

Branch #3 held its 1st annual general meeting, followed by a social evening and dance at the Imperial Club in Davenport on Saturday the 28th of February 1948. A month later branch #5 had a very successful and enjoyable reunion dinner held at the Swan hotel in Chester in November. During the evening the chairman gave details of the post-war activities and some of the well-known EFI personnel were much appreciated. Some months later, on the 6th of March 1948, members met to attend a dance in Northgate Street, Chester.

Branch #7 held the annual general meeting at the Coach and Horses Hotel, Nessgate in York on the 11th of February. The chairman at the meeting, Maj D.G.A. Smith, said that a good deal had been done during the past few months by the subcommittee formed. The foundations had then been laid for steady progress and Capt Blakeway of Darlington had held his 1st subcommittee meeting and a further reunion on the 20th of February In York. Capt Sleep held a games tournament. Newcastle held the largest single membership and the subcommittee and the chairman had made quite some progress where a reunion dinner was held at the Newcastle British Legion where indoor games and dinner were laid on. Further meetings were held every 2nd Thursday evening each month from the 11th of March. Maj Smith resigned as chairman of the branch and Capt. E.M. Blakeway was elected to fill that position.

Branch #8 had yet another meeting in the 'Tuns Inn' in Norwich on the 31st of January 1948. The chairman Lt W.M. Pashley pointed out, with his change of residence, transferred out. He himself was on his way to Grantham so unfortunately with these circumstances a new committee had to be elected and decided that get togethers should be held in the Tuns Inn in Norwich on a permanent basis. On the 1st Saturday of each month the chairman expressed the hope that members would rally round and take the opportunity to spend an evening once a month with their old comrades.

Branch #9 started to get a reputation for the grand dances being held which took place at the 'Golden Eagle Hotel', Hill Street, Birmingham. On Tuesday the 25th of May 'Bobby Ousnam and his band' provided the music.

Branch #11 held whist drives and social evenings laid on. Monday the 29th of March and the function was held at the Masonic Hall, 100 West Street, Glasgow. At the AGM it was proposed they formed a sub branch in Edinburgh with Capt Haldanew who was well known to many of the EFI members as chair. The first subcommittee meeting was held in Edinburgh on the 10th of March; the general support for the branch was outstanding.

CMF branch meetings were held at the Crusader Club, notably on the 1st of December 1947 the following suggestions were discussed and adopted in December. The Oak Carol singers were to visit messes and billets. They would have a Christmas raffle to be organised and sent to Vienna, Graz, Villach and Betfor, where members were stationed. Parties were arranged subject to the amount of space available, dancers were organised and an annual dinner with a bring and buy sale collection boxes to raise funds. In the early part of the year a brand-new branch was formed in Malta due to the amount of people stationed there. The Middle East branch, as a result of the dances held on out on El Alamein night, had raised £159 9s, which was quite something at the time.

Of the success of the branches so far and the wonderful meetings already held, new branches needed to be formed quite quickly so on the 22nd of January 1948 it was discussed about how to split some of the branches up solely for the interest of members, for ease of travelling and accommodation. The general committee unanimously agreed that the decision was that number one branch would organise a big annual reunion in London. This then had the feeling that nobody would miss out on the privileges of the members being invited; that also made it inclusive for them. The new branches were Kent, Bedfordshire/Hertfordshire, Middlesex, Surrey, Essex, and Sussex branch. More donations to the fund started to come in and further donations from EFI PRI fund in Ceylon was £74 11s 3d.

By the Christmas of 1948 the fund stood at over £3180, and already members in distress had received £843 covering 81 separate issues. Following the need for benevolence, the general committee appointed for trustees. One of their 1st approvals, was a £1,500 invested at 2.5% as a war loan. This then left the Benevolent Fund with sufficient to meet the requirements by the way of grants in the short term.

Applications for grants for aid from the fund were dealt with by members applying to the central office or to approach the branch chairman or one of the committee members. Where less urgent cases came about, personnel were referred to the 'Soldiers Sailors and Airmen Families Association' for support. They interviewed the applicants and as they had years of experience, were often able to refer them to different areas for help or send the report straight to that Association. This also ensured that full confidentiality was at the forefront of every application.

Unfortunately, all these years on the early records of the Association have long since been destroyed but every act of benevolence had his case number to be referred to. Many letters of thanks was sent to the Association by members who were very grateful for helping them and gratefully they wanted to help others in return. As today as it was then the Benevolent Fund would not be infinite but to rely on donations and income from the social activity or the generosity of its members.

Copyright Sue A Lowe

On the 13th of November the grand reunion dance took place with 1200 members who had brought tickets for 4 shillings each. The dance was held at the Seymour Hall in London, and started at 1830 hrs; 'The Gibson sisters and buddy' headlined, they were a well known singing act and received a rousing reception at the reunion. The Hall itself was very large with a large dance floor and other amenities. It was decorated with flags, bunting and a large replica of the OCA badge suspended from the ceiling, and a large net containing 700 coloured balloons in a large Union Jack. The Gibson sisters and buddy were accompanied by the Royal Artillery Ballroom Orchestra from Woolwich Depot. With the dancing led by Frank Spencer and his partner all orchestrated by the master of ceremonies Mr A.E. Woolford from the No 1 branch.

The OCA tie had now gone into production and the response from members had been phenomenal – when the first delivery from the manufacturers arrived it sold out within 2 weeks. The fine quality of material and the smart and effective design which had been registered to prevent the duplication looked very smart. The main colour was Navy blue with a double yellow stripe on a single Brown stripe, the Navy blue was to represent the NCS, the yellow and the Navy blue for the RASC/EFI, and the beach Brown single stripe to represent the ATS/EFI.

It wasn't until the late 70s that it stopped being produced. Then after months of conversations with a manufacturer and the committee, in May 2019 at the AGM the tie went back on sale with an additional detail of the Association crest in the tip of the tie.

Memories of the NCS 1948

Friday the 13th of August 1948 would be a day to be remembered. The NCS would be immobilised of all staff enrolled into the Royal Navy NCS, these would be the last uniformed sea going grocers to collect their city suits from the clothing centre and the last shipmate would be CPO Keith Simmons who had recently arrived home from Singapore.

Many of them had memories of being a lone figure waiting for their final instalment of their naval pay. These, however, were all new recruits for the OCA. Notification also came out about applications for war medals for the NCS; this was now made to the director of Navy accounts branch, 3B/Medals, Admiralty, Bath. They were required to send their certificates with their application, so their medals were not delayed.

The fourth new permanent club in Chatham 1948

The Chatham club was the 4th permanent club in the United Kingdom. This was quite a unique club because of the addition in the usual amenities it provided, accommodation for married men and their wives and families. This separate residential wing was included at the request of the Admiralty to meet a particular need. Ships from the home fleet and those returning from overseas did not always come into their home ports and as a result, the married ratings were anxious to see their wives and found it almost impossible to do so because there were no facilities provided. But now, however, they were able to and also know that they would be able to accommodate with that of the first-class hotel at extremely reasonable prices.

In the words in the opening address the commander in chief The Nore, Admiral Sir Harold Borrough, president of the NAAFI council, drew attention to the feature of the new Chatham club. It made a difference from any other club at home although part of the main structure, the residential quarters, were housed in a separate wing in Arethusa house which served its own entrance, reception desk, lounge, writing room and 48 bedrooms, each tastefully decorated and furnished with hot and cold running water and wash basins.

There was also a nursery in a playroom for guests' children. This Grand Hotel for the lower deck cost only 5s 6dper person per night and the guests could also have morning tea served in their rooms. An annex was also being approved to give the sleeping accommodation for up to 200 single men of the three services. The club itself had all the familiar amenities as the other 3 and the opening ceremony was on the 16th of July 1948, which was attended by many distinguished service officers and

local officials. Speaking on behalf of the army and Royal Air Force respectively, the General Sidney Kirkman and Air Marshal Sir Hugh Saunders sang their praises of what the NAAFI had done and was also doing for the ranks of all 3 services. Some days later His Majesty the King visited the new club who spent some time touring the club and chatting with the staff.

The Navy's canteen parliament 1948

The Royal Navy in 1948 was a bewildering blend of old and new ancient customs and ceremonies flourished alongside the most up to the minute ideas in naval strategy, tactics, equipment, and training. Naval democracy was something else and at the headquarters of the naval canteen committee which met twice a year at NAAFI headquarters, the parliament comprised naval ratings with representatives from lower deck from fleets and ports who met senior officers from around the conference table to bring forward their complaints and queries raised by their constituents during the previous 6 months.

The twice-yearly sessions would assemble in the Nissen huts in the grounds of Ruxley Towers. The meetings lasted 2 days and were devoted to clearing the ground and tidying up a fairly crowded agenda. Mr TE Pegg, manager at the NCS with other NAAFI officials met the delegates and started to settle many of the lesser problems early on in the meetings. By the end of the first day the agenda was agreed before the full session on the second day of the meeting. These meetings were laid out with a hint of the Westminster arrangement in the House of Commons – at one end of the room sat the speaker, officially known as the chairman who was the Admiral Sir Harold M Burrough, commander in chief, The Nore, who was also the president of the NAAFI council. Then on either side sat the members of the watch which could be known as the "cabinet" – two representatives from NAAFI and a further two representatives representing the Admiralty. On what would have been the government benches sat several naval officers, Rear Admirals, captains and commanders representing the commander in chief of the ports, fleets, Royal Marines, air, submarines and WRNS.

Facing them across the room where the "back benches", who were there to ask the questions and move resolutions, the lower deck spokesman for the Royal Marines, the Mediterranean fleet, battling twosquadrons, the home fleet destroyer flotillas, The Royal Navy air stations and the WRNS.

Overall, the naval parliamentarians were amongst the finest types in the British Navy, many of them sporting impressive rows of war ribbons, and when they spoke, they did with an air of authority and responsibility. They were able Seamen, leading Seamen, leading Stoker mechanics, electricians, petty officers and Yeoman of the signals; these were a sturdy bunch of sensible men elected by their fellows to voice their wishes and air their grievances of the lower deck on all matters affecting their canteens. And this was something to emphasise this was a canteen parliament and Mr Speaker would only have subjects directly concerned with the NAAFI service to the Royal Navy by the way of the NCS.

It was a free for all discussion with mutual respect between officers and men, they spoke their minds fearlessly and forthrightly but with verbal leg pulling and delight from both sides of the house with the good humour. The debating clash and exchange of points concerning the Admiralty, knowing that they were dealing with men of their own calibre who shared with them one objective, which was the welfare of the service they love.

Much was achieved from these meetings with representatives returning to their constituents with a full brief. And at the end of the business Mr Speaker thanked the representatives to bring in the proceedings to a friendly conclusion. On the 1st meeting of 1948 when it was closed by Admiral Sir Harold M Burrough with these words:

> *'I confess I look forward to these meetings very much. I always enjoy them. The way in which you present your case always gives me a feeling of great pride in our service. We can discuss every conceivable kind of thing around this table quite clearly and without any attempt to hide anything, and the result, to my mind, is excellent. I feel that I'm privileged, as your chairman, in being more in touch with the general feeling in the Navy than almost anyone else is privileged to be'.*

NAAFI news goes on sale for staff 1948

In the autumn edition in 1948 when the editor acknowledges the collectability and need for more copies of the publication to be produced, it is proposed that each copy be chargeable at 6d initially, but copies still sent without charge to the outlying areas of EFI. It was then scheduled the last free issue would be the Christmas edition of 1948 and the first chargeable edition would be spring of 1949. Where all issues sent to the outlying areas off EFI would be issued with a list of names so once each person had read it they were duty bound to pop it back in an envelope and send it to the next person on the list.

Operation Plainfare 1948

During September and October 1948 NAAFI supplies needed to reach Berlin on average 33,000lb a day, which would equal two full York aircraft loads. In fact, so much stock was being flown across to Berlin that General Herbert, the British commandant, said 'we are in a strong position for food. Stocks of rations and NAAFI supplies are higher than they were before the blockade started.' Stores came into Gatow airfield near Berlin, offloading 7000lbs of stores straight out the back of a Dakota.

Mr FW Bell, the manager of the family's shop in Berlin, won a high commendation for himself under staff for the service that they had given the British families since the blockaded had started. This was due to his polite and personal example of the courteous helpfulness; he had made his shop the best of its kind and that any of his customers had encountered. Mr Bell had brought with him 22 years' experience with the company. The first Imperial club in

Berlin was opened in the August bank holiday and all the NAAFI staff would frequently work by oil lamps because of the power cuts. Many of the NAAFI women were mobile canteen drivers and assistance doing excellent work around the clock, making sure there was a service for the aircraft at Wunsdorf. One of the ladies was an ex-dressmaker, Mrs D Hern from Croydon; she swapped her sewing machine for a civil defence ambulance. Another was a Miss D Banks of Hawley, who before joining drove for 3½ years in the WAAF. Mr McGarrell, a charge hand of the Berlin grocery store lift on the airfield, and he was on call night and day so when the aircraft touched down, they were able to unload as quickly as possible. A large canvas canteen was erected on the airfield to provide 24-hour service to the men working on aircraft operations. Mr Withers, the Superintendent, was part of the party that got the canvas up so quickly. In 1944 he was responsible for the NAAFI canvas in the D day camps throughout the southern command so as you can imagine this was a very professional job.

Often staff would go 24 hours without sleep due to the schedule of the incoming aircraft. All this was just to keep the grocery store at Hannover and Berlin with a steady flow of supplies. There was a small tent run by the WVS representatives which had a sign written in bright red lipstick which read 'WVS Kosy Korner' but at least everybody knew where they could get a hot cup of tea and supplies on the long hours making sure all the stores have the groceries that they needed.

A second point of supply was the Royal Air Force airfield at Fassberg near Berlin to ensure the operation of supply went smoothly, again the WVS representatives, a couple of Scottish ladies, made sure that the mobile refreshment van was well stocked to make sure these supplies got through OK.

Christmas 1948

NAAFI started ahead of Christmas; it would only then see if the 18 months' worth of preparation would be enough. They had to obtain the permission from the Ministry of Food to have quantities of product made due to all the shortages and restrictions on raw materials, dried fruit, almonds, sugar, flower, rum etc; all had to be carefully calculated. Including the paper that would be either wrapped around them or made into packaging. The bill of fare for 1948 took shape with 55 tonnes of Christmas puddings, 25 tonnes of mincemeat, 70 tons of turkey and poultry, 25,000 toys, 20,000 boxes of crackers, 24,000 books and manuals, 60,000 tins of biscuits, and massive 200,000 boxes of chocolates. One of the items the company could be quite sure of having ready on time was the cards. Their in-house printing branch worked 15 months ahead. They had accumulated enough materials in small portions over time to be able to fill changing tastes and colours and finishes and quality and size required for their customers.

Ancillary items like boxes, envelopes, printed labels and inks had to be accumulated in the first three months of each year. But the search for materials went on all year round. Every year the printing branch in June was poised with the labour, materials and machinery all tuned up ready to deal with Christmas card orders. At this time, it wasn't just the UK that was being

considered everything had to be coordinated with the export branch and estimating the amount of goods to be shipped with their destinations attached. Arrangements had to be made early on to define the delivery dates to coincide with the ships sailing during August and September, to make sure that the Christmas supplies were on the ground overseas, in every area, no later than the 1st week of November to make sure that the distribution to those areas happened in time for December.

The first of the areas always to be dealt with was the Far East, as this was always the hardest to get supplies to. Some of the issues that they had shipping Christmas lines, was the export of turkey, poultry, mincemeat and crackers. The poultry demanded refrigeration space and mincemeat also had to be handled with great care, particularly in the Far East because of the risk of fermentation. Crackers brought a whole different state of affairs with the heat having risk of extreme danger of fire and this also had special stowage agreements. The easier products to ship were toys, books and annuals, but these were sent to an export warehouse to be packed in the assortment required for each area as the manufacturer refused to do this. Every year Operation Santa Claus – it was an all year-round affair never stopping, you could say some staff were like Santa's elves.

1949

Review on the new club programme 1949

1949 started with a review on the new club programme that had started in 1944. Mr L.C. Wynne-Tyson OBE, who was the deputy general manager, tells of how a permanent club was chosen all the way through to the opening.

The making of a club was essentially a combined operation, all dependent on the skill and energy of a large number of people. The original programme first war clubs were inspired not only by the outside authority, but the company itself and this happened as early as 1944. The initiative had to decide upon where these permanent clubs would be and after the war a number of traditional service centres in the United Kingdom had taken shape. There were obvious sites of which we have already looked at Portsmouth, Chatham, Colchester, Aldershot and Catterick.

Unbeknown to the management at the time, when all of these clubs were in their infancy the success was immediate and it was almost embarrassing for the company as requests for similar clubs were being asked for all the time from a variety of sources, either local authorities, military formations, GOC and occasionally the service ministries themselves. Some of these clubs were easy to dismiss – this was from either insufficient servicemen in the proposed area or there was knowledge of the troops departing and the barracks closing down.

At first glance each club request had to be examined, this was because the executive committee needed to know all of the pros and cons of the situation. The request was then passed to HCS (Home Canteen Service) and S.M. Sowerby, then after the briefing by Chief R.J. Wallace, they would approve and then set the ball rolling with a detailed report on the locality.

The report prepared by them in conjunction with the command supervisor and the local service authorities would be a comprehensive affair showing the number of potential customers within the area detailing from 5 to 25 miles of the proposed club. The report would also detail the existing civilian amenities, local transport with the fares and also the canteen and hostel accommodation already available in the local area. This report would then be carefully studied by the executive committee who would then recommend it to the board of management who would or would not be in favour of such a project. At the time in the post-war period several cases came up for Folkestone, Dover, Gosport, Hull and Edinburgh, but the executive decided that on the evidence at the time these clubs would not be justified for a permanent club and all of the refit or rebuild which was attached to this.

You would assume the executive committee would give an idea of if its blessing and recommendations to the board of management, which would give an idea for what would and would not be approved. But depending on all the details, they would still have to wait for the secretary to inform of the decision from the board. From the moment that the decision was made that it would go ahead, there was no turning back when a new club had been conceived, but at this point many people within the company knew that some long days, weeks and months were ahead.

One of the first people to be informed of the positive decision from the board was E.M. Joseph, the honorary consulting architect, and F.H Garner, the director of works and buildings. Home Canteen Service provided a general picture of the type of club that would fit and the sort of size of the accommodation and the number of sizes of the rooms and any other special features that were required. With this information the Estates team would visit the time and call on the clerk and surveyor and the lead estate agent. Their job would be to find an existing building suitable for conversion or if nothing was available a new site for a new building.

They then reported back to Mr Garner, bringing the answers to many of the questions which had been asked. What building was suitable for their needs? What's available? Were there any existing tenancies? Was it a reasonable price? Was there a town planned in the area? How does it lie regarding to drainage service mains, or neighbouring houses and shops? Each one of the possibilities was considered. The architect would view the proposal with an eye to the levels and orientations and the host of the technical and aesthetic considerations to be considered and also the proximity to local cinemas, railway stations, bus stops, other public houses in the area and other factors which could enhance or reduce its user potential.

Then Mr Arnold would have to instruct and negotiate with the owner for the purchase of the land or the building and if this was the War Department land the secretariat would approach the war office for a long lease. Only after this price was agreed and the executive committee laid the whole scheme before the board of management with an estimate at the total cost. It was then approved by solicitors and instructed to acquire the property. It sure sounded very simple but this over many hours and many days and weeks would create headaches for many of the company's men who ploughed their way through the jungle of forms and permits and claims and licences, and unlike today everything had to be done with pen and paper – not even a fax machine existed at this point, never mind the Internet.

They could waste no time in applying to the regional building committee for the building licences. This would involve personal appearances before the committee to state the case and then the licence seldom was granted once and often postponed for several months or if it was granted, it would carry various restrictive clauses, for example number of local labourers to be employed, fixed number of trainees to be employed, and no work could begin until such and such a date. So yet again delaying even starting.

Permits would then have to be obtained from the appropriate authorities for the amount of controlled materials which could be used in the construction based on the directors' estimate. These permits would need to be granted with certain amendments; this would include things like whether they could use clay bricks or the requests for the way the timber would be cut. Even the steel demands had to be reduced and this is when at the Plymouth club in order to save steel they hoped to use old tram rails.

The planning authorities then had to look at the drawings produced, and for them to assess the nature of the proposed buildings. Only now they could consider if the building or property they were going to use needed a change of user application. Although there was no sign on site of any club developing, months of hard work had already gone in and a great deal of money spent on the process so far. Mr F.H. Crosier, R.J. Wallace, S.B. Martin, S.M. Sowerby, F.H. Garner, E. McGowan and the Dep director all had a task to do. Only now that all the preliminary drawings could be assessed and various suggestions were made, thrashed out around the table to adopt or reject. Through previous experience details like load windows in the billiards room as they may be smashed when the cue is pulled back, the stair treads must be proofed against hobnails from slipping, rises of stairs must be in a dark material so as not to show marks from the toe caps, the bannisters must be impossible to slide down (I always wondered why it was impossible to do so – they actually planned it that way), the precise position for all of the finger plates and kick plates on the doors and that the wash hand basins were required to support because the customers had a little habit of sitting on them. It was at all these meetings that the ultimate shape and style of all the clubs were finally determined and after possibly 2 or 3 months of discussion from long talks and exchanges of ideas the architect would produce working drawings for the approval of the local authority.

At this point they had acquired the land, planning consent, they had a licence to build and permits for certain controlled materials. When and now they needed to find somebody to build the club? Several contractors would be invited in, professional quantity surveyors would carefully check all estimates and during the construction test materials for quality and ensure that every yard of glass and pound of putty was correctly costed. Then finally a contractor would be chosen and the contract for the job would be drawn up and signed for by the contractor and also the secretary of the company. A starting date would then be agreed by the building committee and so the work began.

From the dates the building started, Mr CC Francis, the furnishings buyer would be placing his contract finishes, floor coverings and fabrics all in keeping with the style and look agreed. It was only then that an opening date would be tentatively agreed. Then it was the deputy director's duty to call Buckingham Palace or St James's Palace to agree various details if it was to be a Royal opening with the Equerry or the lady-in-waiting whichever the case may be. Now with the light at the end of the tunnel, Mr EE Warner and Mr W Broomfield would have already decided the type of kitchen equipment which needed to be arranged for purchase, while works and building people carried out its installation. Mr W Broomfield's role was to consult with the local club supervisors and 2 months ahead of the date they began to recruit staff. First and foremost they needed a manager, and only then they could look at canteen attendants, cooks, commissionaires, porters, games room attendants, toilet and cloakroom attendants and others, about 100 in all for each of these brand-new clubs. Most of these would be recruited locally and the club supervisor in certain cases would see that the girls received the first-class training in other clubs prior to opening and not forgetting at this point in time that the WVS chief liaison officer Mrs Cross would need to see the rooms, made available to them and how many members they would need to staff the information Bureau.

From then a meeting, the new club's advisory committee – this was a local body which comprised 102 councillors, the vicar, leading members of the town, WVS and officers and other ranks of the three services. This would go through some of the aims and objectives with the responsibilities of the advisory committee. The invitation list would then be prepared only invitations dispatched. Entertainment would be arranged, an orchestra, a guard of honour, its royalty was to be present would be arranged and special invitation issued to other ranks of the local units of the three services. Approximately 3 weeks before the opening the club manager would be appointed and they would move in. The cleaners would arrive and begin to prepare the building to receive the furniture and basic things like curtains to be hung and mirrors to be put in position and the final parts of the club arranged.

About a week before the opening, Mr W Broomfield would take up residence to complete all the local arrangements, and a few days later Mr H Osmond arrived from the headquarters to supervise the catering for the opening day; this would be followed shortly by the chefs. The day before opening it would be tough to say that the club was always going to be ready, especially after so many goings on and so much planning leading up to it. Everybody as usual would be running around like headless chickens and everything would appear to be a complete shambles; the cleaners would be cleaning, the other tradespeople would be completing the snagging and then masses of flowers would arrive to be arranged.

Then in typical fashion, as with all clubs that had been open previously, it would be expected that the miracle would happen. The last hours before all the dignitaries and VIPs arrived everything would look pristine, even the people that had been running around minutes before would look like they'd been ready for weeks. The vision that had been from the beginning a pristine club with all the amenities and facilities expected of them would look exactly as they expected it to.

All that was left now would be for the guests to arrive, royalty would arrive and the presentations with the opening ceremony and the dedication would go off without a hitch. When then the speeches and entertainment would all go smoothly as finely as it would have been rehearsed and everything timed perfectly. The Grand Tour and lunch would go ahead, and everybody would leave as planned and on time.

The club was born as to those clubs before it until the same as the clubs after it. The day after everything could run like clockwork as if it had been opened for years, and even though the staff would be nearly dead on their feet from the day before and the months and weeks behind them, they would be as neatly turned out after the opening day. There are many things you can say about a team of staff, no matter what level, who worked so hard to make something happen over such a long period of time that no matter what was going on, passion and the dedication today at work second to none, camaraderie and excellence all rolled into one.

Behind the scenes Ruxley Towers Form 1241, 1949

Behind the scenes at Ruxley Towers there was a Department which actually served staff serving services, affectionately known as 'Form 1241'. However, a better description for what they were was the information Bureau for the company. They held the records of all establishments operating across the United Kingdom and Western Europe, together with the details of over 30,000 establishments that had opened and closed during the war years. They had a motto 'quoting registered number or an address and we guarantee to supply information over the last 10 years'; the records included the registered numbers, postal addresses, railway station of every establishment, and the name and the unit using that canteen. In addition to this they held the details of all group supervisors, district managers and other staff members.

Over a long period of time they had become busier and busier up to a dozen calls a day from high ranking officials down to privates seeking the nearest canteen to their home address, often so they could exchange their vouchers for sweets and cheap cigarettes. Over the 26 years with the company one staff member reported they had dealt with so many subjects but none as varied as the present job which is full of interest and an essential part of the NAAFI. What if the telephone exchange got a call and they were uncertain as to where to direct it, they knew full well that they would get a phone call.

One amusing incident which had been documented had occurred just before Christmas 1948. A lady telephoned in from London and said she wanted to send a parcel to her son in 'Blankland', and if she sent it to the office at Kennington would they enclose it with their goods for shipment, as she was so afraid to send it by post just in case it got lost. The member of staff inquired whether her son's unit was actually stationed in 'Blankland' and the lady replied indignantly, "young man, my son is the officer commanding all the troops in that country". It was never certain whether her son's parcel got there in the end!

Everything arrived and Form 1241 section was opened, collated and date stamped twice and all records were kept up to date with copies of all circulars, price lists and movements of the troops. It would seem such a shame that today the hard work of Alban Clark and his colleagues no longer exists as this would be a treasure trove of historical information.

A day in the life of mobile canteen Olive N. Lewin, Combermere Bks Windsor 1949

Olive was a mobile canteen driver in 1949 who had served with NAAFI for 5½ years whose job it was to keep some 300 cavalry men happy with cups of tea and cake. She started work at 0830 hrs and began by checking off the cakes that had been left out for her from the evening before. She collected about 70 dozen, so this took some time and if they had left Swiss roll or slab cake, she would have to cut it into the required portions before loading. At 0930 hrs, she would take the cakes out to the van and collect the rest of her stores for making tea. The most difficult part of the job was starting the van, it was a large Fordson type and very temperamental. The task of starting it normally it took about 15 minutes of persuasion and then with a sudden spurt it would start up like a dream.

Once everything was loaded and the van was running, it was time to go off at a steady speed of 5 miles an hour, which at the time was the speed limit of the barracks. One of the first service points was just outside of the barracks about 3/4 of a mile down the road. She was due to arrive there at 1015 hrs every morning, and there was a very long queue waiting for her, by 1100 hrs the men had all been served and often had returned for more tea or cake. The next stop only required to serve 30 men at the guard room of Windsor Castle, 151 of the guard would come out for their refreshments. She writes that the men on guard had a tedious job, but they were all very cheerful and ready for a joke and a laugh. At 1200 hrs she drove back to the canteen to take lunch and then 1300 hrs until 1430 hrs she cleaned her van to get more cakes ready.

Olive's accommodation was a little room she shared with the counter assistant. They had an open fire, which was well needed during the winter and they had a radio between them which made the afternoons quite cheerful. By 1700 hrs they were back at work and the first task was to light the fires. They used to have to bank the fireplaces and drag packs of coal in from outside.

Again, she loaded her van with tea and cakes, then at 1730 hrs the other girls arrived on duty, one of them helped load the urns onto the van. This time she served Windsor Castle first in the evening arriving at 1745hrs so that she could then serve the relief guard before they take up their posts at 1800 hrs. Then she had to wait until the old guard returned to the guard room and this meant she didn't get away from there before 1830 hrs. Then she would go and serve the other boys who were already in an even longer queue than the morning. In the mornings the van only served tea and cakes but, in the evenings, it also provided cigarettes and other items, only then at about 1930 hrs she was rushed off her feet until she sold out of most items. Thursdays were exceptionally busy, and she needed to carry extra stock as this was payday and often didn't finish past 2100 hrs. When she finished in the evening she'd go back to her room, tired but happy knowing that she was doing a job well worthwhile.

The only woman gunner 1949

At the end of February 1949 Miss Caroline Sutton retired from the company after 20 years as the manager of the canteen at St John's Wood barracks in London serving the Royal Horse Artillery, M, J, F and K Batteries and Battery which then became the King's troop. Miss Sutton saw King's troop move off on a number of historic occasions. She had seen 3 Kings ascended to the British throne and watched the 13 pounders leave the wood to salute 7 Royal babies. In 1939 Miss Sutton watched K&G batteries leave for the 6-year war and she was there to greet them on their return during the war years. The barracks was occupied by the London District Signals and Miss Sutton saw them arrive, young territorials, who in civilian life were bank, clerks, actors, clergyman, sons, but in a few weeks, they were hardened soldiers. In June 1941 she was presented to the Princess Royal who was Colonel in chief of the Signals and in October 1947 the King paid the battery a visit and when signing the visitors book struck out "The riding troop" and wrote above it "the King's troop RHA". The men were lined up on parade and Miss Sutton was called and presented to His Majesty by the commanding officer. She liked to receive a photograph of them shaking hands which was signed by the King at Buckingham Palace. Throughout the London blitz, she continued to live and work as St John's Wood barracks. Various buildings were hit and burned out, water and gas were out of action for 3 months and cooking sausages in the open air became commonplace. She recalls that the quietest two nights in the NAAFI were Armistice night 1918 and VE night 1945, whether men left for parties further afield.

Before Miss Sutton arrived in 1928, she'd served at Purfleet, Salisbury Plain, Sutton Veney, Bovington, Larkhill, Tidworth, Colchester, Camberley and Windsor. Hundreds of counter assistants and schools of cooks and manageresses had passed through her hands and many of her old staff at the time sent her flowers. Even her Siamese cats were famous characters in the club. On her retirement the commanding officer Maj JA Norman DSO, presented her with a charming gold bracelet with the enamel RHA cipher mounted on it with an engraved subscription. This became her most prized possession and upon her death this was returned to the King's troop as it had been previously arranged. She was proudest to boast that she was known to the barracks as the only woman gunner, or in the words of Maj Norman she was the only Horse Artillery man left behind.

Give me 6 pence for a NAAFI News! 1949

Six pence for a NAAFI News was actually going down quite well and many letters were written to the editor to compliment them for the extra copies being made available, even though they had to pay for them this time and they were still operating under the proviso that once they read it they would hand it to somebody else to read, whether they had paid or not. But one lady, a Mrs J Hudson Manageress from registered number 13246R, had to complain; she states: "I am one of the opinions that, at the moment that NAAFI News is not quite worth sixpence. We should like to see a little more news of our local canteens. My 2 girls and myself have worked in an old Nissen hutted camp for years now, with soot, smoke and rain coming in whatever we do. We are quite happy, but in NAAFI News we always see pictures of luxury canteens, where conditions are ideal, and all of the good times they seem to be having overseas. Let us have a little more of the home news and the ordinary working staff, and then we would not mind paying a shilling for a copy."

From the editor: we cannot print what we do not hear about. We have no widespread team of reporters; we rely on people like Mrs Hudson to keep us informed, with paragraphs and photographs of local affairs. In every issue we repeat our urgent appeal for cooperation from all the ordinary working staff in keeping us informed of their local activities. Let us hear from you all keeping in mind that we are subject to limited space, but you will receive a fair showing: Ed.

Tea for 1,000 1949

Consider this; the commanding officer requests tea to be laid on for 1000 people at a sports afternoon. Now you would think that this would be quite simple, but is it?

The district manager requires more precise information the exact date, time and location of the event. Whether it is for officers, other ranks or all 3, and for how many of each grade, how far it would be from the nearest canteen? How many staff male and female will be required? Whether the attendance of the restaurant superintendent will be needed? Nature of the catering required. Would this be a buffet tea, sit down tea, lunch, dance with or without a bar.

Next would be the summary of the special catering costs Then the menu priced and agreed and then form 205A would be filled out which gives the information needed for the coming event. This form then would go to the command office which gives special catering a registered number and forwards a copy to Ruxley Towers. Big jobs of this kind were supervised from Ruxley Towers, but other moderately sized events would fall entirely to the district manager and restaurant superintendent.

The DM now organises the event according to his own timetable. Staff would be allocated from local canteens and necessary equipment would be obtained through head office. Orders for supplies, cakes and pastries, other refreshments must be placed with the appropriate warehouses and bakeries. Flowers and sundry items would also need to be ordered via head office. And when the day came the careful plans would be carried out without a hitch as they would nearly always be.

For larger special events such as Bisley or Trooping the colour, or the sovereign's parade at Camberley, 2 or 3 or more of the catering staff at Ruxley Towers would be dedicated to the job. This would mean a team of experts, 2 catering superintendents, four chief demonstrators, 2 assistant catering superintendents and one assistant chef demonstrator with a wine steward and the leave train superintendent. NAAFI's bigger catering responsibilities would earn the team's recognition but if they would fail this would not be something they would be familiar with at all.

In one year, the company would serve over 600,000 meals of all kinds during these special catering events. In the 6 months leading up to April of 1949, which was a fairly quiet period, they undertook 243 special catering and 154 ordinary catering events. In the summer months from May to October on average 500 functions would be close to the amount catered for. Within the calendar festive occasions were something the company was very familiar with when it came to the services. If the Officer's daughter was getting married NAAFI would arrange the reception, if the OCA had a reunion again the company would do the catering, the station commander threw a cocktail party NAAFI lay it on. In the summer also came the tattoos, cricket weeks, garden parties, reunions, and in the winter they would have a full-service point to point meetings, a variety of regimental dances and balls, Christmas tea parties and then end of year dances.

On the whole 1949 saw a party for the Imperial defence college to visit the Grand National with lunch and a wine bar, a 28 day function for 2000 officers per day, and military police reunion at Woking with 1500 lunches and teas to be prepared and served, the RE's 1400 teas and lunches, RASC 1060 teas and lunches, a national tea cocktail party, The Royal Naval Benevolent Fund meeting, numerous new club openings and to round it all off a garden party at St James's Palace with royalty present and another function at Lancaster House and St James's Palace on behalf of the government hospitality fund for distinguished statesman who had gathered in London for various conferences.

The end of a blockade 1949

On the afternoon of May 11th, 1949, a number of servicemen and officials with press representatives of the world began to gather at the barrier at Helmstedt, when they were served by a mobile canteen waiting to make its first trip to Berlin. As the evening fell that NAAFI roadhouse at Helmstedt, unlike other evenings where they served only about a dozen, at the blockade this was different, 250 dinners throughout the night. This was a busy night for the NAAFI mobile team, and at midnight the blockade ended. The press cars raced to Berlin followed closely by the NAAFI mobile, the first heavy vehicle to reach the capital. It had a successful journey and was greeted by enthusiastic crowds of British and Berliners, with cameras and news reels it reached one of the western zone's points of the city. The trip had taken about 2 hours and 40 minutes. By dawn they were in Berlin at last and one of the most exciting evenings of their lives when the driver Edward Stappard, and Reginald Porter had done

8 years with NAAFI and both Dunkirk veterans who would work nonstop 24 hours to make sure that they arrived on time to relieve one of the old vehicles that had been stuck behind the blockade.

OCA 1949

In the autumn of 1949 Lt Col R Merry OBE, chairman of the general committee, which summarised the annual general meeting.

Thirty-eight delegates, representing branches of the United Kingdom, completed the assembly. The chairman addressed the committee and the members: "It once again gives me great pleasure to welcome you, on behalf of the general committee, to the annual general meeting of our OCA and thank you for your work you have done for the OCA during the past year. Our Association is now firmly established, and I am able to report a successful year working in both the social and the benevolence spheres. There are now 16 branches in the United Kingdom with a total membership of 5278. The overseas branches total nine with an approximate membership of 514. The total home membership fees that have not been paid total 1000 members; these have received a final notice and they anticipate a considerable number of them would be lost. However, these losses largely offset by the fact that 734 new members had been enrolled during 1948. Your general committee are considering promoting a further drive to rope in potential members and our Association has progressed so far since many of them were approached".

Some of the branches that were created out of branch one at the end of the previous year had now requested to be reabsorbed into branch number one; these were the County branches of Surrey, Middlesex, Essex and Bedfordshire and Herts. The reason for this was very simple: they preferred the more social and varied occasions organised by branch one and the County branches were too small to deal with these sorts of events, but still the members had actually increased on the back of the County branches. The OCA, even though it wanted to be all inclusive of all members, would still struggle with this; it was all down to expensive travel and shortage of spending money. So, on the whole this at the time was not due to a lack of initiative by the branch committees. Since the reunion dance was such a success with 1200 people attending the evening, they had already fixed a date at Seymour Hall on the 3rd of December 1949. Since the previous annual general meeting 66 cases had actually received benevolence, this totalled 124 cases that had been dealt with. One of the main suggestions that had come out of the previous meeting was that they would like to have an OCA club in London but unfortunately due to the types of properties and the costs and staffing of such an establishment, it was not going to happen so this idea was then closed. The idea was put forward, yet those keen to use the amenities of a London club solely devoted to the ex-service interests will refer to the victory club in Seymour Street, London which is a stone's throw from Marble Arch. This was an ideal place for ex-service members to meet up.

HMS amethyst Canteen manager John J.S. McNamara 1949

As he stood on the Jetty at Davenport dockyards watching the HMS Amethyst tie up after the 10,000-mile journey home, Lady Astor pushed him politely, but firmly, to one side and leaned forward asking if he'd seen the officers and men. From Plymouth Hoe right along the dockyard to the waterfront was thickly fringed with people who wanted to see what manner of men these were whose behaviour in the Yangtse had raised the morale of an empire and his daring escape had dealt a loss of face to the Chinese communists.

On the jetty hundreds of relatives waved and cheered and cried. Burly men shouted a welcome while tears run unashamedly down their cheeks. Statesmen, Admirals, senior army and our AF officers, civic dignitaries, and other nobilities stood in a glittering array, they lost to be temporarily dimmed by the humble British seamen now lining the rail of their battered little ship. Nearly 200 reporters, broadcasters, newsreel crews and television men recorded the scene, the greatest gathering of newsmen since Princess Elizabeth's wedding. If anyone in their assembly had suggested that "the HMS Amethyst's affair had been overdone" he would have been tossed into the drink.

The relatives surged aboard and to the most hardened of us came an uncomfortable lump in the throat. I saw 100 human cameos to stir the heart. I saw one tubby middle-aged Petty Officer run towards his homely, middle aged wife and sweep her into his arms, raining kisses on her lips and eyes and hair as though he were sweet 17. I saw a cockney mother greet her young son, she put out her hands and touched his face, and her eyes were wonderful to see. Struggling for words, she knew that the great moment had come, and yet she could find nothing to say. Then "you good boy, Charlie?" she piped. The boy hugged her close: "of course, MA," he said a little guiltily.

We went below, representing NCS, George Wood representing Imperial club and I who wanted to hear the first-hand personal story of the NAAFI canteen manager aboard, John McNamara. We had already heard much of this young man. We had heard Mr Pegg's assurance that the commander and the ship's company were very appreciative of the canteen manager's excellent service and assistance. We had seen the commander report in what he stated that McNamara's conduct was of the highest order, and that he carried out his duties with complete efficiency. As an NCS member of the crew, he proved that he was a first-class semen. We found him in his canteen and apartment between decks no bigger than a large cupboard, with his mother, his father who had served 21 years in the Royal Navy, and his fiancée. At age 22 McNamara was a short dark-haired youngster with a firm chin and a steady glance. Typically, although he had served the ordeal of the trip, he was scared stiff of the approaching march through the town and the civic reception to follow. He showed us around the ship and took us into the shell scarred sick bay, where he had tended the wounds, and a chat room where during the HMS Amethyst's freedom, he had plotted the course. Later that morning they stood at the saluting base outside Plymouth Guildhall and watched with pride as this young NAAFI representative marched with his shipmates in an honoured place, carrying himself excellently throughout the parade. And later still at Prospect Row, it took some doing but I managed to drag his story out of him.

McNamara's story

He first joined and NCS in October 1944, a day before his 17th birthday. He was posted to Plymouth aboard the Defiance for preliminary training and then onto the Impregnable for disciplinary training. His 1st canteen was Wembury camp outside Plymouth where he served his time as a canteen assistant. Then he was sent to the destroyer Undaunted for his 1st cantina float, where he served under Mr Hambly; after 2 months he went as a leading CA to the carrier Indominable and went out with her to Australia.

After 2 years in NCS he was demobilised and returned to civilian life for a time. But in April 1947 he rejoined and again came to Plymouth where he was sent by trooper to Hong Kong. In July 1947 in September of that year he joined the HMS Amethyst in Hong Kong as a canteen assistant and later that year became an assistant in charge acting as manager. In April of that year they left Shanghai and sailed up to Nanking where they were to relieve the concert Asgard ship at the British embassy. Their job would have been to stand by in case it was necessary to evacuate British Nationals from the city.

The HMS Amethyst herself was a frigate of 1490 tonnes with the main armament of 6 four-inch guns. The maximum speed was 20 knots, and when they set off, they had 192 officers and men aboard under the command of Lieutenant Commander BM Skinner. At the time they knew there was fighting between the communists on the North bank and the nationalists on the South, and it did not expect trouble as if this was an ordinary trip.

On the morning of April 20th at 0815hrs action stations were sounded. He went at once to sick bay and by 0830hrs they were under fire. They did not score any hits and they hoped it hadn't been a mistake made and they lowered the union jacks over either side of the ship and after a few minutes the firing stopped; they began to think it had been a mistake but at 0910hrs they knew it wasn't – heavy artillery was now blasting away. One heavy shell hit the bridge and knocked out all 5 officers, another hit the wheelhouse and put the crew out of action.

At this time McNamara was in sick bay still, the first casualty a boy Seaman lay in one of the bunks and he was sitting beside him. Something caused him to get up and move to the other side and at that moment a shell burst outside, and shrapnel spurted into the bay. The seaman was killed outright but he escaped without a scratch. It was a nasty messy business, but he had no time to feel really scared because by now the wounded were coming down at regular intervals and his job was to render first aid, bandage them and wait for the doctor. But in a short time both the doctor and the sick berth attendant were killed. Their only hope was to make the wounded as comfortable as possible. By now the ship had stopped moving with the wheelhouse crew gone, the HMS Amethyst had swerved and ran aground on the South Bank near Rose Island and within 400 to 500 yards of the communist guns. They were now a sitting target and 75MM and 105MM shells were hitting them constantly. They had been aground about an hour and the order came to get the wounded on the quarterdeck in order to take them ashore. About 60 ratings were ordered over the side to swim 50 to 60 yards to the shore. The communists opened up with machine guns and several of them were hit, 3 were killed while swimming but the others scrambled ashore into the arms of the nationalists who conducted them to Shanghai.

Then came the order that no more men were to go over the side and that the wounded were to be made as comfortable as possible while they waited for a medical officer and medical supplies. Around midday things quietened down a bit but 2 or 3 hours later they were overjoyed to see HMS Consort, the ship they were sent to relieve, steaming downstream towards them, with all her guns blazing. It was now a grand sight and cheered them up tremendously. But the communist fire was too fierce to allow the Consort to get out of trouble, after the gallant battle she had to steam downstream still under heavy fire.

Once again things quietened down until after dark, they managed to lift the HMS Amethyst off the mud and proceed up the river for about 10 miles under machine gunfire. The next morning April 21st they received the signal that the Consort had been joined by HMS London and HMS Black Swan and they were going to try to force their way upstream to their rescue. But soon they were under ferocious fire again from the North bank and being unable to take evading action in the narrow deep-water channel they suffered heavily. In the end they reluctantly had to turn back, carrying their dead and wounded.

At about 1500hrs that afternoon and our AF Sunderland touched down just long enough to enable the RF medical officer Flt Lt Fearnley to jump on while the aircraft took off under fire. They got aboard safely and at once set about tending the wounded. That night after dark, 12 sampans belonging to the nationalist came along and took off 27 wounded including the CEO Commander Skinner and put them on the last train to Shanghai; Lt Commander Skinner died on that journey. That night was quiet and the next day sometime during the afternoon, a nationalist MTB brought off Lt Commander Karen downriver from Nanking and he took command from Lt Western who, although wounded, had refused to leave until he was relieved. That night the new skipper ordered them to move still further upriver to an anchorage at Tanto Island and there they stayed for 102 days.

With the wounded gone, his duties were now divided between running the canteen and watchkeeping. In the canteen all was well, luckily. He'd left Shanghai with 2 months' supplies and with half of the ship's company gone they were well stocked up; in fact, the only item they ran short of was toothpaste. The food situation was good until the last month when the meat was going bad and they all went on half rations and they were able to buy ashore at great prices certain quantities of fresh vegetables and eggs. And very occasionally they got hold of beer in a bottle. On July 30th at 1940 hrs the commander called the CPO to his cabin and told them he intended to try and breakout that night without charts or pilot and down a river notorious for its sandbanks and torturous course. At about 2200hrs that night the Lieutenant ordered him to the chart house, and showed him the proposed course on the plan of the river and told him that he was to plot their progress so that, in case the bridge was put out of action once more, there would be a secondary check on their position. It was a bit of a headache McNamara says for him as he was quite new to navigation. Then was a very anxious moment when he heard them call from the bridge that they had reached the spot where the river was only 2½ fathoms and they were drawing 2 fathoms. In other words their keel was only 3 feet above the riverbed. It was almost 0500hrs and dawn was breaking when they came in sight of Woosung and a message came from the bridge HMS Consort was in sight and then made it, but still, they had to pass the Forts and it was getting lighter every moment. They held their breath every moment expecting the 6 inch and 9.2-inch guns to open up and blow them out of the water. Instead nothing happened. They slipped past Woosung and the CEO sent his famous signal," have re-joined the fleet. No damage or casualties. God save the King" so this ended the canteen manager story and McNamara said he went below, had a nice strong cup of tea and then when they came alongside the consort he didn't mind saying he had many tots of rum passed from the Consort to the HMS Amethyst. McNamara had become a celebrity with his NAAFI colleagues in the Imperial club and later still that night that they got back they found themselves next to the Lieutenant Commander Karen who said, "Young McNamara, he's alright, he's one of us".

Norwood Depot 1949

As the 1940s drew to a close so did the Norwood Depot. Now with the silence of peace and war some years ago for those people who either became a part of it or had passed through it to the many adventures, tours and exercises Norwood Depot will have held pride of place in many memories of EFI. It is important to record the history of such a place that held so many fond memories of those who pass through it.

The story of Norwood Depot began at the end of 1940. It was previously a Yeoman service and a hastily set up Depot at Imperial Court, St James's Road, Croydon, and the Mitcham sports ground. During those times they were very difficult conditions and many of the pioneers of those early days were to form the backbone of the Norwood Depot staff in the years to come. It was in the dark days of 1940, after the war had broken out, the survivors of RASC EFI of Dunkirk were recovering from their experiences at the Mitcham camp, this is when the idea of Norwood Depot was born. At that time, it was quickly realised that we were up against things in a big way, that the warfare to be waged was in Total War which would revolutionise all preconceived notions and measures of the previous conflicts. It was plain to see that the NAAFI could satisfactorily carry out their commitment to the forces, and many of their employees would be made into equally good soldiers. This included the staff who served in operational areas overseas.

The aim of the new Depot was to achieve a quality training centre for the RASC and EFI for deployment. The first necessary step was to work out a staff establishment capable of training and administering up to a strength of 1500 officers and other ranks. For this purpose, the final establishment approved was that of 10 officers and 96 other ranks. The next thing was to find suitable premises with the requisite training grounds. In this they were lucky as at this time the 'Fidelis convent' at Norwood, with its 16½ acres of ground which had previously been leased by the company for some other purpose, was currently unoccupied and found exceptionally suitable for the purpose required. Over a short time, the necessary alterations, additions, and equipping were splendidly carried out by the works and furnishing branches. When this was done it was plain to see that the establishment now at the disposal was beautifully equipped and a Top-class Depot in every way, now it was up to the training staff to deliver the goods.

During the lifetime of the Depot it was fathered by Mr Stagg and Mr Baker, of OCS, whose inspiration and care it duly reflected. It was on the 12th of March 1941 that they marched in from Croydon and started the training. It has been decided that the Depot must set a high military standard equal at least to that of the regular Royal Army Service Corps training depots; this would be the general lines of how it was intended that it should be run. The purpose of the Depot was to accommodate, train, and dispatch military personnel of the NAAFI, ask RASC EFI for overseas service.

The conference at Norwood was then their military home for the next 5½ years, when at the end of the war they moved further up central Hill and took possession of the Royal Norman college for the blind. From the start they became house proud, taking delight in combining the efficiency with the comfort and good food. The environment of Norwood not only created first class soldiers but also made it easy to maintain good discipline and personal pride.

The training Depot was well organised into a number of training companies, under the able control of Maj W Paterson. The men received at least 4 weeks' basic military training before being posted to draft companies, and eventually dispatched too overseas commands. The thousands of men who passed through Norwood Depot during the war years, whose days will bring back varied and vivid memories, some few men perhaps painful memories, but many more pleasant and some distinctly humorous. Not many will ever forget their passing out parade and the drill competition, only the highest standard to have turnout and drill would win the Drill competition. The high standards were all due to the patience and skill of the staff instructors, and amongst them were Devlin, Fraser, Stubbs, Williams, Burtenshaw, Scott, Goff, Hamilton, White and Middleditch. All of whom have now returned to civilian life – a Maj Paterson returned to his motor business in Preston. Many of the men who left the Depot and are now part of the OCA, flying the flag for camaraderie and the family of which they became whilst serving.

The officers' training and the cadets was 4 to 5 weeks long and based on the syllabus of training used at the Royal Army Service Corps OCTU. The RSM who later became Lieutenant Comrie, was remembered fondly for his keenness to turn them out to be not only a credit to themselves but also the EFI and the British army – after all, 1st and foremost they were soldiers.

Over the life span of the Depot over 800 officers passed through this course. The sole object of all of the Depot training was to instil discipline and morale found on military and NAAFI training, this was to enable the EFI personnel to take their place in the military commands overseas with confidence and efficiency.

After the military training came the main job of the Depot, and that was to prepare and dispatch all of the EFI officers and other ranks to every worldwide Theatre of war, where they were required to carry out the company's business. The preparation and dispatch of these drafts was a complicated and detailed task. It included medical inoculations and equipping them down to the last button and the final documentation. It ended in the transportation, and often waving goodbye on a darkened railway station during an air raid. Documentation was particularly heavy, at it had to include both military and commercial papers. This job was largely in the hands of the successive adjutants, captains Cooper, Edwards, Harrison, Bottome and Pallett and their capable staff.

From March 1941, to the end of 1945, the numbers sent from the Depot to overseas commands were 912 officers, 10,306 other ranks, under 506 operational orders. Included in this number were the North African force, and a Brigadier Hamilton and the all-important D-force which finally left for the shores of France under the command of Brigadier Peters and subsequently came under the command of Brigadier Hamilton, who had much to do in its planning. These 2 forces of considerable numbers were built up, organised and trained the Depot for several months.

From these numbers it was seen that the quartermaster's job at the Depot was no easy task and his Department had to work all hours to keep the faith with the commitments given to them. Amongst his many other duties, the QM SSM Bowen, who then became the general secretary of the OCA, was in 1944 responsible for 122,050 articles of equipment, 141,926 of clothing and 12,867 of special kit, all issued from the stores to the drafts going overseas.

At the peak of the war the accommodation at the Depot was very tight and to ease this a large canvas camp was set up in the Depot grounds, in which a system of air raid trenches were dug. Additional houses and a school was also taken over for temporary use. Separate detachments of the Depot was set up at Hindhead for ENSA, and at the Imperial Sports Club ground at Mitcham for transport. Both were primarily in connection with the activities for

D-Day and after. In 1944 to 45 the number of motor vehicles of all types sent overseas from Mitcham detachment was 1465. Many of these had to be waterproof for the D-Day landings. From the opening of the Depot in 1941 to the end of 1945 the separate entries of officers numbered 1117 and that of the other ranks 18,639 – quite a large family to cater for. For the catering they had the splendid kitchen staff to thank when day after day, under the supervision of Maj John Egerton, originally from army rations was transformed by the magic of the chefs and cooks. Some said it was hotel quality food, like eating out in London.

When it came to being bombed out, they had perhaps more than their fair share as Civilian figures and reports published later, it transpired that the area in which the Depot had been situated suffered more severely than any other part of London. In particular, from the 15th of June 1944 to the 31st of August of that year, they had to cope with almost hourly flying bombs from the coast of France. Up until March 1945 V1s and V2s were still frequent. The Depot in itself, although badly blasted on several occasions, was only severely hit once when in June 1944 a flying bomb fell into the grounds 25 yards from the building, where 10 nuns were still in residence, and it also killed some passers-by. The nuns, however, were very well looked after and had a good night's rest in the air raid shelters; they were served by the boys and chaperoned by Bill the bull terrier with early morning tea. In those hectic days large parties of men from the Depot were often engaged at short notice in digging out civilian casualties and salvaging their goods from their homes. Many letters of appreciation of their work were received but unfortunately none of those exist today.

Despite the bombing, work and play, of which they had plenty of both, went on uninterrupted. Their entertainment also continued and was catered for by Sgt Bentley and later S/Sgt Patterson. They had hundreds of dances, ENSA and the cinema shows all chipped in to keep the morale up. In keeping with military affairs, they had many inspections but the honour of being inspected by 3 successive Quartermaster generals, amongst many others general Sir Brian Horrocks and General Sir Oliver Leese. in 1945 peace came and the machinery of the Depot was put into reverse, demobilisation was the order of the day. For this purpose, they had to leave their wartime home at the convent, and the lease had expired, and they moved not very far to the Royal College for the Blind, which had been placed at their disposal prior to the collapse of Japan. They again found themselves in a beautifully appointed Depot. In many ways it was the realization of the army's blueprint of better living conditions for all ranks and certainly at that time the only one in existence.

During the demobilization the officers and other ranks came through and were dealt with a steady stream. The accommodation and dispatch overseas of civilian company employees was also undertaken to comply with the policy of returning to a civilian basis. The Depot finally closed its door on the 30th of June 1949. The memories forever will belong to those who served and were discussed for many years at the OCA functions.

Sir Lancelot C. Royle 1949

Sir Lancelot C. Royle gave the closing address to the year: "In the closing weeks of 1949 after a careful survey of the problem for over 2 years, the board of management had appointed a general manager. As older members of the staff were aware, the office of the general manager was part of NAAFI structure from its inception in 1921 until 21 years later, when, under the pressure of war, the functions of a general manager were assumed by an executive committee. Few know better than I how well executive committee served the company throughout the crowded and anxious war years, and it is a matter of great satisfaction to the board that the members of that wartime committee will remain with us to lend their support and wealth of experience to the new general manager".

1950–1959

1950

He sailed through a minefield 1950

It was Sunday morning in December 1950. The United Nations troops in North Korea were in full retreat. Only one-week earlier Capt Brian Hislop, RASC EFI, had arrived at Chinanpo, the port at Pyongyang, and now he was ordered to do a smart about turn and report back to Incheon. He was the senior army officer of a small party consisting of 5 men of the Expeditionary Force Institutes, 2 civilians from Cable and Wireless and 2 Australian soldiers which was to make the trip in a fragile looking lighter craft with a Japanese crew and an Australian signal all under the command of an Australian commissioned bosun.

They were tumbled by a bitterly cold wind, the sea tossed the little craft from one wave to another. The commander decided that to avoid taking the lighter too far out to sea he would take his chance among the minefields inshore. Capt Hislop, not a nervous man, recalled: "the trip gave me some of the worst moments in my life. Theoretically we were safe. The lighter only drew about 6 feet of water and the mines were laid 8 or 9 feet below the surface but we could see them quite clearly through the waves and no great stretch of the imagination was needed to picture what might well happen at the trough of the next swell."

They navigated the minefield safely and battled on through the storm. Eventually they overhauled a native junk which the commander ordered to be searched in case it should be laying mines or carrying arms. Capt Hislop, armed only with a revolver, went over the side, he boarded and searched the junk but fortunately the vessel proved innocent enough.

After a rough passage though, the little party entered the Inchon Harbour the following afternoon but even as they were breathing a sigh of relief, they ran aground on the submerged break water. There they had to sit tight for the full tide at 2100hrs where the bigger waves occasionally lifted them clear of the obstruction, only to drop them back with a sickening thump which threatened to break the lighter in 2. When the conditions at last allowed them to attempt re-floating, the tide was running about 7 knots and the tricky manoeuvre of clearing the obstacle without getting sunk was not helped by the knowledge that if they did they could not expect to last more than 3 minutes in the sub-zero waters.

From clerical to canteen, Lillias Bell 1950

Previously working at Ruxley Towers in the staff Department in a clerical job, she decided to change jobs and become a trainee restaurant and welfare Superintendent (RWS). Being posted with a battalion of Scots Guards was quite interesting, so she decided to stay and become a training manageress instead. She was given an overall and a very large white apron, and learnt how to make NAAFI flaky pastry, and then lay it into a large pie dish covered with a white cloth, as this was her 1st attempt. Once they came back from lunch, she found a note pinned to the mould of her pastry which read "in loving memory RIP". Undeterred by the note she then went on to make Apple tarts with shortcrust pastry and tried her hand at making sausage rolls with the legendary flaky pastry.

Next up was her first experience with special catering, this was in the shape of a children's Christmas party; they had to spread the bread for 400 sandwiches, not too thick not too thin seemed to be the order of the day and not too much and not too little for the filling. When the food was finished they had to lay the tables with crepe paper decorations, with the paper being cut into strips and stretched over 2, all 3 times its normal length, and then trying to get it in place with drawing pins which generally did not want to stay. At the same function in a separate room the food had to be laid out for the band.

She caused a few raised eyebrows while at the counter filling the teapots from the urns, she saw one of the lids drop inside one of the pots and promptly announced "not to worry it'll soon be returned for a refill and then we can get the lid out" – this seemed to be a perfectly plausible idea!

The difference between special catering and ordinary catering, was to be made clear when they prepared a chicken dinner for the 60 NCOs at a small and sparsely equipped canteen in the district. They had to borrow extra equipment from various other canteens. She arrived with the RWS the day before the dinner to prepare the trifles and the chickens. Unfortunately, the chickens arrived fully frozen and they could do nothing with them the day before. The next morning, they had to get there really early, to be able to clean, draw and stuff the chickens. They waived the standard rule of no smoking in the kitchen, because otherwise they would have had to have used clothes pegs on their noses! She volunteered happily to pipe the buttercream for the trifles, so she opened the recipe book and with one hand glued to everything else with a mixture of cornflour, sugar and margarine, she worked frantically trying to get the mixture to combine and not curdle, then settled down to piping.

Two more special caterings followed Christmas Teas for the children, both of which were very enjoyable and went off successfully. An hour after one of these was over, the washing and tidying up was well under way, so you can imagine their surprise when a mother with two small boys arrived at the Tea Party. In less than no time, with forced smiles on their faces they had to relay the tables with what they had left. As they sat down they proceeded to devour everything quietly but quickly!

After the first few months she then transferred to a canteen where she could see in more detail the skills to be a manageress which she found highly interesting; even though it was early days for her she felt that she had started to grasp the routine involving the multiple forms, entries, records and returns, which they had to do which was a small part of the manageress's responsibilities. And they also offered a practical course in pastry making so she could finally get her flaky pastry right.

OCA 1950

The OCA was going from strength to strength, with the numbers increasing of people requiring benevolence and in 1949 alone 69 separate cases. They could not have done all this without the SSAFA, whose local representatives furnished detail reports and recommendations to the general committee to assess the merits of every individual case requiring it. To give examples of the amazing work done in the early days it would be good to outline some of the cases.

Benevolent case number 119.

An ATS member wrote, saying that owing to the housing shortage, her family had been living in a furnished flat, and that the Gratuities received by herself and her husband had been eaten up by high rental. They were both orphans and had 2 children aged 4 years and 2½ years. A job had been offered to her husband, including an unfurnished flat. Beds and bedding were necessary. After investigation by SSAFA, who provided a bed and the necessary aid was forthcoming from the OCA. The member wrote: "I thank you so much for the help on the gift of a bed; it has been a God send to me and my children. I thank all members of the OCA who made this possible. It will keep us off the floors and make them tidier."

Benevolent case number 150.

A disabled member had worked only 12 weeks in the past 15 months. He needed to obtain special food ordered by the doctor, to have his shoes repaired and buy some coal. The OCA came to the rescue with a grant and the member subsequently wrote: " I am indeed grateful to the OCA and I trust when my health improves I may be able to assist the OCA if not in cash in some other way."

Benevolent case 154.

Information received from an outside source led to the OCA making some enquiries regarding one of the EFI comrades. An investigation showed that the continued illness, the result of severe wounds received during the evacuation from France in 1940, had caused financial distress. Although he was in receipt of a small pension, he had not drawn full National Health benefit for some time, as owing to his many periods of sickness, his National Health contributions were in arrears. In order to keep the home going – there were two young children – he had sold practically all his furniture and when our representative called, he had just sold his overcoat. The OCA made grants covering a period of 6 weeks. He afterwards wrote: "I am pleased to say that things are thankfully on the up with thanks to the aid of the Association. I shall soon be on an even keel still, thanks again to the Association, the feeling of despondency has gone."

Benevolent case number 159.

A member's wife wrote, saying that her husband had been in hospital for about 2 months, having been ill over 4 months and in consequence they were in strained circumstances. In response to our request, SSAFA reported: "we do consider that they have an anxious, hard time and are worthy of assistance." The OCA has made 2 grants, and subsequently the member wrote, "please thank the general committee for their kindness my wife and I are very grateful."

The OCA did some fantastic work in early 1950s making sure that their veterans were as well looked after as possible. Christmas parcels were dispatched to those members who were known to be in hospital or ill at home. One recipient wrote: "I have to thank you for the parcel which I received today. It came as a pleasant surprise to know that someone thought of me at this time of year. It gives one a pleasant feeling inside as good as many a bottle of medicine. Please accept my best thanks."

As the year ended the final report of the year was released. The facts and figures reported that the present membership for the United Kingdom was 4250 which was in comparison with the previous figure of 5278 at the same time the previous year. The reduction in membership was accounted for by 39 deaths, 84 resignations, 1158 who stopped being members because they were in violation of rule 11 – and this was that they had not paid their subscription for 1948. Included in the present total were 1381 who despite reminders have not paid their subscriptions for 1949 and 350 who we have lost trace of due to the change of address.

Even in the early days, falling membership was always expected and the common factor in all associations even from the early stages. Over the coming years the membership settled down to a good core to be maintained and even in 1950.

With the overseas branches the SEAC and Hong Kong branches had already ceased to exist, this was due to this disbandment of the RASC EFI and the general rundown of overseas branches of the NAAFI commitments. Members that had returned to the UK from overseas branches and any other branches had been taken on in the strength of branches in the UK.

The branches from overseas that had continued to function, BAOR, Bermuda, BTA, Gibraltar, Malta, Egypt, and East Africa. Overall, at this time the Association was proving itself to be well worthwhile in helping to keep alive the spirit of comradeship, which was endangered during the war years, so it was essential that they had a happy community. At this time the bedrock of the Association with the comradeship and also to help the less fortunate comrades which are the two areas of great success.

The president at the time, Sir Lancelot Royle, with thanks for their help and encouragement he had always given, Mr Balfour and his staff for auditing the accounts and Mrs Alderson and her staff for the excellent arrangements that they enjoyed during functions. The success was also due to the secretary, Mr Bowen, and his assistant, Mr Parkin, who had devoted to the foundation of the association.

The general committee had been watching the depreciation of the war stock and taken advice of the trustees as to whether they should sell, and their advice was they should hold the stock. The interest they would have received from the investment had accrued and was free from income tax. The chairman had asked that any delegate had any comments to make about the accounts and Miss Crossfield asked if there was any particular reason for wanting to sell war stock, to which the chairman replied that it was to cut their losses on the investment. Regarding the loss, Mr Crossfield suggested that the interest they were getting would reduce the loss and the chairman said that irrespective of the question of loss it would eventually have to sell to reinforce the Benevolent Fund and were looking for the interest received to make up the depreciation.

The roll of honour was a poignant subject in 1950 and the management had approved the recommendation that a memorial to the members of the staff who had lost their lives in service of the company or as a result of the 1939 to 45 war should consist simply of a subtle plaque to be installed at Imperial Court without the names of the individuals. Then a suitably bound book containing their names of the individuals concerned should be placed on a stand beneath the plaque. Major Patit said that the company had published a roll of honour in 1943 and this had prompted an enquiry from the number one branch. As the record was kept at Imperial Court the branch committees had no list to refer to. The chairman said that once the book was published a list should be taken and copies made for the branch committees.

First into Vienna

Junior commander Miller ATS EFI, the first NAAFI girl to enter Vienna in September 1945. Miss McNaulty was the first NAAFI manageress civilian to go there in August 1945 to open the ENSA hostel. She was posted to the 8th army NAAFI in 1944 and went to help the Fano hostel. As they had no light or water a Lt Col Taylor inspected by candlelight. They later went to Riccione to open a hostel there, and she was at Forli when the War ended. She saw thousands of

Miss M. McNulty

German prisoners entering the town and many of them drove themselves in. One day the admin officer told them that she was to be posted to Krupendorf in Austria and had to go the next day. NAAFI had no transport going for at least a week, so she had to hitchhike all the way there. To her relief the ENSA transport took her as far as Padua, where she spent the night in the new hostel. The next day she got a lift to Maestra.

The driver took her and a major who was sitting in a tent drinking NAAFI beer by the roadside on the way to Venice. He lent her car and a driver to go to Udine. She contacted NAAFI and they told her to spend a night at Natzionale, which was run by the RAF, which was later taken over by ENSA. The next day the RAF would provide her with a truck and driver. She arrived at Klagenfurt at midnight, but she could not find the hostel. She went to the police station of the 6th armoured division and they found her room for the night in an Austrian flat, which was part of the police station. Later when the 8th army entered Vienna she was told to go there and get the hostel ready by September. Capt Swan did not know where to accommodate her. He was the only man in charge of the canteen at Schonbrun Palace, so unfortunately, she was not allowed to stay there, as the Russian troops kept on breaking in and sleeping there overnight. The captain's driver eventually solved the problem – he was sleeping in the NAAFI office until accommodation could be found for him. He gave her his bed and went to sleep at the officer's mess for the night. He also presented her with a rifle for protection, which she did not know how to use.

She recalls that she was awakened by the sound of shooting outside her window and the noise of the men and women screaming. She thought it better to stay in bed and not be curious. She never did find out what it was all about but the next day Capt Swan found her accommodation in an Austrian flat and there she remained until the hostel was ready. Vienna at the time was quite depressing but previously it had been phenomenal. Unfortunately, graves were everywhere, even in gardens and public parks. One of the strangest sights that she recalls seeing was a Russian grave in the middle of a vegetable garden. The British started to clear them away at the end of August 1945. They were told people were buried where they fell during the fighting, this was because of the lack of transport and the bodies had to be buried. She was very happy to return to Austria where she stayed until 1947 when NAAFI stopped running the hostels in Austria. She spent a year in Hamburg and after this she decided to go home to the UK to take charge of Dishforth RAF canteen 1223R where she had trained to be a manageress 6 years previously.

New pay packets 1950

In the summer of 1950, a revolutionary type of pay packet was being issued. At first glance the card resembled something of a shooting target off a drunk rifle. It was clustered in hazardous groups, scattered widely over the card, upwards of 50 holes. These holes were in fact precise accurate informative information. They were the brand-new language of the new accountancy system. This was a brand-new machine office central range wages branch whereby they interpreted it into words and figures for the recipient to read. Payments had to be made to some 17,000 men and women scattered the length and breadth of the country. These meaningless random holes were a simple way of interpreting their pay. There was an office in the warehouse at Kingsway and Mr WB Veal was the accountant in charge of the central wages branch. Mr Veal certainly had the artist's passion for his job. He was a heavily built man, he could talk about his new accounting machines and was very nimble minded and creative. The Picasso of payroll who wholeheartedly absorbed the problems of the people and machines. He had an affection for the mechanical marvels which record, tabulate, add and subtract and sort at lightning speeds.

The new machines gathered some interest from other businesses and even Lions, the London passenger transport board, the allied suppliers, Odeon cinemas and others came to see what all the fuss was about. Many people had already told him that he would never succeed and that NAAFI's pay problem was so intricate that no system of machinery in accounting could cope with it. But he did it and a punch card experiment had begun. Mr Veal explained that way back in 1943 when due to the staff shortage and the interruption of air raids, arrears of work had accumulated until the chief accountant instructed him to examine the possibility of mechanising the whole system of wages payments. After 3 short months and intensive study of various systems of punch counting cards and devising a message to which they might be applied to NAAFI problems, Mr Veal launched the experiment. He started with one clerk who had to train and later took on several juniors then patiently trained each one of them. He admitted that it took 12 to 18 months to train anyone on these machines and nearly all the girls who he trained began as juniors and most of them at this point had been married but stayed on. By 1948 his team was ready to start the larger scale operations; they began with the centralisation of all wages in the NCS. With the support of Mr RJ Wallace and Mr Whitehouse, the same system was applied to the home canteen service weekly wages system.

Shortly after the wages at Kingsway and the transport branch were also centralized, the whole of the weekly pay staff had begun to take shape and this new method meant that it was a slick operation. There was actually nothing wrong with the previous system but before organisation and centralisation, people received their wages just as regularly and accurately as they did with the machinery. But it meant that the manageresses of the canteens had to work out tax deductions, split duty payments and all other additions to or subtractions from the basic wages of each of the staff. Then district managers had to check the tax facts and command officers checked basic wages and deductions. All editions and pay had to be exact. All gross pay and tax added by hand to Ledger cards and then had to write to the district managers on all outstanding points. This almost also made sense with the increase in the number of acts of parliament and various wage agreements affecting the staff; it was proved to be more efficient and economical to let machines and their operators do it in one central office that had previously been done in scores of decentralised establishments.

In the machine room, massive machines, including 12 automatic keypunches, 3 sorters, 3 tabulators, 2 cross adding punches, two reproducing punches and 2 interpreters. All of this was an impressive sight and the noise of the clicking and clattering and the girls moving calmly from one to another feeding cards, making adjustments, watching totals, in an orderly professional manner all alongside the mechanical skill. This was extremely impressive for its time.

There was, however, preliminary human input before the machine started to tick. At the end of each working week the manageresses made up their timesheets which showed in such detail as the basic wage, hours of overtime, split shift duty, holidays, sick leave and so on. All these going to special envelopes which by arrangement with the GPO were bagged separately from NAAFI's of the mail and delivered to the central wages branch at Kennington. All the timesheets had to be arranged and delivered to him on a Monday morning for all of this to go without a hitch. When the timesheets arrived they were scrutinised by the clerks familiar with overtime calculations and the various provisions of the catering wages act, the bakery award, the retail food award, and similar matters affecting wages. The sheets were added up for the gross wage and were then checked against the individual's card for the current week. Basic information on each one was reproduced mechanically from the previous week's card. At this

stage parts for all employees away on sick or paid leave were extracted and separately dealt with. Remainder matched up into 250 and then passed to the machine room. All of this then gave a good idea to the company head office how many staff were off sick, on holiday or on unpaid leave. And that is how wages were done in the 1950s.

Mr Stanley Baker OBE 1950

Mr Baker was educated at Charterhouse and Cambridge, he served in the 1914 War as a pilot in the Royal Flying Corps and the Royal Air Force. After the war he became a traffic officer in Croydon and was for 4 years in charge of the aerodrome. He joined NAAFI in 1926 as a transport manager and was later in charge of the staff branch. Then followed a spell as secretary of the Company. In 1939 he was in charge of supplies then moved over to help Mr Stag in the overseas canteen service and became the manager of the OCS in 1946. He was an original AGM and also one of the original DGMs of the wartime executive committee. He was a popular chairman of the Imperial club. He was one of the most widely travelled members of the company, making hundreds of friends of all grades of staff in parts of the world so in April 1950 it was a real shame that he retired.

Memories of Malta. WM Hamilton OBE area manager Malta 1950

NAAFI in Malta dates from 1921 when it superseded their NACB. Malta was a fortress and the base for the Mediterranean fleet of the Royal Navy. In the interval between the two world wars life in Malta was peaceful and uneventful and the first signs of discontent arising out of the Abyssinian and Albanian crisis.

At the outbreak of war in September 1939 the Navy left Malta, making Alexandria their war base. The RAF also moved to North Africa and the army garrison in the island began to be stepped up, gradually increasing from three thousand in 1938 to about 16 to 20,000 in 1942. In 1941 the RAF came back in some strength from the UK when the island received Hurricanes and Spitfires. In 1939 that NAAFI had 17 institutes ashore but this increased to well over 80 by early 1942. It was not until Italy entered the war at midnight on the 10th of June 1940 that Malta suffered in any way but from 0600 hours on the 11th of June 1940 to May / June of 1942 the island was almost continuously under bombing from the Air Force of both Italy and Germany, the damage to buildings was very considerable but the casualties were not proportionately heavy owing to the deep rock shelters provided for the population.

Before the construction of the deep shelters the Italians were dropping only small bombs, and these were from a considerable height. In consequence many fell into the sea and did no damage. When Germany attacked Russia they could not maintain their Air Force in Russia during the winter months so they were moved to Sicily which was used as the base for elimination of Malta and the tempo of rate and weight of bombs dropped on the island increased considerably. Not a day went without 4 or 5 canteens being damaged, and it was necessary to have 2 rescue squads standing by continuously. The heavy squad under the area engineer Mr FV Catt was ordered that only when a building had a direct hit that the heavy stones used in the construction of the Maltese buildings had to be moved to release personnel and stores. But the light squad under the furnishing's inspector, Mr Guineas, was in constant demand to repair bomb blasted buildings. Unless the raid was particularly heavy and in the immediate vicinity NAAFI staff rarely took shelter; this being the case it was more remarkable that only 2 NAAFI employees were killed by enemy action during the siege.

At the time it was not the policy of the government at the outbreak of the war to evacuate the wives and families of UK personnel on the island but on Italy entering the war these families were concentrated in various parts of the island, each service family being kept separate, and NAAFI ran the catering arrangements for them all. This was not an easy job with the island besieged and supplies being very short, but there is no record of anyone grumbling about the service given.

With the complete destruction of ordinary life in Valletta, a number of cabaret girls found themselves out of business. They were rounded up by the Marshal and with the addition of the male cast of a touring company stranded on the island, NAAFI started the whizzbang concert party. The talent in town was not the high standard that some people demanded but there was not the slightest of doubt that they did an excellent job. Air raids did not interfere with the show and once they were provided with tin hats and nobody ever heard them grumble about the conditions under which they worked. The whizzbang concert party unfortunately wasn't entitled to the Africa star as they did a lot to maintain the morale of the troops.

With the capture of the 'North Africa' the centre of the fighting moved to Italy and many NAAFI Maltese staff did service in Sicily and Italy after enlisting into the RASC EFI and many of them also served in the canteens run by the NCS to serve on ships. Six were killed in action and 13 were missing, 2 became wounded and 3 ended up as prisoners of war. The company was very proud of the service given by the Maltese staff during the 1939 to 1945 war.

As the war came to an end the reduction of personnel of the services on Malta started to take place and the Mediterranean fleet became a fraction of its pre-war strength, the Garrison had also dwindled to practically nothing. With little or no money coming in and profits restricted by the government control of all retail prices, many economies had to be affected and many valued and faithful staff had to be laid off.

Mr Hamilton – he was a Colonel and then subsequently a brigadier EFI – oversaw Malta throughout the aerial bombardment and shared the gallantry of the island which won him the George Cross.

Ghost ship canteen manager, HMS challenger DS Stephenson 1950

He was waiting for the transport home from Trincomalee when the area manager asked him if he would escort NAAFI motor launch called the 'Mercia' to Malta. The motor launch was going to be secured to the LST that would be towed home to be broken up. Stevenson would be on his own for much of the trip.

In March 1949 it started with getting all the necessary equipment together – this meant cooking, utensils, bedding, tin foods all had to go on board. There was 200-gallon water tank which was cleaned out so he could have running water, lighting was 4 hurricane lamps and cooking was done on a Primus stove. He was accommodated in the captain's cabin and made it comfortable with all the things that had been taken on board.

Once the tug had got them under way, 14 days later they reached Bombay. For some of the trip 4 Ceylonese boys were on board to light the navigation lamps, also to keep watch on the tow rope but they were only going as far as Aden. It wasn't long before they'd got to Bombay and they stayed there for 3 days. There was not much to do on board except to swill down the decks and cook food. Unfortunately the Primus stove was very old and many times it would burst into flames, ruining the food that was on it. Like many a good movie, a lone man on a boat would have a fishing line over the side, but unfortunately, he had no luck and caught nothing. The day before they arrived at Aden one of the boys came running up to him shouting there was a big fish on the line, as he approached they had already got the fish on board – it was 4 foot long and weighed roughly 20 pounds. As you can imagine he'd enjoyed his fish supper.

They arrived on the 14th day and said goodbye to the boys, the captain of the tug told him that another tug would be coming out to take him to Malta so he stocked up with food and water and he said better you than me and disappeared. It was then he found himself all alone.

He kept busy as in the evenings he had navigation lights to put on and every hour or so he went to check on the tow rope. He also set many other lines over the side to see if he could recreate his twenty-pound fish, but this was not to be he caught many an ugly fish and decided to throw them back.

Being on your own on ship had made him fairly jumpy and he even locked his cabin door at night expecting somebody to jump out at him with every creak and crack of the boat, even the wind whistling through the sails got the hairs on his neck standing up on end.

Sixteen days later he arrived at the Suez Canal and the tug came alongside and tied up. The skipper invited him onto the top to have breakfast. And that's where they told him that he'd have to take all of his belongings off the LST as it would be classed as a passenger ship if he was on it.

The next day they started their journey and 2 more tugs helped them through; on the same evening they arrived at Port Said. The next morning, he checked on the Mercia but unfortunately somebody had broken in and stolen the mooring ropes and its tools. The skipper of the tug and the area manager went to the police and gave a statement. They should have sailed that evening, but the police wouldn't let them for 3 days while the investigation was on. He was by himself again and he saw a sack that hadn't been there when he first arrived at the canal, he opened it and it contained the missing tools from the 'Mercia' and after searching around he found the rest of the stuff too. The trip from Port Said proved to be the worst of the lot; he was getting sick and tired of tinned foods and being on his own. He was stood on the deck one day when he noted several people waving from the tug, one had a piece of word and threw it in the water, it got closer and he saw some writing on there: "arriving Saturday". The piece of driftwood said they arrived late on the Saturday.

Two tugs came out and helped them onto the dockyard and one of the tugs threw a line. The skipper told him to get somebody to help him and he was amazed when he told him that he was the only one on board – the ship could actually hold 150 people.

NAAFI Memorial in the desert 1950

In the desert 5 miles from Tobruk, stood memorial to the officers, warrant officers, NCOs, the men of the RASC EFI who fell in Egypt, Libya, Greece, Crete, and Palestine during the Middle East campaigns of the Second World War. To the South of the memorial lies the vast desert spaces where the 8th army battles raged in 1941 to 1942. To the West can be glimpsed the blue of Tobruk Harbour and the white bombed houses of the Garrison. Eastwards ran the long road to all those places named which part of the desert campaign – Bardia, Capuzzo, Sollum, Sidi Barrani, Mersa Matrouh and Alexandria. Close by to the North lay the desolate remains of the NAAFI bulk issue store and office compound which operated through the siege of Tobruk.

The memorial comprises an obelisk some 12 feet high and was constructed of smooth cut cream stone, especially quarried at Sollum, on the Egyptian frontier. The 3 main inscription panels were made of polished Botticini stone, beautifully carved and polished. The design was simple and truly noble proportions of the monument are the conception of the Imperial (now Commonwealth) War Graves Commission who undertook the erection of the memorial on behalf of NAAFI.

At the unveiling ceremony a special observer wrote "amid the warm sunshine of a Cyrenaican autumn morning on Sunday the 26th of November 1950, representatives of the British residency, NAAFI, WVS, Royal Navy, army and Royal Air Force and the Imperial War Graves Commission paid tribute to the dead at an exceedingly moving service conducted by the

Copyright CWGC

Reverend Gwyn Lewis B.Ach.D, where senior staff chaplain at GHQ, MELF who during the war himself had laid to rest a number of the men whom the memorial was dedicated."

The chaplain's address was followed by the hymn "Oh God help in ages past". The memorial was unveiled by Mr HG Swithenbank OBE, personnel manager of NAAFI, who had flown out from England for the ceremony. At the dedication the trumpeter sounded The Last Post and the congregation observed 2 minutes' silence. This was broken by the soft strains of "Abide with me", during which the flower wreaths were laid. After this the Reveille was then sounded followed by the hymn "The strife is o'er, the battle is done", followed by the national anthem and the blessing. The service was supported by the regimental band of the 16/5th Queen's Royal Lancers who were joined by contingents of the army and the Royal Air Force personnel from the Garrison and RAF station.

I saw a cloud that changed the world recalled in 1950

This is the story of O.F. Mahoney, Canteen Manager HMS Jufair, Bahrain island, Persian Gulf August 1945

The author of this story was known as Spike Mahoney to all his associates, who was asked for the details of his career.

I joined the NCS when I was 16 years of age under Mr EC Furze, manager. When Mr furze was asked to Commission HMS Prince of Wales at the end of 1940, I was chosen to accompany him. I served in that ship from her commissioning until the order was given to abandon ship somewhere in the China Sea, having previously seen action in the Atlantic against the Bismarck and in the Mediterranean against Axis aircraft. We who survived the sinking of the 'Prince of Wales' and the 'Repulse' were taken to Singapore, where I joined 'HMS Stronghold' as canteen manager. On this ship, after 2 months of constant actions and alarms around the East Indies, we were unfortunate enough to run into a large Japanese task force which sent this brave little ship to the bottom. I survived this second mishap and after 18 hours on a float in shark infested waters, 42 of us were picked up by a Japanese ship for interrogation while the remainder were left to the mercy of the sea. We were taken to the island of Celebes, where we were engaged on the construction of a road through the jungle. After 8 months of this we were transported to Nagasaki to work in the shipyards until The Big Bang ended the war.

We the POWs of Fukuoka #2 camp Nagasaki, Japan, were nonplussed. We could not understand the sudden change in the attitude of the Japanese towards us. For more than 3½ years now we had been kicked and bullied all over this rotten shipyard. Now the Japanese seemed to have had a change of heart, first made apparent after one of the weekly meetings of the Japanese charge men. It was the usual practice after a meeting to force the POWs to work twice as hard as normal, as if they had been given a pep talk and were determined to take it out on us. On this occasion, however, they seemed so busy with their own thoughts that they hardly noticed our presence.

It is said that the face of an Oriental is expressionless, but I think this can only apply if one is not conversant with the Orient. We the POWs were more than conversant with the ways of these strange people and because we understood them, we knew whatever it was that was troubling them in some way affected us. The Japanese charge man of the party in which I was working was one of the older and more sensible types, so we felt reasonably safe in trying to get some information from him. In this respect, however, we were unlucky as he seemed to be too scared of his own countrymen to be seen talking to us in much detail.

On our arrival back in camp that evening we found that some of the other prisoners of war had been more fortunate in questioning the Japanese. One party of men said the Japanese with whom they had been working had told them that at the meeting all the Japanese had been warned that for the next few days they were to expect a lot of danger from enemy aircraft, whilst other Japanese had told some of the other prisoners of war that something of considerable importance had taken place at Hiroshima (at that point nobody quite knew where this was). Exactly what had just happened they were unable to understand, as the Japanese guard was very vague about it himself. When it seemed that there had been a raid causing some tens of thousands of casualties, but when the Japanese guard was asked how many planes had taken part in the raid, he answered 'only one'. This became even harder to understand when he replied to further questioning that only one bomb had been dropped. When our lads had pointed out to him that one bomb seldom caused as many casualties, he stated he became quite upset about it and started raving something about a Tommy. As he seemed to be getting really annoyed our boys thought it was safe as to refrain from questioning him further.

We spent the whole of the evening in camp going over and over all that was said by these Japanese guards in the hope that we might be able to get some glimmer of sense out of the reports. We wondered if the Japanese guard referred to Tommy could have anything to do with the invasion of British troops at Hiroshima. This prospect certainly caused some alarm amongst us, as we had been told all the time we had been in this country that if the allies did invade the mainland of Japan prisoners of war would be executed. We had no reason to doubt that the Japanese would carry out this threat.

I could only imagine how we felt as most certainly wanted this war to end and an invasion of Japan would certainly shorten the length of the conflict; on the other hand, we did not wish to be shot or otherwise slaughtered when liberation was at last in sight. The thought alone was enough to send a man out of his mind after 3½ years of toil and sweat, scrimping and scrounging his way through the hellish existence, watching his chums die off like flies and wondering when it would be his own turn, to be carried out in one wooden box. It served as a coffin until it arrived at the crematorium where the body was burnt, then the box and a few ashes were brought back to the camp by the burial party. The ashes being placed on a shelf in an urn marked with the dead man's number, while the box was returned to the sick room to await the next death. It was of little consequence to us that the war was about to be won by our side if our lives were now going to be brought to an abrupt end.

During the days that followed we became convinced that it was indeed an invasion, and the Japanese soldiers were treating us so strangely, they no longer bullied and beat us; some became almost decent. It was as if they felt sorry for us, that we, who had been their slaves for so long would soon be leaving them to join our ancestors.

The suspense during these days was hardly bearable while at all times we thought the end was not far off. It was plain to see that we the POWs were at the centre of all conversation between the Japanese guards. They watched every move that we made, yet no matter what we did they never even raised their voices in anger at us. We sat down for a rest when we wanted to, and even went as far as to take out our cigarette ends and light them to see what repercussion this would have. It was always the same, they looked and smiled in a sickly way, but never did they beat us. After the treatment that we had been used to this almost seemed strange, we felt the same way that the man in the condemned cell must feel having all their last wishes granted.

It was about 1000hrs or so on the second day after the Japanese soldiers had told our boys that we were to expect heavy air raids and that we heard the sound of a solitary aircraft overhead. It was very high and some of the RAF boys amongst us remarked that it sounded as if it was a bomber. On hearing this our spirits sank to rock bottom, as we had never in all the years that we had been here seen a Japanese bomber around, so we presumed that must surely be an allied plane. This was it, then, we thought. First a lone plane on a reconnaissance mission, then a big raid to flatten the defences, to be followed by the invading force. From now on, we thought, our hours are numbered and we would be lucky if we saw the sunrise once more.

We waited for the siren to sound, but for some reason, unknowing to this day, there was no warning. The Japanese soldiers did not seem to pay any attention to the plane as it flew over, and as the warning was not sounded; we then took it to be that they must have known for certain that it was a Japanese plane. Within a couple of minutes, the plane passed over and soon the sound of its engines had faded in the distance, so we settled down to our work, thankful that we had been reprieved for a little while longer at least.

The work that I and three other POWs were engaged upon at this time consisted simply of unscrewing nuts and bolts, oiling them, and replacing them. It was the sort of work that prisoners of war dreamed about and confirmed our belief that the Japanese were now sorry for us and wished to make our last few days a little better than the rest. As we twisted and turned the nuts and bolts, we talked of our chances of survival if an invasion of this part of the Japanese mainland did take place. As we would be a potential menace to them if they allowed us to remain alive, we guessed that we were bound to be executed, so we decided that the only chance we had would be if we made a break for it and attempted to enter the sea at the first sight of the invading force. Swimming for all of us towards the allied ships was hard. We never really thought we would get very far in this way but at least it was better to try than to wait around for some dirty Japanese soldier to come along and cut one down out of hand. As we worked and talked, we became aware that overhead it was that lone aircraft again, flying so high that it was only by listening intensely that one was able to tell the sound of the engines above the clatter of the yard.

While we were wondering why the Japanese soldiers did not sound off the siren, we were suddenly blinded by a flash of such intense brilliance that no one could say from which direction the flash had come from. It seems to have come at us from all directions, such was the vastness of it. Before we were able to gather our shaken wits about us, we were all sent flying to the ground by the blast from one of the greatest and most devastating explosions that mankind had ever devised. We were smothered in dust and debris, while some of us were badly cut by flying glass. When we were all shaken and bruised from the sudden crash to the ground. As we scrambled to our feet, we made a dash to retrieve our caps, which had blown off by the blast. This move was made instinctively as we were very often beaten to within an inch of our lives for not having on the caps with the vivid red band which let all and sundry know that the wearer was a prisoner of war. We stood trembling with trepidation as the echo of the awe-inspiring explosion came back to us again and again from many hills and crags which were many in this country.

One of our men was facing towards the city of Nagasaki, which is about 3 or 4 miles away from us on the island prison camp. He did not speak but we saw the look on his face and his hand outstretched pointing toward the city. We looked that way and saw a huge mushroom like cloud billowing overhead. It was pulsing and throbbing as if it was alive and the colour changed again and again while we watched, at the same time growing rapidly in size until soon it blotted out the sun.

We watched it fascinated until we became aware that the siren was sounding, as it was with a feeling of impending evil that we made our way to the hillside cave which served as our air raid shelter. We remained in the shelter until 1900hrs and then when the guard eventually let us out our eyes first turned to the stricken city. The whole of Nagasaki seemed to be on fire, the flames reflected on that huge anonymous looking cloud which even now was still hanging over the city as if it was much too heavy for the slight summer breeze to move.

We marched back to our camp in silence, contemplating the course of such a terrific explosion. We did not dare to speak to each other as we guessed that the Japanese soldiers would be so mad after this catastrophe that they were liable to run berserk and cut us down out of hand if we gave the least sign that we were pleased that they had got their just punishment for the inhuman way they had treated us. On reaching the privacy of our rooms, we all started to talk to each other on the possible cause of The Big Bang as we soon called it. Some were of the opinion that it was a large petrol dump that had exploded while the other thought it would been an electrical power plant that had gone up.

The days that followed were spent in the yard, but we found we and our guard were the only people there. Every other Japanese soldier on the island had been put to work on clearing the debris and fighting fires in the city. As the hospitals in Nagasaki had been damaged or destroyed, it was not long before the wounded were being brought over to the island for treatment in the shipyard hospital. We were horror struck as we saw to what degree some of the Japanese were burnt, while the hospital soon became powerless to help them as the medical supplies became exhausted. We saw the men, women and children with flesh burned from their bodies, covered in nothing more than a newspaper and laid out in the caves as there was no room elsewhere to put them. On the 3rd day following The Big Bang we were told by the Japanese interpreter that all men would remain in the camp and have a rest. We were quite surprised at this and we thought that we would soon be given some really heavy work to help them clearing the debris. As it was, we were not even put to work in the camp. The following day we were again told that we would not have to work, so we surmised that it must have been a power station that had blown up and that now there was no power in the yard to work the machines. The day after this, we were all awake and at the usual time of 0500hrs by the Indonesian bugle boy, we noticed something different in the call. We sat in our bunks and looked at each other, everyman knowing that although the call was familiar it was not the Japanese reveille. Then suddenly it struck home. About 5 or 6 men shouted at the same time: "That's our bugle call! That's the English reveille we have been waiting to hear that for the last 4 years almost! Can't you fellows remember it?"

We remembered it, and we waited for the bellow that would come when the Japanese guard had realised what had taken place. No bellow came, and the little Indonesian bugle boy then came along to each room telling us that it was the Sergeant who had told him to sound off The English reveille. What was happening? Could it be that the war was over? No, this was too much to expect, we thought our heads were going around with thinking and hoping. Some of the men became almost hysterical with the joy at the suggestion that the war was over, but the majority of the men were not going to let themselves go so easily; after all, we had seen so many bitter disappointments in the years that we had been prisoners that it was hard to believe that now, at long last, we were to get something for which we had all been praying, daily, weekly, monthly and yearly, hoping all the time the our prayers would be answered but doubting more and more as the time went along our ability to stand the pace. Someone took the trouble to find out the date, as this was the thing that we did not know; in fact, it was the thing that we did not care about these days, one day being exactly as all the others, but this one day was different. Something was happening of considerable importance, otherwise the Japanese guard would not have left the camp in the care of only the Sergeant. Today's date was Aug 14th, 1945. Two days later we found out that the war was indeed over. With tears of joy in our eyes we went around congratulating each other on the fact that we had 'made it'. One consolation we derive from this existence was that we knew that when we did die, we would go straight to heaven, as we had suffered our purgatory here on this earth by the hand of man.

1951

NAAFI In Paris 1951

Early in 1951 the company was asked to organise an accounting service for the personnel of SHAPE; they needed it to be made up of 14 nations represented at General Eisenhower's headquarters outside Paris, although this was officially known as the SHAPE canteen service when it was fully controlled by NAAFI with English and French staff.

Unlike many requests that the company received this came at short notice. A telephone call from the War Office set the ball in motion and the consultations followed which was called 'Operation SHAPE'. Within a matter of hours Mr Lanyard and Mr Warner flew to Paris to report on the existing setup and at that time established in the Astoria Hotel, Paris. The general manager and Mr Barker crossed the channel to survey the size of the operation that was needed. By the end of May NAAFI had been committed to operate a full canteen service in the new headquarters and it was nearing completion. This was now solely the responsibility of the home canteen service and the team immediately demonstrated what it could do under pressure.

The great race was on. With the work being organised at Ruxley Towers and Mr Cooper in charge on the ground, the operation gradually took shape. The British staff immobilised, French staff engaged 2 furnishing fitters brought from Germany, and the furniture arrived alongside them from the UK and Germany. A special plane was chartered to lift urgently required equipment from England. Every other day officials flew back and forth between Ruxley Towers and Paris, smoothing out the 101 problems involve. Constant meetings took place with the members of General Eisenhower's staff, with the French authorities, with architects, financial experts, and others, while the myriad technical questions of the equipment, furnishing supplies, staff and accountancy method were resolved. Day after day the team in Paris worked until midnight or after. Before the opening date Mr Street was brought from his duties as club supervisor, Germany, to take charge on the ground and worked like a Trojan, frequently from 0500hrs until midnight. On the opening day he actually lit the first fires and cooked the first breakfasts. The canteen at Camp des Loges opened in the middle of June. The opening of their Rocquencourt establishments was postponed by SHAPE until the middle of July 1951 – these precious days enabled the company to complete the task in good time, maintaining the highest quality. The old ranks' cafeteria opened on the 12th of July and the officers' restaurant 4 days later. Some 3 months later the general manager received the following letter from General Grunther, chief of staff who stayed on in the same post now that General Eisenhower had been succeeded by General Ridgeway as Supreme Commander. All in all, the whole project involved 110 staff; with the additional services in 1952 a total of 350 staff were required.

A fitting memorial 1951

The unveiling of the War Memorial was held on Remembrance Sunday 1951 at Imperial Court, London. The new memorial had been constructed at a well-chosen site at the head of the stairs leading from the entrance hall to the boardroom, where no one could fail to see the clean lines and simple dignity of the design.

A large bronze plaque inscribed with the words:

In memory of more than 550 members of staff,
when serving the Company, gave their
lives for right and freedom.

Below the tablet was a stone plinth, with the early adaptation of the company's crest in bronze, sitting upon it was a bronze casket containing a volume, beautifully bound in blue Morocco leather, with illuminated pages and hand lettered names of the fallen; each day a different page would be displayed. Below this book was a drawer which held a photographic reproduction of the book for public inspection. The service was large with a marquee and loudspeakers in the forecourt. The chaplain, the Reverend HW Nestling CF, opened the service with 3 prayers, one for the fallen, another for those who mourn, and the 3rd for the work of the NAAFI. The then chairman, Sir Lancelot C Royle, unveiled the memorial and the chaplain raised his hands in benediction and dedicated the memorial with the words: in the name of the father, and of the son, and the Holy Ghost I dedicate this memorial to be a Remembrance of those who gave their lives for King, country and the righteous course. After the service the wreaths were laid by relatives of the fallen, the board of management, NAAFI's chairman, NAAFI staff, the general manager, the Imperial club, the NAAFI staff council, OCA, WVS, and ENSA. The service concluded with the chaplain quoting the famous lines, they shall not grow old, as we that are left grow old. With the sounding of Reveille, the singing of the national anthem and blessing.

1952

NAAFI museum 1952

It was in April 1952 the company recognised, they were not only just serving the services, but also becoming part of history as well. The idea to build a museum archive was now becoming a reality. The only record of the original history had been written by Sir John Fortescue, history of canteens in the British army. There were only traces of the development of the establishment of NAAFI in 1921. It was of the utmost importance that this gap in historical record needed to be filled. They hoped to gain a large collection of books, photographs, curios, souvenirs, interesting documents, letters and records referring to the work of the Navy Army Air force Institutes and its predecessors, the recognition of whether it came from where they'd been and where they were going. The appeal was for suitable materials and anything from the Boer War, First World War, the incidents in Shanghai, Chanak, the Saar, the general strike, the Abyssinian crisis. Reminders from the days that they had catered for the Royal households and provided catering for the Schneider Cup races. They were looking for famous club signs of the desert in the 2nd World War, photographs of the EFI in the Sicilian, Indian and Normandy landings.

They even looked for a full set of the NAAFI tokens and the NAAFI badges and service chevrons which thousands of NAAFI girls proudly sported during the war; they looked for a complete uniform worn by the civilian NAAFI girls or by the ATS EFI.

Some more of the items that they'd looked for were canteen packs which were issued in the first phase of wartime operations, prisoner of war sports parcels, parcels issued to homecoming troops at the docks. Even cut down beer bottles used by thousands in the Middle East as drinking mugs or even the NAAFI stamps and seals used in Egypt.

They understood that a vast amount of the archive information would need to contain historic signals, letters, visitors' books, autographed menu cards of special occasions, reports of Dunkirk survivors, letters from NAAFI prisoners of war. They even looked for three Vellums which had been signed by the Queen, the Queen Mother and HRH Princess Margaret when they visited the Aberdeen club. One of the most sought-after items was a glass paperweight issued 30 or more years previously by the Richard Dickeson canteen contractors. Over time they managed to collect enough to open the museum around a year later.

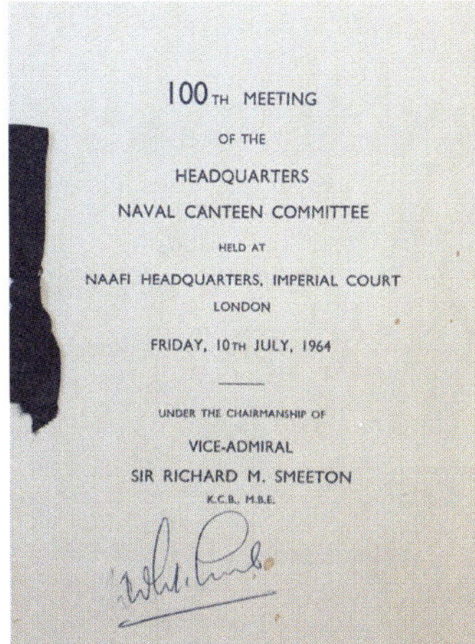

100TH MEETING
OF THE
HEADQUARTERS
NAVAL CANTEEN COMMITTEE
HELD AT
NAAFI HEADQUARTERS, IMPERIAL COURT
LONDON
FRIDAY, 10TH JULY, 1964

UNDER THE CHAIRMANSHIP OF
VICE-ADMIRAL
SIR RICHARD M. SMEETON
K.C.B., M.B.E.

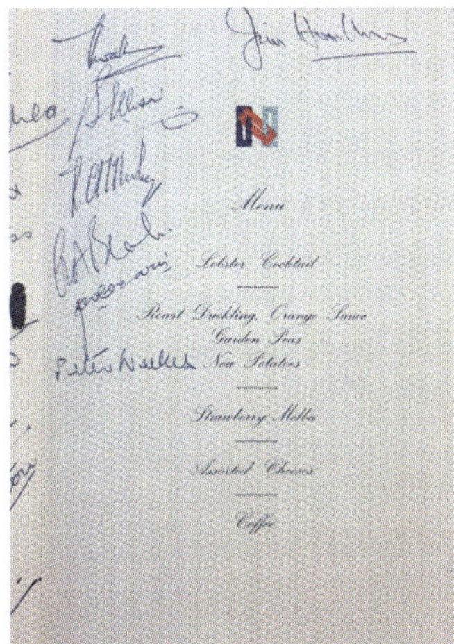

Menu

Lobster Cocktail

Roast Duckling, Orange Sauce
Garden Peas
New Potatoes

Strawberry Melba

Assorted Cheeses

Coffee

Copyright Sue A Lowe

This section has been put together by Mals Tokens

This section has been given to me to highlight the other options to using money during conflict and shortages in coinage.

NAAFI North China; Shanghai.

It would appear c1937 is probably the approximate date of the supper coupons.

(I notice the member's card from the Imperial Club uses this same early logo yet it should have been changed in 1954 when the use of the Queen's crown was authorised. Apparently NAAFI were still using old stock in 1962.)

France 1944

Octagonal Half Franc:

> Type 1 incuse legend. July 1944; The tokens were made of a brown laminated material known as CP 3 impressed with the design by De La Rue Insulations Ltd of Sutton, Surrey. 212,570 issued.

Type 2 font 0.5mm high August 1944; Printed in small letters.5mm high were most unsatisfactory but were accepted due to the urgency of the situation. 1,342,000 issued.

Type 3 font 1.5mm high October 1944; Larger letters 1.5mm high, 3,445,130 were issued to complete the order of 5 million tokens.

Type 4 font 2.5mm high December 1944; A further order of 5 million tokens in a still larger printed design with the value on the reverse was issued and remained in use for several years after the end of the war.

Austria hexagonal tokens 1946

Two tokens issued. 20 Groschen in red plastic and 10 Groschen in yellow plastic; 500,000 of each denomination were produced by Wollen and Co. Ltd. Sheffield.

Egypt 1952

NAAFI Egypt, / 1 Cup of Tea, 25mm brass; this was issued in the 1930s but nothing more is known of this very rare token.

January 1952: 75,000 green plastic tokens were issued as a ½ piastre value with a final total of 980,000 in three orders, as the green blank sample rather than the black sample that had previously been forwarded to NAAFI. However, in October of the same year NAAFI increased the price of tea effective December 1953 necessitating a ¼ piastre token. 600,000 Red ¼ piastre were ordered from British Artid Plastics for Egypt and 20,000 Red ¼ piastre ordered for Sudan. The latter are now very rare.

NAAFI Italy 1970s

Issued at Decimomannu Air Base, Sardinia; 10 Lire uniface tokens, 29mm and 5 Lire uniface tokens, 24mm both in aluminium. c1970s.

NAAFI Beer token

Exact place of use of this beer token, 50 × 27mm, is unknown but likely it was used during the Korean War as the Australian War Memorial has three of these tokens on display in its Korean War section.

NAAFI Malta

NAAFI St James Kavalier, Valletta was opened in 1921 much to the annoyance of the local shopkeepers. I have only the 2/6 Malta token.

Afghanistan / Iraq 2003

The NAAFI had gaming machines in Iraq and in Afghanistan, where the base currency was US Dollars. The NAAFI approached Gamestec to produce tokens and convert all the coin mechanisms on the gaming machines and pool tables that the NAAFI had in use, to accept these tokens, which have a value of US$2.00 or US$5.00 respectively. They were introduced in Dec 2003.

Other

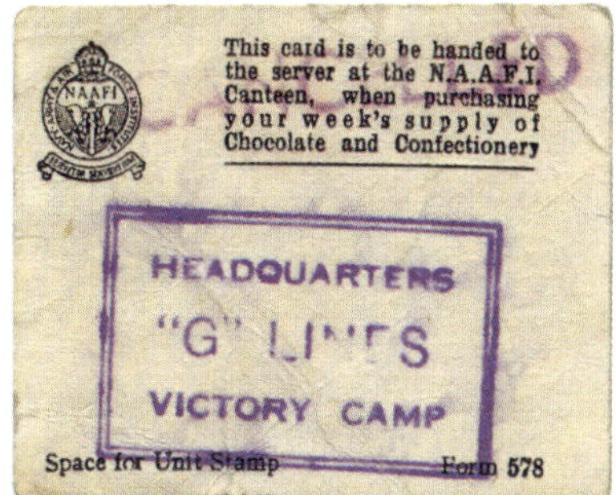

HRH Princess Margaret opening NAAFI club Plymouth 1952

The new NAAFI club, Plymouth, on Friday 18th of July 1952 was opened by HRH Princess Margaret. After inspecting the naval guard of honour, the Princess entered the club where a number of service and NAAFI representatives were presented to her; amongst them was Lieutenant General Sir Philip Balfore, president of the NAAFI council, Sir Lancelot C Royle, chairman of the board of management, Major General RG Feildon, general manager and Miss AI H Fraser, chief R&WS.

Before the opening ceremony, Princess Margaret was taken on a tour of the club by the general manager, visiting the restaurant cafeteria, the spacious walnut panelled tavern, the games room, complete with 3 full sized billiard tables, the lounges, writing rooms, WVS information Bureau and a modern cocktail bar overlooking the dance floor. Princess Margaret was particularly impressed with the residential wing, containing 42 double bedrooms for service married families and 5 first floor bedrooms for members of the women's services. After lunch the Princess's tour of the building, the opening ceremony was held in the ballroom. Princess Margaret said she was very touched by the kindness with which the Lord Matt and the people of Plymouth had received her:

"It is always with the feeling of great elation that I come to the West country, Bristol, Bideford, Falmouth and Plymouth; these and many other West Country ports and Mariners of England put into the narrow waters of the channel to answer the call of duty to set sail across the broad Atlantic. By the great daring, the restless energy, the sailors of Queen Elizabeth succeeded in planting the seed of our empire. Today the people of this empire are United and seek fresh inspiration from that Golden age. The story of Sir Francis Drake on Plymouth Hoe is one that is still there to every Englishman because it is characteristic of the indifference of forces. It was true that this attitude had at times put our island in great danger, but it had never, at least since 1066, being carried too far. It is in the spirit of Drake that we give place to recreation in the life of every fighting man. The grim mechanical nature of Modern Warfare makes him feel greater need than ever for change and relaxation. This splendid new club is an outstanding example of how that need is being realised."

With a new club being designed to be a home from home where soldiers, sailors and airmen could enjoy their off-duty hours with friends, the Princess went on to say:

"All around us we see this brave old City rising up with renewed strength from the devastation it suffered. Its historic association make it most fitting that among the buildings planned for the new Plymouth, my sister, the Queen, opened one like this. I should like to say how much I share her interest in the welfare of our fighting services. I enjoyed so much the opportunity of looking around this club and I have been greatly impressed by its fine appearance. Every praise is due to those who have planned and built it to such a high standard. It is with great pleasure that I now declare the club open and to all who come here I wish good fortune and a well-earned rest."

Shortly after the opening, HRH left the club, having enjoyed her time.

OCA 1952

The 5th AGM was held on the 24th of May 1952. By this point some changes on the committee had been made: Lt Col Merry was still in charge, but now Capt F Cooper, JE Ellison, Esq, Lt J Heald, R.N.V.R., Miss M Murdoch, TE Pegg, Esq, OBE, Brigadier NV Peters OBE MC, RC Petit, Esq, Capt JT Picton, Col E Tanner. Also, in attendance was HW Bowen Esq, the general secretary, Lt RWT Lines as honorary treasurer, A W Balfour, Esq, the auditor.

They reviewed the whole of 1951, with Lt Col Merry OBE as the chairman. It was reported that there had been not much change in the Association financially or in members. They had now got to a point where they were maintaining a hardcore of membership and the benevolent and social side of the activities were now well organised.

The social side of the Association now posted 27 events held by different branches and not forgetting the grand annual reunion and dance at the Seymour Hall. Some of these events were dances, concerts, outings, and social evenings. It was just unfortunate that the attendance of the grand annual reunion had showed a loss of £61. This then prompted the discussion to hold it in a smaller hall so the overheads were not so expensive. The move would now be made to hold this event at the assembly rooms of St Pancras Town Hall, which would be held on the 11th of October 1952. The only 2 major differences being would be the smaller hall and the smaller cost. Price per ticket for the reunion would be Sixpence a ticket.

The membership had now increased ever so slightly from 3014 to 3028. Unfortunately, there were approximately 200 members who had not advised the Association of their new addresses and they had lost trace of them. So essentially gaining just over 200 members in one year. As part of the subscription since they started charging for their NAAFI News it was agreed that all paid up members would receive 2 free copies a year, the first one would be in June and the 2nd would be the winter issue.

As with the drawdown of some establishments across the world, so did some of the branches of the OCA. BTA branch had been wound up during the year and the members were transferred to the headquarters membership list. With the remaining branches overseas being BAOR, Bermuda, Gibraltar, Malta, Egypt, and East Africa, all who still tried to put on dances to retain the camaraderie between its members.

Some of the year's more memorable events were on the 11th of November the War Memorial unveiling at Imperial Court. This was attended by over 400 relatives of the fallen, and representatives of all departments of the company. Not to mention that it was fully represented by the general committee and of the branches who all laid wreaths on behalf of their members. The Benevolent Fund would be the lifeblood of the OCA and during 1951, 33 cases of assistance were dealt with by the general committee. Oddly enough it is also reported that gifts of cigarettes were sent to all NCS&FI ranks serving in Korea and Christmas parcels to all sick members in hospital.

In the early days of the Association it was decided that there should be a general fund and a Benevolent Fund. The division was made because during World War II in many cases surplus money or other regimental funds were donated to the Association on their closing down. The donations were large amounts, and it was decided that this had been mainly given to further the benevolent side of the Association's work. This meant that the general fund would be looked upon as for dealing with the running expenses of the Association. The subscriptions and interest from investments up until this point had been sufficient to meet the expenses, the balance being added to the general accumulated fund. This also meant that the Benevolent Fund could not be touched in regard to any general expenses and would be devoted solely to the assistance of its members. It was then recorded that with the general fund the subscriptions would be enough to continue the running of the Association so any profits from entertainments would go directly into the Benevolent Fund. This started on the 31st of December 1951. By now the investment of the war stock had increased to £2494 with a market value on the 31st of December 1951 of £1938.

1953

Quarterly survey of NAAFI activities, NAAFI review 1953

Early in 1953 behind the scenes an additional publication was in production. The aim was to make people aware of other activities that were going on in the company and the achievements on a quarterly basis.

One of the 1st reports was not overseas or in time of war but in response to adverse weather conditions. The mobile canteens swung into action when a great flood struck Britain. The East Coast from Grimsby to Sheerness was battered by the raging waters. NAAFI staff were alerted alongside civil and service authorities to meet the emergencies. The main aim of the company was to provide hot meals, chocolate, cigarettes, and small comforts to help the victims and rescuers to carry on. Staff were out in their mobile canteens at the main danger points throughout the stricken areas; some of the female drivers had struggled through submerged roads to reach working parties on duty.

At Felixstowe RAF camp the canteen restaurant disappeared under 7 feet of water, although when the first warning was given the staff refused to leave the canteen and continued moving products and equipment upstairs even though the water swirled around their legs. They stayed there until the camp was evacuated the next day by the Navy who came to the rescue with three minesweepers and took them off.

Mobile Canteen driver Ron Gurney found himself suddenly in an ocean-going concern when he set out to search for RAF working parties. It is quoted that Ron said, "I started off in my van but soon found the road was part of the sea. So, I hopped aboard a big matador truck with the tray of chocolates and cigarettes. A few miles further on the water was too deep even for the matador, but from thereon I bobbed about on the sea wall for an hour juggling my tray and there were blokes glad to see me!"

Miss Lina Chaplin, a manageress at the Orsett Army camp near Grays, Essex, on a quiet Sunday afternoon was visited by the commanding officer, to ask them to look after some 100 flood refugees from Tilbury. As usual it was no question and no problem at all, the troops began shifting beds and blankets into the NAAFI dancehall and Miss Chaplin and her staff, even those off duty, were starting to prepare meals for them. They worked through the night to provide hot meals for all 500 men, women and children. Members of the WRAC also assisted.

In total 9 mobile canteens operated from Orsett, taking tea and cakes to members of the three services who were deployed on sea defence work, Canvey, Benfleet and as far as Purfleet. Each of them covering up to 80 miles a day through water and were still squelching through mud after the floods subsided. Volunteers from other NAAFI commands also helped man temporary canteens and extended existing facilities to assist with the crisis. Although this was not a wartime calling, it was with the same spirit and passion the staff had always shown.

Portsmouth memorial 1953

Queen Elizabeth and the Queen Mother on the 29th of April 1953 attended the unveiling of the Portsmouth Naval War Memorial. Six members of the NCS staff were led by Mr JH Ville to represent the company.

1939
ROYAL NAVAL
VOLUNTEER RESERVE
ORDINARY SIGNALMAN
BIRKENSHAW A.
BROWN R.W.
ROYAL NAVAL VOLUNTEER
(WIRELESS) RESERVE
TELEGRAPHIST
GREGORY J.
N.A.A.F.I. STAFF
CANTEEN ASSISTANT
DAYSH A.
LENZ B.H.
O'SHEA M.
WHITE H.J.W.

1940
ROYAL NAVAL VOLUNTEER
(WIRELESS) RESERVE
TELEGRAPHIST
FOX I.G.
GOUGH R.B.
HALL A.B.
MACFARLANE J.T.
MILLS H.R.
PARSONS A.R.B.
RHODES B.C.
WARNER C.S.
ROYAL NAVAL AUXILIARY
SICK BERTH RESERVE
SICK BERTH ATTDT.
LEAH S.
RAMSDEN W.T.
N.A.A.F.I. STAFF
CANTEEN MANAGER
FOXON A.S.
HURDING J.E.
KING A.F.
MILLER L.V.
PARSONS C.W.
PENKSTERMAN C.
PRIOR C.F.
PELETIER F.A.
CANTEEN ASSISTANT
CLARK A.H.

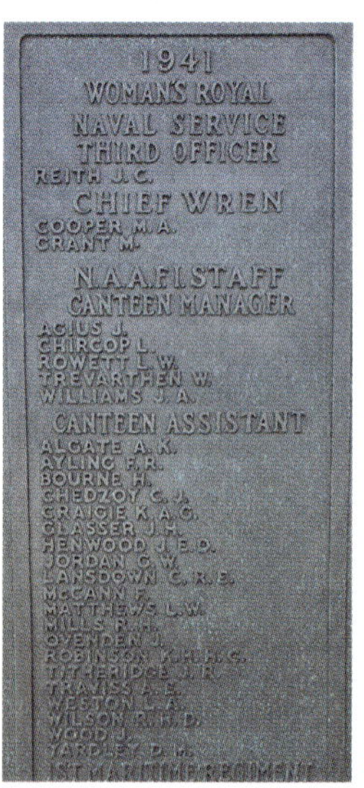
1941
WOMAN'S ROYAL
NAVAL SERVICE
THIRD OFFICER
REITH J.C.
CHIEF WREN
COOPER M.A.
GRANT M.
N.A.A.F.I. STAFF
CANTEEN MANAGER
AGIUS J.
CHIRCOP L.
ROWETT L.W.
TREVARTHEN W.
WILLIAMS J.A.
CANTEEN ASSISTANT
ALGATE A.K.
AYLING F.R.
BOURNE H.
CHEDZOY C.J.
CRAIGIE K.A.G.
GLASSER J.H.
HENWOOD J.E.D.
JORDAN C.W.
LANSDOWN C.R.E.
McCANN F.
MATTHEWS L.W.
WILSON R.H.D.
YARDLEY D.M.

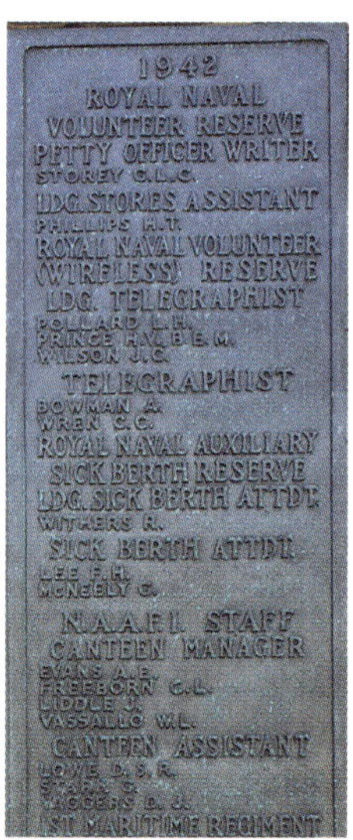
1942
ROYAL NAVAL
VOLUNTEER RESERVE
PETTY OFFICER WRITER
STOREY G.L.C.
LDG. STORES ASSISTANT
PHILLIPS H.T.
ROYAL NAVAL VOLUNTEER
(WIRELESS) RESERVE
LDG. TELEGRAPHIST
POLLARD L.H.
PRINCE H.V. B.E.M.
WILSON J.C.
TELEGRAPHIST
BOWMAN A.
WREN C.C.
ROYAL NAVAL AUXILIARY
SICK BERTH RESERVE
LDG. SICK BERTH ATTDT.
WITHERS R.
SICK BERTH ATTDT.
LEE F.H.
McNEELY G.
N.A.A.F.I. STAFF
CANTEEN MANAGER
EVANS A.E.
FREEBORN C.L.
LIDDLE J.
VASSALLO W.L.
CANTEEN ASSISTANT
LOWE D.B.R.

The Coronation of Queen Elizabeth II 1953

Like with any major event there is a long drawn out build up with a huge amount of preparations. And the Coronation day would be followed by the naval review at Spithead and the Royal Air Force review at Odiham. The HCS and the NCS would be doing the catering, supply, and manpower. Although there would be issues with not enough staff, careful planning and preparation was to make sure this went off without a hitch.

This was started early in 1952 at the command supervisors meeting at Ruxley Towers, they formed the NAAFI Coronation committee. In June 1952 a Coronation conference was called by Mr Whitehouse, manager, HCS and a planning committee was formed. The first full Coronation committee meeting was held at Ruxley Towers on the 27th of January 1953, the level of detail for the requirements was already starting to be set and all the specialists within headquarters were all called on for their skills. Provisional staff arrangements were made and requirements for transport, tentage equipment, stores and supplies were worked out. The task of preparing and packing over 33,000 haversack rations were considered and Kennings Way or Totteridge was chosen as a possible location for this.

At this time 450 staff were borrowed from canteens all over Great Britain; they played an important role in the Coronation by providing food and refreshments for thousands of servicemen taking part. The military camp was sited at Kensington Gardens, marquees were set up covering 6 acres and would accommodate restaurants and bars for 12,000 troops, bars and lounges for 1300 warrant officers and sergeants and 3 full scale officers' messes catering for 700 officers.

Skilled Craftsman at the NAAFI tentage works at Aldershot were hard at work preparing £60,000 worth of tents and marquees, the first of which went up in Kensington Gardens on the 15th of May. By the 18th of May they were up and running and would remain open until the 9th of June. Seventy staff would be living in tents in Kensington Gardens for the duration of the camp and another 280 would be billeted in and around north London. Alongside this was a huge stores tent in Kensington Gardens – this would provide extra messing with fresh vegetables, fruit, fish, milk, and general groceries for 35,000 men including special packs for 1100 Pakistan, Gurkha, Cinghalese and other Asiatic troops who would be camping nearby.

The NCS also had been in preparation for the activities that occurred 2 weeks after the Coronation, on the 15th of June when the Portsmouth staff, assisted by a large group of volunteers from the neighbouring NCS domains, catered for over 30,000 service and civilian spectators lining the shore for the Royal review of the Navy.

The Royal Air Force review at Odiham's, the biggest catering commitment, was held on the 15th of July. Over 300 staff manned a mile and a half of tented restaurants and bars, providing food and drink to the vast concourse of servicemen and civilians filling the public enclosures.

A week before coronation day the NAAFI News went to Pirbright to visit the 2 canteens operating exclusively for the armed forces of a dozen different countries – this also included

Great Britain. Soldiers, sailors, and airmen in a variety of uniforms were hard at work practising for Coronation day – this was a drill sergeant's dream. You could hear commands from various languages all around and of course, with so many nationalities brought so many catering challenges, even the army catering corps had got involved to make sure the Gurkha and Pakistan messes were in accordance with their religious beliefs and requirements.

The major operation in the Coronation campaign was the preparing and the packaging of 33,000 haversack rations for troops based at the new training and collecting centre, Totteridge; a line was formed to ensure it was done with precision.

Eighty volunteer staff recruited from clerical and canteen Departments at Ruxley Towers and Imperial Court arrived at Totteridge early on May 30th for the initial stage of the packaging. Chocolate, barley sugar and apples were packed that day, bread rolls and cakes prepared unwrapped on the 2 days after. The girls worked in teams of six, each in charge of a trainee district manager and did the job well: it was completed within 15 minutes of the schedule of the eve of the Coronation.

The girls and boys in the huge packing tent and demonstration kitchens did the job quickly with a nonstop programme of community singing. Originally it was thought that they would have to work through the night, but this was not so. When the great day came this was enough reward for the work well done. The full ceremony procession was televised on a screen in the modern Totteridge Lodge cinema before a packed audience of volunteers, all who had done their special part towards making the occasion a memorable one.

As far back as August 1952 the first thoughts were given to the pattern and extent of the outside decorations for the NAAFI premises at home and overseas, and the first meeting of the committee appointed to work out these details was held on the 4th of September 1952. The committee outlined the standard of the decorations and possibly using floodlighting for NAAFI premises in prominent positions like town clubs, account offices, warehouses, command offices and similar establishments, together with an estimated requirement of materials. Regular meetings were held to ensure that everything could be prepared in the months leading up to the Coronation. The estimated quantities and placing orders for the materials involved included flags, bunting, streamers, plaques and set pieces; 6000 yards of streamers and 4000 yards of bunting were used in addition to 222 flag trophies, 55 banners, 24 Royal arms and 150 feet of flower boxes. By the end of 1952 there was much material overseas that was already on its way and at home, the material being used sadly distributed and carefully stored in the respective buildings. Ruxley Towers and Imperial Court had special designs made as the two headquarter offices; the main tower of Ruxley Towers a special illuminated crown would sit right on top and on a clear night could be seen from Windsor Castle. It was said that this was one of the 'brightest ideas' in the London Coronation scene and people from miles around came to see it. At Imperial Court the space between the front pillars was attractively filled with a back cloth and large reproduction of the Royal cypher. Both buildings were floodlit. There was also a competition for the best dress clubs without too much extravagance, but it needed to be kept within the financial constraints of each club.

Patronage HM the Queen 1953

After the death of her father the late King George VI who granted his patronage in 1947, Her Majesty Queen Elizabeth II in 1953 graciously granted her patronage to the NAAFI in recognition of services rendered to her majesty's forces.

Sir Richard Burbridge BT, CBE 1953

When Sir Richard was interviewed and asked about his most striking impression of the 10 years he had served as a civilian member of the NAAFI board, his reply was the amazing 'esprit de corps' of the staff. Sir Richard explained that although ultimately the staff had reasonable accommodation, inevitably when a NAAFI moved into a new location there was a short period when there was no proper facilities and the accommodation was well below standard, and yet, despite this the wonderful spirit still existed and all difficulties were faced with a smile and a capacity for work that was truly inspiring.

As another instance of this feeling of loyalty, Sir Richard quoted the recent trouble in Egypt and said that when there was a call for volunteers to work in a dangerous spot, 1000 applications came rolling in and it became extremely difficult to organise sufficient transport to get them to the location.

Sir Richard, with his knowledge of the happy staff relationships in the Harrods group, was exceptionally noteworthy. Sir Richard stressed that the NAAFI does not trade for profit and that its personnel was 90% civilian. Many people thought of the organisation as the place where service personnel gets his cup of char and people failed to realise the full extent of the responsibilities. For example, all the bacon and many of the supplementary rations for the forces were supplied through NAAFI. Since the war the shops catering for the soldier and his family are miniature Harrods. As an illustration of some of the difficulties with which he had contended, Sir Richard recalls the occasion when he and Mr Mills went to Canada to arrange supplies of beer for the forces in the Middle East and Far East. The Canadian Brewers agreed that enough beer would be supplied if NAAFI provided containers.

Bottles being unobtainable in Canada, Sir Richard preceded to the United States where he became involved in endless negotiations. Further difficulties arose because the American authorities treated NAAFI as a civilian organisation and were not prepared to grant any priority in supplies. After much patience it was finally agreed to supply 95,000 cases of 48 bottles a month. Sir Richard then returned to Canada to find that owing to the shortage of malt the supplies of beer had become difficult. Ultimately Sir Richard negotiated successfully, and the troops got their beer. Other memories which were recalled by Sir Richard included the occasion when he discussed with an American manufacturer an order for 200 million cigarettes and the suggestion of supplying ice cream. Two ships were actually fitted with ice cream fountains, but as you can imagine this was not a hot idea.

His 1947 tour of the clubs, shops, and warehouses in Germany and in a lighter vein an exciting trip on the engine of a Canadian Pacific Railway. The enjoyment of the story of the

Canadian official who thought NAAFI was a peacetime organisation for civilians, in time of war ran canteens for the army! He thought that NAAFI would be returning to serving civilian customers when the war was over. Sir Richard corrected him and explained that the organisation was a permanent business.

We were privileged to read much of Sir Richard's personal diary concerned with his 10 years with the company and from it gathered some idea of the magnitude of the task. It was clear that it called for patience and perseverance and long and arduous hours of hard work on his trip to the United States and Canada. Many a day was crowded with appointments with cabinet ministers, embassy and government officials, civil servants, heads of great industrial concerns and service Chiefs; often a day's work did not finish until the early hours of the morning. Decisions often affected thousands of the force personnel serving in every Theatre of war in a conflict that embraced the world, and underlying the notes that he made a sense of his constant endeavour to obtain a square deal for his country and the serving men and women.

His wide experience as the chief of the Harrods group, together with his commercial gifts and flair for leadership, must have been a great assistance to him in his responsibilities with NAAFI. In the birthday honours of 1946, he was awarded the CBE for his wartime services which were given voluntarily during those difficult and trying years. Ten strenuous years of hard work for Sir Richard, in which he loyally lived up to the NAAFI motto, 'servitor Servientium', and for which the culmination was the dinner given to him at Claridge's in his honour, when many tributes were paid to him by his wartime colleagues and those who had served with him.

In subsequent talks with the NAAFI News, Sir Richard said, "I confess I miss those Tuesdays at Ruxley Towers. During the war years and after we held official board meetings once a month, but we met frequently unofficially at other times so that nearly every Tuesday found me leaving my desk at Harrods and driving down to Claygate for conferences. It was refreshing to switch from one's mind from the problems of a London store in wartime to the complicated demands of NAAFI business. It was rewarding to know that one was working in a war job of real value, contributing to the welfare of the men and women of the armed forces. Rewarding too were the many friendships I made in NAAFI. I have already expressed my admiration for the loyalty and the team spirit of the staff. In all the time I knew them they worked hard, played hard. And I cherish the liveliest recollections of the wide variety of Imperial club occasions I attended, sports days, dances and victory ball and various dramatic shows, and the impression those restaurant chairs left on us. I wish there was space to mention all the grand fellows with whom my 10 years with the company brought me in contact. I must content myself with two. Firstly, the chairman Sir Launcelot Royle. A great man and a hard worker! He never stopped and yet somehow he always managed to find the time for the little kindly act of calling in on a sick colleague, or dropping a personal letter of reassurance to a wife whose husband was overseas, showing a real practical interest in the welfare of the humblest of his employees. Many men intended to do such things. Sir Lancelot does them. I count it as a privilege to have worked as his friend and colleague for all those years.

"The outstanding character of my NAAFI memories was Mr FH Crosier. Much of the stability and integrity of NAAFI is merely a reflection of those same characteristics of Frank Crosier. Not that he and I always saw eye to eye. Far from it. We had many a friendly battle across the board table, but never a moment did I cease to admire and respect him for the honest, rugged man of unswerving principle that he was." He concluded with wishing every success and prosperity to the good ship NAAFI and all those who sailed in her.

Exercise holdfast 1953

Mobile canteens in Germany had deployed to service The Rhine army and 2nd Royal Air Force at exercise holdfast held in the autumn. Once the exercise began the mobiles came under stringent security regulations. They were required to camouflage with Nets. They served tea and cakes to the soldiers and airmen taking part in the exercise. The driver had to find a secluded tree sheltered spot hidden from the aerial observation before he could set up to serve the troops. As in all the wars mobile canteens were present so whilst on exercise it should be no different. After all the satisfied smiles on the faces of every soldier or airmen with a cake in one hand and a cup of tea in the other, could be very uplifting.

A visit to NAAFI transport workshops 1953

Workshop manager Arthur Browne at Bielefeld, had a staff of 100 workers; this included mechanics, paint sprayers, metal workers, carpenters, and blacksmiths. They carried out all sorts of major maintenance work on the transport division and ensured that the fleet of several 100 vehicles was kept on the road. Day to day maintenance work and minor repairs were carried out in depots in Berlin, Hamburg, Luneburg, Hanover, Celle, Bad Salzuflen, Osnabruck, Iserlohn and Dusseldorf. Each vehicle underwent a periodic overhaul and it was up to the transport examiners in the districts to decide whether an individual lorry or car should, or should not, be sent for re-conditioning. On average 35 full scale re-conditioning jobs were dealt with every month by the 5 British and 95 Germans employed in the workshops. An engagement of local staff was carried out through the German Labour exchange. Engagements, dismissals, gradings conditions of Labour were all very carefully laid down by the control council law 27. The British army's PCLU was responsible for administering this law and it acted as a go-between for the employer and the German authorities.

In the winter months the vehicles required more attention as the autobahn can be a treacherous place in wet or in frosty weather. Other roads in Germany were often rough and narrow. Many were lined with trees close to the edge and slippery cobbles and bad cambers were commonplace. Huge civilian haulage vehicles with trailers laden with lumber through Norwich village streets would take up most of the room on the road, but in winter a vehicle could easily be written off in bad weather. Whatever the volume of the reconditioning work and however badly a vehicle may be damaged by an accident, the NAAFI technicians remained undismayed

for the machinery at their disposal was first rate. Some machines were requisitioned, others like the boring and valve refacing machines were NAAFI's own property. But no matter, the fleet had to keep on moving, so the transport workshops often spent days and even weeks repairing vehicles to keep the whole machine moving. After all, where would they be if they couldn't get 'char and wad' to their customers.

New bakery at Lincoln 1953

This brand new bakery was built with efficiency in mind; this included offices, and attached workshop and garage, baking hall, receipt and dispatch base, tray washing room, staff toilets and changing rooms on the ground floor. On the 2nd floor was a self-contained manager's flat, a tastefully decorated staff mess and restroom, and a large flour store; the basement housed an oil fired boiler and main electrical equipment.

It had been designed around the bakery equipment, all in the order of baking from the delivery of the raw materials to the opposite end to the finish of the products ready to be dispatched. The proposed area for it to service was Lincoln, Cranwell district, Digby, Waddington, Grantham, Retford, North Coates, Nottingham and all the way to Norton camp. It was that efficient for its time it produced 24,000 small pastries, 3200 pounds of slab cake, 1200 sponge cakes, 3200 Swiss and chocolate rolls and 1800 dozen bread rolls per week. This was the 23rd bakery in the UK and in its 1st year produced a record 2 million pound of slab cake, 8 million meat pies, nine million sausage rolls, 7 million bread rolls amongst other goods. In the UK all the bakeries together employed male and female staff totalling 1600 throughout and also had 18 bakeries overseas.

Operation Hurricane, Anthony Irvin district manager 1953

The district manager took with him 15 NCS staff. Operation Hurricane on the 19th February 1953 at 1100hrs in two of HM ships left Portsmouth Harbour for a secret destination. These ships were the tank landing craft 'Narvik' and 'Zeebrugge'; they were on their way to prepare for the testing of Britain's first atomic weapon.

The course was set for Gibraltar, which was their first port of call. The two ships were flat bottomed, so this made the journey to Gibraltar one of the roughest parts of the journey. The Bay of Biscay lived up to its reputation. Arriving in Gibraltar, some of the lucky ones managed to obtain visas and cross the border into Spain. Malta was the next port of call, from Malta through the Suez Canal, then sailed on to Aden where it was searing hot.

They crossed the Indian Ocean and heard over the radio that the Prime Minister of Ceylon had died after a serious accident whilst out horse riding. On their arrival at Colombo the body of the Prime Minister was lying in state at the House of Representatives. Huge crowds had lined the streets waiting to pay their respects to a much loved and revered leader. Later there was a procession through the streets of Colombo with thousands turning out for the funeral and the cremation, a tribute to this man's greatness.

As they left the island, they set a course for the Cocos Keeling Islands. These islands were covered with palm trees, a real gem in the Indian Ocean. When they arrived on the islands the RAF were busy building an airstrip to be used on the new route between Australia and South Africa. Five of the men had decided to go swimming, unfortunately they got into difficulties, they had been swept over a coral reef and were in grave danger. Several of the Australians formed a human rescue chain from the shore to the reef and rescued all except for one of the swimmers. Unfortunately, two of the Australian air men had also lost their lives in the rescue attempts.

When they had reached Fremantle, Western Australia, they found themselves in the news and there was speculation as to their final destination. They were subject to a very strict security control and no visitors were allowed on board; this was disappointing because the hospitality of the Australians would have been a treat.

As they left, they set sail on the last part of the voyage. The captain called everybody together and told them that their final destination was the remote island of Montebello and would be their home for the next few months. The Montebello islands were numerous and formed a rough circle, they had very limited vegetation and were low lying. But once they had taken a closer look there was an abundance of birds, reptiles and flowers. Fishing became the favourite pastime for off duty hours for many on board.

The army wasted no time in rigging up large marquees which together with a Nissen Hut made the first shore canteen. The staff were quick in stocking it up and opening for business. They made a swimming pool by netting off a small part of the Bay and on the edge of this was the canteen – this showed what could be accomplished with very little in a short space of time. In considering that these islands were uninhabited, it wasn't long until a few weeks had gone by and the fleet was increased by the arrival of HM Campania, Tracker and Plym.

These brought with them the ministry of supply scientists who we affectionately named the boffins. They bought numerous gadgets and apparatus with them and worked exceptionally hard. Two more canteens onshore were opened, and additional swimming areas were made. An Australian frigate joined the fleet HMAS Hawkesbury. Helicopters and sea otters took to the air and the occasional Sunderland flying boat arrived making the operation even more of a combined effort.

Merchant ships arrived bringing with it stores and the latest news and gossip from the mainland. The day came which every man had been waiting for. They all wanted to see the explosion. Everybody was told to have their back to the explosion as the flash could mean blindness for them. As they started to countdown a few minutes before the explosion was due to occur a voice came over the air, counting the seconds as they came and went, until utter silence, immediately after a brilliant vivid flash passed by them. Ten seconds later they were told they could turn around. What they saw was frightening: a huge column had appeared over the lagoon where HMS Plym had been left at anchor. The massive cloud in the sky started to disperse as the high winds caught hold of it and that was the end. Many hands made light work and the ships were loaded from the shore; 1 by 1 the anchors went up and they sailed on to the first leg of their voyage home.

Jungle canteens Malaya 1953

With the fighting in Malaya and the frontline advancing through the jungle the policy had been to keep as close as possible to the troops, opening and closing canteens when and where necessary. This was done by making the best of the local facilities, enjoying the last 6 months of 1952; fourteen new establishments had been opened in Malaya, 7 had closed, leaving a total of 81. At Penang, they had ideal swimming facilities where they ran 2 leave centres, where servicemen could step back from the jungle fighting and rest and relax in ideal conditions.

NAAFI 21 issues old 1953

1953 was a year of celebration; the NAAFI News had now published 21 issues to staff. Between the two wars staff received an excellent biannual publication called the Imperial club magazine. This was printed on good quality paper and sold at sixpence and had a circulation of nearly 3000. This all stopped in 1940 as it was one of the first casualties of World War 2. The lack of paper and shortage of staff in the tiny public relations unit was the main cause. It was a sad blow for staff as they were rapidly expanding from 5000 personnel to over 120,000. So, in the history of the company a magazine for the staff was essential in those war years. Every attempt to restart the magazine failed due to the lack of paper. In 1941 the founder and editor of NAAFI News, Claude F Luke, started a new sheet called NAAFI News; this was a short bulletin which was circulated to some 200 newspapers, giving a brief story on the activities of the company and its personalities. This quickly caught on with only the press in which thousands of stories were reproduced. Although very few stories got through, the popularity of this news sheet was evident with the press. In 1945 the relaxation of the paper control regulations enabled their plans to proceed. It was not only his intention to produce a Journal which carried on from where the old Imperial club magazine left off. But he understood that reading tastes had changed. He knew that it needed to contain more pictures, social gatherings, gossip, and also be brighter and lighter all round and also, to be made relevant to new and old staff.

Christmas 1945, a slim magazine of only 24 pages including its covers was published. This was produced by the material that they had in hand and one of the first quotes from Claude Luke was:

> "We present it without flourish. We seek no bouquets for it and shall be uncommonly surprised if we receive any. None is more aware of the emissions of defiance is of this first number than we who have produced it. This present number merely indicates the shape of things to come."

They'd inserted several features; these included, 'talking shop', the 'honours' page, the 'Imperial club Chronicle'.

The second issue was well illustrated with the opening of the first permanent club at Portsmouth by the then Princess Elizabeth. Sir Frank Benson also celebrated his 50th year in the administration of the service canteens. Later they added sections called 'where's old so and so?' and the 'postscript' pages. Not to mention the 4th edition included the newly formed 'Old comrades Association'.

Paper control was still an issue and with each one the editor was always very unsure as to when it would get printed. This also meant that distribution was an issue, especially when it came to sending it out to Western Europe; sometimes the parcel was unopened for 6 months in the Hamburg warehouse. In the Far East they were lucky to receive the Christmas issue by Midsummer. This is where their very own Searchlight publication eventually came into its own. By the time they'd reached their 10th edition that had so far had been free, they put it on sale for sixpence a copy; they were quite unsure that the readers would be happy paying for it. All in all, from the 10th issue they sold 5954 copies, this nearly doubled by the 16th issue to 9508 and then by the 20th issue they had sold 13,525 copies.

The Coronation issue in 1953, 20,000 copies were printed. It was then estimated that after this approximately 15,000 copies would be sold in the UK meaning that at least 3 out of 4 staff would purchase the issues. Initially the publications had been printed by Messrs 'Samuel Stevens' for the first 14 issues. As the printing branch at headquarters was unable to take over, it was then handed to 'Ditchling press' located in a charming Sussex village which had a reputation for printing high quality publications. This also included colour pages which remained a feature moving forwards. Up until 1953 Claude Luke had been a one-man band doing all the work himself. From then onwards they had become a trio with public relations Mr RD MacBurnie and Mr LH Drake assisting with the copy and pictures and layout.

OCA 1953

The 6th AGM of the OCA was held at Imperial Court on the 9th of May 1953 at 1430 hours. The chairman was still Lt Col Merry OBE.

The Association had grown by 156 new members who had joined from serving in Korea and also men who had joined from the RASC EFI Army emergency reserve. Who would have thought it had now been 8 years since the end of WWII, with all the advancements made and support from the Association had made all the difference?

The annual reunion had taken place for the first time at St Pancras Town Hall which fitted the expectations from the 1952 committee meeting, and they had promptly booked yet another on the 3rd of October 1953.

It was in this year that they introduced the bankers order to maintain the continuity of subscription which also meant they still received 2 free copies of the NAAFI news on an annual basis.

The overseas branches were now down to just 4, BAOR, Gibraltar, Malta and Egypt branches were left. This meant that Bermuda and East Africa branches had been wound up in the previous year. For those who returned home it was heart-warming to be able to gather the members around the new War Memorial at Imperial Court at a service of Remembrance for their fallen comrades.

On the back of the success of their OCA ties and pin badges, it was suggested by a Mr Eaggleton that they have a blazer badge to further publicise the existence of the OCA. It was suggested that they put out to tender and gathered the opinion of other members. It was also suggested by one of the members that an OCA scarf would be produced for sale for members and the chairman suggested the inquiry could be made to the manufacturers of the tie, to suggest what material would be suitable or would there be another option and Mrs Ladd supported the idea of a scarf square made with the tie material.

1954

We are all in it together 1954

NAAFI was as much a part of the services as any of the units within the Navy, Army, or The Royal Air Force. Even in 1953 the fighting men depended on the necessities of life and the little luxuries as well as a large proportion of their daily messing and this is what the company did. Maj General Sir Randle G Feildean, KCVO CB CBE, General manager of NAAFI, said that even though all these things the service personnel have to pay for, the profits are "kept in the family" and not enriching a civilian merchants' pockets so any of the military personnel and their families would know that these profits are returned to them in full directly or indirectly by either way of rebates or via the canteen trade. The unit's funds or a discount on the family shop purchases or the provision of various amenities including the NAAFI clubs all depend on the profits from their spending.

When the servicemen and women go on tours and exercises and the NAAFI canteen goes with them this invariably is always a good service and is only possible by the overall offer, no matter where they go. Whichever way you put it you don't hear any service personnel say 'I'm going to the canteen' but they will definitely say 'I'm going to the NAAFI'. This is because it had become ingrained into military life and not to mention the level of input each unit's committee had in their monthly meetings. The level of input each unit had into their canteen was vast with the ability to air issues or suggestions openly at these meetings. Taking into account the experience this showed, that if a commanding officer convenes a regular Institute or welfare committee meeting and the most important appointment is a senior officer as chairman, if they take a real interest in his men's canteen, then he would regard his NAAFI as an integral part of the military. This was the man's own canteen service organised and maintained with their own money, they ensured that their service personnel had a well-run canteen, with the staff on their toes, eager to give them the best return for their unit's interest and help. In the very beginning this was exactly how it was supposed to be.

40 years at sea Jim Fyfe, BEM canteen manager HMS Vanguard 1954

Few Admirals could claim 40 years' continuous ongoing service with the Royal Navy. James Victor Fyfe BEM served NCS as a canteen manager, first put to sea as a canteen assistant aboard HMS Aurora in 1914 at the age of 16. He had been offered many a chance to take a job onshore, but he didn't think that this was the place for him; aboard ship was in his blood. His father was a captain in the Trinity service and Jim joined up as a canteen assistant as he had been turned down by the Navy due to poor eyesight. He sailed around the world many times and the only countries he hadn't visited were Japan, China and New Zealand. He was a married man in 1954 with sons aged 16 and 28. He was a bit of a stranger in his hometown of Peverell, Plymouth. He had never spent more than 3 months at home.

He was known throughout the Royal Navy as a figure of the NAAFI's NCS, with a reputation for being the perfect canteen manager. For the last 4 years of his career, the commanders in chief of the home fleet insisted upon having him as the canteen manager aboard their flagship. Senior naval officers knew Jim as a good-hearted friend to ensure that stocks were available, ordered to be aboard ship when they were needed. He would often be seen counting stock and even the cakes freshly delivered from the NAAFI bakery at Portsmouth where the HMS Vanguard was then docked.

Egypt's Last canteen standing December 1954

In 1947 when the British army evacuated the Nile Delta, it was a matter of moving from one part of Egypt to another. This time they were leaving Egypt for good. In the years that NAAFI and its predecessors had been there in Egypt, they had served a useful reception area and clearing house in times of emergency. With the evacuation of Greece and Crete in 1941, the departure from Syria and Lebanon in 1946 and the Palestine evacuation in 1948, the furniture and equipment and other assets held by the company in those countries were transferred to Egypt for storage or to be used or transferred to other areas and now one of the biggest projects was to remove everything from Egypt.

There had been nearly 200 establishments to have to be closed – these were everything from warehouses, grocery shops, to officers' clubs and even their own staff hostels. Massive quantities of furniture and equipment either had to be sold or shipped elsewhere. Tens of thousands of chairs, 200 billiard tables, more than 200 pianos, tables, garden furniture, lounge and bar furnishings and hundreds of radios and thousands of pounds worth of equipment. Even though they were drawing down and moving out, they still needed to produce cakes, ice cream and mineral waters for the canal zone Garrison. These were carefully laid plans for reducing the company's strength to meet the needs of the reduced force and then an announcement came. This was going to be a complete evacuation. Mr HG Swithenbank, manager of NAAFI overseas canteen service, flew out to Egypt and formed a special evacuation coordination committee to deal with the task. This all started as soon as the first British troops left and within days 7 establishments had closed; it was decided that only the basics would stay open. The ice cream factory and 2 main mineral water factories were still operating to full capacity and they were especially designed to be easily dismantled. They would continue to produce until the last possible moment and the families' shop would stay open as long as the families were still there to serve them.

Every item of furniture that was in first class condition would be dispersed to other establishments throughout the world wherever it was needed, the rest would be sold off.

Staff training at Totteridge 1954

In 1954 the staff training college had been open a year and during that 12 months 2561 staff of all grades had passed through on various stages of their training; 263 had completed their courses and 250 had come in for refresher. When you included all those who would pass through Totteridge in a transit centre and EFI Depot, you get a grand total of 4582 personnel passing through within the year.

The college was established to make sure there was a steady supply of highly trained staff to meet the company's constant increasing demands, but it was more a place of instruction. They were there to learn in the training school where men and women find the value of service and comradeship and these are lessons that could only be taught by example. This was an experiment which the board of management thought was worthwhile. This gave the staff the best possible facilities and realisation that the high standards the company expected were achievable and they were able to maintain. In the training, of course, nothing was left to chance. Those who were training for the higher grades, district managers, restaurant and welfare superintendents, canteen manageresses and also down the scale of those who would be serving under them, the lower grades, and those who had not been through the mill before. Cooks learnt their jobs in the model of demonstration kitchens containing every type of stove they were likely to encounter and to get the practical experience during training by helping in the house kitchen. Canteen attendants would scrub and polish floors, district managers would teach as well as learn, so that apart from affording the trainees the valuable practical experience, the whole complex machinery of Totteridge could be run with a minimum of permanent staff. The whole atmosphere of the training centre was informal and friendly and there was nothing of the institution about it. One of the principals gave a hint of how they achieved the high-quality training. Mr Lloyd said, 'we don't like to talk to or at people. We like to talk with them.'

Training was only one part of Totteridge's function, there was also an air of toing and froing of NAAFI personnel from all parts of the world coming and going to new appointments. For those that went overseas there were talks about the country in which they were going to and its currency. Female staff that went off to the Middle East were provided with the regulation kit, all staff who went into transit were medically examined and the endless documents had to be put in order.

There was also a canvas site being prepared adjacent to the lodge, so that the canteen staff could be made thoroughly familiar with the hazards of this part of their job and later on in the year the members of the RASC EFI reservists marched in and took over Totteridge for 2 weeks' annual training. The regular army NCOs were attached to NAAFI for the duration of the course to provide the regulation military training and lectures. The first year of the training centre above all proved to be a success and all those who went through there definitely reaped the benefits once they'd got to their own establishments.

Exercise Winch July 1954

On the Belgian coast In July 1954 with 5000 territorials of the 264 Scottish beach brigade Territorial Army 48 RASC EFI which together with their OC and RSM and some 16 NAAFI civilian staff, all of whom were taking part in Exercise Winch.

This was a beach and port landing operation carried out in the vicinity of Zeebrugge, this was just a few miles from the holiday beaches of Blankenburg. For a 3 week period visitors to Zeebrugge found themselves in a captured enemy port with troops working on the cranes and equipment on the famous mole and a fleet of lumbering DUKWS transferring stores from ship to shore; these special mobile cranes loaded a never ending queue of 10 tonne army lorries. Some 8000 tons of army stores were landed and transported by road and rail to the base supply Depot near Antwerp, the army testing its latest port operating equipment and at the same time providing this Scottish beach brigade with a realistic training exercise.

With all this going on the NAAFI provided canteen facilities at the three camps' supper set up on the waste ground in the immediate vicinity of the port. In addition to this they operated 4 mobiles plus a beer bar and grocery shop near the AKC tented cinema. Unfortunately, the weather was very miserable with the wind and rain straight from the UK and the exercise became quite real with the camps being caked in mud. This is where the engineers had to play their part by creating temporary paths and roads.

Practical training and overcoming the manpower problem, it was decided to use RASC EFI reservists, who would normally have carried out their annual 14 day trade training at Totteridge Lodge, these man the canteens with a nucleus of some 16 NAAFI staff to provide the experience and to organise the setting up in the closing down of the canteens. The personnel department had no difficulty in obtaining the required number of volunteers who were mostly young men from multiple grocery firms and by the end of May, 48 reserves had been chosen for the exercise and instructed to report to Totteridge Lodge by 0900hrs on the 17th of July. Two coaches took the men with their OC Maj J Duncan OC EFI Depot, and RSM Marrison to Harwich where they went on the troop transport, Empire Wansbeck, to the location.

Mr JW Hackett, the district manager, raced against time to open up the canteen beer bars and a shop. Mr Withers of the equipment warehouse in Germany and Mr R Lockwood the tent man, had supervised the erection of the canvas aided by 2 NAAFI drivers.

On the 26th of July the camps were at their peak strength at over 5000 troops that were using the canteens and facilities. Unfortunately, the army kitchens were experiencing major difficulties and the EFI cooks, who were railway men, farmers, and mechanics in civilian life, performed miracles in the kitchen which would have been impossible without their training. In one evening, they dished up 19,000 fried eggs across all 3 canteens, to give some idea of the volume of all food which was prepared. At the main camp Mr J Ellis and Mr JE Bradford, both trainee district managers, shared the responsibility for the canteen and the adjacent bar; they served over 28,000 suppers and sold 66,000 cakes, 33,000 cups of tea and twenty one thousand filled rolls, 47,000 bottles of beer and one point 5,000,000 cigarettes. This canteen was taxed to its full capacity at all times and there were 3700 troops in the main camp during the peak period and owing to the fact the shifts were being worked on an exercise.

Mobiles were sent down from Germany and were maintained by EFI drivers and assistants, most of whom were quite new to the job. They provided a morning and evening service to the troops working far out on the mole and on the beaches that were very much appreciated.

Local purchases were arranged by Mr Hackett, general supplies were brought in by road from the Waldniel Warehouse 180 miles away and daily delivery of fresh cakes was made from the NAAFI bakery at Ratingen near Dusseldorf. On the 30th of July the RASC EFI closed down all the establishments except for the main camp canteen. The remaining

NAAFI staff maintained a reduced service in the main camp until the 7th of August for the benefit of the administrative troops engaged in closing down the camps and army installations. By the end of the first week in August all the stores and equipment had been packed away and were already on their way back to Germany after the successful exercise.

7th AGM OCA 1954

The 7th AGM of the NCS EFI OCA was held at Imperial Court, Kennington on the 15th of May 1954 but this time something was a little different. Before I set out the agenda for the meeting they announced the official resignation of Col Merry, who had decided to step down. The OCA was his baby and he was behind the driving force of its formation, his enthusiastic leadership was going to be sorely missed. It was proposed at the general committee meeting that he became vice president and he accepted.

It was now up to the new chairman TE Pegg, Esq, OBE, to lead from the front whilst assuring the committee that he would do everything in his powers to ensure that the OCA was kept very much alive and that the continuance of its good work is maintained. In his opening speech he said, "I hope, with the enthusiastic support of the general committee, officers, delegates and members of the branch committees, to prove a worthy successor to our retiring chairman." He received a rapturous round of applause. The meeting was then open. Since the previous general meeting 112 new members had been enrolled, these were mainly personnel of the RASC EFI who had served in Korea. It was also announced that over 30 entertainments were held during 1953 and again their annual reunion was St Pancras Town Hall, a resounding social success.

The Benevolent Fund continued to assist people and in 1950 326 cases of assistance were dealt with by the general committee. As for the unpaid subscriptions it now totalled 490 for 1954 with the members that had paid at 1515. This meant that the new routine of using a banker's order was taking off. The BAOR branch had also closed down, with the Egypt branch also being wound down.

From the very first days of the Association the branches were laid out quite clearly but after the drawdown in the post-war years, the branches became fewer. In the UK there were now 5 branches: London, West of England, NW England, North East England, and Glasgow and the West of Scotland.

The field of Remembrance for the 2nd year was attended well, and arrangements were made for the NAAFI plot at Westminster Abbey during Armistice week; on this occasion, crosses were planted bearing inscriptions of the various overseas theatres of war in which our comrades served. The plot was tended by members of the general committee and number one branch committee. The large number of British Legion crosses planted in the plot with significance of the number of members and relatives who paid their due to honour the dead.

Sir Launcelot C Royle KBE resigned from being the president of the Association and this also coincided with his retirement as chairman of the board of management of NAAFI.

Copyright Sue A Lowe

Earlier in the year before the retirement took place Col Beale OBE consented to becoming the vice president upon the resignation of Sir Launcelot Royle, he then stepped up to become the president of the Association. Col Beale was the chairman of the board of the management of NAAFI and was a very prominent figure within EFI during WWII, he was very keenly interested in the OCA affairs.

In the past year they'd also managed to secure the ladies scarfs even though this was previously not possible. The first batch of NAAFI blazer badges had been ordered and people had already started to pay for them in advance.

Royal fashion for service wives 1954

British soldiers' wives in Germany and the Suez Canal zone during the summer of 1954 were wearing copies of some of the cotton dresses worn by the Queen during her Commonwealth tour. They were chosen by Her Majesty from "off the peg" stocks of a famous manufacturer of cotton dresses, and NAAFI fashion buyer, Mr JH Jordan, had been quick to follow this Royal fashion lead. The dresses were amongst 20,000 items of clothing which were bought from leading British fashion manufacturers to stock the NAAFI family shops in Germany, Austria, and Egypt and at the time were available at all larger NAAFI shops in those areas.

British women in Germany and Egypt, Mr Jordan found, were particularly fond of sun dresses with matching boleros; with our gracious young Queen setting the example, cotton at the time was more popular than ever. Mr Jordan said, "We have a really marvellous selection of cotton dresses, especially in the lower price ranges." The dresses were for every taste and pocket, ranging from the attractive little dresses to beautiful models for formal or partyware. The buying team started in the early October, attending fashion shows and the leading wholesale fashion houses all day, every day, for a whole month. At the end of that time they had chosen the collection of suits, coats, skirts, cotton dresses, cocktail dresses, knitwear, swimwear, and shoes all priced as reasonably as possible. At the time British women in Germany like pastel coloured suits, coats and dresses in bright, light colours and they very seldom bought navy or black. They also enjoyed separates which rose to popularity that year and became very glamorous.

NAAFI offered customers skirts in a variety of styles, lightweight wools, dupont and cotton bearing famous fashion house labels and to help the customer in selecting their separates, the skirt and blouse knitwear sections of the NAAFI shops had been combined.

Planning the big move by Norman Parkin, Assistant to the secretary 1954

Just after Christmas 1953 they found out the news that the big news was really on. The board of management had decided that a term should be set to the wartime arrangement which had involved the splitting of the management between London and Claygate, and arising from the decision the general manager gave the secretary the 1st of December 1954 as the target date for the completion of the exercise from that onwards that date was firmly in our minds.

Obviously, no planning could be effective until we knew precisely what Department some branches it was necessary to move to London and consequently, groups of staff would have to be rehoused. I sent a note to the heads of Department asking for this information and accommodation ideally would be required. Naturally the responsible officials required time to access their requirements and a few weeks elapsed before it all happened. From summary of those we were now able to arrive at some estimate of the number of staff to be moved and the total area of accommodation to be found in London, not necessarily at Imperial Court.

The next step was to carry out a detailed survey of the existing occupation of Imperial Court and Kennings Way. About this time, we had our first slice of luck. After lengthy negotiations the Company acquired the old YMCA building at 91 Kennington Lane. This was the most welcome windfall, an extra 9000 square feet which, in the end, was enough to house certain offices, the sports showroom and the Imperial club.

Nevertheless, even with this extra space, it was apparent from the start that some staff would be required to move from Kennington to make room for the Claygate influx.

At this stage I began considering Imperial Court as an empty building and then to make preliminary allocations of space for members of Top management and for those Department and branches for whom it was imperative to provide offices at Imperial Court. This involved a long and tedious process of trial and error, trying to match spaces with people, like a gigantic jigsaw puzzle.

Eventually I was able to provide a floor plan of Imperial Court on which was marked a tentative allocation of space for the various departments. This was circulated to the officials concerned and overall, was favourably received though a little subsequent juggling was necessary.

So far, all was theory, no one had to be practical and consider the redistribution of those main branches at present in possession such as HAB, EAB, TAB and Export Branch. Affecting our approach to the problem was the management wish that, if possible, these account branches should be grouped together in London and this meant Kennings Way, which was already fully occupied.

The question was how to then find extra accommodation at Kennings Way? I have mentioned our new premises at 91 Kennington Way and the transfer there of the sports showroom released something like 3000 square feet of potential office accommodation, but this was only a small part of the extra accommodation which had to be found. It was quite obvious that there had to be some fairly substantial movement of clerical staff from Kennings Way. It had for a long time been thought that in the interests of efficiency central wages branch ought to be at Ruxley Towers, alongside the staff branches, particularly as it was also planned to transfer the Aldershot staff records office to Ruxley Towers.

The movement of management from Ruxley Towers presented a Golden opportunity to achieve the ideal in this respect and the opportunity was seized. The transfer of central wages branch from Kennings Way helped considerably in solving the problem of finding the extra accommodation required, although there was still several problems to be solved. For example there was the problem of Kennings Way staff restaurant which was barely adequate to cope with the needs of the staff already employed at Kennings Way and this situation would be obviously aggravated by the additional staff which had to be housed there were transferred. The next step was to look around to see what functions at present carried on at Kennings Way could be more efficiently or conveniently carried on elsewhere; it was finally agreed that the produce warehouse ought to be sited nearer to the produce markets. After a rapid search, suitable premises were found at Fashion Street in the Spitalfields market area, which rivalled Covent Garden as a produce market.

The site of the produce warehouse at Kennings Way was earmarked for a new and enlarged staff restaurant; the area of the old staff restaurant was therefore released for office purposes and this area, together with the other areas which I have mentioned and other minor adjustments at Kennings Way, together provided a basis on which it was possible to work.

We then had to repeat the process adopted in the case of Imperial Court, and by a process of trial and error succeeded in fitting in the various branches into the various pieces of accommodation. The plan was now taking shape and we had at last a clear picture of our final problem. We now knew that we had X square feet available space in which to house 'y' essential bodies and at first sight it seemed we were trying everything to fit them in.

By early summer, management had approved the plans. The big move was complete, but on paper only. Now it was the turn of the works and buildings branch to press ahead with the alterations and adaption, the most urgent tasks being the conversion of the old produce warehouse into a new staff restaurant and reconditioning of 91 Kennington Lane. As soon as the latter was ready the first phase of the move was undertaken and "91" became the new home of sports branch from Ruxley Towers, the sports showroom and HCS wines and spirits sales office from Kennings Way. These moves were completed towards the end of September.

The removal of the sports branch (HCS C3) from Ruxley Towers left a hole in our jigsaw which enabled us to move the eastern command down to Claygate.

Work was also put in hand to convert the old sports showroom at Kennings Way into offices for export branch, the old Imperial club games room to be combined with the existing offices.

By now the summer was slipping into autumn and the tempo of the work began to accelerate. The next major step being the transfer of the export branch from Imperial Court to their new home at Kennings Way. The area they vacated had been allocated to the NCS which Department was transferring from Ruxley Towers. The day came when all was ready to receive them and for the first-time the house managers at Ruxley and Imperial Court would be put to the test.

On October 4th, 1954, MCS moved to town almost without a hitch and expressed their satisfaction with the whole operation and with their new offices. The next move on the chess board was EAB from Imperial Court to Kennings Way. This was followed by the transfer of the central wages branch from Kennings Way to Ruxley Towers. This latter was a fairly formidable business, with many highly costly pieces of machinery to removed and reassembled in time to avoid any delay in the payment of wages. Here the transport branch did sterling work and carefully nursed the machines from first to last.

October saw the completion of the new Kennings Way restaurant and work began at once to convert the old restaurant for office purposes. The three-storey office block at Kennings Way had been completely reconstituted, bringing HAB alongside SAB and his staff who cheerfully worked on while the demolition and reconstruction was carried out all round them. With the movement of TAB from Imperial Court to Kennings Way the way was opened to move the department and branches which had been arranged should be transferred from Ruxley Towers to Imperial Court.

Bearing in mind the target date of the 1st of December, work had been started to convert the old buyers' wing to provide offices for the general manager and senior members of the management and I'm glad to say that the weekend of the 29th November, they and their immediate staff had moved into their new quarters.

HCS and OCS followed together with the chief accountant staff, HQ accounts from a statistical branch. Christmas caused a temporary halt but soon afterwards the HCS supplies moved to London, insurance branch followed, leaving at Ruxley only investigation branch, which would shortly join the Kennington family, when the big move will have been completed.

Amesbury warehouse 1954

Amesbury warehouse was always a hub of activity. A lorry carrying 400 cases of baked beans backed up to the offloading bank at Amesbury warehouse; 15 minutes later the lorry was empty, and the baked beans, 9600 tins altogether, had been neatly stacked in the bulk section of the warehouse. Mr RD MacBurnie tells us what it takes to be part of the Amesbury warehouse: Four men and an electrically powered forklift truck had accomplished the task, quickly, quietly, with the minimum of physical effort.

They showed the benefits of mechanical handling and the reduced strain on the heavy lifting of the warehouse staff. He was guided round the warehouse by Mr RW Hoit, headquarters inspector of HCS warehouses, who'd implemented the use of mechanical handling devices. The job of moving the baked beans would have taken up to 3 hours to complete before the electric forklifts were brought in and every single case would have had to have been individually handled 2 or 3 times to move it into position.

Initially the mechanical handling equipment was introduced to the Stafford Warehouse which opened in 1952; its layout was planned specifically to allow the maximum use of power operated equipment for the moving and stacking of stores. The new system was so successful that within a year the company had decided to mechanise the remaining HCS warehouses at Amesbury, Darlington, and Peterborough. John Simpson on the warehouse floor supervised the arrival of all stores and checked off everything as it came in. As this sort of assistance on the warehouse floor was new to everybody its amazed gliding at A5 mph silently carrying tons of goods where they could be stacked with precision which would have previously taken many men hours to do. Not only did they have the ride on version of electric forklift they also had a pedestrianised one and the noise they made reminded them of the milk cart which delivered every morning. The first type could lift 3000 lbs to a height of 9 feet while the second machine, which was a little more manoeuvrable and good for confined spaces, lifted one to a height of 10ft 10″.

In Amesbury they also had to power operated pallet trucks which lifted 2 tonne loads are few inches from the ground and move it from A to B they also had the manually operated pallet trucks which work on the same system as the big hydraulics Jack's found in the garage is. The manager of Amesbury warehouse at the time was Mr AJ Everett, he had worked at the warehouse since 1948 and used to run his own grocery business in Southend; he took him on a quick tour of inspection. He explained how orders from more than 300 NAAFI establishments in the South West of England and South Wales were made up and moved onto pallets then dispatched by a waiting delivery truck. There were 15 transport vehicles allocated to this warehouse which meant that 2000 tons of a wide variety of stores were handled through the warehouse every month; there was over 45,000 square feet of storage space available and then up to 1400 cases of eggs went in and out of the warehouse weekly. A single consignment could enter and leave the warehouse within 48 hours of arrival.

One of the key areas of the warehouse was in a calm and quiet atmosphere of the offices upstairs, the real backroom boys and girls. It was a large well-lit office where the chief clerk Mr N Thurber who had been with the company 26 years, he managed staff of clerks, typists, invoice machine operators and telephonists. They dealt with a frightening flood of invoices, indents, receipts, ledgers, files and of course HQ instructions and correspondence. All indents from the establishment served by Amesbury were received here, some of them were invoiced and sent out to the manufacturers concerned for direct delivery to the establishments. The reminder was transferred to specially numbered and coloured invoices and issued in duplicates of six to go to the section of the warehouse supplying the stores required.

In consideration that the new equipment had arrived at the warehouse it was received and the staff were full of enthusiasm, the machines had taken the heavy work out of warehousing and it eased the labour issue by making the job more attractive.

We will remember them 1954

On the 7th of November 1954 at the Armistice commemoration service at the Imperial Court, Mr WF Beale OBE, chairman of the board of management, president of the OCA honoured the dead. He told relatives and representatives of the OCA that the memorial at Imperial Court was a constant reminder to all who passed it of their colleagues in NAAFI and their comrades in the NCS and EFI who gave their lives in the great conflict.

On this occasion he urged people that during the 2 minutes' silence, let us think of those who we went out with, but did not return. Let us remember their generosity, their kindness, and their comradeship. Earlier in the week on the 3rd of November the representatives of the OCA headed by Mr TE Pegg OBE, the chairman of the general committee, attended a short service at the Field of Remembrance, Westminster.

1955

NAAFI joint services HQ München Gladbach February 1955

On Monday the 28th of February the new NAAFI HQ was opened at München Gladbach. But some 160 miles away from this new military town, the previous official home for NAAFI controller Western Europe would close at Bad Salzuflen. For 10 years this had been the home of the headquarters in Germany. Hundreds of staff had worked at the HQ offices since it was first opened back in 1946. All the buildings were handed back to the town to be redeveloped. After the initial move, some time later the administration, transport, works and buildings, the offices of the senior R&WS, the WVS administrator and public relations made their move also. By midsummer a new office building and hostel at Waldniel was completed. More than 14 employees uprooted their whole family to make the move from an idyllic traditional German setting to the brand new sprawling concrete purpose-built barracks.

Both British and German staff would find things quite different in their new home. The bleak German-Dutch border country had replaced the rich woodland countryside and idyllic setting. But nevertheless, the usual amenities were available at the new site. Cinemas were nearby and there was a small Imperial club at Waldniel warehouse. The joint service headquarters had shops and education centres with ample sports facilities. The first week of their occupation, NAAFI staff began to make themselves at home. This seamless changeover all happened in one weekend, as usual the whole NAAFI family pulled together.

NAAFI Tea 1955

It is safe to say that a cup of NAAFI tea historically has always kept the armed forces on its feet. But the question is where does it come from? It's quite obvious really: the NAAFI girls make it! Not as in put the tea in the pot and brew it, but actually make the tea to put in the pot!

In spring of 1955 a new piece of equipment arrived, this was an automatic tea packer. For the girls at the NAAFI tea factory at Kennings Way, the girls operate the only NAAFI tea factory in the world and their job is to package and carton the tea. The factory where they work where most of them had spent many years of their career they described as being brightly lit and having a pleasantly full and rich aroma of the teas of the world. The tea came from many of the famous plantations around the world, from the sunlit slopes of India and Ceylon.

In the packing factory it was a real family affair with one of the senior ladies being Ada Norris with her sister Rose also working at Kennings Way where their mother had worked before ill health and their sister Josephine until she was married. The ladies had a uniform which had been specially designed for them; it was a neat blue and beige uniform, the beige overall with trimmed with a blue collar and cuffs and the pockets were also trimmed in blue with blue buttons, on their epaulettes in blue had a white embroidered NAAFI Crest with the King's Crown, meaning that they stood out from the rest.

The job itself was highly skilled, which demanded dexterity of the hands plus a quick mind. Even though Miss Norris liked the aroma of tea she admitted that she rarely drank it, but another member of staff, Vera Cole, 2nd in command amongst the girls, loved it. Vera estimated that she drank at least 10 cups a day, three with breakfast, one at 1100hrs, two with lunch and 4 spread over the evening. Miss Cole oversaw the automatic tea packer, which was capable of turning out hundreds of quarter pound packets. It was a job that meant you had to be continuously alerted all day because an unnecessary stoppage of the machine would result

in an immediate drop of production. The blended teas and wrapping paper were fed into one section of the machine and the finished product came out on a shoot at the other end packed and labelled and ready for dispatch to the establishments and shops all over the world. The staff were so good at their jobs it meant that any fault could be detected before the machine went horribly wrong just by the sound of it.

Other girls in the factory were all trained to work at the tea weighing and packing machines. Amongst them were Miss Mabel Holme and Miss Florence Dunn who had both worked for the company for many years. Mr Banks at the time was the NAAFI tea buyer who appreciated the work that all the ladies did saying they do a skilled job requiring a fair amount of training.

NAAFI revolutionary tea machine 1955

NAAFI special catering advisor Mr EE Warner MVO, during the early months into 1955, had helped NAAFI take the first strides towards the realms of tea making, in 34 years of the company as the dispenser of the famous tea to the British armed forces. They have now found a way of dispensing up to 600 cups per hour from one machine. They heard about the machine many months before while it was in the blueprint stages. They described it as a tea brewing apparatus which, by the simple pressure of a cup to a lever, would instantly fill the cup with hot and really fresh tea. It quoted that the first cup would be as hot as the last and this is what sold it to the company.

The makers of the machine had put some heavy claims about their brand-new revolutionary equipment. Mr Warner had been in the catering business for 35 years and had already heard many claims of machines which did not measure up. They examined the prototype and then it was agreed that NAAFI should be the first organisation in the world to test this new device under ordinary conditions. He decided that such tests would be as thorough and exhaustive as anyone in the tea trade could possibly make them. They tried it out for several weeks, day in day out, at the large staff canteen in the London headquarters. There they could see the problems were very much the same as any other service canteen – how to provide a quick service of tea to hundreds of customers in a strictly limited period. At the same time how to ensure that, despite the rush of service, the quality of each cup remains high and constant from the 1st to the last.

And there was the shock: it worked, all of the customers lined up, each took a cup, pressed it against the lever, and hot tea gushed into the cup. In a few seconds the customer moved on and the next took their place. The makers claimed that the machine could serve 10 cups a minute, under test conditions they reached a total of 12 cups a minute of an excellent standard quality, with no falling off in freshness, strength or heat. This was true when the service was at its peak or at other times of the day, when the demand fell off and only an occasional cup was called for. They were astonished at the performance of the experts of the London Tea Bureau, an independent organisation concerned with the principles of high-quality tea making. After thorough tests, the Bureau reported, "we confirm that the machine will make and serve 225 cups of good tea without replenishment. We also confirm your claim that machine brews a fresh cup of tea every time one is drawn off and the brewing principles incorporated are fully in accordance with the recognised rules of good tea making."

Another decision had to be made on how it would work on a roll-out across the clubs. How did this machine actually work – as you push your cup against the trigger hot tea pours down one shoot and a premeasured quantity of milk down the other from a separate reservoir. Both milk and tea reached the cup at the same time. At the top of the machine there is a rotating basket containing 8 segments into which carefully measured quantities of dry tea are placed. As each cup is drawn off, the basket rotates 1 notch so that the quantity of fresh, dry tea is brought into use with each cup. In fact, while one cup was drawn off, a further cup is made. Every cup, therefore, is actually a freshly made cup; this remained true whether it was the first or the last of the entire brew. After 225 cups had been filled a warning bell would ring and staff must then change the baskets of infused tea leaves; while the 225 cups have been served the staff were able to get on with their jobs. And when she hears the bell, she makes the necessary changes – this would take about 2 minutes and the machine would be ready to get on to the next 225 customers.

The machine itself was very well designed and it even took into consideration the fact that there was a possibility the parts could be tainted or discoloured by the tea; this was not so as various parts were made out of copper, nickel alloy or stainless steel. The electric tea machine maintained a constant temperature in the tea reservoir of 165 to 170 degrees Fahrenheit so that was no possibility of lukewarm tea.

The company were extremely proud of this brand-new machine 'BRUIN Tea Brewer', the product of the London firm Peerless and Ericsson Limited.

HRH Princess Alexandra opens the new Salisbury club 1955

On the opening of the new NAAFI club at Salisbury by HRH Princess Alexandra on the 29th of October 1955 provided a gala day for the ancient city and marked the climax of NAAFI's post-war building programme, this being the 12th club in the centres throughout the United Kingdom traditionally associated with service life. Inside the club HRH was greeted with autumn colours and the beauty of the club's décor, with the traditional atmosphere of the tension of the opening of a club. A guard of honour was provided by the first battalion the Wiltshire regiment, as the Princess entered the club, where she was greeted by NAAFI officials. While the Princess inspected the club, guests including a number of servicemen and women from the NAAFIs in the district, took their places in the ballroom ready for the opening ceremony.

The mayor of Salisbury gave a speech and spoke of the club as a legacy from the man who fought in the last war and to the servicemen of today and future generations, and it was NAAFI wartime surplus that had made the post-war club building programme possible.

Of the welcome that Salisbury had given she went on to give her speech.

> *"I think it would only be honest to confess that, until today, I knew very little indeed about the inside of a NAAFI. I'm sure that my brother could easily supply this lack of knowledge and would be in a far better position than I am to judge all of the rights and wrongs of this sort of building. But the brief tour which I have made this afternoon has shown me how much thought has been given to this, the most recent of many such buildings lately erected by NAAFI in various parts of the country. I cannot help thinking that the care with which the planning has been carried out will be much appreciated by all those who, in future days, will be using this club.*
>
> *"It was, I am sure, a very daunting experiment to introduce into a city so remarkable for its charm, for the outstanding beauty of its cathedral, a brand new building designed for a purely utilitarian purpose. I can only offer my congratulations to the architects for that act and dignity with which they have solved what must have been a formidable problem, in designing something essentially for practical use, yet a building that in no way disturbs the beauty of its surroundings. May I also at this point congratulate all who have been in anyway concerned with the layout and general equipment of the club.*
>
> *"Salisbury House, for many years now, being an important centre for those serving with the armed forces, in the West country, it was accordingly essential that a new and up to date NAAFI should be available. I would like, therefore, to give my best wishes to all who will be making use of this building in future. I now have very much pleasure in declaring open the new NAAFI club at Salisbury."*

Televisions for the Ark Royal May 1955

The television system installed aboard the aircraft carrier HMS Ark Royal to relay entertainment films to the ship's company of over 2000, beamed live programmes through 20 TV sets sited in the wardrooms, dining halls and on individual mess decks. The deputy electrical officer on board HMS Ark Royal had the idea of using closed circuit television systems to relay film shows to the whole of the ship's company. Despite the vast size of the carrier, once the ship's aircraft and crews were aboard, space below decks was so restricted that film shows could not be given to more than 150 men at one time.

The Lt Commander May had passed this idea from the ship's Capt DRE Campbell DSC RN, with the promise of the financial backing from the ship's welfare fund and grants from other sources, an approach was made to a number of the leading television and radio manufacturers. With a few setbacks, the search went on and eventually they discovered a firm specialising in the production of commercial radio and television programmes had developed a similar closed circuit television system on a small scale; this was for the purpose of demonstrating their own advertising films. This was the sort of thing that they were looking for, arrangements were made for the supply of the necessary equipment.

The installation of the new television system had been fitted by the ship's staff in May 1955 and the first BBC television programme was shown to the ship's company over the system on September the 12th that year. The work of installing the equipment was largely a responsibility of Lieutenant FC Regan, one of the ship's electrical officers, who headed a team of technicians.

A small compartment 7 decks down that was originally used as a computer room and was full of gunnery equipment, became the combined control room and studio. The television camera, 16mm projector, control panel and other equipment was ingeniously fitted in an around the bulky computer apparatus. BBC television shows and telly cinema shows were shown to the ship's company with great success. All this had been achieved without touching a penny of the public funds. The initial cost came to £3000 and this was met from the ship's welfare fund, helps by grants from Messrs Lloyds, the naval central fund, the Nuffield Trust, the Devonport fund, and the Wardroom mess.

1956

The Grand Tour of the Middle East 1956: 'Diary of an innocent abroad so this is the Middle East'. By Claude F Luke 1956, chief public relations officer

The last lap home. We are flying from Cyprus to London, now but a few hundred feet above the Alps and from the windows of the Viscount Aircraft I can see the sunlit snow-clad peaks thrusting above the white clouds, like icebergs in a sea of cotton wool.

Two hours later darkness had descended and so have we, coming down through black cloud and lashing rain to the glistening tarmac of London airport. Clear customs, then wait

40 minutes for a car that does not arrive. In the end I climb aboard the airport bus to Waterloo, paying the five-shilling fare with ill grace. Please "incidentals" provide an unnecessary irritation to the air traveller: 5 Bob airport charge, 5 Bob for crawling bus ride. . . A small fortune if your baggage is a few pounds overweight. There used to be a saying which still has a point: "if you've time to spare, go by air." To this I would add: "take more than your fare when you go by air."

Still, it would be churlish to grumble. They have carried me safely and in fair comfort from London to Rome, to Malta, to Tripoli, to Benghazi, Cairo, to Cyprus, to Athens and back to London town, 8000 miles across the sunny lands encircling the Mediterranean without a single hitch and if flying is a bore, at least it gets to the point with speed and precision.

If you leave your desk for a day, you are obviously playing golf; if you leave it for a gruelling week's duty tour, clearly, you are on a Swan; and if you leave it for a month, then you are known to be swanning in the grand manner and the accountants start biting their nails in nervous anticipation of your 43s (expenses claim).

Let's go back to the start of Greenhorns Odyssey. London airport at 0100hrs. With an hour to climb into the air! Even the birds have been asleep for hours. Sleep! Not a wink for most of us from the moment we took off to the touchdown at Rome. The Squadron Leader in the seat next to mine tosses and turns. Finally, we set up, light cigarettes, call for drinks and yarn and you on the night away.

Never realised before how dark Europe looks at night from 18,000 feet, scarcely a pinpoint of light to be seen until we passover Nice, which is at 0300hrs in the morning. Comes the dawn and all weariness is at once dispelled by the glory of a new day.

Now it's Rome and refuel, then aunty Malta, that pinhead, sandy coloured island, smaller than the Isle of Wight, yes, a vital cornerstone of the British naval power in the Mediterranean. The new supervisor, David Shepherd, is at the airport welcoming me with only a broad grin and a broad Scottish accent. Only a week or two previously I had lunched with him in London with his cousin, Herbert Gum, the brilliant editor of the Daily Sketch and a good friend. David was then recently home from Korea where he had succeeded Lt Col Clements as OC RASC EFI. He joined NAAFI in 1941 as a district manager, in Scotland and in his own words, was so green that he thought 220 was the last train out of town. But he soon got the hang of things and during the next dozen years steadily climbed the NAAFI ladder with spells of duty in Palestine, Cyprus, Greece, Berlin, Austria and Trieste, Japan and Korea and now to Malta where he succeeds WA Brown as supervisor.

David is a typical Scot with all the humour of his clan – when he returns on leave to his native Scotland, he solemnly declares that he is going home for "thrift injections"!

Malta greets me with a belated heatwave, 96 degrees, which everyone thinks delightfully cool, except for me. I decided I have much to learn about coping with Mediterranean temperatures, 3 baths today and a similar number of changes of linen provide only part of the answer. If you want a guide to Malta, I recommend the supervisors' driver, J Spiteri. In his 31 years' service he has driven for 11 successive supervisors: Mrs Burke, Butcher, Hamilton, Pegg, Hamilton on his 2nd spell, Holloway, Coulson, Anderson, Redbone, Brown, and Shepherd.

At the NAAFI headquarters at Imperial Court, I am made quickly to feel at home by the officials and staff. Here I meet an old friend, the assistant supervisor, GP Bradley, cheerful and smiling as usual and recall other meetings in his NCS days. Here too is WE Manly, the friendly and ever helpful administrative assistant in charge of accounts, who has served in various account offices since he joined NAAFI 32 years ago. The district managers are Mr V Fava, LG Camilleri, from ships and GC Bush-Harris from the Mediterranean fleet.

Mr Fava began in 1918 with the NACB and served under 15 area managers and supervisors in a variety of capacities including naval stock-taker, naval inspector, fleet canteen Superintendent, naval Superintendent and district manager; his duties have taken him to sea in various units of the fleet from motor vessels to battleships. Mr Camilleri is another old hand with 29 years' service, mainly in HM ships but with sails in Palestine in 1935, with war service in Norway, Crete, S Atlantic, Italy and Malta convoys; he mentions casually that he survived HMS Eaglein 1942. His service in Europe earned him a mention in dispatches. The Abadan crisis in 1951 carried him off to the Persian Gulf and the following year found him in Egypt. In comparison with his two colleagues, GC Bush Harris is a new boy with barely 6 years' service with NAAFI. Before joining us, he spent six and a half years at sea, first in the merchant service and later in their purser branch of the Royal Navy and before going to sea he had 14 years in the hotel business. A new boy in NAAFI but one of the earliest graduates of the trainee district managers' course. Another ex-Royal Navy, official I find is RE Hall who served 25 years in the Royal Navy as a commissioned engineer before joining NAAFI in 1947. He relieved AV Catt, then area engineer on his retirement and is now responsible for maintenance of the bakery, motor launches, ship's soda fountains and general maintenance at Imperial Court; he had assumed responsibility for the furnishing Department, his predecessor being Jay Guineas who retired in 1954 after 40 years' service.

I interrupt the work of the headquarters one morning and gather the entire office staff in the front of Imperial Court for a photograph. We go out to take up our position, the rumour flashes around the island, "NAAFI staff are coming out on strike", someone has seen them trooping out and so the rumour went around.

At a party in the Imperial club one evening, I was called upon to present testimonials to 2 long servicemen. This gives David Shepherd an idea: "let's have a picture of everyone in the room with more than 30 years' NAAFI service." He says how many, do you imagine, answer this call? 5? 10? 20? In fact, no fewer than 34 members of staff stepped forward to compose the group and the photograph is taken. At this party I meet Carmelo Costa, a notable character who has developed a skill in broadcasting that has earned him the name of the "Glendenning Of Malta". As a hobby he writes sports reports for the local press, during the siege of Malta he frequently reported the football matches while the anti-aircraft guns were engaging the stukas. Since 1945 he has turned to broadcast commentaries for the local broadcasting service. His proudest feat to date was the broadcast to the people of Malta details of a section of the route taken during the official visit of the Queen and the Duke of Edinburgh in May 1954

Next a quick look at the establishment serving the Navy, army, and RAF. They come thick and fast: HMS St Angelo, the Corradino fleet canteen, the airmen's canteen and family shop at Luqa and others at Ta Kali, St Andrews barracks and St Patrick's barracks, both army and of course the mammoth shop at St James's cavalier. They leave a kaleidoscope of bright memories, for instance the sunlit steps leading to the centuries-old Fort at Sant Angelo, shallow steps designated for the ancient Knights waited with Armour and besides the steps a ramp for their horses. The ratings bar at Corradino, nicknamed "The lobster pot", where 700 ratings gather on 'Tombola' nights, the large Royal Navy cinema nearby where Max Bygraves is due the following week and was a sold-out event. The canteen there was opened in 1897.

After meeting many more staff, I take to the roof of the shop and after a farewell glance at the fine panorama of Valletta. A great little island and grand people and if they wish to become a part of Britain, why, let them, say I, and welcome.

On the night hop from Malta to Tripoli, I join Mrs HC Stamp and her young son who left England that morning to join the newly installed supervisor, HC Stamp. It is their first flight and they are enjoying it. The boy is flying mad and I win his favour by calling him Jet Morgan after the hero of the radio space travel serial. He honours me by calling me Lemmy. A grand little chap, bright as a button and excellent company so the 90-minute flight passes quickly. Well after midnight, Charles Stamp is driving us through the darkness from the airport to Tripoli. In the headlights, a camel train loops massively by and I experienced a faint thrill. So, this is Africa at last! I find a bed at the officer's club where Ronald Walker, PRO, Middle East stays.

I lie on the bed and pant in the heat. The insect underground movement has been busy today. Clearly the word has gone forth some 12 stone of white English meat is due in Tripoli this night and every insect in Africa has come to join the feast.

Few NAAFI officials have had more varied experience than supervisor Charles Stamp. Starting as an office boy to Reginald Stagg, 32 years ago, he has served as a clerk, caterer, inspector, district manager, area supervisor, group supervisor, a Maj in the EFI. In 1930 he worked for a year at Buckingham Palace under EE Warner, reorganising the catering for the Royal household staff. It was the only time in history that the Royal palaces bought NAAFI registered number R1, R2, R3 and R4 for Buckingham Palace, Windsor Castle, Sandringham, and Balmoral respectively. During the war the Germans seemed to take a special dislike to him, throwing everything at him but the kitchen stove. In his 1st convoy from Glasgow, his ship was heavily bombarded and had to limp back to port. In Greece the following year he was in the NAAFI warehouse when it received a direct hit; several of his men were killed but he was untouched. He moved to Crete and on 4 occasions was in buildings that were bombed. He was evacuated to Alexandria on board HMS Sydney, which again was bombed and later disappeared without trace. In 1943, Charles Stamp was recalled to England and travelled in a French tramp steamer in a convoy which was continuously attacked by submarines and finished with only 45 ships out of the original fleet of 80.

D-Day plus four found him off the Normandy beaches, held up by a storm, but eventually he landed and set up his HQ at Bayeux, which was where I first met him, cheerful, rounded.

At his headquarters I met his two district managers RA Riddell and WH Loxton. Both of these have a personal story worth a page or two of the NAAFI News to themselves and they will be told in future issues. Meanwhile I quote a little gem from each. When RA Riddell was operating the famous canvas, Noah's Ark in the western desert, he did a roaring trade in the sale of local eggs, some 5000 a day which were great delicacies to men straight out of the line. He was amused to read in the suggestions book one day, the entry by a RAF officer: "the 11th egg was slightly underdone". During the war WH Loxton was torpedoed and spent several days in an open boat, eventually he was picked up and taken to Freetown. Walking in a forest outside Freetown, Loxton suddenly came upon a clearing where a number of natives were performing a ritual dance around the fire. He was a little apprehensive when one of the natives, all black and entirely nude, approached him and in a cultured English accent invited him to join the gathering and even dusted a log for him to sit upon!

I tourd the headquarters, meeting the chief clerk P Michaelides, the warehouse manager, FC Yelden, who serves 14 establishments with a staff of 8 Italians and 18 Libyans and in the hot weather disposes of 2000 cases of mineral waters a week, 84 bottles to a case.

NAAFI continues to employ people who have so many different nationalities into happy working families and above all of the friendliness and hospitality of Charles Stamp, his wife and young Jet Morgan and all other officials and their wives throughout my stay.

Next comes a 3-hour flight across the Gulf of Sidra to Benina airfield at Benghazi, with Miss Allison and Ronald Walker as travelling companions. At Benina the heat hits us like a blast furnace but nobody seems to notice except for me. The supervisor and his wife most kindly put me up at their delightful flat overlooking the centre of town. I take a look at Benghazi and quickly decide that you can have this too, a war battered town that has still not pulled itself together. Reconstruction seems painfully slow and depressing, lifeless air hangs over the place, which our staff must find hard. But not all of them do.

At the headquarter offices I do the rounds meeting the supervisor's secretary, Miss Betty Hayward, who is looking forward to going home in a few weeks' time. At first, she found Benghazi interesting, but the novelty soon wore off, she tells me. You tend to lose energy and get irritated over things which normally would not worry you at all. But she would not have missed the experience, she insists. That seemed to be the general attitude of another shortly homeward bound member of staff. Miss Barlow, the accounts clerk, has travelled extensively for NAAFI in Europe and the Middle East and is now watching her opportunity for a Far East posting. A last look in at Benghazi canteens, at Lumsden barracks and into the air once again on another 3-hour flight to Cairo, following the historic coastal road where Rommel and Montgomery fought it out, amongst other conflicts.

I arrive at Cairo airport as the sun sets which was an unforgettable sight. The darkness seems to rush at you across the desert, there is no twilight in the lands of extremes. Ronald Walker, who has flown on ahead, is there to meet me; though I'm old enough to be his father, he treats me with care on this my first and only night in this city. Tonight we break training and go for drinks then end up having dinner at a roof garden restaurant with an open air cinema show thrown in and an hour at the local nightclub, the cabaret, which is so respectful that two of the acts have already been seen on the BBC television. The next morning a couple of hours of sightseeing which takes me to the pyramids and the native bazaars and Tutankhamun's treasures, then by car along the desert road to Fayid on the canal zone.

As I reached the canal zone a warm greeting from Frank Anniss, the controller and his wife, 2 good friends from my first days with NAAFI when assistant Ann Marjorie was secretary to the RAF members. Packing up their belongings to move to Cyprus. Indeed, the entire zone has the atmosphere of moving day, several of the big camps are already closed and the desert sands had started to obliterate the last traces of their occupation. The NAAFI warehouses are steadily emptying, an auction sale of surplus equipment and transport are the order of the day.

I do the rounds of offices and messes, meeting scores of men and women whom I and NAAFI News readers, have known through Ronald Walker's articles and photographs. Several of them tell me an odd thing, 3 or 4 years under the Egyptian sun slows down one's reflexes as the heat affects everybody.

Several of the Egyptian villages are still out of bounds and though I see no signs of actual hostility, I would not care to wander through them at night. To the new, the squalor and insanitary conditions of the native way of life and I am not surprised to be told that if an Englishman happens to fall into the sweet water canal he has to be rushed to hospital and undergo about 14 inoculations immediately.

Sweetwater canal! Was ever a muddy ditch more ironically named? Bloated animal corpses and other unpleasant refuse float on the murky surface of this, the main water supply for the natives' washing and drinking.

To and fro along the treaty road we go, visiting staff and establishments and at the end of it my old friend Warwick Broomfield holds the supervisor position. This is his first overseas appointment since he joined the company in 1940; he has come a long way since those days as district manager, Winchester assistant area supervisor southern area, group supervisor, Wiltshire and then HQ supervisor of clubs until 1944 when he was transferred to the NCS as headquarters supervisor and with the formation of the NCS command, became the first command supervisor, Portsmouth command. But not for long, at 3 weeks' notice he was sent out to Egypt to supervise the evacuation of the Canal Zone. He says I enjoyed all my jobs with NAAFI, but this Egypt assignment has been the most interesting of them all. I inherited a first-class team and although the run down has meant hard work and innumerable problems, we have managed to pull together and mastered the job.

He was still in the thick of the run down. When he arrived in November 1954 there was some 90,000 troops in the zone. A year later they were down to 30,000 and the last of them will have left Egyptian soil by June 1956. Already staff had been reduced from 3700 to 2100.

I am delighted to shake the hand of my old acquaintance, the most loyal Osman, the man who was picked to come to London to represent Egyptian staff at the NAAFI exhibit in the Ideal Home exhibition some years ago, the man who stayed at his post throughout difficult times in the Canal Zone and the man with the happiest smile in all of Egypt.

I now take my final trip a short flight to my final touchdown, Nicosia, in the troubled island of Cyprus. Things are warming up in Cyprus. It is still far from their island of terror as pictured in the home press, but incidents increase in frequency and violence. On the 1st evening we take a drink at the exquisitely scented Jasmine Walk of the hotel. Suddenly shots are heard nearby. Everyone behaves with studied English charm, glasses are raised and conversations continue without the faintest pause. Only the press boys, hard at it in the bar, show the slightest concern; they are hopping mad because of the difficulty of covering the Cyprus story. It's this way, one explains, you stick around in Nicosia and a bomb goes off in Famagusta, you just dash off to Famagusta and there is a bombing in Limassol. You catch up with Limassol only to hear that soldier has been shot in Nicosia. You were never in the right place at the right time; you need a helicopter for this job.

After visiting all of the establishments it was now time to take a last look around this lovely island, a beautiful Eden but marked with the scars of war on every village wall. I get a brief chat with RC Lamb, brother of the controller, works and buildings, along with the manager of the shop in Nicosia. The English style Garrison club in Nicosia, which claims to be the coolest spot in town, the day before my plane leaves for London Lori informs me that within a day or 2 there will be an earthquake. All the conditions, and usual high temperatures point to a repetition of the sort of weather that accompanied a severe quake on the island 2 years previously. They advised me that this could be today or tomorrow. The next morning, not without relief, I climb into the Viscount and we take off. A few hours later a strong earthquake shakes the island and drives the people from their homes.

The verdict of my trip: Malta delightful for work or play, grand for holiday, not so good for 3-year tour of duty. Canal zone, questionable. Cyprus, when things quieten down the most attractive posting in the Middle East and yes, this would be a trip I would like to do all over again.

Canteen revolution experiments successful 1956

At the later end of 1955 there was brought about revolutionary changes in the canteen service. Slowly but surely the results of countless experiments and careful research by NAAFI brought into use. In the early months of 1956, the previous year's challenges became standard routine in many clubs. A a good example of this was the "called order" service. The modern conception of canteen catering enabled the customer to choose the ingredients of his meal and watch it cooked on the latest type of equipment that had been installed in full view behind the counter. A special infrared Ray cooker grill cooked a steak in 90 seconds, a hot plate of fried eggs in a matter of seconds, chips were ready in a deep fat fryer.

The equipment varied according to the requirements of the individual canteens and clubs and could include a salamander grill, a Bain Marie, boiling plate, a hot cupboard, a domestic type cooker and a sunglow counter unit for temporary hot holding. Through this equipment passed many types of cooked dishes. And 6 months before the launch the units had been installed up and down the country as part of a large scale experiment to test the efficiency of different types of equipment and this was also to gauge the reaction of the customer with this new style of catering. The NAAFI experts claimed as a result of an analysis of Supper sales in over 2000 canteens, that elaborate meals cooked in the kitchen were not required by the modern servicemen. They did require quickly prepared snacks and grills which were the choice of the time, with eggs and chips topping the popularity poll.

Careful records were kept at all the canteens with this new equipment and the called to order units with detailed reports flowing into the headquarters, confirmed the success of the new service. The best example of this came from the restaurant and welfare Superintendent at Kinmel Park camp, who reported: "I consider the called to order service is a great asset to the canteen. The supper dishes look attractive and are served really hot. The customer can see that the order is being dealt with as quickly as possible. The reaction of the customer is very favourable. They all agree that this type of service is a great improvement. The general remarks were, that it was a better tasting meal and looked more appetising and it was the types of meal they wanted."

Over 50 units had been installed by early 1956 and others were in the process of being installed, the trials became a success and the scheme was extended to take in all suitable canteens. This also sat alongside the brand-new Brun tea machines that had been rolled out earlier in 1955. So now the service personnel could get hot food and a hot cup of tea in a fraction of the time that they used to.

The experiments had also not been confined to the installation of new types of equipment. There had been tests of a different kind in the past, the use of NAAFI family shops was restricted, with certain exceptions, the service families and a separate small counter in the NAAFI canteen supplied the sailor, soldier or airmen with his day-to-day personal requirements. The lack of space in the canteen net bars restricted the range of goods that could be offered, and this meant that the sales were being lost as service was not always available.

It was suggested that the experiment in the family shops in some 50 Royal Navy stations, army barracks and RAF stations should be made available to all servicemen and servicewomen – this would provide a far wider range of goods for the service personnel and this would enable the canteen to concentrate on daily purchases such as cigarettes and chocolates. This idea had the secondary object of reducing queues in the canteens by simplifying the service as it was. This new arrangement had found favour, with the wives or parents of servicemen going home on weekend leave for many in the instance the husband or son bringing a parcel of groceries with him from the NAAFI shop! The experiment had been highly successful and this which was another innovation NAAFI have had pioneered.

A life of adventure 1956

When he was in school in Clapham in the early 1900s, young Brian Hislop dreamed of a life of adventure and travel. He could now look back on a life of which more than half has been overseas in 18 or 19 countries. Almost straight from school he joined the Roughriders, the City of London Yeomanry, and after training with the 3rd King's Own Hussars, one of Britain's crack cavalry regiments, he saw active service as a cavalry in Egypt, Palestine, Syria and Greece during the First World War.

He fought alongside the 3rd Australian Light Horse Brigade during the campaign against the Turks in Egypt and rode during the time of his campaign, from Suez to Damascus. He saw what the last old-time cavalry charge was probably when the Warwick and Worcestershire Yeomanry rode into the face of some 13 Turkish guns. Though he came through the campaign with nothing more serious than a slight facial wound from shrapnel, he had a high opinion of the Turkish men.

At the end of the war he settled into the city for a few years but the ambition of his youth to see the Far East and India in particular took him to Burma with the firm of the Far Eastern merchants in 1926. Although based in Rangoon, he travelled upcountry as far as Namtu in the northern Shan states and made occasional business trips to Calcutta. It was only in 1939 that Mr Hislop joined NAAFI as an assistant to the manager of the messing store at Fulwood barracks, in Preston and a couple of years later found him in uniform of the RASC EFI bound for Egypt. Egypt was followed by Cyprus and Sudan and amongst other places he made his way to Greece. After a brief spell as a civilian in the United Kingdom he donned the uniform once again in October 1950, and he joined a small party of EFI men in Korea. He returned home in 1952 but left again the following year for Kenya, where he became the district manager of the Mau-mau operational area of the 70th and 39th brigades. In 1956 he was seen briefly at Imperial Court before he set out once more on his travels. At the age of 58 he is headed for Christmas Island where there will be a change of NAAFI services to Operation Grapple.

Korean kaleidoscope written by Frank Edmunds 1956

More than 6 years have passed since the aggression by North Korea shocked the free world. I recall that I was journeying from Hamburg to Milan when I first heard the news, little did I know then that one day I would be treating the country which was to figure so much in the headlines in the months ahead. However, fate and the wheel of time caught up with me and after 2 very happy and interesting years in Japan I am now with the British Commonwealth contingent in Korea.

Through an Azure blue sky, I went across Japan one early morning in June. My thoughts were a mixture of all I was leaving behind and of what to expect on arrival in Korea. Both countries were in the midst of the monsoon season and it appeared symbolic that on the day of departure from Japan the weather was near perfect but began to deteriorate as soon as the plane arrived over the East Coast of Korea. By the time Seoul was reached we had run into a heavy rainstorm.

A bumpy landing was my introduction to Korea, and I was greeted by a sea of mud and driving rain which completely drenched me in the short walk from the aircraft to a reception hut. Before my departure from Japan I had been briefed by old timers on the conditions in

Korea and mentally I was prepared for the very worst. The road from the airport to Inchon and Edinburgh camp, the headquarters of the advance base of the Commonwealth contingent in Korea was scenic. Life behind barbed wire is an experienced common to many NAAFI staff in various parts of the world. However, this place had nothing to offer so being behind the wire was not, after all, too depressing. Some really lovely countryside exists.

Recently I had occasion to visit the NAAFI battalion club operating for troops in the forward area, just 2 miles from the 38th parallel and 5 miles from the North Koreans. The journey took me through Seoul and a large modern city built mainly by the Japanese during their period of occupation from 1910 until their defeat in the Pacific war. On leaving via the northern suburbs the countryside acquires a grandeur that I only previously associated with parts of Scotland. I certainly never visualised that Korea could be so beautiful. Gloucestershire Valley, scenes of one of the Korean war's most glorious actions, was breathtakingly beautiful in the summer sunshine and was looking fresh and green after the recent rains. The club in the battalion area is managed by Sgt E Hughes and is assisted by Cpl Jay Wilson and Mr D Fox who had recently arrived from Japan. Facilities exist for privates, Pier Tavern and a corporal's bar apart from the usual restaurant and WVS recreation room, the latter being cheerfully supervised by Miss Joy Sibbald and Elizabeth Woolmington.

Establishments in Inchon area have similar amenities at present; there are 2 clubs operating, the Rose and Crown in Edinburgh camp and a club in the leave centre on the coast about 4 miles from the town centre. The manager of the Rose and Crown, Sgt F Butler ably assisted by Sgt E Reddick and Miss Christine Cooper, add enterprising charm in running the WVS

room which, to the chaps in the camp, is a haven during their leisure hours. The club and leave centre is managed by Sgt F Kelly and Corporal B Hall. The leave centre was formally a Japanese rest and cultural centre and boasts a lagoon admirably suited for bathing or boating. The whole area is enveloped in parkland of trees of a great variety. The cricket pitch is a beautiful setting, usually associated with a village cricket green and here on many occasions Capt RW Stokes I/C RASC EFI, may be seen lending his skill to the game which is played wherever an English community is established abroad.

At the leave centre club Miss Joan Mann is kept very busy in the WVS recreation room organising competitions, tournaments, and outings, all of which assist in no small measure in keeping the morale of the troops.

OCA 1956 by T E Pegg

One is to associate the phrase 'old comrades' with a collection of grey haired, grey bearded, gnarled old men and women, who to say the least are rapidly getting well past the prime of life.

The intention of the contribution is to endeavour to conceive readers that with the possible exception of the writer, not only is the above description quite erroneous but that our Association is, in fact, a group of men and women who are not only very much alive, but anxious and keen to give the practical evidence of their determination to live up to the principles and upon which The OCA was founded.

It is fitting that some comments should be made on the 9th AGM was held on the 21st of April 1956. Strange as it may appear, the weather was beautiful and invited a visit to the coast rather than a journey to Kennington and an afternoon at Imperial Court.

At the end of the year the membership totalled 2375, during the year 285 new members were enrolled, principally from the RASC EFI, army emergency reserve. Branch and headquarters social activities continued, 27 functions being held in 1955. These including the 9th annual reunion and also the dinner party both held at Imperial Court, Kennington. Everyone will be pleased to learn that the Reverend H Wallis Bird, vicar of St Mark's church Kennington, had become the honorary chaplain of the Association.

The Remembrance Day ceremony on Sunday the 6th of November 1955 was held at Saint Anne's Roman Catholic Church, Kennington. The field of Remembrance at Westminster was well attended by NAAFI and crosses were placed.

The association's first and foremost work is to help those members who are in need and this was continued in 1955 with the result that since the inception of the OCA 366 cases had received financial assistance. Many of our members have volunteered to visit several needy cases, by doing so they have been brought face to face with circumstances which would never have been believed existed but for the personal contact. The considerable number of letters received from sick and distressed members, from visiting the members themselves, are abundant. Evidence of the value of these in providing a cheery word, encouragement, and hope, so essential to the patient and the real pleasure experienced by visiting members.

The OCA ties, blazer badges, scarfs and Christmas cards were still in steady demand, clear evidence of the continued interest of members. The 3rd annual dinner party was held at Imperial Court, Kennington, on Saturday the 21st of April. More than 100 members and their guests were present. Some of the main branches that were still very much active were: London, Portsmouth, West of England, NW England, North East England, West Midlands, and Glasgow and the West of Scotland.

They Blew up De Lesseps, S Vasey NCS District Manager (interviewed R.D. McBurnie in 1956)

When Nasser seized the Suez Canal and Great Britain responded by calling up reservists and augmenting Mediterranean fleet, home fleet and flown out to Malta to "standby" for further action.

After a few weeks of comparative inactivity, I learned that the Mediterranean fleet was getting ready to move off on exercise and made arrangements to travel aboard HMS Ranpura, a fleet repair ship. We sailed up the Mediterranean on our way to Port Said and the only incident on the journey was our encounter with the American fleet which resulted in exchange of verbal broadsides only.

We arrived off Port Said on the 5th of November and to my annoyance HMS Ranpura dropped anchor some 8 miles out and there I was stuck for 4 days, with a grandstand view of our ships and aircraft going in but quite unable to get myself ashore. The annoying part about this was the fact that back in Malta I had made a small bet with Maj Rodney of the RASC EFI detachment, that I would be in Port Said before him. Finally, I got myself transferred to HMS Forth, the HQ ship of the naval officer I/C Port Said, which was birthed in the inner Harbour alongside the statue of Ferdinand de Lesseps, the man who built the Suez Canal. One of my first visitors was Maj Rodney, who came aboard to claim his winnings and incidentally, to scrounge a bath, a haircut, and a change of underclothes.

In the next 10 days the most important task was to distribute canteen stores equally between the 30 British ships operating in Port Said area. Twelve of the naval vessels had NCS canteens aboard, 3 of them had quite large stocks, the others were extremely stocked short of canteen supplies. There was, as you can imagine, a great demand for beer from the cruise and to satisfy it I had to persuade ships' Captains to let me move beer from well stocked canteens to less fortunate ships. Although it was all our beer and technically did not belong to any one ship, it was not particularly easy to convince the responsible officers that some of "their beer" should be handed over to another ship! Fortunately, good reason prevailed and with the help of canteen managers I was able to draw up a comprehensive list of all of the stores available in the Port Said ships and then arrange a fair allocation. All this extra fetching and carrying of stores was made necessary by the non-arrival of the Navy stores ship, which had been delayed with engine trouble at Gibraltar. It was the 18th of November before the stores ship VSIS Fort Duquesne, moved into Port Said, with 200 tonnes of NAAFI stores aboard, as well as general supplies for the fleet.

I moved my quarters from the Fourth to Fort Duquesne, so that I could take over the stores and control issues with other ships. During this I kept in close touch with Maj Head, OC RASC EFI detachment, whose bulk issue store had been established in a Harbour warehouse, and we were able to help each other in many ways. Conditions ashore were pretty grim, for electricity, water and sewage works were put out of action in the early stages and the army lads were having an uncomfortable time of it. Living conditions aboard ship were luxurious in comparison and any hospitality I was able to offer was readily accepted.

When we heard the news that we were going to withdraw there was a great sense of disappointment. There wasn't a sailor or a soldier who didn't want to go on and finish the job that had been started. However, the decision had been made and gradually the perimeter occupied by the British forces closed in on the Harbour itself, while United Nations forces took over in the town. Excited, jubilant Egyptians made the nights hideous with ceaseless rattle of rifle fire and they blazed away at nothing sending curving trails of traces through the thick night sky. A few days before Christmas I learned that Fort Duquesne was due to stay behind with salvage fleet after troops and fighting ships had left. Canteen manager Spiteri, who was with me aboard, immediately volunteered to remain aboard his ship and I decided that I'd better stay too.

Naval uniforms disappeared overnight, the Ensign was lowered and replaced by the flag of the United Nations organisation. To protect us from the local population we had four dour Finnish soldiers, looking a little awkward and uncomfortable in their blue UNO helmets and American type uniforms. As the last ship of the British Navy steamed out of sight leaving us alongside in the Harbour, we had to admit a feeling of apprehension. There was a sudden outbreak of rifle and Tommy gunfire from the Harbour area, but it was only a bunch of Nasser's boys letting off steam with few defiant volleys.

We were quite near the famous de Lesseps statue and had a ringside view of the attempts of a mob to blow it up. The first two charges were too small and failed to bring the statue down. The 3rd charge was too big. The statue crashed down, but the explosion killed at least 2 of the demolition team and injured a number of the cheering mob.

My most pleasant memory was of the efforts of the gang of Egyptians to dislodge a large Union Jack, run up on a flagpole on the jetty by a party of British soldiers just before they embarked. The matelots had carefully greased the pole after running up the flag and the infuriated civilians couldn't seem to understand why their desperate attempts to shin up the pole was always ending in failure. Finally, they chopped the thing down!

I was issued with an UNO armband and thus protected, set about distributing Christmas supplies to the salvage fleet. There were about 1100 sailors and technicians to cater for, but ample supplies had come forward from Malta and every ship was able to lay on a traditional turkey and Christmas pudding meal. There was beer and enough left over to celebrate the new year. On the 4th of January, the Fort Duquesne cast off and left for Malta and I went with her. Left behind in one of the Navy vessels was a canteen manager Caruana, of HMS Striker, who had volunteered to stay. I flew back to England from Malta, arriving on the 11th of January and after reporting to headquarters took a much-appreciated spell of leave, climbed aboard yet another aeroplane and headed back to Gibraltar, where I re-joined the home fleet.

1957

The first NAAFI shop to become self-service 26th March 1957 by R.D.McBurnie

The new shop had been converted into a self-service system which was officially opened at the Royal Marine barracks in Eastney, Portsmouth on the 26th of March 1957 by Mrs EA Brown, the wife of Colonel EA Brown OBE,RM, commandant of the barracks.

There had been a lot of planning that had gone into this at HQ and they had spent a hectic weekend putting the finishing touches to the conversion of the shop and preparing for the opening ceremony. The changeover had begun 3 weeks earlier and the staff had cheerfully tackled the task of packing and pricing all the goods, a job that had to be completed before the conversion. A Sweda cash register was brought in to use and during quiet periods the cashier and her relief were given special training. A week before the opening day the specially designed self-service equipment was assembled in the shop, the normal counters being pulled forward day by day so that the full service to the customers was kept going. The final transformation took place between midday on the Saturday to the Tuesday morning, which meant only one shopping day had been lost. The shop staff, the planning, and the professionalism together with the shopfitters worked long hours to get everything ready in time.

As they were about to open there was the usual hurry and scurry as the final minutes ticked by, everything was ready on time and the opening ceremony went off smoothly before an interested audience of service wives, officers and men of the Royal Navy and Royal Marines, NAAFI officials and representatives of the BBC and the local press. The BBC representative subsequently gave a glowing description of the new shop in the BBC home service lunchtime programme "Eyewitness"'.

Introducing Mrs Brown, Mr Laynard said that self-service shops would now appear like mushrooms throughout the country. There was approximately 4000 which had opened in quick succession, it was now widely believed that in the grocery trade that self-service would be the future method of retailing. He went on to explain the Eastney barracks shop had been chosen as the first NAAFI in the United Kingdom shops to be converted because a minimum of structural alterations were required and the shop provides a typical balance of trade to the Royal Marines and the families.

As soon as Mrs Brown cut the ceremonial tape and had been taken on a tour of inspection, the cashier took her seat at the cash register and NAAFI's first self-service shop in Great Britain was open for business. The first customers moved slowly around the shop admiring all the new 3 and 4 tier fittings, none more than the eye level in height so that goods are displayed to the best advantage. Prices were printed underneath each article except pre-packaged perishable foodstuffs – these all had labels bearing the weight and the price. A small sealing machine is used to cellophane wrap such items as cheese, cold meats, bacon, fresh vegetables and so on. There was nothing but praise for the redesigned shop and its attractive colour scheme of cream ceiling and walls in pastel shades of green and blue. The refrigerated cabinet with its wide selection of frozen foods was the centre of attraction.

The changeover at Eastney had set the pattern for the painless transformation of those NAAFI shops scheduled for conversion to self-service. Work was already in progress at RAF stations Wittering and Wyton, plans were already in motion for Bassingbourn, Henlow and Cardington. Further changes marked down for conversion were establishments serving the army at Catterick, Tidworth and Bulford as well as RFA shops at Hullavington, Coningsby, Cosford and Benson.

The first Middle East service shop had been opened in Tripoli by Lady Borne, the wife of General Sir Jeffrey K borne, KBE, CB, CMG, commander in chief Middle East land forces. Even the shop in Gibraltar was scheduled for conversion in the June of 1957 and the new shop was being built in Episkopi Cyprus whose opening day was in mid-July. The only complaint that they had in the opening of the new Royal Marines shop was by a Royal Marine Sgt, a married man who said, "This is all very nice, but it makes you want to spend more money."

NAAFI woman saved an Army commander 1957

The monotonous journey from Derna to Tobruk for Miss Jessie Allison, NAAFI drapery Superintendent, for North Africa: 34 miles out of Derna Miss Allison came upon the scene of a serious car accident, a Humber staff car, heading to the Libyan army convoy, had overturned. The driver, who had somehow managed to free himself, was staggering away from the car. She dashed to the car and found a seriously injured officer inside. The officers and men of the convoy had panicked and seemed to be unable to do anything for the stricken man. Eventually Miss Allison found one who spoke English and asked for some first aid equipment. Although there was an ambulance in the convoy there was no first aid supplies, so she had to make do with what was available and her cosmetic case. With handkerchiefs, face towels, cotton wool and toilet water, she cleaned and dressed the officer's wounds. He had serious facial injuries and a smashed shoulder with broken ribs. By this time she had recognised the injured man as Brigadier Abdul Qadir Nazimi, head of the Iraq military mission a commander of the Libyan army.

"He was in great pain," Miss Allison said and, "when we moved him, he was hurting very much but once he was on the stretcher he did not murmur." Not one of the officers or men could be persuaded to ride with him in the ambulance so, sending a car back to Derna, she travelled with him, holding him in her arms to cushion the worst bumps of the desert roads. Having at last seen the brigadier safely in the hands of the doctors at the British military hospital, she set off again for Tobruk. He was operated on that night. The following morning Queen Fatima's secretary rang Miss Allison to thank her for her prompt aid and the thanks were repeated later by the British embassy and the Iraqi minister. She said, "I don't know what all the fuss was about, after all, I travel a lot, and I may have need of help myself someday."

NAAFI News summer in 1957

It was an unusual time and as Claude Luke clearly says in the editor's notes: "So speak the old and the bold and we would be wise to heed them. This is no time for depression. Rather it is an occasion for a clear assessment of the problems ahead and a cheerful determination to overcome them. Many of the problems, admittedly, cannot be clearly seen yet. Until our services reveal the details of their future pattern, until we know more precisely the nature, locations and requirements of the new forces, NAAFI present plans must be largely a matter of inspired guesswork.

One thing we are certain, that during the next 5 years the company is going to lose some 46% of its customers. In that we are officially informed, total service strength will drop down from 690,000 to 375,000. Truly a sombre prospect but not without its silver lining.

"The soldier of the new scientific army" was the statement from the War Office, "will be one of the elite. His importance will be fully recognised and rewarded. He will be offered a first-class career with first class conditions, promotion and pay."

In other words, the customers of tomorrow may be fewer in number but will almost certainly enjoy a high living standard and an increased spending power. Tomorrow's service man will undoubtedly spend more and demand more. For NAAFI, then, the present is an exciting time of challenge and opportunity. Better service, improved conditions, and the latest techniques, and ever-increasing efficiency and our determined drive to win and deserve, the last shilling's worth of potential trade from our service patrons, such must be our targets of today and tomorrow. Great strides towards the new look NAAFI have already been taken. More changes will be necessary if we are to build a streamlined, up to the minute organisation to match the scientific armies of our age."

These were the only changes; the summer edition of their favourite publication went up to a shilling, but it was well worth it.

Korea 1957

In ones and twos, the last of the NAAFI RASC EFI consignment in Korea have been arriving back in this country and within the next few weeks a gallant 7-year episode in the post-war history of RASC EFI will have ended. It was late in 1950 that Nutfield Priory stirred into action once again as a RASC EFI Depot. The Korean incident had become an international war and NAAFI staff were needed quickly for active service. There was a call for volunteers, quickly, eagerly answered, and 100 officers and men, led by Maj who became Lt Col FA Bridgett, spent Christmas 1950 in the ice, mud and the confusion of Korea. Fresh drafts followed quickly and soon the whole unit, with headquarters in Japan numbered over 200 men.

In 1951 first-hand reports of the conditions in Korea were brought back to Imperial Court by LC Wynne-Tyson, OBE, a former deputy general manager, who had flown out to see for himself. This is what he said: "Our colleagues serving in Korea have done their duty in circumstances that would daunt all those but the toughest. Most of us at home even now have not the faintest notion of the difficulties and discomfort which our EFI contingent, all volunteers, have suffered and overcome. I would stress that when we call for further volunteers to replace the first attachment, the newcomers should know from the outset they are in for no picnic. No weaklings need apply. Consider first the climate and the country imaginal and similar to the wilder parts of Scotland and corrugated landscape of hills and mountains, except for the plain around Seoul the capital. The only roads run through the foothills, rural roads often a little better than dust tracks, which were never designed to accommodate the heavy military traffic of a full-scale campaign. I saw those roads at the end of the winter when they were a little better than the ditches of glutinous mud. I stayed to see them dried into long ribbons of thick dust, which as convoys moved, billowed up in clouds.. So dark, indeed that truck drivers were ordered to keep their headlights on even in the middle of the day.

"The one railway was of little use to NAAFI, food and ammunition had to come in first and NAAFI stores would often take 3 weeks to cover an 80-mile rail journey. Consider also, the almost total lack of accommodation. At Pusan in the early days the EFI slept in the ordinary ridge tents covered with a flysheet. This was 40 degrees below freezing point. Tarpaulin covered foxholes shanties hastily knocked gather from packaging cases, similar improvised dwellings were the rule. The intense cold and biting winds of a Korean winter had to be experienced to be believed. This weather lasts from November to April. We could not understand the heavy run on for pipes until we realised that the men preferred them to cigarettes because of the psychological effect of closing their hands around a small bowl of warmth. Truck drivers used 75% antifreeze in their radiators. Fortunately, the winter clothing including the string vests and frost proof boots, gave a good standard of protection."

He went on to describe the special hazards, and paid special tribute to the tough, resourceful mobile drivers who had won the highest of praise from the units they served. On more than one occasion a NAAFI mobile had trampled into the thick of a tank battle to bring tea and cigarettes to the weary crews. Commander JC Rowlands, OBE, Commander of the British Commonwealth, Korean based, was the first of many to give official praise to the EFI. He signalled: "NAAFI have been doing a first-rate job here. Staff have remained cheerful, willing and hard working under the most trying conditions." Fifty of the first 200 volunteers stayed on for a further tour of duty, fresh volunteers came forward to maintain the strength of EFI and keep up the good work.

As the United Nations command built up its power, the Chinese and North Korean Red Armies fell slowly back, and the comparatively static nature of the campaign enabled more ambitious welfare and canteen facilities to be planned. The famous NAAFI roadhouses began under the direction of Lt Col Bridgett and completed by his successor Lt Col FG Soden, OBE, earned praise from the troops of 21 different nations. Writing of these eventful days in an earlier article of NAAFI News, Col Soden recalled an occasion when a group of typical GIs swaggered into one of the road houses in the American sector, one of them cried, and a British Tommy leant across the counter to the NAAFI server and said with a sniff, "Bloody dollars won't buy 'um NAAFI!", special praise for the successful direction of the famous road houses due to the late Capt Philip Bernie office works and buildings and his enthusiastic team. They worked under gruelling conditions, against fantastic odds, to provide the troops with something they never dreamt of getting in far off Korea, was a roadhouse, comfortably furnished and provided hot meals, hot drinks, and English beer.

Then came the long drawn out Armistice negotiations and finally the joyous day when the first of the United Nations prisoners crossed under the freedom march in the neutral zone to a tumultuous welcome from the whole of the free world. NAAFI was there too, with a canteen and a wonderful variety of good things for the men who came back. The war became an occupation and NAAFI commitment was still heavy. A leave camp in Japan, a club in Seoul, Gift shops, then the decision to take over from the Australian canteen service, then operating in Japan. The Colonel was succeeded by Lt Col DCH Clements and as the gradual run down of the United Nations and Commonwealth troops in Korea and Japan got under way, so NAAFI's responsibilities lessened. The strength of the RASC EFI unit began to drop. Korea disappeared from the front pages but for the troops still enduring life in a war shattered country, the EFI continued to provide a keen service. In November 1954 Lt Col DE Shepherd took over command and in turn he handed it over to Maj HEG Taylor. A month before we pulled out of Japan, "Tinker" Taylor resigned to re-join the American PX in Tokyo and in August 1956, Capt EA Self joined the small EFI detachment left in Korea. It has been tasked to supervise the NAAFI 7 year stay as it came to an end. So quietly, almost unheeded, NAAFI's part in the Korean War merges into the proud history of the company. For the hundreds of NAAFI staff who served out there no praise can be too high.

OCA 1957

Many changes have been made in the past year and they celebrated many successes. The AGM happened on the Saturday April 13th with the chairman being TE Pegg, OBE. He said that 19 new members had been enrolled during 1956 and at the end of the year the total membership in the United Kingdom was 2194. In the previous year 25 cases of benevolence in all had been required and the new personal accident scheme that was launched in 1955 made its 1st payment on July 25, 1956 – a member of the Association met with a fatal road accident. All the details were collated quickly, and a claim was lodged with the underwriters. As a result, funds were quickly made available for payment to his legal personal representative. In true style with the rules of its day honoured the family.

The general committee was changing and for the years 1956 to 58 would consist of the following: TE Pegg, OBE, chairman, Colonel AC Pritchard, OBE, vice chairman, other members R Baynham, WR Carr, Capt F Cooper, Lt Col JA Hallett, Maj HB Jamison, Maj Rd Lynde, G Macey, Maj JW Martin, RM Oulsnam and Mrs BR Simpson.

Air terminal number one, Harrow Rd, Paddington by RD McBurnie 1957

In a borrowed drill hall in Harrow Road, Paddington, the army ran its own air terminal, number one air trooping unit, where officers, troops and families travelling between a dozen different countries were smoothly and swiftly politely issued with documents, money, travel warrants and where necessary, uniforms or plain clothes. A spick and span NAAFI canteen provides a 0500hrs to 2359hrs service for passengers on the occasional delayed flights arriving between midnight and 0459hrs, the unit's duty cook prepared emergency cups of tea.

RD McBurnie writes after his visit: when I paid a visit to the air terminal shortly after Christmas 1957, I found the lofty Ex drill Hall quiet and almost empty. A decorated Christmas tree, a carpet on the scrubbed polished floor, several easy chairs and a child's rocking horse softened the military atmosphere of the heavily panelled Hall. Behind the long counter the duty reception officer and his staff were tidying up after dealing with a plane load of passengers from Cyprus. I soon learned that number one air trooping unit is proud of its unique role as the British army's airline "travel Bureau".

It was obvious that the peace and quiet of the main hall was a temporary situation and it was liable to be interrupted at any moment by the arrival of a coachload of travellers from one of 6 airports in the South of England. The Major explained that chartered aircraft from Hong Kong, Singapore, Cyprus, Tripoli, Cyrenaica, Malta, Gibraltar, West Africa, East Africa, Caribbean and Aden could arrive at London airport, Blackbushe, Stansted, Southend, Northolt or Lyneham at any time of the day or night. The reception staff worked in 3 shifts to cover 24 hours.

December had been the busiest month on record, over 10,000 people had passed through the air terminal; this figure also included 7000 wives, 1000 children and was one of the most hectic periods just before Christmas. All the effort was made to get the wives and families and troops in Tripoli back for the Christmas festivities. They had all been evacuated from Tripoli a month or 2 previously, Capt Duff said that now we had to get them back again. Between the 22nd and the 23rd of December 1956 they handled over 30 flights, representing more than 12,000 men, women, and children. A plane load of 60 people on average could be dealt with in just over half an hour, while compassionate cases were whisked through the administrative machinery in 2 or 3 minutes. I was told of a soldier and a Scottish regiment on a compassionate posting from the Far East, who arrived in the terminal one Sunday morning and needed transport to the far North of Scotland. He was put on a plane to Glasgow and by the time his plane landed Capt Turner had arranged with the RAF in Glasgow to fly him on to Inverness in a service aircraft. At Inverness an RAF car was waiting to take him on the last stage of his journey.

As I was chatting to Mr D Elsmore, who had been in charge of NAAFI canteen centres opened last October, some 50 sunburnt soldiers, all in civilian clothes, one wife and one 4-year-old child swept into the Hall. They had landed at Stansted in Essex some 2 hours earlier, after 3-day flight from Singapore.

Smoothly, the reception team went into action. Soldiers wearing plain clothes – uniforms were barred on flights across certain countries – were asked to report to the quartermaster and hand in their army civvies. The single compassionate posting, a national service man flown home to his mother who was seriously ill, was quickly issued with a rail warrant, pay, leave pass, and sent on his way. As the groups of servicemen completed their documentation, they moved down the Hall into the canteen where the canteen manager and his staff were waiting to serve them. Mr Elsmore told me that his biggest problem was knowing what supplies to order in. They seldom get more than 2 hours' notice of a flight coming in, and they just have to guess whether they will be catering for 100, 200 or even 500 people the next day.

The summer of 1957, Jukebox earnings

The installation of the jukeboxes in the Navy, army and RAF canteens in the UK happened in the summer of 1957. The use of the income for the improvement of the canteen amenities made possible by an arrangement negotiated by NAAFI with one of the leading Juke box manufacturers and distributors in the country. As a result the company is now able to install these modern music making machines in canteens on terms which do not involve the unit expense or responsibility, apart from wilful damage and we'll arrange in cooperation with the welfare committee, PRI or PSI, for the takings in each machine, less a share retained by the firm owning machines to be used for canteen amenities or improvements.

A senior company official explained that the terms obtained from the machine owners were more favourable than those generally available for individual hire. Those units, mainly RAF, which had already hired jukeboxes under local arrangements might find it worthwhile to change over to the NAAFI scheme.

Jukeboxes were becoming more and more popular and there is no reason why service units should not cash in on this popularity. These machines pay as they play and experience has shown that they can earn an impressive income. Under the scheme they shared the takings of each machine paid to the company by the machine owners which would go straight into maintaining their contents. Standard lamps, loose covers, cushions, window boxes and all sorts of embellishments and refinements to improve the comfort and appearance of the canteen can be obtained from this fund. Or the unit might prefer to spend the money on things like cards, darts, table tennis equipment and newspapers and magazines and so on. The actual expenditure was authorised by the local welfare committee PRI or PSI concerned. There is no reason why a unit should not save the jukebox earnings over a period that funds can be accumulated for an agreed improvement or amenity. District managers up and down the country will be reporting full details of the jukebox scheme to the committees and meetings of the naval establishments, army barracks and RAF stations for the individual units to decide whether they wanted a jukebox to be installed or not.

The company had already ordered 12 jukeboxes for the 12 permanent clubs in Great Britain and the first was installed at Aldershot a few weeks into the summer. The club Tavern where the jukebox occupies was a place of honour and it has never been so busy. The midday session has always been a quiet time in the Tavern but it's bouncing back – rock and roll rhythm draws the regular clientele. At the London headquarters of the Blackpool firm responsible for the manufacture of the distribution of the jukeboxes, they learnt that there would be 2 types of machines available for the canteens and clubs. The most popular type being the smaller units was the Music Maker, a coin operated preselected jukebox giving a choice of 16 records, which would automatically select and play than any desired order. Three penny pieces were used in this purchase. In the agreements the records would be changed every week by the firm's local representative, who would make the choice in accordance with his own wide experience, plus the up to the minute information on the latest hit record circulated by the headquarter office.

For the NAAFI clubs and large Garrison, the jukebox of choice offered 100 selections and used a telephone dial system to select the desired record, and the 200 selection jukebox was already in the making at this point. It would be safe to say that exiting the 1950s the rock and roll years had definitely started.

1958

Farewell to Totteridge written by AC Pritchard OBE, controller of training 1958

Pleasant memories of Totteridge from over 30,000 of them. Many reunions with old friends and the pleasure of making many new ones. They were a complete cross section of the company, men and women in transit, staff and officials under training, visitors from headquarters and from the Admiralty, the War Office, and the air ministry, and of course the permanent staff. Totteridge was the place to get the news, it was a regular travellers club, with gossip rife the sense of camaraderie was always there. The newcomers met the old hands and they felt the first bite of the NAAFI bug. The more a man knows about his job, the more he enjoys discussing it with others, and one of the most important aspects of Totteridge was the opportunity it gave for discussion with the lecture rooms and the lounges. Although some of the old hands did not, at first, take kindly to being sent back to school this was a friendly yet business-like atmosphere which soon sorted them out. Totteridge Lodge was the beginnings of so many NAAFI marriages that at one time we renamed it, "hook em and marriage Bureau" This was a special service we kept up to the end when Miss Joyce Schmidt, our secretary, left us to marry Mac, Mcshea from the Christmas Island. Out of such a crowded, if short, history it would be impossible to pick out the highlights in a few words; every day had its own highlight, every name recalls another. So, I can only with great regret bid farewell to Totteridge and au revoir to the staff – these at least, I am sure I would meet again. But this does not mean farewell to training, it does not mean that, for the moment, they will be no regular training in a residential centre. For the present we must concentrate on practical training in the field and we hope that those who have been through Totteridge will find their duties all the easier.

Management have decided to retain a training advisory committee, a controller of training a small number of staff officials, working from headquarters, to ensure coordination of training in the field. A number of trainee district managers are still working their way through their final practical part of their course, but it is unlikely that any great number of trainees will be accepted until further clarification of the future role of the services and the company's commitments that ought to be given. Courses for officials still will be held from time to time, perhaps on the lines of a business convention at one of our residential clubs. The training of shop and canteen staff is at present being carried out in establishments under the supervision of the local district managers and restaurant and welfare superintendents who can expect the advisory committee to give them every possible assistance with their training programmes. With all the current developments which are taking place with the company it is not easy or even desirable to settle any single definite plan for the future training. All probable eventualities are being taken into account and courses of training have been and are being prepared.

The final outcome of the consideration at present being given to the new methods of training probably will not be known for some months, but wherever the future from the company there will always be sufficient men and women of experience available, ready and willing to train newcomers.

Automatic sales 1958

The latest step in NAAFI's vending machine experiments was the installation of the battery of machines at Chatham naval barracks. Customers at Chatham could now get a hot and cold snack and a drink at any hour. This additional service was particularly appreciated by men coming off watch or returning from the cinema when the restaurant was closed. The machines were also providing a popular service with the army and the RAF, many barracks and camps now had machines selling milk, chocolate, and cigarettes. It did not stop there; NAAFI self-service was still going in a bespoke vehicle especially fitted out. The 100th self-serve shop was opened at Catterick in 1957; it was also the first mobile self-service shop in the home canteen service. Previously a Bedford coach of the type used by many airlines, it was converted by NAAFI transport branch. Customers entered the coach from the front and then had a clear passage through the length of the shop. The cashier sat at a small built in desk by the exit at the rear of the coach and operated a Sweda cash register.

Cyprus emergency 1958

The presence of over 4000 Greek Cypriot employees, 1200 of whom were working for NAAFI, had long been recognised by the military authorities in Cyprus as a security risk. The majority of them had worked for the British for many years and several NAAFI employees had over 18 years' service and their loyalty was recognised, but the possibility of EOKA infiltration was always present. The work they did in barracks, depots, offices, dining halls, ordnance workshops and other service establishments freed members of the security force for more important work. For this reason, because of the practical difficulties involved in replacing them by UK staff, the Greek Cypriot employees had been kept at work.

As the situation on the island worsened and the tension increased, the security authorities began to re-examine the position of the Greek Cypriot employees. An outbreak of arson at camps and barracks, the burning of NAAFI shops and severe damage to the NAAFI warehouse, where a large number of civilian employees had worked added to the growing demand for the dismissal of all Greek Cypriot labour.

Then came the murder of two airmen in the NAAFI canteen at the Nicosia RAF station. A time bomb hidden, exploded on a busy evening. Killing 2 RAF men and severely injuring several others. The first repercussion of that explosion was the dismissal of all Greek Cypriots employed by RAF. This happened on Sunday the 9th of November. Late that night the military authorities in Cyprus decided to extend the ban to nearly all Greek Cypriots employed by 3 services and by NAAFI. There was no question of notifying the 4000 employees concerned. The decision was implemented at 0700hrs the next morning.

Armed servicemen stopped Greek Cypriot staff at the entrance to camps, barracks, NAAFI shops, warehouses, and offices as they arrived to begin another day's work. They were turned away and told to go home. It was a crippling blow to the company's operations on the island, 1246 out of a total Labour force of 1499 was shut out. The 17 NAAFI shops, 46 canteens, 3 clubs, 2 leave centres, offices, transport section, bakery and warehouse were particularly staffed by them. All that remained was some 50 UK officials and fewer than 200 Turkish Cypriot, the majority of the latter being normally employed by labouring tasks.

This was the situation that faced Mr HD Rake, Middle East controller, and Mr HC stamp, supervisor, at 0700hrs on Monday the 10th of November. At 0915hrs on Monday morning the switchboard operator at Imperial Court put through an urgent call to NAAFI's press officer from the Press Association newsroom. "We have just received a message from Reuters correspondents in Cyprus," the caller said, "stating that all your Greek Cypriot staff have been banned from the shops, canteens, clubs, and offices. What are you going to do about it?"

This was the first news received at NAAFI headquarters of the suspension of 90% of the staff in Cyprus. Mr Swithenbank and Mr Barker were immediately informed of the situation and within 15 minutes an emergency meeting of the senior officials concerned was in progress. The war office had no official news and it was not until 1530hrs that confirmation of the ban was received. Meanwhile the telephones in the public relations were kept busy with a flood of press calls. The journalists were told that an emergency meeting at the top of the management was in progress. The loss of the Greek Cypriot staff meant 90% of our total labour force had gone, every effort would be made to provide some kind of service for the troops and families in Cyprus.

After a teleprinter conference with Cyprus in the afternoon the decision was taken to send out volunteers. Press conference at Imperial Court was arranged for 1730hrs at which Mr HP Prideaux, Assistant managing director, addressed a large company of press, radio and television representatives, outlining the situation, calling for 500 volunteers. He answered a barrage of questions from Fleet Street reporters and for nearly an hour gave individual interviews to BBC radio's newsreel, BBC television, ITN and the British forces broadcasting service. The last interview was recorded on the tape flown to Cyprus that evening for used by BFBS.

Half an hour after the last reporter left Imperial Court, Mr Prideaux's appeal for volunteers was heard on the radio news rail and 2 minutes later the first telephone calls from volunteers were received at Imperial Court. Public relations staff helped out by the night security Watchmen dealt with a succession of calls from all parts of the country. The BBC TV and ITN interviews brought more telephone calls and the rate was increased by the hourly BBC News broadcasts. Next day, when the appeal was headlined in hundreds of newspapers throughout the United Kingdom, Imperial Court's 30-line switchboard was swamped. The 5 operators worked at top speed throughout the day and by 1900hrs on the 11th November some 7000 telephone enquiries had been dealt with and hundreds of men and women and girls had called at Imperial Court in person. The fantastic response to the NAAFI appeal made fresh headlines in the national press and additionally publicly brought even more applications. Imperial Court and Kennings Way were in a state of siege.

Police at the Kennington area complained afterwards that they did little else for several days but direct people to NAAFI headquarters. In the restaurant extra meals were served and hundreds of gallons of tea and coffee were provided for the volunteers. Imperial Court post room was soon caught up in a rush. Thousands of written applications followed and telephone calls and special arrangements had to be made to deal with the total of over 6000 letters and completed application forms that arrived. The teleprinter operator Mrs Church found it almost impossible to send an outward message. Her machine was chattering away incessantly spelling out telegrams from volunteers and urgent dispatches from Cyprus. There was even a cable from an Ex NAAFI man in South Africa offering his immediate services. Within 4 days of the launching of the appeal over 17,000 applications had been received by telephone, letter, telegram, and personal visits to headquarters. And still they came. There were queues outside Imperial Court in Kennings Way before 0900hrs to Imperial Court and at 0500hrs one morning volunteers were knocking at the staff entrance and at 2000hrs that night.

On Thursday the 13th of November the managing director announced that no further applications should be received for the time being. He issued the following statement which was widely quoted in the press radio and TV and news bulletins. "I would like to thank the public for the magnificent response to our appeal, which the 17,000 men women and girls have offered themselves for a task which they recognise will be no picnic, is a token of the country's overwhelming support for, confidence in our troops in Cyprus."

This lessened the tension for the telephone operators and lightened the load for the Morning Post van but there was no let up for personnel administration, the Imperial Court health unit, PR, the house manager, OCS, or any other direct concerned with volunteers. Feature writers, TV, and newsreel film units famous for Fleet Street photographers and any agency reporters were daily callers at Imperial Court. Telephone calls received from the provincial papers up and down the country all asking the same question. "Can you give us the name of any of the volunteers from the area?"

Four days after the appeal was launched it was announced that the first plane load of volunteers would be leaving Blackbushe airport on Sunday the 16th of November. Behind that bold announcement would be a story of hectic day and night work sorting, documenting, examining, photographing, transporting, and assembling the volunteers.

Mr John Martin, assistant to the Comptroller, personal administration, gives this account of how the PA mobilised its resources to meet the emergency.

"At a meeting at Imperial Court on Tuesday morning the 11th of November, caller PA was made responsible for meeting the demand for staff for Cyprus and further notice to transfer our office from Ruxley Towers to London. Mr Scott nominated staff we were going to bring with us, including Mr Jones, Mr Grundy, and the reference section, representing PA3. We set up our headquarters at the boardroom in the Imperial Court. In the meantime the staff offices in London, Miss Carr, Miss Bunker and Mr Duran, assisted by Mr Keefe, and Mr Harmon, set about interviewing the personal applicants. Miss P Heath of public relations stepped into the breach when extra interviews were required to deal with the 3rd day of rush. A system for dealing with written applications was set up and placed under the control of Mr Walmsley of OCS.

"The requirements of staff needed in Cyprus were channelled through the manager to Mr Scott who was responsible for recruiting staff to fill vacancies in the priorities indicated. Immediately the first plane load was planned, contact was made with the air charter firms and arrangements were finally made with Eagle Aviation for aircraft to leave Blackbushe on Sunday, 16th of November.

"Mr Scott presided over the daily morning conference in the old boardroom attended by Miss Fraser, Miss Carr and Mr Jones, Mr Keefe and Mr Doran and Mr Dunn of OCS and myself. At this conference the current situation was reviewed, and the plane loads made up. As the requirements for each plane became known, staff were bought in for the medical examinations and were afterwards passed to the documentation section which was set up under the control of Mr HT Bird, assistant male staff officer, before taking over the stewardship of Mitcham sportsground. He was assisted by Mr RC Pettett, and Mr Hooper with arranged allotments and final documentation at Ruxley Towers. Help was given by the passport office and Somerset House made special arrangements for issuing documents outside normal office hours. Mr Manning and his assistant, the local photographer in Windmill Row, worked until 2200hrs at night to rush passport pictures through. The transport branch laid on the Courier service in the passport office, Somerset House, and Harley Street for medical X-rays. The GPO were also extremely helpful in installing additional telephones at Imperial Court.

"To accommodate staff going to Cyprus the training centre in Wingham, in Claygate, was housed at Heathlands, Wimbledon. Both hostels were put under the control of Miss J Rainey, HCS, who was directly responsible to Mr Scott for their administration.

"Everyone concerned in the emergency gave their best and long hours for work, day after day including Saturdays and Sundays. Nobody complained or even murmured. The interviewing documentation systems was working smoothly and by Wednesday the 12th of November when the first successful applications were brought in for medical examination and documentation. The normal health unit team was doubled up and by working from 8 till 8 they were able to deal with large numbers of people."

"Our medical standards of fitness were not lowered in any way," said the chief medical officer Dr Hunter. By the end of November they had examined 322 people and 9 out of every 10 were found to be fit. All those who passed were vaccinated and inoculated.

From the point of view of the national press, the dispatch of the first plane load of volunteers from Blackbushe rounded off the NAAFI volunteers for the Cyprus story which had filled hundreds of columns and inches of the national and provincial newspapers for 7 days in succession. BBC TV, ITV, and the cameras of the national broadcasting company of America were at the airport, together with 30 press photographers and over 20 reporters. Representatives of the Daily Express, star, Daily Mail, BBC television and the American news agency, AP, actually travelled out on the aircraft. The men, women and girls who set off from Blackbushe that evening were given a real film star send off and when they arrived in Nicosia airport, they received a VIP reception. From then on regular flights were made from Blackbushe, Gatwick and London airports and a total of 302 volunteers, many of them chosen from the 402 NAAFI staff who submitted their names, were flown out to Cyprus. With but a few exceptions, they all settled down well and were continuing to do a valuable job in Cyprus. The servicemen out there thought highly of the new canteen staff and the sudden influx of a crowd of cheerful, attractive, and hardworking girls from England was reported to have boosted morale to a new high.

It all adds up to a greater efficiency by RD McBurnie 1958

A silent clinically clean room in the new warehouse at Krefeld in Germany will house the new NAAFI first electronic computer, the Stantec Zebra, which started operating in April 1958. The adjoining room's punched tape machines and a battery of teleprinters will click and clatter in the service of the electric brain feeding information by the way of coded indents and instructions and converting the answers into invoices, stock figures on ledger sheets. A large keep out sign would keep out all but the qualified programmers and maintenance engineers from the computer room. This will be the nerve centre of the new system of the warehouse accounting and procedure, an electronic arithmetical marvel that can be understood and operated only by this specifically trained staff. This was no miracle machine with reasoning powers of a human brain. It can store instructions and fax in an electronic memory and refers to them when necessary. It can solve arithmetical problems at a very high speed and can be programmed or instructed to carry out lengthy series of sums in a given sequence.

It can choose between alternative programs and certain eventualities. But all these activities were dependent on the work of the programmer, the man or woman who feeds the computer with the facts and detailed instructions converting all the problems to mathematical terms.

The installation of the computer would be the climax of more than 2 years' hard work for Mr Emile Kay, a 38-year-old mathematician from Czechoslovakia who as a Postal student gained an economics degree at London University while still learning English. Mr Kaye joined Plans and Methods Department in January 1957 when the possibility of using an electronic computer was under consideration. He has worked directly under Mr RT Edison, the head of the plans and methods. His first task was to decide the best way in which the computer would be put to work. A detailed examination was made of the work and several departments, including the Waldniel warehouse in Germany. The planned move of the warehouse to a brand-new building at Krefeld, some 30 miles away, offered the golden opportunity to introduce a new procedure using a computer which would accurately teleprint the invoices and orders. During the course of the change over from the old warehouse to the new on the computer was able to take over its task by easy stages. This would space out the immense physical labour and programming of supplying the computer with all the relevant information concerning the stocks and their danger levels, the prices, package weights and locations of different items held.

The next job was to pick the right computer for the job. The Stantec zebra, produced by Standard Telephone and Cables Limited, seemed to meet most of NAAFI's requirements. Consultations with the standard engineers at Newport resulted in an offer to make the necessary alterations to the Zebra to suit the special needs of the company, the board of management then decided to place a firm order, with the promise of the delivery within 9 months.

Standard also offered to help with the training of staff in their Newport factory. Mrs J Renton, formerly of OCS, who had joined Mr Kay as his assistant in September 1957, was the first to undertake the programmer's course. On her course were university professors, highly qualified mathematicians, statisticians, and electronic engineers. She was the only woman; the test program she produced was highly praised.

Mr Kay and Mr Renton worked long hours in mastering their new craft and applying it to the particular job the NAAFI computer had to do. These 4 were The Pioneers of NAAFI's computer experiment. Later two more programmers joined the team at Newport. These were Mr JW Evans, previously a programmer with IBM United Kingdom Limited and Mr W Van Warmelo, a South African who was a computer engineer before switching to programming.

It would usually take 2 years to put a computer into operation, but they had to do it in a little over 9 months and train the staff at the same time. They had been working against the clock to be ready to install a computer as soon as the new warehouse was ready for occupation. Standard Telephones and Cables had given every possible helpful every member of the team was full of enthusiasm for the project and they were determined to meet the deadline. The decision to demonstrate a NAAFI program on the Zebra computer exhibited at Olympia in the December was a further challenge that they had gladly met and the demonstrations they'd given on the Standard Telephone and Cable stand aroused great interest.

In the July Mrs Renton began an additional task, training punched tape machine operators. Three German girls all from the Waldniel warehouse were joined by Miss Margaret Lambert who was formerly with NAAFI in Tripoli and at the NAAFI hostel in Cardiff where the machines were installed. They spent nearly 6 months obtaining touch type efficiency on the tape punching and verifying machines used to feed the coded information into the computer. They had to achieve machinelike efficiency to get as near as humanly possible to the absolute accuracy of the computer. The speed was important too for the punching of the coded tapes is ridiculously slow compared with the millionth of a second speed of the computer itself.

The maintenance of the computer and ancillary equipment, which would include at least 4 teleprinters there, would be 2 engineers. The first to be appointed was Herr A Ulrich who was formerly at ECS headquarters. A teleprinter engineer who used to work for the Royal Signals in Germany underwent a period of training on the computer at Newport. Shortly before Christmas, Mr H K Bradley, a trained computer engineer, previously with Messers AV Roe, the aircraft manufacturers, joined the NAAFI team.

The biggest job was then to get everything ready for the installation of the machine in the warehouse and this was due to take place in the early March. They expected to start operating the computer in April and there was still a tremendous amount of work to be done before that could happen. Programs had to be amended and staff had to be trained for the coding section, more punch machine operators would be required and the price, wait, packaging, code number and warehouse location of every item in stock would have to be recorded. They also pointed out that the installation would not cause any redundancies in the warehouse. It would do away with a considerable amount of tedious routine clerical work, but they hoped that it would make up for the present labour shortage in the warehouse. This would leave NAAFI leading the way with new technology.

1959

NAAFI in print 1959

The question here was when did NAAFI start doing its own printing. There had been a printing branch for as long as there had been a NAAFI and even longer if you wanted to look that far. The current printing plant was directly descended from Messers John Dickieson, one of the pre NACB contractors, who had their small printing works in Tooley St, that NACB took over it and then moved it to Kennings Way in 1920 and NAAFI took it over from the NACB the following year. But now many years later the print room of the NAAFI printing branch was the scene of much noisy activity. There was a young man wearing drainpipe trousers with a smudge of ink behind his ear from carrying one of the gleaming black presses. He was 1 of 8 apprentices being trained by the company.

There were tall stacks of paper and shelves filled with various coloured tins of ink on the way to the manager's office. At his desk it was covered with photographs, proofs and artwork which was required for his approval before they sent it to the engraver; the manager was Mr WH Hodkinson. He was the main man responsible for making the branch one of the most up to date printing plants in the country. On his arrival some 6 years previously, he had turned about half of the works over to new machinery and methods and had continued steadily with his modernisation plans.

In late 1959 the branch was the only works on this side of the Atlantic using a thermoplastic bonding film in preparing blocks, engraved zinc, or copper plates, for printing. The machine which set much of the NAAFI forms and books is one of only 3 in the country.

He was proud of his Warner Jones press which occupied the place of honour in the centre of the print room. The massive machine was specifically built to his specifications and became the prototype of a press which was then sold as far afield as Africa, the Far East, and the Americas. Most of these machines which were available at the time were designed for specialist printers, but they needed a press which could tackle a dozen different jobs. This new real fed machine would print on 2 sides of the paper at one time. It would print 3 colours simultaneously or it would print in 2 colours at the same time number the pages in quadruplicate. In addition to this the machine would automatically perforate where necessary, collect the printed sheets and trim them to size. It was probably the most versatile press of its size in the country at the time. This machine would complete an edition of Books such as forms 496 or 497 within 3 weeks, the delivery of the completed books commencing within half an hour of starting the press. Previously it had taken up to 5 months to produce the first books of a similar edition by various machine and hand processes.

It was not only the machinery of the branch which was changing, the products too had changed over the past 40 years. Modernization in other branches of the company was the main factor for the change, as the demand for forms and other printed matter declined so Mr Hodkinson would build up the output of saleable print. These would include Christmas cards, headed or creased stationery, menus, invitation cards, programmes for 'at homes' handbooks, record books and fixture books for service sportsmen, these were amongst the items which brought in the customers' cash.

Mr O H McCormack, the assistant manager, had all the facts and figures of the branch at his fingertips. The average annual output of the branch was some 5000 jobs, and examples of this were requirements of tea labels, four million of them, which would give you some idea of the volume of work they put through the presses. The fact was they fused over 400 tons of paper each year and handled hundreds of tons of metal, not to mention 90 miles of ribbon for nearly 1 million Christmas cards!

In addition to the printing they were also responsible for the buying of all other paper goods the company required, paper bags, packages, cartons, baking cases, plastic film for self-service packs and so on. The branch now prints 5-unit magazines and in addition took on contracts for more. Printing magazines was not entirely new to the company. Mr Holland reminded them that when he first joined in 1926 as a compositor he used to set up the copy for the Aldershot News and clearly remembered working on the first issue of the Imperial club magazine in 1928. He was probably one of the most knowledgeable people who could recall the early days, of the printing branch, he had a fine record for service, nine of the 74 members received long service awards and over the years they had continued to drive the printing business forward.

1960–1969

1960

Developing new business 1960

The introduction of Kodak printing and developing service was one of NAAFI's new ways to help assist the servicepersons and also gaining a bigger share of the business. At the time 600 establishments had been added to the list of customers at the Kodak laboratories in Fulham, about half of them had already started regularly posting films for processing in early 1960s. Each morning these orders were collected from the GPO and then by teatime the same day the orders had been completed and posted back to the establishments.

A Kodak tip which was given by Mr K Reason, manager of the laboratory: "everything possible is done to provide a speedy, fool proof service once the films arrive in the laboratory but the retailer too can play his part by ensuring that he posts the correct portion of the order form within the film and by using the Postal bag which we have provided."

The film processing service was to be a popular addition to the company services and continued for many years until the digital age took over.

Mobile Self Service 1960

The latest development in the field of self-service was a Mobile Shop built on a trailer. ECS had specially designed this model in Berlin, the extremes of weather and summer temperatures were usually greater than experienced in the United Kingdom so this mobile self-service shop was virtually air conditioned. The plant and equipment necessary to keep the customers cool in the summer and warm in the winter had been installed without interfering with the shopping area and the whole interior was a clean and uncluttered space.

The decision to design and build a self-service trailer, as opposed to a powered vehicle, considered the advantages of a minimum of mechanical servicing and the use of a towing vehicle when a major service risk was acquired by another trailer. The entrance to the mobile was by swing doors on the left-hand side, the door opened to the inside and on the right-hand door to the outside. A barrier rail between the doors, leading to the interior helped to keep the customer traffic moving in the right direction. An importance had been placed on the light and cheerful interior and the mobile had five windows on one side and 7 on the other; there were also 7 more in the roof and two at the front and the back. All windows and the walls were fitted with spring roller blinds. The walls in the roof had been insulated and covered with plywood plates. When it was disconnected from the towing vehicle, the trailer would be supported by adjustable hydraulic corner posts. Each post was fitted with a disk base to prevent sinking in soft ground. The towing bar was fitted with a hydraulic braking and lighting system including indicators, all of which were operated from the towing vehicle.

The warm air which was blown into the trailer from underneath the floor was supported by a heating unit mounted on the tow bar. In the summer months the blower can be disconnected, and the equipment used for ventilation purposes. The refrigeration unit was enclosed and insulated, a soundproof container at the rear of the vehicle and when on location it was ran from 12 Volt batteries.

The self-service fittings within the vehicle were of wire basket type supported on metal uprights and securely fitted within the vehicle. The fittings were detachable and could be transferred to the shop for refilling. The customers' shopping baskets were normal service type and the checkout cited at the exit door was fitted with a Sweda cash register which was also powered from the 12 Volt batteries.

The range of goods available in the Mobile Shop was quite impressive for the time and covered general groceries, canned goods, bread, cakes and pastries, chocolate and confectionery, provisions, frozen goods, pre jointed meat, fresh milk and fresh produce. In addition, there were a selection of baby foods, pet foods, minerals, soap, hardware, polishes, a small range of medicines and toiletries. The Mobile Shop served families in locations in four main isolated districts and the daily visit paid by the Mobile Shop was proving to be an extremely popular service. The driver and cashier operated the Mobile Shop which carried approximately 300 pounds of stock. The weekly turnover was in the region of £500 but there were signs that the figure would increase and the service families in Berlin began to make greater use of the shop on wheels.

The wind of change 1960

The winds of change sweeping through the company had already blown away many familiar features of NAAFI Life, leaving in its wake what they believed at the time to be a newer and better conceptions. So, the 60s brought a new name for canteens where these became junior ranks and airmen's clubs. The Crest made way for the new modern symbol of the NAAFI 'N' and Miss NAAFI's uniform became a smart duty dress. The shop counters now became self-service, and uneconomic kitchens were replaced by handy called to order units. Kiosks blossomed into service shops and everything became more convenient. On all sides the old system had changed as it must and new ideas, new techniques came into their own. Even NAAFI News for the last 15 years had stayed pretty much the same but in February 1961 the new style publication would be launched as a monthly staff Journal, designed to communicate effectively to the company's family. This was providing a lively channel of communication between the staff throughout the world, to present the dynamically urgent problems, achievements and experiments of the company at the fast changing, challenging exciting periods of the company's development.

NAAFI would endeavour to recruit a number of correspondents in the overseas area and they would undertake the chore of becoming spare time reporters for that area, which would assist with keeping the monthly publication full of news from across the world.

Preparations had already started for the new Style magazine; the company as they knew it was born in 1921 but established in early December 1920. Almost from the outset there was demand for an inhouse Journal but other more pressing requirements had to come first and it was not till the Christmas of 1928 that volume one, number one, of the Imperial club magazine, the house organ of the NAAFI, saw the light of day. It was launched initially as an annual and eventually achieved two issues a year and commanded the circulation of about 3000 selling at sixpence. In 1940 it was one of NAAFI's earliest war casualties.

In 1941 the company started a new sheet called NAAFI News which was primarily intended for distribution to the press. It contained brief paragraphs concerning the company's wartime activities and the personalities and hundreds of stories appeared in national and provincial newspapers. It also had a limited circulation among NAAFI staff with whom it proved extremely popular, revealing sadly a staff magazine that was missing in those years.

The paper shortage and the control of paper stopped the efforts to revive a proper Journal until the war ended when at Christmas 1945 the NAAFI News emerged for the first time as a printed magazine. It had only 24 pages and appeared three times a year, to coincide with the paper allocation, and later became a quarterly publication, growing from 24 to 48 pages and once in the Coronation year of Her Majesty the Queen Elizabeth contained 100 pages. Its circulation started at 5000 and soared to 20,000 and now with the rundown of staff had dropped back to 8000.

Initially the publication was printed by the company's own printing branch and was one of very few journals which can claim to be written, edited and printed in house. Up until 1960 the NAAFI News had won 4 awards in a national competition which was promoted each year by the British Association of industrial editors and had received favourable mentions. On the cover of the first issue of the Imperial club magazine appeared benediction from the general manager, Sir Frank Benson, who wrote:

> "Here then is the first number of the often discussed and often turned down Imperial club magazine. We shall all have been speculating as to its contents, now we shall wonder what will become of it. Will it grow and become a quarterly or even a monthly? Will it live and die in an have annual? The answer depends not on me, or upon anyone person, but upon the Imperial club as a whole".

Badges 1960

From the very beginning NAAFI awarded badges for various reasons to staff, and it would be right to detail this as much as possible. Up until now the NAAFI Girls wore a blue overall with white piping and crest on the breast pocket, with a head band embroidered also with the crest, which in 1946 they stopped issuing the khaki green kit and head dress. The ladies would wear the uniforms underneath the overall, whilst the gentleman would wear trousers and shirt, under standard white or tan overcoat style overall. In 1960 in, NAAFI reviewed the whole uniform which was changed for the ladies. As did the crest, it had a major overhaul.

Sometime earlier there had been a competition to think up a new Crest, logo or emblem. It was a sign of the times, not only was NAAFI growing it was also modernising to the point where the Crest, which had been used on everything, would make way for the modernization of the organisation.

The Controller of Supplies (later Supplies Director) Norman Webb-Bourne came up with the idea whilst sitting at his desk messing about with some paper clips, he realised that 3 paper clips formed the shape of the N for NAAFI and also was strongly linked together, which symbolised what the organisation was all about. This was part of the drive to modernise the NAAFI image for the introduction of the Own Label range of products.

This new Symbol would be seen everywhere, on stores, lorries, NAAFI wagons, cartons of tea and the cups it was poured into, also flags and plaques outside of the shops. It was a real step forward to a new era. The 1960 NAAFI Review front page was adorned with Miss Naafi and her new uniform and it explained how all through the first 40 years of service, persons to use NAAFI had been used to the Crest made up of the King's Crown, fouled anchor and the wings with the motto Servitor Servientium, it was important to modernize.

The simple shape with clean lines instantly recognisable from a distance, the 3 links in navy blue, army scarlet and the Royal Air Force blue. This would be a reminder of the triple loyalties and unbreakable links between all 3 services. Without the NAAFI motto. This would show the strength and the true significance of the links not only with every member of the NAAFI family but every service member and their families.

The new uniform would do away with the headband and be replaced by a new blue dress made from nylon and rayon which would feature a brooch bearing the new emblem 'N'. For the Navy the brooch would be topped with the Royal Navy Crown, the Army would be the Imperial Crown and for the Royal Air Force the Albatross. This design was taken by Mr Pat Keely, FSIA, AGI and reimagined into the brooch and the stars.

The brooch was inlaid with marcasite and beautifully crafted. While Norman was stationed at Wingham across the room sat John Parry, who thought that for every staff member who worked either on a Naval base, at army barracks or a Royal Air Force station, they had an emblem to symbolise their duty. Wingham was the main training centre for staff and management alike and he felt that the symbol that would best represent their duty at headquarters would be on the same theme but take on the shape of a 'W' and also on its right hand side have a small squirrel; this was also inlaid with marcasite. On chatting with Mr Parry all these years later he still holds a great affection for the Wingham brooch and has his close to hand. He tells me that the Squirrel was because at the rear was a very large orchard of every fruit tree you could think of and numerous Cedar and Lebanon trees in the front garden. With this there was a "very large" grey squirrel population, who scurried around the property and provided entertainment with their antics often. They would come up on the window ledges of the classrooms and if open they would even venture in. They were very tame.

Mr John Perry said: "There is a lovely story about these little creatures that happened during my time at the centre – the cook had just finished baking mince pies for the afternoon tea break and placed them near the kitchen window to cool. She left the kitchen for a short time to find on her return all the pies gone, and one small squirrel was seen disappearing into the undergrowth with his robber mates all carrying mince pies!"

"The gardens were also the site for a large Badger set – staff would put out leftovers in the evening and the badgers would come for supper, with baby foxes waiting in the background. The badgers were filmed by David Attenborough for BBC TV but the location was kept secret to protect them. The staff came up with the idea of using the Squirrel as the Training Centre Logo and the rest is history thanks to Ben White."

The brooch was launched on the front of the 1960 Autumn NAAFI review and worn by Ann Taylor of television's "The Army Game", where she became the first NAAFI girl to be fitted for the new uniform. The official launch was on television's Granada station in September 1960, as part of her role in ITV's very first sitcom. She signalled start of the break for the adverts with a NAAFI Brew for the lads.

Following the successful launch of the new emblem, the uniform and brooches and the system for recognising staff for their hard work and seniority within the organisation started with stars. This started with one-star faux marcasite brooch. Later in 1964 they would introduce a new star's programme to gain qualifications.

Week by week as the new emblem made its debut an increasing variety of media, on forms and catalogues on camp and shop signs including the brooch worn on the new duty dress, and on paper wrappers, labels and on note paper headings. Then vehicles, the first NAAFI vehicle to carry the emblem was a new home canteen service mobile self-service shop, which was showcased in September 1960 at Imperial Court. The new symbol had slipped into place in the public image of the company with remarkable ease and with popular acceptance. Everywhere it was becoming noticed and remembered and liked. It was a success and it last rewarded the 10-year search for a modern sign which would truly symbolise the modern up and coming NAAFI of its day and for years to come.

Copyright Sue A Lowe

The need for such an emblem was recognised soon after the war which had proved that the old Crest, while it was iconic, its use was not ideal as an all-purpose symbol. What was required was

a significant shape which could be instantly identifiable at a distant on buildings, vehicles, and camp signs. One that would symbolise the company's triple duty and close association with the three services.

The last days of Ruxley Towers wartime headquarters at Claygate in Surrey 1960

Ruxley Towers, NAAFI wartime headquarters at Claygate, Surrey was to be closed. Immediately after the decision had been taken by members of the standing committee of the joint consultative council and the headquarter staff council, after the meeting of Imperial Court on Thursday the 26th of January 1960. The news was given by Mr HPT Prideaux, who gave members the background reasons to their decision. Although the sales per customer had increased, he explained that the number of customers was also reducing. The effect of this could be serious unless the trade expanded further. The ever-rising cost of labour in all trades and types made it imperative to management to ensure the administration was organised as effectively and economically as possible. It was only in this way that the long-term wellbeing of the majority of the staff could be assured.

It was a moment of sadness to think that giving up Ruxley Towers would actually be happening and for some time it had been used to its capacity and then had become increasingly expensive to maintain for the company because of the number of staff employed there.

From the wartime peak of 1100 staff employed at Ruxley Towers it had now dropped to just 300. The branches and departments which were then going to be transferred to Kennings Way, these were the personnel and central wages, HQ Cashiers, pensions accounts, the computer unit and the regional manager's office. Some reorganisation at Kennings Way would be necessary in order to accommodate the officers to be moved from Ruxley. The first step was the local trades function and supplies accountings branch was to be transferred to Nottingham where it was expected to operate much more efficiently side by side with the home accounts branch. The accommodation then was made vacant for this move, together with further space which would become available on the removal of certain sections of the warehouse to the old bakery, would provide offices for the staff moving from Claygate.

Everyone in local trades would be given the opportunity to transfer to Nottingham but management realised that for the majority such a move would be not practical. There was, however, no foreseeable risk of any redundancy as a consequence of the transfers because those affected would be absorbed elsewhere in the accounts department or in those branches transferring to London in which suitable vacancies existed. Everyone at Ruxley whose function was being transferred to London would decide, wherever possible, to transfer their job. For those who could not but who were prepared to continue at Ruxley until the data transfer, there would be some sort of compensatory payment.

The plans that were announced were not put into action much before the end of April. It was not expected that the move from Ruxley would be completed by June. The company had bought Ruxley Towers in 1939 and it served as the company's headquarters throughout the war until the management returned to the former headquarters at Imperial Court in Kennington Lane. The house itself was built in the mid-19th century by the then Lord Foley as a plain brick country home of modest design. After seeing Herstmonceux Castle he added the towers, gargoyles and other embellishments which earned it, in some quarters, the reputation of being the ugliest building in the South of England. Staff now serving in many parts of the world would regret the passing of their house in the country but would agree that economically the closure was the right step.

1961

The problems of providing an efficient service for an isolated unit by G Mowforth 1961

Nine miles from Belize, port of British Honduras is the airport. Few travellers arriving in the colony by plane would give a second thought to a cluster of buildings, just discernible through the trees, across from the runway. Others a little more observant might on leaving the airport steal a glance at a notice board which read L Coy. Royal Hampshire regiment.

The board marks the well laid out camp, surrounded by a swamp, of a small detachment of the British army and needless to say serving their needs was a NAAFI canteen and store. The foundation of a smooth running establishment and a satisfactory service to the troops in such a small secluded spot was based on five main things: knowledge of shipping procedure, stock control, grocery business, canteen work and last but not least getting the best out of the local labour under difficult conditions.

Stock control in a small place like this, caused a headache and it is estimated for a period of up to 4 to 6 months ahead stock would need to be planned. A step up in demand at any time could put you out of stock for a couple of months as it takes ships from 6 to 8 weeks to reach them, from England. Help was given by the district office in the district manager in Kingston a few hundred miles away by sea. At Imperial Court there was a complete stock account of what we had on the premises. It had been known for the London staff to spot a forgotten item and plates it on the order and vice versa to cut down on products where they thought it might be overestimating.

When the ship arrived with NAAFI stores, the local manager took a dusty and uncomfortable journey down to the docks in the back of a three toner. They may have to hang around for a few hours until the shipping agent and customs officials decide to cooperate. But then there was the other issue. It came to the job of checking the cases against the waybills and marking down losses through pilfering which unfortunately was quite out of proportion to the amount put on board in England. Shipping claims out there are a full-time job. The shortages are covered by a certain degree by insurance but that does not fill the empty stand. Journeys were made to police at least twice a week for replenishing stocks of beer and many minerals and purchasing ingredients for making sandwiches and for the baking.

During these times you have to depend on the local staff to carry out the work. There is no bus service between the camp and police, so you had to rely on people living around and about for labour. This presented a problem as the local population was only about 150. Mosquitoes and sand flies are every bit as good a fighting force as the army and it seemed just as well organised. No amount of strategy could seem to repel them. The never ceasing attack of the counter attacks takes place at a time during the mango season. Included in this was the field mice who wouldn't restrict themselves to one pack of cornflakes or one chocolate bar; they had to sample a few to see if they'd come from the same batch. Life had its bright side where everybody else would find such wonderful opportunities for skin diving and the study of underwater life. Regular trips were planned by the army and the invitation to attend is nearly always extended to the NAAFI manager. Complete mess dances or socials or another part of the Royal Hampshire curriculum. Periodic visits by the flying district manager keep you in touch with what's happening in the outside world. And his visits were welcome. Even so, it meant getting up at 0600hrs to meet him at the airport and missing your afternoon siesta.

OCA 14th AGM 1961

The chair of the OCA at its 14th AGM said: "No words of mine can adequately express the high esteem in which was held by all members of the OCA, or give any real conception of the tremendous interest and enthusiasm he has always displayed in his affairs, not only as a founder member of the Association but his chairman during the past Seven years." With these words Mr CA Layard, chairman of the general committee of the NCS EFI OCA paid tribute to the work of his predecessor Mr TE Pegg, OBE who resigned in the January of 1961. The new chair spoke in his annual general report and said the attendance of the annual reunion in October was down to its lowest figure ever of 141.

Copyright Sue A Lowe

It was the idea of a substitute function in mind and the general committee had arranged an OCA luncheon to be held at Mitcham gala and sports day on the 13th of May. It was an ideal opportunity for members to meet old comrades and colleagues, both at the lunch and the afternoon and evening's activities. He said that the numbers at the dinner party at Imperial Court in April of 1960 were also down on the previous year but there is no doubt that it was a most enjoyable and successful function. Members of the Association in the UK was now 1972; this was less than in 1959. Efforts were being made to build the membership up to 2000 and more than 1200 members had already paid their 1961 subscriptions.

Due to a further fall in the market value of 3½% war stock it had been considered and advised to allow this further depreciation amount.

It was also at this stage that the functions in the other district had started to slow down but they were all still enthusiastic and ensuring that the core values of the Association were still upheld at every opportunity.

Sir Randel steps down 1961

On the 1st of June 1961 Maj General Sir Randel G Feildean KCVO, CB, CBE would relinquish his appointment as managing director. The board appointed Mr HPT Prideaux OBE as sole managing director on the same date. Sir Randel said, "Although I shall be retiring from the executive I shall be remaining as part time civilian member of the board and in that capacity I shall have the opportunity to keep in touch with you and to help forward the great work which NAAFI is doing. There is thus happily for me, no question of my having to say goodbye but as I lay down my executive duties I am very conscious of the loyal support which you have always given me, I do want to thank you all most sincerely for it. Mine has been a proud and happy task. We have shared much together since I first came to NAAFI as general manager in 1949, we have seen great changes. You have proved equal to every occasion and it has been great privilege to work with and for you."

At age 56 Sir Randel can already look back on three distinct and highly successful careers. Firstly, as a soldier from Eton and Magdalen college at Cambridge, he joined the brigade in 1925, serving in the Coldstream Guards, for 24 years. In 1939 he was a staff captain in the seventh guards brigade but the war brought rapid promotion, and following a spell in the guards armoured division, he became deputy quartermaster general, Home forces, in 1943 and held a similar post with 21 army group on its formation.

He was a member of General Montgomery's planning staff for D-day and played a major role in the vast build-up of supplies for the invasion of Europe, finishing the war as deputy quartermaster general Rhine Army. Two years later his first career had ended and his second had begun when leaving the army, he joined NAAFI first as general manager, then later as chief general manager and then finally managing director. With the rundown of the forces, the company was facing difficult times and Sir Randel had to hold the Organization on a straight course. One of his greatest tasks in the early years was to run down the stocks and reduce the staff, close countless wartime premises and reduce NAAFI field of operations, in order to keep in step with the rapidly demobilising forces.

NAAFI built for the War Office 1961

A unique double handing over ceremony marked the opening of the first shop to be planned and built by NAAFI for a service department and paid for from public funds. On Monday the 19th of June 1961 Mr J Reuben, of works and buildings, handed over to NAAFI War Office clients the self-service shop at the Royal Armoured Corps Training Depot, Bovington, Dorset. The following day the War Office handed the new shop, which replaced the old Hut type shop, back to NAAFI to operate. In many ways this was the perfect shop since it had been built to the specific specifications of the company's own architects. Inside is 7000 square feet of shopping space. Decoration was in a quiet grey and blues, with walls of glazed tiles. The floor was finished in tiles and lino, lighting was fluorescent and daylight poured in through the long high windows.

Shoppers entered through the glass window foyer. There was a pram park and for car owners a spacious car park adjoining the shop. A distinctive tower concealed a tank of fuel for the oil-fired central heating and emblazoned on the tower is the first NAAFI symbol to appear in neon. The shop's functional elegance was highlighted by the surrounding landscape gardens of grass, trees and shrubs. Linked with the new shop was a messing store and local produce store. The same camp is also the same site for the first junior ranks club to be designated and built by NAAFI. It was scheduled to open in early summer 1962. Plans for a second build at the JRC at Larkhill, Wiltshire at this time were only in the planning stages and work was not scheduled to start until late 1962.

Joining the common market October 1961

In 1961 the company started to assess the changing climate and the direction in which the United Kingdom was going. In October 1961 a report was written on joining the common market: the common market has been discussed, diagnosed and debated by all the economic economists amateur and professional and has been talked about, testified and translated in the myriad of manners.

One of the joys of working in Germany was that you were living, with throbbing businesses on every doorstep and we certainly got caught up in many of the national and economic problems of the countries covered by the European Canteen Service (ECS) – West Germany, Belgium and Holland, all staunch members of the common market. They had a good relationship with many merchants in these countries and the subject was raised by and discussed with them on many occasions. They being enthusiastic supporters of the common market were all convinced that the United Kingdom must join? They found the business of colleagues steeped in a subject, surprisingly well informed and quite empathic on the consequences for us to join and if we didn't, their view seemed to be if we don't join we sit on the fence and freeze economically, if we do join, we have nearly 200 million customers on the continent who we can sell our goods to duty free in the majority of cases.

These businesses and men realised the agonising and complex problems they had to solve before they could join. The economic relationship with the Commonwealth countries, some from our continued protection for our agriculture and so on. They were sure that their hopes of a unity of a Western Europe including the United Kingdom would be best defence against communism. The common market had given six economies great impetus and they knew that the buoyant economy in a country improved as standards of living which made for a contented people. Just as a trade depression and the reverse effect with unemployment and all of the factors on which spread communism thrived. These businessmen said precisely what our government was saying that Western Europe, united in trade, is united politically and so would be a more powerful unit, as large, in fact as powerful as the United States or Russia. In the light of these facts continental colleagues could not see the United Kingdom isolated and frozen out of the European market by having to pay import duties, suffer quantitative restrictions on the exports to Europe whilst the six freely exchanged their goods duty free. It was quoted then that they argued that the United Kingdom frozen out of the European markets, outstripped their European competitors, would not be of much use as a leader to the Commonwealth and therefore, the very real Commonwealth problems regarding our joining the common market must be solved in the interests of their survival as well as our own.

He also went on to say, I think that unfettered by any countries' import duties on their present trade restrictive practices, many of our exports will soar to the heights not possible without the common market idea. On the other hand, he supposed that inevitably, some industries exposed to the full gale of the European competition could suffer. Nevertheless, he thought it would be a very mean spirited United Kingdom that could not take opportunities offered. He also felt that a breakdown of the tariffs and quotas will result in an overall tremendous widening of the trade and markets. Even with motor cars he felt that the picture is not as black as a lot of people thought, maybe in the vast duty-free continental market their exports may increase more than imports of the European cars into the comparatively small country. Whether to join or not, NAAFI trading in Europe must be affected. If they didn't join, bearing in mind that ECS obtained goods duty free both from the United Kingdom and the continents, they might lose some turnover and local traders who would be able to sell goods of a continental origin at the same duty free price that they had, but British goods of course would still be subject to import duties and sale in local shops. On the other hand, if they do join, British goods will enter Germany, Belgium and Holland free of tariffs and beyond, and local shops at duty free prices. Their West Coast corporate companies' virtual monopoly for such goods which now the customers would enjoy because of our tax-free position. This could result in some loss of trade. However, knowing the companies' versatility especially when they are up against it they expected it would be fine in the long run that there was no overall loss of trade, particularly as he believed that the EEC rules trade in drink, tobacco and food would be subject to special negotiation. Written by Mr A Frederiksen Results clerk 1961.

There was then a wide selection of people's opinions throughout the business at different levels for and against the joining of the common market, but now looking back in 2020, over 60 years later, you can see why indeed they did join. Although we voted in 2016 to leave once more.

On call 24 hours a day, a day in the life of a ship's canteen manager 1961

One day serving 1700 customers is pretty much like any other to the Naval canteen manager Robert Cameron. Even if the sun blisters the paint work or forces the sailors to take to their bunks, mad dogs and canteen staff work regardless in the heat.

Last month the aircraft carrier HMS Centaur docked at Davenport after four weeks in Kuwait. This month she sails for the Far East and Robert Cameron goes with her. Heat is no stranger to this 35-year-old Scot who spent the last 18 years with the Naval canteen service in many parts of the world.

He joined the NCS after trying to enlist in the Royal Navy and the merchant marine at the outbreak of war. He was too young for the Royal Navy so he went round to join the Merchant Navy. The queue was a mile long and he couldn't wait so he saw a notice about the NCS so he thought that he'd find out something about it. Eighteen years and several ships later, he thinks he has. For the past 15 years he had been a canteen manager, graduating steadily to bigger and bigger ships until now he is in the big-League aircraft carriers. He joined Centaur eight months previous from the cruiser Gambia and quickly jumped to the head of the NCS League table of his division for instalment of credit sales and agreements, notching a total of 563 agreements.

Mr Cameron and his staff of 13 learned that they were Kuwait-bound a few hours after they left Gibraltar on the 30th of June for a six-week goodwill tour of the USA. They docked at Aden to take on supplies, but they couldn't get all they wanted because they were up to their eyeballs in crisis. What they didn't get at Aden they made up when they met the Royal Navy supply ship at sea and took aboard 1500 cases of beer. Ten days later they arrived at the Persian Gulf and relieved HMS Victorious patrolling the coastline. The temperature hit 110 degrees regularly and it wasn't dry heat, it was very humid. Everything you touched was wet. The manager's day started early, working in the tropical routine meant opening the canteen and sub bars at 0615hrs and he had to be around to see that they were all stocked up.

His other responsibilities included the soda fountain, book stall and gift shop, a senior ratings bar, 2 cold drink automatic machines and a Barber service. After prowling the bars, he usually returned to his office to deal with any outstanding paperwork. The advantage of this place, he said, his arm sweeping the cabin, is that he can roll straight off his bunk and onto his desk and no walking to work. The bars were open again from 0930hrs to 1315hrs. The NAAFI team had a two-hour break from 1330hrs to 1530hrs when they opened the shutters until 1800hrs and from then again in the evening from 1900hrs until 2030hrs.

The canteen manager also had to be on hand for the beer allocation which was handed out to the caterers of the ship's 48 messes. Each man aboard was issued 2 cans of beer a day which meant that 100 cases of beer had to be taken out of the ship's fridge and cases from 3 beer stores at different levels on the carrier and had to be transferred to take their place in cold storage. During the four weeks off Kuwait they sold thousands of pounds worth of beer and more than that had they been in home waters. Soft drinks, orangeade and lemonade were as popular as the beer. There was always a big queue outside the bar especially when they made ice cream. Although they couldn't make milkshakes but some ice cream in the drinks went down very well. The 'jacks' could get through 15 gallons of ice cream a day. A lot used to drift away and bring their glasses back later. But a lot didn't, and 1400 glasses went missing. They not only sold paperback books but also LPs and EPs from the shop.

In a ship although you might finish in theory at about 2200hrs in the evening also you were on call 24 hours a day. If the commander wanted to see you at 0200hrs you would have to see the commander at 0200hrs. The heat at night made sleep impossible belowdecks, he added. Sometimes the staff used to go up and sleep on the flight deck when there was no night flying. One thing he regrets about moving onto a bigger ship is the loss of personal touch with his customers. In a ship of that size a great deal of his time had been taken up with paperwork. The disadvantages were offset by the way in which the team pulled together, and the murderous climate, and he was full of praise for them.

E H Cherry, CBE 1915 to 1961

In 1961 saw the sudden death of Edward Hazlehurst Cherry in the August at the age of 79, this severed one of the few remaining links between NAAFI and its predecessors and he was taken from us, one of the leading pioneers in the development of service canteens since the First World War. In January 1915 Edward Cherry, a War Office civil servant of great promise, was appointed secretary of the Board of Control of regimental institutes and the following year became assistant secretary of the newly formed Army Canteen Committee (ACC). This body eventually developed into the Navy and Army Canteen Board (NACB) of which Mr Cherry became the general secretary in November 1920. Two months later he was appointed the first secretary of the new-born NAAFI becoming assistant general manager in 1922 and deputy general manager in 1934. He retained his latter appointment until retirement in December 1944, and during the war years he was one of the members of the six man executive committee which collectively discharged the duties of the general manager. From the company's earliest days, he identified himself closely with the welfare of the staff. He was the father of the Imperial club and served as the chairman continuously from his inception in 1921 until his retirement.

Mr. E. H. CHERRY, M.B.E., Assistant General Manager.

He was also one of the enthusiasts who succeeded in launching NAAFI's first house Journal, the Imperial club magazine, the forerunner of NAAFI News. He was tall, good looking and with a commanding presence, he could have made his mark in many fields. His brother was Malcolm Cherry, the actor – one wondered sometimes whether Edward Cherry himself was not an actor. Certainly he was a devoted student of the Theatre, constructed model theatres as a hobby, wrote plays and radio scripts in his retirement and during his longest time in the Imperial club established a fine reputation both as an actor and producer and was known for his performances in Ambrose Apple Johns adventure, and the Barracks of Wimpole St and many more. In his tastes and conversation, he displayed a wide variety of intellectual entertainments, he was widely read and widely travelled and thought nothing of going to a Garrison overseas. He was a true legend, a forerunner and visionist, who could see the potential and acted upon it.

1962

At the start of 1962

More progress overseas with a brand new modern factory site at Terendak camp, Malacca, Headquarters of the 28th Commonwealth brigade; it was completed in late October 1961. The new site had a modern bakery, milk plant, butchery, a grocery store unit and mass requirements and transport Depot. With the completion of this factory site, the officers' mess was situated near the beach club, the construction of the NAAFI facilities at the base was virtually complete. Troops and families from Australia, New Zealand and the UK are pouring in every week to bring character, colour and life to this thriving service township. Eventually, there will be nearly 10,000 people living in the camp. This was equipped with the latest plant and packaging machinery, the bakery will produce a full range of cakes, pastries and bread. The ovens which are fully automated an oil fired were capable of baking up to 6000lbs of bread a day. The official in charge was Mr Peter Williamson who was previously at the Singapore bakery.

From the bakery, bread and cakes will be distributed daily to all NAAFI's establishments within the camp. A door to door delivery service was also starting to operate to every house in the base. Later, daily deliveries will also be made to Tampin, Seremban and Kuala Lumpur. The butcher would supply all the NAAFI establishments in the camp with a wide range of meat products. In addition, meat and provisions for the supermarket will be prepared and prepacked with a butchery which is equipped with modern bandsaw, vacuum packing machinery and a sausage making machine.

The mechanical cow, as it was affectionately known, was the milk plant and would produce reconstituted milk for all the residents. It could produce 240 gallons of milk in an 8-hour working day. Specially insulated vespa delivery vans have been designed and will carry supplies straight from the cold store to the housewife. The grocery store supplies, and all the Commonwealth units stationed in the camp with all types of missing items. Adjoining the grocery store was a transport Depot complete with a petrol pump, service bay and inspection pit. This was to meet the needs of the service community; there were no fewer than 17 specialist vehicle operators from the Depot. Delivery vans, an ice cream mobile, mobile refreshment vans, bread, mineral and beer delivery vans. Later a mobile fish and chip van would be added to the fleet. The transport was controlled by Mr White, the transport manager in Malaya.

In consideration, this was 1961 but you could say it sounds like a modern supermarket.

Cyprus gets a mobile fridge 1962

In the heat of Cyprus it was good for getting a tan but this was also bad for the fresh meat so to guarantee the service to families and NAAFI clubs, the shops around Famagusta, Cyprus, get fresh from the carcass joints, NAAFI shipped a new refrigerated meat van to the island.

The 7 ton diesel engine vehicle built to NAAFI design and specifications, left the UK in January of 1962. The most expensive single parts of the van was the American pattern Thermo King refrigeration unit, which was made under licence in Britain – instead of cooling plates the unit worked by blasting cold air into the body and recirculating it. The meat was kept at the temperature of five degrees when the temperature outside was 104 Fahrenheit.

The refrigeration unit was powered by a separate, almost vibrationless, petrol engine while the van was on the road and it operated for 18 hours on approximately 6 gallons of petrol. In the evening and overnight it was plugged into a 440 Volt, three phase circuit to keep it running. The unit defrosted automatically every two hours. The driver could keep an eye on the temperature inside the body by the thermometer gauge mounted outside and visible through the rear-view mirror. This was the thermostatically controlled unit and was chosen by the man who designed the body, Mr Hearn, assistant controller of transport, for the maximum efficiency in relation to its weight. The meat was carried in 108 anonised aluminium trays which left the joints unmarked. The widely spaced shelves ensured that the cold air fully circulated around the products.

The interior also included a novel air lock with a special ventilator through which cold air from the deep freeze can be drawn off so that the dairy produce and eggs can be stored at a higher temperature towards the back of the vehicle. The body was insulated with a type of polystyrene, 6 inches of it on the side, front and rear and seven inches on the floor and roof; the installation was completely vapour sealed. The roof was protected from the sun by an aluminium visor which also helped with the flow of air over the roof surface. The body was finished with an olive green, was built by Sparsholt Limited of Portsmouth, it was mounted on a Thames trader chassis. It was a unique design of its time.

Decimalisation 1962

The government set up a committee under the chairmanship of Lord Halsbury, to inquire into the question of the decimal currency, whereby general staff were asked for their opinion. AV Barker, OBE, CA. Joint general manager, had this to say: 375 years ago, the Dutchman invented a simple notation for decimal fractions. He was so struck by the simplicity and the usefulness of this invention that he announced that the universal introduction of the decimal coins, weights and measures could only be a matter of time. The British government had taken little time to convince but towards the end of 1961 it was announced the decision in principle to switch to the decimal currency system. Before this was done a committee of the inquiry under the chairmanship of Lord Halsbury, he was first to investigate the form of the new currency, the phasing of the old change and the costs to the economy. Now that was a decision that had been taken, other suggestions had been made. One is that it becomes computers count in twos, we should count in eights. This eight would be written 10 and 64 be written 100. Yet another proposal is that we should count in twelves, while eight is only devisable by four and two, 12 can also be divided by three. Since most of the rest of the world had adopted, or are in the process of adopting a decimal currency, it seemed probable that we were to do the same. So as far as NAAFI was concerned, the problems of switching from Sterling to a new decimal currency in the UK.

The main costs to NAAFI would arise from converting accounting and the calculating machines of the cash registers. It was estimated that to convert the cash registers would be £65,000. There would be other costs, of course, such as reprinting a price lists, but this would be a job which would be done fairly frequently as it is already. If the units of currency were changed there could be considerable expenditure and adapting the slot machines that they used. Many people think that the population will have difficulty understanding the new decimal currency, and this may be so. But he was convinced and confident that the NAAFI staff concerned would adapt their counting of currency correctly in a very short period of time. Certainly, it would not have had any troubles over the NAAFI balance sheet, which didn't show any shillings or Pence.

Charles Day, the location manager of SHAPE canteen service: the pound Sterling became a great and powerful currency unit in direct competition with decimal currencies. To dilute our splendid currency with these damned dots is to take yet a further step towards the destruction of the traditional ways of life. The protagonists of pan European pennies would have us adopt decimal currency because it is more economically practical than our duo decimal system. They could no doubt make out a similar case for communal living, communal feeding and all the things that make a 1984 system so efficient. They may care to consider that while 1/3 of a pound is 6 shillings 8d.

Johnny Bradford, location manager, Fontaine blue: I welcome the idea of a decimal coinage for England. During my time with SHAPE canteen service in France I've found it much more efficient than Sterling. Its introduction is in keeping with the common market theme.

WJ Nelson, assistant to the produce branch manager 1962

It was hard on the 15-year-old boy walking into a new job. He didn't know that the Naval parade ground, which he had to cross, was sacred during the morning "divisions". Nor did he know that the man had to cross it at the double. His respectful walk was interrupted by the appearance of an angry officer who yelled at him, "Who the hell are you and where do you think you're going?" My name is Nelson and I'm joining the Victory, the boy replied. The answer was enough to sink the sailor and William J Nelson walked on to the canteen of the Royal Navy barracks, Portsmouth, HMS Victory and into the trade in which he would work for 47 years, 41 would be with NAAFI.

Mr Nelson, assistant to the manager, produce branch, started in the forces messing as a junior clerk with Richard Dickeson, canteen contractors. When he graduated from the Royal Navy barracks to the firm's head office, the jump to it attitude of the junior clerk caught the attention of the managing director, Sir Alexander Prince, who was later the first general manager of the army canteen committee. An encouraging chat with the managing director convinced the young Nelson that it would not be too many years before he would be filling the old man's place.

A little later William Nelson felt he was not making much headway where he was, so he left for the junior army and Navy stores, a firm with several ships' canteen contracts. When the Admiralty decided to join forces with the ACC his firm was absorbed into the new NACB.

Wanting to be as closely connected with the Navy as possible, he took a clerical job on HMS Vernon, which, like Victory, was a relic of the navy's past glories. He was not in the job long before he had the urge to travel. He volunteered for sea service and his first posting took him to Rosyth, where he became a clerk in HMS Crescent, working on messing accounts for the ships and craft attached.

During his five years in Scotland, Mr Nelson carried out various relief duties, both at sea and ashore. In 1923 he was appointed canteen manager in HMS Weymouth, which was then refitting at Chatham as a trooper. As Mr Nelson looked back, he recalls the work, "Seven days a week and no bad results accepted".

He was about to sail in the Weymouth when he was suddenly withdrawn and sent to the Portsmouth Depot office to be an assistant to the late Mr Freddie Thorndike, clerk in charge of one of the sections. His work brought him in touch with Mr HL Allensbury, local produce buyer, who later helped as an assistant buyer. Eleven years later William Nelson was appointed area produce buyer. Based on Chester in the western command, he travelled 350 miles a week by car and train, buying produce, visiting NAAFI establishments and growers.

In 1938 he came to London as an area produce buyer, headquarters, with an office at Covent Garden. He went shopping at the main London markets, Covent Garden and Spitalfields. His job grew more difficult with the outbreak of war. The forces swelled, food was in short supply and London was the target of mass raids. Mr Nelson's job of finding enough fruit and vegetables for the service customers was made easier by the growers. "NAAFI received almost preferential treatment from growers and merchants into the market. They would say, I've got a boy in the RAF, my boy is in North Africa or my son is in the Navy, when they let me have some fruit which was in particularly short supply." At times when people went from merchant to merchant, begging odd cases of fruit, there was one man who had a great pile of crates of apples. To save people pestering him, he had a board in front of them reading 'these are for NAAFI'.

In 1947 Mr Nelson was appointed assistant to the supervisor, local produce, a job he still retained in 1962 although his title was different. His appointment to the job 15 years previous revived memories of his early career in Portsmouth because the man he succeeded was Mr Allensbury, his former chief. Looking back on a long and busy career, Mr Nelson, a youthful 60, said that if he had his life over again and there is no such thing as a produce branch in NAAFI then he would like to go into catering. He was something of an amateur cook and although he didn't know much about cooking in his older years, he certainly didn't do his family any harm. His sons and daughters thrived on his cooking or in spite of it.

A little Nepal takes shape at Tidworth 1962

The exotic fragrance of incense mingled with the scent of eastern cooking at Tidworth, Wiltshire, where the advance party of 63 infantry brigade group, including over 50 Ghurkhas were settling in. NAAFI help them to feel at home to the extent of flying special rice enricher in from America. The arrival of these fighters from Nepal was being spread over three months by the end of May 1962, the Gurkhas' contingent would number about 1700. With them will be about 480 wives and children. This is to be the first time a Gurkha unit has formed part of strategic reserve based in the UK. The Gurkhas would be accompanied at Jalalabad barracks, Lucknow barracks and Mooltan barracks in Tidworth.

They used the junior ranks clubs exclusively and would share the Mooltan junior ranks club with the British troops. For the arrival of the Gurkha families the services shop at Jalalabad will be converted to cater solely for them, stocking native food and items used in their religious rites. NAAFI planning has taken many months and most of the everyday needs of the newcomers have been anticipated. Most of the supplies for the family shop had been brought through a London importer. NAAFI had to make special arrangements for the vitaminized rice the Gurkhas are used to. It was discovered that the enricher was processed in the USA, so a consignment was flown in. A great deal of research into the dieting religious customs of the Gurkhas, who were Hindu, was made before orders were placed with the London merchant. When the Gurkhas' wives went shopping to buy native ingredients of familiar dishes, among them: garlic, cumin seed, coriander seed, turmeric, whole black pepper, Cassi, cardamoms, till seed, tamarind, together with vegetables, similar to lentils and split peas, of the dhal group. Also specially ordered had been the supplies of vegetable ghee, equivalent to the native cooking fat. The produce branch had arranged supplies of chilies, fresh lines, 100 weight of fresh coconut, extra milk, potatoes, and fruits and vegetables. The Gurkha's diet would also be supplemented by barley wheat seed and millet.

All other aspects of their diet were catered for. They would also be able to worship In England as they did at home. To ensure this orders had been placed for any items that they would need.

OCA 1962

Sir William Beale, former chairman of NAAFI, resigned as the association's president. His resignation was announced by Mr CA Layard, chairman of the general committee, at the 15th AGM of the OCA. Mr Layard also announced that the managing director, Mr HPT Prideaux, had consented to succeed Sir William as the president.

In the annual report, the UK membership was now at 1875; this was a drop by 97 members on the previous year's figure. This could be for a variety of reasons but a steady decline in membership was expected. So, the ambition to raise the membership to 2000 was implemented. Mr Layard addressed the meeting and added that he thought the target was possible to reach, if each person and member could introduce five eligible personnel, they would be on their way to hitting their number.

The previous year's events had reflected to the Armistice ceremonies held in the UK and in Malta. Fewer applications had also been submitted for benevolence and assistance. This was actually put down to the sign of the times, welfare state, in a position to provide a greater measure of help for ordinary causes, the chairman said. Turning to the revenue account, he reported that the year subscriptions were slightly less than in 1960 and reflected the drop in membership.

Farewell to Ceylon And Jamaica 1962

The holding down of the white Ensign over HMS Highflyer and the raising of the Ceylon national flag marked the end of a 31-year-old link between NAAFI and the island. When the last British forces, a Royal Navy contingent, pulled out, NAAFI India's district manager Mr Frank Mullins went with them.

After spending four years in the climate averaging 80 Fahrenheit all year round, on an island where a pint of beer costs 7 shillings 6d and the cinema seat costs 6 shillings, Mr Mullins was glad to be arriving back to storm-lashed England.

He brought with them memories of beauty and boredom. To him it was refreshing to look at mile-long beaches fringed with palms, native huts nearby and not a hot dog stand in sight. Upcountry where Mr Mullins spent his leave, the climate was cooler. He said he found himself reminiscing of home with green trees, fields and a cool climate. But there was another less picturesque side of the island as Mr Mullins discovered. It was just as well that the picture postcards so beloved by tourists did not show the squalor and poverty inside the quaint thatched huts, you could not picture the ever-present threat of infection and the high cost of living. Even though the cinemas were expensive the nightlife was virtually non-existent with no television. Radio programs were a far cry from the BBC. And many people on the island thought that the frequent thunderstorms were nature's retaliation for programmes sent into the air by the local radio stations.

As British forces left the island and it gained its independence, NAAFI staff dwindled from a peak of 352 just before the departure to only 30. Two years ago, Mr Mullins and his staff provided a service for nearly 400 RAF and Naval personnel and their families, then in June 1960 350 RAF men and their families left, leaving only the small Naval contingent. One of the major problems was the delay in getting stores unloaded from ships. He said that there was sometimes delays of up to four months in offloading cargoes but despite the delays and setbacks that customers received the normal service from NAAFI, and the name will not be quickly forgotten on the island.

The Queen's Birthday celebrations in June marked the end of over 300 years' association between Jamaica and the British army. The association was celebrated with the reception at King's house at which the ceremony of the beating of the retreat was performed.

NAAFI catered for the reception, which was attended by over 3000 guests and was the largest ever held there – over 7000 drinks were served in 70 minutes. Appreciation was received from the governor Sir Kenneth Blackburn, GBE, KCMG, in which he said, "I write to express the most grateful thanks to my wife and myself for the magnificent job which she did on Saturday evening at the King's house. The Queen's Birthday reception this year was the biggest which has ever been held, I know that you were operating under difficulties because of the uncertainty of the weather and because we did not have the usual help from the military authorities as waiters. Despite these difficulties the supply of drinks was quite admirably carried out and at no time after the first few minutes did any of the guests experience any difficulty in obtaining what they needed. This was due entirely to your excellent organization, we are more grateful than words can say for the most excellent way in which you and your staff helped us on this occasion." The last official engagement at the King's house would be a reception in the August to mark the granting of independence to Jamaica, at which Princess Margaret and Lord Snowdon were expected to be present. NAAFI has been asked to provide the service for one last time.

The Pack Horse, the first NAAFI pub 1962

In Larkhill in 1962 a new private pub was opened. Previously NAAFI had opened a trail of luxury clubs, but this was very new, a pub outside the wire just for service personnel and their families.

In Salisbury Plain Garrison of Larkhill, the first services pub called The Pack Horse had opened. The retired Garrison commander Col Brian Cocks cut a red ribbon across the wide glass doors of this first all ranks, pub styled club, he was witnessing the fruition of his own suggestion. It was he who had originally thought of the idea of building a servicees only pub in the isolated Garrison.

His suggestion was sent to the War Office and 18 months previously the building began on what would be the first in line of new clubs for servicepersons. The colonel's verdict on the club was: "Super. I really think it's super. Two things stand out in my mind. First, it was only a comparatively short time ago that we were discussing things like this with drains and boundaries. The speed with which The Pack Horse had been built was amazing. Secondly the decor, furnishings and fittings are the best I've seen in a pub anywhere. Everything is bright and fun and warm and friendly. It has a built-in atmosphere."

The Pack Horse comprised a public bar, with a country pub interior, natural pine and brick, from which a lobby led to the cocktail bar and lounge bar. The adjacent cocktail bar is decorated in red and gold. A novel feature is the bar, fronted with illuminated panels. The lounge bar was split level and is panelled in light oak. Above the club is a flat for NAAFI's first host and his wife, Mr and Mrs Herbert Pratt, who reported good business as soon as the doors opened. A fortnight earlier Larkhill was the scene of another opening of another Garrison landmark, the social club, Wagon Lines. The club was the 2nd to be designed by NAAFI and completed by the company as agents to the War Office.

Lt Col Sir Robert Bray, GOC in C, southern command, turned the golden key to open the club and then had the Grand Tour, starting from the services shop leading off from the tiled foyer. Here was the restaurant, finished in white plastic wall covering, the TV room with cinema style seating, the social activities room with its hard-wooden dance floor, the beech panelled lounge bar and the two billiard rooms. Outside the club run a slab terrace which was ideal for summer functions to have drinks on. The new club was easily picked out at distance by the curtain of glass windows which ran 165 feet in length of the building.

Edmond Jackson from the Navy to the Naval Canteen Service 1962

After a career on the high seas Mr Edmond Jackson retired in 1962. He had served 36 years with the NCS, but this all began in May 1929 as an assistant steward at the Vernon club in Malta, although he had sailed before. At the age of 15 he left his Dublin home and joined the Royal Navy serving in the final year of the First World War. He remembers 1919 very clearly as this was the last year the straw hat was used in the British Navy.

Mr Jackson left the senior service in December 1928, then was introduced to NAAFI by the man who was to become his brother-in-law and who was already working for the company in Malta. It was as easy as signing a contract and then starting work the very next day. The Burning club was where it all started, he went as a canteen assistant from there, on board the Queen Elizabeth a ship he was to serve on twice. In the mid-30s Mr Jackson was promoted to canteen manager following an interview before the board at Ruxley Towers. By that time that he had married a Maltese girl and set up home on the island of Hamrun.

His first ship is canteen manager was HMS Ormond. Later he then joined the 'Maine' which was a hospital ship, working in partnership with that was to last throughout the Second World War, for more than a decade. The ship was based at Alexandria and was then used to follow the 8th army picking up the frontline casualties. In 1941 the hospital ship suffered a near miss from 1000lb bomb dropped by the enemy above. Four people were killed and 40 injured. After the raid Mr Jackson found a small piece of shrapnel stuck in his neck; if it had moved just a fraction of an inch deeper it would have pierced the jugular vein.

Then in 1948 found Mr Jackson still serving in troubled waters, first on the 'Charity' and then on the 'Cheviot', during the 'Haifa' emergency. After that he lost his sea legs for a while, working at a shore canteen in Cyrenaica at Benghazi and Derna and at the Malta shore base. Then in 1954 he took over as canteen manager on the HMS Meon and remained on her until the summer when the Meon sailed to Portsmouth at the end of his career. Edmond Jackson at that time was age 62.

The HMS Meon (L369) was a frigate of the amphibious Warfare squadron, had seen active service in the Suez campaign of 1956, in the Persian Gulf, before being eventually paid off in 1965.

In 1962 his exemplary service was rewarded with the British Empire medal and during this much travelled career he had five passports, he earned commendations from commanding officers far and wide. His working philosophy was 'patience and goodwill to others. Put yourself last it always pays in the end'.

1963

Bushfire in Brunei written by JE McMullen 1963

A message in a bottle dropped into the Limbang River in Brunei led a 20 strong party of rangers to a rebel hideout near the village of Danau. In an armed attack on the hideout an isolated house in the jungle, one rebel was killed, and two others wounded before the remaining five had surrendered. The all-important message had been dropped from an Army Air corps aircraft, the only way of contacting the Rangers. Such hit and run actions were typical of the Brunei emergency, an emergency which necessitated the movement of a large number of troops from Singapore in early December 1962. It was vital that NAAFI provided a service as quickly as possible in both Brunei and the base area at Labuan, a neighbouring island, from which all supply and maintenance operations were conducted.

To this end, following a hurried meeting at NAAFI Singapore headquarters, Mr Jimmy Duncan, who was then an assistant command supervisor Singapore, and later in Hong Kong, and Mr Tony Irvine, district manager, left by air to make the necessary arrangements to open a bulk issue store and a junior ranks club at the start-up of a mobile refreshment service in the base area.

A landing ship tank, the empire, arrived in Labuan harbour on the 14th of December with the first NAAFI stores: cigarettes, toiletry articles, Gurkha rum and, the most important, beer. By 2200hrs the same evening, Mr Duncan was able to signal to the brigade commander in Brunei that NAAFI BIS operative was open from the 15th of December. The next task was to takeover a small unit run canteen at RAF. Before the emergency the canteen catered for 28 airmen and now some 500 were using it. With the arrival of the volunteer NAAFI staff from Singapore, the canteen and two mobile canteens were quickly in operation. The staff worked from early morning until late in the evening to provide beer and refreshments for the airmen and the troops who were working around the clock at the airport.

Mr Duncan then returned to Singapore and after reporting to the commanding supervisor, Mr Hudman, I fear the plan of action was decided on and the command supervisor left would provide together with the Far East PRO, Mr James McMullan. Their first call was at Brunei airport, the nerve centre of the communications and the operations. It was number one priority to establish service for 500 people based around the airport.

The airport buffet was provided and was the perfect answer. By 1900 hours on the 19th of December an officers' bar and other ranks bar were open for business. Two Chinese staff, who had made their own way to Brunei from North Borneo together with Irvine, McMullen and Hudman, they were soon busy at both bars serving refreshments. They only stopped when further staff reached Brunei from Singapore. A small temporary bulk issue store was also established at the airport to meet unit requirements, mainly beer and cigarettes. The diet of the troops and airmen based in Brunei was at the time compo and biscuits and any variation in diet was a very much welcome. A visit to Brunei town provided some meat pies and cakes, while a local baker started turning out dozens of Curry puffs, which soon became a top favourite at the airport bar.

With the assistance of the Army, NAAFI then set about establishing BIS at a requisitioned Malay girls' school in Brunei. By Christmas Eve it was going great under the direction of Mr Stanley Head, ACS, Malaya, who had arrived from Singapore. Stores reaching the island were quickly distributed to the units based in Brunei. Rebels or no rebels the boys are going to have Christmas, declared Mr Head. By the 27th of December further staff had arrived at the junior ranks club which was established in the Malay school.

Meanwhile Mr Tan Pung Kean, the bulk issue store manager and his staff, together with Tony Irvin worked long into the night arranging supplies for air and parachute drops to the troops deep in the jungle and hard in pursuit of the fleeing rebels.

Christmas fare was of a vital importance and the refrigerated van, normally based in Singapore, was stocked with turkey, chicken, fresh fruit, frozen vegetables, nuts and Christmas puddings, and shipped on LST, with Mr Paul Cheong, traffic foreman, Singapore, in charge. It arrived safely and the distribution of the supplies by air went off rapidly and smoothly. An ITV team were on hand to film the scene as Christmas turkey and the puddings were unloaded.

Mr Nair, assistant district accountant, had volunteered for service in this new trouble spot and arrived to give Mr Irvin invaluable aid in the BIS, establishing records and generally assisting with day-to-day supervision. At the other end of the operation in Singapore, Mr Tannock, the newly arrived supervisor, was working with his team, ensuring the build-up of supplies, staff and equipment for both locations. Supplies included not only food, beers and cigarettes, but furniture, bedding, mobile canteens, vans and other vital stores. One gratifying aspect of the Brunei emergency was the wonderful spirit of the Asian staff, who did not hesitate to volunteer for service at this vital moment. With the hostilities abated, NAAFI's role became of paramount importance, for Brunei is a wild country of swift flowing rivers and impenetrable

jungle. NAAFI staff and officials are seeing that everything that was possible would be done to make life more tolerable for the men of the Royal Navy, the army and the Royal Air Force.

The end of an era March 1963 by Ronald Walker and Claude Luke

The 60th issue of NAAFI News was published in March 1963 by the editor Claude F Luke. The 60th issue Claude handed on the editorial control of NAAFI News to Ronald Walker.

In the production of 60 issues Claude said he had interviewed most of the NAAFI men of the moment, with many of NAAFI's biggest characters, and talked with thousands of NAAFI staff in many countries. I have watched and reported on the momentous changes in the company, in its structure, its trade and its methods. NAAFI News itself had not been immune to change. It began life as a 24 page quarterly, although even my first editorial I foresaw the time when it would become a monthly publication.

I still remember with tremendous pleasure the excitement, the sweat and the labour, the last-minute panics which went into the first issue in the winter of 1945. I recall with appreciation the flood of generous comments with which the readers greeted the appearance of the magazine. As time went by, we were able to improve upon the first issue, as post-war paper restrictions eased we increased the number of pages and used a better-quality paper. We changed from gravure two letter press, which gave the news a brighter, crisper appearance and in 1951 we introduced the first of our photographic supplements as a showcase for the Imperial club photographers. We continued to grow in size until 1954, when we were regularly printing 48 pages.

In the autumn of 1955, we changed printers and NAAFI News became an all in NAAFI production when our own printing branch at Kennings Way undertook the production. In 1960 one NAAFI News achieved its ambition to become a monthly publication. Later that year it changed from the letterpress process to a photo lithography when it became the first magazine to be printed by the new forces press. In the issue for spring 1956.

Ronald Walker, fresh from a tour as a Middle East PRO, joined the editorial staff. In the same editorial I went on to say, the gap between the upstart 20s and the downstart 50s is one that can be bridged only with courtesy and respect on both sides and a humble acknowledgement that none of us is too young or too old to learn from one another. In the case endpoint, bridging the gap was an enjoyable and mutually beneficial experience. But what of the future? I can only reiterate what I have said in the past: the success of any magazine depends more upon the quality of its readers than upon the quality of its editor. Unless the magazine has the support, and active support, of the members of the NAAFI family it is doomed. I have had this support in the past from everyone from the newest recruit to the managing director. I hope it will be given the full measure by my successor.

CLAUDE F LUKE MIPR, a well known Fleet Street freelance feature writer, joined NAAFI in 1940 as the company's first press officer. With the late Col C Fraser, he built the public relations Department and took charge on Colonel Fraser's retirement in 1943. He launched NAAFI News in 1945, NAAFI Review in 1953 and NAAFI Reports in 1956. The first 2 have won Seven awards in national competitions for house journals. Until recently he served a four-year term as chairman of the suggestions committee. He was a member of the managing directors' committee, the merchandising committee and the joint consultative council of which he has been appointed member since its inception.

RONALD WALKER MIPR, went from provincial journalism into the RAF, where he served in Cairo as a features editor of the Air Force News. He took charge of publicity for combined services entertainments, Middle East successor to ENSA, and after a spell with the British transport PR he joined NAAFI in 1952 as PRO Middle East with a parish stretching from Tripoli to East Africa. He returned to headquarters in 1956, he then paid a brief return visits to Tripoli with an ITV production team and Cyprus where he completed a sales promotion assignment. He was appointed assistant editor, NAAFI News in 1957 and NAAFI Review in 1960. His duties include press, radio and TV liaison.

Now over to the new guy. If I feel less nervous, less of a new boy, perhaps even a trifle confident as I try the editor's chair for size, this must be attributed entirely to the retiring editor. This is not so much a stepping into a new job as taking up the last bit of slack for, in recent years, my editor and happily he will continue to be my editor on the NAAFI Review, the annual report and other publications. Slowly but surely, he built up my responsibilities and allowed me to grow into the job.

When I first joined the editorial staff of NAAFI News there were certain aspects of journalism such as print and design in which I felt I had the edge over my editor. On the other hand, there were fields of crafting of writing, for example, in which I knew he left me far behind. Under his guidance the latter gap had narrowed but more than I expected it could as my confidence that there was a balancing gap in other areas diminished. With this sureness that comes from experience and flair he has picked up his way carefully through a wealth of suggestions, adopting, adapting and rejecting. I have watched and hope learned from this process. For this reason, readers need not fear any massive radical changes in the form of content for the magazine. Changes must come, for no two individuals ever think exactly alike. Changes would have come without any editorial change, for our staff magazine, like the company itself, must keep in step with the times.

It is certain that the development I most want to see is one which he heartily approves, greater reader participation but more of this in later issues. The relinquishing of his editorial chair of our magazine by its founder editor is not merely the end of a chapter, it is the end of a volume or rather of three volumes which is why the next issue will appear as volume 4 #61. Fortunately, this is not the end of his active association with the magazine. I sincerely hope that many articles in the future will bear his initials CFL. No reader will welcome them more than I.

Pressing on, at Aldershot the closure of the printing works in Kingsway, London ended the branch's 40-year link with the headquarters building. During January and February the NAAFI lorry shuttled back and forth from London to Aldershot nearly two dozen times with very important cargo. The activity marked the end of an era, the final severing of the printing branch with London. Since its inception NAAFI had a printing works to provide essential forms in domestic stationery.

As the years passed the factory took on more work, including a limited amount of service printing, booklets, handbooks, personal stationery and Christmas cards. Publications such as NAAFI Review, the annual report, NAAFI News and the durable goods catalogue attracted the attention of the services and drew enquiries from the service editors. As a result more and more service magazines were being printed by NAAFI. Two years ago, it was decided that the whole range of service printing was a legitimate field for NAAFI expansion, hence the opening of a modern forces press in Aldershot. It was to employ offset lithography, an entirely different printing process from what was used at Kennings Way.

In place of the familiar heavy lead type the new factory would use photographic film instead of using the old technique of engraving photographs on blocks and a remarkable electronic engraving machine would produce plastic blocks in a fraction of the time, anodised aluminium plates would replace the cumbersome printing forms and high speed presses would print two colours simultaneously.

The first of the new presses began to turn just over a year before and since that day the new equipment had slowly been added, more and more work was undertaken. As the volume of work grew in Aldershot, the usefulness of the Kennington plant dwindled and it was recognised that the branch would operate more economically if the two plants were housed under one roof.

The result was the transfer of the machinery and equipment from Kennington to Crimea Road, Aldershot. The move itself was supervised by Mr Edwin Bacon, a work study official. The task confronting him and the team working with him was the dismantling, transfer and installation of 60 tons of machinery, equipment and printing metal.

The team worked until late at night, seven days a week, for over three weeks. Also involved were NAAFI drivers and staff of the works and buildings. Engineers assembling machines also had problems to overcome, the great presses weighing 12½ tons and a six-tonne guillotine had to be moved. Special arrangements had to be made to store the tonnes of metal type shipped from Kennington.

As the last stages of the transfer were being made in the March of 1963 the result of the efforts made over the 18 month period to transform the bakery into a modern printing plant could be seen – a factory of 20,000 square feet capable of an annual turnover of £500,000 to £750,000 worth of letterpress and lithography equipment for printing.

Coinciding with the move was the opening of the forces press reception room. A close carpeted room where prospective customers could see in comfort, examples of NAAFI quality printing, anything from full colour magazine to a visiting card.

From the reception room it is only a short walk to the factory floor where some of the most technically advanced machinery and equipment in Europe produced work of the highest quality. The pride of the printing works was two giant, two colour offset litho printing presses rolling out 10,000 sheets an hour, 16 hours a day. Working alongside them were smaller offset printing presses and letterpresses plant transferred from Kennington.

The forces press had been planned for a smooth flow of jobs from the paper store where the rolls and sheets of paper were maintained in perfect condition by a thermostatically controlled heating system and humidifiers. These were then taken to the printing machines and on to the folding, gathering, stitching and cutting sections before being sent to the dispatch bay.

Situated strategically, so that the various stages of the copy preparation can be fed into the machine room at the appropriate moment, are the film setters, art studio, composing room, camera and darkrooms, electronic engraver and platemaking equipment. Since the forces press opened the number of service journals bearing the NAAFI imprint has more than doubled. One of the major contracts signed was for Soldier magazine, which had a monthly circulation of 70,000 in 1963.

In addition to magazines, the demand for a wide range of other printing was growing. From the despatch bay pulls a steady stream of personal stationery, menu cards, invitation cards, sports programmes, posters, leaflets, camp guides and brochures.

At the time the potential was almost limitless. Mr WH Hodgkinson, manager of the forces press, put it: "Now that the move from Kennington is complete, the capacity of the press has increased and our sales staff is looking round hungrily for further orders. All NAAFI staff who are in direct touch with the service should remember this important source of revenue and keep an eye open for any talk of printing requirements amongst their customers. The press will be happy to quote full jobs, large or small, simple or intricate dance tickets, menus, invitations,

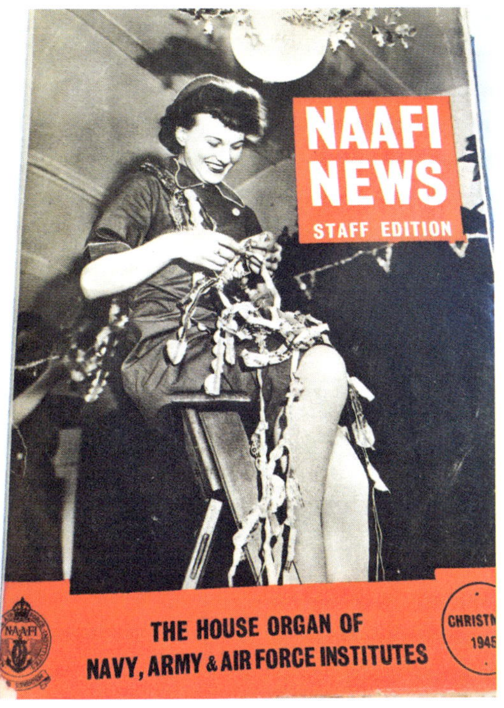

station magazines, posters, programmes, guidebooks and all mass accounting stationery in colour such as mess account books and the waiters' bar books. A letter addressed to me will be bringing a quick quotation for the job."

Farewell to NAAFI review 1963

1963 The winter issue. The much loved NAAFI Review would publish its last issue. The editor Claude Luke would bid a second farewell.

This will have to be the last time we talk it over in quite this way, for the decision has been taken that after 41 issues and 10 years of vigorous life, NAAFI Review must close down. It was not an easy decision to arrive at and in fact a close investigation of all the relevant factors together with several reprieves, preceded it. But now it is felt the axe must fall.

We have talked over many things during the past 10 years, from the effects of blue language in the canteens to the high rate of marriage between Miss NAAFI and the customer. We have discussed NAAFI's policies, principles and prices. We have explained again and again the cooperative methods by which NAAFI operates and ensures that all trading surpluses, or profits, are distributed sooner or later in cash or kind to the only people entitled to them and that would be the military personnel and their families.

No newspaper or magazine folds without a pang of regret from the loyal readers and those who produced it. So why has the Review come to an end? There are several good reasons but the main one is that it has completed the job it set out to do. Older readers will recall that this publication was originally launched at the request of the services, as a medium through which the company could keep staff and service personnel and their families aware of recent activities and achievements and its future plans. It was also desirable that the scores of thousands of national servicemen who were still joining the forces each year should be given some insight into the workings of their own trading organization, with due emphasis on the fact that NAAFI was and always has been, their safeguard against exploitation of the serviceman, the custodian of the profits delivered from his trade.

Other objects of the magazine were to inform customers, both regular and national service, of any new ventures in trading or facilities which is why we devoted considerable space to reporting such events as the introduction of dividend, instalment credit, car hire purchase and NAAFI petrol stations, to mention but a few. We regularly featured such items as the opening of new clubs, pubs, shops, shopping centres, mobile shops, bowling alleys and similar amenities.

Today the picture's changed; the influx of drafts of national servicemen has stopped and the need of repeat explanation of NAAFI policy and practice to these new customers no longer exists. It was not easy for the editors to say that there is not a real need for this publication, the regular professional servicemen would be kept constantly in the picture particularly concerning NAAFI plans which may affect the comfort, welfare and bank balance of them and their family. But these matters are already covered in the other publications. Not long before 'wise buys',

Navy, Army and Air Force
Naafi
Review
A Half-Yearly Survey of Naafi Activities

No. 1 — Published by Naafi — APRIL, 1953

NON-STOP NAAFI SERVICE IN FLOOD AREAS

"Ocean-Going" Mobile Canteens

"OCEAN-GOING" mobile canteens, 24-hour day and night service, the feeding and accommodating of hundreds of refugees were all just part of Naafi's "bit" when the great flood struck at Britain.

As the raging waters swept in over the East Coast from Grimsby to Sheerness, Naafi staff were alerted along with civil and Service authorities to meet the emergency.

CATERING FOR THE CORONATION

66,000 ROLLS and 33,000 SLICES of CAKE

Six Acres of Canvas

FOUR hundred and fifty Naafi staff, "borrowed" from canteens all over Great Britain, will be playing an important role in the Coronation drama by providing food and refreshment for the thousands of Servicemen taking part.

In the military camp to be sited in Kensington Gardens, Naafi marquees covering six acres will accommodate restaurants and bars for 12,000 troops, bars and lounges for 1,300 Warrant Officers and Sergeants and three full scale Officers' Messes, catering for 700 officers.

Skilled craftsmen at Naafi's tentage works at Aldershot are hard at work preparing £60,000 worth of tents and marquees, the first of which will go up in Kensington Gardens on 15th May. Naafi restaurants, bars and messes will be operating there by 18th May and will remain open until 8th or 9th of June.

Strange Cargo

from NAAFI, provided up to date news and all the latest NAAFI bargains, special offers, and sales news for the family man. And this was available in every shop, all I needed to do was ask for a copy. It was free. Another one of the publications which detailed new ventures in the trading field and new establishments and their annual publications was called NAAFI Reports. Every club had one of these available and if somebody wanted to read it, they were able to ask for a copy to borrow. It included full details of the company's finances and it showed how much was earned during the past year and how the profits were distributed.

That wasn't the only way to keep updated with all the news, keeping the customers informed with articles in the press, broadcasts on the forces radio, advertisements in the unit journals, to units and wives by NAAFI staff and the occasional production of leaflets and brochures. They really did keep their customers informed.

So twice in one year the much loved editor of NAAFI News and NAAFI Review would bid farewell as he sent his warmest thanks to the loyal readers whose letters often proved to be so valuable and the advertisers, and support in the early days of the production of another loved publication. Everybody was involved, it varied from generals to privates, from cabinet ministers to canteen staff. This time he affectionately signed his farewell: the editor.

1964

Central London district 1964

The Household Cavalry, the guards and the Royal Horse Artillery are an integral part of London's pride. Inside some of the most historic buildings conditions were austere, their decay added to the difficulties of providing an efficient service for small, but elite units scattered throughout the city. For one of the military showpieces in the capital, the gleaming Chelsea barracks, where there was a NAAFI club and shop were among the best to be found anywhere. There were a dozen other establishments where NAAFI operated in these conditions. Most of the barracks were scheduled for demolition or rebuilding during the decades following 1964, but this did not stop NAAFI staff who had to provide the service to a high level. With only a limited life for those buildings the best they could do was to patch here and a little paint there to bring them up to scratch.

In the heart of the city with unprecedented rivalry from restaurants, cafes, coffee bars, shops and Department stores, the staff got on with providing a first-class service. There had been dramatic improvements in both the standard of the clubs and the trade in recent years and the conditions were improving all the time.

At Hyde Park barracks, the home of the Household Cavalry, the club was sandwiched between the married quarters and the stables. To get to it you have to go up a flight of iron stairs, behind the tall wooden doors lay a high ceiling club managed by an ex wing commander Kenneth Bransby. He had been to many RAF units and now he was working among cavalrymen at Hyde Park, but he was shortly to leave for a new post in Aldershot. With just 135 troops he was kept working long hours; they could have done with more staff but unfortunately the numbers didn't warrant it. The busiest time of day was morning break and later in the evening after dinner.

Half a mile or so along Kensington Road was one-woman club which was run by Miss Florence Hyde, who had been serving the redcaps of the London district provost company. She had been with the company 22 years and was previously a cook at Wellington barracks. And to the boys and girls that she serves gallons of tea and coffee to and dozens of filled rolls each weeks she was called "Flo". Flo had joined EFI during the war, intending to leave after the hostilities ended, but when they did, she found that she had got into the swing of things and stayed on. When she pulled the shutters down in the evening there was little time for leisure but what there was, she spent knitting, reading or watching the television, all of which have allowed her to put her feet up after a long day. Eventually she moved across London to manage the club at Regent's Park barracks and was succeeded at Kensington by Miss Ellen May.

Miss Olive M Adams took over the families' Shop at St John's Wood barracks; at the time they were occupied by King's Troop, Royal Horse Artillery. She also had a storeman Terrence Deeming and the till operator Miss Jean Stains. After 20 years as a manageress in Europe, North Africa and the UK she was now pleased to have her own shop in London. Her immediate job on arriving at St John's Wood shop was familiarising herself with the pet likes and dislikes of 120 troops and some 70 families who would use the shop regularly. Across the parade ground tucked behind the administrative building was the junior ranks club on the first floor where Miss B Saunders and Mrs Gladys Luther and Miss Sheila O'Connor provided the service every day of the year. They even worked Christmas Day, they felt they had a duty to serve the men who stayed behind to look after the horses. The busiest time was in the evening when the TV commercials were screened.

Across London to Regent's Park barracks, Miss Dorothy Packham was the manageress at headquarters, The Royal Army Service Corps, London district, junior ranks club, who was to retire by the end of 1964. She enjoyed her role and had been with the company for 23 years. She believed that after the war the lack of appreciation for the service was the reason that she had decided to leave.

Kelvin House, where there were 30 or more RAF personnel, the whole kitchen had a low ceiling, and without adequate ventilation it made cooking a difficult operation. Mrs Mabel Tilly who since the mid-50s had managed the club and sub bar at the Royal Army Medical Corps college and hospital, the two buildings flanked the Tate Gallery, overlooking the Thames at Milbank. The club was scheduled for alteration, when she first went to Milbank, she was told it was going to close so she agreed to stay on and made the best of it. It wasn't till some years later she realised that the iron posts which went from floor to ceiling, where the horses used to be tied up, meaning it used to be a stables, but the horses had long since gone. One member of staff who worked with her was Savvas Partasas, who operated the bar in the Queen Alexandra Royal Military hospital in the morning and then wheel the trolley back round in the afternoon. She had later then been promoted to Imperial Court.

Wellington barracks, where the guardsmen were up against Miss Winifred Eastman, a manageress whom the guardsmen were aware of. Even though it was a stone's throw from Buckingham Palace she stood no nonsense from the men who called her jokingly 'Ena Sharples'. She originally wanted to be a nurse, but her doctor had told her that she wouldn't be strong enough to stand it, so she joined NAAFI because she looked and thought life would be easier!

The restaurant at the Central London recruiting Depot in great Scotland Yard and the sub bar at Horse Guards were the joint responsibility of the manageress Miss Evelyn Ford and her girls. The recruiting Depot was a stone's throw from the War Office, the air ministry and Admiralty, they provided home cooked meals and snacks and light refreshments, and they also served breakfast too.

Across the road in the silence of Horse Guards, Miss Ford shared her routine with club assistant Miss Millie Nimz, who joined NAAFI in 1943. For 13 years she served food and beverage to an assortment of military and civilian personnel. The biggest advantage to working at Horse Guards, was being right on top of big events such as the Coronation and it was exciting to be so close to the traditional ceremonies like Trooping the Colour. One of the best images of what NAAFI could do given the right surroundings in London, was seen at the then, newly built Chelsea barracks where the club manageress Mrs Phyllis Broomfield and a dozen of her girls served the guardsmen. Mrs Broomfield had grown up with the guards, having been nine years at catering in the former guards Depot.

The man in charge of all of this and the daily routine of the central London district was the district manager John Whitehead and R&WS June Robinson. The majority of Mr Whitehead's service had been spent with the NCS and overseas. He returned to England after six years abroad, and he took over the district in August 1963. He enjoyed the efficiency and the greater interest in increasing sales with the challenge to do the job the way it had been done for years. The team that he had measured up to every problem which presented itself. Miss Robinson was a domestic science teacher in her past and enjoyed the challenges of the continuous 'special catering' in central London.

Mr Bill Turner, who was a sales representative, had been selling to people in the capital since January 1963. His schedule took him to the army sports Control Board, air ministry, and the army cadet headquarters, the headquarters of the Territorial Army, in addition to the military establishments. From visits to the army sports Control Board he had been tasked to sell badges for the army skiing championships which was billed to be held in 1964. Yet another special order had been fulfilled and more to come; these included plaques which each arm of the service would be presented with as a mark of gratitude for the club's interest in the service events.

The general picture of the central London district was rounded off by the South East regional manager, Mr George Rogers, who thought of the district as unusual because of the many small clubs and other services. There was considerable prestige, and this set the district apart from others.

A walk in a minefield 1964

The district manager, Frederick Cook, in the wartime uniform as an EFI officer, was seeking a site for a NAAFI Roadhouse. After examining a large, roped off compound for half an hour, he decided he had found the ideal spot. He stepped back over the rope boundary and a soldier spectator asked how old he was. Mr Cook asked why. With a quick reply: "because you are not going to live much longer if you carry on like that. You just spent the last half an hour walking through a minefield."

The minefield incident was the second time that Mr Cook, now the senior district manager, Hounslow, nearly lost his life during the war in the desert. His first brush with death came as he was driving from Cairo to his first assignment.

He suddenly heard a drumming sound then he saw a ME109 swooping down with guns firing. The driver and Mr Cook hurled themselves from the car as the plane dived almost to ground level. He had said that if he had not been so stunned after falling from the car, he could have shot the pilot he was so low. Fortunately, neither the driver or Mr Cook was hurt apart from bruises.

His stepfather wanted him to join the RAF but he had other ideas as his stepfather was with the First Gloucesters but then was seconded to the RAF whereby he insisted that he had joined the RAF cadets which had opened his eyes. At the time his stepfather was stationed at RAF Holton and had introduced him to the canteen manageress Miss EV Jones, who offered him a job as a general assistant at 14 shillings a week. At this point he was only half a mile away from home, it was far enough to decide that he preferred administrative, or office work. While he was at Holton, he learnt all the secrets of running a canteen and organising the kitchen side of the job. Which stood him in good stead for the future as he was then to stand in for the manageress for three months during the time that she was ill. He was only 15 at that point.

During the outbreak of war Mr Cook was appointed the district manager in charge of a dozen company supply depots based on the Ruislip area. At the outbreak of war, he volunteered for the RAF as a gunner. He enlisted and went to Cardington. He was eventually deferred and discharged because of his work with NAAFI, where he then enlisted in EFI and was commissioned as second Lieutenant in 1942. Mr Cook's primary role in the western desert was the provision of canteens for the troops and during their Alamein offensive, he was opening them up at the rate of half a dozen a time, aided by the staff of 50 Europeans and an army of 1000 Arabs.

Later in the campaign Mr Cook was handed the task of salvaging equipment from the NAAFI mineral water plant at Mersa Matruh. The time to change hands during the fighting and where Mr Cook reached the factory, he discovered that the Germans had installed machines of their own. He'd arranged with some soldiers to dismantle the machines, German as well as his own. They loaded them onto 8 wagons and off they went back to Cairo. When Mr Cook returned to the UK in 1946 with the rank of major, he took with him the commendation of the CNC, Middle East, for good service.

On his return, he joined the home counting services district manager at Leighton Buzzard before attending Ruxley Towers administrative course and being promoted to senior district manager. His first appointment was area supervisor for the eastern command. Two years later in 1953 he took charge of the administrative side of NAAFI's mammoth arrangement for the Coronation. It was a hectic period, but his most difficult job was persuading his wife that he had to sleep at Kensington Gardens which was only 14 miles from home at Hillingdon. Mr Kirk had been with the South East region since 1955 and at Hounslow from 1960 to 1963. His service to the company was 40 years and when asked which were his most enjoyable years his reply was the time he "served with EFI". The satisfaction from that side of the job meant that job was well worth doing.

The founder and editor last farewell, by Ronald Walker March 1964

1964 the March issue of NAAFI News came with some sad news. The founder and editor Claude F Luke had passed.

In the very first issue of the magazine Claude Luke wrote in his editorial: "we present it without a flourish. We seek no bouquets for it and shall be uncommonly surprised if we received any."

But surprised he was, for the bouquets of flowers flowed in when as a member of the Association of industrial editors, was inducted to enter the magazine in two competitions against the country's best, the bouquets were justified by the professions. In the years from 1954 to 1963 he was five times awarded the certificate of merit for the magazine and on more than one occasion was runner up to the first prize winner.

Throughout his career Claude Luke regarded himself as, first and foremost, a journalist. Before he joined NAAFI as its first press officer in 1941, he was a well-known contributor to the national daily, Sunday and magazine press. He succeeded in his field; this was due not only to his acknowledgement as a writer and his ability as an interviewer but to his interest in and liking for people.

He was a champion of youth in any discussion on teenagers and their ability to twist and jive, their passion for hot music, and their ever changing language delighted him, but he warmed to the aged and enjoyed seeing life being lived at any age. His ability to find something likeable in almost everyone he met. To find some merit in all those who worked for him, meant that he in turn was liked and admired. He died a man with many friends and few, if any, enemies.

The only respect in which he may be said to have been old fashioned was in his strict regard for his honour and integrity, he was not to be deflected from saying or doing what he believed to be right.

It could be said that Claude Luke created public relations so far as NAAFI was concerned. When he joined in the early days of the war NAAFI was victim of an almost continuous stream of ill-informed criticism and also from the press. Typically he set himself to establish, to his own satisfaction, whether or not this was justified and then when he found out that the company was working with outstanding devotion to meet the needs of its vastly expanded commitments and, most important, was the honest institution and not, as the press had suggested, something of a racket, he became the most articulative advocates on its behalf.

His Fleet Street background and the respect in which he was held by the national press stood him in good stead for the hostility of the press gradually evaporated. Eventually NAAFI got the fair treatment it deserved. He always claimed that a PRO could never create and maintain a good image which was false, he could only make sure that when a good image was justified it was put across.

NAAFI was not only the child of his creation in the field of NAAFI publications. He founded NAAFI Review which he did a fantastic job of for the 10 years of its publication. He introduced NAAFI Reports, the NAAFI illustrated catalogue and Wise Buys from NAAFI. He was the inspiration behind the Rank "look at life" film on NAAFI and television and radio programmes on the same theme.

It would be difficult to catalogue completely the contributions he made to the success of the company and to the pleasure of the members of the staff who knew him. Those who remember the place and reviews which he produced at Ruxley Towers during and after the war, the famous entertaining quiz programmes in which he was the question master and many other fantastically conceived and carried out projects, the company would always be grateful to him.

Stars for club assistance 1964

After the introduction of the news badges in 1960 with the new uniforms it was now time to implement a new training programme. This would ensure better prospects and pay for over 2000 UK club staff. Winning proficiency stars, they would be able to improve their chances for promotion. The new scheme was proposed by the home service club study group which in October 1962 had been making recommendations on the planning, organization and operation of the junior ranks and airmen's clubs.

This would be the first time that there had been a clear ladder of progression from the lower ranks of club staff. They would pass tests and obtain three stars then staff would qualify for promotion to assistant managers. Once they obtained their three stars they would be known as the senior club assistants, this new title would supersede the existing position of a charge hand. The title of assistant manager or manageress would apply to an assistant personally graded as a senior club assistant who also acted as his deputy manager or manageress.

The tests would include an induction for new staff, based on the training manual for chargehands and would be supervised by R&WS held together with the club manager. The induction test would be planned and would be held between one and three months after the staff joined. They would then be determined by general suitability and given an indication of the future potential. This test would cover 3 separate phases of the club routine, for the right star it would cover the restaurant, the left star would be the bar and the central star would be the services shop. Each time a star was won their salary would be increased. They would then become responsible to whichever level they had qualified for. The key thing to remember at this time was nobody would lose any money under the scheme and their present rates of pay would continue for existing staff, the only change was the opportunity to gain more through learning more about the job.

Copyright Sue A Lowe

There would be no time limit on taking these tests and it would be dependent on personal factors and previous experience, and they would complete the training on the bar concerned. A Bar would hold each of the stars, one star, two stars, three stars and would be worn on their own and not together. The stars would be firstly produced in the traditional Marcasite and then a year later in faux marcasite, and it would be in this year that the Navy, army and Air Force brooches would also become faux marcasite due to the cost of making them.

It would be soon after that a four star and five-star brooch bar would be produced for the next two stages up.

The Cyprus troubles by TD Loughlin OBE 1964

The day by day account of NAAFI's role during the troubles as told by the command supervisor.

The recent disturbances began on the 21st of December 1963. I had met an assistant commander supervisor BJ Howard, on his return to Nicosia from England and we were discussing problems in the Ledra Palace hotel when the trouble erupted around us. That evening I returned to Episkopi, on the following day went to Dhekelia, to attend the Christmas party we were giving for 300 orphan and underprivileged Cypriot children at the Saint Georges club. At the last moment, the Turks prevented their children from attending.

On Monday the 23rd of December I managed to ring Famagusta before the telephone blackout. The services were operational by this time but communications between East and West of the island had ceased to exist. I was told I could not travel to Famagusta because the roads around Nicosia and Larnaca were impassable, but I tried to make the run in that afternoon. I called various establishments en route and it was clear that the panic buying by the services was mounting. Many families who had planned to go away for Christmas were now relying on the Company for goods. Regular customers were stocking up in case of the breakdown of order. Others who normally dealt with the little grocer around the corner, suddenly found the shutters closed.

On the evening of the 23rd I held a conference in Famagusta and made an assessment of the position. Nearly all points were functionally fairly normal. Among the exceptions where Pergamos shop and Dhekelia bulk issue store. Access was through a Turkish village which was cordoned off by Greek Cypriots. Eventually, the district manager Jaune Salmon and Jeffrey Windebank got through and opened the shop with a volunteer staff comprising the district accountant John Field and his wife. The district manager of the bulk issue store was unable to report for work, so the door was forced by assistant command supervisor Ray Bolton and the store was opened by Miss Thora Williams.

Other places affected by the nonappearance of local staff included the roundel club, Nicosia, the bakery and Famagusta headquarters. On Christmas Eve we learned that all Christmas supplies had been issued by shops that morning. Christmas Day and Boxing Day passed without incident and by the 27th of December arrangements were all well in hand for the opening of the two additional canteens at Elizabeth camp, Nicosia and Anzio camp, Dhekelia. The only shortages at the time were vegetables and eggs. On the 28th December, I travelled to Nicosia with the district manager EK Redpath and Miss Williams. I left my driver behind as there was an alleged kidnapping of Greeks by Turks en route.

Mr Bolton and Mr Salmon did the groundwork for the new canteen at Elizabeth camp and did a good job under very difficult circumstances. The canteen had opened on the previous day on a restricted basis. With additional supplies arriving, a full service was possible. I left Miss Williams to help and went on to the joint HQ and spent the rest of the day visiting the other establishments in Nicosia. On the next day, the 29th of December, Mr Howard and I visited the OPS room in Dhekelia, then went on to Anzio camp where the other canteen had been organised by district manager SE Underhill, which was then giving a satisfactory service. One of the club assistants made his own way to the RAF stations through the fighting but on arrival the acting CEO refused to allow his car on camp. He parked it next to the guard room; the next day the car was stolen.

Communications had become very bad, the civilian population ran short of such essentials as petrol, which affected the deliveries from the merchants particularly deliveries of beer and minerals. At the time we could not access our full casualties. A driver, Darvish Akhmed, was shot dead and chief clerk Phedon Soteriades who is the brother of the High Commissioner for Cyprus in London had been kidnapped. Later that day I had received a cable from army HQ: "Our most grateful thanks for the speed in establishing NAAFI canteen facilities in camps at Nicosia and Dhekelia. Well done NAAFI."

I had received an urgent request from NEAF for 500 feeding bottles and 500 tins of infant dried milk for the Romeo Alpha Medical team attending casualties in the Turkish quarter of Nicosia. The majority of the consignment was driven, in staff cars, by Mr Bolton and Mr Salmon. I also heard that we had to open another canteen in Nicosia, at the old RAF number two site. Arrangements were immediately started, and staff stocks and equipment were on site in less than 24 hours, despite the transport difficulties.

The news reached me on the 30th of December that our long-distance lorry drivers had refused to take their vehicles out because of the alleged kidnapping. They had worked hard and courageously up until then and the disappearance of our chief clerk must have had some effect on them. After some effort, we obtained WD lorries with enlisted drivers. The transference of loads from our vehicles and the urgent assembly unloading of supplies and equipment for the new canteen at RAF number two site, plus bumper stocks had been built up in Nicosia, made it a hectic day. The convoy was escorted to Nicosia by senior investigator F Corpe. Unfortunately, we had no means of transporting such perishables as meat and bakery products to Limassol, but the district manager JG Agate brought what we could locally. At the request of the GOC they organised a Mobile Shop and visited marooned service families in the city. The following morning our long-distance drivers again refused to make the journey, but we managed to obtain 10 RASC lorries. Most of the convoy travelled to Limassol, Akrotiri, Episkopi Districts, escorted by Mr A E Snelling, a sales representative. Perishables were delivered to all establishments.

New Year's Day was a public holiday in Cyprus, normally our shops would have closed. I decided to keep all establishments open as a morale raiser for customers and staff alike. We managed to create buffer stocks in Nicosia and Akrotiri, a move intended to prevent difficulties arising from short term dislocation in deliveries. That day I decided to go to Nicosia with Mr Bolton, to wish the staff happy new year. When we arrived, we found that the trouble had broken out again. Smoke from burning houses on the skyline made my compliments of the season to the staff sound quite tactless but it was quite extraordinary how cheerful and industrious most of them were.

Our mobile van was visiting various points in the town, driven by our service driver with Miss Williams and Mr RC Best, official in charge of the bakery and factory serving. The mobile canteen was transformed into a Mobile Shop on alternate days for serving isolated families. Both services were highly appreciated by the families. The next day, on the 2nd of January, we persuaded our drivers to make the run to Nicosia. After reading a batch of the English newspapers that had arrived, I noticed the reports seemed to range from the mock heroics of the authors to an accurate account of the situation only in Nicosia. But few of them had referred to the turmoil and tension throughout the island and this was a predicament which had the greatest impact on the service throughout the island.

Apart from the isolated farming communities, the whole island was on the threshold of civil war, with the threat of invasion hanging over all. All of the main roads had roadblocks on the outskirts of each village, manned by armed civilians with sometimes a sprinkling of police. After each outburst of violence, scare or rumour, the civilian traffic disappeared, and the roads became deserted except for NAAFI and service vehicles. Officials driving cars found it unnerving at times when they approached stone emplacements, where guns were levelled at their cars, despite the Union Jacks on our windscreens. Travelling was only permitted during daylight, which restricted the operational capacity on deliveries and shop opening hours. Shops had to close early to enable staff to reach their homes before nightfall.

Fortunately, most people's utilities contained the telephone, but because of increased use and wire cutting it was unreliable and frustrating means of communications. Rumours of massacres and atrocities were quickly exchanged and had a more demoralising effect than the plain truth. There were no incidents reported on the 4th of January but there was no significance in the fact. I went to the Turkish quarter or Famagusta to receive 150 old blankets, from our almost extinct furniture and equipment warehouse and these were donated to the refugees. The misery, suspicion, hostility and bitterness of the Turks besieged in the old Venetian Fort was something I will definitely remember. I visited the canvas canteen and opened the previous night in Dhekelia, for the arrival of the parachute brigade. Mr Underhill had done a wonderful job, keeping open all night for their reception. It was bitterly cold, as it had been the previous few days, colder than England.

The Bristol hotel at Kyrenia had been cut off for a fortnight. I decided that on the 5th of January I'd go there with Mr Bolton and Mr JC Galley. The manager had stocked up for Christmas bookings, which had been cancelled later. I did not expect to find any food shortage. That part of the country was held by the Turkish army but apart from the numerous roadblocks the journey was uneventful. As the coastline of Turkey could be seen from Kyrenia, there had been a part evacuation of most of the Greeks, but our manager and his staff stayed, and they were overjoyed to see us.

By the 6th of January, 3000 additional troops had arrived. Their speed of arrival was quite fantastic and after arriving they were constantly on the move. This meant that the situation changed hourly. We had now opened five new canteens across the island and a bulk issue store in Nicosia. Every establishment was operating, except the Roundel club, which opened only in the evening and this was one run by Mr Galley and Miss Williams. Nearly all officials had been working day and night as drivers or working on the mobile, anything in fact to keep the service going. We were 20% short on our original numbers and had additional commitments.

The Turkish communities now had been encircled for over 2 weeks and efforts by the army to reopen movement failed. We lost the service of 21 Turkish Cypriots from installations in Famagusta, and a fact which gives us some idea of the burden borne by others. I visited the Turkish culture of Famagusta, where 5000 Turks were besieged, with the aim of persuading some to return to work. A total of 26 Turkish staff reported to the furniture and equipment warehouse, the balance of 35 Turks employed in Famagusta could not travel from homes outside the walls. They gathered round me, bewildered young girls and old men looking for some hope out of the chaos. Through their trade union secretary, I explained to them the conditions of work; one point was that all grades would work as laborers for the first few days but would be paid on their employment grade. Eighteen men and women were to sort and load furniture and sweep up broken glass and, work as unloaders in the warehouse.

Four officials were involved in the operation all day. I led the convoy of cars and despite prior agreement with the authorities, there was an embarrassing search at the border. I informed local army commander and the Turkish district officer that I could not again participate in a similar exercise and proposed to set up a temporary furniture and equipment repair shop in the Turkish quarter, in order to provide some of our employees with work. One of our Turkish staff marooned in the old city whose family lived in the village about 35 miles away had not been able to make any contact with them for the previous three weeks and they did not know if he was alive or dead.

By that stage most of the officials were beginning to feel the strain of very long days and nights. They had all worked so wonderfully well during the previous three or four weeks doing everything conceivable to help. Over the following few days, the situation began to ease. The removal of the armed roadblocks and replacement in many instances by UK forces, enabled traffic on the roads connecting the main towns to circulate more; this eased tension in parts of the island in which we operated. An uneasy calm prevailed. Twenty-six Turkish Cypriots returned to work at the Famagusta headquarters on the 10th of January without incident. Travel between towns at night was not recommended by the government although not enforced. Our shop hours were still open early and closing early basis.

Towards the end of January, we were visited by the managing director, Mr HPT Prideaux, and the RAF director G/Capt FS Wakeham. About the same time, we learned that another of our Turkish Cypriot employees had been killed a month previously during the fighting at Larnaca. Such a sad time in the history of Cyprus but a great show that no matter what, the company did everything possible to assist our British forces and local people during a crisis.

Army council hands over March 1964

After 60 years the army council was superseded by the Army Board of Defence Council and bid farewell to the Army Council past and present members who attended the War Office for this auspicious occasion. Mr James Ramsden, who was the Secretary of State for war, and the full council including the guests of the Earl Attlee, 6 government ministers and 4 field marshals who held the appointment of Chief of the Imperial General staff: Lord Montgomery, Lord Harding, Sir Gerald Templar, Sir Francis Festing and William Slim. This was only to pave the way for a new operation moving forward and again with the truly modernising NAAFI and all that it entailed.

NAAFI EFI first line 1964.

1964 a change in the emergency reserve grouping of NAAFI's EFI, these were the soldiers that went anywhere at any time when they were needed, by any means. This change meant that they could now be called out at a 72-hour notice without the Royal proclamation. They went from a category 11(b) to the EFI reserve, regraded to enable them to achieve a greater degree of readiness to meet emergencies. The current EFI establishment would be six officers and 61 junior ranks, at the time there were just 4 officers and 30 junior ranks. The plan was to ensure that they could divide the 30 into separate groups for different overseas areas. Each man, medically fit and fully kitted out, would be available for service anywhere. The first team of 30 reservists would be backed by a shadow group which could be called on if ever required.

Bounty payments were subject to tax but to offset this they put them on a par with the regular army reservists' wages, to the NAAFI man they were substantially greater than the salary that they were on. Each year if they were still in service, they would be paid a retaining amount and also a small amount on enlistment for a compulsory two years of service. The work of the uniform staff would depend largely on their NAAFI jobs and the demands of the situation. The rank would also depend on the EFI duties that they would need to carry out. In addition, pay would be granted where applicable to bring the service pay up to the NAAFI overseas service rate for the job.

Each service member would be required to undertake 15 days' training each year which was compulsory and would be held at the RASC TA headquarters at Bedford. At Wingham, NAAFI Surrey training centre, which was the original nucleus of where the EFI volunteers would meet. The change in AER grouping was outlined by Maj JP Dunn, OC, EFI. They were told that the 15 days' annual training would be used to obtain the knowledge of the military procedure and get to know the other members of the RASC EFI reserve with whom they would be serving.

Many of the RASC EFI service members were previously regular service and many had served during the war. Throughout the history of EFI this was often the case, people joining because they missed the service or that they didn't know any other way of life.

1965

Around the world on sea and shore Edward Rayner, 1918-1965

The sun blazed out of a cloudless Sicilian sky. Before getting into his car outside the Naval headquarters, Lieut-Cdr Edward Rayner, RNVR, paused to admire the blue sky. As he did so there was a tremendous explosion and the day was turned into night. He and his driver dived for shelter under the car as blazing oil from an erupting fuel dump poured down on them. When they scrambled out, the daylight Raiders had flown away. In the building they had just left, internal walls had collapsed, roof and windows had been blown in and the interior was smothered in fuel oil. Despite this devastation no one was injured. This was May 1943, only a few months after Edward Rayner had received his Commission in the RNVR. He had been serving as a Naval Superintendent Northern Ireland when a telephone call from headquarters instructed him to kit up as a lieutenant commander and go to Portsmouth to join a special party for unknown destination. After 10 days with the 8th army in Sicily his party moved into Syracuse. He had 24 hours to find storage accommodation before the first supply of ships arrived. Mr Rayner said this was the start of a period of providing canteen facilities up both sides of the Italian coast as each area was taken.

Mr Raynor joined NACB in 1918 at the age of 16. His first appointment was to HMS 'Dido', a Depot ship berthed at Harwich and later served in HMS Hecla, he was subsequently transferred to HMS Renown and served in her for about 18 months. During this time, the

'Renown' joined the 'Prince of Wales' for a tour of Canada, West Indies, the United States, Australia and New Zealand.

Mr Rayner later joined HMS Repulse, sister ship to HMS Renown, and remained with her for 10 years. In 1924, a special service squadron was formed, consisting of 'Repulse', 'Hood' and five light cruises. The squadron sailed round the world showing the flag in the Commonwealth ports. In 1926 he and the 'Repulse' again in the company of 'Prince of Wales' visited South Africa and South America. In 1932 he travelled to Malta to take over accounting in HMS London, flagship of the first cruiser squadron. His passage through the Bay of Biscay and the Jarvis Bay was extremely rough. He said that he was the only passenger in the dining room for Christmas dinner. He was still serving in HMS London during the Spanish civil war when, in 1936, the ship spent three months off Barcelona evacuating refugees.

At the outbreak of war World War Two Mr Rayner was serving with HMS Ramillies, which sailed from Scapa Flow on the eve of the war and after various duties, arrived unannounced at Melbourne on Christmas Day. As preparations had not been made for the ship's arrival, storing was impossible for three days they spent there, as all shops and stores were closed. Similar conditions prevailed in New Zealand when they arrived in Wellington on New Year's Eve. When the festive season was over, they managed to take on stores and fuel the ship, escorted the first and second echelons of ANZAC to Suez for the North African campaign. After the war, he worked in the UK and eventually served in Germany from September 1946 to 1948. He was then appointed to the NCS central district at Swindon. He went to Gibraltar in November 1952 and stayed there until April 1956, returning to the UK by road. His next appointment was to Londonderry, Northern Ireland. In March 1959, Mr Raynor was appointed district manager, South Africa, where he remained for four years before returning to the UK again.

From Kennington to Krefeld 1965

Two members of staff that were integral to the operation of transporting goods with Jock Blackie and Dries Raadsen, but these two men had never met and probably never did. They were both key figures in the transportation of NAAFI goods from Kennington to Krefeld. Jock, originally from Edinburgh, lived in London working for the company, he joined in 1950 and by 1965 he was driving 16-ton NAAFI lorries full of goods out of Kennings Way. He called at London Wharf for a consignment of orange juice for collecting NAAFI tea, sports goods and fashion clothing at Kennington. His load might have all been tinned food or perhaps beer, NAAFI sent around 310-gallon kegs to Germany every week. Tilbury to Kennington where Jock lived was around 25 miles. and on the quayside where he pulled into were for lorries and trailers already lining the quayside. From there it was a matter of presenting the documents and clearing customs then waiting.

Sending goods to Germany was re-examined by the Supplies Department and it was decided to send some of the merchandise by road. NAAFI called in the British European transport organisations who started off the service with only two runs per week. Within months this had reached 8 trailers a week involving some 120 tons of goods. Once a week, refrigerated lorries made the trip from the company sausage factory at Portsmouth to the European service carrying sausages and other products that required refrigeration. A second vehicle was introduced to complete the movement by road for the transportation of frozen goods from the United Kingdom to Germany. At the Tilbury dockyard the trailers were unhitched, and the dockyard vehicles took over to guide it through the cavernous turn doors of the Cerdic ferry. The hold of the ferry could take up to 70 vehicles and a further 30 on the upper deck.

The vessels sailed to Rotterdam or occasionally Antwerp in time for breakfast. Passenger accommodation was a maximum of 35. The 2500 tonne ferry, named after a Teutonic King, reached Rotterdam usually on time. And this is where the handover took place. Dries waited for the lorries to disembark and The British European transport would then take the goods the rest of the way to Krefeld. As soon as the ship was offloaded the customs men had to do their checks.

European transport had NAAFI as its biggest customer on the ferry service and everything was geared up to deliver the goods as quick as possible. Once the trailer had been checked off it was Krefeld bound cargo and this would take around five hours to arrive. From start to finish this whole journey took 36 hours until it was in the hands of the warehouse staff in Germany. And the very next day it could be in any one of the 65 NAAFI shops in the European service.

On the run to Berlin April 1965 by Roy Hume

A redcap barked "follow the NAAFI wagon". It was not the beginning of a wild police chase, just MP spotting the easy way of directing a stranger to Berlin. "That often happens," said the NAAFI driver Tommy Scott. He had guided a few people to the divided city and out of it. Its job for which he was well qualified, for three times a week Tuesday, Thursday and Sunday the NAAFI lorry made the round trip from Herford, in the European service's central region to Berlin.

Tommy and his fellow driver Taffy Roberts had been on the Berlin run, for more than three years, taking on each trip some 9 tons of urgent orders of fresh produce for NAAFI establishments in the city. The cargoes supplemented the 250 tons of NAAFI goods carried from Krefeld to Berlin on fortnightly military trains. Starting from Herford in the early afternoon Tommy and Taffy headed first to Hanover, some 60 miles away, to pick up the supplies of milk, cream and yogurt which came from Haderslev in Denmark. They would then head out on the autobahn once more to Helmstedt, the door to East Germany.

Helmstedt, which marks the halfway stage of the 225 miles from Herford to Berlin, it is there that NAAFI has its only roadhouse, a wooden building erected in 1945. It's managed by a Mr Jack Tappenden and open from 0800 till 2200 seven days a week. The roadhouse is a welcome sight for the travelling servicemen. Most of the trade is done in the summer and they have to cater for the unexpected at any time in any season. After all a busload of troops could have arrived anytime. The roadhouse itself had a bar and restaurant for officers and other ranks. They'd introduced a range of gift items for the passing trade and because of this it started to pay dividends. Sighted behind the roadhouse which was the Berlin bound NAAFI where they would drop off the rations, a detachment of the Royal military police, which performed the documentation for the British vehicles moving in and out of Berlin. It also housed a 26 tonne recovery vehicle which was used to bring back any British, French and American vehicles which broke down up to the halfway point in the 102-mile-long Berlin corridor. But if they broke down over that line they would still get to Berlin, but the Americans would tow them the rest of the way.

Just up the road from there was the first checkpoint. You would stop at the allied barriers and present your documents. At this point anybody behind you would be given the command to follow the NAAFI wagon. Then across some 200 yards of no man's land to the Soviet checkpoint where a young fur-clad Russian looked over your passports. They were so strict at this checkpoint that Taffy once had a 't' left off his name and was sent back to the allied checkpoint to have it corrected. In East Germany the autobahn deteriorated and traffic permitting they were able to pick their route carefully across the broken road. In the darkness headlights picked out some cyclists and even pedestrians, something unheard of in West German autobahns.

Once the vehicles had passed over the Magdeburg bridge which passed over the Elbe River was soon the halfway point along the corridor. They were safe so if they broke down, they would still get to Berlin with the goods. At the last checkpoint a signal was sent to Berlin which gave the approximate time of arrival and speed the vehicle would be travelling at which meant they would be discovered even if they did break down.

The drive was 2½ hours to Berlin and then on to another checkpoint; these German guards spotted the Union Jack on the side of the lorry and this was the point where the barbed wire on walls started. The documents had to be gone over before we were then moved on to the allied checkpoint, they drove past the West German lorries queuing up for a more thorough examination. Civilian cars had Arclights blazing on them, and huge mirrors pushed underneath for further checks. Before midnight they generally got into Berlin after driving past a sign which said, "for the next 2 miles you will be in the Soviet zone", and then on past the Berlin bear, into the British sound, across the part of the Avus racing car track, 3 green traffic lights to Summit House, the NAAFI headquarters in the Charlottenburg district of Berlin.

The OCA 1965

News of the formation of a new branch of the NCS EFI OCA was given at the AGM on the 24th of April by Mr Swithenbank; he was now the retiring chairman of the general committee. But a new branch was being organised with great success in West Germany by Mr Wheatley-Perry. Mr Swithenbank gave the current and total membership of the Association at 1726, including the active Malta branch under the chairmanship of Mr Gore. The Association and its various UK branches held 23 functions during the year, including the usual Remembrance ceremonies. The Reverend CFI Scott, vicar of St Mark's church, Kennington, conducted the service at Imperial Court and the address was given by the personnel director Maj General Robertson CB, CBE, DSO. The two-minute silence was observed followed by the laying of wreaths at the two memorials. Mr Swithenbank told the meeting that since the last AGM Mr Wallis Bird had retired from the honorary chaplaincy of the OCA and the appointment had been accepted by the Reverend Scott.

In proposing a toast to the association, Mr H PT Prideaux, chairman and managing director of the company and president of the association, paid tribute to Cannon Bird for his services to the OCA for so many years and also welcomed the new Chaplain, the Reverend Scott and Mrs Scott.

It was his sad duty, the chairman said, to record that this was the last time that Colonel HG Swithenbank would be present at one of these functions as the chairman of the general committee of the Association, he was due to retire at the end of June. The new chairman would now be Sir William Beale, a former president of the Association.

Referring to the Association itself, the managing director remarked that the membership today was only slightly lower than that of 10 years previous and this was a matter for congratulation. He welcomed the new branch that was opening in Germany. He went on to say that the Association was not solely, nor even primarily, an opportunity for social gatherings, although these were of great value. The principal objectives were those of companionship and service in the spirit which gave the Association its birth. These were very much more important than in the long run and were the things that mattered most.

The 20th anniversary at the end of the war in 1965 would also mark the reformation of the western European Branch of the OCA. At a recent meeting of the representative members Mr Wheatley Perry first proposed the branch should be reformed and the motion received unanimous support. A provision committee was elected to launch the new branch. The new branch covered an area roughly the size of England. Periodic functions would be held at convenience centres and the inaugural dance would be at Krefeld on the 16th of June 1965 when it would hope that the old comrades would attend. The branch already had more than 70 members, but the committee would be delighted to welcome any member of the staff currently employed in Western Europe who served in the EFI or who belonged to the RASC EFI Army Emergency Reserve.

Automatic vending for the NCS 1965

In 1965 auto vending became accepted by customers and staff alike as an essential part of the NAAFI trading, but few would have imagined such a growth in mechanise selling in the pioneer days of 1958. The NCS was chosen as the Guinea pig for the vending machine schemes and the services of the firm of industrial caterers called Vendepac, were required to provide a service on behalf of the company. It had become an arrangement that had continued satisfactorily. The first venture began with a bank of machines at Chatham. Soon the coin in the slot trade spread to two further strongholds of the senior service, Portsmouth and Plymouth. During the time the new vending machines were being developed in these two areas, an experimental vending route was started in Scotland, a vending machine engineer was appointed to maintain the machines in ships and on shore, and at the same time an engineer was employed for similar services in the Portland area. These two members of staff were engaged until the latter part of 1959 and were still with the company in 1965.

The first machines were installed on the Royal yacht Britannia and aircraft carrier HMS Bulwark. Since then the vending machines trade had developed throughout Her Majesty's ships and is an integral part of the service that they now provide. Hot and cold drink machines form the basis of the vending machine service afloat and where a ship had sufficient men to warrant several machines an operator mechanic would be part of the canteen staff. Where this was not available the ship's electrical staff could access the machines and fix any faults.

On ships where there was limited space, the sighting of machines was of prime importance. Positioning could be influenced by several factors, the role of the ship for instance, but generally speaking and in the words of Mr Moss the man responsible for NCS vending, "we endeavour to site the machine where there is the greatest customer potential and also give maximum service".

Mr Moss said the thing that keeps the machines going was the confidence that the customer had in them; however, 8 times out of 10 the machine failed to deliver the goods, and this was partly the fault of the customer. With this relatively new technology in 1965 the coin had to have gone fully through the machine before the customer tried to operate it, often the customer would press the buttons before the coin had fully dropped resulting in a miss vend.

The first experiment with a fully automatic cafeteria was at HMS Ganges, at Shotley in 1960. It was sited in the tenpin bowling alley and it was extremely popular. Since then the automatic cafeteria is developed on a larger scale and the best example of this at the time, was at HMS Collingwood 12 miles outside of Portsmouth. This was a project that was once the services shop. This was a seven-day week, round the clock venture, giving Collingwood club freedom to concentrate on its social events. One of the biggest problems when planning a fully automated cafeteria was to calculate the number of machines needed to cope with peak periods. There was an incredible amount of research done at HMS Collingwood to find out, and the way they finally came to a decision was to look at the current sales and relate these to the average sale of each machine.

In the home service from 1963 to 1965 they saw the most development in the automatic catering for the army and the Royal Air Force. Home service formerly ran auto vending in partnership with NCS and then employed outside contractors to provide the service in some of the larger canteens.

Mr WT Fishwick and his team of advisors built up the home service's own specialist organization and by the end of 1965 they will have established 19 vending routes in operation. A further 12 routes were planned to be installed by the end of 1966. Staff for this job were recruited mainly from within the company and from the services. They were attached to a qualified route operator for three months, if they had previous mechanical or electrical experience. The fully automated cafeterias were thriving with sales well up on the former counter service. This was not surprising for they could feed 500 men or more in just one 15-minute break. At the time this was also reported by Mr LG Waters who looked after the automatic cafeteria at Cove near

Aldershot. No sooner did they fill the machines that they were emptied again and of the most popular items the prewrapped hot meat patties, chunky pies and filled rolls were always high on the list of favourites to the service personnel. The original cafeteria at Cove went up in smoke on bonfire night in 1962 and in a ballot the men voted for an auto cafe.

The next advancement in the auto cafe was a portable cabin unit built specifically for a wide range of machines. This was considered a good investment as it would be open 24/7 and available when its customers needed them. Not only was this one of the main advantages but the cabins could be delivered power and water connected, then open for service the same day. In the winter they also served as a warm shelter where the customers could satisfy their thirst or hunger at the drop of a coin and should the station or camp close down overnight it was a relatively simple procedure to remove the cabin and deploy it elsewhere.

Over the years several changes had taken place in the automatic selling and NAAFI developed along the lines of the best suited to the service conditions and customer requirements. Factory visits, trade experts' exhibitions and conferences kept the headquarters expert abreast of the latest trends. New drinks machines offering orange, lemonade, grapefruit and lime was on trial at the Royal tournament. It proved very successful and would be the basis of the refrigerated cold drinks service in 1966.

With any new machinery there would be quite a few technical problems with the cold drink machines, but the new one answered most of their questions and proved to be a great success. Experiments also took place with new lines and constantly endeavoured to satisfy the tastes of NAAFI slot machine customers. Wide interest in these developments had made customers and staff alike love the auto vending and the regional and district managers' stations and camps themselves approached the experts at Imperial Court with their own suggestions. One thing was for certain, remarked Mr Fishwick, the automatic vending had come to stay and it was a big part of the future of the company and he was right – the automatic vending machines would play a massive part in the company moving forward providing the additional service and minimal staff hours.

EFI exercise dazzle. A report on the desert operation by JC Whitehead 1965

Early in 1965 word was received in headquarters of overseas operation that a large-scale exercise called 'Ex Dazzle' was to be held in Cyrenaica, in the summer. The 3rd division, army, and 30 eight group, RAF, combined headquarters had requested NAAFI service for the duration.

With up to date local information provided by Mr Barton, supervisor, the preparation work began. This is the story of the part played by the RAOC EFI who immobilised for the exercise together with one club team from Malta. Maj Freddy Bridgett, OC RAOC EFI Depot and his assistant Mr Wynne, began selecting EFI men to man a field bulk issue store and two tented junior ranks clubs. This exercise within an exercise would test the mobilization procedure of EFI.

I met the rest of the advance party at Bordon. They were a selected band of EFI veterans from the exercise held in 1963 WO2 Frank Bullen, Sgt Ken Machray, Cpl Reg Arminson, and Cpl Peter Hudson along with Pte Terry Slater but when I met them first off, they were all called Mr. And when I met them the following morning, they had all been given their service ranks.

We were to be followed 2 weeks later by Lt Arthur License, Sgt Wynn Davis and the remainder of the team of storm and cooks, waiters, furnishing fitters, drivers, canteen and shop assistants, clerks and warehousemen, most of whom were for the next 8 weeks to carry out unfamiliar work as counter assistants in the tented junior ranks clubs and the bulk issue store.

On August 21st we flew from Lyneham to RAF El Adem, arriving at 0430hrs in the morning. We were met by the district manager Mr Barry Underwood and after brief discussions we set out at 0600hrs in the morning for Bomba camp. On the way we passed a number of cemeteries of war dead, British, German, French and Australian. All beautifully tended. We rode through miles of desert scrub, the sun getting higher and hotter all the time. Stray herds of camels followed our progress with unblinking stares. We left the roads for rough desert tracks and eventually no tracks at all. Suddenly tents seemed to mushroom out of the desert and at 0930hrs in the morning we were at Bomba.

Two 7-ton lorries from Benghazi were waiting for us, having travelled overnight with our equipment and saleable stock. So, the goods, equipment and staff were in the right place at the right time. Maj Vernon Sudbury, whom I had last met briefly at Bulford two weeks before, greeted us and apologised for only having two of our tents ready for use. On being told we needed the 3rd for our gift shop he produced Maj Ronnie Fisher of the Middlesex regiment, who was in charge of tent erection. He had, he explained, a full programme to complete before he could tackle such 'frills'. 'Would you like a beer, Sir?' asked Cpl Arminson. 'Thank you, Corporal,' replied Maj Fisher. His eyes open wide as he tasted his first ice cold beer since he arrived at Bomba.

Things happened so fast in the next few hours and the sequence of events could not be recorded. I remember being most impressed by Pte Slater and Cpl Arminson showing the regular soldiers how to wheel 420 cubic foot refrigerators into the marquee using 6-foot tabletop running on tent poles over a road of tabletops. Mr Paterson, the furnishings inspector for Cyrenaica, with his fitter, Tommy Anders, made the show stands at shelving level and straight, hoisted our flag, erected signs and the dart board cabinet. The goods were unpacked, checked and priced, the electricians brought in the power supply and the water Bowser was provided, later to be replaced with a static tank when the field kitchen shelter was erected. By 1600hrs in the afternoon everything was ready for opening and we knocked off for a swim. One of the only amenities at Bomba was a beautiful beach, clear blue sea and perfect sunshine.

After two days of travelling and labouring in unaccustomed heat we enjoyed that dip more than any which followed. At six in the evening we began our service and from the small advanced party of 40 men, we took £60 in our first evening. The morale of the troops increased fourfold. The heat was the newfound source of energy. Our service opened at 0930hrs every morning and continued without a break until 2200hrs in the evening, the staff working shifts and relieving each other for meals or a swim. The remainder of the EFI party arrived at the beginning of September and we opened up a bulk issue store in Bombay and two extra tented clubs at RAF El Adem. One of these was staffed by a team from Malta led by the manager Frank Gails. With the same enthusiasm as the advance party had shown, the rest of the establishments quickly made themselves the off duty focal point with cold mineral water or beer always available, a cheery word and a quick come back to any quip without getting their knees brown.

Our part time soldiers were, in fact, mostly long service employees with 10 or 20 years in the army before they joined NAAFI. This was a great help to the younger members of the team when it came to learning how to live under canvas. It is never a comfortable life and the heat and dirt make the unaccustomed life even harder but there are lots of little ways of reducing the discomfort. Having someone there who was done it all before makes all the difference. The exercise troops arrived, and we had four weeks of hectic trading before they left the camp for the desert. Then followed quiet days whilst the war was on, followed by the Stampede for the NAAFI when the men returned thirstily to the camp.

Then there was a buying of gifts and souvenirs to take home. We have a gift shop at each of the clubs and the supervisor provided us with a superb range of goods. On the 29th of December we were visited at Bomba by the army director on the board of management, Col A Hogge, accompanied by Mr Barton. They both spent the night under canvas and called on the unit officers before going on to Tobruk and El Adem.

Between Tobruk and El Adem is the War Memorial to NAAFI staff who gave their lives in World War Two. It stands apart from the war cemeteries on a site where so many worked during the desert campaigns. The Colonel told all the permanent establishments in the exercise area and heard praise of the service given by the Tobruk district manager and his team. Our activities came to an end during the week ending October 16th. We flew home between October 17th and 21st and returned to Borden for demobilization. After a few days leave and a debrief at Wingham, we returned to our normal work and the mothball army became a memory, until next year's training.

1966

Farewell Tripoli 1966 by GG Whittle 1966

Twenty-three years previously the 8th army, in its historic march along the coast of North Africa, entered Tripoli. By April 1966 the only British servicemen left in Tripolitania will be airman serving at the Royal Air Force station Idris, some 16 miles from the town of Tripoli, elements of the Royal Navy and the army still serving the Naval and military missions to Libya. Except for a small family shop and airmen's club at Idris, NAAFI will also have withdrawn from the area. In terms of hard cash this represented quite a large turnover to the Corporation per year in an area where the service has enjoyed full duty-free facilities.

Many employees would have served or passed through Tripoli during their careers. The last supervisor Mr HF Frankland first made his acquaintance with Tripoli in 1945 when he was a member of the inspection branch. For those who remember the town in the immediate post-war years, Tripoli today would be full of surprises. Libya became an oil producer of some importance, being the 6th in the League of oil producing countries. Of the total export for 1963 oil accounted for £117½ million. Naturally the discovery of oil had its effect on the economics and the living standards of the country, especially in Tripoli where the majority of oil companies had established their local administrative headquarters. It was now a thriving town whose indigenous population swelled by expatriates from many nations.

No longer are the roads the exclusive preserve of donkey carts, camels, but a few military and NAAFI vehicles. They became filled by the 500,000 cars which then had become registered. With this expanding community the British forces had, over the previous few years been gradually contracting, and so did NAAFI. In December of 1965 the district comprised a district office, distributing warehouse, bakery, transport section, F&E Department, and officers, SNCO and OR club, two family shops, four junior ranks clubs, a drapery shop and a central services shop. The starting gun for operations to close down was after business on Christmas Eve when the drapery and central services shop closed and on New Year's Day 1966 the officers, SNCO, OR club closed. Later in the January the families' shop and one of the junior rank's clubs closed. The junior ranks clubs at Prinn barracks and the British military hospital were expected to close in the February. Allied to the closure of the trading establishments was the rundown of the non-trading establishments and the district office services. However, although closure is the operative function, a new service was opened for those officers, NCO and soldiers concerned with the final details of the army's departure. This was being provided by Kassala barracks and would continue until the 31st of March.

Providing a service for those who remained behind, are larger services shop and the airmen's club at RAF Idris opened in the mid-January and the existing family shop would be wholly responsible for the requirements of the Air Force remaining at Idris. These establishments would come under the control of Cyrenaica, from where they would receive their supplies. A supply line of some 650 miles. Closing an area that size posed many problems. Detailed planning was essential, and the run down would be achieved efficiently and economically. But there was another side to the story, a human one, 255 employees in Tripoli, 202 were local people of Libyan and Italian origin. Many of the staff had seen 20 years plus service and all of them would be losing their jobs, although they were wished good luck in their future as the services moved out of the area.

As the local staff would miss NAAFI so many of the contract staff would miss Tripoli. Several members of the UK staff were now in their second tours, all who would miss Tripoli's delightful climate.

On ship and shore in the Naval Dockyards in Singapore by AE Self NCS 1966

In 1966 Singapore was the 5th largest port in the world. In the beginning the jungle was cleared in 1942, the swamp was filled in and the construction of the base started. With the modern dock installations, workshops, living accommodation, clubs, cinemas, swimming pools, churches, and other welfare facilities, it was one of the finest and most modern dockyards in the world. This was where the stage was set for this story.

The leading character in this Naval spotlight is a man who, nearly 30 years previous, was on the first ship to enter Singapore Naval dry dock and who had just celebrated his 40 years' service with NAAFI. His name was Jack Holness. His job was a supervisor for the Naval canteen service in Singapore. Jack had served in many ships in peace and war. He had served ashore; however, Her Majesty's Ships had dropped anchor. They had known earthquakes in Greece, civil war in Spain and Naval actions at sea. He was on one of the early ships to France during the D-Dday landings and was believed to have been the first NAAFI official to land in Normandy.

In 1966 he headed up the NCS contingent in Singapore under the overall control of the command supervisor, Far East, Mr WGT Duke. Sharing the spotlight with him was his friend and colleague Richard West, district manager Far East fleet. Broadly speaking, Richard West made sure that the men of the fleet had everything afloat and Jack took care of them ashore. Richard had served for 32 years. His first sea trip was to Cowes with the late King George the fifth. Since then he had seen service on many vessels in many places, including seven years aboard HMS Hood.

He was the first official to hold the title of district manager home fleet and had now added that to the first-time title of the district manager Far East fleet. In this assignment he had the task of looking after the needs of 24 assorted ships with canteens, a large number of smaller craft without canteens but which required NAAFI supplies. One of the largest and most famous of the ships in port as the story was written was HMS Ark Royal, now one of the veterans of the fleet. In charge of the NAAFI activities onboard was manager R Henderson, a comparative newcomer with only 23 years' service. He served on a number of ships up to cruiser class before the Ark Royal and he was an experienced seafaring man.

Rich Henderson was ably assisted by an Australian assistant manager called Mal Martin. Mal had only been with the company for eight years and had served with the home service during that time, joining NCS in 1960. The NCS had many other staff on board the Ark Royal, all working at different stations to give the sailors exactly what they needed when they needed it. The commando carrier the Albion, nicknamed HMS trouble shooter, the Manager was called Maurice Mullings and was helped by assistant manager W Goodall, he was known as the old grey ghost of the Borneo coast. As this ship frequented the hotspots because these are the places where the human cargo operates. The supply ships for Fort Charlotte and Fort Dunvegan had managers Goh Hen Suan and Wong Liang Kiang in charge – who but a sailor knows the tremendous relief of the replenishment at sea. Other famous ships such as the Ajax, Bulwark, Triumph, Blackpool, Devonshire and many more with NAAFI men aboard, including the Giant of them all, the aircraft carrier, HMS Eagle, anchored in these waters. They were part of the Far East fleet, and here today and gone tomorrow to some likely trouble spot where NAAFI supplies were the only luxuries available.

So much had to be accomplished during their brief visits to Singapore! Sometimes they cannot get back to port and the store ships then become a floating warehouse. On the 8th of December 1965 the store ship Fort Dunvegan loaded 13,114 packages of NAAFI supplies between 0730hrs in the morning and 2130hrs in the evening during the emergency exercise. This was a little above average, said Mr Holness.

For every ship at sea a number of people must serve ashore. Engineers, fitters, technicians, signallers, clerks, medical staff, school staffs stores and equipment specialists and many others exist in support of the most important Naval base. And NAAFI is concerned with these too. To begin with, ships without canteens aboard needed a ration store, although these had been in existence for nearly three years and newer and larger store was almost ready for occupation. Also, in the dockyard area, serving seamen who had not at the time got to the city, or to visit HMS Terror in the base itself, was the first fleet canteen. This was not structurally one of the best canteens in the world, but it was a place where senior and junior rates can have a drink and relax, a welcome haven for many sailors visiting Singapore Naval dockyard. Manager Wong and his staff were used to the Navy, the fleet canteen performed a very valuable function. Outside the dockyard area but still within the base was HMS Terror.

In the dockyards resided the famous Armada club, recently back in full service after a major improvement scheme. This was now one of the best Naval clubs outside the United Kingdom. It had air conditioning, restaurants and a cocktail lounge, and men only bar, snack bar, quiet lounge and a roof garden. Adjacent to it was the Armada pavilion where all the social functions were held. There was also a services shop, run by a charge hand Loo Tian Woo. A short distance away was the milk bar and soda fountain and a little further on, the Tropicana bar, also air conditioned and a popular retreat for many families and unaccompanied personnel who liked the infectious smile of the barman, Tan Kar Heng. Supervising this network of pleasant relaxation, good food and excellent service was club manager Ken Lampey, an old NCS hand with 24 years' service, ably assisted by duty manager, Cheng Heng Tong.

Ken was a Cornishman from Launceston who joined NAAFI in 1941. He had served in most classes of Naval craft. His assistant had served several stints in the company establishments in Thailand and also took part in the major SEATO exercise 'Air Boon Choo' a couple of years previous. He was presented with a certificate for his contribution to the exercise by the exercise director. There was yet one other establishment on the Dockyards outside HMS Terror, but within the Naval base, this was a self-service shop. This was small compared with some of the supermarkets at the time but one of the most attractive shops in Singapore and run by Jimmy Goh, who had only been with the company seven years and had served at sea on the Fort Charlotte.

The Naval base shop was one of the happiest shops in Singapore. Eleven of the staff had been in the establishment since it opened in 1957. No reference to any base would be complete without the mention of the automatic vending machines mechanic Tan Chen Swee. Tan joined NAAFI in 1946 as a driver and had been looking after vending machines since 1959. He nursed them as a mother would a baby and he was certainly a round peg in a round hole. Finally, there was Rosie and Lucy, two delightful young ladies who were the favourites with all visitors to supervisor Jack Holness's office or the same ration store, which are in the same building. Rosie's name was Miss Sim Lian Neo, who worked as a clerk typist assisting manager Wee Ah Tee in the ration store and Lucy was Miss Lucy Lum, typist to the 2 NCS officials. Both girls joined the company in 1955 when Lucy was 15 and Rosie was 16. After 10 years they are part of the NCS scenery, popular with both visiting managers and ships' representatives.

This was the Naval canteen service in the Naval base. There were other Naval establishments in Singapore, HMS Simbang which housed the Naval Air station and when they were not hunting terrorists in Borneo 42 commando, and the RNW/T station at Kranji. This was the story of the Naval base, a self-contained, bustling, thriving community at the northern end of the sea town. NAAFI's role was a vital one in almost all places where British servicemen were stationed. Nowhere was it more important or more honourably carried out than in this strategic centre in South East Asia, where ships returned from a long and lonely vigil in the certain and comforting knowledge that they will find rest and relaxation and a NAAFI team ready and eager to serve them ashore, as they had been served at sea.

EFI home from Norway May 1966

In February of 1966 EFI went on exercise 'winter express'. After working for two months in the Arctic conditions Capt WA J License of the RAOC EFI flew back into Lyneham to be greeted by yet more snow! Of course, they thought they'd seen the last of the snow in Norway but already being acclimatised this was no issue. Capt License, who headed the EFI team that manned the bulk issue store and a dry goods store shop for the troops on the NATO exercise was an old hand. After all, EFI had been participating in the exercises in Norway for some time.

The temperature at Bardufoss was around 38 degrees below, their winter clothing was more than adequate and assisted in their acclimatization. Once the men had settled in, they were able to take time off to indulge in the local sports. Under the expert guidance of Norwegian children, two adventurous EFI man tried their luck on the nursery ski slopes. They managed to give a credible performance and after a while could stay on their feet for most of the way down.

WO2 Frank Bullen accepted an offer from the local postmaster Mr Svendsen, to go fishing. A 40-mile drive through rugged and beautiful country took them to the small village of Naveren, the temperature was 20 degrees centigrade below freezing and the fishermen had to cut holes in 12 inches of thick ice to reach the water. After each catching 18 fish, Cod and Haddock, they decided to call it a day and Mr Bullen returned to his host's home for a warm cup of coffee and some of his wife's special cake.

After every exercise EFI took part in, on returning back to the United Kingdom a review of the events and service given was essential before demobilization. Everything was looked at: the type of products, the money taken, even comments and requests from the service personnel; not one thing was left out – as with all military exercises everything had to be looked at to ensure that next time there would be a vast improvement to ensure that the correct service would be given at the correct time.

Early days in Zambia 1966 by Sgt AP Crouch and Pte CA Hudson

On the 6th of December 1965 at 1530hrs in the afternoon a VC10 bound for Aden lifted clear of Gatwick runway and set course on its 3000-mile journey. Among the passengers were four men of the RAOC EFI, Capt JJ Roberts, Cpl Reg Arminson, Pte Ian Lawson and Pte CA Hudson. On standby at Back Down were Sgt AP Crouch and Pte RR Hewlett. Six and a half hours after leaving cold and wintry Gatwick the aircraft touched down in Aden, the EFI contingent was greeted by temperatures in the 70s.

The party stayed in Aden for three days before flying with RAF transport command to Nairobi, where Mr JC Whitehead, supervisor for East Africa, was waiting to meet them. After one night in Kenya's capital, the captain, the Corporal and the two privates flew out for Lusaka. Soon after arrival they began work on a marquee that was to be used as the NAAFI club. The layout was carefully planned, and 100 beer crates were stacked for the moment when the club was officially opened. A shop was set up in the buildings of Lusaka college, a temporary measure until college reassembled. To help with these preliminary operations two men were flown in from Aden, Mr DJ Hammond and Mr RM Bowser. The Captain, Corporal and private then moved off to Ndola, a car journey of some five hours. Meanwhile Sgt Crouch and Private Hewlett had left Black Down. Once at Aden they grabbed a meal in the NAAFI before flying on to rock Nairobi and then onto Zambia.

They arrived at Ndola and were driven to Zambia showgrounds. There they spotted a cafe called Isola Capri, a NAAFI club, shop and store. Here they were met by Capt Roberts' party who would arrive the day before. A truck was converted into a mobile canteen and was soon dispensing cold drinks, meat pies, cigarettes and confectionery to appreciative customers. Supplies were ordered from local merchant by Capt Roberts and Mr FB Tanner who had been called from Nairobi to Zambia. Mr Tanner had been acting as a temporary supervisor for East Africa and was, in fact, the first NAAFI man to reach Zambia. Christmas products started to arrive, crackers, nuts, dates, figs, slab cake, and other items from Nairobi. Then came duty free spirits and cigarettes from Aden. Beer was not flown in as a local brewery could meet the demand. All the time more and more RAF men were arriving. With them Christmas arrived and the EFI Men were invited out by civilian families but had to decline as work came first.

The RAF laid on an excellent Christmas dinner at Lusaka and the EFI were invited. Television cameraman were there too. After the Christmas rush, clothing, film, paperback books and other goods began to arrive. In January 1966 another 2 EFI men arrived to join the contingent. They were Sgt DR Sadler and Cpl CK Croker who had flown in from Lyneham. Sgt Sadler stayed at Lusaka while Cpl Croker went onto Ndola. At this time the club and the shop were given a permanent home at the Jubilee Hall in Lusaka showgrounds. All the EFI men were in good spirits in good health and they also acquired the inevitable suntan. One evening

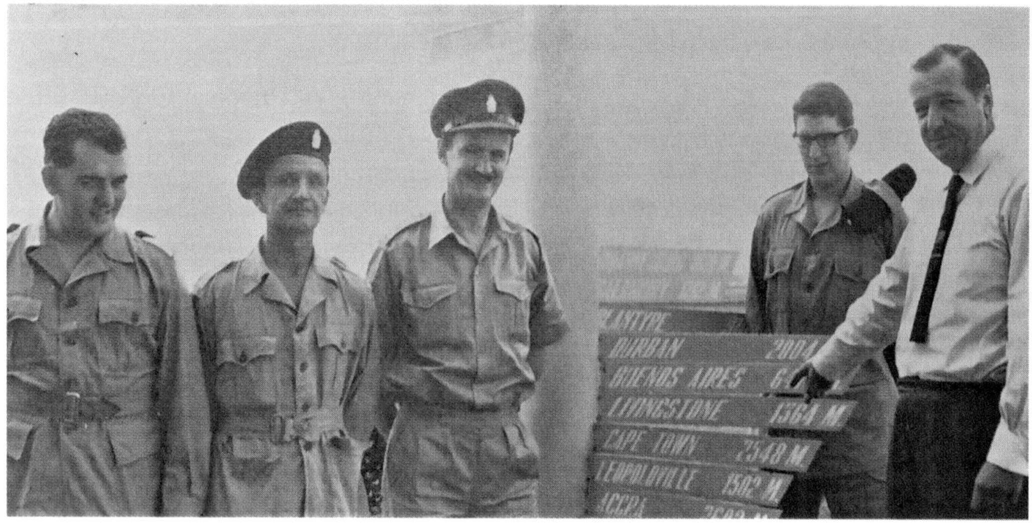

a man had the dubious company of a snake which eventually was caught. As a result, the EFI was issued with a cat. It was a female feline so no doubt there were several more potential pest deterrents in the near future.

The 100th issue 1966

The 100th issue of NAAFI News was issue number 40 volume 5, September 1966; the editor was Ronald Walker who had correspondents in headquarters, the home service, accounts offices, European service, overseas service, and the Naval canteen service. Particularly the overseas service correspondence was based in Aden, Benghazi, Bermuda, Cyprus, East Africa, Far East headquarters, Gibraltar, Hong Kong, Malta, Persian Gulf and Tobruk.

They went back to remember by D Owens, district manager, special duties ES South September 1966

When Mr JA Smith a divisional head in European service, asked me if I spoke French, I had a pretty good idea I would be heading for France in the not too distant future. It was only a matter of a few weeks earlier that I'd entered the same office and was asked if I had my combat kit handy. On that occasion I quickly found myself under canvas on a RAOC exercise, so it was natural for me to jump to conclusions when asked if I spoke French. I don't, incidentally, but that made no difference.

NAAFI had been asked to provide a service to over 300 officers, senior NCOs and junior ranks who were to take part in the commemoration of the 50th anniversary of the battle of the Somme. The NAAFI team consisted of Mr TM Byrne, BM Bed, D Cardwall, AW Whyman, Jane Morgan, JL Meadows. We were to provide a restaurant and Tavern service for senior and junior ranks and operate the officers' mess bar, accommodation being provided in the Lycée at Albert, some 250 miles from my normal base at Dusseldorf.

A reconnaissance of the accommodation was undertaken first and then what was needed for saleable goods and equipment prepared. The supplies were transported by road from Krefeld warehouse to Albert on Sunday, June 26th, in readiness for the opening of business on Monday June 27th. And so, NAAFI found itself on parade with today's service representatives and those of yesteryear including many Somme veterans.

Looking around Albert and the peaceful surrounding countryside it was hard to believe that this was the place where, on the opening day of the battle on the 1st of July 1916, 13 divisions attacked on a 15-mile front astride the Albert-Bapaume road. The battle lasted 4½ months during which time Britain and her allies suffered 600,000 casualties for an advance of about 6 miles. It was interesting to talk to some of the survivors who came back to pay homage to fallen colleagues and to remember their own personal experiences. Most of them, then in their teens and 20s, were now in their 70s. They proudly wore their medals, hard won in one of the bloodiest battles of World War One.

The commemoration service took place besides the 150-foot-high Thiepval Monument and was conducted by Venerable Archdeacon JR Youens, OBE, MC, honorary chaplain to HM The Queen, chaplain general to the army. The tone of the day was set by Field Marshal Earl Alexander of Tunis who spoke to the parade of troops and veterans: 'let us not forget that brave foe we fought against whose losses were at least equal to our own and who sacrificed their lives for what they believed was a worthy cause. Can we not honour them too? On this hallowed and solemn occasion let us honour all brave men who fought and died on this ground on which we stand, and pray that future generations will never again try to solve their problems by fighting it out, as we did at the battle of the Somme'.

Copyright Sue A Lowe

1967

Sunday in Aden, by GT Caddey 1967

When strikes and other circumstances such as the lack of public transport rob NAAFI establishments of the local staff, UK personnel irrespective of their normal jobs, fill the breach to the best of their ability. The fact that they have no training, or liking, for the tasks they are undertaking is disregarded. Thus, furnishing, accounts and personnel staff man the bakery and maintain production of bread during the strikes of the past two months, and the United Kingdom team of drivers delivered each new batch of bread to the shops manned by other volunteers. In a two-day strike at the beginning of February 1967, bread issued by the volunteers equal to production of a normal week.

The difficulties are increased by the shortages of supplies, particularly of meat and vegetables, due to staff shortages in the Aden cold store and the cancellation of flights into Aden from East Africa. But the service kept on going.

It was 1730hrs, Sunday 12th of February. Sitting on the balcony of the Crescent hotel looking out at a peaceful scene, black crows are settling down in the trees of Tawahi as they have done for centuries. Scavenging cats are looking around the rubbish heaps for a titbit before starting their evening prowl. The difference between this Sunday and the last is the curfew. There was one yesterday and who knows there may be another tomorrow and Tuesday. I don't know why there is a curfew. It has something to do with the strikes that periodically occur, but why they care and what they're expected to achieve is a mystery to me. FLOSY And the NLF might be able to tell me, perhaps the High Commissioner too, but I doubt if the water seller, the sweeper or the clerk could. All that man in the street knows is that at the end of the month his pay packet will be a few pounds less and he'll have to economise on an already tight budget. He can't understand why he isn't allowed to walk along, or even stand about, the street. Nor why there is no football on the Crescent, they normally play there happily if not too skilfully, every day of the year.

I'm alright, the hotel people see to that. But the sweeper in the camel cart drivers aren't. The curfew is on and no one has been able to shop since Friday. The prudent have got in reserves of bread and rice and other necessities but whoever heard of a prudent sweeper? Troops are consistently passing in trucks or on foot with guns at the ready. Healthy, sunburnt, but are really clear what is all about? The trouble spots of Maalla and Crater, inoffensive curfew breakers are dealt with in the same way as their more offensive trouble making brothers. A grenade explodes in the street and another innocent bystander or soldier is taken off to hospital, or to the Mortuary. The Mortuary is overworked and full up, I am told, so the resources of Aden Coastal have been listed. Room for bodies must be found, food storage takes 2nd place.

After nearly a month of the sunshine I am looking forward to the rain, snow, gales, even fog, of London. In NAAFI officials who have to soldier on until the end of the year may envy me. For the life in Aden, 1967 is a constant state of improvisation. Their concern is to keep the service going, a good service too. To maintain such a standard in the face of frustrations in Aden and with the staff of the Somalis, Yeminis, and Adenis who knew that their job would last for a year at most, is a task that calls for a lot of hard work even in peaceful times.

The command supervisor and his team will indeed have achieved something if they leave Aden with the NAAFI flag flying as high as it is now. There is of course a lighter side and a typical Aden special occurred while I was studying the implications of the run down. The warehouse on the Wharf side is plagued with rats and the manager sets traps for them. On the first day seven rats were caught, on the second 10 and on the third day 14. Mahomed, the warehouse labourer, was ordered to dispose of each catch and it was assumed that he'd drowned them. On the third day the manager happened by chance to follow him and saw him go behind the nearby building open the cage and release the rats. The warehouse labourer no longer performs this particular chore and the daily catch gets progressively less.

SHAPE 1951-1967

The Supreme Headquarters Allied Powers Europe, SHAPE. This was the headquarters of one of three NATO military commands. The three commands are Allied Command Europe, ACE, with its headquarters, SHAPE, located until April 1967 at the Rocquencourt, about 10 miles North West of Paris. Allied command Atlantic, ACLANT, with headquarters in Norfolk, Virginia, USA and allied command channel, ACCHAN, with headquarters at Northwood, England.

The three commands came into being as a result of the North Atlantic treaty which was signed in 1949 by 12 sovereign nations: Belgium, Canada, Denmark, France, Iceland, Italy, Luxembourg, the Netherlands, Norway, Portugal, the United Kingdom and the United States. In 1952 Greece and Turkey joined the alliance and then in May 1955 West Germany became the 15th member. SHAPE came into being on the 2nd of April 1951, when General Dwight D Eisenhower assumed command as the first SACEUR, Supreme Allied Commander Europe. He has been succeeded by the American generals Ridgway, Grunther, Norstad and Lemnitzer. In essence, each of these generals had the same mission, to defend the NATO territory in Europe.

Last year the French government gave notice to the NATO countries that NATO and SHAPE must be removed from France. On 1st of July 1966 France withdrew its personnel from the military structure of NATO although she still remains a member of the alliance. With the removal of SHAPE to Belgium, the Alpha FCENT to Holland, so the NAAFI offered SHAPE canteen service has begun its run down. A service will still be provided for several weeks to the caretaker elements and the families temporarily left behind.

So where in or less does NAAFI fit? General Eisenhower, President Auriol, field Marshal Montgomery and a host of other nobles, NAAFI might never have received the compliments that have poured into Imperial Court since setting up the SHAPE canteen service in 1951.

In the setup of this new canteen service numerous investments were made but it was not only the kitchens. There were also restaurants, cafeterias, wine bars, staff quarters and offices to be equipped and staffed. If the truth be told, the inventory of equipment for this endeavour totalled 14,459 items, this was from chefs' hats to flower vases.

It all began on the 14th of March 1951 when Colonel Jay Howard Jones, deputy HQ commander of SHAPE, called on Mr L Philbin of NAAFI home canteen service to ask if NAAFI would provide certain services to a dozen or more nationalities to be employed by SHAPE near Paris. Their requirements, explained Colonel Jones, were free clubs for some 2000 other ranks, enlisted men in the SHAPE American terminology in or near SHAPE, a cafeteria and liquor bar for 600 all ranks, a grocery shop for families of service personnel of all nations, and officers' mess for about 150 people including special rooms for VIPs and VVIPs and a club for about 500 officers. No accommodation existed for any of the services required, but Colonel Jones thought SHAPE might provide premises and possibly furnishings for the proposed cafeteria and liquor bar and for the officer's mess. No staff quarters were included in the plans and since SHAPE had no funds, financial provision for these and other buildings could not be promised. Office accommodation, however, would probably be provided rent free. The decision to approach NAAFI had been taken after first considering a plan to have SHAPE personnel conducting the various establishments or a proposal favoured by the Americans, to employ concessionaries.

On the 15th of March NAAFI secretary passed Mr Philbin's report of the meeting to the chairman and with the comment that the provisions were not attractive. They wrote to Colonel Jones the following day which gave a glimpse of his reasons for that comment. After saying that the proposal would be submitted to the board of management he went on to point out that apart from the question of whether or not NAAFI should service non-British personnel, the proposition raises the matter of the employment of NAAFI funds to provide the capital assets required. As you are doubtless aware NAAFI funds are for the benefit of her majesty's forces.

Mr CA Layard, who at the time was assistant to the manager of the NCS, visited SHAPE on the 1st of April to make an on the spot inspection. He reported that SHAPE, because of their lack of funds, would be unable to indemnify NAAFI against loss. The PX had declined to undertake the commitment and believe that British prestige as SHAPE would be greatly enhanced if NAAFI took on the job. A meeting of the NAAFI board of management on the 3rd of April gave approval to the provision of a club and shop subject to the satisfactory safeguards against loss by SHAPE. A day or two later Mr Layard revisited Paris to make more detailed investigations and to discuss the proposals with officers of SHAPE. Following this visit the secretary of the company was able to write to SHAPE on the 15th of April and say that NAAFI was prepared to undertake the service and proposed an all ranks cafeteria at Rocquencourt, SHAPE HQ, 2 clubs for other ranks, catering and a bar Service in the officers' mess and a shop for SHAPE personnel and their dependants. It was on the 2nd of May that the secretary's letter was acknowledged and said it was being studied with a view to meeting the conditions stipulated. Meanwhile at a meeting of the NAAFI board management held on the 1st of May, the principal administrative officers of the three services limited their approval of NAAFI undertaking the SHAPE commitment. It was then on the 22nd of May, Maj General Randle Feilden, NAAFI general manager and Mr AV Barker, AGM, had visited SHAPE and reported to the board that they had met all the conditions laid down and that only matters still outstanding were exemptions and amenities still being negotiated with the French authorities. The general manager had therefore instructed that detailed planning should proceed.

While during his visit he had agreed with SHAPE that the service to be provided would be referred to as the SHAPE canteen service. On the 23rd of May SHAPE wrote to the French Minister of Finance putting forward the proposals for a NAAFI service and seeking certain concessions for the organization to provide the service. Following that on the 27th of May Mr W Whitehouse, then manager of HCS, left for Paris to organise the new canteen service. With him went Mr W Warrener who was to be directly responsible to headquarters for the new service. At a board meeting on the 5th of June the general manager reported that progress had been made towards setting up the SCS but advised that certain conditions regarding the amenities to be enjoyed had not been accepted by the French government.

A satisfactory settlement of the outstanding points was, in fact, to take a considerable time involving mountains of correspondence and tough negotiations at meetings between SHAPE, NAAFI and the French government. Nevertheless, professional agreements on the catering side were reached as early as June and the SCS was able to inaugurate its service at Rocquencourt, in all ranks' cafeteria on the 12th of July and in the office's restaurants on the 16th of July. It was a service designed to spread to camp Voluceau and to the satellite headquarters of allied forces central Europe at Fontainebleau, to diversify and grow into a 2 million a year business. At the first chief of staff's conference following the opening of the service, a French general recorded that the food and the service were of the highest quality. Praise came from high and low. General Eisenhower inspected the officer's restaurant and cafeteria and pronounced his satisfaction with service in both.

In his first report to Imperial Court Mr Warrener acknowledged that the praise is lavish but warned that suggestions and criticism may follow. He went on to say that unseen by the customers the kitchen and storage spaces were pitifully inadequate, and the workmen were still mingling with the kitchen staff. Nevertheless, the first taste of NAAFI service was enough to bring requests and undertake special caterings rolling in, lunch for General Eisenhower and 25 US senators, catering for President Auriol and other VIPs after the raising of the flags of the nations of western alliance and the official opening ceremony of the new Headquarters on the 23rd of July, a cocktail party for the chief of staff on the 27th of July.

Summing up on these early days, Mr Warrener claimed that the service was not perfect, but it was good. Conditions behind the scenes are bad. Storage conditions are poor that frequent interchange of stock between restaurants and cafeteria was inevitable. You may be assured that NAAFI prestige is extremely high at SHAPE. On the 27th of October, General Alfred M Grunther, then chief of staff and then later Supreme commander, wrote to the NAAFI general manager, "now that SHAPE Canteen Service (SCS) has been in operation at this headquarters for approximately 3 months, I consider it appropriate to express to you my appreciation of the service provided and especially the loyalty and hard work of your staff in building up such an efficient organization in so short a time. It is realised that in the view of a very brief interval between the decision to inaugurate SHAPE canteen service and the opening of the headquarters a very special effort was necessary to provide an adequate service without which the work of headquarters would have been seriously hampered. I should be grateful if you would convey the Supreme commander's appreciation and thanks to all concerned". But although the service appeared to progress, NAAFI had still not been able to negotiate final terms on which the service would be provided. Correspondence and meetings on this matter and on the various concessions requested from French government continued. On the 4th of March 1952 it was reported that, at a meeting held at SHAPE, discussion had taken place on the modification of the original conditions on which NAAFI undertook the canteen service. They satisfactory verbal agreement had been made and a draft agreement with SHAPE.

Almost a year after the service began, the allied headquarters canteen service board (AHQSCB) was set up. It held its first meeting at SHAPE on the 28th of July under the chairmanship of the Admiral Ferrante Capponi of the Italian Navy. It was on the 31st of October at the second meeting of this committee, that Mr Barker asked to know precisely what conditions of operating SHAPE could agree to and which they could not agree. The committee agreed that the draft contract should be drawn up and this would be ready on the 10th of November. This draft was ready on the 28th of November and a second draft appeared on the 3rd of December and then on the ninth it was reported to the NAAFI board that the last process was apparently being made towards a firm contract. On the 18th of December, however, a meeting of the NATO budget committee turned down certain important sections of the contract. In a letter to General Grunther on the 1st of January 1953, NAAFI's chairman warned that, if agreement could not be reached, NAAFI would reluctantly have to withdraw its service with effect from the 30th of April 1953.

The general then wrote to the NBC asking them to review their decision but at a meeting following receipt of this letter that NBC failed to reach decision and put certain new proposals, forwarded by the general to the GM on the 12th of January for NAAFI views. Then on the 23rd of January the GM replied to General Guenther stating the terms upon which NAAFI would be prepared to continue its service and agreeing to withhold NAAFI formal notice of withdrawal until after a further NBC meeting in the early February. Eventually the NBC had agreed to meet with NAAFI conditions providing certain points could be satisfactorily resolved with the French government. Many meetings then took place. And eventually confirmation of what SCS could and could not import duty free had been given on the 18th of November 1952. On the duty-free list, the important items were beer, spirits, cigarettes, cigars and tobacco. Soaps and soap powders were allowed in the duty free, but clothes lines and clothes pegs were not. Maps were permissible, rooms were not. Duty was waved on teeth but not on teething rings. The barriers were down for toilet paper but up for chamber pots. Nor would the authorities allow the duty-free import of corkscrews, flycatchers, jam pot covers, reins, or tea bags, but they would allow putting cloths, string, Emery cloth and hot water bottles.

The list was considerably curtailed in the following year at a meeting of the AHQSCB on the 9th of July 1950; three NAAFI officials pointed out that the new restrictions, if they remained in force, would increase the budget of the average family at SHAPE by 25%. Furthermore, the loss of concessions was sure to result in a loss of trade to the SCS and therefore, a loss to welfare funds. The board therefore decided that a new approach should be made to the French government.

On the 28th of July at a meeting with the French authorities SHAPE pressed strongly for an extension of the duty-free list in accord with the NATO agreement. The manager of HCS reported that the meeting was not entirely unsatisfactory. It was not until December, however, that a more liberal list was eventually implemented but these were to have a significant effect on the profitability of the service and of course on the money available to the welfare funds of SHAPE.

The various no actions went on until the 5th of May 1956 when the NAAFI -SHAPE contract was finally signed by General CVR Schuyler for SHAPE and Mr EW McGowan for NAAFI. It had taken NAAFI less than four months, from the date of the first informal request, to set up the service and begin operations but it took over five years to complete the contract on which the service was based. These were mixed years of frustration and success of a hard negotiation. The 10 years or more since the signing of the contract have, by contrast, been comparatively smooth. The files show that the main traffic between SHAPE and Imperial Court had been in the one decision, a flow of requests for profits to be paid to the various welfare accounts and in the other direction, drafts for considerable sums to meet those requests.

The next really significant communication was received at NAAFI headquarters in July 1966 when SCS deputy chief of staff, logistics and administration, gave notice that NAAFI services which had been given in a satisfactory manner, would no longer be required at Rocquencourt, Voluceau and Fontainebleau. The formal NAAFI -SHAPE contract was to be terminated with effect from the 31st of March 1967.

It's a man's life, 1967

They are on the march again, our man in EFI uniform. During 1967 NAAFI servicemen had been active on three fronts, in the United Kingdom, Germany and Greece. On the home front two basic training courses for new EFI recruits were held at the RAOC trade training school at Deepcut, Camberley. The type of NAAFI staff that would attend this course where from bakery departments, canteen managers, training shop managers, clerks in overseas accounting branches and staff from Imperial Court headquarters. Having joined the two weeks at Deepcut, the recruits were taught drill, weapon training and first aid. They also learned about nuclear, biological and chemical warfare. At the end of the course it was commented that they were keen, enthusiastic and hardworking and they would be an asset to the EFI RAOC.

Some of the recruits that were taking part in these training courses would be on deployment within the year. Capt Arthur License, normally a district accountant at Bath, was leading the EFI party. Greece was a change for him at his last EFI exercise, in January, took him to the Arctic regions of Norway. The party was made up by Sergeant David Cook, shop manager at Odiham, Private John Salter, billiards table mechanic in South West region, and Private Paddy Botell, warehouseman at Amesbury.

They drew their kit at Black Down and then moved on to HQ logistic support company at Parham Down where they had two days' training and made final preparations to move to Thessalonica. On the Friday evening the 25th of August, they arrived at RAF Lyneham. There were two flights out, one at midnight and one at four in the morning. Both flights ran into a storm over the Adriatic, but landed safely at Thessalonica in blazing sunshine. The camp was about 3 miles on the other side of town where there were approximately 400,000 inhabitants. A few tents were already on their way up when the EFI detachment arrived. But soon they run into their first problem, Capt Licence had difficulty clearing goods at the docks and coupled with this, there was a shortage of transport. Despite these headaches they began a service on the Saturday evening. Then spent the Sunday unloading the stores and equipment from Greek army lorries, the heat was terrific.

The following day the commanding officer asked some of us to take the stores to the forward supply element some 40 miles away. This was done on the back of a 2½ tonne lorry and on reaching the new camp they unloaded the supplies into the tent which was to be a third NAAFI. This was opened in the early evening and proved to be very popular. Among some of the customers was 4 Sandhurst cadets who were on their way home from Tehran. They were surprised and delighted to find a NAAFI and drove off in their long wheelbase Land Rover, happily clutching duty-free cigarettes and whiskey. They also had a visit from the Canadian general who they were providing the service to the NATO troops. The service seemed to please them too, particularly when they were able to refill his cigarette lighter.

Camp is only half a mile from Stavros beach, and they were able to swim in the blue Aegean Sea, a welcome change from the heat and the bustle of working in the confined conditions of the tent. Maintaining the supply chain between base and forward units was the main problem and estimating demand was made even more difficult by regular visits from nearby gunnery units. The link was stretched further on the 3rd of September when the forward camp was moved again, this was time to site about 5 miles North West. During the move they fell victim to travel sickness due to the appalling roads and heat and dust. They spent the next few days in a German field hospital. Meanwhile they were told by the forward party that they were to make two more moves and at the second site there was a heavy downpour lasting 30 hours, the tent which was full of stock was threatened by flooding.

A good proportion of the EFI service personnel had already seen service with the regular army, whereby one of them decided that it was a good idea to dig a trench around the tent and this is what saved them from flooding. On the 8th of September the forward party returned to base and four days later the exercise finished and three days after that they flew home via Malta.

The following month another EFI party, led on this occasion by Capt Roy Arthur, was operating a tented canteen and bulk issue store for the army and RAF contingents on 'Exercise Overdale' in Germany. They were at RAF Gelsenkirchen, the supply base for the exercise, which was staged at the Eifel Hills, South of Aachen. The special thing about this exercise was that this was the first time since the end of the war that EFI men had returned.

A second contingent had joined the exercise from the European service team headed by district managers Mr Reginald Slatter and Mr Tony Irvine, along with Miss Margaret Aitken. This team operated a tented canteen at Gelsenkirchen and two tented canteens and five battle mobiles in the battle area. The planning and supervision of the joint EFI and ES effort were in the hands of Mr EA Self, manager, South region. About 6000 strategic reserve troops were on exercise and a further 1000 RAF personnel were responsible for the 90 aircraft taking part. The troops started moving out on the 14th of October at the rate of 1000 a day and this meant around the clock service by the EFI. The service was halted only once by gale force winds, a temporary service was set up in a storage unit and the marquee was put up again. The battle lasted about a week. Clearing up operations was expected to take another two weeks and the EFI men expected to be back to their normal jobs in early November 1967.

1968

New man at the top 1968

New Year's Day 1968, NAAFI had a new managing director, he was Mr EW MacGowan; he stepped into the managing director seat taking over the role of chief executive of the company from Mr HPT Prideaux.

Mr Prideaux was appointed managing director in 1960 and took on the additional duties of chairman of the board of management on the 1st of January 1965. He now gives up his appointment of managing director but continued as the chairman. He remained closely involved in all major policy decisions. He was appointed deputy chairman of Liebigs Extract of Meat company, best known at the time for Oxo and Fray Bentos products; he was also vice president of London Life Association, a leading life insurance office.

Mr MacGowan was a qualified solicitor and joined NAAFI in 1939. He was commissioned in the EFI in 1940 and served in France before the evacuation. On his return to England he volunteered for the Royal Navy as a rating and was commissioned in that service in 1943. He was then appointed as assistant secretary of NAAFI in 1949 and secretary in 1952. He became the joint general manager in 1962 and two years later was given the seat on the board of management as administrative director in 1966.

He was a new face at the future board meetings as will be that of Mr JE Ellison who had been appointed administrative director. Mr Ellison qualified as an accountant in 1937 and joined NAAFI as a member of the chief accountant staff in 1941. He was appointed assistant chief accountant in 1948 and became chief accountant four years later. In 1955 he made assistant general manager and was appointed control of supplies in the same year.

Sailors praise NAAFI at lower deck meeting 1968

Chief Petty Officer DEA Dennison said, 'I have gained the impression that NCS constantly strives to provide the best possible service.' The chief Petty Officer reported to the 107th meeting of the Naval canteen committee after his first six months as lower deck representative for the Portsmouth command and western fleet. He went on to say, 'they could only take out of the organization a fair proportion of what they needed to put into it, therefore we must support on our side to reap the benefits of better service and amenities.'

Chief Petty Officer DJ Cooper, lower Accra representative for Plymouth command and Scotland, had particular praise for the facilities in HMS Neptune, Faslane. 'This is the first NAAFI set up I have seen anywhere, with first class lounges, bars, service shop, tailors, barbers, post office, and a receiving centre for laundry, dry cleaning, and shoe repairs catering for all the needs of the busy base.' CPO Cooper went on to mention the excellent service given by the majority of managers aboard HM Ships. 'I must mention particularly the Maltese managers whose high standard of service is beyond compare.'

Chief Petty Officer JD Hoodless, representing Scotland and Northern Ireland, singled out the NCS staff of the fishery protection squadron, 'They're doing such a grand job and like the windmill they never close !' The round the clock service in the Gulf, the food at Penang leave centre, supplying furnishing officials, including many more came in for a share of the commendations from the various representatives at the meeting.

Chief electrician D R Waterhouse, lower deck representative, Far East station, said that the closing down of property in overseas bases was almost bound to have an adverse effect on NAAFI's turnover which, in turn, may similarly affect rebate, discount, or extra rebate. It was therefore in the interest of not only the Navy but all services to help minimise this as much as possible by supporting the company. Changing circumstances were not new to NAAFI and the closure of overseas bases did undoubtedly have to be accepted as yet another challenge to the company's versatility. No one pretends that it was an easy phase, but they were confident that given the maximum support of the services the obstacle would be overcome.

Mr F Anniss, manager, Naval canteen service, stressed the need for such support and said that NCS sales for the six months that ended October 1967 were only just above those for the corresponding. In 1966, preliminary accounts for that half of the year showed that, because of the increased expenses, the trading surplus was approximately half of that for the October 1966. The level of sales since the October, he continued to say, had improved, mainly due to the ships of the task force being at sea for longer periods. The expenses, he warned, included an increase in allowance to sea going staff, this had risen too, more steeply. He also added that the emphasis that was needed for the fullest support from the fleet to enable them to maintain and improve the standards of the Naval canteen service. He went on to tell the meeting that development and modernization of NCS had been maintained and went on to give examples of this in clubs, canteens, and shops.

He said that the Naval canteen service had offered to provide canteen service in Polaris submarines but unfortunately this had proved impractical. Capt FA Bland, Naval director on NAAFI board of management, amplified the ways in which the Navy could give more support to NAAFI. He suggested that there was untapped opportunities going for the company for wines and spirits. Not only are prices competitive, he emphasised, but on top of that the company offers various good rates of discount. He also recommended that families should give full support to the growing number of NCS family shops, then made the plea that the company should be considered part of the Naval family.

Swansong in the Antarctic, an account by the last Commission in the 32-year career service by the training manager Mr T Lewis 1968

The day we joined HMS Protector, it seemed the gods smiled on us, the number of months to be served was short and the list of ports to be visitors was long. The grey funnel line was about to provide us with the experience never to be forgotten.

After my boss, Mr Ernie Winskill, and I arrived, we got on with the job of squeezing supplies for the 7th month voyage into every available nook and cranny. Soon we were leaving behind the majestic chimneys of Portsmouth power station and were on our way to Gibraltar. We arrived amid signs of 'keeping the rock British' and had time for some sightseeing and visits to the casino before setting out for the West Indies on Friday the 13th.

On the 12th day out of Gibraltar we anchored off the island of Tobago and with the aid of the ship's helicopters, set up a beer bar on the shore. The following day we docked at the Port of Spain, Trinidad, where for four days we enjoyed the delights of the silver sand beaches, nightclubs, calypsos, and the Limbo. It was less than a month since we had left Portsmouth and already, we were very brown. We crossed the equator heading for Rio de Janeiro, a journey which lasted two weeks. For amateur photographers, Rio was a paradise with an enormous statue of Christ on the Corcovado mountain a favourite subject. The shops overflowed with souvenirs, the best buys being pitchers and trays patterned with butterfly wings. The SS Arcadia and the RMS Queen Mary arrived while we were in port and we were allowed to look over both ships.

From Rio we sailed for Puerto Belgrano in Argentina, a purely Naval port where we saw the aircraft carrier HMS Warrior and visited the local brewery.

Next port of call was the Falkland group of islands, based in the South. The only town was port Stanley with a population of around 2000. There was detachment of Royal Marines on hand with helicopters and hovercraft to help us arrange orders and pay and collect bills. After a few weeks sightseeing around the island suite whilst survey work was going on, we sailed further South to the almost uninhabited islands of South Georgia. The change to snow and bitter winds was sudden after the sun and warmth of the South American countries. But despite the cold we were glad of the chance to stretch our legs and snap the photogenic seals and penguins. It was here that one of the crew became seriously ill and in need of an operation. At the same time, one of the Queen's helicopters crashed in Britain and our helicopters, the same type, were grounded. We returned to Port Stanley to await instruction, but the invalid became worse and we sailed urgently for Montevideo, Uruguay, where there was a hospital. The operation was successful, and the patient was flown home to recover.

After 10 days in friendly Montevideo, we sailed back to the Falklands and stayed a month while the surveyors carried out their work. Most of the crew employed their time giving the ship a lick of paint, 350 gallons of it. It was an ideal time for my boss and me to carry out a stock take and prepare the stores for which we were due to arrive on a merchant ship. During the preparations we discovered that the beer tank was slowly filling up with fuel oil. We called the stokers and they bailed out about 40 gallons. When the stores arrived and were loaded, we set out to continue our journey and began with another quick trip to Montevideo.

When we left Montevideo, we sailed South once again, loudspeakers blaring out the military music and people on the jetty waved to us, for the HMS Protector was leaving for the last time. After much careful navigation we anchored at the South Orkney islands. Ashore we met 20 dedicated men who carry out research for the British Antarctic survey, they had spent two years on these desolate rocks. They gave us a hearty greeting and an invitation to look around.

All over the island we saw penguins, which always seemed to have smiles on their faces. There was an abundance of wildlife on the shore with birds and seals all willing to have their photographs taken. After a few days, the Royal research ship Shackleton joined us to carry out seismic research. This involved dropping depth charges and measuring the sound waves to plot the contours of the seabed. For those not connected with the operations, it meant that the size of the charge could be judged by the number of items which fell off the shelves and tables. The days passed quickly, and we were soon heading back to Stanley to restock before setting off for Chile, and the Punta Arenas.

The ship was alive with rumours that we would be called upon to accommodate the second lone yachtsman, but we were told that the job was being left to the Chilean Navy. We arrived at Arenas to find that was a dying port. There was not much to see, but plenty of local wine to drink and aspirin sales increased daily. After picking up a detachment of Marines destined for the Falkland Island base, we left for Port Stanley. We stayed only a short while on this occasion and after all the final farewells, steamed proudly out of the Harbour heading home, HMS Protector's last voyage.

Wagons roll for the Royal Air Force 1968

Three mobile canteen mobiles, wartime, and pre-NAAFI, appeared at the 1968 Royal Tournament from the 26th of June to the 13th of July. They formed part of the RAF 50th anniversary display. The idea that NAAFI could take part in the show came from Mr Turnbull, assistant chief public relations officer. The suggestion was received with enthusiasm by the Squadron Leader J Read the RAF display organiser. Mr Turnbull said, 'getting hold of vehicles to represent NAAFI in the two wars was a bit of a problem. Mr MacDonald, control of transport, spoke to Mr Sparshatt, chairman of a Portsmouth firm, whose hobby was collecting old commercial vehicles. And he very kindly provided them with a 1916 Vulcan van and a 1947 Albion lorry and agreed to reconstruct them to look like NAAFI mobile canteens.'

The Crest of NAAFI predecessor, that Navy army canteen board, which appears on the side of the Vulcan, is a colour reproduction of a Crest which was eventually tracked down in Ludgershall warehouse on an ancient note paper rack. Twins Ada and Mary, both club assistants at Catterick, travelled on the two old vehicles. Mary served teas from the Vulcan van and Ada served from the Albion lorry. The girls' uniforms were replicas of those worn in 1914 and 1939. The modern mobile was manned by a WRAF driver.

For several weeks the twins and the mobile canteens took part in rehearsals at RAF Cardington, Bedfordshire, where 50 years ago the R101 airship was built. In the display, the NAAFI vehicles were seen with an array of famous aeroplanes, cars, and vehicles spanning 50 years of the RAF. There was a 1914 motorbike, Rolls Royce silver ghost armoured car, Lord Montgomery's Humber and Scout, Sopwith Camel, Avro 504, Spitfire and Harrier vehicle lift off planes.

1969

NAAFI stores ablaze 1969

Early in 1969, NAAFI goods were destroyed when a stores' ship caught fire on the Rhine. The ship was engulfed in flames after a steam crane driver emptied hot ashes into the river at Parallel Harbour, Duisburg. The glowing hot ashes ignited an oil slick. The full part of MS Markab, including the hold which contained the NAAFI stores bound for Krefeld warehouse, was completely gutted. The crew of six and the Rhein fire brigade fought the blaze for six hours, but the heat of the inferno lifted the steel plates and brought down the mast. The wind fortunately confined the blaze to the front of the vessel and saved an oil tanker lying only 50 yards away. The repairs to the ship, just one of two general steam navigation ships which make weekly deliveries to Krefeld, would take three months to complete. This was the world's largest inland port.

EFI fly to Anguilla 1969

EFI men flew to Anguilla providing a NAAFI service for the British troops on the island. These were Capt John Mileham, a supply official in the overseas service at headquarters, Sergeant Bert Mannion, an administrative official in marketing Department, Cpl George Pearson, furnishings fitter from the northern region and Cpl Louis Wilson, administrative manager at Tidworth Department store. Capt Mileham flew out from RAF Fairford just before Easter in an Argosy aircraft carrying men from the 33rd field squadron, Royal Engineers. His job was to contact service officers and commissioner Mr Tony Lee to assess the need for NAAFI service on the island. Sergeant Mannion, Cpl Pearson and Cpl Wilson left Lyneham on the 12th of April in an aircraft carrying NAAFI supplies of tea, coffee, evaporated milk, crockery, sweets, and paperback books. Drinks, cigarettes, toiletries, stationery, and many other items for the troops on the island were being bought locally.

An unexpected bonus for the EFI men was a 24 hour stop in Bermuda while awaiting their plane connection to the island. All in all, 1969 promised to be one of the busiest peacetime years on record for the EFI.

In addition to Anguilla the unit had been providing a service to the 'Exercise Hardfall 3', which ended in Norway in the April. EFI had seven further commitments on its calendar, running through 1969 into 1970, only a two-month respite in the summer. These exercises took EFI to Holland, Greece, France, Denmark, Libya and Norway. Maj DW Joyce, OC of the unit: 'Anyone volunteering for the EFI in this year can almost be guaranteed a trip abroad and such a trip would add to the usual bounty of payments. There is every indication that the demands for this particular type of service will continue to increase, and I am looking forward to the recruits of all ranks.'

Further to 'Exercise Hardfall 3', the four-month exercise ended with a tribute being paid to a handful of the EFI men, the first battalion Coldstream Guards presented Capt RM Arthur of the EFI contingent, with the regimental plaque in recognition of the EFI service during the operation.

Sales in Norway included 420 ski sweaters, gifts and souvenirs and 4300 picture postcards. The EFI had another important assignment come up in June: they provided a service for the holding unit which was to prepare the ground for the 25th anniversary celebrations of the Normandy landings. They would also provide a service for the bands taking part in the celebrations, some 1000 men in all. The EFI force will be made up of one officer and six other the ranks.

The bumboats returned by William C Fraser 1969

NAAFI took the boats when 62 ships of the NATO fleet visited Portsmouth for the review by HM the Queen. For almost a week it seemed that the bumboat days were back again in the shadow of Nelson's victory. Her majesty's dockyard buzzed with the activity as goods were unloaded and Harbour vessels bustled up to pick up their cargoes and then head for the open water and the massive fleet.

In the complex exercises the logistics afloat, NAAFI Naval canteen service were assisted by the Royal Navy, who made available 6 harbour motor vessels, 2 marine high speed landing craft, and 50 sailors, to ferry the goods to the ships anchored off Spithead. The two faster vessels were essential for the ice cream run. Portsmouth commanding supervisor, Mr J Rangecroft, explained: 'The US Navy requested 745 gallons of ice cream early in the exercise. Normally delivery by motor vessel is out of the question because the ice cream would have melted within an hour of being unloaded from the freezer trucks. We estimated that it would take at least three hours to make the rounds of the American warships, which were scattered throughout the NATO fleet.

'We eventually solved the problem by packing ice cream in special bulk containers filled with dry ice. The entire unit was then lifted by crane, one of the three cranes we had at our disposal for the four days from the dockside, into one of the waiting landing craft. Once clear of the dock area the landing craft were able to make a high-speed run to the fleet, where delivery was carried out very quickly indeed.'

Assisting Mr Rangecroft with the supply arrangements was Mr RJR Atkins, Ship's district manager, Portsmouth. 'All the supplies are obtained through the Portsmouth warehouse,' said Mr Atkins, including fresh vegetables and fruit and pasteurised milk.' However, much of the credit for the efficiency of the operation was due to Mr Syd Edwards, the warehouse charge hand. 'While the fleet was in, our day started at 0630hrs in the morning on the dockside and finished whenever the last order of the day had been delivered. Because of the complexity of the deliveries, each vessel had an experienced senior NAAFI manager on board. His job was to check that the right goods reached the right ships and to see the necessary paperwork.'

On the dockside were Mr Freddie Brown, senior produce buyer, Portsmouth and his assistant Mr Ian Whalley. Mr Brown said: 'By the end of the week we had supplied provisions to ships from Belgium, Denmark, Germany, Italy, the Netherlands, Norway, Portugal, the USA and the Royal Navy. Almost all of the 12 nationalities were represented in the fleet. The goods delivered included 7300 gallons of milk, 4800 loaves, 24 tons of fresh fruit and vegetables, almost 3000 packs of quick-frozen meat and hundreds of chickens.'

On the Saturday and Sunday following the Royal review, 20 of the warships docked in Portsmouth to allow inspection by members of the public. The weather was wet and only a trickle of sightseers took advantage of the occasion. 'In good weather,' said Mr Rangecroft, 'the public swarms all over the dockyard for this certification. But although Portsmouth did not turn out to see the fleet the fleet turned out to see Portsmouth.'

Exercise Cunningham by KVB Emery 1969

The RAOC EFI have a saying: 'where there's muck there's gilders'. They had not had the saying long, and it came from exercise Cunningham at Vlissingen, Holland.

A combined team of EFI and European service personnel took part in a six-week exercise in some of the dirtiest, wettest conditions they had ever experienced. The purpose of the exercise was to stimulate the reinforcement of a beleaguered Holland, by bringing in large quantities of stores and ammunition from England. At one point over 3000 TA troops were engaged in the exercise. Although, financially, NAAFI participation in the exercise was a huge success, it was against the background of miserable conditions and backbreaking work that the young, in many cases inexperienced, staff had to operate. The biggest single problem was the very nature of the ground in which the exercise took place.

The advanced party led by the district manager Derek Bottomley found a suitable hard standing for the 9000 square metre tentage, but a local farmer disputed their choice of site with a shotgun to back up his argument. The farmer won the day and the NAAFI team had to resign themselves to using a lower site. When the NAAFI tentage experts Lofty Lockward and Michael Gribben arrived they were horrified at the conditions. They had never erected a tent on anything like this before, they had to dig a foot down into a mixture of sand and seashells that comprised the soil. They had to use 6-foot poles reinforced with three-foot pegs and hope that the gales didn't blow up the tentage. After the erection of the NAAFI village of tents, staff living quarters, kitchen, bulk issue store, junior ranks club, gift shop and restaurant, then came a disaster: torrential rain and blustery winds had the whole complex under 18 inches of water in a few hours. It was at this point that the eight strong EFI contingent arrived under the command of Capt Eric Carruth, district accountant for Northern Ireland. After the initial shock of seeing the living accommodation and the rest of the canvas underwater, the captain set his men to help in the mopping up operation. For two days solid they dug drainage trenches in an attempt to dry the area, but this did not work. There was simply nowhere for the water to drain to as the land was only 18 inches above sea level. In the end the army's fire service came to the rescue and pumped the water out of the tents. The NAAFI men had to abandon the idea of having a separate gift shop and the stock was transferred into the JRC.

They were now ready for the build-up of the main body of troops taking part in the exercise, and all problems seemed little ones after the flood. The state of affairs did not last long. Allori arrived with stores from Krefeld warehouse, 150 miles away, the driver was unaware of the previous problems and tried to get close to the tent to avoid lugging the stalls. The rear axle of the trailer disappeared into 3 foot of mud and the vehicle tilted to an alarming angle. The driver's consideration cost them a lot of effort and they had to carry the stores 40 yards to the tent.

When the main body of the troops left it looked as if they might have time to relax, but even then, the weather had to have the final say. One evening there was an anonymous greenish tinge to the landscape and the wind dropped completely. Suddenly, we noticed clouds appearing and the next minute we were in a howling gale. The main danger came from the walls of the tent. Once they lifted they knew the tent would take off – it took 40 men to hold the tent to the ground while others rushed to lash the failing guy ropes to the trucks and other heavy objects within range.

This near catastrophe marked the end of the problems and the rest of the exercise went smoothly. Mr LR Rodway, regional manager ES South, commented at the end: 'The most impressive aspect of the exercise was the morale of the combined team. The men never ceased in their efforts to give first class service to the TA troops. Although there were times when it seemed they would crack under the strain, their resilience and sense of humour pulled them through.'

EFI would have its own regulars 1969

A special character of RAOC EFI man was being formed to deal with the increasing number of exercises involving NAAFI services. The purpose of the special court squad was to provide instant reservists for exercises or emergencies without disturbing normal work. Three officers and nine men would be recruited for the special squad, a minimum period of one year. During that year they would be EFI man first and departmentally man second.

Maj Douglas Joyce, OC RAOC EFI explained: 'So far this year the EFI had been involved in eight exercises in Europe not to mention the Anguilla emergency. In earlier years the average has been three exercises. We anticipate that this would increase rather than decrease in the future years.'

Any man who elected to join the special squad for a year had an excellent chance of doing three or four exercises visiting countries and collecting reasonably sized bonuses. In 1968 the exercises covered Norway, Greece, Germany, Denmark, Holland and France. Their main aim was to try and attract some of the men already in EFI. This would not affect the men seniority in the Department but it was expected that the valuable experience gains would improve the prospects of promotion in the future as they entered the 1970s.

1969

Bombs and tornadoes Cyprus 1969

A bomb shattered windows and wrecked fittings and furnishings at the shop at RAF Nicosia, Cyprus, on a Friday evening before Christmas. The bomb had been planted in front of the shop and the blast did considerable damage to the shop front and destroyed stock, but nobody was injured. Shortly afterwards a bundle of dynamite was found lying outside another company building. It had not been detonated and was removed before any damage was caused. The explosion took place at almost the same time as another bomb blast outside the British High Commission. The manager, John Mavrides, and his staff, with the help of MPBW, had the shop back in action within 2 hours of Monday's normal opening time. The Cypriot government and press condemned those responsible for placing the bombs as the acts were against the island's interests.

The bombs were not the end of Cyprus's pre-Christmas troubles. On the Monday following, a tornado swept over the island leaving behind a trail of devastation. At one point the freak wind lifted a car over a service family's house and deposited it in the back garden. The worst hit area was the town of Limassol, where cars were overturned, and more than 100 people were injured. The district manager, Mr Sayer, returning to his Limassol home after visiting the bombed Nicosia shop, found his entry to the town blocked by fallen trees and building debris. The whirlwind struck at 1600hrs but at 1900hrs before Mr Sayer managed to reach his home only 100 yards from the storm's path and reassure himself that his family was safe, Mr Sayer said that his next thought was to check the NAAFI establishments. But fortunately, the Limassol shopping club was intact without electricity, but the RAF did not fare so well. The families' club at RAF Akrotiri was in the direct path of the tornado and suffered considerable damage to the roof, whilst the patio awning was completely destroyed. The RAF regiment sub bar popularly known as Charlie's place was completely destroyed and only the foundation and a few chairs remained of this once popular bar. Some severely damaged stock and furniture was subsequently recovered from up to a mile away, some £100 worth of saleable stock and the walls of the building disappeared without trace.

The Peninsula club was fortunate the whirlwind passed on the opposite side of the road and proved to be the main attraction of the children's party then in progress there. By 2000hrs Mr Sayer had completed his check of the establishments and with his wife and daughter returned to the island club where the manager Mr E Charalambous, greeted us. The next morning was spent laying on emergency mobile services for the RAF married quarters, which were being evacuated, for the RAF regiment who were adjusting themselves to life without their bar, Charlie's place. By the time Mr Morris, the command supervisor, arrived for on the spot inspection, activity was gradually returning to normal. Within seven days Charlie's place had been re housed in a temporary location with the prospect of a more permanent building in the offering. The families club was first estimated to be closed for 10 weeks but was reopened on the 4th of January 1970 only two weeks after the storm. Incident three was not so violent but still caused quite a bit of disruption for NAAFI. It took place when 232 Cypriot staff decided to strike for a midweek afternoon off. The staff stayed out for two days then returned pending discussions.

1970–1979

1970

The last days of Tobruk by John Whitehead 1970

It seemed appropriate that the last British servicemen in North Africa should withdraw from the continent by the way of Tobruk, the port they gave up so reluctantly and finally took during the war. NAAFI, of course, withdrew at the same time. The events of these days are recounted by Cyrenaica's last NAAFI supervisor, John Whitehead.

I had a shrewd idea that we were going to withdraw from Cyrenaica before even the British government or the services knew. After all, the revolution occurred on a public holiday, 1st of September, while I was taking over as supervisor from Bob Lintott. On Tuesday the 2nd of September 1969, the MPBW began to redecorate my shop. I said, at the time, it was a sure sign we're on our way out, an opinion which was strengthened when workmen began to lay new electricity cables in the unmade Garrison Road and eventually transformed it into a made up, well-lit highway into town.

What happened in the weeks immediately following the coup had already been covered in previous stories. That first emergency was followed by the planning and launching of our Christmas trading programme. At the same time, we were casting our minds forward to the merchandising programme for January 1970 onwards, as I get had given an undertaking to the station commander at El Adem that NAAFI was shown no signs that we were preparing to withdraw.

District manager John Minns, in his weekly program over BFBS, made a point of talking about such things as Valentine's cards, Mother's Day cards, Easter eggs and so on. This was deliberately intended to allay rumours that we were going to withdraw in January. However, Colin Simpson, our supply official, acting on my instructions at the beginning of November, had already adjusted our orders so that stocks coming in were an absolute minimum and could be cut off or diverted to other areas should withdrawal be confirmed. Six members of our staff had arranged to take advantage of an RAF charter flight to get home for Christmas leave. Whether the trip was on or not was no matter of conjecture for most of the latter part of November and early December, but when an announcement of the withdrawal was made in the middle of December, I had the unpleasant task of telling the staff that it would not be possible for them to go home. They accepted this with as good a grace as was possible. I was thankful once again for the personal qualities and the kind of people who work for NAAFI overseas.

Finishing fitter Bob McKay, who had come over from Cyprus to improve the appearance of the bars in our clubs at El Adem, Tobruk and the beaches ended all construction work with the announcement of the coup. The remainder of his time was spent taking down signs – all evidence of English occupation had to be removed, package equipment for shipments to other areas needed to be available. One person who deserved a special mention at the time was Tony Peppi, the manager of the team of Cypriots who were running the club at RAF El Adem. They were due to be repatriated at the end of January but shortly before Christmas, Tony came to me and said that, apart from one or two, who had urgent family commitments in Cyprus which they could not delegate to another member of their family, he and his team were prepared to stay.

Andy Caruana, the Maltese manager of the Churchill club in Tobruk, was also due to be repatriated at the end of January and he too sent me a note before Christmas to say that he would be prepared to remain until the end of our time in Libya. Tragically he was not to see Malta again – it was with great sorrow I had to report Andy's death to headquarters in early January. I had been able to see him on the evening of Christmas Day when, over a Christmas drink he had reminisced about his 46 years with the company.

Cyril James, assistant Comptroller of supplies, arrived in December and we discussed the various draft plans which I had been drawing up since September to meet any contingency. As soon as the announcement of our withdrawal was made, Cyril, with typical energy and his knowledge of the commodities aspects of various countries, set about leading our team in the dispersal of assets, sending stock to Germany, Cyprus, and the UK. We still did not know the final date of our withdrawal so it was necessary to act as though the worst possible predictions would prove true and the move would come immediately after Christmas. Mr James cabled to export branch produce a ship specially chartered for our cargo. We subsequently received compliments from the commander in chief and AOA for the prompt way in which NAAFI had got off the ground in disposing of assets and re-exporting and by disposal to the Libyan army and local merchants.

As no new families had been sent to Cyrenaica since the 1st of September, we found that, by Christmas, we were 200 families short. Orders placed earlier in the year had catered for those 200 families who had been repatriated without replacements. A snap merchandising meeting decided on the unusual step of opening our winter sale on the 21st of December. The additional discounts on clothing and durable goods had a tremendous effect upon our customers, particularly those with young children who were being repatriated in January. They were delighted to have the chance to an additional price reduction when it came to kit themselves out and their children with winter clothing in readiness for the premature return to England.

The turn of the year saw his settling down, after the Christmas trading, to set up disposing of the remainder of our assets before the end of March. The Libyan Arab Republic Army's Garrison commander Capt Sallah, and his officers, came to discuss with Mr James and me the possibility of the Libyan army buying stock from us. Protracted negotiations had hard bargaining over a period of some 14 days eventually found us at a point of agreement in respect to considerable quantities of stores. One of my memories is the surprise that I had when going around family shops with the Libyan army representative to discuss which types of goods were acceptable. We were fortunate throughout these negotiations having Peter Dunbar on hand, he had spent many years in North Africa, and he was quite fluent in Arabic.

On the 17th of January we heard that Capt Sallah, the Tobruk garrison commander for the Libyan army, had been promoted to Major. Libyan army Majors and above had been imprisoned at the time of the coup on the same day, all Lieutenants became Captains and

Captains became Majors. Mr James and I went to the offices of the new Major to convey our congratulations and found him seated in front of a revolutionary flag showing off a liberated eagle with a picture of a dog. It was most impressive. We were treated with a customary cup of Turkish coffee, having paid our respects, and Mr James was presented with a star like those used by the American army and offered the title of honorary officer of the Libyan army. He politely declined the honour as, being an Ex-Naval man, he felt his allegiance would be strained.

By mid-February, having dealt with the disposal of the majority of NAAFI's assets, it was time for Cyril James to return to London. He commented before he left that not having been concerned with an evacuation since the withdrawal from Aden, he felt that Cyrenaica had provided a good opener for the Gulf and the Far East, both of which would be occupying a good deal of time in the next 2 years.

All service and civilian families had to be evacuated from Tobruk by the end of January and from El Adem by mid-February. The district accountant's family was the first to go. They left in the beginning of January so that they could get settled into a school in England for the beginning of the spring term. Next to go were the supply official's family and the transport manager. The rest of the NAAFI families had left by the 16th of February. With their departure Tony Whitehead, shop manager at El Adem, his assistant Frank Stevenson and their staff were able to head for home. Then the rest left on the 23rd of March on the last plane out.

Back to the jungle by TH Gore 1970

It was June. And for some it will be reminiscent of that other June. Commonwealth troops would once more feel the ground tremble as the guns thunder and the shells crash. Commandos will storm the beaches. Aircraft will scream overhead. Helicopters will drop into clearings. Armoured cars will patrol. Infantry men will force their way through the jungle, wary of an ambush and crack of the sniper's rifle. This time, thank God, it is a game but a deadly serious game.

With an eye on the withdrawal of the British forces from Singapore and West Malaysia area by the end of 1971, the British Commonwealth governments have mounted a five nation exercise intended to demonstrate Britain's ability to reinforce the capabilities of their allies in the Far East, after withdrawal is complete.

'Exercise Bersatu Padu' which was Malay for Complete Unity, has involved the movement of the Army brigade and equipment from the UK to the Far East, numerous Royal Navy vessels and the RAF Far East command. The UK elements were flown out by the Royal Air Force support command over a period of some 10 days, many lessons on their physical movement of troops and their effectiveness after rapid movement in Asian conditions will be learned. The forces involved are from Great Britain, Malaysia, Singapore, Australia, and New Zealand. The first part of the exercise takes place in the southern tip of West Malaysia, in the jungle warfare school area, to consolidate and acclimatise the forces taking part. The war games began on the 13th of June when the men of 40 commando, Royal Marines, leave the comparative comfort of HMS Bulwark and launch the amphibious attack on the beaches of Trenggaun. The landings will trigger often extensive allied ground manoeuvres against their 'Ganasian' troops occupying the area, Ganasia was an imaginary country situated between West Malaysia and Thailand. Enemy troops will be played by two Gurkha battalions and the British commando unit.

The 40-commando objective is the landing strip at Penarek. On the 14th of June, a joint Malaysian Australian New Zealand helicopter assault will be launched into the jungle and on the following day British and Singapore troops will fly in to Penarrek airstrip. Meanwhile, allied ships will engage enemy submarines off the Trenggaun coast and after mine sweeping exercises, begin surface attacks. Air defence exercises will take place over Butterworth, Singapore, and the fleet.

NAAFI participating in the exercises meant a great deal of study and planning with the exercise planning staff to provide a service for all five nations. In the jungle warfare school at

Kota Tinggi area, where many of the troops are billeted before joining the war games, will have converted an old kit store at Tebrau into a JRC and services shop. Nearby, in the jungle warfare school headquarters the existing club at Kenny camp has been reinforced by reopening the old JRC at Burma camp. Both locations have full canteen facilities and service shops.

Supplies for officers and sergeants' messes had been attained from nearby shops. During the active part of the exercise in the jungle off the North East coast of the western Malaysia, they operated three tented bulk issue stores and a tented canteen. Supplies would also be augmented in the permanent bulk issue store at the RMAF base in Kuantan and this would be the base Depot for supplies to the Malaysian, Australian and New Zealand forces.

It is expected that part of the supplies for use in the exercise will be transferred from Singapore, along with military equipment, by landing ships taking part in the exercise. These tools would be landed over the beach head and will most likely happen in a real emergency. From previous experience of exercises in this part of the world, we expect the troops involved to consume more than some 140,000 gallons of beer, 175,000 gallons of minerals and some 250,000 packets of cigarettes. All the beer and minerals were to be moved from Singapore by rail and sea into the jungle area of the North East coast. Besides these fundamental items, of course, a wide range of general items troops would expect to find at any NAAFI establishment.

The staff involved in the exercise included three district managers, one accountant and some 74 local staff managers, chargehands, cooks, clerks, and assistants. Some of the local staff are obtained on loan from permanent establishments in West Malaysia, others from closest establishments at our old base at Terendak and if you have been temporarily re-engaged.

This five-nation exercise comprised some 25,000 servicemen which also involved 50 ships from submarines to commando carriers and some 200 aircraft. The central control headquarters for an exercise of this size was a very complex undertaking. Granada HQ was located in the beautiful East Coast town of Dungun. When I visited it, the town throbbed with activity and preparation of the two-pronged invasion, the villagers were all set to receive the tourists who arrive here every year to watch the turtles lay their eggs. Over 200 tents had been pitched in the coconut plantation. These would provide the accommodation for the controllers, umpires, observers, and visitors. The soldiers had made this camp by the sea into a Colony with all the comforts of amenities one could think of. Perhaps, one might say, a little unrealistic for a war exercise but it would make life a little easier for those VIPs who would be visiting to see the games in progress.

The setting was typical Southsea island, palm trees, coral sands and beautiful breakers diving onto the beach. Alas, the sea is dangerous the current is extremely strong and the sea snakes aplenty in the deeper water. The troops could bathe only at certain times and then with the lifeguards standing by. District manager Mr Tim Elliott had made himself comfortable in a tent amid these delightful surroundings. Delightful, that is, but for the intense heat and dust everywhere. In the centre of the camp a canvas bulk issue store and canteen had been erected to look after the requirements of the control staff.

I've visited headquarters with Mr Elliott and the transport manager. The NAAFI staff were in good humour and seemed to be enjoying their hard tasks despite the trying conditions. All those things a soldier would expect in a canteen were available, tea, sandwiches, eggs, chips, beer, minerals, toiletries and even gifts. The most popular item on the menu being 'Chip and egg banjo's'. Supplies of spirits, beer, cigarettes and so on were being issued daily for the officers and sergeants' messes. 100 miles or so further north at Kuala Trenggaun I met district manager John Emuss who was in command of our activities in the enemy area. He had come over from his Penang district to take part in the war games. The bulk issue store was well established in two tents in the dust and heat alongside the main road which led to Thailand. Here the temperature was soaring into the 90s and over 120 degrees in the tent. Luckily, our staff only had a short walk to the sea to cool down at the end of the day.

Units tucked away in the jungle paid frequent visits to stock up on their NAAFI supplies. These were the enemy, who would shortly be hounded out of their hideaways by the planes and helicopters and defending forces. South again to Penarek with John Emuss and Tim Elliott to an old disused airstrip from the days of Malaysian unrest; this was where the thunder of the guns and bombers of HMS Bulwark, would be heard as she rode offshore and the commandos prepared for a beach landing for the capture of the strip. As the landing craft and helicopters arrive so would come NAAFI stores across the beach head. Tentage would go up to house the BIS and issues would commence before all the guy ropes were down. In this huge exercise we had to ensure that NAAFI stores were on the ground in enough quantities to meet any emergencies. To this end we had established a base canteen Depot in the rear maintenance area at Kuantan. I called at Kuantan to see the Depot, located in a small hangar lent to us by the Royal Malaysian Air Force. It was, as the saying goes, bursting at the seams, already to make issues to units operating their own canteens to refill our own BIS.

Later, command supervisor Jim Tannock flew north in an Army Beaver aircraft to pay a further visit to all the NAAFI locations. He reported that, at the height of the exercise, all was going well and our service was as expected. Great credit he said was due to all our officials and staff taking part, not forgetting Mr Pink, regional accountant, Mr Webster, senior district accountant and others of the established accounts branch who worked such long hours. Soon after the drawdown of the exercise a draft report would be discussed amongst the planners and then a final appreciation would be scrutinised by the five nations, Malaysia, Great Britain, Singapore, Australia, and New Zealand. But even before that comes it is clear that a formula has been found for the Commonwealth nations to work together in matters of defence in this extremely tough jungle area. We in NAAFI played our own part to ensure the success of Exercise Bersatu Padu.

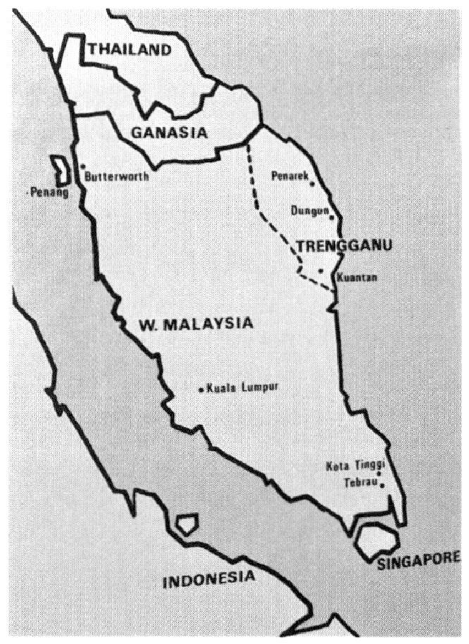

Memories of Ex Bersatu Padu 1970 memories by Tim Elliott 2020

In 1970 I was district manager for the central part of west Malaysia, based in Kuala Lumpur, and had been warned of the big reinforcement exercise in late June 1970, but not as EFI. We were in civvies. My wife returned to the UK in the May and I concentrated full time on the exercise.

I was there for about 6 or 7 weeks in a tent at Kuala Dungun on the Malaysian east coast. I was one of the first occupants of the tented exercise HQ mess and so had a choice of tents. I was going to share with an English engineer captain that I knew from Kuala Lumpur (we had both been on the exercise HQ co-ordination committee in the Malaysian MOD). We agreed that I would choose the tent and ensure a ready supply of ice and he would supply the haybox (insulated container). Thus, we had a steady supply of cold beer etc in our tent for the whole time we were there. The situation was idyllic. Our tent, at right angles to the beach, was in the front row just off the beach and under the palm trees. It faced due east, so we were awoken by the rising sun every day. I was given temporary membership of the little Dungun Golf Club which had an (empty) swimming pool, so I used that as my office. Sitting in the open-sided clubhouse to do my paperwork, looking out across the beach to the South China Sea was one of the best offices I had in all my Naafi years.

In one of the many discussions in the MOD, Kuala Lumpur, the planning committee chairman, a British group captain, raised the question of the showers etc for the officers' mess – always very important. It was interesting to see what different ethnic groups perceived as being important. The Brits were anxious about how the 'thunder box loos' would be screened for privacy, whilst the Muslim element were far more concerned about screening the showers, a matter of complete indifference to the European group!! The result was that the loos had sacking walls and doors and the showers were communal and the Muslim blokes wore their swimming trunks.

In the planning, our regional manager, Ken Hempstead, had told us to use 2 cans of beer/man/day to stock temporary mini warehouses in Malaysia from which the exercise BISs and JRCs etc would draw their stock. The strength figures were given to us by the exercise planning group and they included a sizeable contingent from Australia. You can imagine the jaw-dropping reaction to the Australian commander's advice, on arrival in Malaysia, that his troops would be dry for the whole of the exercise. We had lorry loads of beer waiting for them!! All exported from Singapore.

The visit of command supervisor, Jim Tannock, to the exercise, I remember it well. He was quite a stickler for standards and so, whilst I normally wore shorts, short sleeve shirt and desert boots, for his visit, I climbed into long trousers, long sleeved shirt and a tie. My opposite number up north of the exercise area, John Emuss, came down to see the CS but he decided that there was no need to make any concessions, and so arrived in shorts etc. Raised eyebrows???

Once the exercise was over and all the F&E and saleable stock had been distributed, and the staff sent back to their normal locations, I finally left Dungun for the 350-mile trip to Singapore in my trusty non-aircon Ford Anglia. About a 6- or 7-hour trip. I had asked the admin staff in the HQ office in Singapore to book me into the Lady hill Hotel whilst I waited for a flight home (the RAF flights were full of returning exercisers). I felt I had earned a spell in a posh hotel, but my arrival there in a filthy dirty Anglia car, dressed in exercise gear gave the concierge a bit of a fright!! However, I scrubbed up OK eventually.

There was a plaque manufactured by Naafi for sale in outlets –

Their last tot 31st of July 1970

For the last time British sailors all over the world saluted the passing, on the 31st of July 1970, of the Naval tradition which had been their heritage for almost 250 years. They had swigged their last tot of rum. 2020 marks the 50th year since this tradition ended.

For landlubbers browsing in London Street markets the end of the rum ration meant no more than an opportunity to buy an attractive ornament, the rum barrels, bearing the legend 'The Queen, God bless her' were selling for about 5 pounds each. Rum had been the spirit of the Navy since sailors captured Jamaica in 1655. The secretary of the Admiralty finally made the rum ration official in 1731. In that bygone age when ships relied on the wind and tide, sailors were allowed half a pint of rum a day to help them forget the bad food, the foul water, and the savage discipline. The rum heritage died hard, condemned by the last need for men to have completely clear heads when operating today's complicated ships' equipment.

On the frigate HMS Andromeda, the crew, wearing black armbands, gave the last solemn toast, 'The Queen God bless her' and threw their glasses overboard. The fleet air arm at Yeovilton, Somerset, saw the last tot out with a funeral procession. A draped rum barrel was born ceremoniously through the station on a yellow Rolls Royce, with a young sailor masquerading as Lady Hamilton in the passenger seat. HMS Dolphin used a more traditional gun carriage. Pipers from the second battalion Royal Irish Rangers played for the departed spirit at the Interment of the rum barrel at HMS Jufair, in the Gulf. HMS Dido, off the coast of Scotland, sealed the last tot in a bottle and threw it overboard, a message inside asked the Finder to drink them to the navy's health and write to the ship.

At Portsmouth even the post office caught the air of nostalgia. They franked all letters sent from the main office 'last issue of rum to the Royal Navy 31st July 1970'. The boys onboard HMS Belfast, last of the big gun's cruisers, now used as a floating hotel for men maintaining the ships in reserve at Portsmouth, pooled their last tots into a giant Christmas pudding. No spoon large enough to stir the 168-pound pud could be found, so the captain and his wife used paddles from one of the ship's lifeboats.

In the naval canteen service too, there was nostalgic regret at the ending of a great tradition, a tradition which NAAFI canteen staff have shared for the past 50 years but the NCS regret was tempered by the knowledge that the treasury is paying the fleet so that the daily beer ration for each man afloat had been increased from 2 cans to three cans per day and that POs and CPOs' messes are now to be allowed to serve spirits. These were to be drawn from the ship's canteen.

The money saved from this would form the capital of a new sailors fund, the grants committee of which decided, at their first meeting, to make regular grants to welfare committees so that each ship could decide for itself how to spend the money. An allowance of one extra can of beer a day may not sound like much potential new business, but ships such as HMS Ark Royal had more than 2000 ratings on board. Before she sailed, her canteen manager Mr Phillips must stock up with enough beer to last the crew for three months.

Mr Phillips expected to get through 320 cases of beer a day when they were at sea and 105 cases more than they were used to before the rum ration had finished. On this first trip out after they would take 8000 cases aboard before sailing and replenishment at sea with a further 12,000 cases. Finding storage for those extra cases in the confines of a fighting ship was not easy, not even on a ship as big as the Ark Royal. With the arrival of the new spirit ration for Chiefs and petty officers, Mr Phillips would be supplying 65 bottles of spirits every day. Spirits, he points out, usually require minerals to mix with them, he would take 5600 dozen bottles on board before leaving port and would restock with further supplies at sea.

In addition to supplying the new Beer and spirit rations he would still have to store enough stocks on board to supply for three months. Just how much extra trade the new rations would entail for NCS afloat was still a mystery at this time, but it was known that the Navy drank 150,000 gallons of rum in a year.

The men behind NAAFI big tops 1970

Through the history of the company a lot of events were held under canvas, so the big question is, what does it take to build 3/4 of a mile of canvas walling? A complete camp perhaps of washing facilities, bars, dining rooms and sleeping quarters? Or a single marquee as long as a destroyer?

The services frequently had three stores of needs, as often as not, they would ask Len Kingston, manager of NAAFI canvas warehouse in Aldershot, to supply canvas and Antoni Brudzinski, the official in charge of campus teams, to erect them. For eight months of the year from February to October the team and management and the tent men travel from site to site, erecting, and dismantling marquees for shows, exhibitions, at homes, summer camps, dances, and weddings.

It was a tough job, sometimes involving as much as 12 hours of hard work a day for seven days a week. A 100 foot by 40-foot marquee weighed about 1½ tons, erecting it involved swinging a 14 pound hammer to drive in 78 iron stakes, each 3-foot-long and weighing 11 pounds. Direction and assembly of the tent this size took a four-man team about five hours. First it was the frame, the uprights and the ridges are put into position then the distance for the pegs are mashed off. The guy ropes are laid out and the canvas is now taken and spread over the ridge poles and laced along the side. Now the marquee can be lifted 8 feet off the ground while the supports were completed and the guy ropes tied.

With the ridge up to full height, the canvas spread out on the wall posts were put in, the side lines in and attached, finally the canvas walls will be put up. The 100 by 40, as it is called in the canvas warehouse, is the largest marquee in stock size but further spreads of the canvas can be laced into the centre of the tent to extend its length. And on a number of occasions they erected a marquee measuring 400 feet by 40 feet.

After five hours' work, one marquee would be standing waiting for the counters or show stands, tables and chairs, kitchen equipment or whatever was needed in it. Installing the heavy equipment most of it stored at Ludgershall, was also the responsibility of the team. At the end of the show, the marquee would take another three hours to dismantle and load onto a wagon. But a great many shows needed more than one marquee. At the army's new envoy display at Aldershot in 1970 the marquee team erected 34 marquees, the biggest spread of NAAFI canvas to be raised on one site. At the Biggin Hill air show, the second largest spread of the year, NAAFI canvas covered a total of 34,500 square feet.

In the summer season the team would have to move fast between the jobs. This was hard work, it was OK if the weather was fine and they had good facilities around them. But if it rained or if it was windy like at the Chelsea Flower Show in 1969, it made it much more difficult. A good wind adds about 2 hours to the time it took to put up a 100 × 40 and the weight of the canvas can go up two tons if it rains. The tentage team always carry a propane gas cooker with them for brewing up tea, when they go to sites such as West Mailing, where there is no convenient place to get a meal, they would cook their own food. One thing was for sure, the team were not very keen on camping holidays.

Camping in the Antarctic buy MP Mulvey canteen manager HMS Endurance 1970

On the 27th of October 1970 HMS Endurance set off once again for Antarctica and it made a pleasant change for me going with her to visit a place I had never seen before. One of the high spots of the trip was a visit to Elephant Island where, according to the official records, only two landings had been previously made. The first landing was made by Sir Ernest Shackleton after the first Endurance had been wrecked in Antarctica.

We spent several weeks in the waters around Elephant Island, using the helicopter to drop off a joint services expedition and enough stores for them to survive for five months. We also landed our own ship survey team on various islands for a few days at a time. I decided to ask the captain for a chance to go ashore with one of these teams to see what went on. To my surprise he agreed and within 90 minutes I was kitted out in all the appropriate clothing. On top of my normal clothes, I had a large Kapok jacket and trousers. A Survival kit was added to this, consisting of a red plastic suit worn over the top of my other clothes, an inflatable life raft strapped on my back and a life jacket on my chest. The reason for this, of course, is to protect the wearer from the icy temperature of the water should the helicopter be forced to ditch. I could hardly move, and felt a little apprehensive at carrying my special sleeping bag. I boarded the helicopter and flew towards some high cliffs covered in snow.

Deep snow and glaciers covered most of the rocky island and from the air, made a beautiful scene. What rocks we could see seemed like very much like slate. We landed on a patch of firm snow, where I joined PO Elton and LS Champion, the two-man survey team. Off went the helicopter and then away went HMS Endurance, and we were left to our own devices, but we were at least in radio contact with the ship.

First, we put up two tents and then erected a large bamboo pole with a 16-foot flag on it. This, I later learned, was to serve as a marker for the surveying. I certainly would not relish the survivor's job in such cold, but for this was an experience I will never forget. All seemed so peaceful, as if the outside world had ceased to exist. The only sound came from the albatross and other large birds nesting near our camp, and from the penguins or the elephant seals nearby.

later that evening we had time for a 2-hour walk, during which we came across a penguin colony. I found the penguins very amusing, and I was able to photograph some of the hundreds of seals.

I slept fully dressed in my sleeping bag on the snow inside my tent after a good meal from the special ration packs we had. These packs seemed to have everything one could possibly need, including a plastic top for the coffee tin after it had been opened.

The following day the wind had risen, and it was bitterly cold. By 1730 in the afternoon the ship had still not reappeared but then the helicopter flew in to pick me up, leaving my two pals to finish their work. It was nice to return to the warmth of the ship, and brandy but I would not have missed the experience for anything.

1971

The Golden Jubilee year by Humphrey Prideaux, chairman 1971

In January of 1971 NAAFI celebrates its Golden Jubilee, having first officially come into existence on the 1st of January 1921; it was a momentous milestone in their history. Certainly in 1921 nobody could have foreseen the enormous advance which had been made in the standard of amenity operated by NAAFI for the forces. The canteen of 1921 bore little resemblance to the social club of 1971, nor did the family shop of those days look anything like the modern self-service store. Who would have believed in 1921 that, 50 years on, NAAFI would have been deeply involved in the sale of cars or the many other luxury articles which are commonplace in our transactions of the day?

Despite all the change there has been one consistent factor throughout the 50 years and that is the spirit of the men and women who worked for NAAFI. We all know the old joke about getting the NAAFI bug. There was a NAAFI bug and it does infect people, raising them to new and unexpected heights of enthusiasm, determination, ingenuity, and devotion. It manifests itself in many different ways. It shows up, for example, in a wonderful record of continuity of service. In other organisations 20 years' service is hailed as an achievement, so it is, but in NAAFI it lacks the lustre it deserves in the face of other sheer numbers of those with 30, 40, or even 50 years to their credit. It shows too in the response which always comes to the need of the crisis, of which there have been many in the last 50 years. That had always been then a fierce determination and defiant ingenuity in the aim of maintaining our service to the customers, often themselves hard pressed.

So, what is the bug which produces these admirable virtues? It is, I suggest, the example handed from each generation to the next, often established in the process and its need in our priceless heritage. While we keep this intact, we may be sure that in the next 50 years will be no less glorious than the last.

The biggest building Programme for 20 years 1971

NAAFI works and buildings branch was currently supervising projects worth over 1½ million, the building budget higher than at any time during the previous 20 years. The biggest of the five major developments in hand was the new headquarter office block at Kennington Lane. Work was now going ahead on the site clearance and the building was due to be completed in the spring of 1972. Another large development in the UK was 101,000 square feet extension of the central distribution warehouse at Amesbury. As well as adding 50% to the present storage space, the new building would provide offices, wine bottling plant, a canteen, a shop, and tea and coffee factory.

The cost of the Amesbury extension, which was nearing its completion in March 1971, would be £400,000. Like all other projects in hand it was designed by William Crawforth, assistant control of works and buildings. Another major warehouse project expected to cost in the region of £100,000 was the new equipment warehouse at Ludgershall. This was in the planning stages.

The largest task in the European service was the extension to the centralisation of the shopping facilities in Rheindahlen. This involves building a 14,000 square foot food hall and converting the present food hall into a gifts and durables department and a sports shop. The clothing store, at Collingwood Road, was to be moved into the central building, an added feature will be a customers' cafeteria equipped with a bank of vending machines.

Additional first floor accommodation would provide the facilities and on the spot location for the thriving ES car hire and purchasing section. The food hall, which would be double the size of the existing one, was expected to be ready for occupation in July 1971. The extension and modification of Krefeld Bakery to allow for the installation of automatic bread production plant which was to supply sufficient wrapped and sliced bread to meet the demands. Work started in February 1971 on a 45% extension to the existing building. In preparation for the big move and to make room for the new ovens and ancillary equipment, interior walls had been removed, and machines used for a cake, pie and bread roll production had been temporary re-sited. The problem facing Mr W Ward, senior bakery manager at Krefeld, was to maintain the normal production during the transition period.

A vehicle washing plant at Krefeld transport Depot was expected to be in operation by March 1971. The equipment, which was capable of thoroughly cleaning a 10-ton lorry in six minutes, was installed in a prefabricated building earlier that year. Previously the ES fleet of 190 commercial vehicles had been cleaned by hand, a task taking up to four hours for each of the large trucks. NAAFI was always developing and finding new ways to streamline the service.

Big ships little ships by Michael Walker 1971

The love of the sea and a fascination of the furthest corners of the world, attract many men into the Royal Navy. It is the also the lure for the handful of civilians who serve in HM warships, the men of NAAFI NCS.

Life with NCS afloat is not just one long cruise. For some recruits, one look at the crowded living quarters is enough to send them running to the post box with their resignations. Others stay for one year or two, see a bit of the world and then opt for life ashore. But for some, it becomes a way of life from which they find it hard to breakaway, like 62-year-old Benny Goodman, manager on HMS Forth, Bill Hatton, who at 63, was about to leave for a cruise onboard HMS Minerva. With them he faces the cold of the Arctic, the heat of the tropics, or the discomfort and sea sickness in a storm in the Bay of Biscay. During a 'thimble hunt', when a man is reported missing from the ship, everyone onboard, including the NAAFI man, goes through the search routine and reports to the bridge. When the crew go to action stations, canteen managers and assistants join stretcher first aid parties.

Carl Rust, canteen manager on HMS Tenby, would get up at around 0700hrs, grab a quick breakfast, open the canteen at 0730hrs; at 0830hrs there was a stand easy and then the canteen reopened at 1130hrs for an hour and a half. The canteen would open again for an hour and a half during the afternoon when the ship was in port, he would then finish work at around 1700 hrs. At sea, there would be an additional hour opening at 1930hrs.

He lives in a mess which is the home of 18 CPOs. They eat, sleep and relax. There is a bar, a dining table, easy chairs, a television for use in port. For his clothes and personal possessions, Carl had three drawers, a suit locker, and a place to hang a coat. Wall to wall carpeting and curtains gave the place a homely air, but with 18 other people in a confined space it is essential to be a gracious type.

The mess had to be kept spotlessly clean and tidy and Carl joined with the CPO in their housekeeping duties. Once a week the captain visited the mess, on his rounds to make sure that all was in order. They also shared with their customers the ship's entertainments. In their spare time they did a lot of reading or playing cards and once a week the ship quiz programme and competitions between messes.

The ship also had rugby and soccer teams, and they played local teams when they visited port. There was not much space on the ship, so they tended to get out of condition, so sometimes they joined in the physical training classes with the ship's PTI.

Twice a week they had films shown in the mess, in 16mm cinemascope. They managed to watch most of the latest releases at the time. For people interested in photography, there was usually a developing room or a darkroom on board. One hobby that many had taken up was fishing.

What sort of qualities does it take to be a ship's canteen manager? You had to be an easy sort of person to get on with as it took time to adjust. The first thing you have to do is find a couple of friends, otherwise there is a danger that you will always be an outsider. Cole spent four years on HMS Ark Royal and found life on the frigate very different.

There was much more of a personal touch on a ship of that size. On a big ship you just cannot give customers so much personal attention. Of course on the Ark Royal they hardly knew you while you were at sea, while the ship had the habit of rolling around a bit, it can be quite a job trying to serve sailors who are feeling seasick when you are feeling the very same way yourself, and there are cans and things falling from shelves all the time.

There was a massive difference between a frigate such as the Tenby, only 2100 tons and 370 feet long, with a complement of 200 and the massive aircraft carrier of HMS Eagle, 43,000 tons, 803 feet long, with a complement of over 1300.

The manager on the Eagle with Tom Holland, who joined NAAFI in 1942 at the age of 16, he had been at sea all over the world ever since. Mr Holland who had two assistant managers, one charge hand, two hairdressers, 9 assistants, and one vending assistant to help him. With the turnover set staying very consistent in Harbour and out at sea. In addition to the main canteen there was a bookstore, a cigarette bar, 'goffer' which was the soft drink bars, a Barber shop, and four cold and one hot drink vending machines.

There was reasonable business in messing supplies, such odd individual items as chocolate for the Wardroom for the pilots, who are entitled to a block of chocolate every time they fly. As a manager on aircraft carrier, Mr Holland lived in his own cabin, which is about 8 feet square, it had an adjoining office of a similar size. All the NAAFI staff ate in one of the ship's three dining halls, one for CPOs, one for POs and one for ratings.

Judging what would be needed in the way of stores for a cruise is quite an art. Space is limited, so the requirements of the ship's complement must be estimated with accuracy; there was rarely a chance to take more stores at sea. Stores for the cold drink vending machines on the Eagle for a cruise to Singapore, for example, amounted to some 720 gallons of syrup and 140,000 cups. Alcohol for that matter was a simple question, as it was rationed, and the ration per man can be used as an estimate to requirements. But the canteen manager must be prepared for the unexpected.

To be an NCS manager takes special qualities, an ability to mix with people, adaptability, resolution in the face of difficulty, and independence. In return for this he can look forward to the comradeship of naval life, a chance to see the world, the extra pay and allowances awarded by the company to the NAAFI men at sea.

Our biggest ever food Hall yet 1971

Rheindahlen Food Hall opened on the 1st of September 1971. The manager, John Fisher, reported that weekly sales were more than 11% up. On the opening day customers and staff found the new checkout system a great improvement and even on a busy Saturday the queues had been greatly reduced. The food hall covered an area of 14,000 square feet and gondolas have been widely separated to allow ample room for customer circulation. There were 400 heavy duty trolleys available for them and an impressive row of 12 Sweda checkouts, incorporating the quick load principle, they spanned the path all the way to the automatic doors.

Speaking at a joint services customer relations committee meeting, Mrs VT bridge, NORTHAG, said it was good to see that customers' suggestions and recommendations had been taken into account. I would like to say how much very many of us appreciate the food hall, a great deal of thought had gone into its planning.

As soon as the food hall had opened, all the stops were pulled out to convert the old one into a spacious gifts, durables, and sports department. Hard work paid off and the second stage in the creation of one stop shopping centre opened at the beginning of November 1971. The former gifts and durables area was currently being used for a toy fair, but after Christmas it would then be converted into a clothing shop to replace the one operating in Collingwood Road.

Stocking up for Christmas by Ian Whalley 1971

The island of St Kilda lies some 50 miles west of the Hebrides, a submarine mountain poking its head 1000 feet above the rolling Atlantic; apart from the 300 yard beach, it rises as a cliff out of the sea. Its 2 square miles is a wildlife sanctuary with everything, including the grass and heather, protected by law. It boasts an abundance of puffins and gulls, 40 odd thousand pairs of gannets, a colony of seals, the wreck of a Liberator bomber, bus stop, zebra crossing and 30 soldiers from the artillery range at Benbecula.

These men are now the only inhabitants of St Kilda, deserted in 1930. Their job is to operate and maintain the radar equipment used for tracking missiles fired from the range at Benbecula. The small but well-equipped campsites where a tiny jetty accommodates nothing bigger than the average size lifeboat.

There is no NAAFI on the island, the supplies, including fresh and frozen food, are handled by Bob Fraser, the NAAFI manager on Benbecula. Deliveries are made by army tank landing craft as the only place to unload at St Kilda is the beach. High winds and tide prevent the use of the beaching procedure after October, so it is necessary, by then, to ensure that the island has fuel and food for three months.

The responsibility for delivering the NAAFI goods in perfect condition lies with Mr WDB Taylor, Scotland's area produce buyer. The ship had to be accompanied on its last trip to St Kilda for 1971 and looked after the produce. HMAV Audemer had commenced embarkation of supplies when I arrived at the RCT base. Apart from 2 trailers of food she was carrying two staff cars, tyres, fuel oil, scaffold poles, an elevator, and a concrete mixer. She was commanded by Maj Mike Randall Smith, RCT, veteran in LCTs and an accomplished Mariner.

With loading completed and the bow doors shut tight, we pulled off the concrete ramp and headed through the rain to Gairloch. We arrived at our first port of call, south ford, after some 20 hours of steaming, Anchor Dan waited for the tide. Then the doors were opened, and an army of men unloaded the stores required for Benbecula, unloaded more equipment for St Kilda while I made a quick trip to the Fraser emporium for a few extra items.

The following day, the vessel was rolling madly, and the water poured over her bowels. Looking into the glum faces of the watch, I knew that the weather was bad on St Kilda. Only 8 miles from the island, we turned about, and headed back. Heavy seas with winds gusting 70 knots made it impossible to put the craft on the beach.

My stock of ice already four days old was diminishing rapidly and I did not have enough to hold the stock frozen for another attempt on the island. I contacted Mr Taylor in Edinburgh by ships' radio and he arranged to fly fresh ice to Benbecula. By the time we arrived at Loch Farnon, the ice was waiting for us. During the night we slipped away and headed once again for those elusive mountain peaks. On a magnificent morning, with no trace of the previous day's storm, we crunched onto the tiny beach of St Kilda.

The doors opened and unloading began; huge tractors hauling the heavy-laden trailers onto the sand. The NAAFI container was soon outside the unit cook house. Swiftly, the meat, fish, vegetables and Christmas turkey, were squeezed into the army's fridges. After a welcome 'brew' I was given a tour of the island. Every visitor has a strange feeling when standing on the top of the island and looking west, knowing there is nothing between St Kilda and NYC except a lot of sea.

All too soon, the tide was back, and the ship had to leave. With engines running, and the kedge being slowly hauled on board, we retreated from St Kilda's beach. Chased from the bay by 1000 sea birds, Audemer headed for the mainland, home, submarines, F.2278s and the Helensburgh duty cloud.

1972

Half a century in Malta 1972

NAAFI's 50 year occupation of St James's cavalier in Valletta, Malta, has ended. Whatever the outcome of Malta talks with the British government, St James's cavalier is lost, the NAAFI shop which it housed, closed after the withdrawal of British service families from the island. The cavalier was built in the 16th century by the grandmaster Hughes Loubeux de Verdalle to guard the Porta San Giorgio, the main entrance to the fortress. The engineer for this sturdy redoubt was Giro lama Cassar. In 1775 Maltese rebels captured St James's and held it for several days during the Maltese revolt against the Knights of St John. During the early part of the British occupation the cavalier was somewhat neglected until the Royal engineers began to use it for storage of equipment.

The exact date of NAAFI takeover is vague, it is believed to have been 1921, although one retired member of staff thinks it was used by NAAFI's immediate predecessor around 1918 to 1919. NAAFI shared the building with the services and at various times it has housed map stores and other military and naval requirements. The first sight of St James's cavalier reveals it is an imposing building but also betrays at once its great drawback as a trading establishment. Throughout its 50-year history, though many have tried, no one has been able to find a way of getting provisions in and out of the buildings without negotiating 48 giant stone steps. The steps were constructed to allow the Knights of St John to take their horses up into the cavalier from the square below. They serve that purpose well, but too many staff who have worked at St James's; they were an overwhelming disadvantage that was never overcome.

Mr W GT Duke, manager HS North, who was supervisor in Malta from 1958 to 1962, was one of many who tried to get around the problem of the steps. He discovered an air vent which he traced down to an admiralty map store below. He conceived an idea that lorries might enter the map store so that the goods could be hauled up into the shop. Nothing came of it, however, the 48 steps remained the only means of access. St James cavalier is a giant rabbit warren. The huge 9-foot-thick surrounding walls lock out the heat and the light. Inside, myriad arches provided difficulties for shop fittings.

It is rumoured that ghosts haunt the ancient passages and groans and noises have been heard, much to the concern of the female members of staff. Mr Duke had some fond memories of the building. During his stay on the island, the Royal Navy made great use of the grand Harbour. At a later stage they were replaced by the NATO fleet. The comings and goings of the fleet were not only movements that St James's cavalier witnessed. Mr Duke recalled one fateful day arriving at St James is to find some 40 American tourists waving their blue cards, convinced that the NAAFI shop, as an ancient building, ought to be open to the public.

In addition to its ancient heritage, St James's cavalier had one proud claim to modern fame. It was the first shop on the island to go self-service. Mr Duke recalls that this move caused some excitement and local businessmen came from afar to see the wonders of modern self service, displayed in a building 4 centuries old. In its time St James's cavalier had housed the Malta area office, a grocery, sports, and services shop. It was certainly NAAFI's busiest establishment on the island and its ideal location at the gates to Malta, close to all bus routes from various parts of the country, was a considerable advantage.

At the time of its closure the shop employed 28 staff and served a large part of the service community with bread and general deliveries. Services shop manager Vincent de Giovanni joined NAAFI as a delivery man in 1939 and his colleague Savior Borg, who was in charge of gifts and durables, would have completed 25 years' service with NAAFI in 1972, all of them at St James's.

Perhaps one who will feel the loss of St James's cavalier more than most is Frances Saliba, his 46-year service with the company took him back almost to the date when NAAFI first made any use of the cavalier. Between the years of 1954 and 1964 he in turn served as manager and official in charge of St James's. He attended the closing down of the building as district manager and took away the great key that locked the entrance doors for the last time.

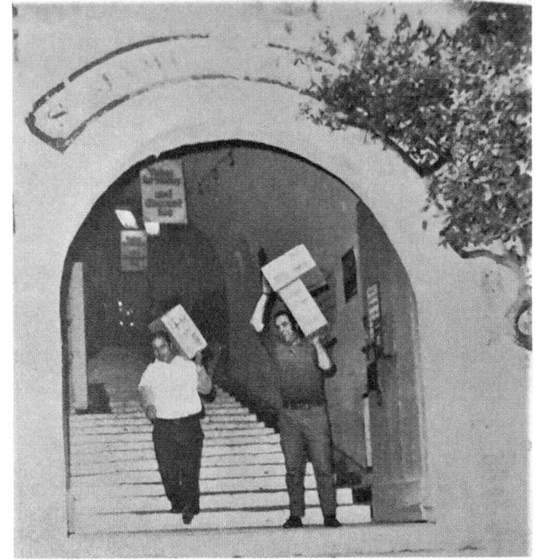

Despite its awkwardness and complete unsuitability as a modern self-service store, St James's cavalier drew great affection from all NAAFI personnel connected with this unusual establishment. Mr Duke said, 'Everyone spent so much time trying to think of ways of converting this great clumsy building, but St James would not be changed. I think we all had a soft spot for it. It was unique and always kept its marvellous character.'

Farewell to the Gulf by Mr A E Self 15th of February 1972.

The crunch came on Tuesday the 15th of February 1972 when a bearded Arab climbed into my Austin, pulled his cloak around his knees, straightened his headdress, and drove off. The last of the NAAFI vehicles in Bahrain had been sold.

I gazed after the car as it disappeared in a cloud of sandy dust and the lines of Caroline Norton came into my mind. 'Fret not to roam the desert now with all thy winged speed, I may not mount on thee again! thou art sold my Arab steed'. She was writing about a horse, but you can be fond of a car too. And so, another chapter in NAAFI history had been completed, another overseas area had closed down. Not many on the western side of Europe know much about the Arabian Gulf, as it is now called. Even the old name Persian Gulf meant little to most people, except perhaps, that there are a fair number of barrels of oil lying down below and British servicemen were stationed there. Yet the Gulf is one of the oldest sea routes in the world with historical connections going back to 3000 BC, the sight of Bahrain is believed to have been the garden of Eden. Today there is not a fig leaf to be seen.

But why was the Union Jack flying and what were we doing there? The answer lay in the need to protect British interests and in particular British shipping. Back in the 18th and early 19th centuries the Arab rulers in the area along the entrance to the Gulf extracted tolls from ships passing through and continually brawled with each other in their competition for dominance in the area. A number of military excursions were launched by the British against the warring states – in those empire days that was the right and proper thing to do. The culmination of the argument was the signing of the perpetual maritime truce by each of the states concerned. That was 120 years ago and the origin of the Trucial states of Oman (not to be confused with Muscat and Oman which is outside the Gulf waters). Since then, although the Trucial states have been largely self-governing, Britain has been responsible for their defence.

Further up the Gulf from the states is the Peninsula of Qatar and just above this lies Bahrain, an island of about 300 square miles and 200,000 inhabitants, with a few smaller islands scattered around Bahrain and Qatar also came with a defence commitments of Great Britain. That, briefly, is the background to the British link. For many years now there has been a small and unobtrusive British presence, consisting of a token Royal Navy and RAF units in Bahrain and RAF and army installations in Sharjah.

A local force was set up by the British government in 1951. It was then known as the Trucial Oman levees but had since been renamed Trucial Oman scouts. This force, recruited in the trucial states, had a number of seconded personnel and its command by the British Colonel. In 1972 the scouts consisted of about 2000 all ranks, and the headquarters stood on the outskirts of Sharjah on the road to Ajman.

With the discovery of the large deposits of oil in the area, the fortunes of some of the states began to improve. Dual carriageways with modern overhead lighting, air-conditioned luxury hotels and international standard airports, schools, and well-appointed hospitals are accepted features of the Gulf life now and with the exception of Qatar and Kuwait, the thirsty expatriate may take his pick of several well stocked bars. There are even nightclubs mushrooming in Abu Dhabi and Dubai.

The system of government is authoritarian. The ruler's authority is absolute, yet they are accessible to any of their subjects who may wish to see them, whether within a petition or complaint or merely to pay respects. There is no parliament or elections and most of the ministerial appointments are held by ruling families. But the guidance that has been given by successive British residents and political agents over the years, coupled with the enlightened and educated outlook of most of the ruling sheiks, is producing a standard of life which may soon rival that of some more developed countries.

Now Britain has withdrawn, a union Defence Force is being formed. Based in Sharjah it will eventually be the joint Defence Force for the combined trucial states. Six of the seven states have formed a union of Arab Emirates. They are Dubai, Sharjah, Abu Dhabi, Umm al Qaiwain, Fujairah and Ajman. The 7th state, Ras al Khaimah, was, at the time of the British withdrawal, expected to join soon. Thus, although each state is intensely jealous of its separate identity, the likelihood is that the merged Emirates will become an integral independent whole with common boundaries, law, and tariffs. Bahrain and Qatar are now quite separate independent Emirates but work in close cooperation with their neighbouring states.

The affair of NAAFI in the Gulf in the early post-war years was controlled from Iraq. When we withdrew from Iraq the area came under Aden, however, until 1960 when Bahrain became an independent NAAFI district. It remained so until the end of 1967 when, with the rundown of Aden and building up of the forces in the Gulf, it became a separate command and took over responsibility for the two root stations at Masirah and Salalah in Muscat and Oman. The latter have now moved into the administrative orbit of NAAFI in Cyprus. Over the past three years the Gulf contributed more to the NAAFI pool than any other overseas area. Although it may be argued that the trade is now merely transferred, it is an unfortunate fact that per capita spending with the company by those same customers in other areas is unlikely to be nearly as high.

The main consideration of the service personnel from 1968 to the end of 1971 had been in Sharjah and Bahrain where some 6000 personnel have been deployed. In Sharjah about 3000 army and RAF servicemen were stationed without families and with virtually little else but their NAAFI clubs and service shops to relieve the boredom and frustration of their celibate existence. The Malcolm club and MMG Club and bookshop provided the only alternative facilities, unless one had the cash for a 10-mile taxi journey to Dubai.

In Bahrain, the total numbers were about the same but about 600 of the men were accompanied and life generally was much more comfortable. There was also a small but important naval presence in the shape of a frigate and six minesweepers with supporting short installations. Bahrain was a more sophisticated area, the presence of families made it more satisfying and a more commercially rewarding centre. NAAFI command headquarters was located there and the spread of the operations covering Sharjah, the trucial Masirah and Salalah, in Muscat and Oman, entailed considerable travel usually accompanied by several tons of freight in the belly of RAF Argosy.

Unlike some of the other overseas locations, the British were well liked and relations with the local population were cordial and friendly. The build-up in the Gulf in late 1967 and 1968 indicated a prolonged unhappy stay for the British forces in the area. The announcement of the withdrawal was received with amazement and not until it got underway did the irrevocability of the decision become clear. To the end, the friendly, hospitable behaviour of the Arab population did not change. The Amir of Bahrain continued to make available his private beach for service families and the open-hearted traders in the 'souk' continue to slip an apple or a few grapes into the hands of children accompanying mums to the market.

Then, on a breezy sunny day in October, the last of the minesweepers sailed majestically out of Bahrain harbour. They were escorted to the harbour limits by The Commodores barge with the commander, British forces, Gulf, and other VIPs aboard, several other barges filled with waving and smiling, but sad eyed local well-wishers. This set in train for what from then on became a speedy uneventful withdrawal. By the end of November all the families had departed from Bahrain. On the 17th of December, the final RAF VC10 left Bahrain airport with the commander, British forces Gulf Maj General RC Gibbs and his staff on board.

NAAFI service went on until the 19th of December and it was perhaps fitting that it ended almost where it began, about 37 years previously. The first establishment to operate in the Gulf was a fleet canteen in Jufair back in 1934 or 35, to cater for the Royal Navy stationed in the area. The last NAAFI to close in December 1971 was the two seas club in Jufair which remained open to provide a service for HMS Intrepid, which slipped quietly away bound for the UK on the 20th of December.

So ended the British presence in the Gulf, although a small military assistance team will continue to operate in Sharjah and NAAFI will provide a service. The last NAAFI staff to leave Bahrain, apart from myself, were supplies official Bri Gibson, senior district accountant Jim Penford, and establishment official Ernie Rudd, who comprised the final disposals team, plus sponsored foreign Nationals. The Bahrain flag was kept flying by long serving Nasser Mohammed Khalifa and Sultan Ali Kahn, both of whom received certificates of commendation from the commander, British forces, Gulf, presented by the command supervisor.

Many NAAFI staff sales serving may also look back on their years in and around Bahrain and Sharjah, when conditions were much less civilised and comfortable than they are now. They will think of sand, of ill lit streets and camels, donkeys. They will think of the Speed Bird, the nearest approach to a hotel that Bahrain possessed, the old Fort in Sharjah which was the hotel.

The memories of those who saw the Gulf of the 70s will be very different, the booming future is brightly indicated everywhere. Only in one sense will recent memories be linked with the old, and that is the genuine goodwill of the people of those lands, and of Bahrain in particular.

New uniform for 1972

The last uniform change was in 1960, and now there was another change for all the girls. The first of 4500 newly designed overalls for the NAAFI girls were dispatched to the clubs from the

Ludgershall warehouse in April of 1972. The overalls, the result of 18 months' backroom work, had been made in a neat check pattern with blue trimmings and three-quarter length sleeves. They were made of a knitted nylon and should breathe much better than the old woven type.

It had been 12 years since the previous type was introduced and the divisional buyer for clothing and cosmetics, Mr BF Clow, knew they were ready for a change. The prototype was tested for some months at three establishments and the only change that was made was the trimmings went from white to being blue which made them easier to wash. The open collar and half buttoned overall made it easier for the wearer, to wear appropriate clothes underneath.

It's time for another change says Sir Charles Hardie May 1972.

I suppose it is natural for all of us to regard our own particular span with NAAFI as the most interesting and formative part of the company's history. Certainly, when I review my 20 years on the board, I've found it difficult to believe that so much change could have been packed into any other double decade.

The year of my arrival in 1952, was itself a year of change, a forerunner of what was to come. Edward McGowan had taken over as secretary. Eric A Ellison was the new chief accountant. Sir Richard Burbage of Harrods had just retired from the board and Sir George Erskine handed over the deputy chairmanship to Sir William Beale. The first meeting of the NAAFI joint consultative council was held that year and it was at the meeting of 'AOs' (administrative officials) came into existence as such. At that first meeting it was announced that the company was studying all aspects of office operations with a view to increasing efficiency and eliminating unnecessary paperwork. Now there's one thing that still sounds familiar today.

At this time NAAFI was building town clubs not closing them and that year Princess Margaret opened the new Plymouth club and the Duke of Edinburgh opened the Lincoln club.

NAAFI was at war in Korea, there was trouble in the canal zone of Egypt, in Malaysia, and in Kenya. The district manager and 15 NCS managers and assistants were providing canteen facilities for servicemen and scientists taking part in Britain's first atomic bomb test on Montebello. At home, NAAFI was preparing to play its part in the forthcoming Coronation of Queen Elizabeth II.

At that time NAAFI had more than twice the customers it has now, at much more than twice the staff. The dramatic run down of the immediate post-war years was over but a much longer period of retrenchment lay ahead as troop strengths were further reduced and Britain withdrew from various overseas areas. Within a year of my taking a seat on the board, Sir Lancelot Royle, chairman through the momentous years of war, retired and was succeeded by his deputy. At this time, I was proud to become deputy chairman. A young Humphrey Prideaux arrived on the scene as NAAFI personnel manager and in the following year was appointed joint general manager.

It was about this time that the company, among the leaders as ever, began its experiments with self-service and seriously began to take advantage of mechanical handling in warehouses. During the remainder of the 50s there was a small but steady rise in the per capita spending of NAAFI customers, but this was to be accompanied by a small but steady fall in turnover as our area of operations and our customer potential shrank. We pulled out of Trieste, The Sudan, Rhodesia, Egypt, Japan, Korea . . .

It was in the midst of these troubled times that NAAFI began its long-term plans for the 60s and 70s. On the management side, NAAFI executives were given seats on the board for the first time, a move I had long pressed for. Sir Randall Feilden, who until then had been chief general manager, was appointed to the board as managing director. Humphrey Prideaux also joined the board as assistant managing director.

On the operation side a great deal was happening. The conversion of shops to self-service was being pushed ahead as rapidly as possible, we made our first venture into contract catering, services shops then known as walk in shops made their appearance, our first experiments with the vending age got underway. The social club concept was introduced, regional management replaced the command structure, the company installed its first computer, and the instalment credit began to feature in our turnover figures. That is a lot of new thinking to pack into one paragraph in a few short hectic years.

As NAAFI entered the 60s, Humphrey Prideaux became managing director. The experiments in operation tentatively began in the previous decades proved their worth and were now vigorously promoted. Change no longer seemed strange and alien, it was welcomed as the right road to a more efficient and vital organization. Then the company adopted the 'N' symbol, car hire Purchase was introduced, and NAAFI buildings began to take on a new look as new shops and shopping centres opened from Aldershot to Terendak.

When Sir William Beale relinquished the chair at the end of 1961, the appointment of Sir (then Mr) Rex Cohen, chairman of the Lewis group, and his successor was an acknowledgment of the increased importance of the shopping side of NAAFI business.

For the first time the activities of the company were separated into two board divisions, merchandising and administration. Edward McGowan relinquished the secretaryship of the company to take charge of administration as joint general manager.

He had accepted an appointment for a period of three years and at the end of that time Humphrey Prideaux took on the chairmanship. At the same time NAAFI representation on the board was strengthened by the appointment of Edward McGowan as administrative director, Harvey Swithenbank as merchandise director, and Jim Robertson as personnel director.

After the 60s began with changing progress, so they continued. We saw the steady widening of the range of NAAFI own label products and their rapid achievement and success, the introduction of dividend stamps, the arrival of 2nd and then third generation computers, the development of aid to ordering system, the NAAFI petrol stations, a new accent on staff training, proficiency payments for club staff, the introduction of bonus schemes for various other jobs, and the buy British campaign in Germany which led among other things to the present status of the butcheries and Marks and Spencer's style clothing shops there.

More changes were taking place on the board of management too. Austen Layard had joined the board in 1965 as merchandise director and then, in 1969 when the chairman now Sir Humphrey, gave up his role as managing director, Edward McGowan assumed the mantle. Eric Allison was appointed administrative director and James Spooner, now to be my successor as deputy chairman, arrived on the scene.

The events of the early 70s, job evaluation, the Amesbury extension, the Rheindahlen centre and so on, would seem to indicate that the progress of the 60s will not be lost in the 70s. I shall of course be sorry not to play a part in the progress which I am sure will continue to be made, but I am convinced I am right, at this juncture, to make the way for a younger man. Happily, James Spooner and I are partners in my chartered accounting firm, and I am sure he will keep me in the picture, so I am able to say farewell in the knowledge that I shall not be completely out of touch.

I am on record elsewhere as having said that NAAFI is the best run business I have been connected with and that joining the board was one of the most significant steps in my career. This stems from NAAFI discipline (gleaned from the services) and commercial attitudes, the former is so often lacking in industry. I stand by that today. Any help that I have been able to give NAAFI has been amply repaid in what I have personally gained from the example of NAAFI and its people.

They answer the call of the sea, by Mike Pheasant 1972

'You've got the brains of a bloody rocking horse, laddie!' The angry instructors' words are cracked across the rifle range. 'Don't you realise that if we had an idiot on the end of this line, which we probably have, you could have been shot' The recruit, who had wandered dangerously close to the firing bullets, paled and another instructor, accepting his cue with the timing of a comic, approached the last man on the range. 'Are you an idiot?', 'no, Sir'. 'Alright, just checking.' This is HMS Raleigh, Torpoint, Cornwall, training place for naval recruits, where discipline is strict but is tempered with humour, sometimes.

Raleigh stands on a slope of a hill, its one storey huts spread out and down to the River Hamoaze. The day starts at 9 with divisions. Markers for various classes take their place on the parade ground. Orders split the air and everyone else doubles into position. The band of the Royal Marines plays itself proudly onto the scene. Hats are removed and the Padre's prayer echoes through the public address system and across the damp, still square. Then as the last strain of the national anthem is played, the white Ensign flutters into place on the Flagstaff. The band strikes up again and the class march past, eyes right, for the salute. First come the old hands, recruits have almost finished their training. They are slick and well drilled. Bringing up the rear are the freshman of the ship, trying hard to maintain some sort of formation.

Recruits spend their first week at Torpoint, across the road from Raleigh, in HMS Fishguard, the naval artificers training centre. There they fill in forms, collect their uniforms and learn how to wear them. They spend those first 7 days of their career confined to the barracks, only when they cross the footbridge to Raleigh are they free to sample the delights of nearby Plymouth.

The new boys spend a minimum of six weeks at Torpoint, doing part one naval training. This involves instruction in such things as naval discipline and organisation, drilling, firearms, first aid, firefighting, and damage control. If they elect to become Seamen, they stay on for a further nine weeks of more intensive Part 2 seamanship training after which they go to places like HMS Vernon, for anti-submarine torpedo work and HMS Cambridge, the gunnery school. But many ratings want a career in a more specialised Navy activities as they leave Raleigh after the initial six weeks for Part 2 training in other establishments. The marine engineer mechanics train at HMS Sultan, the electricians go to HMS Collingwood and the cooks and stewards and writers to HMS Pembroke. But all get their sea legs at the earliest opportunity.

Two miles from Raleigh, at Jupiter Point, blue Navy buses regularly disgorge recruits onto a slipway. The lights line-up, orange life jackets strapped tightly around them, ready for the first taste of handling a boat, some have been no closer to the sea than a school outing to Margate. They are shown how to rig a variety of craft and within minutes, are launched onto a swift running tide into a stiff south-westerly wind with orders to fend for themselves; an instructor sails in each vessel but he acts only as an emergency. The instructors have discovered that the recruits quickly learn how to master the elements, or at least compete with them, when they are thrown in at the deep end like this.

The same applies to damage control lessons; the ratings are put into huge tanks and have to stop water pouring in through the gashes and holes in an assortment of gear including planks, ropes, and sheeting.

Three times a year naval recruits at Raleigh are joined by NCS assistants on a crash two-day course which follows a week's classroom tuition at Wingham. In July 1972, Tony Whettam from HMS Sirius, Mike Hillier from HMS Plymouth, Alan Leach from HMS Ark Royal, and Peter Smith from HMS Defiance took their turn. They had general interest lectures and films, a damage control session, a day on firefighting training, a few hours at Jupiter Point, and a target practice on an indoor.22 range. The most spectacular of these lessons was the firefighting school where they charged at tanks of blazing oil with both foam and water extinguishers. They donned breathing apparatus and climbed a ladder into the first floor, smoke chamber, a maze of doors and walkways with a yawning hole in one section of the floor, one false move and it would bring them crashing to the ground 12 feet below. 'I was doing alright,' said Peter Smith, 'until my tanks ran out, by the time I got out of the smoke chamber I was gasping for air and could hardly wait while Tony tore my mask off.'

EFI in Arctic saves 9 NATO nations 1972

Just like the wartime Windmill Theatre, the EFI service on Exercise Strong expressway, never closed. The eight-man team was operating in Bardufoss, northern Norway. A tiny town several 100 miles inside the Arctic Circle. Their job was to carry on the NAAFI in the tradition of serving troops wherever they may be, regardless of the conditions.

The weather was bad in Norway. Statistics had shown that rain could be expected on 16 September days but the EFI man swore that the full ration fell in the first couple of days, and the rain continued for the remaining 12, transforming the terrain into a mud swamp. 'Exercise Strong Expressway', one of the largest exercises in the history of NATO, it involved 64,000 men from 12 countries. It covered the whole of the North Atlantic and included carrier-based aircraft operations submarines and anti-submarine warfare. Minelaying and mine countermeasures, amphibious operations by 4000 strong Tri-national marine force and ground operations by the allied command Europe, mobile forces 5000 men backed by 5000 Norwegian troops.

Working from 4 tents at the logistic support battalion headquarters in the field, the EFI men, Sgt Maj David Sadler, Sgt Gordon Begley, and Cpl Vic Bonner, Ian Davidson, David Kennedy, Ian Stirling and Mike Turner, under the command of Capt David Sizmur, gave a nonstop service to the men of the ACE mobile force and the Norwegian troops in the area. Their customers included troops from Belgium, Canada, Denmark, Holland, Italy, Luxembourg, Norway, the UK, and the United States of America.

The conditions proved a tough baptism for Iain Davidson, Ian Stirling and Mike Turner who were on their first EFI exercise. They must have been surprised to be building houses inside the tent from tri-wall cartons. They were a great help in keeping belongings clean and gave them a bit of privacy. NAAFI sales exceeded expectation and approximately 10% of this was locally produced knitwear and gifts. They sold a lot of spirits but then at the time was 85 pence a bottle, so this was hardly surprising. Spirit sales generally far outstripped the forecasts and an extra 200 cases had to be flown in from Lyneham and Brize Norton.

Three hundred ships were involved in the Ex Strong Express and the Royal Navy contingent comprised HMS Ark Royal, Intrepid, Albion, Fearless, Blake, Fife, Norfolk, Achilles, Juno, Phoebe, and Brighton. The exercise meant an even busier time than usual for the ship's canteen managers who although didn't experience the adverse weather conditions on land they got the full experience whilst on board.

Kennings Way the end of an era by Tim Roberts 1972

When Lambeth Council contractors demolished NAAFI Kennings Way property to make space for multi storey flats, they will be finishing off a job that Reichmarshal Hermann Goering tried to do in the early 1940s.

It was not a particularly heavily bombed area of London but of the bombs that did fall on the locality, a fair percentage found their way to NAAFI in Kennings Way. Some 30 bombs and an uncounted number of incendiaries fell on or near the warehouse. One incendiary canister fell through the roof of what was the games room at Kennings Way and dropped clean into the corner pocket of a billiard table. 'It didn't even touch the sides of the pocket, a lovely pot,' recalled Alfred Woodward, who was then the foreman Porter, who was a firewatcher at the time.

Much of the early burden of setting up ARP control and organising fire watching fell on Mr JF Pond, the then manager of the printing branch. Mr Pond, who in 1972 was a fit 86-year-old, he still lived in New Eltham from where he used to travel daily to Kennington. He recalled the blitz well. In neat, precise handwriting he kept a complete air raid record for Kennings Way. It made interesting reading, although some of the more humorous tales to be told are not recorded there.

Mr Pond was the chair for the first meeting of the ARP committee on 6th of June 1940. The minutes record how the system of Volunteer Fire watches was set up and a control tower established in the North East end of Kennings Way in what was still known at the time as the new building. Fire watching was later made compulsory and the sum of 4s, 6d was paid for each night worked, though out of this had to come a charge for breakfast.

Three main air raid shelters were established, one in the wine cellars, one under the restaurant and one under the old printing branch. Air raid warning practices were regularly carried out and blackouts put into operation. First aid posts were organised, and Kennings Way prepared for the aerial onslaught.

In August 1940, although there were no significant raids, the shelters were used for the first time on the first day of the blitz, 7th of September, the first bombs were dropped nearby on the night of September came the first direct hit on a NAAFI property. A 100lb bomb fell near the oil stores at the back of the bacon stoves. It was defused by a bomb disposal expert but much of Kingsway as it then stood would have been blown to pieces if it had exploded. On the 11th of September incendiaries were dropped on the warehouse. One penetrated the tea department and tobacco room where sprinklers, set off by the bomb, caused more damage than the bomb itself. The fires were dealt with by NAAFI owned firewatchers, armed with stirrup pumps and buckets of sand before the auxiliary fire service arrived on the scene. Later the Germans were to develop a bomb that exploded when sand was thrown on it. A NAAFI worker was the very first victim of this type of bomb; he suffered facial injuries when he threw sand on a bomb in order to stifle it.

Bombs, incendiary canisters, fell regularly on the warehouse. St Mary's Church at the back of Kingsway was set ablaze by an incendiary attack and the Elephant and Castle was badly damaged during many heavy raids. The shelters were now in constant use and Mr Pond had resorted to sleeping in a large armchair in his office. 'I used to go home about once or twice a week for a bath,' he recalled.

On the 25th of October, a bomb sliced through part of the new extension and hit a surface shelter in Cottington Street, killing seven local people and injuring many others. Clifford Wawn, now warehouse manager, Kennings Way, recalled coming into the building after the explosion – 'the damage was amazing, I saw ordinary wooden pencils driven through the steel spinning by the force of the blast.'

Jack Sharp, now in charge of the purchase tax section of supplies accounts branch, was on duty as a member of the Home Guard, when an oil bomb fell on the roof of the new extension. 'I had just checked the roof with Charles Jolly, and we were halfway down the stairs when "boom" the thing landed,' he remembers. Fortunately, it did not explode but nevertheless Charles and Jack ended up on their backsides at the bottom of the stairs such was the force of the impact. They were lucky not to be injured because they were carrying rifles with fixed bayonets at the time.

The bomb dropped at 0400hrs and Mr Pond recalled trying to get back to Kennington from his New Eltham home. At Peckham there was a German plane across the road and then at Camberwell the police stopped him and said that if he wanted to go any further, it would have to be at his own risk.

As Mr Pond pressed on, a falling block of masonry crashed onto the back seat of his Lanchester car. There was some respite in the November although many high explosive and incendiary bombs fell nearby, and one demolished a 5-tonne lorry parked in the warehouse. At the beginning of December a high explosive bomb fell in Cottington Street blowing in many of NAAFI windows, the nearby telephone exchange was damaged, and a host of incendiaries gave the firewatchers more work to do. On the 11th of January, a total of 12 bombs and incendiaries fell on Kennings Way but the fire watching teams soon dealt with them. The following night some 14 incendiaries also then fell on the warehouse.

In the following months though the rest of the London received nightly treatment, Kennington suffered little and the worst had passed. NAAFI was fortunate in having both a first-class air raid warning system and excellent shelters. However, many people preferred the underground. Mr Pond recorded: 'when I used to leave late at night, I would have to walk over sleeping people to get out.'

The fire watching teams were supported in their work by the men of NAAFI 50 strong, Kennings Way Home Guard unit. True to the Dad's Army tradition, the men were first equipped with sharpened metal spikes to keep off the enemy. Jim Jolly, warehouseman and brother of Charles Jolly, who was a private in that NAAFI unit, recalled: 'I suppose we had a laugh about the spikes ourselves, but they were all we had at the time and they were better than nothing.'

The Home Guard were based in the lodge where the one 'Bren gun' was kept under lock and key. Capt George Ellis who was a former branch manager, Capt Douglas Bolingbroke, former house manager, Lt Harry Hornsey, former transport stores, Lt Wally Pierce, former warehouse manager, from the offices of the Home Guard. They were ably supported by Sgt Maj's Green and Robertson.

Wally Rose, a member of the Home Guard and now a section leader in the overseas accounts branch, recalled witnessing a portly Sgt Maj Green attempting to shin up two drainpipes to get at an incendiary bomb. Cecil Bevan in a battle dress made for someone else, and an army greatcoat that came down to his ankles, had the unwelcome task of checking people in the main gate as they arrived for work. There were people that had worked there for years but they had to be checked and a few unprintable suggestions of what to do with my metal spike were suggested.

Geoff Farrar, assistant manager prices branch, another member of Kennings Way Home Guard, had earlier been a member of the LDV, the Local Defence Volunteers, known somewhat unkindly as 'the look, duck and vanish brigade'. He recalled, during a mock invasion exercise, being sent out on a tram car to attack some guardsmen posted in a Vauxhall pub. One of Capt Bolingbroke's duties was to take crates of Spanish oranges down to Kennington Park and sort through them and check that no pro Axis Spaniard had slipped in a bomb or two.

Despite the Dad's Army approach to the NAAFI Home Guard, Staff Sgt Jack sharp recalled: 'Sgt Maj Green and Robertson took things very seriously and NAAFI was definitely one of the better Home Guard units.'

Mr Pond was similarly proud of his firewatchers: 'They were a fine team of men. We never knew what a full night's sleep was in those days, but we got used to it, we handled most of what came our way.'

With the demobilisation of Kennings Way and the approaching retirement of a few remaining staff who worked there during the war, the memory of Kennings Way and the blitz are, like old soldiers, fading away.

Royal opening for Edinburgh House 1972

His Royal Highness the Duke of Edinburgh, with a broad smile, said, 'I had no option but to accept the invitation to open this building, the name of the building is an inducement, the property is on ground virtually owned by my son, as past and serving members of the forces we have both used NAAFI, as the chairman and I served together at one time.'

The Duke, opening NAAFI's new Kennington offices, went on to congratulate NAAFI on its contribution to service life. As a serving officer, he said he had learned what rebate meant to the service units and how much they depended on it. He then unveiled a commemorative plaque saying with another grin: 'in case there is any doubt about it, this place is now open.'

Some 1700 headquarters staff watched the ceremony and the rest of the hour-long visit on closed circuit television which had been installed in Edinburgh House and in Imperial Court just down the road. They had seen the Duke arrive by car to be greeted by NAAFI chairman and the managing director. The board of management were presented in the ground floor entrance hall where the chairman welcomed His Royal Highness officially and invited him to open the building.

After the unveiling the Duke was whisked up to the penthouse snack bar where the department and managers were presented. It was there the Duke made his first unscheduled detour, going out onto the roof to view the London skyline, before setting out on his tour to meet Edinburgh House staff in their offices. Fourteen people had been selected for official presentation, but the Duke made many unscheduled stops. Staff who came to work expecting only to see him on television or, at best, bypassing them went home that evening with exciting tales of the day that they spoke to royalty.

Edinburgh House still stands today and has been turned into workspaces with its entrance moved to a more central point in the building. But before NAAFI, Edinburgh House stood on the footprint of Kennington Palace's old stables. In 1346, Edward, the third eldest son, dubbed the 'Black Prince' had started work on the Palace, from the early 1340s until about 1350. It was then demolished by Henry VIII in 1531 and used the building materials for the Palace at Whitehall. Even though today the old exterior looks as fresh as the day it was opened by the Duke of Edinburgh, the interior and the roof have somewhat changed.

1973

Brize Norton, Heathrow of the military by David Lloyd 1973

Everyday tonnes of food and equipment and hundreds of servicemen and families passed through RAF Brize Norton bound for British bases and military exercises throughout the world. The station whose motto is 'Pass through confidently', nestled in the quiet of the rolling Oxfordshire countryside; this is a vital link between Britain and the forces overseas.

In 1973 scheduled passenger flights had been stepped up to operate 24 hours a day, and at the beginning of May NAAFI extended the opening times of the refreshment kiosk in the departure lounge to provide around the clock service for departing servicemen and their families. The services were provided by a dedicated team of eight NAAFI girls working shifts. One of them, Jenny Herbstreit, work the night shift. She had got engaged recently but didn't celebrate. She had to go to work. Jenny started work at 2200hrs and served tea, coffee, sausage rolls, sandwiches, pies, and sweets throughout the night. Occasionally she would also give words of reassurance to worried mums making their first flight. She said that she enjoyed working this shift as it was interesting observing the different types of people as they passed through. She was so busy that she never had the time to feel tired.

When the announcement of the next incoming flight from Berlin came, tearful, smiling reunions were made with returning heroes. There was usually time for a cup of tea and a bite at the NAAFI before driving home through the night. Jenny a few times had to stock up again before 3 coaches pulled up outside and more servicemen and their families flooded into the lounge. Some were off to a posting in Gan, others were returning to Hong Kong and Gibraltar after leave. There would regularly be a queue of 50 deep from the kiosk. Jenny worked flat out, and all had been served by the time their flights were announced a few minutes later.

The procession continued, the boredom and the discomfort of waiting eased by a cup of tea and a friendly word. Gradually darkness gives way to the dawn and Kay Bishop and Rose Wigley arrived to work the 0600hrs to the 1200hrs shift.

RAF Brize Norton began life in 1937 as a flying training command training school. In 1942 the heavy glider conversion unit took over and used the station as a base for wartime parachute and glider operations. In December 1945, the station became the home of transport commands' development unit and the school of flight efficiency later joined by the army airborne transport development unit. Flying training command returned in 1949 until two years later when the United States Air Force formally accepted control of the station. They extended the one runway and built taxiways, hardstandings, and accommodation. Jet bombers, bombers, and refuelling squadrons were based there until, on the 1st of April 1965, the station was handed back to the RAF, eventually becoming an airfield with 46 group, strike command. The development of the station since then has been extensive.

The station was organised into three functional wings, operations, engineering, and administration. It boasted the single largest span cantilever hangar in Western Europe covering 5½ acres and capable of servicing, at one time, 3 VC10s and three Belfasts, or 11 Britannias.

In 1973 it took almost 5000 officers, airmen and airwomen to run RAF Brize Norton. The majority, whether married or single, lived on the station and NAAFI was there in strength to cater for their needs too, and the requirements of their families. The social scene for the permanent staff centred around the 'Spotlight club', opened by Her Majesty the Queen in March 1971. It is there that the majority of the airmen relaxed away from the seriousness of business and keeping the planes flying. Over 12,000 pints of draught beer were pulled in the club's 3 bars every week. The busiest night was Saturday when a dance, for station personnel only, was held with a big-name group providing the music.

The Spotlight had a restaurant open to all ranks, services shop, and automatic cafeteria, colour television and games room. Vending machines were provided at several locations around

the station including the crash training centre, the education centre, the unit run 10 pin bowling and in summer the ATC cadets' quarters.

RAF Brize Norton also had a NAAFI petrol station. They prided themselves on having cheaper fuel than anywhere else around and the manager Barbara Hayward estimated that there were 4500 car owners on the station and that there existed quite a potential for car sales. During the previous year, the manufacturers lent NAAFI an Avenger and a Victor 2300 SL for display in their showroom, which they had an encouraging number of inquiries for. Many of the airmen didn't realise at the time that they could buy a car from them. But they are beginning to realise that they can get more from NAAFI than pint and a roll.

The station's deputy commander at the time, Group Capt Deryck Groocock said that the NAAFI facilities were a boost to the community and the extensive range of goods and services were appreciated by all. The company's reputation was considerably enhanced by the efficient way emergency refreshment services were mounted during the previous year's evacuation of service families from Malta to Brize Norton. Everybody was impressed with the service.

NAAFI stars at the Army show 1973

63 NAAFI marquees and tents covered 150,000 square foot of grass in the 1973 Aldershot army display, it was NAAFI's largest ever spread of canvas. This tented Township was erected to house NAAFI catering and bar facilities, regimental recruitment displays, and civilian traders.

The marquees ranged from 120 foot by 40-foot to 22 foot by 12 foot. They were erected in just two weeks by NAAFI's 7-strong canvas team. The same crew also assembled thousands of feet of canvas screening and walling, hundreds of floorboards counters and so on.

Over 250,000 people visited the four-day display held at the Rushmore arena. The main attraction was the gymnastics, Land Rover dismantling and reassembling, freefall parachuting and motorcycling. The equipment of the modern army was also on show and regimental displays depicted the many roles and opportunities to today's professional soldiers. NAAFI takings were recorded for this annual event. It produced record sales and at the end a rebate was paid to the army Benevolent Fund, the display's beneficiary.

During the Saturday and Sunday, the public catering marquees served 6416 cups of tea and coffee, 1600 rounds of sandwiches, 7000 filled rolls and 19,440 pints of draught beer. Over 1000 cases of minerals and 250 gallons of orange squash were used. All the food was prepared on the spot. Over 100 staff including casuals provided service under Aldershot district manager Barry Lodge.

NAAFI played a vital part in its success of the show, said Colonel JF Dixon-Nuttall, Controller of the display, the caterings facilities were mounted and run with expertise that only NAAFI can bring to a job of this size. The excellence of NAAFI catering did not go unnoticed by the public and even the tea was complimented as the best cup that they had tasted in years and the queues were kept to a minimum which made the service speedy.

Right dress! 1973

Newly designed dresses for club and shop managers and assistant managers would be introduced in October 1973. Other staff would also benefit from the smarten up campaign, later in the year shop assistants would get a blue check uniform identical to the new ones worn by club assistants, the club staff would be supplied with a plain blue bib apron.

The new managers' uniforms were cream, trimmed with brown. Assistant managers would wear pale blue trimmed with brown. That for the manager is an A line with front plate and back fastening, replacing the full pleated skirt and button up front. Assistant managers would get a straight-line front fastening step in style. Both uniforms are in polyester linen and have matching brown bib aprons. Staff have a choice of two hem lengths. The choice of colour is limited, explained Miss Jean Rainey, chief R&WS. For instance, we didn't choose green because many people are superstitious. It is surprising how quickly the choice is whittled down. They also had to consider how the uniforms would wear, if they were smart, easy to launder and not too hot or not too cool. The clothing buyer was Bertie Clow and they had to bear in mind that the ladies' fashions were becoming more casual and length is very important.

Considering criticisms of the old uniform, they pored over their ideas to produce samples that were given to a number of managers to try out. Generally, they proved popular, but criticism led to the changes in the belt, sleeves and the pockets. After a fashion parade at Imperial Court for the trading and marketing eepartment managers, the final go ahead was given by the managing director and the results are modelled in the pictures by Mrs Sybil Riddell, manager of the shop. Her opinion was that she thought they were gorgeous, and that NAAFI could produce anything so stylish for the staff.

20 years on the Royal yacht by David Lloyd 1973

Instead of spending three weeks in the Caribbean and Pacific with Royal newlyweds, Douglas Jackson had been recovering in Gravesend from an operation to remove a stomach ulcer. Unless Doug made a quick recovery, he might also miss the visit by the Queen and Prince Philip to New Zealand, New Guinea, Solomon Islands, New Hebrides and Indonesia.

But Doug wasn't too despondent, as a canteen manager for nearly 20 years in the Royal yacht Britannia he had seen most of it before. During that time, he had travelled nearly half a million miles with the Royal Family, including three around the world trips and had visited most countries of the world. He had accumulated a wealth of memories. Memories of meetings and conversations with the Queen, Prince Philip, and the Royal Family and of state visits to dozens of countries. Britannia was anchored off Whale Island, Portsmouth. The Royal yacht was linked to the shore by a 600-yard-long floating pontoon. Even in the austere setting of the dockyard she looked a ship fit for royalty. Her gleaming slim Royal blue hull and delicate looking white superstructure contrasted sharply with the grey no nonsense shapes of the neighbouring destroyers and totally dwarfed a tug with a crane unloading machinery alongside.

Doug was relaxed and cheerful despite having had little sleep for eight weeks because of the pain from his ulcer. He was remaining on board until entering hospital to show his relief, Roy Massey, the Portsmouth based canteen manager the ropes. He was naturally disappointed he wouldn't be making this trip but if everything went well, he was hoping to be flown out to join the yacht in New Zealand.

Doug said that the job on the Britannia is basically the same as any other canteen manager's job: hard work. It may be the Royal yacht but still I humped beer about. I'm very much a working manager. My job is to provide a service to the ship's 250 men and when The Royal family's entourage and the Royal marine band are on board it went up to 350. But there were compensations and privileges, the travel and occasionally meeting famous people; he loved it. With Doug leading the way, they went on a tour of the ship, except Royal apartments which are out of bounds. The final touches were being put to the £1.7 million modernization of the ship. This included the installation of bunks instead of hammocks for all ratings. The separate dining halls, recreation rooms, air conditioning, improved bathroom facilities and a thorough overhaul of all the mechanical and electrical systems. The NAAFI canteen was also improved, with a new deck head, illuminated showcase, floor tiles, carpet, and office furniture. These were installed by the furnishing branch at Portsmouth.

Wherever we went Britannia was spotless. The corridors are light and airy and uncluttered by pipes and cables. Personally, signed informal photographs of the members of the Royal Family and mementos of Royal visits, hang everywhere. There are no loudspeaker announcements giving orders, these were given personally, and important messages were written on a red-hot notice board so that disturbances to the Royal quarters was kept to a minimum. Britannia was more like a five-star hotel than a ship.

During voyages, the Royal guests tend to stay in their quarters which occupy an area from the funnel aft. But they usually go on at least one tour around the other half of the ship accompanied by the yacht's commander, Rear Admiral Towbridge. When they do, they usually stop at the NAAFI canteen. This way Doug has seen the Queen six times. The most memorable meeting took place, however, at Buckingham Palace in 1963 when Doug received from Her Majesty the Royal Victoria medal in recognition of outstanding service to the Crown. It was a great honour and a great day for him, the high spot in his life.

Doug said the essential qualifications for his job are a willingness to work hard and a respect for the Royal Family. Also, this is no job for a married man. You are very rarely at home. Doug was 55 and a bachelor. He had joined NAAFI in 1939 as a trainee canteen manager, after

2½ years with a Meadow dairy shop in Chatham High Street. He had two stepbrothers who were canteen managers and they persuaded him to join. If someone had said that It would lead to him travelling the world with royalty, he would have said they were mad!

After training his canteen manager at the Royal Marine barracks, Chatham, Doug joined HMS Hambledon at Gillingham. Other postings followed including a spell with HMS Ivanhoe from which he narrowly escaped with his life when it went down off Holland during the war. Postings to HMS Queen Emma, India, Scapa Flow, Gibraltar and Plymouth followed until 1953 when he was offered the job on the Royal yacht.

He still remembered vividly the day the job came up. He was at one of NAAFI's annual sports days at Mitcham. Cyril James, who was now assistant Comptroller of supplies, but was then with NCS, asked how he'd like to manage the canteen on the yacht. He was looking for a move but really after a job on something bigger like an aircraft carrier. Later in the afternoon he bumped into an old district manager friend from Chatham and he said that he should take it. At first, he was nervous at the thought of meeting royalty, but you soon get used to seeing them around.

When at sea Doug and his assistant Stephen came under the jurisdiction of the Navy, Doug wore the new uniform of a chief Petty Officer, Stephen that of a junior rating. They were the only canteen managers in the NCS to wear uniforms. Part-time sailors they may have been but both men still got seasick. After many years it still gets bad when the going gets a bit rough, and they usually go along to the medical centre to get some tablets and hang on. He was once ill for 9 days when they hit a terrific storm in the Pacific. Stephen had been with the NCS for a year, but he joined Britannia in the August from HMS Hampshire.

Old men serving on the Royal yacht are specifically selected and are in some way the cream of the Navy. Yachtsman wear uniform similar to the normal Navy dress but with their trousers, which have a black silk bow at the back, being worn outside their jumpers so they also wear plimsoles and their working dress badges are white instead of red. Every man is trusted and expected to behave well at all times, and they do, said Doug.

According to the Royal yacht commander, the canteen had always given Britannia excellent service, and invariably met their many requests, managing to obtain the seemingly impossible.

Fifty per cent of the crew were permanent. The other half, mainly officers, do two years on the yacht. Many of the men catalogue their lives by Royal events. They talk about the car they bought after getting back from the honeymoon cruise of Princess Margaret and Lord Snowdon, or the holiday they had after the Queen mother's convalescent crews. The crew isn't changed around too much as the Royal Family like to see familiar faces when they come aboard – it is, after all, their home.

When Britannia is not at sea the canteen opens seven days a week. It stocks all the usual items but not beer, which is supplied directly to the messes. The day starts for Doug and Steven at around 0700hrs and they get up to get the canteen ready for early customers for the 0745hrs to 0830hrs session. They then have breakfast and restock for opening intermittently from 1015hrs to 2100hrs in the evening. The schedule when Britannia is in dock is a little easier as they get Sundays off. But they always try to open every day because the lads appreciate it.

The worst part of the job was actually getting the goods on board before the start of a very long voyage. They came from the stores at Anson Road, Portsmouth and are delivered to the end of the pontoon. It was then their job to bring them on board from there. We go out with a wooden barrow and haul them down 600 yards or so to the foot of the gangway and then have to carry them aboard. Which is not very pleasant when it rained.

The day before David Lloyd's visit, Doug and Stephen had finished loading the last delivery, which included 6000 cans of beer, 140-5gallon barrels of beer, 1,000,000 cigarettes, and 5000 cases of minerals. More stores would be taken on at Singapore and in Australia. All the beer was brought out by boat but provisions we bought on board in the barrow. It meant about 100 journeys backwards and forwards along the pontoon, nearly 35 miles.

When the stores eventually get on board, they are distributed to 8 storage locations in varying sections of the ship. They were better off for storage space than the canteens on fighting ships where space was at a premium. The canteen does its best business when Britannia docks for a Royal visit, particularly when homeward bound. Despite the attractions and festivities onshore, Doug always opened the canteen for the men remaining on board. It's business as usual for us, he said; his dedication paid off and did record trade when Britannia was moored at Singapore on her way home from the Royal Family's visit to Bangkok. All day sailors queued to order stereo equipment, radios, cameras, food mixers and watches, presents for the folks back home. Doug's most consistent sellers are goods that have the Britannia Crest. Things like lighters, ashtrays, and postcards. They sell like hotcakes wherever they are in the world.

When royalty is on shore on official visits, the host country usually invites the crew of Britannia, including the NAAFI staff, to sightsee tours and receptions. During his 20 years with the Royal yacht, Doug had been to many places way off the beaten track and once spent a week on an Australian sheep farm in the Outback. His favourite countries were Australia, New Zealand, and the West coast of Canada. But he says there is no place like England with its green fields and trees.

In his off-duty hours at sea, which he says were rare, he sunbathes, reads mainly autobiographies and plays deck tennis. When he gets back to England and goes on leave, he heads straight for his house at Gravesend. "After all the travelling I do during the year it is great to just be in one place for a while and relax."

1975

Inflation kills sausages and savouries 1975

After 22 years of sausage and savoury food production, NAAFI is to close its meat factories at Portsmouth and North Hykeham. The closures at the end of August 1975 had been made necessary by the increasing inflation, which has made it uneconomic for the company to produce its own sausages, sausage rolls, pasties and so on. The closures brought redundancies of 114 NAAFI full-time factory staff. Bill Crawling, executive director, said, 'There has been a considerable amount of light-hearted comments in the media about the closure of these factories and the disappearance of a NAAFI "Banger". For the managing director and for all of us in the NAAFI management team, the redundancies which in some measure inevitably result from the closures. 'Our factories have an enviable record of efficiency and the products have been first class, naturally, we have given the most serious consideration to their future.' Unfortunately, overall economic circumstances in the UK at that time, required regarding trade generally, meant that smaller producers such as NAAFI could not manufacture products as cheaply as the giants of the trade. By buying from one of these giants, they are obtaining products more cheaply than the cost of those they were manufacturing themselves. This they did if they were to preserve their profitability and the interests of the forces of whom they existed to serve.

Concerned about the redundancies, NAAFI management met representatives of the union of shop, disributive and allied workers, together with Mr Earnest Fernyhough, MP for Portsmouth, in the June of 1975. Among the questions raised were those of terminal benefits and these were discussed further as redundancies started to happen.

As far as the company's customers were concerned, they will still be able to buy first class sausages and savoury products at the family shops and NAAFI clubs. However, the only difference being that they were produced by an outside company but one that had a high reputation for its trade.

Production of cakes ends 1975

Production of cakes and pastries at the Hereford and Krefeld bakeries had ended. This movement that the only NAAFI bakeries still baking cakes at that time with those in Berlin and Malta. Cake production in the UK had already ceased in June of 1974.

The end of cake production in Germany was a matter of economics, said Paul Beerli, controller of bakeries and factories; once again inflation had taken another great part of the company. Rising costs meant that it was now cheaper for them to buy cakes from Cadbury's or McVitie's, who have the facilities and the market to make the long production runs.

Krefeld and Hereford would continue to produce bread, bread rolls, fancy breads, meat pies and savoury products, and also handle the distribution of Cadbury's and McVitie's and Dutch products. The end of NAAFI cake production in Germany meant, however, that they had to re-examine the position of the bakeries there. The decision then was made to close the Herford bakery by the January of 1976 but then they also had to decide to invest more modern machinery to streamline production and facilities in the Krefeld bakery.

The news of the closure of the NAAFI cake filtered through to the customers in ES where there was a flurry of last orders for specials. The last cake to come off the Krefeld production line was for an order placed by a NAAFI employee Jane Turk of the ES marketing Department. Jane ordered birthday cake for her God-daughter. When Jane took delivery of the last NAAFI cake, the first delivery from Cadbury and McVitie's was being offloaded at Krefeld for distribution to shops in Germany and Belgium.

EFI serve five nations in Turkey 1975

A 7-man EFI team, led by district manager Mr Gallagher, operated a shopping club from the cover of a couple of army tents and ran a bulk issue store from the back of a four-tonne lorry on the exercise in Turkey. With 5000 troops from 7 countries they were taking part in 'Exercise Deep Express', which simulated a war on Turkey's northern border. Although the American contingent came equipped with a PX store, they would accept only dollars so the Belgian, Dutch, Turkish and German forces joined the British troops in the NAAFI, where all types of currency were welcome. 'The Turks wanted to barter for everything,' said Peter Webb of the central administrative service, 'so we played along by quoting vastly inflated prices then letting them knock us down to the true price!'

Conditions in the arid wastes of the Turkish Thrace were rather Spartan, TMO Richard Illesley reported. 'You had to take a shovel with you to the toilet, so you could dig your own hole. We did have a day off to go to Istanbul,' added Peter who was taking part in his first exercise with EFI. 'We managed to get a lift with a Land Rover, so it only took about an hour and a half to get us to the city for the exercise area near Corlu. We had to return by chat train – for some reason Turkish stations aren't in towns, they're in the middle of nowhere, the journey took 5½ hours, and the train stopped miles from Corlu. We have to hitch a lift into town and then get a taxi back to camp.'

After nearly a month of battling with sandstorms the EFI men flew home all except Amesbury driver Roy Baines who got the job of driving a Land Rover back across Europe.

Dividend stamps proved popular with customers 1975

Customers at the family shop, RAF Henlow, were no longer asked stamps or discount as they pass through the checkout. For the next few months, it was a case of stamps only as Henlow's shoppers test the new dividends savings card scheme. Instead of sticking their stamps into the traditional savings book customers used a stamp card which took 90 pence worth of stamps. The full card was worth £1 if it was used to buy goods in the shop and that included groceries, cigarettes, wines and unlike existing bonus dividend certificates which can only be exchanged for non-grocery items. Alternatively, filled out partially filled cards can be exchanged for the face value of the stamps.

The shop manager Kingsley Bryant found that the majority of the customer approve of the new scheme: 'Many customers used to complain about the bonus certificates couldn't be used for groceries, in fact some of them preferred to cash the stamp books at face value rather than take the certificate. Before the experiment started, we explained the scheme to the customer relations committee and the wives club and also sent an explanatory and savings card with along with the regular 'Wise Buys' leaflets distribution. So, most customers knew all about the scheme when it started, and we didn't get too many problems.'

Unlike savings books, which had to be cashed in at the office, the completed cards were accepted at the checkout. It was just like taking pound notes to the till, commented the Sweda operator Ann Twigg. The customers like being able to spend the bonus on groceries. NAAFI staff get double stamps and had completed 4 cards in just over 2 weeks.

There had been a few complaints from customers who preferred discount, one man even walked out of the shop in disgust on the first morning, said Mr Bryant, but he was back the next day and started saving stamps. A few shoppers also remarked that the new scheme gives less bonus, 11% instead of 25%, given the bonus certificate for two full stamps books. 'They were generally satisfied when I explained the groceries and wines carried less profit than the durables,' commented Mr Bryant.

Mrs Winnie Hamilton, married to a Sergeant at the station, was shopping with her two small children and thought it was very useful to be able to spend the bonuses on groceries she said but apparently it is not really enough, she'd rather save for two or three pounds.

The trial continued until April 1976. The Henlow shop was a favourite with research and development experiments and there were generally half a dozen ideas under test there.

EFI men keep step on the inside right 1975

Britain went to war in October 1975; thousands of reservists throughout the country received urgent phone calls and telegrams instructing them to report immediately to the unit's headquarters, and just as in 1939 thousands responded to the call.

The practice mobilisation, codenamed 'inside right', involved 30,000 of British reserve forces including 40 NAAFI men of the Royal Army Ordnance Corps Expeditionary Force Institute, who gave up their weekends to take part in the exercise.

Maj Bob Randerson, officer commanding RAOC EFI, who called out his men on G Day 1 (Go Day 1), explained: 'the exercise was designed to test contingency plans to mobilise regular and reserve forces in the event of a war in Europe, to reinforce NATO forces, and to allot home defence tasks.'

The EFI men were all at the Mobilisation centre in London less than 24 hours after the call out to members. Andy Dungay and Ken George, who were NAAFI NCS drivers, had to make their way from Davenport, while district manager Richard Gaymer, EFI newest commissioned officer, had to come from Edinburgh. Richard Gaymer had a special problem getting to London on time: 'Fog at Edinburgh Turnhouse airport grounded all flights and I was delayed 3 hours, but I still managed to get to the centre on G Day 1,' he said.

Club manager Gerry Feber, who recently had taken over the junior ranks club at RAF Hendon, had to be at his club until the late hours for a regular Friday night disco, but he still arrived at the mobilisation centre in the early hours of Saturday morning.

After everyone had reported at the centre, the documentation and issuing of uniforms had begun. 'I wanted to make the whole exercise as realistic as possible,' said Maj Randerson, 'so I instructed certain people to present the reception staff with some of the problems they might have to face in a real situation. One chap had to ask to be excused as his wife was expecting a baby, while another was to say he was to appear in court on Monday and therefore could not serve. I'm glad to say that the reception staff dealt with all the problems efficiently and with good humour.'

The fully kitted and documented unit were then formed into five sections. One section was dispatched into a temporary mobilisation centre to be issued with EFI entitlement to weapons, ammunition, tentage and transport, the remainder moved off to Wingham, NAAFI training centre in Surrey, where they set up camp in a field adjoining the training centre. 'For some this was their first outing with EFI,' said Eddie Gallagher, district manager for Camberley who was messing and canteen officer on the exercise, 'so they were able to practise more simple tasks, like putting up tents and cooking with Primus stoves.' Although Capt Gallagher described these tasks as simple, there were more complicated tent erecting efforts and several portions of baked beans were served flambe.

The climax of G Day 2 was a get together around a blazing campfire. 'An important aspect of any exercise is to foster a spirit of camaraderie. After all,' explained Maj Randerson, 'some of these chaps may find themselves having to work together in the future on exercises, it helps if you are already friendly with the chap whom you might be stuck with in an isolation station up a Norwegian mountain for a long period.'

This spirit was fostered by plenty of beer and the camp comedian. 'Every exercise produces a comedian and when people's spirits are getting low, the comedian in the party can always be relied on to show himself,' said Maj Randerson. The jester of 'inside right' turned out to be storeman from Amesbury warehouse, Nigel Kent. He was soon generally known by his nickname Betty because of the impressions of an actor Michael Crawford's character Frank Spencer (who stage wife is called Betty). When it came to encourage the singing, Betty was quickly on his feet giving a unique rendition of Old MacDonald's farm.

The last day of the exercise started earlier than expected. The majority of EFI members were just getting used to the canvas camp beds and sleeping bags, when there was a bomb alert which proved to be a false alarm. That was 0400 hrs. At reveille, 3 hours later, it was obvious that a few had not been able to get anymore sleep.

The unit assembled in the nearby woods for the day's exercises organised by ex-RAF man Liam Doole, Electra at Wingham. These proved to be an initiative test/obstacle course. An area was marked off in the woods and designated a minefield. Each unit had to work out how to cross the area carrying a 55-pound Jerry can of petrol and using a combination of fallen trees and ropes. Another complication was that only two members of each unit were allowed to use fallen trees to get across.

Derek Howard Bud, district manager for Thetford clubs, was the first to lead his group across a minefield. 'I think everybody thought it was easier than it looked,' he said afterwards, 'but then I think some of us made heavier weather of it then we should have done.'

'The exercise may have provided many of the EFI members with a great deal of amusement, especially at the expense of one or two of the groups who got themselves into all kinds of trouble, but it taught me a lot about the men, our organisation, and our procedures,' said Maj Randerson.

1977

On a rock in the mid-Atlantic March 1977

Sunday the 27th of March marked a new era in NAAFI history. For the first time, NAAFI staff would be providing a service to a basically non-military community, the residents of a small, almost barren island in the South Atlantic.

In 1501 a Spanish Explorer by the name of Juan da Nova first sighted the lofty peaks of a volcanic rock we now know as the Ascension Island. Lying between the continents of South America and Africa, roughly equal distance from the coast of Brazil and Angola, the island was found to be abundant in bird life but low in Equatorial vegetation.

Some of the names later given to places on the island, like hollow tooth, bears back, devil's cauldron, conjure up visions of Pirates and buried treasure. Indeed, the island had an interesting history with Pirates once plundering a British ship within sight of the Garrison.

William Dampier's ship, the Roebuck, was wrecked at Dampier's drip in 1701. A Dutch sailor was castaway on the island in 1725 and survived five months on turtles and goats. Capt Cook called at the Ascensions for turtles in 1775 during one of his voyages in HMS Resolution. A British Garrison was established in 1815 to prevent attempts to rescue Napoleon Bonaparte from exile on St Helena, to the South East.

In 1836 Charles Darwin visited the island in HMS Beagle. In 1899 the Eastern Telegraph company, now Cable then Cable and Wireless limited, laid the first cable from the Cape of Good Hope to Ascension. British servicemen were withdrawn from the island in 1922 although British administration continued.

The island had changed little over the years. Turtles, yellow and purple land crabs, lizards, clawed toads, scorpions and large centipedes are common sights on the rocks and beaches. The extensive bird life included noddies, petrels and frigate birds. Cable and Wireless, the British government owned company at the time, continued to provide the bulk of the island's population but had now been joined by the BBC, the PSA (property Services Agency, previously the ministry of public buildings and works), the composite signals organization, Bendix, NASA, and an American Air Force unit.

The principal British organisations joined together from London Uses Committee (LUC) to run 2 shops, the butchery, bakery, slaughterhouse and a farm complex in 1974, the LUC asked NAAFI to examine the operation and advise. In February 1975, at the expense of Cable and Wireless, David Newman (who became assistant regional manager in European service) flew out to make an on the spot assessment.

Mr Newman reported that there were three main areas of habitation: Georgetown, two boats and the base (manned by United States Air Force personnel who had their own PX store and clubs). At the time there were 1200 people on the island. Georgetown was the centre for Cable and Wireless employees. This company was responsible for maintaining the web of submarine telegraph cables linking the United Kingdom to the Cape of Good Hope, West Africa and Central and South America. The main shop was located there. Two boats were some 10 minutes away by motor vehicle. The smaller shop here was used by the employees of the BBC and PSA.

To operate the two shops, bakery, and butchery, 12 staff were employed, of whom three worked full-time at two boats. Many of them did more than one job – assistant manager Michael Vincent, for instance, doubled as a slaughterhouse and butchery manager. Derek Lupson was then a district manager, South Wales who went out to Ascension early in 1977 on attachment, to supervise the shop and bakery operation for a year, during which time NAAFI would be able to obtain first-hand experience and formulate plans for a takeover.

John Morris, manager of the overseas service, flew out in the December to finalise these plans. He met the heads of the organisations on the island and worked out the final plans for NAAFI to take over the shops, butchery and bakery on an agency basis from the 27th of March 1977. The company would not be involved in the farm operation. Mr Morris returned to the UK and Mr Lupson just before Christmas when district manager Eddie Right flew out to take charge of the operation.

Mr Morris reported on his return that the shops were well laid out and stocked and attractive. The bakery and slaughterhouse, he noted, were equipped, and the butchery had an excellent display, serving into the self-service area of the main shop. Some 15 local sheep and five pigs were slaughtered, dressed and butchered every week for the island's population. Beef was imported from South Africa. The bakery in Georgetown produced 300 lb of bread each day but did little in the way of cakes and bakes and rolls. All of the currently employed staff that worked in the areas being taken over by NAAFI would then become fully employed personnel for the company.

The supply of goods was as it had always been, 60% from the UK, 30% from South Africa and the remaining 10% from the island's farm on Green Mountain. The UK's supplies arrived quarterly by ship although top up supplies were delivered by Mail vessels which visited the island every three weeks, or chartered aircraft which fly to Ascension a few times a year, carrying mainly fresh fruit and vegetables from the UK. Just about every item offered normally to service personnel by the company would be sold in the shops on the Ascension Island, including clothing (from Marks and Spencer's) which were previously not stocked. They will be able to have access to the Littlewoods catalogue and the NAAFI catalogue.

Sales drive by Jeremy Dennis About Eric Hicks 1977

It takes character to build a working environment which includes a raptured hunting horn, cream doughnuts, pictures of nude young ladies, and a pink potty. One such original is to be found on the NAAFI mobile canteen located in the middle of the beautiful Norfolk countryside at RAF Coltishall. He is Eric Hicks, who has been driving round the station for 26 years. Covering over 200,000 miles and using up 9 vans in the process. His first mobile was a 3-tonner from which he sold only the basics, tea and cakes. This was in the days when there were no private cars at all at Coltishall, only bicycles and a few service vehicles. The extravagance of his present stock, everything from fresh fruit, cakes and hot pies to pencils, cigarettes and postage stamps, is now displayed in a Ford Transit van which carries its own gas fired oven.

Shining through all of Eric's work is a rounded sense of humour. In his never-ending efforts to increase turnover and bring in more business he has developed a number of gimmicks. This explains the role of the brass hunting horn – it was once used to terrorise people into making purchases or, as Eric puts it, attract them to the van from further flung corners of the station.

The pink plastic potty was a conversation piece which made his exchanges with his customers somewhat different from those of the average Vendor and purchaser. He confides that it also has a subsidiary use. Eric's sense of humour is a vital part of his character and it must be for any ardent Norwich City supporter. He said that he will do anything for a laugh and, in support of this, there is a selection of jokes, cartoons, and photographs pinned up on his notice board for the entertainment of his clientele.

The jokes, many of them made by the customers, are changed every day so that there was always a fresh incentive to visit the mobile. When people are queuing up for service their attention is drawn to the board which has brought together many a potential buyer and seller. There can be few of the mobiles which are responsible for the sales of televisions and cars. When they are there, there was even a notice advertising a modern semidetached bungalow in a quiet cul de sac. Now if only Eric were to charge the agents commission for this service.

The working day is a long one. The baker makes his delivery at 0630 hrs and the rolls have to be filled before Eric has started his rounds, so the club staff started early to get it all done in time. At 0830hrs Eric departs and does not get back to the club before noon. Then the morning's takings are totted up and the van restocked for the afternoon session which began at 1430 hrs and ended at 1645 hrs. Somewhere in between Eric had to find time for his lunch.

The first shop of the morning was outside the airfield at the NAAFI shop where the school children congregated on the way to lessons. Eric describes this as one of the highlights of his morning. 'You should see the kids, it's a really nice way to start the day.'

The next stop is the guard room and the hangars, towers, radar huts and so on. He stops at over 20 sections which means that he opens up between 50 and 60 times in one morning or afternoon to approximately 500 people. He had a fairly regular timetable. 'I keep to the same route and they come to rely on me for their breaks in the morning' but it is subject to fluctuations because he will always wait for latecomers and revisit sections where the internal response to his call has been small.

Through it all he managed to keep a smile on his face, even when the desperately hungry resort to blocking tactics. While we were with him, Eric tried to move off from one section only to be stopped by a towering truck parked directly in front of him, forcing him to open up once again without a hint of complaint. Eric's relationship with his customers accounts for much of his success, if at some stage he hasn't got what somebody wants, he makes a point of getting it before his next round. 'I enjoy the job mainly for the company. They all know me, I make it my business to know people.' He managed to deal with all of his customers with maximum speed and yet stays on first name terms with many of them.

The customers have a soft spot for Eric too, and some have made their presence felt by painting squadron badges on the side of the van when he wasn't looking. His popularity can

be explained by his attitude to life. 'If I can help anybody, I will. And I like to have a laugh and a joke.'

Club manager Rosemary Norton said that when Eric goes on leave, the takings drop dramatically no matter how hard the other staff tried to make up for his absence. He has now been made responsible for the ordering of his wares because he knows better than anybody what demand for any particular item is to be like.

His involvement with the job is such that he made some modifications to his van which could not be done by outside contractors except for at great expense; he went out of his way to get a cold storage space fitted so that he can provide ice cream in the summer. This will increase his workload even further but there would be no complaints from Eric.

Eric has built up quite a service which has earned him renown and praise from customers and from other NAAFI staff. Yet, despite his fame and popularity, Eric shuns the publicity. He told me, 'I'd rather do things behind the curtains.' So although he was reluctanct to have this article done on his contribution, he allowed it to be published in the May edition of NAAFI News 1977.

The Royal Connection1977

NAAFI had had a long and happy association with royalty. Since its inception in 1921, the company had served the forces of the Crown under 4 monarchs: George V, Edward VIII, George VI, and Elizabeth II.

The earliest recorded Royal visits to NAAFI establishments took place in 1927 when the then Prince of Wales visited the Kennings Way warehouse. One year later, King George V and

Queen Mary visited Kennings Way and Imperial Court. The interest of the Royal Family in NAAFI became particularly keen during the war years, when members of the Royal Family visited many canteens and clubs to talk to the sailors, soldiers and airmen and they usually had some words of appreciation for NAAFI staff.

It was early in the war that Queen Elizabeth II was introduced to NAAFI when, as Princess Elizabeth she and her sister were taken, by their mother, to spend an afternoon at NAAFI training centre, Woking. In January 1946 Princess Elizabeth opened the Portsmouth club, first of the post-war town clubs to be built on wartime profits. The association was a notable 'first' as it was the princess's first solo public engagement.

In the first ever NAAFI News the Princess was described as a radiant young girl of 19, with eyes of English blue, and a lovely complexion with an enriching smile, looking upon us with a gracious friendliness as to put us instantly at ease. In two minutes, Princess Elizabeth had conquered us all.

A year later His Majesty King George VI granted his patronage to NAAFI in recognition of its services to his majesty's forces. In the same year Her Royal Highness the Duchess of Kent opened the Colchester club. In 1948 the King visited the recently opened Chatham club and HRH the Duke of Gloucester opened the Roundabout Club at Aldershot. The Catterick Club was opened the following year by HRH the Princess Royal who had been one of NAAF India's most frequent Royal visitors during the war.

When Elizabeth succeeded to the throne, she followed the precedent by her father and graciously bestowed her patronage on the company. In the first 25 years of her majesty's reign not a year had passed which NAAFI had not had the pleasure of welcoming a Royal visitor formally or informally. And the occasions almost without number on which NAAFI had served a Royal luncheon, tea, or dinner. There was a consistent connection between

NAAFI and the Royal household through the service the company provides to the Palace staff canteens.

As Prince Charles, Princess Anne, and Princess Alexandra reached maturity they too started to take the same interest in the company which was shown by their parents, aunts and uncles.

Some of the more notable events that NAAFI provided was the catering in the Great Hall of the Royal Hospital, Chelsea, when the army council held a dinner in honour of the Queen in 1956. The Queen was seen at the centre of the Royal table with the Queen Mother and Princess Margaret.

Princess Anne opened RAF Honington's new shop shortly before her marriage in 1973. At the Aldershot horse show a year later she watched her husband, Capt Mark Phillips, competing in the NAAFI service team jumping competition at the Aldershot horse show. Capt Phillips' team finished third.

The first Royal visit to a NAAFI shop by Prince Charles was Montgomery barracks in Berlin. His Royal Highness asked 'could I have a look around? I have never been in a NAAFI shop before.' It would be safe to say he enjoyed his visit.

Silver Jubilee medals 1977

In 1977 the Silver Jubilee year, 14 NAAFI staff had been awarded the Queen's Silver Jubilee medal in recognition of long, faithful, and distinguished service. Previously the Coronation medals were awarded to 88 members of the company, these included a typist, or waitress, or lorry driver, club and canteen managers, clerks, a bakery inspector and a field and headquarters official. Only three of those who received the Coronation medal were still with NAAFI. They were Edward MacGowan, managing director, EJ Bill Crawley, executive director in charge of administration, Western Europe and William Hall, shop manager at RAF station Leuchars in 1977.

1978

New Managing director 1978

As Edward MacGowan stepped down as managing director, Brian Whitaker stepped in. Brian had been with NAAFI for some 25 years at this time and although by now he had a touch of grey his philosophy had developed, and his attitude matured. Although these two were quite different people and undoubtedly would have differences in style and emphasis, their objectives were the same: prosperous company, satisfied customers, and happy and contented workers. He believed these objectives were completely independent.

The changes which would undoubtedly happen in subsequent years with the utmost respect of the changes his predecessor had already brought. He was basically a trader, the appointment of a trader at this time was undoubtedly a calculated move to bring the right kind of change at the right time. so as from the 1st of January 1978 Brian Whitaker would represent a breadth of experience in trading, administration and the law, finance, marketing, and supply. He could only build upon the successes that came before him.

New outfits for shop and club staff 1978

The shop management staff at RAF Wittering had given their approval of the latest design of overall for the shop and the club staff and a dress for the management and assistant managers. They thought their dresses were a vast improvement on the old design and A line was so much better than the pleats of the old style as they found them more flattering to the larger figure. The dresses themselves were 90% polyester and 10% flax, the pockets were outlined with a saddle stitch and the dress zipped up the front and belts were optional. Shop assistant Eileen Broom, Margaret Canham, Shirley Campbell, Diane Johnson, and Julie Pennington found the new assistant overalls more practical. The girls said that the zip at the front saved them losing their buttons when loading shelves or carrying boxes. The Royal blue check overall is made of the same nylon material as the previous one, but the hope is that it would be changed to polyester cotton at a future date.

After the trial period Mrs Rockett, who is a member of NAAFI protective clothing committee, made some recommendations. These included cutting the armholes of the overalls and the dresses one inch deeper to allow for easier movement, and supplying belts for larger dress sizes.

Cool customers, Exercise Hardfall 1978 by Suellen Butler

Orders for the army on 'Exercise Hardfall' were much the same each year but supplies for the Marines in this year could not be based on previous experience. 'The needs of the commandos on 'Exercise Mainspring' were arrived at by an educated guesswork,' said Mr Caddey. They had to rely on their estimates when it came to ordering supplies. Goods sent to Exercise Mainspring North, included 182,000 12oz cans of beer, 17,000 cans of minerals, 30 1½ lb tins of N-symbol coffee, 1440 4oz packets of tea, over a million cigarettes and 1000 bars of chocolate. It was important to strike the right balance, even NAAFI oversupplies, then the return cost of the freightage falls on the company. If there was a shortfall, then NAAFI was failing in its obligation to provide the right service, potential sales are lost, and then there is the added expense of resupplying if possible.

In addition to the experience needed to estimate quantities, NAAFI must try to anticipate tastes. Bacardi was the 'in' drink for several years, with NAAFI hard put to supply sufficient for everybody's needs in the first year. Then there was a sudden switch to vodka and NAAFI was left with cases of rum while the men on exercise only ordered vodka.

All supplies are carefully and individually priced in the marketing department and costed under the supervision of senior group leader 'Bunny Burrows', Fred Narbrough, administrative official and Sidney Barnard, manager of export branch. Those for the advanced parties go out with the first troops on an RAF flight. Most items then were obtained from Amesbury or the Portsmouth warehouses and include such delicacies as water chestnuts and bean sprouts.

Duty free supplies of toiletries and perfume came from Germany and customs documents must be produced at the port of shipment to prove free exportation or the company becomes liable for the duty. Chris Christie was responsible for invoicing all supplies and Nancy Gryphon detailed the shipping arrangements. This was ensuring that the right orders reached their respective locations on time.

A major setback was caused by a dispute at Grimsby docks. The supplies for the Exercise Mainspring would jeopardise only for one week before they would do in Norway, but export branch managed to take delivery on time by rerouting them through Felixstowe. The inevitable losses through the breakages and theft were dealt with by Reggie Mears, who looked after the marine insurance. When the excitement of the exercise was over it was Mr Bernard's task to arrange the reimportation into the UK of any goods which had not been sold. These were sent to the Portsmouth warehouse for manager Stan Luff to sort out, which could prove difficult when cardboard containers had become damp from the Arctic.

Choosing men for these exercises was not easy. Maj Bob Randerson, OC EFI, was briefed by Mr Caddy on how many were needed, and he made the selection from those willing to be away from the UK for between one and three months. The difficulty of replacing staff for such long periods, especially during the winter, is a headache for home service North and South, European service, the controller of training at Wingham and on this occasion NCS. Replacing district managers was particularly difficult – where possible training management officials, near the end of the training, were used. They also had to consider the men's careers as well. The exercises provided valuable experience but would have to be careful not to have particular people away for too long or too often.

Before going to Norway, NAAFI EFI men received training in the technique of Arctic survival from 48 (ACE mobile force land) company, RAOC, to prepare them for severe conditions in which they would be working. It was essential for the men to learn to live under canvas and adjust quickly to freezing conditions. The reservists themselves thoroughly enjoyed these exercises. It gave them a chance to meet their customers face to face whilst on exercise. Where possible, NAAFI stores were placed in buildings. This is not for the comfort of EFI men but for security reasons and to ensure that the beer and minerals remain drinkable. The accommodation on Exercise Mainspring South was a condemned building. Capt Kevin Storey, district manager Cambridge, said, 'There was no hot water at first and then even the cans of beer froze.' There was plenty of physical work involved too. 'When stores arrive, they all have to be manhandled which isn't easy in Arctic conditions,' said Capt Storey. The truth of this statement was brought home to him when a pallet of beer crushed his foot and he had to be prematurely flown home suffering from a broken foot.

Salalah Shop switches to a do it yourself operation. 1978

The NAAFI shop in Salalah, Oman, was given a facelift. The Salalah shop, with another store at Masirah, supplied groceries and household goods to members of the sultan's army and Air Force plus a sprinkling of Britons on secondment or contract. The district manager David Stevens said the shop was closed for five days in June, so that it could be redecorated and refitted as a self-service store.

In those days there was no team of shopfitters or furnishing inspectors in attendance, But Mr Sammy Anthonipillai, finishing fitter, rose to the occasion. He was from Sri Lanka (Ceylon), and a jack of all trades; he was ably assisted by Ken Rockett, the district accountant, who gave a credible performance as a carpenter and electrician. All the salesman chipped in to help. The team worked through the Friday and the Saturday until midnight. At 2300hrs on the Sunday it was agreed that they had finally finished the self-service shop, and all that remained to do was to stock the shelves and arrange the displays and advertising literature.

An official opening ceremony happened at 1030hrs the next day, so the working party carried on until 0200hrs before taking a break. They started again at 0700hrs and had every packet and tin price ticket in position before 1015hrs. After the opening ceremony by the Wing Commander Martin Bee, officer commanding the Sultan of Oman's Air Force, staff member Sammy switched hats and became the driver of the store's Mobile Shop, and makeshift van conversion that was another recent introduction.

Sultanate of Oman. Memories by David Stevens 1978

In 1978 I was posted to Oman to look after NAAFI's activities for the Sultan of Oman's Forces.

My military 'boss' was a real life-like Lawrence of Arabia character. I was based in Salalah in the south of Oman and used to have to go additionally to Muscat, the capital, for military liaison and to Dubai on buying trips. At that time Dubai was literally a desert with only limited buildings – one hotel etc. Not like now!

My staff were mainly from South India and Sri Lanka. Assisting me was a NAAFI District Auditor.

It was really seat of the pants stuff with one visit during my 15 months there from the head of NAAFI Overseas Department. I was responsible for basically everything, to do with our operation where we had shops and clubs, for both local Oman staff and the various nations that had been seconded to the Sultan's forces.

Being based in Salalah it was basically a war zone as they were being attacked from time to time by South Yemen. It was also the time when the Sultan of Iran was deposed and many of his Iranian troops had also been seconded to Oman. They were unsure what to do when the revolution took place.

Interesting times. Oman was progressive but deep down in the South of the country there were rigid rules re alcohol, and I had to ensure that only entitled personnel – i.e. foreign nationals – could obtain such supplies. Twice we were "prosecuted" at the local religious court – once because somebody who was not entitled stole a bottle of whisky and once for being accused of selling a watch that did not work! Scary moments.

EFI take on NATO exercise 1978

Thirty-six EFI men spent a month on a NATO exercise in Germany in the autumn of 1978. They were giving the same support they would be expected to give to troops during wartime. They supplied such items as postcards, paperbacks, razor blades, soap, polish, dusters, radios, beer, wine, spirits, and tobacco. The British element of the 100,000 strong NATO force on 'Exercise Bold Guard', and 'Exercise Provident Gesture'.

Capt Richard Illsley, a district manager in Northern Ireland, and Capt Dave Satherly, a trainee management official, set up and ran a bulk issue store and nine shops for the 9000 British troops on exercise 'Ex Bold Guard' in Schleswig-Holstein.

Twenty-four reservists from the UK and European service helped run the shop and store. They included NAAFI drivers Ken George and Taffy Davis, from Plymouth and Amesbury respectively, who took 2 four-tonne Bedfords across to the exercise area and drove them in a continuous shuttle service between the store and shops. Demand for NAAFI goods was so great on 'Exercise Bold Guard', that an extra shop was operated from the bulk issue store itself.

The 6th field force, the land component of the UK mobile force, was a major customer. Its presence on the exercise, where it appeared in full strength for the first time was to practise the defence of Schleswig-Holstein and Jutland, the key to the Baltic entrance to the North Sea and to promote an effective working relationship between NATO forces.

When they arrived at the location allocated to EFI, Capt Illesley and his team were confronted with an empty field. The building which had been selected on the recce was no

longer there. By the end of the day they had managed to secure a hangar opposite the German army barracks and were providing a service to units the following day. Typical enthusiasm shown by EFI men, despite tough conditions. They kept their shop open throughout the night and on one occasion to provide a service for troops returning from the field and moving out within a couple of hours. The 6000 British regular and TAVR servicemen from 7th field force on 'Exercise Provident Gesture' were also served by a team of EFI reservists near Soltau.

Life changed on exercise from normal shifts to a 12-hour day, seven days a week but the morale of the staff was very high, and people seem to thrive on more work and these sorts of conditions. For many of the EFI staff that had gone out on this exercise, it was their first time, but in true style they responded remarkably well despite the conditions that they had to work under. EFI had given a splendid service under the most trying conditions, working long hours, cheerfully without seeking recognition, was the compliment given by the UK mobile force news sheet called Guardian.

1979

The Malta Story 1979 by Fred A Court

The tiny sun-drenched Malta island, that strategic spec in the very centre of the Mediterranean, had been like a mighty magnet to the maritime nations of the world.

Britain won the last great contest, in 1800, when they drove out the French with a little help from the Maltese themselves. Britain had defended the island ever since, notably during the Second World War when 16,000 tonnes of German and Italian bombs rained down on the island and its people in just two years. For bravery in the face of such an onslaught, the whole population was jointly awarded the George cross. But now the British had left. The final farewell was marked by fireworks which paled in the echoes of the Second World War bombs.

When the 5500-tonne destroyer HMS London sailed majestically away from the island on the 1st of April 1979, the only foreign force left on what had been called the world's greatest natural fortress was a helicopter group of 60 Libyans. The sailing of HMS London was the final scene in the 179-year story of the British Malta Association. The NAAFI thread in that story had, of course, been much shorter, just 58 years, although the NACB and the ACC operated on the island before the company was formed in 1921. Before those organisations, the British contractors Richard Dickieson were supplying service canteens on the island. It was known that the Corradino canteen was built in 1897 at a cost of around £7000 back then.

NAAFI presence had been comparatively short, but the influence and effect it had on Malta had been far from insignificant. Not only had the company, over the years, been in the forefront when it had come to introducing new ideas and modern concepts, such as self-service shops and frozen foods, but at the time of the withdrawal, the staff probably had more years of service than any other company on the island. Underlying the fact that the company's island headquarters was called Imperial Court also, for 30 years this had dominated a prime site at Marsa, just two miles from the capital Valletta. It looked out over the island's main port, grand harbour; the NAAFI headquarters was built before Mersa begin to grow into a thriving commercial and business centre.

Overseeing NAAFI operations in Malta for three years prior to closure was John Fisher. He had the difficult and delicate task of winding up the company's affairs before March. When he arrived on the island in 1976 many clubs and shops were still in full swing. Headquarters was buzzing with the hectic activity of over 60 workers, 30 of which were administrative officers and the rest in the adjoining warehouse and other support services. A fleet of over 20 NAAFI vehicles was still running. The large Royal Navy hospital at Mtarfu was still operating, and consuming large consignments of goods delivered by NAAFI. The Royal Navy ships were constantly sailing into Malta and taking on supplies. Last but no means least, the NAAFI bakery, situated just down the road from the headquarters, was baking over 3500 loaves of bread and 1250 cakes and savouries a day for consumption by service persons and their families.

John Fisher was tasked with winding down all operations on the island: 'My role was to run down NAAFI service in a phrased operation according to the requirements of the services. We had to link our closures with their withdrawal, and so it was necessary to work with the services planning staff under the commander of British forces Malta and air commander Malta.'

Throughout Mr Fisher's time hardly a week went by without the closure of some of the services installations or shops. As a result, scores of buildings were vacated and people posted elsewhere, which meant, in turn, less demand for NAAFI services.

As a result, the need for accurate assessment of stock requirements to meet the falling demand and warehouse manager Franz Muscat explained: 'It was a question of slowly cutting away the quantity of stock but always having enough to keep going. Eight weeks' supplies of imported goods was always kept at the warehouse to supply all NAAFI establishments. It meant at the end relying on goods produced locally rather than from the United Kingdom.'

The Royal naval hospital closed in 1977. They had been supplying several services to the hospital. There was a ward service for patients, cafeteria, and a shop with a delivery service. They were also operating a club for the hospital staff. Three major closures were HMS Saint Angelo, which had been used as a base shop for the Mediterranean fleet since 1912, St Andrews barracks, home for Royal Marine commandos and St Francis Ravelin, at Florianna, used by various services. Several clubs and shops were run in all three establishments. By mid-March only one club, the Gladiator at RAF Luqa, was still functioning. It was under the management of Vincent Degiovanne who joined NAAFI in 1939 as a bread delivery man. This wasn't the first time that Vincent had seen the closure of a shop; he was the last services shop manager at the famous St James' cavalier in Valletta before it closed. As well as supervising the closures of clubs and shops, Mr Fisher had to dispose of all NAAFI equipment and transport and help settle the future of his staff.

The staff on Malta, a large number of them long serving and many of them second generation NAAFI, are sad that the company's long association with the island had to end.

When all the packing had been done at Imperial Court, the office equipment removed, and the warehouse emptied of the few remaining items of stock, Mr Camilleri took a final walk around and reflected on the past. The footsteps and voices echoed around the empty shell. 'I started work for the company in 1928,' he said. 'In those days the Mediterranean fleet consisted, if I remember rightly, of four battleships, four battle cruisers, five light cruisers, 2 aircraft carriers, repair ship, a submarine depot ship and about 10 submarines, plus supply ship which NAAFI had a share in. At that time NAAFI had two main buildings on Malta, St James's cavalier and Santa Vennera, which had the warehouse, meat factory, the original bakery, and mineral water factory, furnishings, and transport section with equipment section. '

The billiard table mechanic who was based in Santa Vennera, serviced 80 tables on the island in NAAFI establishments. The Malta Imperial Club, which was formed in January of 1929, was particularly strong in billiards and during its first year beat every ship in sight with the exception of the fleet champions, HMS Resolution. They had only lost to them by 770 to 782. Mr Camilleri clearly remembered the opening of Imperial Court in 1949, which replaced the Santa Vennera complex. The opening was performed by Brigadier WN Hamilton and the building was blessed by the Vicar, Admirals, generals, and air marshal were there, plus a good selection of leading Maltese businessmen. The building itself was probably the most impressive in the area at the time. On the ground floor was the duty-free warehouse which supplied the fleet, together with furnishings and equipment stores and the local produce store.

On the 1st floor was the administrative offices, another duty paid warehouse which supplied the land-based clubs and shops. On the top floor was Imperial Club and the staff canteen. From the balcony there was a panoramic view across the grand harbour. The view was even grander from the flat roof. Channels were built along the roof to pipes which run down into a well underneath the building, providing the builder with his own water collection system.

There were many tense and hectic occasions, the Suez crisis was one of them. The troops were flown there before going on to Suez; nothing was known by the staff until the 11th hour. They were all recalled from leave and told what was happening and they remember with satisfaction that NAAFI was ready and waiting to serve the troops as they flew in at 2200hrs. Every time there was a crisis in the Mediterranean it affected Malta, this was probably because the island was so central, and Britain was then a very important power.

Mussolini's invasion of Albania in 1939 was one of those occasions. In 48 hours, the fleet was supplied. They worked day and night. The Second World War, of course, saw NAAFI at its most active on the island. From June 1940 to June 1942, the island was almost constantly bombed by the Italian and German air forces. Although the damage done to the buildings was considerable, human casualties were few, but George Tabone, a district accountant who had worked alongside Mr Camilleri during the withdrawal, was one of them. In 1942 he was in EFIU working as a shop clerk. He said, 'I was going on duty at 0700hrs at St Andrews barracks when there was an air raid without any warning, it was just one aircraft, I remember seeing it dive and I thought it was going to crash.' Then he saw the bomb drop. 'There wasn't time to dive for cover. There was a tremendous explosion. I was taken to the blue sister's hospital which was very near St Andrews. The next morning, I was transferred to the military hospital at St Patricks because I was EFI. I was there for 10 months with a broken leg. It didn't heal any quicker because we weren't getting any proper food. There simply wasn't the food available. I was lucky to be alive.' Mr Tabone had a permanent limp as a result of his injury.

The manager of the NAAFI bakery at Marsa has for 17 years been Joe Cassar who joined NAAFI in 1942. The bakery supplied bread, cakes, pastries, and savouries to families, shops, visiting ships, and other service establishments. For 15 years before it closed it also had messing contracts with the army and the Navy. It continued to supply bread for the services right until the final withdrawal. The bakery's busiest time was in the 1950s when 10,000 loaves a day were being produced. At that time the bakery operated 24 hours a day with 80 staff working in shifts. During the Suez crisis, bread production rose to 20,000 loaves a day. During the 1970s the figure declined but two years previously, during the strike by local bakers, the Malta government through the British High Commission, asked NAAFI for help with essential bread supplies.

Approximately 50 extra people were taken on and bread was supplied to hospitals, orphanages, and similar organisations. During the three-week strike, 300,000 loaves of bread were baked in addition to the normal services quota. The bakery continued to employ 10 people, baking bread for the services, until withdrawal deadline; it was handed over as a going concern to air supplies, the catering subsidiary of Air Malta, the national airline.

Malta, the government owned shipping company, were taking over the Imperial Court building. Their withdrawal had been very well organised, the operation between NAAFI and the services before John Fisher left the island at the end of March had meant that the run down had gone smoothly and was on target all the time.

When Belize breezes Blow by Dudley Williams 1979

Belize is land of wide brown rivers, palm trees, lagoons, and orchids, bound by Mexico to the North, Guatemala to the West and South, and the Caribbean to the East. Inhabited by sand flies, caiman, armadillos, land crabs, mosquitoes and possums, to name but a few of the residents. Its human population was a colourful mix of Mayan, Carib, African, European, and Garifuna. They are happy-go-lucky people known for their friendliness and great hospitality.

Formerly known as British Honduras, the country is roughly the size of Wales, and by coincidence its highest peak, Mount Victoria, is the same height as Snowdon. Much of the land is low lying scrub or mangrove swamp and the remainder is jungle covered mountains with a few pockets of cleared areas growing citrus crops, sugar cane or rice, and some cattle ranching.

Located in the subtropics the temperature in Belize is usually in the 80s or 90s throughout the year. It is very humid and has a hurricane season which lasts from June to November. The last hurricane before I left was called Greta. It left behind a trail of devastation and floods. The airport camp escaped the brunt of the wind's force, but at holdfast the roof of the club was blown off. In Belize City, the ensuing tidal wave broke the sea wall and flooded the city to a depth of four feet. When it receded, it left behind a thick layer of black, stinking mud. Some houses were washed off their timber stilts and one was left high and dry in the middle of the road.

The evening before Hurricane Greta struck, I had crossed the Hawksworth suspension bridge into San Ignacio. The wide, brown river flowed quietly some 80 feet below. By 2300hrs that night, trees were flying through the air horizontally and the rains poured down. Shortly after dawn I drove back across the bridge, but now the waters were around 4 feet below the bridge and downstream, many square miles of countryside were covered with swelling torrent.

Many memories of Belize will remain with me. There were, for instance, the four burly, bronze Scottish Sgts bounding through a field of waist high bracken very intent on catching their prey, one of the thousands of butterflies that abound in Toledo district. There was the annual crab walk in October when the land around the airport camp became a seething moving carpet of land crabs making their way from the swamps to the coast. All shapes and sizes, with shells of many colours from purple to yellow, from blue to olive green. Last year an extra-large one invaded the NAAFI office and took refuge behind a filing cabinet. Its waving claw just daring to attempt any removal. Lastly, there is the memory of the beating the retreat in the floodlit lawns of the governor's house in Belize City. The band of the first Royal Welsh Fusiliers in white uniforms with scarlet sashes. The white timbered old colonial mansion and, beyond, the lawn with its torn flag post, the open bay with the ship's lights twinkling in the harbour. One felt as if one had stepped back into the pages of history in the old empire days.

EFI give frontline service to 'Exercise Steel Trap' 1979

The frontline service NAAFI gave during 'Exercise Steel Trap' was a new experience for customers and RAOC EFI men. The exercise, in Germany, was the first in which NAAFI territorials had been asked to serve in the 'war' area of an exercise (as opposed to general war situations). Most of the trading was done at the basic camp in Reinshlen where Capt John Williams and 18 men run a bulk issue store, 2 shops and a Mobile Shop, for members of the logistic support group and for all 7000 of the exercise training troops passing through the reception and transit camp.

A two-man team, Cpls Gordon Sweeney and Larry Todd who ran the reception shop at Reinshlen, opened at 3 in the morning to supply a convoy that was passing through. With the names of Sweeney and Todd their partnership was inevitable as the teaming up of a horse and cart. Shops were open on a 24-hour basis and on the run down of the exercise, said Capt Williams, to ensure the troops were catered for before they return to the UK.

The EFI men were, as usual, ready to provide a 24-hour service and in addition to long working hours, they were expected to 'stand to' with all the regulars at any time of the day or night to repel invaders. The order to ship goods to the frontline was received at 2000hrs and chocolate, cigarettes, mineral waters, and 1000 cases of beer were assembled and loaded at night. Cpls Mike Andrew, Bill Nimmo, and John Logan rushed three loaded full tonners to the forward maintenance area to deliver the goods before dawn.

A bulk issue store and shop was set up and run by WO Russell Smith and Sgt Nigel Silveston to sell these items to the frontline troops. EFI's role in peace time is to practise giving a service to the troops in war situations, and the NAAFI territorials who for the rest of the year are storemen, club assistants, drivers, and district managers. They make the most of these opportunities to show just how well NAAFI can supply the services under war-like conditions. They fully justify all the work that goes on behind the scenes ordering the supplies and getting them to the exercise areas on time.

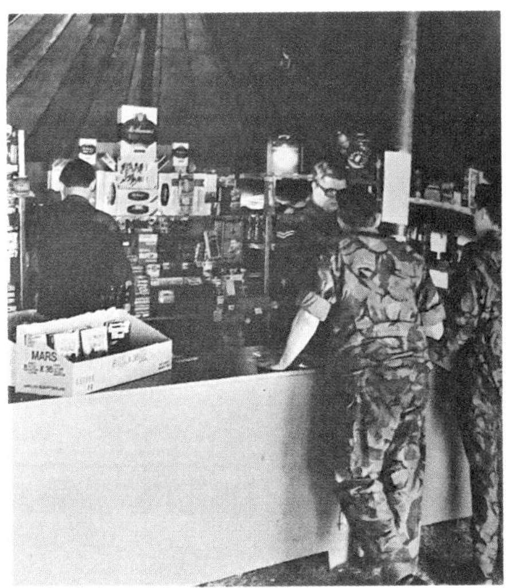

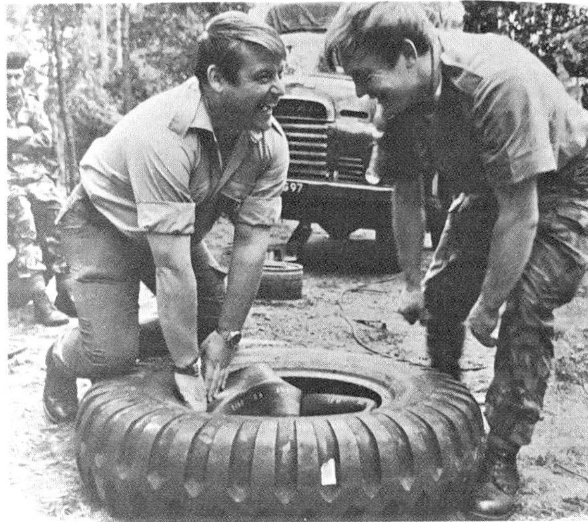

1980–1989

1980

Furnishing. The forgotten branch by Colette Warner 1980

The ambassadors of the furnishing branch are the furnishing inspectors and the teams of fitters. These are the people in the firing line when units are unhappy about some aspect of club furnishings, or when headquarters are worrying about the budget, or a club manager wants to know when his new bar stools are going to arrive.

Ron Miller, who covered the South Central, looked at it in this way: 'We are usually the first NAAFI people in the clubs, and the last out. While the building is still a shell, we are discussing decor with the unit and with property services, planning furnishings for staff living quarters and keeping an eye on how the club will take shape. When the party is over and the club is closing down, we are still there sorting out all the equipment we installed, way back, and finding a new home for it even if only a temporary one at Ludgershall warehouse.'

Keeping track of furniture once it has been issued could be a problem. In an article on Belize in the December NAAFI news, finishing inspector Howard Streeter had mentioned that chairs disappeared from clubs and were rediscovered in the backs of army trucks. Soldiers were using them to make their forays into the jungle more comfortable. In the UK, bar stools have been offered as prizes in clubs' darts matches. They also had the problem in the clubs which was shared by two units, each with its own inventory holder. The first service man checks the furniture on his side, finds that he is missing a few chairs and helps himself to the other side. When the second inventory holder finds himself low on furniture, he starts looking at his colleague and takes him back and so, it went on.

Stocking and ensuring timely developed delivery of all the other items of furnishings and equipment required by NAAFI clubs was a demanding task. The catalogue of items at Ludgershall warehouse ranged from a teaspoon to a snooker table. Over 200,000 beer tankards would have to be replaced every year and there were 25 other types of glasses in use in addition to crockery and cutlery, kitchenware, curtains, carpets, and lino. Some 800 snooker tables were in use by servicemen around the world, over 300 custom made table tennis tables and almost 200 pianos. Besides clubs there were all NAAFI shops and offices and staff quarters to furnish, equipped and maintained, not to mention all the crockery and equipment needed to cope with the hundreds of caterings NAAFI undertook each year or the glasses and crockery hired to messes for their special functions.

Steve Markham looked after NAAFI Financed furnishings unsaleable, he would find anything the unit required. Peter Robinson concentrated on the general equipment and also monitored the club's cleaning scheme, which would be administered by furnishing branch but paid for by the MOD.

At the warehouse Tony Budzinski and a team of 10 were always available to supply tentage for summer camps, open days, caterings, and other outdoor events. Amusement and gaming machines were also provided by the furnishing branch, were an increasingly popular source of entertainment and a source of welcome welfare funds for units. With the help of Dolly Morgan, and Chris Russell, they looked after something like 850 gaming machines, 2000 amusement machines and 350 jukeboxes: 'The great success of the 70s was the introduction of video machines,' he said. 'In the 80s their use will certainly boom.'

Everyone in finishing branch were certainly looking for a way to improve the overall image, to keep up with the current trends. Ken Radford, assistant manager of the branch, explained if the customers liked the atmosphere in a club they would come back, and this branch's major contribution to the atmosphere is the colour schemes and finishings. However, there was a limit to what they could do. 'We work to a strict budget from the MoD at present. It pays for all that goes into the servicemen side of the counter through the ISFS – interservice furnishing scheme.'

Each finishing inspector works to annual budgets, the size of which is decided at the beginning of each financial year. He then has to deal with requests from any number of units and field officer officials, who feel that their own needs are the greatest. As a vital part of the job it is the responsibility for establishing priorities and selecting furniture clubs according to their individual needs. His choice was made from a range of carefully chosen with young, energetic servicemen in view. Mr Bradford pointed out some of the things that had to be borne in mind when selecting new furniture for clubs: 'It was no good choosing button backed chairs; they would soon be buttonless. Foot rails on tables quickly get scarred with heavy boots. Wooden top tables are a terrible temptation to carvers. Vinyl covered chairs get picked out, and stuffing pulled out. The use of long bench seating required careful choice of situation – you only need one rip in the cloth and the whole lot has to be replaced. Bowlegs have to be avoided as they are not strong enough. So do wheel back chairs, which are easy to break and hard to repair. Really the list is endless,' he said.

Colin Smith, furnishing buyer, puts it more emphatically: 'nothing is servicemen proof and there are always a few vandals, phantom carvers, flashers, and scribblers. Some units pose more problems than others and furnishing inspectors are always aware of this when they are choosing new schemes. The club attached to a vehicle workshop, for instance, had to be greaseproof, and pattern fabrics are used to hide stains. The club attached to a hospital is invariably kept clean, servicemen who spend their days crawling under tanks are supplied with robust furniture.'

Mr Miller again: 'We are low priority in the MOD's eyes, so we don't get enough cash to be adventurous. However, the money would go further if it wasn't for the damage done by the customer. Call it vandalism, call it high spirits, either way it costs money. It is hard to convince the service man that he is not helping his own cause, that he pays in the long run. In one club, I recall some scratchproof Formica tables were installed. Unfortunately, the label stating that the Formica would not scratch was left on one of them – you can guess what happened. Soon the Formica was riddled with scratches. The unit had to pay for a new tabletop from the welfare funds, and the OC posted the old one up as a notice board, explaining how much it costs for the boys to have their fun.'

But David Liddiard, manager of the furnishings branch, had observed the current beginnings of a change in attitude: 'Men would like to bring their wives and girlfriends into the lounge bars in evenings, and we are trying to cater for their tastes, their greater acceptance of responsibility for their clubs.'

The Pegasus club, Lyneham, the idea was encouraged by manager George Aqualina. The result is the new bar, which is proving a great success, has become the blueprint for a new bar at South Cerney. However, shortage of cash meant that nothing could be replaced when it is still in good condition, even if a new scheme is being designed by Bob Fowler, the PSD designer. So, Mr Fowler often had to compromise in his schemes, to include some fabric, for example, that could not be dispensed with.

Nevertheless, the clubs of the 1980s were a far cry from the wet canteens of the early days, with their long refractory style tables and benches. The best of them had bars designed on the same lines as pubs in Civvy Street and the restaurants had been replaced with the popular vending and pub grub served from behind the bar.

Records set at arms exhibition and Army show 1980

Prince Philip was among the VIP guests entertained under NAAFI canvas at Aldershot during the British army equipment exhibition. For the headquarters catering team, the occasion set a new record: it was the biggest ever event with 2500 lunches served over 2 days.

The menu included such delicacies as Scottish salmon fruit savarin with rum, and strawberries with cream. Catering Superintendent Stanley Kennedy was busy seeing to the particular needs of foreign delegates and ensuring that the waitresses did not offer any alcohol to the teetotal Arabs. In the troop tent the regional team served the men who were at Aldershot to set up the army show. Two days later the same team opened their doors and the doors of the now vacated VIP tent to serve the thousands of members of the public who went to the show.

The district manager Mike MacDonald and RWS Angela Cockrill were convinced that NAAFI was the only company willing or able to operate to such scale: 'Who else would provide all the facilities necessary from tentage through to silver and glasses at those prices?' they asked. Tony Budzynski, manager of the tentage warehouse Ludgershall, providing a total of 120 tents and marquees for the show, as well as floorboards, show stands, boilers, and counters.

Miss Cockrill clearly saw the event as an opportunity for pleasure as well as for hard work: 'Many of the casual staff come every year. They take their annual holiday so that they can come. It isn't money that draws them because they really enjoy the event. One girl had travelled all the way from Worksop to be here. We are operating an officers' tent, a troop tent, and a public tent so we won't run out of things for the girls to do!'

NAAFI girls invited to join TA 1980

NAAFI girls who envy their male colleagues the adventurous EFI life will be happy to hear of the latest recruitment moves by the Territorial Army. Basic training experience meant they could enrol with the catering corps volunteers, enjoy varied training programmes featuring weapon training and tactics, and spend time on exercise with the Territorial Army units. There are promotion prospects too. After two years with catering corps most girls will have reached the rank of L/Cpl. And there are further rewards in the shape of bounties. Tax free bonuses of up to £300 could be one for loyal and continuous service in 1980.

The 15-day training programme, held at St Omer barracks, Aldershot, began soon after enlistment. Students visited the catering colleges throughout the country, given presentations, and learned basic military skills. The assault course and weapon training are optional for female students, but all the girls invariably join. After training, the volunteer will usually spend a minimum of two weekends and one fortnight with the Territorial Army at their training camps or on exercise, helping to supplement any catering staff shortage.

Contracts are for three years but there is an opt out clause should a volunteer decide to leave. Their initial contract, volunteers are enlisted on a yearly basis. Female applicants, who must be aged between 17 and 35, needed to contact the headquarters for the central volunteers' details at Aldershot. This was a massive step for women and this meant finally female EFI staff could join their male counterparts.

NAAFI on Crusader 1980

Over 18 NAAFI men donned the uniform of the RAOC Expeditionary Force Institutes to practise their wartime role in Crusader 80. Supported by other NAAFI staff throughout northern Europe, they provided a 24-hour service to the 86,000 men and women who took part in what was the biggest peacetime exercise involving British troops. The RAOC EFI contingent was also the biggest ever mobilised for manoeuvres.

The crusader story began in Britain as thousands of troops converged on transit centres near airports and docks to await transportation to Germany. Wherever they gathered, and whatever time they arrived, they usually found a NAAFI canteen or mobile waiting for them. At Victoria barracks, Windsor, a team led by manager Isabella Brampton kept the club open for 72 hours nonstop as more than 4000 soldiers passed through on their way to Heathrow.

It was a similar tale across the country at Shorncliffe where Dibgate summer camp was opened up for 1000 servicemen bound for the ports of Dover and Folkestone. Alan Evans, district manager, Hazel Jones, RWS, John Morris, trainee DM, and Nancy Barnett, manager at Howe barracks, supervised a two-day shift system to give the troops a continuous service.

At Cavalry Barracks, Colchester, a former NAAFI club reverted to its former use, temporarily. The building, recently a thrift shop, became for a few days a canteen shop for the crusader troops. A team led by the district manager Dave Drury provided a day and night service there for the soldiers en route to Harwich, with a total of 30,000 men passing through on both outward and return journeys.

Down at Harwich docks, a six-man team complemented the NAAFI service with two mobiles. As the troops returned, several days later, the mobiles were once again there to greet them. The staff are exhausted but pleased that the service had been appreciated, said Mr Drury. When the hard work was over, they got together for a celebratory fish and chip party.

A NAAFI tent was pitched in the old airfield at Normandy barracks, Leconfield, to serve the 3800 troops travelling to Europe via Immingham docks. Disaster almost struck when fierce winds flattened the tents during the busiest weekend, but the staff quickly transferred to a former air traffic control building and the business was resumed under supervision of management team Jim and Jean Thornton, and RWS Jane Whitelock. Troops returning through Leconfield were met by three mobiles sent from RAF Binbrook. Further north in Cumbria, 'Exercise Square Leg' part of Crusader, meant a busy time for Catterick staff.

An aircraft hangar was transformed into a canteen at 48 hours' notice to serve 1000 soldiers passing through, and at Catterick, staff gave a service to battalions of paratroopers on their way to a mock 'communist infiltration'. Meanwhile more civilian staff in Germany were already busy catering for the first arrivals. During the months that followed, temporary canteens were manned, long hours were worked in the club's backing up the EFI canteens, and bulk issue stores provided immediate service to units arriving for the exercise.

Warehouse deliveries were made to strange places along muddy tracks which exercised the skill of the drivers to the utmost and officials who had laboured long in preparation for the exercise were on constant alert, changing plans as the army's requirements altered.

Life in the field for the majority of EFI was less than glamorous, working all hours of the day and night in muddy tents, sleeping in the back of the tented bulk issue store, shaving in cold water in the darkness of a chilly September morning. But whatever the difficulties, beer, food stuffs, cigarettes, all the home comforts reached the troops wherever they were exercising at whatever hour they needed them. As a contrast, the allied press Information Centre at Heildesheim, EFI run a bar for the hordes of international newspaper, television, and radio correspondents covering the exercise. It was also a visiting port for innumerable VIPs including Francis Pym, the minister of defence.

The EFI press centre team, smart in their red dress trousers, white shirts, and bow ties, never departed from the high standards despite long hours, and Capt Gordon Vaughn had every reason to be proud of his detachment and their efforts. NAAFI used Crusader to flex its wartime muscles. EFI troops were controlled from a marquee in the Waldniel Compound, manned for 24 hours a day throughout the exercise, where Maj Bob Randerson, OC EFI, and his headquartered detachment established their troop mobilisation centre.

Immediately the HQ was established, Maj Randerson and his staff began work. Marquees were erected, uniforms and other military equipment drawn, and drivers sent to Antwerp to collect Land Rovers and 4-tonners, so that everything in the field was ready to greet troops as they arrived. EFI men arrived one day, were kitted out, documented, briefed and, when necessary, given final training before being dispatched. They manned locations from Het Loo in Belgium, to Hildesheim, 425 kilometres to the east, they ran canteens, services shops, bulk issue stores, and mobiles.

Crusader comprised two principal exercises, 'Exercise Jogtrot', the reinforcement of NATO forces in Europe from the UK and 'Exercise Spear Point', the culminating battle fought by

1 British Corps. 'Jogtrot ' involved moving forward 10,000 regular reinforcements arriving from the UK during the 1st to the 11th of September, followed by 20,000 TA from the 13th to the 15th of September. The huge influx of troops had to be sent to the battle zone, and NAAFI service in the area was vital. It was best demonstrated by events on the Dutch-German border some 3 kilometres from the village of Leuth, a convoy point where a stop was made for refuelling, rest, feeding and buying personal supplies.

At 0300hrs in the dark of Tuesday the 2nd of September, the full EFI contingent was at stand 2, awaiting the imminent arrival of 137 vehicles. Tea and coffee were ready, rolls filled and wrapped, tills primed with plenty of change. The EFI waited until 0800hrs when the weary troops eventually rolled in after endless delays. They refuelled and parked and were overjoyed to find EFI tents in attendance. Colonel A Robertson, deputy commander of the Rhine Army, was delighted and surprised at the depth of service provided.

There was no respite for EFI. Before the last of the convoy one was rolling away, convoy two drove onto the site. Later a line of vehicles pulled in with 400 unscheduled passengers on board. Arrangements had been made to accept Sterling cheques and notes, in addition to German deutschmarks and American dollars, but some soldiers were also trying to change Danish bank notes (received on the ferry), a problem that was not foreseen. Another problem presented itself, when almost without fail, the troops offered large DM notes for small purchases, and eventually the float of change run out. WO Ray Docherty sped away to a nearby bank to rectify the shortage, but eventually even that source dried up and the manager was forced to call on other banks further afield for fresh supplies.

Leuth was planned for closure on the 11th of September when EFI Capt Brian Newland and his detachment deployed to Het Loo in Belgium, but a change of army plan brought more TA convoys through on the 13th to the 15th of December. At short notice another EFI team was raised to continue service under Capt Kevin Royle, just arrived in Germany as a district manager. A few days later, an EFI detachment headed by Capt John Williams from JHQ shopping centre was serving yet another convoy making its way home at the end of the exercise.

The army began work on the plans for Crusader in 1978 and it was March 1979 that NAAFI administrative official Eric Golding first heard the exercise mentioned during a routine conference. 'Over a long series of meetings at HQ BAOR, the army's plans gradually crystallised,' he explained. 'By February 1980 we're at a stage where "recces" could be made to the various locations to determine what kind of service would meet their requirements. In some places the local junior ranks' club or shop would cope, in others the EFI would be required. The picture gradually evolved into a plan of action in which every Department and resource of NAAFI ES was a part.'

Torches, vacuum flasks, razors sold well at the convoy resting points. Despite the presence of a field kitchen, rolls, sandwiches and pies were bought in hundreds as well as trays and trays of minerals. A particularly good seller was produced, a Crusader T-shirt but, as always, demand was unpredictable – one detachment at Leuth bought so many that an EFI Cpl was occupied solely on selling them. Another, a few hours later, bought scarcely a single tee shirt, but left the shop with boxes of 50 King Edward cigars, which they bought 4 at a time.

A special service was the dispatching of processed films direct to home addresses, a scheme later extended to the New Zealand, Australian and USA. Scharfoldendorf, a remote and hilly site where the second battalion Royal green jackets were based, epitomised all that was best and worst about living on the exercise. Heavy rain and clay subsoil made the whole area a quagmire.

WO Dave Ryan was supposed to be running a services shop, but when the travel weary battalion arrived late on the first night, he and three staff ran a canteen service for the men from 11 in the evening until 0400hrs. They continued to supply the troops with filled rolls and pies for several days. Their service was so much appreciated, said C/Sgt Payne of two Royal green jackets: 'NAAFI had really done us proud. We'd be in an awful state without them. The EFI team couldn't have done a better job.' Cooperation was excellent and the battalion lent a ready hand to help unload fresh supplies.

One army catering Corps officer, delighted with the service he had received from the management team William and Winifred Fullerton, commented: 'never a demand refused, never "come back later". Even the US forces are using the Hameln BIS,' he added. 'They were tickled pink to be told that if they waited a few minutes their order would be ready for them. They expected they'd have to submit demands 3 days in advance.'

An emergency gift shop, manned by Cpl Steve Emery from Scharfoldendorf, was set up at bridging camp for 36 hours before the battle. It proved to be a welcome surface and exceeded all trade expectations.

At Tofrek barracks, Hildesheim, Capt Barry Starck ran a tented BIS store, a gift shop, and a tented canteen, looking after thousands of exercise troops using the base. They were forbidden to use the normal facilities but club management team Terry and Susan Mould were kept busy preparing rolls and sandwiches for the field locations. All at the Hildesheim EFI bases were featured on a TV report on BFBS. The canteen was also flooded and the floor reduced to a muddy swamp. Happily, a nearby field had just been harvested and there was plenty of straw so the enterprising EFI lads turned cleaners and a makeshift carpet soon covered the floor of the canteen tent. A television, installed by a local unit, turned the tent into a popular recreation area. For those troops who couldn't reach the Tent, a mobile service was provided by Klaus Blancbois, the same mobile that provided a touch of humour amid the stark realities of war.

The world's press had been happily popping off flashbulbs at all the sophisticated military equipment on display. But when the NAAFI news photographer decided to take some shots of Herr Blancbois on his mobile, the military police were quickly on the spot to ask if they had permission to photograph the vehicle.

At Rheinselen, EFI, headed by Capt Ian Clarke, manned a BIS and 2 tented services shop selling gifts.

In Bloomberg, Mike Simpson and his team ran a BIS and shop. They arrived on site to discover they had no tent but until the canvas arrived, they ran a makeshift service from the back of a lorry. In Sennelager behind the firing lines was a combined EFI and civilian establishment, with district manager Roger Fisher in charge. At Staumuhle Camp a few kilometres to the north of Normandy barracks, the home of HQ Sennelager training centre, WO Dave Rackham and

Martyn Willey set up a canteen and shop for the deployment phase. For the recovery, Dave manned a tented gift shop at the main barracks next to the JRC.

Another change in the army's plans required an extra canteen and gift shop at the air movement centre in Normandy barracks, so an EFI team, under WO Tim Bennett, was formed. All the facilities operated 24 hours a day during the deployment and recovery stages. When two of the men were given a day off, they stayed on to lend a hand. The flexibility of NAAFI was on trial from day one. A call from BAOR announced that they needed a refreshment service at Recklinghausen, a vehicle park with no NAAFI facilities. An Army furniture van was padded with stocks from Wulfen club and was manned by district manager Pat Lafferty and Wulfen shop manager Trevor Underwood with EFI under WO John Lake taking over for the night shift.

Although EFI played a major role throughout the exercise, civilian NAAFI staff are always ready to lend a hand. At Dusseldorf district manager Alan Mayor, RWS Elizabeth Wallace, and staff from the local club stepped in to run the canteen in a garage. At Curtis Lowe air movement centre, manageress Jane Thomas realised that many reinforcements were moving direct from aircraft to the railway station, so she packed supplies onto a trolley and took the trade to the customers. And staff under district manager Christine Harrison operated two mobiles for convoys resting after the Rhine River crossing.

The army's constant changes of plan caused a few headaches, but problems were solved quickly and won admiring comments from the services. On Saturday, sixth of September the ACC suddenly demanded 2000 haversack meals for Sunday and Monday. Colin Foster, regional manager Rhine, called Ken Gwilliam, Krefeld bakery manager, on the evening, and ordered 2000 pies. Other items were obtained from shops at Dusseldorf and Bracht and 1000 apples taken on Sunday from the Krefeld fresh produce warehouse. The haversack rations were delivered on time. To cope with many changes in plans, Maj Randerson was kept busy reforming teams, calling out further EFI men and even using his own staff at Waldniel to keep the field service going.

More unforeseen orders for haversack rations came flooding in. Original orders for Sennelager were for 12,500 rations, but a further 13,500 packs were demanded for convoys leaving the continent. Even so, by the time the convoys had travelled from Sennelager to Leuth or Oevel, the 10-hour rations had long disappeared and there was a rush to the 24-hour EFI canteens to buy fresh supplies to sustain them on their way.

Throughout the exercise both EFI and NAAFI staff adapted to altered plans and seemingly impossible tasks with unfailing enthusiasm. They worked long hours with little regard for fatigue and gained respect and approval for their efforts. Maj Randerson said, 'It was a total NAAFI effort, both EFI and civilian staff worked together for the same cause, we are extremely pleased with the Exercise and the excellent liaison between NAAFI people; the troops were the most appreciative too.'

Lieutenant General Sir Peter Leng, command of the first British Corps, echoed his troops' comments. 'Thank you for the tremendous service you and your staff gave us throughout Crusader, you met all our requirements admirably. Do please pass on my thanks to everyone;

we are often not as appreciative of them as we should be but we would all complain if you were not here to serve us so well,' in a letter written to ES Jimmy Tannock.

Maj General R Guy, chief of staff for the British army of the Rhine, said, 'The EFI operated under difficult and trying circumstances, their enthusiasm and professional attitude throughout was the subject of much favourable comment.' The final accolade came from TA soldiers Phil Crane and Dave Cudworth, usually found in the car sales and internal audit office in Nottingham. The two NAAFI men, members of RHQ troop were among the thousands of soldiers travelling to Germany. And wherever they went, they were impressed with NAAFI. The canteens always seemed to be open, commented Mr Cudworth, even three in the morning the EFI lads were cheerful and welcoming and we found the same standard of service wherever we went.

1981

Royal visitor for renovated corporal's club 1981

Early in 1981 after several months of extensive renovation work, the corporal's club at Bhurtpore barracks, Tidworth, had been re-opened by HRH the Duke of Edinburgh. The club serves the Queen's Royal Irish Hussars and as Colonel in chief of the regiment, the Duke officially opened the transformed premises on the 16th of March 1981.

He unveiled a commemorative plaque before moving on to spend about 40 minutes inspecting the building and chatting to representatives of the regiment, and to NAAFI district manager Gordon Vaughan, and the club manager David Knapp. The Duke was interested in how the alterations had been funded and Gordon explained it was a joint venture between NAAFI and PSA.

About 80 representatives of the regiment attended the opening ceremony and the Duke made a point of chatting to as many of the men as possible. Once work had started on the club's facelift the project took about seven months to complete so Mr Knapp said the scheme had been on the cards for eight years.

Where the club was just one room it now offers a snooker room, lounge, and a large bar area. Ladies' stall toilets had also been added. Mr Knapp went on to say 'a complete wall was taken out to extend the club, the original bar was also taken out in a new one fitted'. Bob Fowler, NAAFI interior designer, was responsible for the cream and maroon decor.

NCS HMS Collingwood Club 1981

A beautiful building with lots of potential, that's how manager John Bailey describes his new club at Collingwood, Fareham. The new Collingwood Club was one of the biggest at NCS, is part of an attractive 2-storey sports and recreation centre built to serve the largest naval shore establishment in the country, catering for well over 3000.

HMS Collingwood is a naval training base with courses running from six weeks to two years, but despite the transient clientele, the Collingwood Club has always had a good atmosphere. Now in its new building, the disco nights, three times a week bring in up to 600, filling the upstairs disco area to capacity. The club had brand new sound and lighting equipment, serving the disco area, the comfortable carpeted lounge and two bars. On the ground floor the Tavern bar had carpet, paid for by club funds.

The services shop attracts customers throughout the day from them those using the sporting facilities. It is the second shop on the base and Mr Bailey was well satisfied with its turnover. The automat with its five vending machines was also attracting some good custom, having

doubled the turnover of the old premises. Mr Bailey was particularly pleased with the automat's success since there are other vending facilities available on their base, at the southern club, in a well-established canteen refreshment bar for junior ratings, and in the swimming pool area.

He said: our automat is conveniently placed for the classrooms and a lot come for their morning and afternoon breaks. The new building was not only providing a better club facility but also improved accommodation for staff. 'It must be among the largest and best staff accommodation in the country,' said Mr Bailey. He lived in a two roomed flat, annexed to the staff hostel which had 11 bedrooms and a spacious lounge. At the back of the hostel, a walled garden combined a pleasant outlook with privacy. And, said Mr Bailey: 'it's really something of a sun trap in the summer.'

Only nine of the 45 staff lived in, but the hostel could accommodate 10 more quite comfortably. In their spare time the staff had access to the sports facilities, including the large indoor swimming pool. Mr Bailey spent some of his free hours keeping fit in the gym, which was only a few corridors away from his office. Kevin Holland, one of the newer members of staff who often trained with him, said over the weeks he had been there he had become very fit using the facilities.

Working conditions were equally pleasant. The kitchen, in which an increasing number of buffets and meals were being handled, was in assistant club manager Julie Nally's words 'all MoD cons and very nice'. The only complaint about the centre among staff and customers was that when something was new IT takes a little getting used to. But everybody who worked there enjoyed the facilities and were intent on building up a good atmosphere.

1982

UK staff beat the blizzards 1982

The worst weather to hit Britain in a century posed a few problems for NAAFI staff. Throughout the country they struggled through blizzards, snowdrifts, storms and floods to keep the service going.

Former Royal engineer George Coulson, who ran the combined shopping club at Hempton Close, Hemswell, Lincolnshire, camped in his office for a week. The roads were so bad he just had to stay there and keep open the shop. Like at many other establishments, Mr Coulson and his assistants, Christine Hotchin and Gwen Blow, saw sales jump as service personnel stayed on camp.

Their efforts won praise from Margaret Wilson, district manager Finningley. All of the staff struggled to get through, but they managed extremely well. Another manager to sleep on the premises was Margaret Hayward at the family shop 'Worthy Down', Winchester. Mrs Hayward was registered as disabled, as a result of a car accident four years previously. Mrs Hayward praised her shop assistants, Irene North, Jean Holloway, Grace Medland and Shauna Brooks, after 27 years' service she didn't mind a little bit of inconvenience.

Cyril Isaacs, serving his 41st year with NAAFI, stayed at the Sgt's mess at RAF St Athan, South Glamorgan to keep his shop open. His wife Charlotte was not happy with him being away, but he could never have made it the five miles home. Wales was the hardest hit area, first came the snow, then the flooding. As district manager David Satherley, South Wales, said, 'Everyone had to forget about wheels and use their legs. They all made a tremendous effort.' He had to walk to work on 8 days, abandoned the suit and wellingtons in favour of his EFI kit! It was the warmest clothing he had and despite the weather in Wales they managed reasonably well. Bob Lintott said that all of his staff coped come what may.

Manager Beatrice Price, after being cut off for two days, walked the five miles from her home, to find at the shop at Wilcot camp, Nesscliffe, had been kept open in her absence by her assistant Dorothy Walton. When the freeze caused leaks in the ceiling at RAF Sealand shop, Clwyd, manager Kathleen Hislop stayed on duty all night so that the workmen could repair the damage.

Joyce Mitchell was called to attend to burst pipes at his shop at Dering Lines, Bracken at 4:00 o'clock in the morning. Dave Thomas managed his club bar for 18 hours, single handed, When the all arms training area, Sennybridge, Powys, was cut off, John Buy, after four days without electricity, telephone, or water, opened his shop at Merion camp, Castle Martin on a Sunday to help his customers.

In Yorkshire too, flooding caused havoc. Troops were called out to rescue stranded families from their homes. That brought a boom to business for Wendy Moran, of Checkers club, Imphal barracks, Fulford. She praised her staff Margaret Grennan, Liz Richards who were absolutely rushed off their feet. The troops came in from all over the place and they stayed open on their day off. By the end of the week they were so tired. But they managed to keep the service open.

The Argosy at RAF Benson was busy because none of the service personnel could get off camp. Peter Callow, manager of the family shop, RAF Benson experienced a similar boon in sales to the manager Lucy Ball. 'Everybody simply invaded the shop,' he said, 'it was an absolute madhouse. We were nearly cleared out.' Unit cleaners Betty Copeland and Maria Silk struggled 9 miles through the ice and snow from their homes to work at the Green Mole club, Oakington Barracks, Cambridge. The journey took them over 5 hours. 'The fact that people struggled into work was reflected in their figures. Everybody did really well,' said Albert Chantler, district manager Huntingdon.

There was praise from the trading department managers for all staff whose stories came to light and for the many whose tales didn't reach headquarters. There was praise from the regions of NAAFI transport and distribution staff who managed to keep most shops well stocked.

Mike Long, transport manager, Amesbury, reported that a few vehicles were stuck in the snow because their diesel fuel turned to wax at temperatures below 9 Celsius. Some drivers slept in their cabs, one was trapped at RAF Brawdy, Haverfordwest for a week. 'They did very well in the conditions, we only had two drivers involved in accidents and neither was serious.' Mike McCue, assistant manager, Aldershot distribution depot, said some perishable goods had to be thrown away when lorries were stranded but this had been minimal. Keith Beavers, transport charge hand at Aldershot, added: 'I've been with NAAFI for 15 years and, though I've seen snow and ice before, that was the worst winter I've ever experienced.'

Queen Elizabeth 2 set sail for the south Atlantic 1982

As 3000 uniformed passengers embarked on The QE2, Southampton docks echoed to the sound of military music. The dockside was alive with loved ones and well wishes. They were brave smiles, cheerful waves and not a few tears. For many there was tender kisses, farewell hugs, and parting words and because they were British, there was a last cup of tea, shared beside the NAAFI mobiles standing in the shadow of the great ocean liner.

Pressed 3 deep against the ship's rails, the men of the Welsh and Scots Guards and the Gurkha Rifles craned to catch a glimpse of their nearest and dearest. The multi-coloured streamers that normally go hand in hand with a cruise liner's departure were missing. Instead, her rails were lined with sheets and placards bearing menacing slogans directed at the Argentinians, between messages of love and the promise that 'Bill Bailey will be coming home'.

It was proving a long day for the small team of RAOC EFI men who manned the mobiles, Capt Pat Lafferty, Sgt Andy Dungay and Jimmy Nicholls, and Cpls Paul I'Anson, Mike Hammond and Mark Dale. They were among the first on the scene and were ready for business by the time the first contingent, the Welsh Guards, arrived with the dawn. Business continued steadily throughout the day as the rest of the troops arrived to claim their berths.

A week before 'The Queen' sailed, the plan to provide a mobile service was drawn up by Portsmouth district manager Dennis Lafferty, Pat's brother, and Irene Bardsley, manager of the excellence steps club and shop at Portsmouth. Visiting the docks to arrange for water and electricity supplies for the mobiles, Mrs Bardsley was delighted to be given a guided tour of the ship. 'It was an unexpected pleasure, I was very impressed; it didn't look like a ship inside, more a floating hotel of unashamedly luxury.' Mrs Bardsley is herself a service wife, husband Frank was in the Red Caps and an army careers officer and had been at Portsmouth for seven years.

The day before the QE2 sailed, the staff were kept busy making sandwiches from 50 loaves, loading 1 mobile and preparing stocks for the second mobile and a Transit van. The Lafferty brothers were working together for the first time. Only brother Tom was missing – he was attending a Wingham Seminar.

At 2 minutes past four, QE2 slipped her moorings to the sound of the military band playing 'we are sailing' backed by an impromptu chorus of sirens from the ambulance and fire engines parked on the dockside alongside the ship. A flotilla of small boats escorted the liner out of the Harbour as she sailed for less friendly territory, while helicopters hovered above her.

On the dockside, those left behind waved and cheered until they were hoarse, and the ship was out of sight. The EFI team soon found themselves serving queues of people who needed to calm their throats and emotions. At last, only the NAAFI mobiles and supply van could be seen on the deserted dockyard.

Our man hailed a hero of HMS Ardent June 1982

National press and television hailed a NAAFI canteen manager as the hero of the task force sent to the Falkland Islands. After the British landings at San Carlos, they heaped praise on 32-year-old John Leake for his part in the battle to save the crippled frigate HMS Ardent from further enemy attack after a savage pounding.

As Argentinian war planes continued firing at the burning, sinking ship, Mr John Leake, who had 'death before dishonour' tattooed on his arm, was reported to have led his team of machine gunners in the last act of defiance. In the Times newspaper he was dubbed a NAAFI Tiger, while the Daily Express called him a civvie hero of the Ardent. Similar headlines were used in other papers and on the BBC and ITV News bulletins

Mr Leake's moment of glory came almost three years after he joined Ardent, his first posting as a canteen manager, and added to the proud record since he joined NAAFI in 1977. In 1979, he was commended together with his then assistant Gerry Downing, for the excellent service provided during a 10 day 'Exercise Highwood', when the canteen was manned around the clock. Popular with the crew, he represented the ship at rugby and hockey. Also, in 1979 Mr Leake, who completed his training aboard HMS Hermes, now the task force flagship, HMS Charybdis and HMS Arrow, won a £20 NAAFI award for suggesting a cassette display rack for use in ships canteens.

His career before NAAFI included spells as a security guard and a storeman and, for a year, he ran his own retail record business. He previously served with the first battalion Devon and Dorset regiment from 1966 to 1973. Undoubtedly, the weapon training he received then came in useful as he fought the Argentinian aircraft.

When the frigate finally went down, he and his assistant, Nigel Woods, were amongst 178 survivors; 22 members of the crew were missing presumed dead. He was commanded in the House of Commons by Sir Peter Emery, which followed in the traditions of ships' canteen staff, many of whom were awarded medals for brave actions during World War 2, including the youngest ever recipient of the George medal, 16 year old Tommy Brown.

Preparing for an emergency by Liz Hutton 1982

The RAOC Expeditionary Force Institute's first permanent peacetime force had been established at Wingham, home of NAAFI TA unit. The eight-man team, drawn from throughout the company, is known as the EFI cadre. Its members have exchanged their family homes for two years under canvas and postponed their civilian careers in favour of an intensive military and administrative training. They will form a highly trained EFI nucleus, capable of quick response to all foreseeable emergencies in peacetime and in war.

In 1983, they will be joined by 6 more men, and will use their newly acquired skills to train and instruct those recruits. In 1984 they will return to civilian life, the new recruits will take their place, and the third group of EFI men will become part of the cadre to be trained in turn. And so, it will go on. Plans for a cadre were planned several years ago. Explained Maj Bob Randerson, OC EFI: 'Trading Department have always found it difficult to release men for exercises, which might last 13 weeks. The point was emphasised two years previously on exercise Crusader when 80 men were called into EFI service. It was obvious then that one of the answers should be a permanent EFI team.'

He launched an appeal for volunteers through the pages of the EFI newsletter. The response was tremendous – about 40 men applied for the positions. And he had to choose whom he felt would work together as a team. The temperaments had to be a blend if the cadre were going to succeed. The composition of the force had been predetermined. At the head would be a district manager, followed by a district accountant and a variety of staff ranging from club managers to a driver. Extensive EFI experience was not essential, the main qualifications were compatibility and enthusiasm.

Pat Lafferty, the Dusseldorf district manager, 13 years with NAAFI and an EFI Capt, was chosen to lead the group. His 2nd in command, WOII John Perrott, a district accountant in the European service. They were joined in the March of 1982 by Plymouth HGV driver Sgt Andy Dungay, Stanmore shop manager, Sgt Jim Nichols, Cpls Paul I'Anson, Catterick shop assistant, Mike Hammond, store man at Hounslow, Golden Sweeney, storeman at Dortmund, and Arthur West, a barman at WRAC college, Guilford, who at 20 was the youngest member of the team.

Each of the men was totally enthusiastic about his new lifestyle. It was a marvellous compromise between the army and civilian life, explained Cpl West, Sgt Andy Dungay former soldier with the Royal engineers, the cadre provided the perfect outlet for his army training. It had given him the opportunity to use his background to the full advantage and hoped that the experience he gained would be a boost for his career.

Maj Randerson was determined that enlistment would not jeopardise their civilian careers. Although the men will be away from their usual jobs for two years, they will be learning subjects which will be a great benefit to them, accounts procedures, how to run a store and a host of administrative tasks. The training and experience they gain should prove considerable assets to them in the future. While civilian skills are nurtured, there is also a heavy emphasis on the military know-how. It was essential that the men became well trained soldiers and it would make more efficiency in the field, and win the respect of their service colleagues. During their two years' service, the cadre attended courses run by the regular army; this included weapon handling, nuclear defence, first aid and will be encouraged to develop their initiative.

Their initiative had already been put to the test at this point as their home was a large tent alongside EFI headquarters, but the interior would be all their own work. The tent was divided into 3 areas, a bar lounge lecture room, cooking and dining area, and bedroom. Many of the materials used inside could be found on Exercise or Operational service. The floor was covered in old packing cases and the attractive screens around the bar and dining area were made by weaving branches scavenged from nearby woods.

There were concessions to creature comforts, settees, armchairs and standard beds. And while the tent was far from luxurious, it was comfortable. Maj Randerson said, 'Just because the men are living under canvas, they don't have to live like pigs. They use their brains to make the place more homely, pictures on the walls and carpets.'

Further opportunity for initiative came three weeks after the formation of the cadre, when they were joined by 10 EFI colleagues for 'Exercise Undergrowth', a survival and defence weekend in the nearby woods. Part of the group established and operated a bulk issue store capable of serving 7000 troops. The rest became customers and were given paper money to authenticate transactions. There were no goods to buy, but administration was realistic.

The customers based themselves in the woods where they were set up defences to prepare for unexpected enemy attack. They built camouflage look out points, dug trenches and planned strategies. On the Saturday night, the enemy team, led by Maj Randerson, crept through the woods to seek them out in a battle which ended in a draw. Maj Randerson was delighted with the exercise: 'It was extremely valuable for both administrative practice and military skills. The lads in the woods picked up some tips about defending positions and spending a night out in the open, they slept out after the attack. The men back at base had first-hand experience of running a bulk issue still, coping with all sorts of problems that arise in the field.'

Half a World Away Falklands Campaign Memories by Rodger Seaman 1982

Having recently returned from EFI duties in Norway (Arctic Express) I was not totally surprised when I received a call from Major Bob Randerson, advising that he had been asked to build a team to be the advance party for EFI in the Falkland Islands and asked if I would consider volunteering . . . It didn't take me long to accept, stating: "If I was prepared to practise for a situation like the Falklands, I should be prepared to do it for real" and that was that. The team – Captain Pat Lafferty; Sgt Jim Nicholls; Sgt Larry Graves, Cpl Mike Hammond, Cpl Mike Nicholson, Cpl Trevor Reoch, Cpl Mike Burke and myself.

Within a few days I met up with the remaining team at Wingham, we were kitted up, including with our SLR rifles and dispatched to Brize Norton for a flight to Ascension Islands, where we awaited a merchant ship to take us south.

It was whilst on Ascension that the gravity of what we had embarked upon became apparent, as we supported the local NAAFI guys by meeting survivors from the sinking of HMS Sheffield (10th May – 20 fatalities) at the airport – they looked wrung out, bedraggled and relieved to be heading home –any hint of 'glamour in war' quickly evaporated that night..

We were finally helicoptered (& abseiled) onto a diving support vessel – British Enterprise III – and once we took on an extraordinary amount of "post", we headed south toward Stanley.

Within a few days, the nature of the post became more apparent – it was mostly in fact a philanthropic gift from one Paul Raymond of endless amounts of pornography, to boost the . . . war effort. We joked that the course of the campaign could have changed dramatically had it reached the front line, as the task force would probably have been too tired to fight.

The Enterprise was powered by an ex U Boat engine and was less than reliable and broke down numerous times but finally, after a diversion with post (?) to South Georgia and nearly a month at sea, we were towed into Blanco Bay, off Port Stanley on 3rd July 1982 – those historians amongst you will deduce this was nearly 3 weeks after the ceasefire.

Having spent the 1st few nights sleeping on top of the stock in the temporary Bulk Issue Store (BIS) set up by 2 Naval Canteen Service guys (sorry, names escape me) our enterprising and seriously persuasive CO – Capt Pat Lafferty – got us all billeted with local families, which proved to be a genius move and seriously enhanced our island experience, as we were able to get an appreciation of life pre-invasion, under temporary Argentinian rule and through the liberation.

One of the most amusing local stories was regarding the large screen TVs that were offered to the islanders on generous HP terms, by the Argentine leaders, hoping to win the hearts and minds by piping in Argentine TV from the mainland. The islanders were not stupid and were confident the Argies would be gone very soon and never even paid the 1st instalments on their new bright shiny TVs, which they showed off to anyone who expressed an interest in where they came from.

We were joined shortly after by 2 more EFI personnel – Capt John Perry and Lt Jeff Soughton (both auditors in their day jobs) who flew straight into the newly opened airport from the UK – we never forgave them for not having to endure a month at sea!

Inevitably there were many moments of humour and others that defined our individual roles within the team. My defining moment, other than gaining the nickname "Spunky" (not used since school) for the duration of the tour was when we moved the BIS to a new bigger warehouse.

There had been numerous incidents of booby traps having been left in homes and buildings by the retreating Argentine army and although our building had been cleared, we were not taking any chances. There was one room adjacent to the main building which we couldn't gain access to, as the door, whilst unlocked, just would not budge. Eventually I was sent, via a serving hatch, into a pitch-black room to unblock the door. The nature of the blockage became quickly apparent. The room was in a fact a shared toilet with the warehouse next door. This had obviously been very popular with the Argentine conscripts who had slept there, too popular actually, as even though the water supply had been switched off (or frozen) they continued to diligently use the toilet until it overflowed the toilet bowl, then the floor & ultimately half way up the door. Suffice to say it took an iron stomach and gallons of water to clear the debris, whilst I gained the lasting respect of my fellow EFI troopers (and a wide berth for a few days).

There were many other examples of the guys expressing more of their personalities as we got to know each other better, offering support and encouragement where needed, the occasional rollicking, showing grit and determination when needed and lots and lots of laughter.

Thanks to Pat Lafferty, we all developed a love/hate relationship with the music of Abba, which he played incessantly.

Major Bob had promised us that we would be home by Christmas, a promise he couldn't possibly have been able to guarantee in May 1982, BUT we eventually got notice of our departure, which was scheduled for 21/9/1982 – so we obviously needed to organize a farewell party!

Pat Lafferty excelled himself again, no scabby warm cans of Hofmeister in the BIS for us, our farewell do was to take place in the Governor's Residence and all the families who had housed us were invited. It was a suitably grand affair; we even had a disco and a Gurkha curry. Unfortunately, my host – Gladys Almonacid – and her knitting group girlfriends took to the fruit punch with a little too much vigour and after feeling very sick, she managed to flush her only set of dentures down the Governor's toilet. (I spoke to her years later and she told me it took 6 months to get a replacement set from the UK.)

We all flew home to Brize Norton, arriving on the morning of 22/9/19 and were quickly debriefed, collected by relatives and went our separate ways. I subsequently met Trevor Reoch in Canterbury in 1984/5 (he was working for Safeway by then) and I later worked with Pat Lafferty, who was my DM Aldershot in 1985/6 BUT I haven't seen the other guys again since. I left NAAFI in 1989 but will never forget my 9 years' service and hold my EFI time in particularly high regard. I was, with the benefit of another 38 years' life experience and hindsight, a boy when I started out and it was those experiences that helped define the man, husband and father I eventually became.

A Royal welcome for Falklands survivors on the QE2 1982.

They came sporting red, white and blue coloured bottles of champagne. They met in a frenzy of excitement on the dockside, nervous and elated, the mothers, fathers, sweethearts and friends. Their welcome home banners were lifted high, their eyes bright with anticipation. With those three unmistakable siren blasts echoed the length of Southampton water, they cheered, shouted, waved and cried. The Queen Elizabeth 2, pride of the Cunard line, came home from the Falklands, dirty and worn, to a Royal welcome.

Boats of all shapes and sizes went out to meet her and from the deck of HMY Britannia, HM the Queen Mother waved as the great cruise liner went by. You could see their faces lined every railing, too far away to be individually recognised. But the crowds waved regardless. As she tied up at pier 39, the red carpet was unrolled, and the waiting families and friends moved towards the door of the terminal building.

They came from the ship almost at a run, 255 survivors of HMS Coventry, 177 from HMS Ardent, and 197 from HMS Antelope.

Telepathy seemed to draw the families together, through the crowds. There were tears, kisses and hugs, weeping children and ecstatic wives. And there were copious cups of tea from the NAAFI buffet to help settle excited nerves. Among the first to disembark were Coventry canteen manager Ron Fletcher and his assistant Anthony Oliver. With a Cheshire cat grin on his face, Mr Fletcher retold his story, surrounded by his mum, sisters and brother-in-law, who had left their Cleveland home. Coventry had been blasted by a wave of Argentine bombs as she sailed north of the Falklands. Twenty men died and 20 more were injured. 'The ship began listing almost immediately, their only thought was to get off quickly,' recalled Mr Fletcher, 'she seemed to go down so fast.' 'It was terrifying, you didn't have time to think, you had just been told to abandon ship, and that's exactly what we did. I don't think I'd ever been so frightened,' admitted his assistant. 'It was only when we thought about it afterwards that we realised what was happening and how lucky you were. It's great to be back now; all I want to do is get home and have a few "wets" and relax.'

John Leake, the canteen manager in HMS Ardent, was also on board; he hit the national headlines when he led a machine gun team against the Argentine Skyhawk jets. 'I didn't see myself as a hero,' he said, 'I'm a trained soldier and I did what any other trained soldier would have done. All I could think of was hitting the aircraft. I hit one and saw the bullets entering the wing. I didn't see the plane crash, but the lads told me that the pilot would never get home.'

The third ship's company to disembark was that of HMS Antelope. The type 21 frigate was seriously damaged by Argentine Skyhawk jets in San Carlos Bay and later sank. She was hit by at least three bombs but, miraculously, they crashed through her unarmoured decks without exploding and her crew was transferred safely to other ships. But there was a casualty a bomb disposal expert, who died when a 1000lb bomb, unexploded, blew up as he attempted to diffuse it. As the Antelope struggled to survive, canteen manager Gerry Downing and his assistant Colin Digby, were safely transferred.

As the last of the survivors walked out into the sunlight, to the cheers and claps of spectators, the NAAFI team began the task of clearing out. This was led by Dennis Lafferty, district manager, Portsmouth, and Lew Williamson, district manager, Portsmouth ships – they had been working from early that morning, preparing snacks for service families, pouring gallons of tea, at a NAAFI mobile canteen outside on the dock.

No one had stood idle. When Ray Vardon, manager home service South and naval, and Richard Hoskyn, personal officer, HS (S) and naval, arrived to meet the survivors, they helped distribute food; 3000 sausage rolls and Scotch eggs and 8 pounds of apples were just some of the items consumed. Irene Bardsley, manager of the club at Excellent Steps, Portsmouth, and one of the key figures in the catering for 5000, stood exhausted, hands on hips, as she watched the last of the survivor's families depart.

Canteen paperwork saved on HMS Sheffield from Argentine missile 1982

Canteen manager David Hesketh missed death by minutes when Argentinian Exocet missile destroyed HMS Sheffield. The missile struck its target at 1400hrs, exploding amidships, just 20 yards from the NAAFI canteen. 'The ship gave a shudder and I realised we'd been hit, but I thought we'd been torpedoed; the canteen was demolished. Luckily I had just left to fetch some paperwork from my cabin.'

As part of the medical team David and his assistant, 21-year-old Reg Caligari, who was resting in his cabin when the missile hit, went immediately to their action stations. Thick black smoke was everywhere as the crew fought the blaze for five hours. They spent most of their time treating minor casualties for shock, burns, cuts and bruising. 'We just couldn't reach the badly injured men,' said Reg.

Meanwhile, David and a few crewmen set up an emergency sick bay in the helicopter hangar. 'The smoke was so thick on Deck 2, we had to bring the injured into the hangar until the helicopters arrived and winched them to safety on the Hermes.' After Capt Sam Salt gave the order to abandon ship, David was one of the last off and he heard men shouting jump as HMS Arrow, one of the two rescue ships, started pulling away. The last thing he remembered was somersaulting into the scrambling nets put out by HMS Arrow and heading away from the wreck. From the Arrow the 260 survivors were transferred to Fort Austin and British Elk which took them to the Ascension Island from there they were flown home. They arrived at RAF Brize Norton, to discover that the world's press had gathered to welcome them.

The diary of a canteen manager 1982

Wednesday 2nd of June: signal received aboard HMS Invincible from task force commander calling for NAAFI volunteers to run a BIS until EFI teams arrive. We volunteered (Higton and Panther).

Monday 7th of June: issues with cold weather clothing and transferred to Fort Grange which would provide essentials (soap, razors, toothpaste etc.) for 5000 men for one week. Helped RAF staff in making up supply packs for replenishment for Invincible, Fearless and others.

Wednesday 9th of June: replenishment at sea of Invincible commenced 0500. Completed assembling loads for Falkland Islands by 2000.

Thursday 10th of June: air raids at 1400 and 1730. Issued with atropine injectors and tablets for defence against possible Argentinian gas attacks. First loads centre short a landing zone (LZ) at red beach. Sea King dropped us with kit into muddy bog. Given hot tea. Taken to BIS accommodation, old Nissen Hut, part of abandoned refrigeration plant. No windows or doors and many roof panels missing because the building next door was bombed by the Argentinians. No movement of stores possible from LZ to BIS, fork trucks unable to work in deep mud in dark.

Friday 11th of June: slept on floor with only ship's internal sleeping bags. Impressive view of star systems, through large hole in roof, interrupted by rainstorm which froze around us. Up at dawn. Search for more suitable kit unfortunately found colour Sgt Sandy McLeod, who I know from HMS Hermes where he was Sgts mess president. Our survival depended on the amount of helping kit he could provide, given hot food, camp beds, bedrolls, Arctic sleeping bags, boots, extra clothing, cooker, mess tins, compo rations, sheets for holes in roof and much survival advice.

Most stores from LZ to BIS. Some inaccessible due to mud. With just two of us security couldn't be a problem. P.M: Higton to Fearless. Find 11 further loads of supplies transferred aboard before Fort Grange left 'bomb alley'. Two NAAFI staff, Chris Foulkard and Ken Simpson, offer help for a couple of days. Load brought ashore by landing craft. They built a temporary house inside the Hut using mineral cases and Kip sheets. Fast and almost six successful attempts cooking hot meal from compo rations. Pressure from shore to obtain further stores, particularly cigarettes and chocolate. Surprise expressed about non availability of beer and spirits.

Electric light fitted, a welcome bonus in finding and checking stock, though outside generator thundered away throughout the night. Check LZ for one pallet of minerals still on hills, stores okay but Higton and Chris Foulkard blown into mud by helicopter. Two dubious overnight visits by customers, who left rapidly on finding out we were sleeping with our stores.

Saturday 12th June: find, much to our delight, that old hospital building, 12 feet away from us, contained two unexploded bombs, one suspended by parachute through a hole in the wall. Ate loads prepared for flying to Teal and Fitzroy by 1400. Many smaller units supplied. SOS2 fearless for forms A71. Overnight snow. Many casualties flown into the field hospital.

Sunday 13th of June: Chris to blue beach (San Carlos) with loads ordered by two paras. Mark flies to frontline at Teal and returns after delay caused by Argentinian bombing raid. Ken Simpson to Fitzroy, less successful. Helicopter load hook breaks and drops most of stores over mountain side. Two red alerts during the afternoon. Supplies to several other units and small amount of cash sales. Virtually all stores accept soap, soap powder, toothpaste and minerals exhausted.

Monday 14th of June: usual force 10 Gale through the end, reduced to force 5 by rebuilding wall and blocking off door. Mark and Ken to Fearless for mail and a shower. Argentinian prisoners start to arrive.

Tuesday 15th of June: snow overnight again. Received last 11 loads from Fort Grange. Told to have 17 packs ready for distribution 1400hrs tomorrow.

Wednesday 16th of June: No load sent forward, no transport. They heard Argentinians had surrendered the Falklands but to expect air attacks from disgruntled Argentine Air Force. Fresh chops for supper courtesy of colour Sgt McLeod. At last, a bottle of whiskey from Fearless. Several hot toddies make us feel warm enough to go to sleep.

Thursday 17th of June: Christian can fly back to Fearless. All bulk stores exhausted except minerals, toothpaste and Daz (does nobody wash on this island?).

Friday 18th of June: all remaining stores palletised, together with five remaining loads, for transfer with us to Stanley.

Saturday 19th of June: embark Elk 2 at 0000hrs. Sleep on car deck along with three hundred others.

Sunday 20th of June disembarks Stanley 0830hrs. Find unloading of beer from resource already in progress. Given half ground floor of Falkland Island company (FIC) bonded shed. Obtain forklift and driver to bring beer (46 pallets) from jetty to safety. Receive 4 landing craft full of stores overnight and finished storing 0335hrs. Issues made all day and late into the night while storing.

Monday 21st of June: issued all day from 0800. No lights from midday throughout the night because the power cuts. Still no stores off Elk, including petrol cooker and much personal kit. Mail arriving for EFI, their whereabouts being investigated.

Tuesday 22nd of June: first mail from UK for RAOC EFI turns out to be establishment rubber stamp, no inkpad and no invoices yet received (no EFI either). Back to paraffin heater and camp bed.

Wednesday 23rd of June: Stromness sends 22 'try walls' of stores by boat. Use Sir Bedivere's crane to hoist onto jetty. Issues as normal. Fresh steak for dinner, courtesy of HMS Fearless CPO cook.

Thursday 24th of June: 3 finals trials from Stromness. New task force commander promises to try and obtain price list or invoices for goods from RFA, detail of stock and RFA about to descend on us before they arrive, and whereabouts of elusive Capt Lafferty and gang. Warehouse, now three parts full of NAAFI stock, will be required by FIC when their store ships arrived Friday 2nd of July. Supply St Edmund, Ocean Trading and Saxonia, and the Ghurkhas at Goose Green, by helicopter. Our first early night. Both in sleeping bags by 2130hrs, British Elk stores finally arrive at 2230hrs finished at 0015hrs.

Saturday 26th of June: notified EFI are embarked on Rangatira. Put up opening hours to discourage late night customers who are making our days long and meals few and far between.

Sunday 27th of June: closed pm went walkabout around Stanley. Viewed Argentinian defences on Murray Heights. Impressive positions with tremendous amounts of ammunition around. Serve 3 units just returned from surrounding hillsides.

Tuesday 29th of June: Shawn proposed new warehouse, totally unsuitable while just two of us and stores have to be got up and down steps. Also, half full of government stocks. Offered to take 50 loads of beer, 40 minerals, 7 tobacco and 16 of spirits from Geestport Purser.

Thursday 1st July: minerals arrived from Geestport. Told EFI expected between 14-16 July. Trying to store an issue at the same time, down to one proper compo meal a day. Living in a warehouse with no washing, toilet or heating facilities is wearing thin. Sir Bedivere's offer of occasional shower and laundry facilities beginning investigated as clothes brought ashore for the original week are continuing to walk around when we take them off. Request Garrison orders published open hours as too many customers assuming we are open day and night. Stress we will continue to serve emergencies.

Friday 2nd of July: finished storing spirits, beer and tobacco from Geestport 0030. Ghurkhas collect biggest order to date.

Saturday 3rd of July: warehouse full again. Mail arrives from Invisible, 1st for three weeks. Capt Lafferty and seven EFI arrive late pm.

Sunday 4th of July: EFI shown present and proposed warehouse. All amazed by amount of work done by two and by number of accounts (90 plus) to be sorted out. Decision made to go for new warehouse.

Monday 5th-10th July: EFI found accommodation over next two days. Office set up in new warehouse. Run down BIS at old warehouse. Capt Perry and Lieutenant Stoughton (EFI) arrive from UK.

Thursday 15th of July: storing from Astronomer and Geestport.

Friday 16th of July: Mark to field hospital with good helping of 'Galtieri's revenge'. Kept in bed without food for two days.

Wednesday 21st of July: flown back to Invincible. We both consider the time on FI well spent despite the atrocious conditions. The number of customers who went out of their way to thank us before leaving for the UK was pleasing. Haven't learned much, particularly about survival. Although confusion resigned from the first, the sense of achievement against all odds.

HMS Invincible canteen manager David Higton and Mark Panter, his assistant, were the first NAAFI staff ashore on the Falkland Islands. As battle raged, they landed at Ajax Bay to establish a bulk issue store and for almost two months work from makeshift premises in appalling conditions; these were extracts from David Higton's personal diary.

Taffy (Allen) Davies MBE a photographic record of the Falklands 1982-1986

"I did my basic EFI training in Dulmen, Germany and thoroughly enjoyed my whole career of thirty years in NAAFI and within RAOC/EFI and RLC/EFI. Whilst in NAAFI I was fortunate to work in different departments ranging from Transport, Distribution and Warehousing, Export, Overseas Division then International and Export and Logistics. Whilst not actively serving with EFI in uniform during the Falklands Crisis or immediately thereafter, I travelled to the Falklands and Ascension Islands many times and came to know the personnel who were serving thereon.

"I also became known to the majority of people within the company because of my sitting on the Pensioners Advisory Committee, from its inauguration in 1981 until finally retiring as a Pension Fund Trustee in 2003. The Company closed its warehouses at the end of 1997 and Transport in early 1998. At that time Bob Lewis became my new boss, as Manager International Division. When Bob retired, I inherited all his paperwork etc. That included a large number of Falkland Island and Ascension Island photographs. They, together with photographs of my own, plus pictures taken by various others, make up the collection presented."

Falklands Islands

KELPER STORE

CXU 299848 5

CANACHE
SERVICES
SHOP

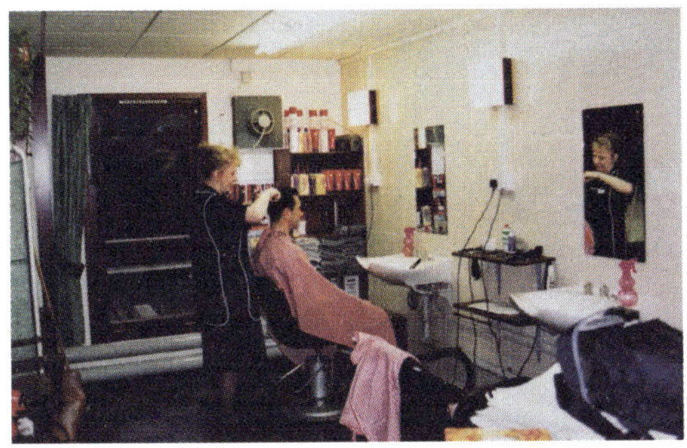

Barbers Shop
Mount Pleasant
tel. 3039
Hairport
appointment
here

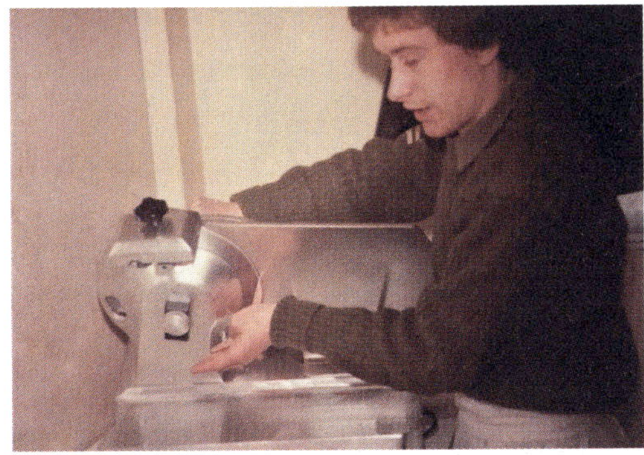

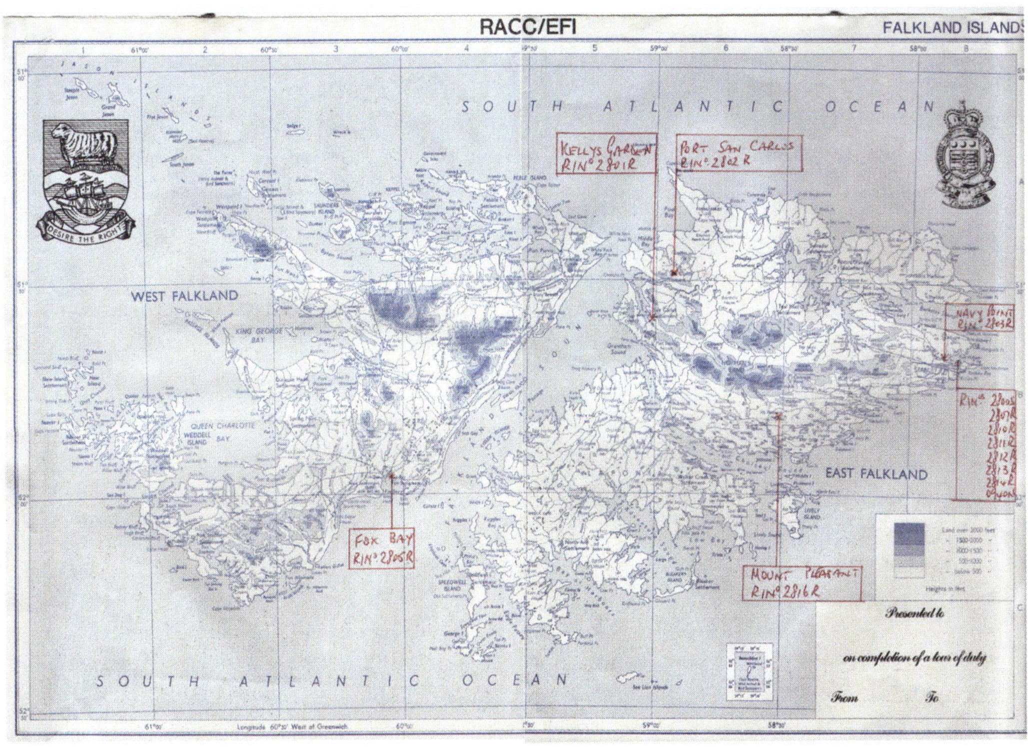
RACC/EFI
FALKLAND ISLANDS
SOUTH ATLANTIC OCEAN
KELLYS GARDEN
RIN° 2801R
PORT SAN CARLOS
RIN° 2802 R
WEST FALKLAND
KING GEORGE BAY
QUEEN CHARLOTTE BAY
WEDDELL ISLAND
EAST FALKLAND
FOX BAY
RIN° 2805R
MOUNT PLEASANT
RIN° 2816R
DESIRE THE RIGHT
Presented to
on completion of a tour of duty
From
To

SECC

Ascension Island

Over 100 staff honoured 1982

Over 100 NAAFI men received the South Atlantic medal for service with the task force sent to recapture the Falkland Islands from Argentinian invaders. Three members of staff received special recognition for valuable roles they played during the emergency. Canteen manager John Leake, the hero of HMS Ardent, is awarded the distinguished service medal for leading a team of machine Gunners against the Argentinian jets strafing the stricken ship. Graham Lloyd, assistant manager warehousing and distribution, is made MBE for his part in coordinating the efforts of hundreds of staff involved in supplying the task force. Irene Bartley, manager of the HMS Excellent Steps club, Portsmouth, who organised dockside refreshments for troops leaving for and returning from, the Falklands, receives the British Empire medal.

1983

Getting to grips with the Falklands 1983

Life in the Falklands was no picnic, a fact which registered very clearly with Peter Lucas, manager of the overseas service, on a fact-finding mission to the islands. He wanted to see first hand the conditions under which NAAFI staff in uniform lived and worked.

'The first priority after setting up the service had been to find the staff reasonable living conditions,' he said. Some of the men were now living in Kelper House, Port Stanley, which was next door to the store that NAAFI took over as a service shop. Mr Lucas explained: 'We have now obtained additional accommodation in another house nearby which will eventually reduce the numbers of EFI staff who are billeted by the army with local families. Overcrowding was a problem in Port Stanley for all the services and will only be overcome as the tented camps are occupied, later in 1983.'

Staff are working seven days a week without a break, moving from job to job, this was commonplace. Two things that impressed Mr Lucas was firstly how serious the locals and the troops still consider the island to be at risk, and that comfort and welfare are very much second to defence. 'The other is that whenever the forces are put under trying conditions, it brings out all their cheerful qualities and determination to make the best of it. This makes the job we're doing so much more worthwhile, and our own people respond.'

NAAFI staff on the island currently change over every four months, but Mr Lucas expects eventually to have up to 50 civilian staff working there, on yearly contracts to provide the continually needed to carry out the job once the accommodation problems have been resolved. Among the problems staff have to contend with is a shortage of beer for the troops. Mr Lucas commented: 'There is space to hold about 30,000 cases, but we need nearer 50,000. However, the arrival of the warehouse ship at the end of February was expected to provide the answer.'

Popular buys in the services shop include pre-recorded cassettes – they supplied over 5000 a month. Other popular items are crested tee shirts, toy penguins and cameras. They were hoping then to expand the range to increase the sales as they opened clubs in the hutted camps. Mr Lucas flew over the whole of the islands, and visited every service location except Port Howard.

Six UK breweries set up a fund off money, the bulk of which was to be used to provide projector television equipment. Watching video films is the main off duty activity on the island. The Falkland Islands situation had given the forces a chance to see NAAFI in another light, and how useful they could be to them. This did that image an awful lot of good. They were doing as much as they could in the prevailing conditions. Winter was fast approaching which didn't make their job on the island any easier.

Summer had not ended when Mr Lucas visited the penguin colony, 14 miles west of Port Stanley, with Capt Eddie Gallagher OC RAOC EFI and Lieutenant Mike De Caux, the supplies officer. Mr Lucas recalled: 'The countryside is rather like the Hebrides and it was a lovely and warm sunny day. There was close to 1000 penguins, sharing their colony with sheep and seagulls. Parent penguins were running backwards and forwards to the sea, catching fish for their fluffy little youngsters. But it's hard countryside, and troops must have found it near impossible to jump across in winter conditions. It really brought home to me what they had achieved.'

Edinburgh House, sale ends era 1983

A multi million pound deal had been completed for the sale of NAAFI former London offices, Edinburgh House in Kennington Lane to British Telecom. The sale, the most lucrative single property transaction ever completed by the company, ended the reconstructing of headquarters offices between London and Nottingham.

Edinburgh House, a four storey building with almost 70,000 square feet of offices, which the company built in 1970, became surplus to requirements after the refurbishment of Imperial Court. This followed the transfer of some departments from London to Nottingham, and the earlier moves from Kennings Way to Amesbury in the early 1970s. Ted Legg, assistant manager property services Department, explained: 'Our aim was to find good tenants for Edinburgh House, and then sell it as an investment to a big institution. As it is, the tenants we found, British Telecom, have now bought the building.'

NAAFI had also sold its leasehold interest in 91 Kennings Lane, former home of the London Imperial club, to Lambeth borough council, who plans to use the building for neighbourhood and community facilities.

Imperial War Museum, a seat with a view 1983

In 1983 members of the in NCS EFI old comrades Association donated a bench seat for the grounds of the Imperial War Museum, London. Bill Jouxsomn, Dicky Bullen (retiring chairman), Eric Peterson, Maj Henry Jameson, Ken Hempstead, Doug Stapely and chairman designate Tommy Booth.

The suggestion that the OCA should donate a seat came from members Bill White and George Caddey, who on regular visits to the museum found that there was a lack of seating for the public. Then deputy director of the Imperial War Museum, Robert Crawford, said that this was a generous gesture and was very much appreciated.

Unfortunately, in 2020, no trace remains of this donation, for reference made except for this article in the 1983 June July NAAFI News on the back page.

A new lease of life for a dear old friend by Vic Walters 1983

A convoy of WWII vehicles that paraded through Weymouth in June 1983 to commemorate D-Dday was a small, drab olive van. It looks surprisingly unwarlike among the jeeps, trucks and armoured personnel carriers. But when that vehicle passed the reviewing platform, the assembled top brass led a spontaneous standing ovation, as the crowds recognised an original wartime NAAFI mobile.

Enthusiasts have described it as the rarest of all historic military vehicles currently making the rounds of shows and rallies. Yet just a year before, the object of all this interest and affection was rusting quietly into oblivion, emblazoned with nothing more honourable than a Mr Kreamy sign.

The born again mobile, registration number JNO665, owes its new lease of life to the retired butcher Burt Conroy, and wife Lil, both members of the Dorset branch of the military vehicles conservation group. Their enthusiasm, hundreds of hours of painstaking work, and a substantial amount of money had restored this little Ford 10h.p. to the task for which it was built. They heard about the van through contacts in the group, and it had been used for years as an ice cream van and was really a wreck. They payed £275 for a heap of rust with a clapped-out engine. That was only the start of the outlay. The upper, wooden body was replaced, countless layers of paint and rust removed. The inner wing panels were welded, and the engine was totally rebuilt. They worked in a yard near Ringwood in Hampshire, home for almost a year, to bring the mobile back to its original specifications.

Ford supplied just 350 of these mobiles to NAAFI from 1939 onwards, and the Conroys' vehicle was now believed to be the only one left in Britain. As such it is a collector's item, and already the Conroys had turned down an offer from a Dutch enthusiast. But they wanted it to stay in Britain, so they did not sell it. They thought of the van as a travelling NAAFI museum anyway. Going to these shows, it gives younger people who do not remember the war a chance

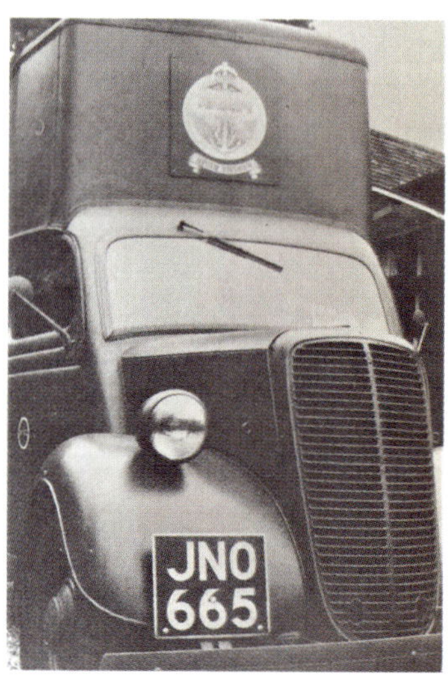

to see something of what things were like in those days. The Conroys spared no effort to make JNO665 as authentic as possible.

The NAAFI emblem was commissioned from a specialist artist, and even stencilled letters NAAFI on the van side are authentic, with small diamond shaped separators between each. After Weymouth, the first outing for the reconditioned mobile, it appeared at many shows all over the South of England. Visitors were able to lean on the counter and drink tea from the authentic NAAFI urn, and study the bill of fare that included fly pie (rock cake), bride's cake (bread pudding), and the ever famous 'wad' (just a sandwich). They were amazed at how many of the older people came over all tearful. Lil who ran the refreshment service raised charity funds. They leaned on the counter and suddenly were transported back 40 years.

Still earning her living, JNO665 dispensed tea, refreshments, and nostalgia thereafter. Having virtually completed the restoration, the present owners were anxious to hear from anybody with knowledge of a mobile which went into service in 1942. The vehicle itself now resides in the National Army Museum where it is looked after and kept in good condition alongside many other items.

Farewell to Chatham by Eleonore Kostur 1983

The ships are gone, the crane stand idle, the quayside desolate. Chatham dockyard as closed down. The death of this once thriving Medway port, steeped in history, marks the end of an era for the Royal Navy and for NAAFI.

In Chatham's heyday, hundreds of ships and thousands of sailors benefited from the services provided by a NAAFI bakery, bond store, warehouse and clubs and shops. The last of these, the Pembroke club, closed in August of 1983. The only NAAFI service in evidence when NAAFI News visited was a bar being operated in the Wardroom of HMS Pembroke for the regard of ratings and officers who were administering the last rites to the dockyard.

Outside, Eric Peterson, the last NAAFI manager in Chatham, was on a farewell tour of the yard. With him, reminiscing, were two retired colleagues Bill Ward and Ted Cossey, between them the trio boasted nearly 150 years' NAAFI service, the majority of it was spent at Chatham. Mr Peterson led the way into the defunct ration store and shop he managed for half of his 45-year NAAFI career. His office had already started gathering dust and cobwebs.

Mr Peterson first entered the dockyard when, as a trainee assistant in the Gillingham warehouse long since closed, he had to make deliveries to the shops on a box tricycle. Little did he know then that he would go on to manage the shop and store and help supply the HM ships, Royal Fleet Auxiliary and ships of foreign navies, which called into the dockyard. He recalled how a bugler piped him aboard the Polish naval destroyer each time he called to discuss messing demands. 'But the oddest sight of all was watching the officers peeling potatoes with the ratings,' he said.

On board the US Navy's only square rigger, the Coast Guard 'Cutter Eagle' which was originally the German cadet training ship Horst Vessel, during World War II.

Gone now were the days when Mr Peterson could involve Navy and NAAFI staff, including those visiting ships, in fundraising efforts for the children's Peanut Ward of the Queen Victoria Hospital, East Grinstead. 'Such cooperation was typical of the relationship NAAFI enjoyed at Chatham over the years,' said Mr Peterson. He also recalled the Navy days when they used to cater for 30,000 people, starting at 0600hrs and finishing at 2200hrs. 'The Christmas season was another busy time,' recalled Mr Cossey who berthed in Chatham after 18 years' afloat with the naval canteen service: 'We were all roped in to help the ration store staff prepare 400 turkeys, ducks, chicken and geese for Christmas dinners. It was known as the Turkey trot.'

'We would involve the whole family,' added Mr Ward, who spent 37 of his 51 years at Chatham with inspection branch, and often worked until 0200hrs. They had quite a shock when they heard that the dockyard would close even though the NAAFI operation had grown smaller over the years. Under Nore command (which ceased to exist in 1961) there were canteens and shops at the Royal naval hospital, the barracks, the East camp 'Wrenery', Collingwood block, and the Royal marine barracks, In addition to the St Mary's island canteen.

In Gillingham there was a warehouse, bond store, bakery, and the Chatham town club, which opened on the 16th of July 1948. With its residential wing where wives often welcomed sailor husbands home from sea, the club became more popularly known as 'honeymoon hotel'.

Navy operations included refitting and modernization facilities for fleet submarines and certain frigates, an inshore survey squadron, routine maintenance and the running repairs shops, and a base for coastal minesweepers and other smaller craft. But as defence cuts began to bite, NAAFI and the Navy began to run things down. By 1961 only the ration store (opened when the Gillingham warehouse and bond store closed), a services shop, the family shop, and the Pembroke club remained. But right up to 1974 there was an attractive Imperial club branch.

Over the years the winding down of operations had unearthed so much Naval history, said Mr Cossey, who managed the Pembroke club for 21 years. 'So many great ships were built here, HMS Victory which was now berthed at Portsmouth, HMS Warrior, the first ironclad vessel, and the Medway Queen, the paddle steamer famous for its part in the Dunkirk evacuation.'

The Cunne, the first ship launched here in 1586, Francis Drake learnt to sail here, so did Horatio Nelson. Lieutenant Commander Mick Poole, the man who will close Chatham's gates for the last time on the 31st of March 1984, when the winding down staff will leave, said, 'NAAFI provided everything we needed and its staff are always helpful.'

The old Chatham club provided the essential service. It had always been clean and comfortable, and what people needed. Around the NAAFI world, men and women who have served at Chatham will find memories in the news of the dockyard's demise. Stan Alsop, assistant manager of the home service South and naval supplies pointed out: 'All NAAFI staff who wore their NCS uniform in the last war were Chatham ratings. Those who lost their lives have their names inscribed on the Chatham War Memorial.'

Doug Stapely, assistant manager, was fresh out of Navy training when he first saw Chatham as a naval rating. 'That was September 1941. First impressions of a NAAFI canteen were formed at morning break when we could buy a cup of tea, 2 doughnuts, and three cigarettes for six old pence.'

EFI girls are needed for the Falklands September 1983

An advertisement was put in the NAAFI News in 1983 calling on NAAFI girls, in uniform for the first time since World War II. They required a dozen volunteers to go to the Falklands as members of the EFI where they would serve in NAAFI clubs in and around Port Stanley. Many more will be needed and the volunteers will be the first to wear the EFI uniform since the demobilisation at the end of the Second World War when NAAFI girls were known affectionately as 'Effies' who served as ATS (EFI) in Europe, North Africa and the Middle East.

They were looking for experienced female club management and assistant club managers with a sense of adventure. Maj Bob Randerson, OC RAOC EFI said: 'They should be aged between 18 and 40, medically fit and it would be useful if they had knowledge of clerical work. I'm particularly interested in hearing from those with previous service or territorial experience.'

The volunteers would be enrolled in the women's Royal Army Corps (WRAC) EFI and will undergo a short period of training at Wingham before going to the Falkland Islands via Ascension Island.

Some months later a team of six who had been enrolled in, and wear the uniform of, the women's Royal Army Corps, left RAF Brize Norton on December the 28th 1983 to go to Port Stanley. The girl's Sgts Patricia Cunane and Francis Bowler, Cpls Mary Gallacher, Mandy Simmons, Kay Winfield and Jill Wright, would join their male counterparts in the EFI, manning bars, clubs and shops, in and around the town.

The girls attracted a great deal of attention when the media were invited to meet them at EFI headquarters Wingham in Surrey. They were inspected by Mary Joy, the last commanding officer of the Auxiliary Territorial Service (ATS) EFI which was disbanded in 1949. 'The girls are extremely nice and I'm sure they'll be well received in the Falklands,' said Miss Joy afterwards. 'I was very impressed. The uniform is a lot smarter than ours was, much more comfortable and flexible for the job that they have to do.'

In preparation for the five-month tour, the girls had had three days' crash course at the WRAC training college at Guildford. They studied Army ranks, military law, first aid, map reading and drill. They were also kitted out with all their bottle green uniforms. They were also issued with a book on how to stay healthy in cold climates, including tips on how to avoid frostbite, snow blindness, sunburn, windburn, and chilblains.

Among the civilian clothes the girls packed were jeans, anoraks, shoes, swimming costumes, tracksuit, wellingtons and thick tights. They were also advised to take hair conditioner, torch, clock, camera and a penknife. Everyone was looking forward to the EFI girls arriving. The weather was unpredictable. Lieutenant Dehnel who, before she went into uniform, was a restaurant and welfare Superintendent in the South eastern region, said: 'One day we are in shirtsleeve order, the next, complete combats. Bring plenty of hair conditioner and face cream as weather and dust take its full toll. Suggested you would also bring good walking shoes as the roads are virtually non-existent.'

The girls were chosen from 120 applicants. Maj Bob Randerson, OC RAOC EFI said: 'They are a very good bunch and coped very well in training. In my view they will be well treated on the island, as they should be. I think they're great. We are also now able to look for a limited number of shop staff, particularly those with clerical experience, to join the WRAC EFI. Drafts were going to the Falklands at regular intervals.'

Staff who opt out to spend more than the standard five-month tour including travel time, on the Falklands duty will receive a bonus payment for three-month extension. Additional payments for every month thereafter for up to one year.

Lieutenant Jophy Dehnel, 27, was the first commanding officer of the WRAC EFI. She held the qualification of hotel management and secretarial duties and joined NAAFI in 1981 as a trainee RWS. In 1982 she was posted to South Central region as RWS, and in July of 1983, moved to the neighbouring South eastern region. She was settling down in a new role when she volunteered to go into uniform. She spent a week at the WRAC college, Guilford, before flying to the Falklands.

She followed Mary Joy, the last CO of the ATS EFI, who joined in 1942 and in August of 1943 she led the third draft of NAAFI girls to North Africa. After a spell in Algiers she went to an officers' training unit in Palestine. Passing out as junior commander, she was posted to Italy where she was awarded the MBE (military division) for gallant and distinguished service in Salerno, Florence, Milan and Naples. In January of 1948, after appointments in Padua and NAAFI HQ in Austria, she was appointed officer commanding the ATS EFI where 18 months later at the last ATS EFI commander she was demobilised. Miss Joy continued to work for NAAFI as an RWS and later as senior tutor at Wingham until her retirement in 1975. She was on the committee of the NCS EFI old comrades Association.

During the Second World War NAAFI girls stepped out in uniform of the ATS EFI. The ATS was formed in September of 1938, but NAAFI girls were not in listed till December 1942 when it was decided that NAAFI girls posted overseas should be listed as members of the ATS EFI. Like the ladies who are now posted to the Falkland Islands the first draft of 100 strong ATS EFI sailed to Egypt in the May of 1943.

Earning my stars from the beginning, Memories by Jane Kierstenson 1983

I served at HMS Warrior Northwood 1983 where I gained the 1- and 2-stars Marcasite brooches and also the Navy 'N' brooch then I moved to Inglis Barracks Mill Hill 1983-1984 Gained 3,4 and 5 stars, alongside the Army 'N' Brooch.

The following year had the call up from RAOC/EFI Falkland Islands and served from 1984 to 1985 at 'The Stables' (aka The Canache Club), Town Club and Kelper Store as deputy manager.

21st birthday in the Falklands, kept quiet about. Somebody found out at Lookout Camp where we lived. Shots were only 6p. I was trashed in less than half an hour apparently. Ended up in the FIGPU bar, escorted out. Found following morning asleep in a bath in an Ablutions ISO block by an officer. Oops. Not charged thankfully.

Casevac back to UK from Falklands with trashed back, unable to walk after lifting boxes of spirits for CBFFI's order in Kelper Store. First flight in helo, high on morphine from BMH FI to Mount Pleasant airfield. Threw up over RAF doc on TriStar back to UK. Refuelling at Ascension Island, had to stay on plane as could not be moved. Remember a very handsome bronzed, blonde RAF fireman being on the plane with me and the doc. Maybe the morphine played tricks on me.

When returning to the UK the next postings were in various locations, then in 1988 I was manager of HMS Royal Arthur Corsham 1988 before I left. These were some of the best years of my life and the fond memories will stay with me.

1984

Bad weather and Dinner with Jim. Memories by Sharon Dutton 1984

I was about 24 when I went to the Falkland Islands as part of EFI. I remember picking up my uniform and being told yes that fits, even if the crotch of the combats were halfway down my legs, I wasn't going to argue, I was quite scared. I did a week in Guildford for basic training, which was quite intense as we had to fit about six weeks of training in. The thing I hated most was getting the toilets ready for Captain's Rounds. Anyway, completed that and the time came to leave. If my memory serves me right we left from Brize Norton, and had to stop at Qatar to refuel, and as we were in uniform we had to stand on the side of the runway and wait, we were not allowed into the airport there. The humidity was very high, and I was looking forward to having a cigarette as I smoked in those days, but it was such a let-down due to the humidity. Anyway, we flew to the Ascension Islands, I'm pretty sure we had an overnight stop and then we boarded a helicopter that took us to the MV Keren. I spent two weeks on the boat sailing to the Falklands, it was a good two weeks dressing for dinner each evening.

We arrived at the Falklands and we couldn't leave the ship as the weather was too bad; personally I was quite pleased about this as when I took a look at the Islands I thought what a bleak place, what am I doing here!! Please let the weather be bad for ages. Eventually we managed to disembark onto I think it was the 'black pig'. I was quite homesick and thinking I had made a mistake. The next few months home was a portacabin which was filled with bunk beds and quite cramped, also the toilets and showers were in a neighbouring portacabin so was quite cold. I remember a crosswind all the time and four seasons in one day.

So, I'm pretty sure it was the 23rd September, but we had to go and attend Jim Davison's show – he was over recording his Christmas Special – in September!! As you can imagine I wasn't feeling in the least bit festive as it was September and I was still feeling homesick. So, I sat in the audience and watched Jim perform, the show wasn't too bad, and when I finally saw the final cut, I managed to catch a glimpse of myself in the audience – not looking too happy. After the show somehow a few of us managed to have dinner with Jim, I have no recollection of how this event happened as I am 59 now and my memory is not what it used to be!! Anyway, we went to the canteen and there was Jim in his combat jacket – looking absolutely knackered – I do not think he'd been in town for long. So we all sat down and had dinner, Jim told lots of stories, we took a few photos, unfortunately I cannot remember any little ditties, but it certainly cheered me up, and after that I started to feel a lot better about being there. I found I was able to phone home after that day, as I hadn't done in case I started crying.

I had a lot of adventures whilst there, some were good, some were bad, lots were happy, and some were sad. When it was getting towards the end of my tour, I was quite sad; I really wanted to stay, but also really wanted to go home if you know what I mean. Obviously the airport wasn't built at that time so we had to go home the same way as we had got there, and I remember arriving at Ascension and the bags being transferred to the Helicopter, and only I could have the suitcase that opened on the deck with all my smalls and everything falling out – very embarrassing. Our luggage was transferred first in a big net being carried under the helicopter. Then we got on the helicopter and eventually transferred to the plane. I enjoyed my time in the Falklands, met lots of amazing people and made lots of friends and had an experience that not many have had.

HMS Illustrious visited New York by Bob Wilder 1984

We were greeted by sub-zero temperatures, and the sight of a fire boat spouting a welcome as we sailed past downtown Manhattan to dock at a pier normally reserved for the QE2. It was 0730hrs when we docked, but from our berth we could already hear the bustle of traffic and people moving around the city. We spent our time visiting famous places of interest such as the Statue of Liberty, a must see for everyone who goes to New York. Getting to the statue was easy enough – a short tube journey and a ferry across to the island. Then we had to climb the spiral staircase 18 inches wide with hundreds and hundreds of steps to the top. Luckily, there were seats at intervals to rest on, fortunate for those of us not fit or young enough anymore.

The World Trade Center with its familiar twin towers, Macy's, the world's largest store, and the Empire State building also visited. The Empire State building reminded me of Hollywood film era, maybe because of the film King Kong. While you're on top, you can almost imagine him climbing up. Macy's was a spellbinder. Once you get in, you have trouble finding your way out it's so big. There isn't enough time or space to describe all the fantastic things we saw and did, but I must say something about Chinatown. If it hadn't been for the cold wind, I could have almost believed I was in the Far East. The lights, the bustle, the beautiful, spicy, and exotic aromas made it an exhilarating experience.

The service in New York is among the best in the world. You can eat, drink, and see a movie or be entertained, 24 hours a day. The people were altogether very friendly, and then it was back to the ship.

Two unique ships of the Royal Navy with very different roles and needs by Patrick Breen 1984

Her Majesty's Yacht Britannia.

Canteen manager Dave Atkinson has had a lot to live up to aboard the Royal yacht Britannia. Not only as he followed in the footsteps of the popular predecessor Douglas Jackson, who ran the canteen for 30 years, but has also had to master the protocol involved. Mr Atkinson joined the yacht in 1982 after experience in a number of Her Majesty's ships and had served 4½ years aboard the ice patrol ship, HMS Endurance.

Members of the Royal Family, heads of state, members of government, and other VIPs are occasional visitors to this small (8 feet × 10 feet), tidy, and recently refurbished canteen on the yacht's main deck. Their Royal Highnesses the Prince and Princess of Wales were among his most recent visitors. 'They were particularly interested in the books on sale,' recalled Mr Atkinson. 'The Princess admired the cover picture of herself which she didn't know had been taken. She was great to talk to, very natural and pleasant. So is Prince Charles, a real gentleman and a scholar.'

Collar and tie must be worn at all times, even off duty when members of the Royal Family are on board, and plimsolls are the only footwear acceptable on deck. Jeans and tee shirts are taboo.

Nancy Reagan, wife of the American president, was shown the canteen when the yacht docked in San Francisco on the Queen's Pacific tour the previous year, ex-King Constantine of Greece called in at Cannes, and the president of Mexico left with tee shirts for his children.

Nearly all visitors to the canteen want souvenirs of the yacht to take home, so Mr Atkinson keeps more than 1000 crested items, spoons, plaques, T shirts, ladies' compacts, etc. His regular stores include everything from soap to books, sweets to biscuits, for the yacht's 275 strong crew. This number is increased by some 60 or so staff of the Royal household when the Queen is on board the yacht. 'There are big differences between my canteen range and that on grey funnel ships,' said Mr Atkinson. 'For instance, I must stock hairspray for maids in the Royal household. Crested items sell like hot cakes, framed pictures, clocks, mugs, anything with a Crest on it, I can sell. Books on the Royal Family are also popular.' This kept Mr Atkinson and his assistant, Pat Walker, on their toes. Normal opening times with six periods each day go by the wayside when guests come on board and snap up mementos from the canteen.

Rebate has paid for sports and other equipment to keep the ship's company entertained. A committee, which comprises a member from each mess, organises activities. 'Everybody is treated the same and there's a great loyalty on board. The crew is just like one big family,' said Mr Atkinson. Nothing demonstrates the family spirit of the ship's crew more than Sunday 'church' service is held when the Royal Family are on board. A member of the Royal Family such as Prince Andrew or Prince Edward often reads the lessons, just five seats in front of Mr Atkinson in the Royal dining room. The services are one of a number of occasions when the crew get close to the Royal Family. Others are the 'piping board' ceremony on Royal walkabouts. The state apartments are all exquisitely furnished.

'Of course, at first, I was very nervous and excited at the thought of meeting members of the Royal Family, but I soon overcame the butterflies,' he said. 'It hasn't been easy following in Douglas Jackson's footsteps, Douglas had his own way of doing things and the crew have had to get used to mine. Mind you, I think I've got over that. I'd like to be doing this job in 15 years' time. But, on the other hand I don't want to hog the post, I'd like other people to get the chance.'

HMS Endurance

She is known affectionately in the Navy as 'red plum', and certainly, as she lists heavily out of port to start a voyage, HMS Endurance looks like an over ripe fruit in the water. But set against the wild, white waters of the unwelcoming Antarctic, the 3700-tonne ice patrol and survey ship gleams bright as a beacon. Her 130 crewmen live on board for eight months each year while they chart the waters and ice floes, and complete other studies in the South Atlantic and beyond.

In those remote, cold conditions, the work of the canteen manager Ian Gregory and assistant Ashley Sanders is vital to morale Whether it be giving each man his beer ration, or making sure a gift reaches his wife back home, the success of their efforts is laid well before Endurance leaves her Portsmouth berth. While the crew prepared the ship to sail, the 2 NAAFI men are also making ready. Top priority is ordering and storing supplies.

Mr Gregory joined Endurance after 9 years with NAAFI serving in HM ships Norfolk, Fife, Intrepid, and Achilles. Even with that experience, and one Antarctic Trip behind him, stocking for such a cruise can be a problem: 'We take on board some 4550 cases, and 500 barrels of beer and minerals known by the Navy as "goffa". Every man's favourite "bevvy" is supplied. If only one individual drinks Guinness, we will stock it. Similarly, we carry whatever range of cigarettes we need to meet each month until we stop; that is no mean feat when 50% of the crew changes between trips.'

During a typical deployment, the crew will get through some 106,800 cans of beer, 650 litres of spirits, 650,000 cigarettes, 32,500 cigars, 580 tubes of toothpaste, almost 6000 Mars bars, hundreds of boxes of Maltesers, smarties, and 15,000 bags of assorted sweets.

The canteen, just aft of the midships, is small and crowded, but enormous storerooms, starboard side, hold many tonnes of NAAFI and other stocks, which accounts for the ship's list when fully loaded. 'We are meant to be totally independent for supplies and we don't draw from any ships in the Royal Fleet Auxiliary,' explained Mr Gregory. 'We shouldn't run out, at least in theory; if we do, we could pick up stock from the Falklands, where we are about to establish boat camps.'

Endurance and her crew always get a good reception from the Falkland Islanders who hold the ship in great esteem. They had 2 wasp helicopters, normally used to find a pass through pack ice, have ferried patients from outpost to Stanley hospital and her crew have assisted with house school repairs and given practical help to farmers. These activities were recognised with the award of the Wilkinson sword of peace to the ship in 1982.

Visits to the Falklands and other natural landmarks, such as Christmas Island and St Helena, are often highlights of the long voyage. Another, before the Falklands invasion, was calling at Mar del Plata in Argentina. Playing football and other games on the ice also provides physical recreation, while sights of penguins, albatrosses, petrels, shearwaters, cormorants, whales, and seals, provide a spectacle.

Mr Gregory has come to terms with the atrocious conditions that must be faced: 'Endurance was once trapped for five days in thick pack ice. An iceberg cut a gaping hole in her hull. During a storm, the ship rolled 42 degrees, stocks were sent flying. They were breakages and write offs, and the store was flooded when water poured in the ventilation shaft. Living conditions on board, however, are better than those found on grey funnel ships, the crew cabins, wood panelled, are nicely decorated and comfortable.'

The large ship's library pleases Mr Gregory, a keen reader. Currently he's reading an account of Elephant Island,, famous for its seals and bird colonies. There is a great sense of camaraderie among the crew. As Mr Gregory said: 'We are cooped up together so long, we just have to get on. There has got to be a friendly and relaxed atmosphere, and NAAFI is making a valuable contribution to that in more ways than one.'

Stores are all at sea 1984

In the Falklands from the very beginning of the conflict there had been storage issues but that had been resolved with a floating warehouse on the Canache where thousands of tonnes of NAAFI goods are housed in bulk issue stalls. These were named the Coastals, Esperia, Dominia, and Pursuivant. This warehousing system, known as FIPASS (Falklands intermediate port and storage system), comprises six barges, each approximately 300 yards long by 99 yards wide, anchored to the seabed and can handle ships up to 1000 feet long.

The NAAFI Bulk issue store covered some 8000 square feet in area where the EFI team consisted of a Warrant Officer, two sergeants, one in charge of operations, the other responsible for shipping and accounts, and five Cpls. The movement of stock is assisted by electrical power pallet movers and forklift trucks, to move the vast amount of stocks around.

The operation was becoming more sophisticated and the volunteers prided themselves on being able to offer high standards of service. They knew they were doing a worthwhile job and their efforts were greatly appreciated by the servicemen stationed on the islands.

In addition to the floating warehouses NAAFI operations on the Falkland Islands included five clubs, 3 coastal facilities, and a town club, 2 mobile vans, to shops all supplied from the FIPASS.

Anyone who'd been down there in recent months had come back pleasantly surprised at the working conditions. Many had gone back for a second tour.

Exercise Lionheart 1984

Britain's biggest troop movement since the Second World war, Exercise Lionheart, provided NAAFI with its toughest ever peacetime test. The company came through not only with flying colours, but with a healthy balance sheet and a wealth of invaluable experience, particularly where the EFI were concerned.

The five-week exercise in Germany, civilian staff along with 86 EFI personnel (operating in 13 locations) provided shop canteen and bulk issue service. They catered for some 50,000 regular and reserve troops from the UK, 20,000 of whom went through British seaports Zeebrugge and Ostend and met up on a stretch of autobahn where they were marshalled into convoys.

From the early planning stage NAAFI's aim was clear: to demonstrate the vital part NAAFI would play under war conditions. Inevitably, the EFI became the glamour end of the operations, though few of the EFI themselves would describe their efforts as glamorous. Bedding down in the end of a storage tent, grabbing snacks or meals when possible, wading through a sea of mud and running a full 24-hour service to meet widely fluctuating demands do not rate high in the glamour stakes. But genuine appreciation for their activities, openly expressed by the services, and the knowledge that they were playing a vital role in the whole exercise were compensation enough.

Glamour was also noticeably missing at the temporary mobilisation centre at Waldniel, except for that provided by Sgt Julie Ward, where Maj Bob Randerson, OC RAOC EFI, controls his team operations from the tented complex. Early in the exercise torrential rain and very high winds flattened one of the marquees, but without affecting administration.

EFI facilities were supplemented by the service in the family shops, service shops, and clubs much visited by exercise troops and called upon for backing them up. Along with their uniformed EFI colleagues, civilian staff arranged some peculiar opening times to meet troop movements, often at very short notice. In Munster, larger shops stayed open later in the evening to service a territorial Highland battalion on their way back to the UK. This was service to the services indeed, from a shop manager Norman Cubitt and his staff.

Such field efforts would be impossible without the backing of transport, warehouses, and ES supporting staff. The initial NAAFI involvement was at Jabbeke, the first point in the line of communication just outside Ostende and Zeebrugge, where 2 EFI mobiles, under the control of Sgt Glenn Jones, provided refreshment while the convoy sorted themselves out. From here convoys moved via Het Loo, and EFI shop, mobile, and canteen supervised by Sgt Idris Hammett to the first major refuelling stop, in Leuth. The EFI, under Capt Richard Gamer, provided a 24-hour canteen and shop facility. Capt David Satherly had two shops and a canteen at Salaga, Warrant Officer Alan Bishop had a canteen and shop at Rheindahlen.

All along the line, of communication, via Reckling hausen and halten to the battle area, resources were tested to the limit. To supply 5000 apples for haversack rations at 24 hours' notice was satisfied.

At Mons Bks, a vast, tented camp, Capt Barry Smith and his EFI team, included Sgts Mick Whatron and Laurie Gravestock had an order for 5000 packs of liver sausage, only to see it cancelled and changed to 5000 pork pies instead! Capt Smith also looked after the allied press centre bar where amongst the EFI staff was a contingent of ex Falklands EFI WRAC, including Sgt Fran Bowler and Cpl Jill Wright. Sgt Bowler, normally manager at the junior ranks club, Aliwal barracks, Tidworth, said: 'There's no comparison between Ex Lionheart and the Falklands. At Port Stanley we had proper accommodation, in Germany the tent fell down on top of us.'

Sgt Bowler's most memorable experience of Ex Lionheart was driving to Belgium to serve troops through the night from a mobile, then drive all the way back. It was at Hildesheim that army Maj Gwynne Chipperfield, from the UK as part of the press briefing team, commented, 'There are two brilliant parts of this Hildesheim set up, the army catering and the NAAFI service.'

Perhaps the most romantically located EFI unit was the bulk issue store under the command of Capt Mike Simpson at Walsede, in particular the derelict courtyard and over 300-year-old baronial estate, with a 200-year-old water wheel.

Here initiative typically prevailed. Discovering that local detachments were not being catered for by their parent units, Capt Simpson, normally officially in charge at Hereford, loaded up his Land Rover, turned his BIS into a Mobile Shop, and sold over 10,000 items of drinks, confectionery and other necessities over the tail board. Further detachment of 24 EFI catered for 12,000 troops on Exercise Bold Gannet in Southern Denmark. Although the EFI attracted much of the limelight, civilian NAAFI staff worked well.

Hilda Jones, club manageress, arranged for the telephone to be manned continuously and had a ready constant supply of sandwiches, filled rolls, pies and other items. George Goodman, the mobile charge hand, was joined by Sue Fisher, club assistant from Napier barracks, Janet Backstrom from Barossa barracks, and Ian Wilson from West Riding barracks, to keep the convoys happy.

At Iserlohn, the smallest establishment in Dortmund district, Keith and Andy Arundell and Irene Moore saw an 83% increase in the usual sales when TA hospital facility was set up, manageress Irmgard Langer and her staff at Minden matched these efforts by increasing sales by 119% at another TA hospital. Club assistant Fiona O'Brien contributed to this with sales in the Tavern bar up an astounding 300%.

At Gorunna barracks, the SAS invaded the NAAFI and declared everyone dead even though it was full of TA suppers at the time. The Rhine region proudly boasted, looking after much of the lines of communication and many logistic units in the rear combat zone. Such was the pressure of the regional manager Pat Corlett, was put to work washing up when he visited Olen club near Brussels, especially reopened for the 40th anniversary of the liberation of Brussels and the exercise. Shop manager Allan Robertson and his team ran this temporary facility.

In the midst of all this active service, a VIP luncheon was laid on at the ammunition Department of Bracht for a party of 180 visiting members of the House of Lords, MPs, and senior officers of many countries, including China. Charles Hill, district manager, Rheindahlen, and Maureen Freeman RWS headed the team; a buffet was provided by HQ official Roger Gilbert and the chef Alphonse Dunebacher and other assistance came from staff throughout the region. The QMG, general Sir Richard Trant, made a special visit to talk to all staff involved.

Buschof Shop manager Bill Spragg and staff were active in support of the Army Catering Corps throughout the exercise, actions rewarded by certificates of commendation. Perhaps their supreme effort was arranged for fresh, well not frozen, kippers to be flown in by produce branch. It was a fishy tale indeed. Yvonne Simpson, clothing manager at JHQ and her staff did not miss a chance of extra sales when they arranged a special display of perfumes and other items, relieving the VIPs of their cash.

Wherever service was needed it was provided, whether planned or emergency. No one waited for the okay from on high, they just got stuck in. Both NAAFI and EFI reputations were immeasurably enhanced. 'The EFI acquitted themselves very well and became very much part of the services. The exercise did show us, however, that our training could be more comprehensive and that's something we will work on. But we did iron out and improve on Crusader four years ago,' said Maj Randerson, who praised other links in the NAAFI set up, particularly transporting supplies.

'We didn't have to wait longer than 18 hours for resupply on demand anywhere in Germany. I've never seen anything quite like it. I think we came out of it as well if not better than any other unit.' It is not possible in an exercise of Ex Lionheart's dimensions to mention everyone involved, but the efforts of all those NAAFI and ES staff were summed up by one comment: 'They are worthy successors to a great tradition'.

1985

Falklands Memories by David Stevens 1985

I was OC EFI (rank of Major) from February to October 1985. Sir Peter de la Billière was Commander British Forces Falklands and I received the best annual report I ever had in my 32 years with NAAFI and the EFI. At the time of my arrival we had the famous Court Martial of 15 EFI Personnel for me to sort out and our image was at a very low ebb. Therefore, we had unprecedented shortages of staff and many of the administrative personnel and supply functions were in disarray.

Despite all that, along with another officer, from the RLC plus five others, we managed to put on two productions at Government House during our leisure time – looking back that might have been the reason why I now work in theatre with the Royal Shakespeare Company! Certainly, our evenings of Entertainment for Sir Rex Hunt and Lady Mavis as well, then Sir Peter and Lady de la Billière kept us away from the Coastal 2 Bar. it was the time too that we started the plans to move to Mount Pleasant.

I have many memories of the Falklands including, HQ London asked me to make a video film of our operations both at Port Stanley and the Islands. Goodness knows whatever happened to it. It was the subject of a cartoon in the Penguin News (Major Spielberg Stevens).

Looking at what I have kept there are some photos – mainly of seals! Sammy the seal used to come on Coastal 2 (the floating barge where we lived) to bask in the sun. Port Stanley appeared to be the only place where you can have all four seasons in one day! I have fond memories of the Falkland Islands Logistics Battalion Officers of 1985 and the opening of Mount Pleasant with Michael Heseltine (Defence Secretary), Rex Hunt, Peter de la Billière.

We tried to improve our image in Port Stanley – still have the Penguin Passport which we sold with a giant soft toy penguin. It was necessary for the passport to be signed confirming that it was hatched at the 'Olde Bakery Number 7, Fitzroy Road, Port Stanley' to prove the penguin had been registered and had full right of abode in the UK prior to departure. I don't have my penguin as my dog took a fancy to it but still have the passport!

We did a weekly offer which we highlighted on the radio with a five-minute slot – like we did in Germany on BFBS.

It was strange and difficult times – working nearly every day but still having time for some fun especially in the evenings. Even played golf once with Sir Rex Hunt, the Governor – the world's worst golf course, you had to leave your ball if you went into the rough because of the mines!

Meeting the Princess of Wales on HMS Beaver Memories by Kevin O'Kane 1985

Meeting the Princess of Wales. On HMS Beaver, during a trials period at Portland, Dorset, Diana, Princess of Wales toured the ship and stopped off briefly at the canteen where Kevin O'Kane was the Canteen Manager. Kevin is seen in this picture answering a few questions from the Princess who was impressed by the display of 'nutty' as chocolate is known in the Navy as her love of chocolate is well known. She also spoke to several sailors in the queue and congratulated them on their hard work and dedication before moving on to tour the rest of the ship.

Behind the wire at RAF Molesworth 1985

Under cover of darkness in February 1500 Royal Engineers and hundreds of police officers arrived at a derelict bomber station in rural Cambridgeshire and began erecting a 7-mile-long barbed wire fence around its perimeter. CND supporters, who had vowed to make RAF Molesworth the focus of anti-nuclear demonstrations during the current cruise missile debate, were foiled by a massive security operation.

Construction work was continuing, and the job of feeding hundreds of contractors and security staff was currently testing the capabilities of NAAFI manager, contract catering Clive Hall, and his team. He landed the catering contract at Molesworth just before Christmas. But the task was not without problems. 'The main one was security; this had to be kept under wraps right until the last moment. We had a tremendous problem, supplies could not be told where we were going, staff could not be told where they would be working, very few people knew about the operation at all,' he said.

Contract manager Dave Saunders was brought back from European service to handle the day-to-day running of the contract and he arrived, together with 36 staff, at 0800hrs on the day of operation. The RAF provided an empty hangar in the middle of Molesworth for NAAFI use. Mr Saunders' team had four hours to set up the tables, chairs, services, and cooking equipment, before the 1st 1080 customers arrived for a hot lunch.

During the first few days, in blizzard conditions, the hangar was shared with RAF motor transport section. NAAFI staff cooked and served food at one end and the mechanics serviced earth movers and trucks at the other.

Thankfully, a partition wall was soon built and conditions inside the canteen rapidly improved. Generators were brought in to provide electricity and propane gas space heaters brought the temperature indoors, at least above freezing point. 'Conditions were terrible when we first arrived, there was nothing on site except for an empty building. There was no electricity, no water, no heating,' said Andy Sargent, a kitchen porter. 'We were running with plastic bins for firemen who were filling them with hoses and then we carried them back to the kitchen. Until then we couldn't even start cooking. Conditions were gradually improving with the arrival of gas bottles, generators, portacabins for sleeping; until they arrived, we were hot-bedding it with one shift getting out of bed and the lads coming off duty climbing in.'

Staff were serving up 2250 meals a day and the mess was open 24 hours. Staff from near RAF Wyton were running a club service in one corner of the building. Reaction from the civilian labourers, soldiers and police alike had been very good. All appreciated the hot substantial meals served under very testing conditions and more than a few made their comparison with the EFI service on the Falklands.

In a letter to the managing director Brian Whittaker, Air Commodore John Barney of HQ RAF support command said that NAAFI contribution at RAF Molesworth was valued and appreciated. The company's involvement in the provision of catering support under such trying conditions was crucial to the success of the operation.

Berlin a city of surprises by Roy Gabriele 1985

The city of Berlin was misunderstood, so the family shop manager Roy Gabriele, who after 4 and half years there, gave a quick guide.

West Berlin was a surprising city, a cosmopolitan metropolis surrounded by forests, rivers, parks and lakes, and not the concrete and steel jungle generally imagined.

Its streets alone were lined with more than 200,000 trees. Over 1/3 of Berlin was parkland or waterways. Within its walls, there were 100 farms and huge lakes, with their 180 miles of beaches, providing it for many sports. Nearly 2 million people live there, and they could enjoy a lot in the way of entertainment. There were 5000 restaurants, cafes, pubs, and night clubs, more than 50 art galleries, museums and more than 20 theatres and opera houses, including the home of the Philharmonic Orchestra.

The most infamous and famous landmark was the Berlin Wall; this was 165 kilometres long completely encircling West Berlin. Before their escape route was finally sealed off in 1961, 2½ million East Germans fled to the West sector, 73 people have been killed trying to get over the wall. Among their obstacles, dogs, mines, tank traps, tripwires, 289 watchtowers with armed guards and 124 km of electrified fencing.

Only two miles long, however, is Kurfurstendamm, West Berlin's main shopping street, full of people day and night. Its parade of shops, theatres, restaurants, night clubs, and cafes are complemented by street performers, clowns, jugglers, pavement artists and musicians.

Just past the end of the Ku'damm as the street is known locally is the Kaufhaus-des-Westrens, a massive store covering 43,000 square metres, which, after Harrods, is the largest store in Europe. It receives between 70 and 80,000 customers who can choose from more than 250,000 items. The city had many other attractions. The Berlin zoo, opened in 1844, and one of the oldest in the world, it was virtually destroyed during the war. Only 91 animals survived. In 1985 it was home to 7500 animals over 74 acres. The botanical gardens covered 100 acres, had 45 greenhouses, and some 18,000 different species of plant, including some found in Egyptian tombs.

The Olympic Stadium, built to house the 1936 games, is 300 metres long, 230 metres wide and seated 100,000 people. Around it is a riding arena, swimming complex, hockey field, tennis courts, and a sports ground for rugby, football and parades. West Berlin had two airports Tegal and Templehof, the latter used in 1985 as an American military base. Templehof was originally used as a parade ground during the days of the Kaiser, was an important airfield in the First World War, and in 1923, it was the world's third largest airport.

During the 1948 1949 Berlin blockade, aircraft landed and took off every 90 seconds bringing 2 million tonnes of supplies in a total of 280,000 flights. The city was steeped in history and wealth of interesting places.

1986

Bakery's rise to success 1986

The rising success of NAAFI's first in-store bakeries in the UK shops led to more openings that year. The two bakeries, at Shute Road, Catterick Garrison, and Station Road, Tidworth were installed with the twin aims of providing experience for staff in their operation and to stimulate customers' visitation. George Waller, manager at Shute Road, said: 'It's too early to judge whether the bakery is increasing customer loyalty, but the signs are encouraging. The real test comes with this winter weather. If the Garrison gets cut off, the customers will have nowhere else to go. Once they've turned to us, we hope to keep them.' Mr Waller explained that the bakery took a fortnight to install, involving staff in re-merchandising operation to make room, but little inconvenience to customers.

Its operation is in the capable hands of shop assistants Maureen Cranney and Allison Prescott, who are helped when needed by Mr Wallace's wife. Their initial training was given by Baughans Limited, suppliers of ready to bake bread, cakes, etc. The equipment was supplied by Fair Deal Equipment limited, of Northants.

Mrs Cranney, four years at Catterick, described the work: 'When the uncooked bread is delivered, we pack it straight into our freezer. The night before baking we take it out to defrost. In the morning, it is proved to permit the yeast content of the dough to work and expand. Then it's straight into the oven for about 30 minutes to bake.'

Customers are also tempted with fresh baked rolls, buns, Cornish pasties, sausage rolls, custard pies and other delights. Preparation and baking times vary, as many items did not need proving before baking, some needed to be glazed like the savouries with egg before they were cooked. Otherwise the bakery was easy to work on, and enjoyable for the staff. In a typical day, the shop would clear three dozen loaves and French sticks, 300 rolls, 180 savouries, 250 doughnuts. The latter come ready made, do not have to go in the oven, and are either sugared or iced prior to going on display. Customers started to buy their rolls and bakery goods regularly as they could smell a freshness as they walked in the shop. Being freshly baked made all the difference to the customer, as the taste was much nicer.

The success story was the same as Station Road commented with: 'Customers snap up 240 doughnuts, around three dozen loaves, scores of savouries, rolls, and pastries every day'. The shop assistants Beth Finnigan and Jessica Campbell are kept busy, especially during the troops' morning break when it is a rush for hot snacks. They both said it was hard work especially when they are trying to bake and serve at the same time, but they enjoyed it.

Bob is honoured 1986

Throughout the whole of NAAFI history many men and women have been honoured by the Queen, but one man stands out above all. The commanding officer of NAAFI's own Territorial

Army, EFI, was made an MBE in the Queen's birthday honours. Maj Bob Randerson, OC RAOC EFI for almost 14 years, said he was delighted and surprised to receive the award but added: 'It is really an award for the whole of EFI, for the NAAFI staff who volunteered to serve the services in uniform. It rewards their efforts for me and the company.'

Maj Randerson was attending their NCS EFI OCA reunion at Wingham, the day the award was announced. He was overwhelmed by the congratulations and the special presentation made on behalf of the OCA members. He received a framed limited edition print of the evacuation from Dunkirk.

Maj Bob Randerson MBE will always remain one of the EFI legends of all time; he was favoured by all and his previous experience in the armed forces stood him in good stead for all the development and successes of EFI.

Accepting the challenge by Malcolm D Field taking the role of chairman 1986

As a member of the board of management for 18 years, 13 of them chairman, Sir James Spooner made a major contribution to and had considerable influence on NAAFI. During that time, Sir James also enjoyed a most distinguished business career and yet was always able to find time to devote to NAAFI affairs. No one knows more than I do how difficult it will be to follow him as chairman. The progress made by NAAFI under him and the two managing directors who served during his period of office, namely Edward MacGowan and Brian Whitaker, must be maintained.

I accepted the council's invitation to become chairman because I believe that NAAFI has a valuable and important contribution to make to the quality of service life. Over the past 15 years as a non-executive director I have been impressed with the spirit, enthusiasm, and the commitment within NAAFI to make this contribution, I am honoured that I should be asked to take this post. The role of chairman of any board is to select the right strategy for the future of any business and to ensure the board works as a cohesive unit. In reaching his conclusions the chairman should bring together the wisdom and experience of the board members.

In respect we are fortunate to have a high quality of successful businessmen as nonexecutive directors and your deputy chairman, Jeremy Hardie, whose father was also a member and then deputy chairman of NAAFI board, has a wide field of experience through the many appointments he has held in the financial world and through his involvement as deputy chairman of the Monopolies Commission.

On the trading side we have Sir Adrian Swire with his deep knowledge and experience of the Far East, John Bartholomew as a Brewer, and Colin Cullimore as managing director of Dewhurst and president of the Multiple Retailers Association. The recent appointment of Air Chief Marshall Sir David Evans, previously president of the NAAFI council, has brought a knowledge of the MoD which has already proved invaluable. Finally, we have the service directors with their first-hand experience and understanding of the services requirements.

I am very fortunate to have such a distinguished group of nonexecutive directors. I look forward to working with them and the executive directors and with James Rucker when he takes over as managing director. In accepting the post of chairman, I believe, perhaps immodestly, I can make a contribution to NAAFI for I see so many similarities with my own company. In WH Smith we have the same concern and caring attitude for our staff and customers, which is such a strong philosophy within NAAFI. I'm often asked how I find the time to do these different jobs. Of course, it is sometimes very difficult, but I remember that I am a non-executive chairman and my role is to give advice and steer the future course for the NAAFI business.

It is in the managing director's interest that his executive director who would be responsible for executing the strategy agreed by the board. I believe that it is good for directors of public and private companies to have business interests outside their own companies and to have the benefit of their experience to another organisation such as NAAFI. It is a two-way arrangement, and many of the nonexecutive directors would be the first to admit that they have learnt a great deal about managing business from their experience as a non-executive director of NAAFI.

Prior to my joining of the board, NAAFI in 1973, my only experience of the company was during my national service days at the guards depot, Caterham. Thereafter my services took me to Cyprus where, as a second Lieutenant in the Welsh Guards, I learned how important the company was to the wellbeing of the service community in providing what the services require. NAAFI has proved that it can do this and make a profit to ensure the future development of the business.

The climate in which we trade today is very different from what it was then. More and more, service life has come closer to Civilian life. NAAFI finds itself competing, as far as its shops are concerned, with successful High Street retailers. Customers' requirements in NAAFI are very wide. We are asked, for example, to run supermarkets and the equivalent of village shops. Success depends on the managers and staff who work in those shops.

On the club side, we faced competition from numerous different leisure interests, which leads me to the point of view that, if we want service people to look upon our clubs as places in which they would like to spend part of their leisure time, we have to offer very high standards of service, comfort and entertainment. We need to show the services, through what we do now, how we can improve the quality of service life, generate a rebate, and make an increasing contribution to service welfare funds. I want to see this contribution increase so that our customers recognise that this is the services' own organisation and our Motto 'serving the services' is what NAAFI is all about.

1987

Operation Oman Ex Saif Sareea 1987

Winter weather provided a stark welcome home for EFI lads on their return from serving 1800 troops involved in 'Exercise Saif Sareea', on the island of Masirah, off Oman.

The eight-strong team got back to freezing temperatures after running a bulk issue store and canteens in temperatures which averaged 25 degrees centigrade each day. The 19-day exercise involved troops in five airborne brigade, two Parachute Regiments, and the Omani armed forces. Despite being in a Muslim country, EFI were able to sell duty free alcohol but only to British customers to bring back with them to the UK. Sweets and peanuts, cigarettes and other goods provided the bulk of the sales; 200 pairs of men's flip flops were sold in just four days.

Local goods such as prayer mats bought specifically from Oman's capital city, Muscat and Shemaghs, worn as a traditional headdress by the Omani men, also provided popular buys – 200 of each were sold. Additional revenue from a kiosk Which the EFI team ran at the base camp mess on film nights.

Surprisingly, demand for soft drinks in such a warm climate was lower than expected, averaging only three cans per man per day. The officer who led the EFI team said that all eight of us, at one time helped by a service forklift truck driver, working hard throughout.

On the days when troops arrived and left Oman, the EFI lads ran a 24-hour service in shifts and for the duration of the exercise, opened from 0700 to 0000hrs each day. Their efforts were very much appreciated, and as they left, the RAF officer in charge of the movement said that they didn't know what they would have done without them. The officer in charge's team comprised Sgt Dave Forster and Paul I'Anson along with Cpl Stan Goodwin, Ian Yarnton, Chris Webb, Bob Lawrence and Andy Moore.

Maj Bob Randerson, OC RAOC EFI said: 'We were invited by 5 brigade to provide our service in Oman, the first time we had operated in that area of the world in many years. Our lads did a fine job, I'm sure it was tremendous experience for them. We are now looking forward to running a service for five brigade when they exercise in Galloway, Scotland, later this year. I'm sure they'll receive the same good service.'

All changes civilians take over the Falkland Islands 1987

Civilians would take over the running of NAAFI facilities on the Falklands from the uniform staff of the EFI. The move follows the establishment of a new Tri service base at Mount Pleasant airfield, 30 miles from the capital, Port Stanley. The new civilian team will comprise 13 staff recruited in the UK and 12 recruited from the Atlantic island of Saint Helena. The Saint Helena staff arrived on the island at the end of April 1987 and will progressively replace EFI volunteers. The UK staff will start to arrive in the June and the transition from uniform service to the more usual civilian operated service would be completed by the end of September.

Pat Wilcox, manager of the overseas service, said: 'The establishment of a steady pace presents an ideal opportunity for NAAFI to turn to its civilian role. The premises at the airport at Mount Pleasant are a vast improvement on the rough and ready facilities they first encountered and are more appropriate for civilian staff. Since the outbreak of the hostilities in 1982, EFI have had 500 men and women serve on the island. Some had even completed a second and a third tour of duty.'

Maj Bob Randerson, officer commanding RAOC EFI, said, 'The last five years have been a memorable part of EFI history. We thrive under difficult conditions, but now there are clean, modern clubs in use, our presence is no longer needed. Some of EFI have enjoyed their tour of duty, others have found it hard going but none have regretted the experience. I'm sure that everybody that goes to the Falkland Islands as civilians will find it just as rewarding.'

Arctic training pays off for EFI in Norway 1987

This year had been no different to every other year EFI had supported troops in Norway. And every year they excelled their numbers to a new record.

A 25 strong team of EFI ran the service for 10 weeks throughout the five-troop exercise in Norway. The EFI lads, operating from 7 bulk issue stores and shops with two canteens, on mobile shops in scattered locations, in below zero temperatures kept the allied command Europe (ACE) mobile force and Royal Marines supplied with refreshments, snacks, cigarettes, chocolates, gifts and durables with souvenirs.

The NAAFI team, volunteered from the UK and Europe service establishments, they were well prepared for that Norway task after a weekend's Arctic training at Wingham in November. Many of them found the freezing conditions extremely hard work, even Capt David Satherly, who was on his first visit to Norway, he was commanding the EFI detachment. 'Breathing was difficult, temperatures were so low down to minus 35 degrees centigrade we could only work outside for 15 minutes shifts. I even got frost nip on my toes, which thankfully cleared up,' he said.

Taking NAAFI to Norway did not mean that they didn't take part in any of the exercise, several of the EFI lads learned how to prevent similar ailments from expert Marines who taught them survival techniques over three days and nights spent in a snow hole. Richard Illsley said, 'It wasn't pleasant the long dark nights, with nothing to do for hours but watch candles burn, was boring. In the few hours of daylight, the Marines taught us a great deal.'

Operating as the service, provided many an incident, perfume solidified in the cold, soda bottles exploded and equipment froze, and Capt Satherley's record, reaching Lom with his team two days before 42 commando advanced party: 'They were amazed we were there before them'.

Cpl Ross was greeted like an old friend by customers of 42 commando, who he went on to serve for a third year in a row. Sgt Dave Foster occupied the same desk, in the same office in the same location (Bomoen), as he had on 12 previous occasions. Warrant Officer Andy Dungay re-joined the Andalsness indoor football team for the fifth year in succession: 'I even had my own locker!' he declared proudly.

As normal, Maj Bob Randerson OC RAOC EFI congratulated the lads that had done a job they did so well and in the manner that they did it. They were also congratulated for raising £300 for the Zeebrugge ferry disaster fund.

HMS Sultan club June 1987

A new NAAFI club, heralded by sailors as probably the most prestigious in the South, opened in May 1987 at HMS Sultan, Gosport, with a sparkling cabaret night. Dave Lee Travis, popular Radio One-disc jockey, led celebrations as hundreds of sailors from the Royal Navy marine engineering school and their guests packed the disco club and marvelled at the latest in high tech sounds and lighting equipment.

More than 90 neon strip lights, two mirror globes spread their light show to the disco beat, giving way only for an equally impressive display of stage lighting when Pop group Greengage stepped out to perform their set. 'You have to travel quite a way to find anything like this,' said chief Petty Officer Alan Pennifold, chairman of the club committee which plays an integral part in planning the new facilities. 'The club is spacious, modern and well equipped for our needs. Measurably better than anything we had before.'

In fact, the new club was a centrepiece of a leisure and recreation centre, which took nine years to get from the drawing board to reality. Planned and built by Property Services Agency, in consultation with NAAFI property services Department, the centre includes a post office, bank, barbers, and tailors, and other shops, as well as a NAAFI club.

At the naming ceremony of Sultan club, Rear Admiral John Burgess commanding officer at Sultan when building work began, said: 'The club is a great credit to all those involved in its planning and construction. It had good architecture, a clever design and surpassed most service clubs I'd seen.' The club wasn't short of all the usual grandeur invested in our armed forces service clubs. In addition, two rooftop gardens where barbecue pit pits were fitted for use on warm summer nights for major events was a real stand out feature. There wasn't one aspect or age group left out.

Gulf call met by swift response 1987

A six-day deadline was beaten by staff at Rosyth who worked determinedly to stock 4 minesweepers and a support vessel, HMS Abdiel, to sail to the strife torn Gulf of Oman.

Geoff Duncan, district manager Scotland (naval), and cantina warehouse staff swung into action immediately as notice was given that the ships were to join Royal Navy vessels on patrol in troubled waters outside Iraq-Iran war zone. Andrew Inglis, manager of Rosyth ration store planned the storing operations with the canteen managers Geordie Boaden, of HMS Abdiel, and Gary Murphy, of HMS Rothesay. The due were in the middle of exchanging posts when the emergency call was raised. 'Our initial problem was uncertainty, and asked what other ships, if any, might sail to support the minesweepers, as a precaution, we decided to load as many stores as HMS Abdiel could carry. Additional stories were released by the ship supply officer to take an extra 2000 cases of beer and 2500 cases of minerals. Three days after we were given notice the stores had to be loaded aboard by Mr Murphy and canteen staff. The emergency couldn't have come at a worse time for us,' said Mr Duncan. 'Given that we were right in the middle of the summer leave, we were short of manpower.'

With HMS Abdiel at sea, Andrew and his staff at the ration store was still faced with the problem of storing major refurbishment ship Royal Fleet Auxiliary Regent with, among other things 72,000 eggs, 1260 cases of own brand minerals, and 12 pallets of dry stores. 'That operation took three days,' said Mr Duncan, 'a task made more difficult since with ammunition on board, Regent was moored out in the Forth. Goods had to be taken out by supply boat.'

The Fleet Inn Tavern opened its services shop, normally closed at weekends, for sailors to buy their essentials and extras before sailing. The staff worked magnificently to beat the deadlines we faced, they had good reason to be proud of their endeavours.

Dressed for the 90s October 1987

Fresh, attractive and in keeping with NAAFI's modern approach that the look of the new staff uniforms was set to make their debut in the UK and Germany around Christmas time. The uniform issue had been extended to include blouses and quilted body warmers for female staff, and trousers, shirts and jackets for men. Another first for the introduction of a uniform for male clothing, and all gifts and durables staff in Germany.

The range is strong on detailing with attention given to comfort and practicality. A new hat had replaced scarves worn during food preparation and serving. On the tabard, Velcro had replaced the buttons for easier removal. Pockets have been added to the front which was one of the points praised by staff at the Pegasus club, Lyneham, who previewed the range during a photo call at the club.

'It's useful to have a place for notebooks, keys,' said Helen Blackwell, club assistant, 'but the neckline is a little high for wearing in hot weather. The hat is a good idea, it won't fall off, it's definitely more the modern image.'

June Fullwood, assistant club manager, agreed: 'It's the nicest uniform I've seen since I joined NAAFI in 1961. The dress is of a good washable material, slightly longer than before, and more fashionable.' Hugh Cowley, manager of the home service South and naval, and chairman of the staff clothing committee, said the new look is more in keeping with the

NAAFI modern approach. 'I am pleased we can now issue a complete uniform. Management will ensure NAAFI presentation in shops and clubs is continually reviewed, with the object of improving our image with customers. The clothing committee will meet regularly to make sure the uniform is kept up to date.'

Shirley Roberts, buyer, stressed that a great deal of thought went into the colour scheme chosen to replace that of the navy blue one introduced in 1981. The new house colours of orange, brown and cream made the choice of colour for dresses and suits difficult, bearing in mind the uniform had to be worn by all skin tones and age groups. Brown was felt to be too drab and cream was out because it stains easily. The texture of the polyester fabric had a good colour retention, crease, and tear resistance. It was easy to wash, and it wears well.

Mrs Roberts explained that the old pinafores were designed to be worn with ladies' own blouses, which led to a range of looks and colours. All the outfits complement each other, and their surroundings. The new styles have been designed to flatter the female wearers whatever their size. We were pleasantly surprised by the samples made up in larger sizes. The manufacturer reshaped the garments with extra darts and pleats to suit the larger figure. The skirts and jacket could now be ordered separately, to allow for a mix of sizes. The suit has been very well received by the staff who have seen it. It is more appropriate for meeting suppliers and customers.

The new look could start to appear in clubs and shops in the UK and clubs and shops in Germany towards the end of 1987. Clubs in Germany would follow in 1988. It was important that all the staff in each establishment would wait until every member of staff was fully kitted out with the new uniform before they were wearing it. This was to ensure that there was not a mix of Old Navy blue and new rust and brown in the same location.

Exercise Keystone in West Germany 1987

NAAFI was on hand to serve 30,000 troops before, during, and after one of the biggest army exercises since World War II, 'Exercise Keystone' in West Germany. Staff in northern and western region ran services for troops travelling to and returning from the exercise while the EFI were present to serve them in the field.

At Newcastle airport, Tony Bleathman, district manager Catterick South, his wife Camille and staff from Allenbrook barracks, Albermarle barracks and the RAF regiment depot at Catterick, operated a canteen service in an aircraft hangar. They worked 12 hour shifts for five days selling teas, coffees, and snacks. They also showed video films. The men really valued the service especially the videos. They were bored waiting to fly out – a cup of tea and a film was just what they wanted.

At North Shields docks, Tyne and Wear, Lou Milstead Williamson, district manager Catterick North, with staff from the Harden club, Catterick Garrison and from Wathgill training camp, operated a similar service and two mobiles for 3600 troops. The four strong team, based in a disused car import warehouse, closed the bar for only four hours a day, to grab some sleep. As the territorials didn't often come into contact with NAAFI, this was a good exercise to let them know all about us.

Derek Lupson, district manager Finningley, led a 6 strong team operating two mobiles at Immingham docks on the Humber, from where 1600 troops and all vehicles for the exercise were ferried to West Germany. At the air mounting service South Cerney, Gloucestershire, Dennis Lafferty, district manager Worcester, and staff from western region ran a 72-hour restaurant service for 6500 troops during the exercise.

Troops arriving in Germany were met by NAAFI mobile supports and airports. In the exercise area a 30-strong EFI team, operating from two bulk issue stores, three shops and a canteen, and several mobiles, kept them supplied with sweets, soft drinks, cigarettes, and durables. At Bonnien, a disused cowshed was the site for a shop and bulk issue store which was up and running in under 24 hours and open from 0800 to 2200hrs each day of the exercise, although a knock on the door ensured a 24 hour service. One of the best sellers was an Exercise Keystone mug and tee shirts which proved to be popular for the soldiers to take home with them.

1988

Exercise Snow Queen 1988

The first customers feeling the benefits of the new family shop and bulk issue store at Sonthofen, in Germany, were our troops on exercise Snow Queen which got underway in December 1987. The facilities set up following a request from HQ 1 British Corps, for the exercise which ended in March 1988, they will stay open thereafter for volunteers undergoing adventure training. The army used to make its own arrangement but made an approach to NAAFI through John Fisher, regional manager 4 Div. The premises were leased and then used as a store for traffic signs and, after the landlord carried out alterations, moved in and fitted them out. Not surprisingly as Snow Queen largely involved troops using ski equipment, the new shop offered a range of ski wear and accessories. As well as traditional goods, confectionery, groceries, dairy produce, frozen foods and duty free. Also available was beers, wines, and spirits. The home and leisure section offered an assortment of personal audio equipment, household goods, toys and games.

The shop also had video films for hire, and customers could take advantage of a three-day photographic printing and development service. They could use their NAAFI budget account or charge cards, Access and Visa to pay for goods. Unusually, but at the request of HQ 1 BR Corps, no discount or dividend on purchase, instead a 4% rebate on sales goes to the unit to improve facilities at Sonthofen.

Exercise Purple Warrior 1988

A 30-strong EFI team were on hand to serve some 20,000 troops involved in 'Ex Purple Warrior', the biggest Tri service exercise held on British soil. The EFI men, living in tents inside an aircraft hangar at West Freugh, Stranraer, West Scotland, operated out of mobiles and 24-hour bulk issue store, shop, and canteen. Over 11,000 cups of tea and coffee and 2500 sandwiches were sold during the 16-day exercise.

Sgt Dave Forster, who managed the EFI operation, said it was hard work and the men were working 10-hour shifts, and noise in the hangar made it difficult to sleep. The only major issue was flooding which could have damaged the power points. On one occasion the water was four inches deep and they had to call the fire brigade in to pump it dry.

The Darlington warehouse was the main centre for the supply of canteen and mess hall items to Ex Purple Warrior. Their trucks made 6 trips to fill up with groceries, messing goods, and such personal items as soap and toothpaste. Jack Hardy, warehouse assistant, had extra interest in loading supplies before the exercise. He was a Cpl in the EFI, and Purple Warrior was his first exercise.

Mill Hill IRA bomb 1988

A NAAFI driver was the first to rush to the aid of the victims after the IRA bomb blast at Inglis barracks, Mill Hill, London, which left one soldier dead and nine others injured. Frank Townley, from Aldershot transport department, was about to make his early morning delivery to the NAAFI club when the bomb went off at an accommodation block nearby, reported Helen Walkey.

I was about 50 metres from the blast, I could feel the shock waves hit my Ford cargo lorry, said Frank, who served in the army for 18 years, including Northern Ireland. 'I could hear the screams and the injured among the rubble. When you hear someone screaming like that it remains with you forever. I ran across to see what I could do, it was terrible, rubble everywhere, like being back in Northern Ireland. I helped a man for 20 minutes, pulling three men out from the debris. I never found out who they were. I didn't have time to think of the consequences, speed was of the essence. At first, half the brief was holding up, but later pictures on television showed it caved in. After making my delivery it took 45 minutes to get out of the barracks. All traffic had to make way for fleets of ambulances and fire engines. By the time I got to the NAAFI shop down the road I was grateful for a cup of tea.'

Frank who had been with NAAFI for two years, received a letter of thanks for his swift action from James Rucker, MD. Mr Rucker had congratulated him for 'being so quick and that there were people out there working for the company like myself'.

Quick action by 5 live-in staff who were shaken from their beds by the 0655 hrs explosion. Hillary Hiett, manager, Lyn Turner, family shop assistant manager, and club assistants evacuated their quarters over the club and joined the military personnel in the safe area of the barracks.

The staff were given emergency issues of tracksuits and toiletries to tide them over, and temporary accommodation at RAF Hendon until, after routine questioning, the police allowed them to go home. 'Large numbers of panes of glass in the club were shattered in the blast,' said Tim Bennett, district manager Halton. 'The girls had to pick their way down glass strewn stairs to get out. Once out, no NAAFI staff were allowed back into the building until the following day. We had no idea of the extent of the damage until then. We offered the commanding officer an extended service on the Tuesday evening, which he was happy for us to provide. The lads at Mill Hill were sorely in need of a quiet drink. We are part of the camp and we would have liked to have provided a service on the day of the bombing, but we couldn't get back into the building until the Police forensic team had done their work. When we did, at around noon, the staff here did a tremendous job clearing up the debris ready for opening late that afternoon. All the lads who had been living in the bombed block were given temporary accommodation at the Mill Hill Postal Depot about a mile away, where we run a 24-hour Vending service. Normally it was staffed in the morning, but during the upheaval we had staff there throughout the day providing a limited counter service and keeping the vending machines stocked,' said Tim Bennett.

'We provided an extended bar and restaurant service, from 0900 to2230 hrs for a week after the incident,' said Miss Hiett. Reflecting on events of Monday the 1st of August 1988, Mr

Bennett said: 'You never received training for an event like this, and don't know how to react when it happens. My first concern was for the staff, I made sure that they told their parents that they were alright. My thoughts then turned to resuming normal service as soon as possible. The shock only set in later.'

NAAFI issued a security notice, by the central administrative services to all departments at headquarters Imperial Court, London and College House, Nottingham, asking staff to ensure safety, wherever they were based. Tim Elliott, manager CAS, said 'It's everyone's personal responsibility to take precautions to ensure they don't put themselves and their colleagues at risk.' He warned that if they notice anything unusual that you must look twice because it must be reported to security staff. Security within all bases was increased immediately and NAAFI staff increased their vigilance for things out of the ordinary in the clubs.

My Far East Voyages by Tom Holland 1988

My recent retirement brought back memories of a long career with NAAFI which started out on a cold morning when I set out at 0630hrs to walk for miles to Crediton station to catch the train to Plymouth. At 1130hrs I arrived at Prospect Row, Davenport, and I was sent to HMS Raleigh, Torpoint. I was on my way to Chatham to sign on for the Navy and six weeks training.

My next stop was a draft to HMS Newcastle. On the 1st of March 1943 we sailed for the Far East, not knowing when we would arrive home again. That turned out to be May 1945. The two years and two months were spent mostly in Burma area, which gave us the Burma star.

Back at Rosyth Seaport I was on draft again, this time to a minesweeper, HMS Ossory, and spent the next nine months running in and out to Londonderry, Northern Ireland, sweeping mines in the Irish Sea and Atlantic. I was sent to Portsmouth, only for a month, and then back to Plymouth, changing ships every few months: King George V, Newfoundland, Comet, Vancouver, and several others. I joined HMS Jamaica in June 1949 for a two-year tour of the West Indies, After only four months we were off to Hong Kong, a trip which took six weeks. We were just in time to escort HMS Amethyst from China back to the colony.

During our trip to Japan, the Korean War started. The first day up the East Coast we were hit by shellfire from ashore and 5 were killed, and 7 hurt. Later we joined the American fleet and stood off, letting go R6 inch guns. Our luck ran out and we were hit by a shell from the Korean aircraft, one killed. But the day was not lost. We shot the aircraft down, the only one downed by a ship in the Korean War.

Back into Susako, Japan, I left the Jamaica for HMS Ladybird, the Chinese gunboat we had taken over. After two years and four months on Jamaica and Ladybird, I was sent on leave. A telegram from London interrupted my break. I was given a railway warrant to Plymouth and told to go and find HMS St Brides Bay in the Far East.

First test was to find a ship going my way. I managed to take a trip on HMS Bermuda to Malta, where I was stuck for a fortnight before jumping aboard HMS Unicorn, on which I slept on the flight deck on a camp bed. Unicorn took me as far as Hong Kong, HMS Ocean to Susako, and a Navy railway warrant to Kuri, where I joined HMS Bridesway four months after leaving Plymouth.

My next ship was HMS Salisbury on which I spent five good years of which the highlight was 2000 mile trip up the St Lawrence seaway. With Salisbury paid off I was sent back to the Far East to join HMS Woodbridge for two years. By now the Far East was like a second home to me, so it came as no surprise when I was sent to Plymouth to pick up HMS Eagle, which was going out to the Far East for 12 months before being paid off back in Portsmouth. I felt I'd run out of ships, NAAFI decided it was time I came ashore. I was sent to Whale Island, but not for long as I had a heart attack, and it was touch and go for a while. After six months I returned to work at home in Portsmouth, where three years later I had another heart attack.

Back at work I moved to HMS Dolphin where I spent a very good 10 years, made a lot of good friends, and it is from HMS Dolphin that I said goodbye to NAAFI. Finishing off my time, I had a surprise. Commander Davies, Capt of HMS Newcastle at the time, having heard about my first ship, sent me an invite to go to sea for a day. I was in the dockyard by 0700hrs on the 21st of May and sailed at 0800hrs returning at 1700hrs. My first ship, HMS Newcastle, also became my last; it was a wonderful day and made it all so worthwhile.

1989

The Duchess of York visits Amesbury 1989

A morale boosting visit by the Duchess of York, in March of 1989, delighted staff at Amesbury warehouse. The Duchess took time to meet as many staff as she could within her tight schedule and surprised many by being so relaxed and informal as she chatted to them.

The Duchess was greeted by the Vice Lord Lieutenant of Wiltshire, Field Marshal Sir Ronald Gibbs, and was guided round the warehouse by Tim Best, distribution manager who programmed the visit. He said: 'She seemed a little bit nervous at first but quickly settled down and was very spontaneous. A visit like this was very good for morale. It was a very happy day.' The chief constable of Wiltshire, Walter Girven, James Rocker, managing director, Mike Henebrey, supplies director, and three service directors and other senior staff were presented to the Duchess. In the blue room the Duchess signed the visitors' book and was told, over refreshments, about NAAFI and the role of the warehouse.

Her tour which followed, took in the general office, the computer and stock control sections, the extended range operation, export, traditional goods, packaging, assembly, dispatch, transport, loading sections of the warehouse and the staff restaurant in the tea factory. In the tea factory, the Duchess heard from Bill Payne, tea buyer, how they buy and select. She saw blending drums, and machines packaging tea bags. Mr Payne said: 'She was very interested in NAAFI tea and recalled how she used to drink it as a young girl with a spoonful of sugar as a treat. She'd always wondered how tea bags were produced and asked questions.'

At the end of the tour, the Duchess was treated to a farewell line-up of nine forklift truck drivers, including two ladies, Sue Richards and Angie Jones. Before leaving for another engagement, she was presented with a toy bunny for Princess Beatrice by Debbie Campbell, 21, an assembler.

In the tea factory, the Duchess was presented with a framed photograph of the Queen Mother taken in 1943 during the visit to NAAFI training centre, then at Woking in Surrey. The photograph was used in the 1953 Coronation issue off NAAFI News. A copy has hung in the historical collection at Imperial Court, and another copy was hung in the office of Bill Payne, tea factory manager, for more than 36 years. Mr Payne recalled that the picture was presented to his predecessor Neville Banks. A copy of the photograph appeared in the Times on 2nd of January 1988.

Infused ginger was the duchess's favourite drink and thanks to a tip from Buckingham Palace, Alec Clayton, restaurant manager, was well prepared. The Duchess was generally surprised when she was offered her favourite brew while the other guests drank tea and coffee during the break for refreshments. The drink was made by pouring boiling water onto grated root ginger, is left to stand then strained, it reputedly settles the stomach and is drunk by the Duchess on long flights.

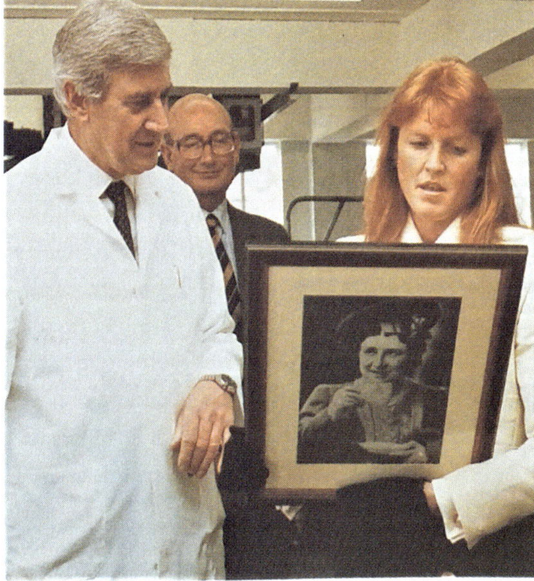

The Queen Mother had a lovely day at Sir John Moore barracks Winchester 1989

Her Majesty the Queen Mother took tea in the NAAFI Green Light Club at Sir John Moore Barracks Winchester, when she visited the light division Depot.

She joined soldiers and their families in the club, recently refurbished. The new lighting fixtures, paid for by NAAFI and the unit, impressed Her Majesty. She described the club as spacious and airy. Preparations for the visit took many days, even the chair legs were varnished. Staff prepared the refreshments for 200 guests.

Susan Lindsay, club manager and Martyn Wiley, district manager. The Queen Mother was impressed that the club was so large and asked how many staff it had. Her Majesty thanked them for the tea and said she was having a lovely day. Most of the staff were noticeably nervous but the Queen Mother did her best to make you feel at ease.

Her Majesty also shook hands with Bridget Cox, assistant club manager, and spoke to June Dalton, senior club assistant. Mrs Dalton, who arranged flowers on tables, said: 'She asked me how long I'd worked here, I said since the club opened. She looked lovely.'

The Queen Mother, Colonel in chief of the Light Infantry, planted one of eight trees in memory of soldiers from the regiment killed at Ballygawley in August 1988.

Sara Alexander visits HMS Dolphin to find out how they kept the submarine supplied 1989

The phone rang at 1000hrs one Monday morning. Sue Davis, manager of HMS Dolphin services shopper messing store, answered. The request was simple: three submarines had to be issued stores for war that day.

The call marked the start of an exercise to see how quickly UK submarines could be stocked and put to sea and fully tested. Aldershot distributive Depot had delivered goods to HMS Dolphin in Gosport, Hampshire at 0800hrs. Two hours later Mrs Davis was back up on the phone for more supplies. The Depot arranged special transport to deliver the goods, issues with warehouse made extra deliveries necessary, and some were made direct from merchants. Previous order-related deliveries were used to save extra time, extra orders were taken over the phone. By 1800 hours all three submarines had been fully stocked and were underway.

Ian MacFarlane, commander of supplies at HMS Dolphin, later wrote to thank the staff for their efforts. One of Dolphin's submarines, HMS Onslaught, was the first to set sail. Miss Davis said, 'Both the warehouse and the Depot pulled out all the stops. They understood the problem and acted quickly. It was a marvellous effort from everybody.'

Supplying submarines at Dolphin can be an unpredictable task for Mrs Davis and her assistant manager Chris Roebuck, and their staff. They met the demands of HMS Otus, HMS Olympus, HMS Otter, HMS Onslaught, HMS Onyx, HMS Osiris and HMS Opossum.

Orders covered food, from the dry store to frozen stores, and fruit and vegetables and wardroom stocks, beer and minerals, tobacco and sweets. The team handled the accounting because the submarines, unlike ships, have no canteen manager on board. Goods to delivered direct to the submarines at the dockside but ward room caterers can often be found rushing to the Dolphin store, just a few 100 yards from the dockside. Traditional requirements, boxes of confectionery or cases of cans, for example.

The 13-strong NAAFI team have a good relationship with the submarines they serve, extending to the Atlantis junior ranks club which has two Automats. The priority is the Navy and keeping them happy, said Mrs Davis, they have good links with the submariners and they even had postcards sent from all over the world to them. Although the ward rooms could buy from anywhere, they were using NAAFI more. It was because they were easy to work with and they knew who they were dealing with.

Imperial Court closure announced 1989

Headquarter offices were about to be relocated from Imperial Court, London, to a new building erected on the company's existing site at Amesbury. The court would be closed and sold.

The decision, in principle, was taken by the board of management at a meeting on Friday the 27th of October and was expected to take two years to take effect. The trade unions were told the following Monday in advance of meetings at which departments and managers were informed. A letter outlining the decision was posted on the staff notice boards at Imperial Court and elsewhere.

A letter signed by James Rucker, managing director, explained how the decision had been arrived at and outlined the Board's aims in reconsidering the merits of relocation. Mr Rucker wrote:

> 'In the past few months, much effort and activity has gone into analysing the possibilities, a number of locations have been considered, including those where NAAFI already has a face. In view of the importance of the exercise, we felt it right to engage the service of a consultant who, with the support of management staff, compiled a detailed report covering the key factors involved in a headquarter move. The report was considered at a meeting of the Board last week and I'm pleased to be able to announce that the decision in principle has been taken.'
>
> 'To gain maximum advantage in terms of efficiency, the Board decided to reduce effectively the number of major NAAFI centres from three: Imperial court, Amesbury, and Nottingham to two, this would be Amesbury and Nottingham.
>
> 'As a result, NAAFI headquarters will move to a new building to be constructed on the existing NAAFI site in Amesbury, Wiltshire. Most functions currently undertaken in Imperial Court will move to Amesbury. A number may be better relocated to Nottingham, but no firm conclusion has yet been reached. I expect the precise location of all departments and branches to be known before Christmas. I realised that decisions in principle, by their very nature, leave unanswered questions and concerns the staff quite naturally, to how the move will affect them individually. I must ask everyone's patience until these questions can be answered, as and when we develop the precise plans for relocation. I envisage that personnel department will, within a short time, set up a unit to deal with these enquiries.

'There is now much detailed work to be undertaken. A working party will be set up to initiate detailed personal plans, flow charts and property designs. Although the aim is to proceed with dispatch, I do not envisage project completion in less than two years.'

NAAFI print works, why the presses had to shut down by Sara Alexander 1989

The force's press, which printed thousands of publications, millions of forms, and sheets of stationery, had rolled for the last time. The closure of the print works at the end of October 1989 marked the end of an era.

While news of the closure announced in May 1989 surprised some of the 32 staff, others admitted they half expected it. Marion Dear, sales official and secretary, is one who says the closure came as a shock: 'Forces press was not just a place to work, it was like family. The people were magic. When you joined, you belonged straight away. The closure was sad because we produced first class work. I never hesitated in trying to sell our products because I knew they were good.'

Peggy Marlow, print finisher, who started at Forces press in 1961, echoed her sentiments. Operations at the print works, once a hive of activity, were scaled down in the last few weeks before the closure. When the machine stood silent, workmen moved in to dismantle them for sale. David Newsome, sat as he surveyed the deserted print works on the day Sara Alexander visited, said it was the end of an era. The folder operator and stamper are now looking for new employment after 20 years with Forces press.

Brian Underwood, manager of the forces press, was then a print buyer at Amesbury, like many loyal staff at Forces press the holder of 25 year award, said: 'The decision was not good for a lot of people but they accepted it. They knew in their hearts the closure was going to happen.'

The reasons for the closure were economic, the high capital costs to replace a slow and labour intensive ageing equipment, increased services costs, and reduction in NAAFI's own stationery needs, and the ability of high tech equipment and commercial printers to meet NAAFI new requirements at lower costs. Mr Underwood explained that the work had changed, and this was a fact of life that they had actually passed their sell by date. They used to print thousands of forms, and now they were down to 760. The more NAAFI switched over to computers, the less forms were needed.

Die stamping, the specialist printing used for decoration, was dying out. They used old fashioned methods and would have had to bring in computers to go forward. A special committee, chaired by Ken Newens, controller supplies, was established to smooth the closure and transition to alternative sources of printing matter. In the meantime, many Forces press staff had to be moved on to pastures new, many left within weeks of the announcement that they were about to close and found other jobs. Some were close to retirement like Len Foley, composing room overseer, 42 years with NAAFI, he could remember the printing branch based in London in the 40s and the 50s.

Bob Geere, foreman, who started as a guillotine operator, spent 29 years with the forces press, John Spencer, order processing buyer, 26 years. Arnold Perera, assistant manager, at Forces press for 29 years, planned to work from home as a print consultant due to his wide experience and expertise gained over the 38 years in the trade, he felt it should not be thrown away. As a printer all of his life he was one of those who moved with the printing branch from Kennings Way in 1963. Forces press was housed in a building once a NAAFI bakery, which was one of the most modern of its time. Offset lithography was used to prepare such publications as NAAFI annual report, NAAFI News, and the durable goods catalogue. These attracted the attention of service editors who turned to Forces press to print their journals.

When the last edition of the Craftsman, the magazine of the Royal electrical and Mechanical Engineers, rolled off the presses, an 18 year association spanning 223 issues came to a close. Just days later the end of an era for NAAFI printing branch followed.

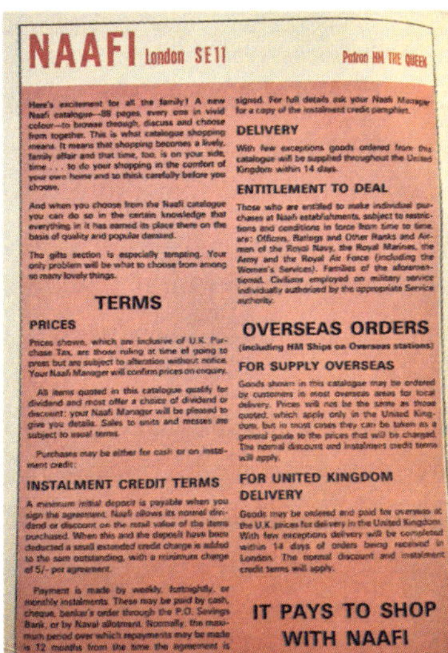

NAAFI London SE11 — Patron HM THE QUEEN

Here's excitement for all the family! A new Naafi catalogue—88 pages, every one in vivid colour—to browse through, discuss and choose from together. This is what catalogue shopping means. It means that shopping becomes a lively family affair and that time, too, is on your side, time . . . to do your shopping in the comfort of your own home and to think carefully before you choose.

And when you choose from the Naafi catalogue you can do so in the certain knowledge that everything in it has earned its place there on the basis of quality and popular demand.

The gifts section is especially tempting. Your only problem will be what to choose from among so many lovely things.

TERMS

PRICES

Prices shown, which are inclusive of U.K. Purchase Tax, are those ruling at time of going to press but are subject to alteration without notice. Your Naafi Manager will confirm prices on enquiry.

All items quoted in this catalogue qualify for dividend and most offer a choice of dividend or discount: your Naafi Manager will be pleased to give you details. Sales to units and messes are subject to usual terms.

Purchases may be either for cash or on instalment credit.

INSTALMENT CREDIT TERMS

A minimum initial deposit is payable when you sign the agreement. Naafi allows its normal dividend or discount on the retail value of the items purchased. When this and the deposit have been deducted a small extended credit charge is added to the sum outstanding, with a minimum charge of 5/- per agreement.

Payment is made by weekly, fortnightly, or monthly instalments. These may be paid by cash, cheque, banker's order through the P.O. Savings Bank, or by Naval allotment. Normally, the maximum period over which repayments may be made is 12 months from the time the agreement is signed. For full details ask your Naafi Manager for a copy of the instalment credit pamphlet.

DELIVERY

With few exceptions goods ordered from this catalogue will be supplied throughout the United Kingdom within 14 days.

ENTITLEMENT TO DEAL

Those who are entitled to make individual purchases at Naafi establishments, subject to restrictions and conditions in force from time to time are: Officers, Ratings and Other Ranks and Airmen of the Royal Navy, the Royal Marines, the Army and the Royal Air Force (including the Women's Services). Families of the aforementioned. Civilians employed on military service individually authorized by the appropriate Service authority.

OVERSEAS ORDERS

(including HM Ships on Overseas stations)

FOR SUPPLY OVERSEAS

Goods shown in this catalogue may be ordered by customers in most overseas areas for local delivery. Prices will not be the same as those quoted, which apply only in the United Kingdom, but in most cases they can be taken as a general guide to the prices that will be charged. The normal discount and instalment credit terms will apply.

FOR UNITED KINGDOM DELIVERY

Goods may be ordered and paid for overseas at the U.K. prices for delivery in the United Kingdom. With few exceptions delivery will be completed within 14 days of orders being received in London. The normal discount and instalment credit terms will apply.

IT PAYS TO SHOP WITH NAAFI

Life changing, Memories by Ron Leacy 1980 to 1989

So, there I was, 17 years old, just left school and living with my military family in Germany and let's say job prospects were minimal but a chance visit to my local NAAFI shop changed the course of my life.

A speculative enquiry to the manager got me a part-time storeman job; shortly after it was made full time. I had a great 18 months working there and when I asked about career opportunities the option of transferring to the NCS was brought up. Four months later I arrived at NAAFI HQ in London and was told I was on my way to Portsmouth to become the "Canteen Assistant" (Can Ass) on board HMS Nottingham.

To say it was a culture shock would be an understatement; my main workplace was a 12ft × 12ft space that served as a shop, an office and a storeroom, serving the ship's crew through a shutter in a side wall. Main storerooms that could hold 6 months' supplies were deep in the bowels of the ship meaning a daily effort of manhandling stores through various levels to get the shop replenished.

I very quickly settled into life on board and got used to living in a mess with lots of other people who quickly became my friends. They soon accepted me as one of "The Lads" and I joined in and was included in everything that went on.

Being a sporty type I tried out for the Rugby team and was recruited as a full team member, I also turned out for the ship cricket team and a bit less energetically for the darts team.

I had 3 deployments on the Nottingham, the first to the Falklands about a year after the war had ended, the following year it was off to the Persian Gulf and the last main trip was to the USA and Bahamas as escort ship to the Royal Yacht Britannia. I always say how lucky I was, I have travelled and seen more of the world than most people dream of and got paid to do it.

My biggest honour was getting awarded the Ship's Company man of the year award, unheard of for a civilian to win and to say it was a huge surprise when it was announced would be an understatement.

So, what did I do to win the award? As far as I was concerned, I was just being a part of the crew and doing my bit, but I guess I was doing enough to be recognised? When away from the UK I ran the ship's radio and TV station, organising different wives and girlfriends to record various shows on video and send them in the mail, I then collated them all into nightly TV shows so everyone still got their fill of Match of the Day and Neighbours, I would also do a morning radio show and each day get the news ticker tape and make a news bulletin that I would read on camera during the TV broadcast.

When in defence watches the crew worked shifts that included a 2am shift change, so I would make sure the canteen was open at that time, I even had a wooden tray made, think 1980s cinema sweet sellers, and I would walk around the ship so people could get their fix of "Nutty" (Sweets) and "Goffa" (Canned Drinks). I also trained as the ship's First Aid State Board operator so when at action stations I would be in the sick bay coordinating all the info coming in from the first aid teams about casualties etc. Luckily I only did this during exercises and not for real.

I found life on board to be a great life, and the crew were my family and you do anything for your family, right? I made friends on the Nottingham that are still friends now, was best man at one wedding and a guest at a couple more.

After becoming a manager, I moved onto other ships, eventually moving from Portsmouth to Plymouth, meeting my wife and settling there. Retail and customer service stayed as my career and it's still what I do nearly 40 years later, so like I said at the start, that chance job enquiry as a 17-year-old, did really change my life.

1990–1999

1990

HMS Fearless and HMS Cardiff Memories by Stephen Watkins 1990

It was August 1989 and my A level results had proven to be a huge disappointment. I had already secured a job in the local supermarket but wanted to get out and see the world. Friends had gone on to University, but others were taking a gap year and travelling. That was when I decided that what I needed was a job that paid me to travel. That was the start of my journey.

Crediton is a small market town in Devon. It's a beautiful area to live in but in 1989, the job market offered a very narrow choice. There was no internet at that time and so my job search was limited to newspaper adverts. It was my parents who excitedly shoved a newspaper clipping under my nose one evening and that was the first time I had ever heard of NAAFI.

The advert sounded like a dream. See the world! I wanted that job so bad! I sat down and handwrote my CV as neatly as I could and posted off my application to Imperial Court. It was several months before I received a reply and I was convinced it was a rejection. It wasn't. It was a medical form! I had to see my GP for him to complete the medical before my interview in London. I was so excited!

Now, going to London was not an everyday occurrence for me back then. It was surreal that I was heading there for a job interview. My mum drove me up and my sister came too. We got lost trying to find Imperial Court and decided to park up and get a taxi. They dropped me off and headed for Oxford Street for some retail therapy.

I can remember standing outside and staring at this wonderful old building. I was late and I was nervous. I walked in and straight away was made to feel at ease and offered a cup of tea. At the age of 18, I hadn't travelled outside of the South West very much and certainly not without my parents. Looking back, I was quite immature for my age but here I was, in this massive building in what felt like very formal surroundings being offered tea and biscuits!

The interview began with several written tests both in English and Mathematics. There followed a formal interview panel and then I was asked to wait in a side room. After what felt like an age, I had several informal discussions with various people. One was outlining career opportunities at Imperial Court; another was a fast track management training programme for shop/club management, and one was about EFI/NCS. I was hooked, I wanted to go to sea!!

Afterwards, I was told someone would be in touch and was reimbursed my taxi fare. Mobile phones didn't exist, and I had no way of contacting my Mum, so I headed to the nearby pub and had a couple of pints. Being used to Devon prices, I was astounded when the barman asked me for £1.36 for a pint of Fosters.

On the way home I couldn't stop thinking about what life at sea would be like. I was both nervous and excited at the same time.

Again, it was several months until I heard anything. I came home from work and there was a letter waiting for me. A few months before, the Gulf War had started which added to the nervousness. I was to report to Imperial Court on 12th November 1990.

I handed my notice in the following day. My manager was Ex-Army and was proud for me. Others were excited for me that I was getting to do something I really wanted to do. After the obligatory week of winding down, I took a week off to sort myself out with everything I might need. To be fair, I didn't really have a clue what I needed.

On arrival at Imperial Court, I was told I was to join HMS Fearless in Portsmouth that afternoon. I was issued with my ID card and my parents drove me down. We said goodbye at the gates and my NCS journey began.

Charles 'Charlie' Hill came to collect me and explained, to my disappointment, that there had been a mix up and that I should have joined HMS Fearless in Portland on the following Monday. So, I joined HMS Intrepid for a few days with Andy Kirk and Dave Kirman. Within a few hours, I had experienced the joy of seeing cockroaches crawling over dinner before going out for a 'few' beers. Also, with much hilarity was the look on Dave Kirman's face when he drank a coffee and discovered a cockroach in the bottom! On the Thursday, I was sent on long weekend leave before joining HMS Fearless in Portland.

I knew Portland reasonably well as I was born in Dorchester and I had an aunt in Portland. Again, my parents dropped me off and I made my way to the club to meet Dave Frampton. HMS Fearless was at sea and due alongside that afternoon. When she berthed, I was taken over to HMS Fearless and introduced to my new colleagues. The ship was in the middle of sea trials following a major refit and the decks were covered in firefighting kit, the air reeking of smoke after an exercise. My first thoughts were 'what have I done!' but I was made really welcome by everyone. After meeting my new colleagues, I was taken to my living quarters, 2G1 NAAFI mess, by Paul Wilkinson who had joined just a week before me from NAAFI HMS Culdrose, the RN Air Station near Helston in Cornwall. Paul and I would go on to form a friendship spanning 3 decades (so far) and he became my best man, almost 25 years later.

It was a case of 'in at the deep end' as the following weeks were made up of intense operational sea training. This included a swift introduction to 'Thursday' war where training scenarios were so incredibly realistic that eventually, your actions became instinctive. Ballast tanks were flooded to make the ship list, water and smoke were pouring into the passageways, theatrical makeup was used on casualties, charges made the ship shake as planes flew overhead. The training was hard, but it did exactly what it was intended to do, we all knew what to do if it all happened for real.

Just before Christmas, we had a little light relief as we went to Rotterdam for a few days before Christmas leave began. This was my first time abroad as an adult and although it was 'just Rotterdam', it felt amazing that I was following my dream of travelling. I had learned a huge amount about myself in a very short space of time. My dad often says that I went away a boy but, after a few weeks, I came home a man.

Just a few weeks after Christmas leave, HMS Fearless was sailing for Norway. In preparation there was a period of storing ship. This was when I began to learn how to utilise every nook and cranny. Space was precious but stock still had to be stowed safely and securely for sea. My manager was Steve Appleby, a Falklands veteran and a highly experienced manager. He soon realised that I was neither small nor agile and so we would usually utilise Paul for accessing the smaller and tighter spaces! We bonded well as a team fairly quickly. Steve recognised our individual strengths and as such, Paul and I would go on to work with Steve on HMS Fearless for several years.

Cold Winter training with the Royal Marines was an amazing experience and I would go on to repeat this deployment again, several years later. Sailing through the narrow fjords surrounded by snow covered cliffs and mountains was spectacular. We visited Narvik and Trondheim; sailed into the Arctic Circle through sea ice; saw the Northern Lights as well as taking part in beach landings. The second time, we went to Bergen and I was lucky enough to go skiing at Voss.

After a couple of months back in the UK, another store ship and we were off to the Caribbean. Talk about weather extremes! On our way there, a big storm hit during the night. Next morning, I was on the upper deck with my bacon roll and cup of tea watching bananas float on past and flying fish were jumping out of the water in between them! Apparently, a Fyffes banana ship had lost part of its cargo in the storm.

We stopped at Beef Island in the British Virgin Islands and anchored off. I can remember being transfixed at what seemed to me to be this tropical paradise. As I was taking in the view, a large ray left the water and rolled just in front of me. Amazing.

We were going to have a ship's Banyan which is essentially a beach party. With Dougie Reekie and Brian 'Scouse' Nugent, we loaded beer onto an LCVP via the tank deck and set off for the beach. The Chefs had built a BBQ, so we found some shade nearby and set up the bar. It was a welcome break after a long voyage across the Atlantic.

A few days later, the Royal Marines were taking the LCUs and the LCVPs on drug patrols. They needed volunteers to act as first aiders, so I volunteered to go. We had to carry minimal kit as we needed to take camp beds and sleeping bags with us as well. At about 3am I was woken up by the Colour Sgt asking if we could sneak some beer on board as I had been allocated to him. Around half a dozen of us quietly spent the next hour or so chaining crates of Grolsch and Red Death through the tank deck before unbolting ballast tank covers and stuffing the beer into the voids. After breakfast, we flooded the stern with the stern gate open and sailed away for a week. That night, we met up with the others and tied up in a row whilst at sea. With music on, BBQ lit and bar open, we had passing yachts stopping for a chat and a burger! With the first Gulf Conflict having just finished, many Americans assumed we were on a jolly after being out there (we hadn't been) but we just went along with it as they just thought we were being modest.

The following night, we found a small beach on an island called Van Dyke Island. There was a reef and shallow waters meaning we had to anchor off and wade ashore. We were all in combats or 8's and were warmly greeted by the local police. The beach had a small hotel, police station and a bar with a jetty for small motor launches. The bar manager ushered us over and we spent the rest of the day drinking at a bar which was allegedly owned by Phil Collins. As the day rolled on, Foxy, the bar manager said he had just spoken to Phil Collins and he had paid our bar bill and suggested we had dinner. Bonus!

We were making our way back to our boat when we were ushered into the only other bar on the beach, the hotel. Again, we were told drinks were on the house and I was shoved behind the bar and asked to mix a NAAFI cocktail. I called it 'Poison' because I was far too drunk to know what I was putting in it but I do remember it was green! (Crème de Menthe I think!) The hotel offered us all a burger each which we ate whilst walking back.

Next morning, I woke up with water lapping at my feet, face down in the sand with a half-eaten burger in one hand and a glass of something green in the other. I felt rough. As I glanced around me, I noticed most of my shipmates were in a similar state. As we all came around, we noticed some coconuts floating in the water. After gathering them up, we waded out to our boat. We all had a raging thirst and decided to open up the coconuts to drink the milk. Little did we realise that they had soaked up seawater and it tasted vile!

When we returned to HMS Fearless, we conducted several drills such as gas mask testing and NBCD training. To test your gas mask, you had to walk into a chamber of gas and if you could taste pear drops, your mask didn't fit properly. As an upper deck first aid team member, I had to wear a rubber suit in 40 degree C heat on the upper deck for several exhausting hours as part of NBCD training. We just hoped we never had to do that for real. After several other stops such as Montego Bay, Aruba and Cancun, we headed back to the UK and our families.

I returned to the Caribbean again a few years later. One memorable stop over was Guyana. We had to use the ship's LCU's to get ashore due to offshore sandbanks and the condition of the jetty. This was probably my first experience of abject poverty. We were met by plush modern vehicles and escorted by armed guards to local hotels. On arrival at the Georgetown Hilton, women were begging for food and trying to push through the cordon to touch us in the hope we would donate. Some carried deceased children as if to demonstrate their need. It was heart-breaking. We were there to deliver a large aid package and for this, HMS Fearless was awarded the Wilkinson Sword of Peace.

On one visit to Curacao, I was 12th man for the cricket team. I ended up playing for Curacao as they were short of players. We were astounded at how old they all were and there was talk of going easy on them! The pitch was a dustbowl and HMS Fearless were all out for just 22. A total that, of course, Curacao easily reached.

On another visit, this time to Bermuda, Paul and myself went for a Sunday walk. After a while, we were stopped by a guy on a moped and asked if we liked cricket. He then rode on ahead and sent a car to pick us up which took us to a local game. Bermuda is split into counties just like England and each one is named after an English county. This game was Somerset v Warwickshire. We were invited into the President's tent and told that we were their guests, and everything was complimentary. Beers, sandwiches and cakes! After a wonderful day (on best behaviour) we were taken back to the ship.

On our return to the UK we were met by our families who were allowed on board for a day at sea. My parents had brought my grandfather who was eager to see what life was like on board ship. We had always been close but my time at sea brought us even closer as I would often stop off and stay the night on my way home for leave. We would pop down to the Working Men's Club in Stoke Sub Hamdon, Somerset where I would be grilled by his friends about where I had been and what I had been up to. Many of them were D-Day veterans, just like my grandad. He was in the 7th Battalion Somerset Light Infantry and if I remember correctly, he landed in France on D-Day +6.

As a surprise, I had arranged with the Royal Marines, 4ASRM, to take us out on an LCU. We managed to get him into it and as soon as we hit the water, his face lit up. It was an incredible feeling, experiencing this with my father and grandfather.

Several deployments to the Mediterranean followed, one of which saw us visit what was then the USSR or Soviet Union. We sailed through the Dardenelles, the scene of an infamous naval battle during WW1. We held a remembrance service to honour the dead before heading for Sevastopol in the Crimea. We were greeted my thousands of people as it was unusual for the Royal Navy to enter a Soviet port.

We were only allowed ashore in uniform so that we could be easily identified. Only being allowed to exchange £10 of local currency, we all thought we would have no cash left within minutes, but it transpired that this was a huge amount to the local people. A few of us began loading bags of treats like canned drinks and chocolate to hand out to the children. A simple gift of a few bars of chocolate and a can of Coke was apparently worth a month's wages on the black market and this left some parents overcome with joy. Some parents would chase us down the street and try to give it back saying it was too much. This really made us realise how much Western Society takes these things for granted.

Vodka and Armenian brandy were readily available to us in the local bars at around 15p a bottle! Caviar on Melba toasts went well with it and to us it was astounding how inexpensive these treats were compared to home. One evening though, guilt set in as we walked down a street and realised there was a queue nearly 500m long. The butchers had just received a delivery, the first for a month and meat was rationed. This was 1991 and none of us could believe what we were seeing.

We sailed from the Crimea to Constanta in Romania where we were to assist with the humanitarian aid delivery. What we witnessed was horrific. The institutions had been abandoned by the authorities, in fear of reprisals following the overthrow of Ceausescu and the patients in care homes and the children in orphanages had been left to care for themselves and each other. Whilst the ship had allocated teams to carry out essential maintenance, others gathered together unwanted clothes and spare toiletries.

We were due to sail to Venice for some cultural R&R but the unrest in Yugoslavia began and we had to spend some time close to Dubrovnik. You could hear the artillery in the distance and see the occasional flash. Sometimes a gunboat would come out to take a look at us. I was a designated upper deck first aid comms runner and can remember one night being able to see the faces of the gunboat crew as they passed so close by.

Venice was a complete contrast to the relative stress of the preceding month or so. It was the first time I had ever visited and was in awe of my surroundings. One day, I stood and watched a street artist paint for a while. I ended up buying the painting and it is hung in my lounge at home.

A Royal Navy deployment to the Mediterranean wouldn't be complete without a visit to Gibraltar, which I visited many times. We all walked up the rock and took in the views, visited the military caves, walked across to Spain for a day, watched in hysterics when a seagull pooed in Dave Wood's pint of Stella from a great height, and experienced the horrors of a bottomless jug of Sangria.

In 1995, HMS Fearless was in a major refit so we reduced to a skeleton crew. Paul Wilkinson had been promoted to manager and left HMS Fearless, but I was living in quarters at HMS

Nelson. During the summer were the VE Day 50 Celebrations at Southsea. I was asked to help at the reception for dignitaries at Southsea Castle having spent the afternoon serving tea to veterans at the main celebration on the common. What struck me was how grateful the veterans were for the very presence of NAAFI and how pleased they were it was still going strong.

In 1996, I was officially made a Trainee manager. Steve Appleby had been training me unofficially for a while anyway, but this meant that I would be guaranteed to be on board for the deployment of a lifetime, the Far East to cover the handover of Hong Kong to China. We sailed early January 1997 and stopped in Greece before transiting the Suez Canal. I had never realised how narrow some of the stretches are and we would have barbers and traders coming on board selling their wares on the flight deck.

Whilst away, we visited some places I had only dreamt of visiting. In Goa, I took a few days' leave and travelled with some Petty Officers as I had been moved from 2G1 up to O1H1 Petty Officers Mess. We stayed in a hostel and visited markets and off the beaten track restaurants. In Kota Kinabalu, I joined a tourist trek to the summit of Mount Kinabalu, the highest peak in South East Asia. The tour was timed so that you could watch the sun rising and could see the islands appearing from the horizon.

Another visit was to Brunei. The British expats were glad to see us as there were restrictions on alcohol consumption due to the strict Muslim laws. The flip side was there were no drink drive laws either as the local population were not permitted to consume alcohol. When attending a party, conveniently a bring a bottle or 2 party, we were offered lifts back to the ship which we politely declined in favour of the sobering but much safer long walk back.

My birthday that year was spent in Singapore. We went to Raffles Hotel for the obligatory Singapore Sling before having a party at the dockyard sports facility pool. It rains every afternoon in Singapore, and it is accompanied by a massive thunderstorm. I had to be dragged from the pool as I didn't realise the danger of being in water in a storm!

There was also a retirement party for Harry who had worked for NAAFI most of his life in Singapore. This saw Charles Hill fly over from the UK to join all the staff off the various ships that were docked in Singapore at the time. It was more of a feast/banquet to be honest, with dishes such as suckling pig and so on.

My mess had an official mess dinner whilst alongside. It was my first real taste of Senior Rate traditions such as how to pass the port, etiquette for leaving the table and so on. I had to borrow a cummerbund off Steve Appleby who gave me a quick rundown on what NOT to do! Steve was the king of trying to catch you out with things like asking for a left-handed screwdriver or a glass hammer, but I was wiser by now and survived the event unscathed.

When it came to the ceremony to hand over Hong Kong, we didn't even see land. We stayed out at sea and were on standby in case of civil unrest. When the ceremony passed without incident, HMY Britannia sailed past all the guard ships and gave the order to 'Splice the Main Brace'. This caused momentary panic as we were not sure if we had enough Rum!!

We were off to the Maldives when I took advantage for the first time of 'hands to bathe'. This is essentially when marksmen scan the horizon for sharks whilst the ship's company go for a swim! Access was via the tank deck and the stern gates opened to allow easy access to the water. Not being a strong swimmer, I panicked when I turned to see that the ship was moving away from me. I managed to make it back but that was the last time I did that!

The welcome we received on our return to the UK was immense. We had just been on my longest deployment and for the first time ever, on occasion, I had really missed home. We came alongside and the gangway went down. It was obvious where my family were because it was like the parting of the Red Sea! Not long before we had sailed, my parents had been in a serious car accident and when I had left home, my mother was still recovering but here she was, walking with sticks through a crowd of around 2000 people! She was one of the first aboard, helped down the steps by the Captain himself. I was expecting an icy look, but he simply said 'Neither Man nor God himself should ever get between a Mother and her Son' then smiled and winked at me.

Because my family, including my sister, had met the ship, I volunteered for second leave. During these first few weeks back, I was offered my first managerial posting, HMS Cardiff. I was sent on leave and told to join her on my return. I was apprehensive as I was considering moving on and finding some roots back home. I had spent a huge amount of time away since joining and knew HMS Cardiff had a hectic schedule when completing her sea trials.

After mulling things over, I decided to give it a go. I hadn't worked hard to pass up the chance of becoming a manager, even if it turned out to be for just a short while. When I boarded her, morale seemed low. The ship's company looked like they needed a lift. When I entered the NAAFI, I could see why. Empty shelves, sparse opening hours, bad state of repair. The workload was huge. I was immediately impressed with my new assistant, Nathan. He was enthusiastic and keen, he just needed guidance and he explained there had been a high turnover of managers. I decided to look at stock levels and found that plenty of stock was in the storerooms. We spent the day restocking the canteen and sat down to look at the opening hours. We decided to open in line with larger ships' opening times, altered slightly to account for the fact there were only 2 of us.

After meeting with the supply officer and ship's captain, I felt more at ease. They were very welcoming and offered me all the support I needed to turn things around. All the NAAFI areas needed a huge amount of work to reach the standard required by Flag Officer Sea Training (FOST) inspections. Steve Appleby had demanded, quite rightly, high standards and I wasn't going to let those standards slip. I called in favours from a lot of people to get up to scratch and we sailed through initial inspections. Then the bombshell, Nathan had been hospitalised following an assault whilst on weekend leave. He was desperate to get back on board, but I told him not to worry, his health was more important.

I asked NAAFI for some assistance as FOST training is exhausting when fully manned, let alone being a man down. The ship's company were brilliant though. I had help to bring stores up and there were no complaints when I had long queues. By this time, I had established a great relationship with the ship's Captain who wrote numerous letters to NAAFI requesting help on my behalf. At this point, I was also in regular contact with Bob Talboys, Area Manager in Portsmouth as after 3 months, my pay still hadn't reflected the fact I had been promoted.

The ship was in Plymouth a lot throughout FOST so my parents had the opportunity to see what a Type 42 Destroyer looked like. They were amazed at how low the stern sat in the water and I explained that you could literally pat the passing dolphins on the head if they came close enough. One of the Chief stokers whom I knew from HMS Fearless gave my dad a tour of the engine spaces while my mum, who had to be helped down the ladders, enjoyed a 'wobbly coffee' made by the Chief Cook. When he asked if she wanted a double measure of rum in it, she didn't realise a Navy measure is already a double! After a couple of these, she was rather merry!

After successfully completing FOST training, we had a brief trip to Cherbourg just before Christmas. Myself and a few Chief Petty Officers and Warrant Officers decided to utilise the space in my storerooms and do a few trips to the Hypermarkets. We were loading up trolleys and pushing them back to the ship. One afternoon, we counted up our purchases and realised we had bought too much to bring back so decided to have a big cheese and wine party on the way back to Portsmouth. This made quite a dent in the surplus, but the mess fridge stank of French cheese for weeks.

After Christmas leave, I managed to meet with Bob Tallboys about my pay. I was not prepared for the outcome of that conversation. I was informed that my pay was being backdated with a pay CUT! Apparently, at that time assistants on Capital ships like the carriers and Fearless were paid more than a junior manager on a small ship. Therefore, I was to be paid less as a manager than I would have been as an assistant on HMS Fearless. I was furious. I handed my

3 months' notice in there and then and busily got job hunting. Fortunately for me, my good friend and ex NAAFI colleague Tim Gibbs knew of a job for me and a place to live so everything was put in place for me to leave.

Unfortunately, when at sea and on our way back to Portsmouth during my notice period, HMS Cardiff was diverted and was at sea for longer than anticipated. When the captain realised, I was no longer a NAAFI employee as my notice had expired, he had no choice but to get me off the ship. I packed all my belongings and said my goodbyes. A helicopter was sent out to pick me up and drop me off on the Isle of Lewis. I managed to get a Bristow's helicopter to take me to Aberdeen airport where I hired a car and made the long journey back to Devon.

A few weeks later, I made my way to Portsmouth Dockyard to collect the rest of my belongings. It was a weekend, so nobody was around to say goodbye to. As I drove out those gates for the last time, it felt like a huge part of me had been left behind. I have no regrets about leaving, I have had a wonderful life since, but I regret the way I left.

Since leaving, I have managed to get back in touch with a lot of old colleagues and have attended Royal Navy and NAAFI reunions. The bonds you form with people you share that time with are priceless. One of my favourite experiences since leaving was being given the chance to represent NAAFI at the Cenotaph Remembrance Parade, an emotional and proud moment. The NCS will remain a huge part of me and the people will remain my friends for the rest of my life.

NAAFI made me who I am today. I joined as a shy, introverted adolescent and left as a confident man with a unique skillset, work ethic, and a whole heap of amazing memories and the friends that come with them!

Aldershot Depot to close January 1991

The closure of the Aldershot distribution Depot, which had been open since 1976 and the relocation of its functions to Amesbury warehouse in Wiltshire, had been announced. The move scheduled for January 1991, will follow the extension of Amesbury to fulfil an expanded distribution role and precede the relocation of the London headquarters support services to the new offices that were being built nearby. Ken Newens, control of supplies, explained there were two main reasons for the closure. The first was insufficient refrigeration capacity and equipment at Aldershot to deal with the ever-increasing demands for chilled and frozen supplies from establishments and units in the South of England. The second was the inability of the depots inadequate computer systems, which were in need of renewal, to effectively cope with an increased workload.

Additionally, significant rises were expected in the rents paid by the company to lease the Aldershot premises. Mr Newens said: 'The computer was installed in 1978 and is not up to modern standards. Management services had recommended it for replacement since too many faults were occurring on the system. In fact, people are keeping their fingers crossed that the systems used for telesales, ordering, invoicing, and inventories, do not crash before we are able to relocate.'

Management decided to inform staff immediately rather than wait and give them only six months' notice. I sat down in the job, security agreement signed with trade unions. It was felt by telling them early that they were giving them plenty of time to make their own plans for their futures.

New EFI HQ (Originally written by Sarah Wintle) 1990

The EFI was at the sharp end of the NAAFI stick, and part of the company most appreciated by the service. The RAOC EFI is the military unit for which NAAFI staff may volunteer to provide a service to the services on exercise or emergencies, in times of war and peace.

After basic military training, recruits are ready to join military units wherever the need arises, and to set up and run bulk issue stores, shops at mobiles and canteens. In 1989 alone, EFI sold record sales of goods on Arctic exercise in Norway, and others around the globe including: Ave Express in Denmark, Armada exchange in Italy, Plain Sailing and Grand Canyon in Germany and Ardent ground in Sardinia.

In order to train and coordinate the activities of EFI 250 members, and eight men of the permanent cadre, based at EFI headquarters at Wingham, NAAFI training centre in Surrey. They trained personnel from raw recruits to more experienced hands, prepared supplies and equipment for field Ops, provided cover in emergencies, and administered the daily running of EFI.

This was no mean feat and they also tried to educate military units about the specialised services that they provided. Neither the military, NAAFI or EFI had any doubts that they could prepare and run an efficient Op in times of war. In 1990, the Cadre, as well as running the unit's complex activities, and racing around the world, took on the complicated ambitious project to rebuild their headquarters.

Maj Randerson said, 'The old headquarters was terribly cramped and with increased workload and visits from military personnel, we needed something better to project a professional image.' Cramped was an understatement, the main office was situated in a converted garage and the EFI bar and lounge in a shed no more than 20 feet square. Although none of them had any previous building experience, they set to work digging foundations, installing a water drainage system, constructing wooden framework, laying floors and roof, putting up walls and room partitions and decorating throughout. It took 15 months to complete, The HQ known as the Goodwin block. The cadre moved into the new building complete with QM store, three offices, lecture room, before starting work on the garage to convert it into a bar, lounge, kitchen, games room for leisure. It had been a real labour of love, fitting the work in and around everyday duties, but spent abroad, and working at weekends paid off in the end.

However, they did not work alone in their efforts. Any EFI member at Wingham during construction was set to work, even if only for a few hours. The enthusiasm clearly demonstrated the dedication of EFI members who had to rough it with the forces on exercise elsewhere. As a result of this Sgt Stan Goodwin said that they got a lot of respect from the army from the work that they did. They treated them like equals because they work and live in the same conditions as they do. And the job was satisfying although you did look forward to coming home.

Ian Honeywood, a S/Sgt explained why he joined: 'I was a club manager but became bored with the set routine. The EFI offers me a chance to do something different and worthwhile. I plan our part in an exercise, order supplies and dry messing, deal with customs and shipping, as well as working in the field. We supply troops with what they want. From Mars bars to crystal animals and cuckoo clocks, even if abroad we have to go to local suppliers.'

Logistic Support battalion AMF/L had been supported by EFI on many exercises. Lt Col Paddy Henderson, CO, said their capabilities were always in search of excellence and that's what they offered. Even services as far north as Norway reminded service personnel when Valentine's Day was approaching when they haven't sent their wives or girlfriends a card. EFI produced a card and stamp and an order form for a bouquet of flowers which were delivered on the day and saved them. Staff Sgt Honeywood's agenda, six months in advance gave an indication that EFI's hectic timetable on exercise in Germany for the month followed three weeks in Sardinia, a week at EFI HQ before joining an exercise in Norway for six weeks, a week's Christmas break, and then back to Norway for two months. To help with the enormous amount of planning and paperwork they had a new computer and VDUs.

Staff Sgt Gary Roberts, a former storm and now a clerk in charge at the office administration and recruitment, explained why a computer was needed: 'Paperwork has to be completed for the army and NAAFI, rail warrants, travel orders, military identity cards, and transport forms to be issued to name but a few. The computer also gives a record for all EFI members.'

Although staff Sgt Roberts joined EFI for travelling fieldwork, he, like others in the cadre, thinks the adventure is just one of the benefits for members. Recruits learned about responsibility

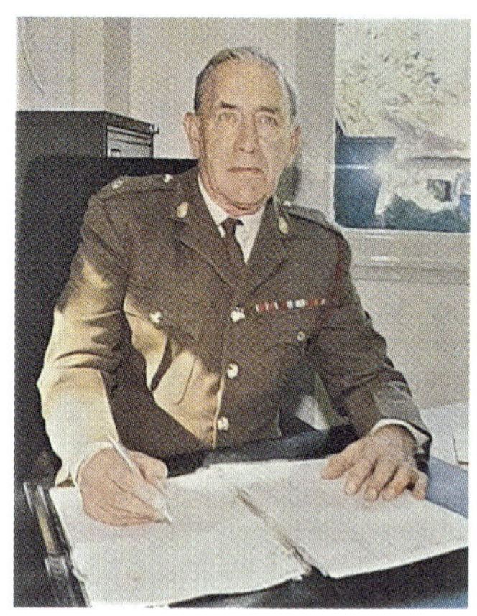

and discipline after an exercise, which helps build character and employees are more efficient. Maj Randerson elaborated on this and said that unlike any other TA units EFI was doing its job 365 days a year, whether they are working in a shop or helping a warehouse. The job was to transfer a mix of skills into a military environment.

RAF Leeming (Originally written by Graham Stirling) 1990

After six years work the transformation art NAAFI RAF Leeming has been hailed the best RAF station. The turnaround followed the upgrading of the North Yorkshire station in 1984 from a Sleepy Hollow, pilot training school to a frontline NATO base. The arrival of three tornado squadrons and personnel, boosting the station's population to 4000 by the end of 1990 prompted the action.

The arrivals at the station have for their wellbeing, a purpose-built family centre including bowling alley, refurbished family shop within store bakery, and an improved club, the Swordsman. Tony Bleathman, district manager York, commented: 'I can't think of anywhere that is better served by NAAFI. The services here are very good indeed. The RAF Corporation and understanding have been excellent.'

The RAF worked closely with property services, specifically Peter Closier, chief planning officer, in drawing up plans to update facilities to meet the expected Station strength. Throughout 1987, while work took place, club staff ran a service in the Sgts mess, coping with such problems as lack of customers, no beer sellers, and little storage space; it was all worth it in the end – the unit had a plush modern club finished to a high standard. The club had a Cpl Bar, a junior ranks bar with pool tables and dart boards, and an upstairs entertainments area, with dance floor, disco lighting, and a main bar. A raised seating area was added as a finishing touch.

There was little fear of anybody experiencing claustrophobic crush associated with many city night clubs since the Woodsman centre had been provided. Built outside the inner perimeter, the new family centre, especially in times of increased security, gave the off-duty personnel and their dependants a place to spend their leisure hours. Beneath the Woodsman's high wooden ceiling lay a large dividable leisure area, plentiful seating, wooden dance floor, bar, pool table, and darts area.

The centre was already used for bingo nights, and a social club and for various functions large and small. Richard Gaymer, regional manager northern, described the centre as nothing short of luxurious. The family shop had new flooring and decoration, 13% more retailing space and in store bakery; this meant that customers had a pleasant and convenient place to shop for their household needs. The bakery, NAAFI's ninth in the UK, produced fresh bakery goods including bread rolls, doughnuts, Danish pastries, pies, and sausage rolls. The shop was officially reopened by Group Captain John Rooum, station commander, and his wife. The nearest shop was some 6 miles away and the facility was very much needed with the staff and manager Vicki Pickering being immensely proud of the facilities and the rise in turnover with still more families to move into the area. One of the biggest additions was the bowling alley and this was incorporated with an excellent design which took six months to complete, it had four lanes with room for two more. It was more than just the preserve of bowlers, and people could simply pop in for a drink, to watch TV, in the lounge with the comfortable seating area or take advantage of the catering facilities with an American feel.

Tina Larkin, who had been with NAAFI for eight years, managed the Swordsman club, and the bowling alley and family centres. She said: 'It was a very good posting, all three facilities and their customers, junior ranks, families, and all ranks have very different requirements.'

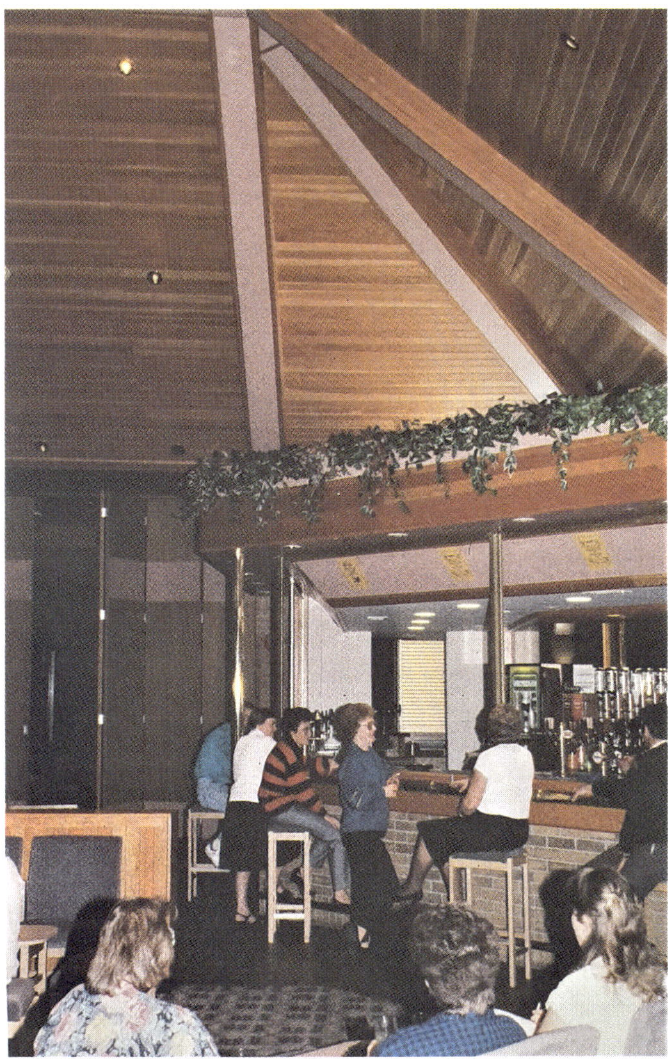

Exercise Saef Al Had (Sharp Sword) Egypt 1990

Daily temperatures over 31 Celsius proved no problem for the Expeditionary Force Institutes, on Exercise Sharp Sword in Egypt. S/Sgt Ian Honeywood, Sgt Stan Goodwin, Cpl Gary Smith, and Brian Hermon set up shop in a truck for 40 commando Royal Marines, The first British military presence in Egypt since 1956.

Staff Sgt Honeywood said: 'We helped set up 200 tents for 700 chips in the middle of the desert and operated from 0730 hrs, to 2300 hrs. The range of stock was quite unexpected, included electrical goods, film, sweets, and soft drinks, the latter being the best seller. The biggest difficulties were keeping sand out of the stock and the lack of change. The return trip was not without problems either, as Cpl Smith explained that they crossed the Mediterranean to Cyprus in landing craft in force eight conditions, it was like sailing in a messed tin. They landed 36 hours later to an invitation to take a boat trip around the island. Needless to say, at that point all four of them opted to stay on dry land.

The Model T Ford delivery van 1990

A leaflet sent out with the budget card and charge card statements offered customers a beautifully detailed replica in miniature of a 1915 Model T Ford delivery van, typical of the commercial vehicles used by NAAFI during the First World War. But it had escaped somebody's historical knowledge whilst creating these perfectly formed replicas that NAAFI only came into being on the 1st of January 1921 some three years after the end of World War One.

The van's insignia should have either been the Canteen and Mess Cooperative Society up to June 1917 or the NACB thereafter. Although this is a small point to make, the company had always taught staff history during induction training and now it seemed that they were trying to change history. The Crest that was used on the side was not the original Crest from 1921 ether, the addition of the motto came some years later.

Wingham Reunion 1990

One hundred and fifty members of the NCS an Expeditionary Force Institute's OCA gathered on the lawns of Wingham in Surrey, for their reunion. They travelled from all over the country to enjoy a buffet lunch, strawberry tea, and refreshments served by current EFI members, house staff, and volunteers.

For many, however, the highlight was a selection of photographs from The NAAFI historical collection, and autographed Korean flag, a pair of binoculars, liberated from the Germans by Maj Ben White, during the North African campaign. These provided a source of memories, not least of all for Frank Clements who served in the NCS during the Second World War on board HMS Anthony, Highlander, and Exeter. At St Lazaire he took the only photographs of the tragic sinking of HMS Lancastria. His pictures used around the world at the time were on display.

Mr Clements' wartime adventures did not end there. HMS Exeter was sunk in the Java sea on the 1st of March 1942, exactly one year after his wedding. Taken prisoner by the Japanese, he spent 1264 days in captivity before his release on the 25th of September 1945. Two other prisoners of war, Bert Simms and Albert Mudge, attended the reunion. The first two met in 1938 when they were sent to the Middle East, on a French boat, recalled Mr Mudge. Mr Mudge was taken prisoner when Crete fell to Germany in June 1941, Mr Simms was captured at Tobruk in June 1942. Both were released in May 1945. They had kept in touch since 1938 and met up at the reunion for the first time in eight years. A call for ex staff from Christmas Island to get in touch was made by their former manager William Davis. He and his team of eight served Forces on the island in 1960 during the nuclear testing.

Entertainment at the reunion was provided by members of the district managers' training course taking place that week. The participants formed two teams, NCS and EFI, to race each other to pitch 12 foot by 12-foot field tents. NCS won the challenge.

The Gulf 1990

Three ships sailed fully stocked for the Gulf within 48 hours of placing their orders thanks to a new back office computer at Rosyth messing store, Scotland.

The demands of HMS Cattistock, Hurworth and Atherstone, were telephoned to Darlington warehouse, over 150 miles south of Rosyth and next day, delivered, priced, invoiced, and dispatched in two hours. Andy Inglis, messing store manager, explained that with manual systems, the stores have taken longer to complete the necessary paperwork.

As it was then price changes were fed into the computer each morning, so it was only a matter of printing an invoice and checking it off. The computer, a Tulip AT compact 2, had significantly improved the efficiency of the establishments, which served up to 50 Navy vessels. Balance sheet and summaries were now calculated and processed in minutes, and credit sales form A51 in just 15. Generally, an A51 used to take the whole afternoon to write out if you got it right first time. The computer made it a lot easier to find the information because all the records are on the system, backed up five times a day. Gene Blackadder, clerk, commented: 'It had taken time to adapt, especially for those with no computer experience. However, now the system is used so frequently we want another terminal so pricing and invoices can be done simultaneously.'

While all this was going on EFI Cpls Paul Brown and Paul Jennings sampled the grown up spread, sent to boost morale among troops in Saudi Arabia. The duo helped unload 12,000 free jars of Marmite, one for every soldier on Op Granby, at Portsmouth warehouse from where the products were dispatched. The next day 2 uniformed volunteers flew to the Gulf to join their colleagues running a bulk issue store and spread the news of the tasty treat which would follow.

Hard work serving troops in the hotspot that is the Gulf crisis were EFI. The first nine-man team, running a shop canteen BIS in Saudi Arabia, had been joined by two others, bringing the EFI number up to 27. More EFI taking a total to more than 60 would follow as Four armoured brigade were deployed to join the desert rats of Seven armoured brigade on Op Granby.

The sizeable army commitment involving 28,000 personnel, was backed by RAF Tornado and Jaguar squadrons and support staff, almost all from Germany. The adverse impact on the trade is now being felt in the European service. Colin Foster, manager overseas service, had been to Saudi to see first-hand how the services' needs were being met. The EFI were doing an excellent job inside difficult circumstances and they were operating the BIS, shop, plus tented canteens. Sometime later a second BIS was being opened before Christmas. Mobile van services were provided using army trucks and Land Rovers. A converted refrigerated truck, purchased from the army welfare funds, is used to sell cold drinks. En route to back them up four mobile vans, Ex-ES, were about to arrive and the vehicles were being purchased locally in order to provide a comprehensive service in rear forward areas.

James Rucker MD was due to see NAAFI Ops in the Gulf as NAAFI News went to press. The troops were being supplied with everything from toothpaste and soap, through to shaving cream and suntan oil. Amongst other items were sweets, paperbacks, stationery and Christmas cards and they could also order gifts by post and flowers through Interflora, so loved ones were not forgotten.

Initial stocks were shipped out in 31 containers with others following. Supply official Tony Storey had returned from Saudi and briefed management on the future demand and what goods could be obtained through local merchants. Mike Henebrey, supplies director, said: 'The shop is obviously just a hut with shelves and a table. The canteen is tented, open around the Clock, with EFI sleeping with their stock.'

The range was rather restricted, but they have met the most important requirement, and that was of liquid refreshment. Initially shipped out were large quantities of minerals such as Coca Cola and Pepsi. One of the larger tasks NAAFI had undertaken with supplying the army with traditional Christmas fare. The only thing missing would be wine and beers, alcohol was banned in Saudi Arabia.

As EFI left for the Gulf confident that they could do their job well, Maj Murray Smith 2IC said that their personal quick kit weighed 80 pounds including lightweight combat clothing, water bottles, emergency rations, S10 respirators, and nuclear and biological chemical suits. Each member was fully trained to react in any biological or chemical attack. Some having experience serving troops on exercise Sharp Sword in Egypt earlier that year, the first presence in the Middle East since 1956. Maj Smith: 'Many had served in the desert conditions and so are probably better prepared than Seven armoured brigade.'

1991

HMS TIGER to The WO and Chief Petty Officers Mess on HM Royal Yacht Britannia

Memories by Dave Atkinson 1972-1991

My life onboard HM Ships really started when applying for the role as a canteen assistant with NAAFI within the NCS.

I first applied in 1972 after going to London for an interview. Within three weeks I was posted to Portsmouth, staying overnight in the home club and being picked up in the morning, by a Mr West, district manager for Portsmouth ships. After being taken to his office in the dockyard, I was then transferred to HMS Tiger, a Royal Navy helicopter cruiser. After meeting the manager I met Mr Gordon Cousins. I was taken down to my mess which was the electricians mess 3G1 where 40 other people slept.

It was a very daunting experience for me as a person who had left home for the first time. We had a ship's company of over 800 sailors, our duties were to serve in the ship's canteen and cigarette kiosk. Daily tasks included bringing up the stores and serving the sailors, at the morning stand easy, dinner time, and afternoon stand easy and then in the evening. The days were long, and it was very hard work. The mess-deck life was fun – during the evening we would watch a film on the closed circuit television, listen to the radio, sing, and obviously drink beer.

In 1972 there was no mobile phones, no Internet, television and so we made our own entertainment. My first trip was a six-month tour of the Far East visiting places such as Gibraltar, Singapore, Hong Kong, the Philippines, Diego Garcia, and other stops on the way. Before joining the NCS I was a member of the St John's ambulance, and whilst on board ships I became a member of the first-aid team. On our return to the UK I went on a course to HMS Raleigh and did a course in firefighting as well as sea survival. My first-aid knowledge was kept up to date by ongoing training on different ships and became very useful to me in later years.

As a first ship HMS Tiger had a great impact on me and I decided that I really wanted to stay with the NCS. I was also taught how to canoe and used to go canoeing as part of the Royal Naval kayak team and then in 1974 on a visit to Kiel in Germany I canoed the Kielcanal with three other canoes for charity which was great.

After leaving HMS Tiger in 1975 I joined HMS Sheffield, the new type 42 destroyer. HMS Sheffield was then brand-new but very sadly in 1982, the Sheffield was sank by the Argentines. I served for 12 months on board HMS Sheffield and in 1976 joined HMS London as a trainee canteen manager. During my time on HMS London we visited the Caribbean.

In 1976, being the Bi-centenary year of America's independence, we sailed into New York and into Providence, Rhode Island with the TALL SHIPS, under sail, which was a great sight. During my training on board HMS London my trainer manager was a Mr Don Luckett, whom I feel was one of the best teachers anybody could ever have; then he sadly passed away but what a great guy he was. After leaving HMS London in 1977, I became the manager of my first ship HMS Dundas, a Portland training ship for officers. I was only on-board HMS Dundas a short time.

HMS Dundas was lucky to be one of the ships, at the Spithead review for HM the Queen's Silver Jubilee and it was a great honour to me, to see the Royal yacht sailing past with the Queen on board – who knew what the future would bring. At the end of the Spithead review in Portsmouth I was transferred to Chatham to join HMS Eskimo, where I was first introduced to a Mr Eric Peterson BEM for the first time. Eric was the NAAFI manager, at the Ration store in Chatham dockyard. Whilst in Chatham, all the stores for your ship, came through Eric; he was also heavily involved in the peanut ward, which was a children's burns unit at East Grinstead hospital. He got all the ships involved and helped to raise thousands of pounds, for the charity.

I began to become a good friend of Eric's and did many charity events for him. We cycled to East Grinstead for charity, we canoed it, also with the help of Ian Perks, canteen manager, and Malcolm Mason, in London, Linda Probate who both worked in Imperial Court and other members of the NAAFI staff. I can remember paddling with Ian, in single canoes towards East Grinstead and Ian said, 'let's take this little river to the left' and we ran out of water, we had to carry the canoes for about a mile back to the river.

After leaving HMS Eskimo in the summer of 1978, I joined HMS Endurance, the Royal Navy's Ice patrol ship. This was going to be a certain experience for me, a ship which I will never forget and had many great memories. On joining HMS Endurance I was in a senior rates' mess and somebody was talking and I remember, somebody said oh we are off to the Falklands in a month's time and I thought a couple of weeks up in Scotland sounds good, little did I know, at this time, it was 8000 miles away. We were an independently commanded ship, and were on our own, for most of the time after leaving the UK.

I stored the ship up for six months' stores for 150 crew – although there were not 150 crew on board you need those extra stores just in case. Our ship would take us down South America, visiting places like Santos in Brazil, Rio de Janeiro, Montevideo in Uruguay, down to the Falkland Islands, and then into the Antarctic to do our surveys in. Our base would then be in Port Stanley, the Falklands, where the governor of the Falklands resided. I spent some four seasons on HMS ENDURANCE, going through to 1982; during the 81 to 82 season something happened to change my life and everybody else's life forever.

On our last visit to Port Stanley in March 82 we were playing football against Port Stanley, when we were all recalled back on board Endurance; instead of going northwards towards home we were heading south towards the island of South Georgia, with extra forces from NP8901 Royal Marines. The Argentines had landed a small party of scrap metal workers, on the island of South Georgia, but had landed them by military transport and had raised the Argentine flags, without permission; this was the beginning of the war.

On arrival at South Georgia, we landed the Royal marine detachment, plus troops from the Falklands MP8901, to protect the people that were there at King Edward point. We then heard that the Argentinian invasion of the Falkland Islands itself, was imminent and we headed back towards the Falklands to try to see if we could do anything. Before we could get back to Stanley, they had invaded, it was too late; we turned round to sail back towards South Georgia to see if we could assist our troops on the ground, but anyway by the time we got there, the troops had done a fantastic job but sadly had to eventually surrender, not losing one man.

Keith Mills, and his detachment did fantastic, holding out at King Edward Point, but eventually taken to Argentina as prisoners of war. We were then alone in the South Georgia area, waiting for the decision by Margaret Thatcher, to send a task force to assist, we were the only Royal Navy ship within the Falklands, after being chased by the Argentine submarine, the Santa Fe and overflown by Argentine air force, Hercules aircraft. As we had already been down on patrol, for some months our stocks were getting low, we would have to check our supplies and we started rationing food on board Endurance, until we knew there was a task force on its way.

This was quite a scary time for us as we did not know what was going on, or what would happen next. I was called up to Captain Barker's cabin and he asked me to sit down. He poured me a large rum and said, he had something to ask me, but he said, 'I already know your answer'. He then said in three days' time, we will be going north to refuel and meet up with a store ship. As myself and my assistant were civilians, we could leave the ship and go home if we wanted. My answer was of course, we are staying, our joining papers were signed and we both joined the Royal Navy there and then, first civilians to do so in decades. After meeting the store's ship, we went back south, into battle, I was the leader of the after first aid post. My assistant Tony Weighll was also a first aider.

After embarking forces of the SAS and SBS, we eventually took South Georgia back. The retaking of South Georgia meant we were dispatched to the South Sandwich Islands, where there were Argentine soldiers who had raised the Argentine flag. On our way to Southern Thule, Captain Nick Barker was going over to HMS Yarmouth by helicopter, whilst at sea, to talk about the plans to retake the islands. He asked me if I wanted to go over to speak to the canteen manager, Ian Perks, so I did. After putting on my once only orange suit, my life jacket and flying helmet, off we went to HMS Yarmouth. On arrival, I was taken down to Ian's canteen and when I knocked on the door and opened it, he looked at me with all my flying gear on, said flipping heck Dave how did you get here. Well after a few drinks and then back to Endurance, the following day they surrendered.

The rest is history, and as they say we could write a book. Before I leave the Falklands may I say how privileged it was to have served on HMS Endurance (The Red Plum) and an honour to be part of the ship's company, not forgetting the ships and armed forces lost, and still on patrol, we will always remember them.

After being there before and after the conflict on board HMS Endurance, being the longest serving Royal Naval vessel through the Falklands, we then returned home to Chatham. The night before arrival into Chatham Naval base, we were boarded by government officials, and told anything we saw or heard prior to them invading, we were not to talk about it as a D notice was placed on us for 25 years; this has since passed. After a hero's welcome back to our naval base, we all went on leave. For me, what to do next? The Endurance was paying off and so I needed another ship.

They were looking for a canteen manager to take over on the Royal Yacht Britannia from the manager, I was to take over from Dougie Jackson, he was retiring after 28 years' service. I went down for the interview on a Friday, after a couple of other people were interviewed, they came down to the Warrant officers' mess and said you have the job, go back to Chatham, pack your cases, join here first thing Monday morning.

I joined the Yacht December 1982 until August 1991. It was a totally different job on the Royal Yacht from the other Royal Navy ships, first of all you always wore uniform and from that day on we could never wear jeans, it was always jacket, shirt and tie, as you were always representing HM the Queen. We were away from England between 6 to 8 months of the year, on Royal tours and duties; it was hard work and very hard on your families, but very enjoyable. You got to meet all the Royal Family and many other kings and queens around the world.

I met the king and queen of Spain, the president, and First Lady of the USA, the Reagans, to name but a few. I have been to Buckingham Palace many times. It was a great time in my life, being able to serve the Queen and Royal Family, to whom l remain true and loyal to this day, I took early retirement in 1991 due to my sight loss and had a private audience with HM The Queen AND HRH the Duke of Edinburgh on the yacht in August 1991. I was presented with a signed photograph, from them both. During my time on Britannia, we had circumnavigated the world and there were not many places I had not been to.

The yacht carried on for another six years after I left, and I was invited back for its decommissioning in 1997. The last canteen manager was Steve Cooper, a great friend of mine for many years. In my 19 years with NCS, I had been to many places and met many people, it's been a memorable career. I would like to thank Dave Frampton, my District manager and good friend for all his help along the way. My 3 most treasured possessions: My personal signed photograph from this Queen; my S Atlantic medal presented to me by His Royal Highness the Duke of Edinburgh; and my commendation from the Falklands.

EFI parade after returning from the Gulf December 1991

The Gulf war once again showed how vital NAAFI was to the services. There is not another organisation that could step into the role EFI filled, said Maj Bob Randerson, commanding officer. He stood and watched the Gulf reunion parade, at Wingham in Surrey, to mark the contribution of NAAFI volunteers in uniform to Op Granby, on land and sea and to Op Safe Haven which followed.

'I am enormously proud of all the lads and it's a great relief to have them all home. We brought them altogether as a mark of our appreciation of their work,' said Maj Randerson.

Over 70 men from UK and Germany, dressed in either desert combats or NCS uniform, assembled with those they had served within the Middle East. Before he took their salute, Maj General David Botting, direct general, Royal Army Ordnance call, told watching friends and relatives, 'Congratulations to the EFI on their contribution to Ops in the Middle East. I thank you for all of what you did for the services in the Gulf. Once again EFI went to an area of conflict at a moment's notice. Your contribution continued and enhanced your predecessors for an example.'

Maj General Bottings singled out one man for particular praise: 'Although EFI work as a team, one member, Warrant Officer Dave Forster, was mentioned in dispatches. That award not only credits him and his men, but all EFI in the Gulf. And his team was supported by the permanent cadre, and staff behind the scenes in the UK and throughout the world.'

He also took the opportunity to explain EFI's evolving role in the new logistical corps which will emerge following troop reductions and Ops for change: 'The confirmation of cuts to troop numbers will, of course, have an effect on NAAFI and EFI. The RAOC will become the new logistical corps incorporating RTC, ACC, pioneer Corps, and the Postal and Courier service. I can assure you that the only difference this will make to EFI is that they will have to wear a different cap badge.'

Before presenting commemorative certificates and speaking with each volunteer, General Botting continued: 'The Gulf, northern Iraq, and Turkey had been a major Op and I'm sure that you were all proud that you were there and played a part in history, you really will have stories to tell your grandchildren. Your continued dedication and enthusiasm was clearly shown in the Gulf. Your wonderful support has made me extremely proud that you wear the RAOC cap badge.'

As volunteers and guests settled down to afternoon tea on Wingham's lawn listening to the RAOC band, Dave Frampton, district manager Plymouth ships, told NAAFI News that he was delighted that members of the NCS attended in recognition of their work.

They were usually at sea, but they are easily forgotten, and the lads appreciate the invitation. Most of them went back to the Gulf on deployment so this was to show our thanks to help them on their way.

Richard Burton, district manager Munster Germany, who served on Ops Safe Haven, spoke of his time in the Middle East: 'To begin with the Royal Marines didn't want our support but we soon broke down the barriers and have since had letters of thanks for the help,' he said. His experience has affected him on his return to district: 'Seeing so much suffering of the Kurdish people suddenly put my life into perspective. I realised how lucky I am to have the job, home and family.'

In this he echoed many of the volunteers' thoughts. Brian Hamilton, broadcaster at the time for British Forces Broadcasting Service (BFBS) made a half hour programme on EFI and NAAFI for a radio series called The Fringe, which truly opened the eyes about the breadth of service that EFI played.

The truth of it was that post-WWII the Gulf was the first time the armed forces truly appreciated everything EFI could do and did do for regular serving personnel and this was being duly recognised.

The Gulf reunion parade also marked the end of an era; this was the last day Maj Bob Randerson, officer commanding, would wear the uniform of the RAOC EFI. Maj Randerson had retired in just one month before the parade but waited to see the lads come back from the Gulf reunited and honoured before saying his final farewell. 'I wouldn't have felt happy leaving unfinished business after seeing them go through such hardship in the desert,' he said.

In recognition of Maj Randerson's 18 years at EFI headquarters, Surrey, James Rucker, MD, presented him with a miniature uniform statue. Mr Rucker said that: 'The remarkable OC, on his career first in the Royal Navy in the Second World War, and then with the Royal Pioneer Corps before taking charge of EFI's 250 personnel. Everyone will remember him for his sense of humour and leadership, and the good work he has done making EFI the efficient unit it was.'

1992

EFI ladies join the ranks 1992

The first group of female staff to join the ranks of EFI since 1987 were ready for action and completing their basic training. Diane Kerry, Brenda Hodgson, Nikki Stokes, and Debbie Mawhinney, Karen Kilburn, joined a lone male volunteer Peter Nicholls at Prince William of Gloucester barracks Lincoln, for a gruelling week at EFI headquarters, Surrey.

Basic training began each morning at 0600 hrs with 45 minutes of physical exercise. And lights out was at 2300hrs. The bulk of the week was spent, learning military law, badges of rank, drill, map reading, first aid, field survival, and defence against nuclear, chemical, and biological attack. All of which was examined during a written test at the end of the course. The group also spent a full day at the RAOC, Deep Cut, Surrey, learning how to handle weapons.

Warrant Officer Andy Dungay, leader of the course, made it apparent that it was not easy to grasp these skills in such short time when regular soldiers get six weeks' training. The girls are treated like the same as the male volunteers because they do the same job as the men on exercise, unloading lorries and carrying boxes and equipment as part of normal duties.

Sgt Nigel Hall, EFI trainer, showed troops how to use the breathing equipment in the gas chamber. He said: 'I released CS gas pellets, which makes the eyes and skin sting when inhaled, and ordered troops to take off their masks, shout their name rank and number, before walking out. It's a very unpleasant experience, but they coped well, and none of them panicked.'

The new recruits' 3-year EFI commitment meant being ready to mobilise with troops at any time, in the event of war or to serve with HM forces on exercise in the UK and abroad. Maj Marie Smith, officer commanding EFI, said: 'Clearly women can cope as well as men. Now we have more trained staffed immobilised in emergencies.' This was one of the biggest step forwards in terms of equal opportunities within NAAFI, which meant this was an historic moment. The first intake of female officer recruits would be in June 1993.

EFI UN Christmas spirit 1992

British troops deployed to the former Yugoslavia will have a Taste of Home Christmas 1992 thanks to NAAFI. Former members of the Expeditionary Force Institutes have left home shows in support of the British troops taking part in 'Op Grapple', the United Nations protection force guarding the convoys in the war-torn republics. The men, Captain Andrew Parkinson, Sgt Nigel Hall, and Cpl Brian McCourt and Cpl Richard Starkey, had to set up a shop at the former seaside resort of Split, on the Adriatic coast of Bosnia.

They were attached to 31 Ordnance Company, a bulk issue store and shop, keeping over 2400 troops supplied with everything from Mars bars to a bar of soap. Should the services request it, two men are on standby to move forward to the town of Vitez, in Croatia, to run a similar service.

Before leaving for Split the men underwent two days' military training at the Sun Lager in Germany. They took part in live firing of SA80 rifles, heavy machine guns, and anti-tank weaponry. They were also taught how to handle grenades and other Army training.

For Cpt Parkinson the call up came as quite a surprise – his only experience with EFI was when he did basic training in Deep Cut in Hampshire 2½ years previously. When he was asked to go to Yugoslavia, he was very shocked, but relished the chance to go. The two days were very educational, apart from the initial basic training, he had never fired a weapon until he'd gone to Santiago. For Sgt Hellen, Cpl McCourt and Cpl Starkey, the Split venture is their second tour of duty with EFI in a warzone, all three spent six months in Saudi Arabia with troops during the Gulf conflict.

Sgt Hall said: 'We sell everything the troops need, even Christmas cards, and all the things that make the Op a bit more bearable. We look forward to going but the risks, which are very real, have been emphasised. The dangers in Yugoslavia, that of sniper fire, will be very different from the Scud missiles we faced in the Gulf. Our training has been thorough, and we were able and prepared to defend ourselves.'

The EFI Op at Pleso air base, near Zagreb in Sylvania, had gone from strength to strength since Cpt Andrew Cowen and Sgt Chris Webb set up shop there in the summer.

Maurice Madelin, manager overseas service, visited the men on a fact-finding tour, accompanied by Maj Murry Smith, OC EFI. Everyone they spoke to were very impressed with the work done by Cpt Coenen, Sgt Webb. In fact, the Chief of general staff, General Sir Peter Inge, said in his report of the army's Ops there: 'I was pleased to hear considerable praise for EFI whose service was proving indispensable with an effective resupply system.'

Supplies to the Pleso base and the local population were then sent on a regular basis from Kempen distribution centre in Germany. One driver, who had made the 2.569 km round trip was Tim Cooks. He said that he'd heard artillery fire on his journeys to the base, but the worst part of the trip was dealing with three different languages and three different borders. Staff had to travel through a potentially hazardous journey, the professionalism and commitment of the drivers had meant that they had had no problems so far and the vehicles closely resemble commercial vehicles, so they do not attract undue attention.

EFI role in the new Corps 1992

It was farewell to the old and greetings to the new when EFI took part in an open day to herald the formation of the Royal Logistic Corps in 1993.

The Corps will replace the RAOC, as part of the army's restructuring following the options for change defence cuts. Since 1965, EFI had worn the cap badge of the RAOC in campaigns as diverse as the Falklands and the Gulf.

The display, held at Andover airfield in Hampshire, brought together all aspects of the new Corps, including transport, engineering, bomb disposal and communications. Over 2 days guests were shown how the new Corps would work, and the role it would play in the military Ops.

Guests included the undersecretary and state for defence, Lord Cranbourne, and the chief of general staff, general Sir Peter Inge. Representing EFI were Cpl Brian McCourt and Warren's officer Andy Dungay, both from the Cadre at EFI headquarters, Wingham, and Cpl Brenda Hodgson, employee relations, Nottingham, one of the first female recruits to EFI. At the display volunteers manned a mobile serving cups of tea to guests, and a tented shop and bulk issue store, set up in a shipping container. The display gave people an idea of the role EFI played in Ops, and to show off the facilities and goods that they could supply.

There was a lot of interest in the display and how EFI could help. Amongst the other displays for examples of the facilities provided like showers, Postal Service, local liaison office, and bomb disposal.

Op Grapple 1, Croatia/Bosnia, Attached to 360 Supply Company RAOC Memories by Nigel Hall 1992

The EFI Cadre, based at Wingham in Surrey, was a core team of more experienced personnel who formed the basis for most operations and exercises and were supplemented with volunteers from the wider EFI ranks.

As the situation in the Former Yugoslavia deteriorated in 1992, we were on stand-by to deploy as part of the UK contingent to United Nations Peacekeeping forces.

First to deploy were S/Sgt Chris Webb along with Capt Andy Cowan who set up a service at Pleso camp just outside Zagreb airport. The rest of the cadre staff stood by ready to go.

When we learned of our impending deployment, life became extremely busy. I, along with Cpl Brian McCourt and Cpl Richard Starkie, first attended a 7-day training course at the Light Infantry Depot in Winchester. There, we brushed up on our weapons, first aid, NBC, warfare drills and radio skills, ending with a 3-day exercise on Salisbury Plain. In early October 1992, we deployed to Munster in Germany along with Capt Andy Parkinson (NAAFI District Manager, London) and met up with our unit, 360 Supply Company RAOC.

After a further 2 weeks of training, we finally flew to Split, Croatia, arriving on October 27th. We learned that our base would be in 2 large warehouses (Shed 6, Shed 7) within Split North Port where we were to be accommodated on board a Royal Fleet Auxiliary ship, RFA Sir Bedivere.

Our first reaction to the port area was one of shock. The warehouse we were to use had to be cleared of 38,000 tonnes of flour, and its resident rats, before we could move in. An open sewer to the rear of the building along with large piles of rubbish dotted around the place added an interesting aroma!

Winter was extremely cold and thermal clothing provided much needed warmth. At times though, it became difficult to write invoices as our hands were so cold.

While the main supply routes into Bosnia itself were established, initial deliveries to the troops had to be made to Tomislavgrad (the base for HQ UK National Support Element and two squadrons of Royal Engineers) in our Land Rover and trailer.

On one occasion, Cpl McCourt and I led a convoy to the base – an experience not to be missed. Fortunately, I only made the one wrong turning!

As the EFI service had been established, business has nearly trebled. We now run 64 wholesale credit accounts for various units of the British Forces as well as the Canadians, Dutch, Americans, French, Danish and Norwegians.

We stocked more than 400 lines and sales have included 1.57 million cans of beer and minerals, 430,000 bars of chocolate and 160,000 bags of crisps.

Life had improved considerably since our arrival. We now have a computer to run our accounts and an office to replace the tent we started in. In between the snow, heavy rain and gale force winds, the weather is gradually getting warmer.

Apart from Croatian troops occasionally shooting into the port area and rats that will eat anything not stored 6 feet off the ground, our biggest headache is power cuts which occur from 0630 to 1700 every day. Batteries are a very popular item in our shop!

Goods are supplied from Kempen Distribution Centre in Germany, every 2 weeks with 2 and sometimes 3 lorries making the trip. David Moth (Customer Accounts, Warehousing & Distribution, Kempen) and his team have played a vital part in the success of our operation. Orders are often needed at very short notice and they cope extremely well with any problems.

Customer orders have certainly been varied, including industrial washing machines and driers, a 12-foot inflatable shark, Matey Bubble Bath (there is only one bath here!) and a BMW car for a member of the UN High Commission for Refugees (UNHCR).

As our tour draws to a close, we are looking forward to some well-earned leave. We depart knowing that we have contributed a great deal in support of the UN peace effort, and to the welfare of the troops who face a demanding task in often hostile and arduous conditions.

1993

War touches EFI 1993

EFI men serving in Croatia were victims of violence when two grenades exploded outside their shop in Split. Andrew Cowan, formerly 2nd in command EFI cadre, explained to NAAFI News on the return from the warzone: 'The shop was only 10 metres from the perimeter fence and bordering road. Two grenades were thrown over the fence and they landed at the side of the building. The first we knew of it was when they exploded seconds later. As duty officer that evening, I was in the building opposite and rushed out as soon as I heard the bangs. The EFI lads did the same and saw just how close the explosions had been by the debris. It was 2100hrs and because the shop was closed, and no one was outside the building, no one was hurt. However, the incident was the first reported act of aggression within the United Nations compound at Split.'

The attack was the closest the EFI had come to the war. Although small arms fire often skimmed over the port area, and a gun battle occurred outside the harbour's back gate. 'Obviously, you are always conscious of your military role because you are in uniform,' continued Mr Cowan. 'For instance when we travelled upcountry to Vitez we carried loaded weapons and wear flak jackets to protect us. However, this incident brought it home to us the danger we all served in.'

Training for troops on their way to Bosnia had been taking place since June on Salisbury Plain. In Split, EFI were still busy serving troops taking part in Op Grapple. Cpl Karen Kilburn said: 'I'm now halfway through my six-month tour and I'm loving every minute. Even my boots have broken in now and they feel more like slippers. The main thing happening at the moment is the Christmas pantomime. It is still in the early planning stages, but it should be good fun. Insect bites are a problem and I miss being able to have a bath but apart from that everything is well.'

1994

A ship to shore service (Originally written by Tina Merrifield) 1994

The Navy dates back as far as the 13th century when Edward I assembled the first national task force to sail for South West France.

Even in 1994, 7 centuries later, Plymouth was still a thriving naval base with ships and submarines regularly leaving on deployment worldwide, from its dockyard in Davenport. HMS Drake, situated in the heart of Royal Navy Ops within the dockyard, had also evolved into one of the most well equipped and modern technological refitted facilities in the world. Following the Argentinian invasion of the Falklands in 1982, warships were dispatched from Davenport to defend British territory and more recently to fight in the Gulf war and The Bosnian conflict.

Another important part of Ops at Drake's presence since World War 2, is, of course, NAAFI which over the years has helped sustain morale by providing a unique service for those stationed and visiting the base. Drake itself, which covers an area around 2 miles long and half a mile wide, is a sure establishment and accounting base for ships and submarines on refit. It provided accommodation, and victualling, pay, Family Services and amenities for the Royal Navy and the Royal Marines personnel serving there. Situated in Devonport dockyard, West of Plymouth town centre, Drake was home to around 2000 service personnel ranks.

In charge of NAAFI Ops was David Frampton, district manager, Davenport, who had worked alongside the Navy for over 30 years. It was his responsibility to oversee the day to day running of both NAAFI ship and shore establishments. The ship work added a different dimension to the role at Drake. Mr Frampton explained: 'My staff are always on the move and it can be difficult to keep track of them while on deployment. Staff were on 27 ships and you can only be contacting them through letter or signal when away, and I also supply 12 submarines. Right now, I have staff on deployment in the Gulf, S Atlantic, and outside Croatia. Generally, I am only in contact with them if there are any problems, such as low supplies or out of date confectionery. When necessary I can authorise, the canteen manager to go ashore and purchase items locally to keep the stocks full until return to Plymouth or I can ask the supply officer on the vessel to help out. I am also the middleman in cases of real emergency. For example, last month one of the managers became sick on RFA Fort Austin and had to be flown home. I informed the captain and the supplies officer and quickly found a temporary replacement and had to ensure the personnel Department at Amesbury made transport arrangements.'

As soon as the ship comes into dock, Mr Frampton's main work begins. He has to make initial inspections of the NAAFI canteen stores to see if the standards of hygiene are maintained and the accounts are in good order, and staffing levels are adequate. The ships dock three times a year for refitting, at Christmas, Easter and in August for summer leave, which were the busiest times. While the ships were in dock, they keep a close contact with the supply officers to see if they are satisfied with the standards of service from NAAFI. Supporting Mr Frampton was Steve Timbrell, who managed the shore establishment with his staff of 43. On land, NAAFI is still very central to the wellbeing of the service personnel and played a very active role in maintaining them all. The service that was provided was essential to personnel at Drake as it was not so easy just popping into town. Customers needed somewhere to relax and a place to pick up a few supplies or a bite to eat. They were always busy.

The service is well situated within Drake, offering customers access to a whole range of durable and non-durable goods without the inconvenience of a two-mile track into the city centre. The facilities comprised a financial centre, post office, shop, hairdressers, automat, food bar, and a club and function room. The financial centre adjoining the shop was opened in 1991, the first naval centre of its kind. Tony Tomlinson, manager said: 'The centre is responsible for generating excess commission per year to cover costs and meet expected profits which we always achieve. Our main business was personal loans, mostly for holidays, household items and even educational courses. Customers use the centre because it is easy to pop in for advice. We get a lot of impulse inquiries when customers wander in for a look around.'

As an added convenience, Roy Alesbrook, the centre's personal financial advisor, went aboard ship to speak to customers, although when aboard he was always still in direct competition with High Street financial advisors. Most of the business was done there as well as generating custom for life insurance and pensions, he also redirected many customers on to the centre for other requests or enquiries.

Other popular financial services were an immediate access to new budgeting charge card accounts which customers could open in the shop. Customers at the time liked to have such items as HiFi equipment to take on board with them but didn't have the cash available. For them, instant access to credit is a real bonus and it was not just British customers that NAAFI attended to.

It was always difficult to accommodate a large amount of stock in the shop as the storerooms were always too small, or goods were ordered from Amesbury, and although they had a delivery by lorry once a week, goods could still take some time to arrive, especially when Amesbury was out of stock. This meant that at busy times such as Christmas, when many more customers are ordering goods, they sometimes lost sales. This was changed as a major refurbishment in the shop and store solved the issues and the difficulties in holding the stock.

Next door to the shop was the post office; every Friday, you would see canteen managers banking their week's takings with Henry Finnamore, manager. He was an old hand at the job and a familiar face to all on the base as he had worked there for 10 years and it ran like every other post office.

Just nearby was the hairdressers which never saw a quiet moment. Carol Roberts, senior stylist there, looked after both male and female customers. Brought up in the Naval environment after her father joined the service, she was used to dealing with all types of service personnel. Customers were on on their best behaviour when they came into the salon and a lot of the time it was the regulation haircut and if a customer was not keeping to them, she suggested they had a little bit extra snipped here and there. To cope with the demands an average day saw them seeing 80 customers and she was helped out on a part-time basis by her assistant Angie Pollard. One of her customers explained to her that they needed their hair very short as they were about to go on a sub for two months and they wanted to keep their hair within the regulations. Unfortunately, at the time the hair could not be trimmed on a submarine as it clogged up the ventilation.

The thriving area of NAAFI's facilities was the 'Drumbeat' club where customers could relax after a day's work. The introduction of regular club promotions meant they could coincide these with function nights. They would also try and organise events when they knew ships were in dock to improve sales. They were informed of incoming ships by a circular produced by staff within the admin block every week. For NAAFI, life at Drake was not just busy ashore, aboard ship it is just as hectic, and staff do their best to meet demands and limited accommodation.

HMS Beaver Memories by Dean Kelly 1994

I joined HMS Beaver as a NAAFI Can man. I spent time at the battle of Atlantic celebrations, and after a few weeks of training, we got ready for our Bosnia/Adriatic tour.

I was given a new assistant, who turned out to be a senior manager from Germany, Michael Reynolds; it was decided that we would both fill in the manager role, which was great for me. We sailed, first stop was Gibraltar for 4 hour fuel up, we then proceeded to Cagliary, we spent 3 days on the beach before going to the Adriatic for 3 weeks and 3 days of patrols. With stops in Venice, lots of stops in Naples and Capri to top up stores and fuel.

Then after the next patrol we were given 2 weeks off in Corfu, which was fun. During that time the rest of the UK task force arrived, part of NATO Task force. One morning I got a call to the flight deck to be surrounded by lots of can men and can'ass, all the other ships had sailed in, to do a peace conference on HMS Illustrious. Whilst they were all on a night out, they all needed money to stay in hotels until the ships came back. Which I was only happy to then be back on patrol after 6 months we headed back to the UK.

On our first day back we were told there was going to be a photo shoot in 2 days' time but we were empty and needed to top up. Once we were done we headed out to the bar, then back to the ship in the early hours of the morning. We had to be ready for the photo shoot by 0800 plus the captain was also involved so we had to be smart! To say it was a struggle would be an understatement.

The fearless few (Originally written by Sarah Wintle) 1994

An emergency at sea meant all hands-on deck, including those of canteen men who live and work alongside their customers.

The steel hull of HMS fearless shuddered as a muffled roar announced the ship had been impacted by missiles. Lights flickered and dimmed, the ship listed as the water flooded in, the tannoy barked orders, and the crew that had been silently waiting in anticipation sprang to action stations' duties. The Iraqis had fired, and this was war.

This sounds like a scene from the Gulf war. Far from it, in this instance the crew of HMS Fearless was fighting to save their badly damaged ship just off Portland in the English Channel. The rogue Iraqi aircraft carrier and submarine that were closing in for the kill were imaginary players in a damage control exercise.

In the Royal Navy world, Portland was the base all vessels check into for regular overhaul of equipment and personnel. It was there that men and machinery were put through their paces to ensure that they were up to the standards demanded by the service. It was on her last exercise before the final inspection that NAAFI News joined the HMS Fearless. During the next three hours the crew, including five NAAFI canteen men, would be stretched to their professional limits, as active members of the crew they had an important role to play during action stations. Steve Appleby, canteen manager, said: 'I secure the canteen with Andy Meikle, trainee assistant canteen manager, remaining there. Canteen assistants Paul Wilkinson and Steve Watkins help the emergency medical teams, and Phil Gale, canteen assistant, acted as a runner for the sick bay.'

Primed and ready, then NAAFI lads reacted instantly to the call for action stations. Quickly pulling on heavy protective clothing, anti-flash masks, and emergency life support apparatus equipment, the men dispersed to their assigned locations. Back at the canteen, mesh was hurriedly fixed over the shelves of stock. 'The last thing you needed when the ship began to list is stock rolling around the floor; that would be hazardous if it got under foot or potentially flammable if near fire,' said Mr Appleby.

Once secure, the two men waited for further orders. The canteen manager explained: 'If the state of emergency were to go on for some time, for example during war, the captain might give the command to release 'action snacks'. As the crew would be unable to stand down for food and drink during conflicts, we would then issue drinks and chocolate to sustain them during the physically draining action stations.'

The rest of the team were already finding out how draining the exercise could be. Wearing heavy, constrictive clothing, and making their way through the maze of dark narrow gangways, the atmosphere was both hot and claustrophobic. Emergency lighting meant vision was restricted, especially in areas now filled with acrid smoke, and the temperature quickly rose as their air conditioning stopped. The exercise was meant to recreate the type of conditions a crew would have to work in during conflict. Starting with thunder flashes over this side of the ship and smoke bombs inside to simulate the explosions, the ship's ballast is then altered to make it list, electricity is cut so lighting, communications and air conditioning are lost, and volunteers 'wounded' for the medical teams to rescue.

The results were frighteningly realistic. There was a makeshift emergency room, medical teams were tending to their casualties. Even though they're outside of the normal sick bay surroundings, they organise some sort of system to deal with their worst cases whilst improvising with their minimal supplies. An update on the deteriorating situation has to be passed to the central point in the emergency operating Theatre. NAAFI runner, Mr Gale, made his way there past firefighting teams, electricians trying to establish emergency power lines, and the wounded. His part in the proceedings was vital. Even though communications were down the different parts of the ship still needed keeping into contact to gauge damage and number of injuries. The runner's job was to keep information flowing which meant running miles to deliver messages. Mr Wilkinson updated the detailed plans of the ship with the latest damage information. They had to coordinate the activities of the medical teams, so it was important for them to know where they were and what state the ship was in. The canteen assistants could also administer first aid in emergency.

Needing to be in touch with the sick bay, an exhausted canteen assistant was ordered on to arrive just in time to be told that the area had been taken out in the latest attack. He was the only survivor. This is all happening while the ship was under a constant barrage of fire, many of the crew and equipment were out of action, but they must battle on to save the ship. It was

at this point that their determination was really tested. The crew bravely carried on through the repeated assaults until the end came some 3 hours later – after the first impact HMS Fearless had sunk.

Unfortunately, this was the end result and it was inevitable on the exercise that this would happen. It was up to the ship's crew to keep the ship afloat for as long as possible, which they did. The NAAFI men were important members of the crew; everybody had a role to play during, and outside of, action stations, and the canteen men did their part with great professionalism and dedication. Without the support of the NAAFI crew they would be unable to do this job as efficiently.

The Call of Duty soon came. The NAAFI canteen opened for business immediately, following stand down and the canteen assistants made their way back to start their duties on the other side of the counter. But have they enjoyed the exercise? They had, explaining that being so involved meant they felt a real part of the crew and the team spirit. Although their ship had sunk, the canteen men's spirits were not dampened as the fearless few lived to fight another day.

End of an era at joint HQ 1994

Wingham training and development centre was sold to a developer and the site was to become an 80-bedroom residential nursing home.

Staff that were currently located at the centre, business development trainers and EFI Cadre, were anticipated to leave the premises by mid-April 1994. London regional office staff would remain in situ for up to six months while the new headquarters for them was being found.

Although a headquarter location for business development trainers still needed to be found at the time, regional training centres for on the job training in the field had already been established. Designated sites in the first wave include HMS Raleigh, RAF Cosford, RAF Brize Norton, RAF Lyneham, Wellington barracks in London, HMS Cochrane, and Alexander barracks in County Antrim.

Centres had been set up for assistant club managers' training but could also be used by regional training and catering supervisors for both shop and club training as appropriate. First to move from Wingham was the EFI who would be based at Ward barracks, Bulford. Maj Murray Smith, OC EFI RLC, said: 'It would be better for us to be nearer the centre of military Ops and our customers in the South of the country such as RAF Brize Norton and RAF Lyneham and South Cerney. In fact, we will be in the same barracks as mobile land forces (MLF) who we were often mobile with on exercise.'

Another plus point was that the location made it much more secure. The EFI was a military unit and as such they had been very vulnerable in such an open location as Wingham. The services personnel would become aware of EFI and its role as a result of seeing us based within a military environment. All EFI requirements, such as training and accommodation would be met by local army facilities, wardrooms, and messes. Those currently living at Wingham will either commute daily or live alongside then military customers.

Members of the cadre served three years then returned to the original establishments, whilst with EFI they spent nine months overseas and at the time it was six months in Bosnia and three months in Norway, plus their leave entitlement. This left members very little time to actually be based at headquarters. Maj Smith was also the chairman of NAAFI OCA which traditionally held an annual reunion at Wingham. In 1994 the get together would be held at Chelsea barracks, London on the 30th of July 1994.

The location of future reunions on the Remembrance Day service would be decided at the association's AGM in April of that year. Maj Smith said: 'Although I am sad at this passing of an era, we must look to the future, the modern-day role and demands on EFI meant that relocation to Bulford was beneficial to the cadre, customers and NAAFI.'

Catering for Royalty in 1994

Catering staff worked round the clock to prepare food for over 4000 guests attending the bicentenary celebrations of the Royal Yeomanry, Health Wintergreen Park. As well as saving food, 65 staff from Kent and London establishments also run a beer tent for a further 4000 guests.

NAAFI services on the day were organised by Andrew Parkinson, district manager north London, and Lisa Shire, club manager Victoria barracks, Windsor. The food was prepared by John Flew, Catering advisor, and catering staff from Amesbury, who worked 24 hours in the HQ restaurant kitchens to get everything ready.

Mr Parkinson found this the most difficult catering event that he had organised for some time. The size of the celebrations and the location of the various serving points, and the sheer number of people involved meant it had to be planned to the smallest detail. That involved meeting with event organisers 2 months in advance. Among the staff drawn into help were Cathy Hopkins and Glenys D'Arcy, both club assistants from RAF High Wycombe. They started work at 0630 hrs preparing food and drink in their location. They found this very difficult to get ready but once all the problems were ironed out it went without a hitch.

The event was attended by Her Majesty the Queen, the Queen Mother, and the Duke of Edinburgh, so it was a very memorable occasion for all involved.

First EFI girl to serve in warzone since World War II, 1994

The first EFI girl to serve in a warzone since World War II returned from her six-month tour in the port of Split, Croatia. Cpl Karen Kilburn helped her EFI colleagues to run a shop and bulk issue store for the United Nations troops based there. When she arrived in Split the first thing to hit her was the strong smell of sulphur around the docks. Although it was unpleasant, it took time to get used to it. The accommodation for staff was on board a naval ship in the Harbour, with the other army women. Although she became very good friends with a number of them, the long working hours didn't give much time for socialising.

When she started behind the counter some of the lads found it funny to see a woman serving them for the first time, as they weren't used to it.

Once Cpl Kilburn had returned, she went on leave before going on exercise in Germany. It was then she was promoted to Sgt and took 2 EFI team members to Gioia Del Colle, Italy, serving members of the RAF in 'Op Deny Flight'. This was going to be a challenge for her but she was more than happy to take it on.

As two of NAAFI's finest were flown to Italy to serve airmen on Op Deny Flight guarding the no-fly zone over the former Yugoslavia. The departure marked a double achievement for NAAFI. It was the first time the RAF had requested NAAFI service, and the first time the service had been provided by an all-female team.

EFI Sgt Karen Kilburn and Cpl Carol Fowler volunteered to run a bulk issue store and shop for the airman based at Gioia Del Colle, in southern Italy. The service kept the men supplied with everything from razors and crisps through to washing powder, chocolate, and souvenirs. Sgt Kilburn said that NAAFI service in the area had been used to two-man Op, and now it had a two-woman Op. Cpl Fowler was usually found filling the shelves in the family shop at RAF Brize Norton. Her first tour of EFI duty began and she was looking forward to providing a much-needed service. It was a real challenge for them both and they could live up to the expectations easily. The girls took over from Sgt Chris Webb and Cpl Fred Merrington. Their tour of duty lasted four months, bringing them home just in time for Christmas.

From Major to Lieutenant Colonel 1994

The rank of commanding officer, Expeditionary Force Institutes, Royal Logistics Corps, had been upgraded from Maj to Lt Col. Lt Col Murray Smith, OC EFI RLC, followed the formation of the RLC. It took into account the increased role EFI played in areas such as Split, Croatia, and Gioia Del Colle in Italy.

Lt Col Murray Smith, having joined the Parachute Regiment in 1958, embarked upon his career with NAAFI in 1989 when he took up a post of 2nd in command EFI. Now based at Ward barracks, Bulford, he was responsible for ensuring EFI had sufficiently trained staff to mobilise in the event of war, or limited ops as currently being seen in Croatia. He selected teams for deployment answering to the administration of EFI assisted by a permanent cadre.

His main aim was to ensure EFI is issued with the right equipment and stores and get them to the right place at the right time. He was very pleased to be the first OC EFI RLC to reach this rank, and the job had been judged by the Ministry of Defence to be so valuable.

EFI team makes its mark in Croatia 1994

EFI soldiers in Croatia had their work cut out for them, with relocation to another warehouse at Dalma taking place in the middle of that deployment. The warehouse was purpose built near Sandy Beach. It was clean and spacious with excellent facilities throughout. The move, however, did not go without hitches. First of all, the ferry carrying the lorries with supplies from camp was delayed for 36 hours. Then the forklift truck Cpl Darren Smith was using to load the supplies broke down and could not be repaired. Despite the problems they were open for business within days. However, living accommodation was hard to find so Cpl Smith, Gary Britt, Declan Pickup, and Brandie Baxter dreamed up the little house in the warehouse project.

They made their own living space among the containers, and decorated it to look like home. It was officially opened by the commanding officer, Lt Col Steirn, who liked the picket fence! Cpl Britt also took the opportunity to travel in convoy into war-torn Bosnia itself. They often sent supplies to units inside the Bosnian border and had heard of the terrible road conditions the convoys had to negotiate to reach these units. He had to go and see them for himself.

As they approached the border between Croatia and Bosnia they couldn't help but think how peaceful it was. The driver then pointed out that the building on their left was a training section for one of the warring factions. They then arrived at Gornji Vakuf in the afternoon to refuel. They were amazed by the destruction around them as they drove through the town. It brought home to them what the war was doing to those involved, and how important the United Nations' presence was there.

Once they arrived at Vitez, their final destination at 1430 hours, they then accompanied another vehicle on the convoy to the town of Zepce. This was a different drive altogether where they could see the improvised armoured vehicles that local forces had designed to use against their enemy. They stayed overnight and returned the following morning to re-join the convoy back to Dalma.

On the journey back it took them past 'bon bon corner'. This is where the local children would stand at the side of the streets asking passing convoys to throw sweets at them. But this wasn't as friendly as it sounded – some had been known to throw bricks through the lorry windows if the requests were not met. So, they were pleased to get the chance to go upcountry and it helped them understand the logistics of the Op. It showed them how well the service was received in the forward locations.

Storm in a teacup 1994

The force's best kept secret was finally out in the open. The liquid lifeline that kept the troops going in the trenches had left the battlefield for the frontline of the High Street supermarket shelves. NAAFI tea had appeared on the High Street with shoppers lapping it up.

For the first time in the 73-year history, the NAAFI tea company was selling its famous brew to civilian customers through Nisa shops. The historic move followed an unprecedented public reaction to NAAFI commemorative packs of D-Day Tea and media interest from the Times and BBC Radio 5 Live to Sky News. The decision was made mainly by Ian Whalley, deputy manager, of the food division; this was due to the public interest and then they decided to market the tea on the right basis. Many people have fond memories of the tea from their service days and were over the moon to find it available to them again after all those years. Customers old and new, who preferred the type of strong tea the NAAFI blend delivered, loved it.

NAAFI's Wiltshire based factory had been buying, blending, and packaging quality tea for the armed forces since 1921 and each year sent hundreds of tonnes of tea to service bases around the world. During the Second World War, NAAFI tea was regarded as a lifeline for troops and the tastes of today's forces have not changed. In fact, NAAFI received letters every year from ex-servicemen and women asking where they could purchase the tea.

Steve Cooper, who worked at the tea factory at the Amesbury distribution centre in Wiltshire, produced seven different blends: traditional, breakfast, premium, special, 1 Cup, Earl Grey and Supreme. The tea was so good because there was a lot of care into the selection and the blending, it had bags of flavour and plenty of colour to ensure you get a great cup of tea every time. Mr Cooper explained that buyers travelled to London to buy different types of leaves imported from Kenya, Tanzania, Rwanda, Malawi, Sri Lanka, and India to name a few. Buyers had to know what made a good tea.

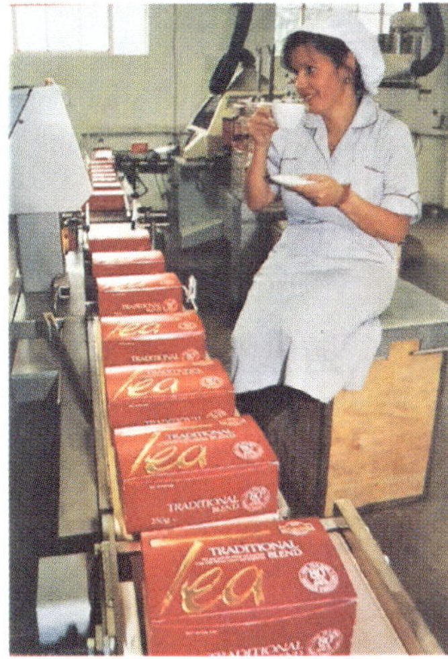

Everything from the look and smell of the dry leaves, their taste when in boiling water, when it is added to make an infusion and the colour and taste when milk is added also. To get a blend tasting as it should, up to 18 different teas are blended by giant machines at the factory, a tonne at a time. NAAFI sold 53 tonnes of tea each year, of which bags in 1994 account for 90% of that production.

In 1994 to make the bags, the measured amounts of tea were dropped between large sheets of porous paper. The paper and the tea was then heat sealed, making up to 1200 bags a minute which accounted for 280 million bags a year. A magic eye counted for the correct number of bags into boxes, which was sealed to ensure the freshness.

James Rucker retires 1994

James Rucker, NAAFI managing director since 1986, had taken early retirement from NAAFI for health reasons. In a letter to the board of management Mr Rucker wrote: 'After nearly eight years as managing director of NAAFI, the stress and planning of the implementation of public funding messing, I have asked the board if I may take early retirement as allowed under my contract. With the additional volume of the food supply contracts, and the likelihood of my having a hip op in the near future, I'm sure it will be the best interests of all concerned for the appointment of a younger person.'

Mr Rucker had joined NAAFI following a successful military career that saw him reach the rank of Brigadier. Following national service in 1955 to 57, Mr Rucker joined the family firm of Rucker and Bencroft before returning to the army, the 5th Royal Inniskilling Dragoon Guards, a 2Lt in 1960. Promotion and postings throughout the world followed with Mr Rucker filling the post of director (land), at the Ministry of Defence prior to his move to NAAFI.

His eight years with the company had been eventful. Set against a backdrop of fast changing environment globally, and within the forces, NAAFI had to tailor its services accordingly. And throughout, Mr Rucker had been a guiding influence.

In that time NAAFI headquarters had relocated from London to Amesbury, the European service warehousing operation had moved from Krefeld to Kempen, financial services had introduced in store credit facilities, armed service numbers had reduced significantly because of options for change. NAAFI had joined the NISA buying group, NAAFI had traded with civilians for the first time through its subsidiary company NAAFI commercial enterprises (NCE)and the EFI had seen action during the Gulf war and in Croatia. They had also changed their cap badge to that of the RLC, and allowed women back into their ranks.

The closing sentence in his letter of resignation showed the depth of feeling Mr Rucker held for the company, by his years at its helm: 'I would like to thank all members and staff and my many close friends in NAAFI for their loyalty, friendship and support. I wish the company every future success and good fortune.'

Voyage into turbulent waters Memories by Michael Reynolds 1994

As a canteen manager on board HMS Brave, I came face to face with the reality of war in Bosnia when I took part in the foreign exchange with a difference. The ship was patrolling in the Adriatic and, in common with other Royal Navy units, had been taking part in exchanges with the army units in Bosnia. This time, however, the opportunity arose for a NAAFI canteen manager to take part. I spent five days with the army in Bosnia and although shocked by the horrors of war, found the experience very valuable.

The countryside was stunning, but with the way the population is destroying it and each other, it's quite depressing. I now have a much better appreciation of why the troops are on the ground and why we are patrolling the Adriatic to help enforce the embargo. I would recommend that anyone who gets the opportunity to take part in an exchange like this grasps it with both hands.

DAY ONE: an intensive briefing on what to do if the helicopter ditches between HMS Brave and land wasn't the ideal way to complete preparations for the trip. It did, however, bring home some of the very real dangers associated with my adventure. A Sea King from 845 squadron landed on the flight deck and we were quickly ushered onboard and strapped in. Forty-five minutes later we touched down in Split and I met my host for the visit, Sgt 'Taff' Stock, from the Royal Logistic Corps.

Being in Croatia and away from the frontline, Split is relatively secure. It provides the base for the UK contingent of the United Nations force in Bosnia. The army had been there for some time and it was well established. I arrived on Sunday and I was promptly invited by the unit to a barbecue, which proved a marvellous opportunity to meet the team informally.

DAY 2: after an early breakfast, we changed into army topicals complete with UN blue beret and then we were off. We went up country with a store's convoy, delivering food and equipment to the many outstations in Bosnia. Having arrived at the Croatia-Bosnia border in good time, we were then delayed for an hour while the convoy leader negotiated our passage.

As he travelled into Bosnia, the effects of the fighting quickly became apparent. The contrast between the lush, gently rolling countryside and the bombed, burnt out shells of villages was stark and depressing. We passed through Mostar, once a scenic town but now strewn with demolished houses, where people still live. We had intended to stop so that I could take some photographs, but the convoy drove straight up.

Later I discovered the reason why – the convoy leader had noticed that there were fewer people around than usual, a sure sign that trouble was brewing. The flak jackets and helmets that had seemed so uncomfortable in heat were suddenly very reassuring. Nine hours and several deliveries after we had first set out, we arrived at Bugojno camp, our destination for the night.

The campers likened it to a prison with barbed wire fences, armed guards, and searchlights. Even in the camp, buildings showed signs of recent fighting, some partly destroyed, and many with splinter and bullet holes. On arrival we were thoroughly briefed on what to do in the event of activity during our stay.

DAY 3: sleeping in the cab of an 8-tonne lorry is, to say the least, uncomfortable, so I didn't mind the 0600 hrs start too much! We backtracked to Gornji Vakuf, where I said farewell to the convoy as it headed north east to other outstations, then I headed back to Split in a Land Rover.

The UN roads in Bosnia were divided according to the location and codenamed. Around Gornji Vakuf the roads are named after shapes and we returned to Split via roots, diamond, triangle, and circle. In stark contrast to the outward route, these roads were built into the sides of cliffs and were often little more than tracks. It was, however, worth suffering the bumpy ride and threat of sheer drops for the views.

Back in Split, dinner of a pizza and a bottle of wine in a pavement cafe seemed like normality.

DAY 4: this was my last full day ashore and I went to see the EFI lads running the Op in the hub area in Split. Six staff under the direction of Captain Simon Davis, who had relieved Captain Tom Lafferty, run what must be one of the largest NAAFI Ops outside of Amesbury! They supply NAAFI goods to the entire shore based UK contingent of the peacekeeping force.

That is more than 3500 uniformed personnel at more than a dozen locations, some of which were in hard to reach, isolated locations. I also took the opportunity to renew my acquaintance with Brian Whitaker, canteen manager on RFA Fort Grange which, based alongside Split, supports the army ashore.

DAY 5: after final goodbyes it was back to the airport for a flight home to HMS Brave. The UK element of the UN Force now is absolutely well organised and doing such a great job.

1995

The annual Norway exercise 1995

21 EFI staff travelled to Norway to support the annual Royal Marines and ace mobile force (land) exercise, which included many first timers. Before leaving the UK, they were given a taste of the skills they would need when they underwent Arctic training, including skiing, at Bulford. They were also issued with Arctic Survival-wear to combat the sub-zero temperatures they would face.

Lt Col Smith, commanding officer EFI, said: 'The training that the staff underwent before leaving for Norway was vital. It taught them the skills that enabled them to cope with some of the difficult situations they found themselves in, such as driving in hazardous conditions, and sleeping in tents in sub-zero temperatures. We were careful to ensure that all the staff sent to support the exercise were able to look after themselves as well as the business.' One newcomer was Karen Hicks, from Wellington barracks. It was her first time in Norway and the training in Bulford prepared her for the conditions.

The EFI team set up bulk issue store and shops in five locations across Norway in buildings ranging from a farmer's garage to some holiday villages and a Norwegian army camp. Driving in the snow was tackled for the first time when they reached Norway. An airport runway was commandeered as a skid pan and EFI staff were instructed in the skills they would need to cope with the thick snow they would be soon driving through. Because of the extreme cold, many of the goods were specially insulated for extra protection against freezing.

Cpl Hicks took a turn at providing mobile support selling from the back of a Land Rover and some teams visited locations 200 kilometres from the base, often driving through blizzards. It ended with the NATO exercise involving more than 4000 troops. EFI staff were not told where it would be held until the day before. The location was a shopping precinct at Surnadal and their only means of communication was a mobile phone.

To feed the troops taking part, BIS and a shop was set up in a disused shop. Total sales for the exercise again surpassed expectations, including 500 Interflora orders. This compared well with sales from two years previously, the most recent exercise with such a large number of troops taking part.

Thanks for EFI's service were sent to Lt Col Smith by Lt Col S. Tetlow, logistical support battalion, AMF(L). He said: 'EFI provides an excellent service throughout their deployment. Their positive attitude and ability to adapt underpinned the services they provided. They were a credit to the service and did much to improve the morale of the soldiers.'

Dalma Wearhouse, Memories by Kevin Mingham 1995

In 1995 we were serving on Op Grapple7/Op Resolute, based in the Dalma Warehouse Complex in Split, Croatia. We were co-located with the guys from 12 supply regiment who were normally based in Dulmen, Germany. Our Officer Commanding was Capt Tim Bennett, who in normal life was an area manager for NAAFI in Germany.

The Dalma Warehouse Complex was just that, a huge warehouse consisting of 2 floors. The lower floor was where the EFI had its Bulk Issue Store (BIS) and the supply unit did most of its work from other parts there also. The upper floor was accommodation for about 300 junior ranks as the officers and senior ranks had Corimecs outside.

One night in the officer's mess Tim was bragging to the commanding officer how much favour he had with chefs on camp and could get anything he wanted and ended up inviting the CO to a BBQ the following day.

The following day Tim arose, realising what he had said and immediately set us all tasks to fulfil his promise. Someone had to find a pioneer to build us the BBQ, whilst someone else had to find the charcoal, someone else had to see the chefs for the food and cooking utensils, all of which had to be paid for in the usual currency: crates of beer.

The stage was set, all the pieces were in place and we started cooking outside at the back of the warehouse and the guests started to arrive, the commanding officer, the OC of the supply squadron, and various other officers all being entertained by EFI.

Then the worst possible thing happened: it started to rain; all our plans were about to be ruined. Then somebody was heard to say as quoted by someone we all knew: "improvise, adapt and overcome". So, the idea arose to have the BBQ indoors in the EFI area of the warehouse and the BBQ and all the equipment was moved indoors, and the party was recommenced.

After about 30 minutes the smoke from the BBQ was getting thicker and thicker and the huge steel door to the EFI section slid open and the huge booming voice of the Regimental Sgt Major was heard booming "what the hell is going on here?". A very coy Tim Bennett goes over to him and casually says "we are having a BBQ. Would you care to join?" to which the reply comes "who the hell gave you permission for this?" and from the back of a group of people a low quiet voice comes back "me, RSM" and there at the back was the commanding officer to whom the RSM says quietly "that's ok then" and the RSM promptly picks up a beer and joins in for the rest of the party.

This has got to be one of the best times that we have seen, that as long as you are the commanding officer you can do whatever you want. A day I will never forget.

Take stock publication 1995

Catering officers in the services now receive their own newsletter providing them with news and information about the PFM contract, NAAFI, and general industry issues.

The first quarterly edition of 'take stock 'was launched in March 1995 and included information about Easter delivery dates, the food service challenge, a catering competition partly sponsored by NAAFI, the rising UK potato prices, and the army liaison teams based at NAAFI sites to assist with the smooth running of the contract.

The start of the public funded messing in October 1994 was a historic move for NAAFI and the services and communication was essential in getting the relationship right. Take stock had the backing of Directorate of food service Management and aimed to promote the communication between the company and its PFM customers.

Chief executive, John Busby said: 'NAAFI intended to develop a good working relationship and take stock is the forefront of this drive.' The newsletter covered both NAAFI and the catering industry in general and also provided a forum for the feedback from the catering officers who worked depended upon the service they received from NAAFI. Flight Sgt Mick Green from RAF Cromwell liked the mix of information contained in the newsletter. It was informative and interesting, and the chefs were keen to read it.

Small force 1995

In 1995 the new children's section, Small force, was one year old. NAAFI's special club for service children all over the UK had his birthday. Characters Jet, Dek, TT, Mike and Bird had battled against the incredibly bad people for over 12 months, and regions were hooked. The comic moved to the centre of the NAAFI break magazine, providing further incentive for customers to pick up the magazine and find out what was on offer in NAAFI shops.

In its first year it attracted 3150 members of the Small force gang. They all received Small force goodie bags, including a badge membership card, yo-yo, poster, rubber, and pencils, when they joined. Their badge entitled them to a special offer, goodies, and competitions. Ferris Jones the family shop manager said: 'Small forces are hit here. We recruited 150 members when the comic was launched last year, but now we must have at least 300. It is an excellent way to encourage parents into the shop and spend money. As a retailer, I believe in NAAFI making the right impression on the children, they will be our customers in the future.'

The original idea for the club came from Sarah Wintle, former publications manager CAP Bureau (communications, advertising, and publishing). Robert Duncan, cartoonist, brought the characters to life, while Robert Howell, publishing and public relations manager, launched and developed Small force magazine. The huge response to Small force far exceeded the company's expectations. And the letters and pictures received seemed to have caught the imagination of service children throughout the country. Developing the personalities of the Small force characters was one of the most interesting and enjoyable exercises to really capture the imaginations of the children. But the club went one stage further – from July of 1995 members of the gang would be able to make a purchase of various items featuring their favourite character from selected NAAFI shops.

EFI moves to new headquarters at Bulford camp

The headquarters of the Expeditionary Force Institutes (EFI) had been relocated to a permanent base at Double Hedges, a building within a compound on the outskirts of Bulford camp, in Wiltshire. Following a move from Wingham training centre in April of 1994, the EFI had taken temporary accommodation at a messing store in the centre of Bulford camp. Now the Cadre had traded in its makeshift base for more comfortable surroundings.

Lt Col Murray Smith, OC EFI RLC, explained: 'The new building offered a far better working environment. Compared with our temporary base in Bulford this was luxurious. We had all got our own offices, and it made a change not to be covered in dust!' After a short time they began to settle in and it was nice for them to have more windows as well as lit offices to work in. The new HQ buildings would eventually house 9 EFI staff, five of whom were currently serving troops in Italy and Split. Unlike the Wingham base, this location had been allocated specifically to the Cadre staff, with all supplies being held at Amesbury and Kempen distribution centres.

Training awards for staff 1995

Just three months after the new 3-tiered training scheme was launched for field staff, 120 club assistants and 34 shop assistants passed their bronze award. All shopping club staff had to take the award before they can progress on to silver and gold. Business development trainers, Juliet Smith (club and wholesale), and Steven Booth (shops), were delighted with the results. Miss Smith said that the general response to the new award scheme was very positive.

The general response to the bronze award was very positive and now they could move onto the silver and gold which was due to be launched at the end of 1995. The initial response from the managers was that their staff had started doing things they hadn't been taught in store and trainees that filled their workbooks in found it a great reference. Chris Dawson, club manager at Flower Down, near Winchester, had seen all her staff collect their bronze awards.

The initial training had a major impact on the establishments and more suggestions were coming through to add more tasks to ensure efficiency. The key thing was that everybody would be trained to the same standard, so if a club assistant was transferred to another location, they would know they had a basic level of training.

Sally Buchanan, a club assistant at Flower Down, had four stars under the old system. She had to take her bronze award though, in order to qualify for the silver. So, she'd found this quite easy and could not wait to get on with the silver award. The bronze award would take a minimum of three months to complete and required learning on the job to be signed off.

This new system would replace the old Marcasite brooches and bars, which replaced a previous system of a simple circular badge with NAAFI Crest.

NAAFI News late anniversary issue July August 1995

The publications of NAAFI started with the Imperial club magazine, which first edition was launched at Christmas 1928; this was an in-house publication launched by the editor Lt Col C Fraser.

With the outbreak of the Second World War the paper shortage caused the closure of the new magazine in 1940. A year later a news sheet was produced solely for the purpose of keeping the press informed about the company's activities, and to stave off ill-informed criticism of the valuable activities and contribution NAAFI made to the war effort. Although this was woefully inadequate it did keep over 200 newspapers informed at home and overseas. The editor Claude F Luke was not impressed with the lack of paper, but the news sheet would have to do for now.

As the paper shortage eased off the very first edition of NAAFI News was published Christmas 1945. Depending on the availability of paper and stories to go inside, the idea was to publish four a year. Between the 1st edition and the autumn of 1949 11 issues were printed. Christmas 1949 they started to be marked volume one with an issue number, and although this was not a regular publication a special edition for the Coronation in 1953 volume 2, 22, was produced. In 1961 volume 3, issue 39 started the production of a monthly issue although not regularly every month, this was the aim as the paper shortage eased and ensured that they could reach staff at home and overseas.

March 1963, Claude F Luke retired and handed the ropes to Ronald Walker who had been assistant editor for many years. As Ronald Walker took over, he started volume 4, issue 1, until 1983 issue 206 but it was actually issue 266 as he had restarted the issue numbers when he took over as editor of NAAFI News. For a few issues the editor became Tony Flood then in September 1983 Patrick Breen became editor and, unwittingly, in February 1987 was the true editor for issue 300. Patrick would retire at the end of 1990 with issue number 275 (331). In the next year only two issues were produced and in December 1991 issue 278 (334), Sarah Wintle took over as editor until the end of 1994 with issue 296 (353). Robert Howell then without his knowledge produced issue 300 July August 1995, which in actual fact was 357.

NAAFI News would then go on to be edited by Georgina Marlow from August-September 1996 until September 1997. Julia Heaton from October 1997 until October 1998. Unfortunately, at this time until June 2000 the editor was not listed when Simon Monkman took over, where he started the numbers again from issue 1 (which was issue number 389) only several issues had him listed as editor. It was not until February 2008 when Layton and Sarah became joint editors and issue number 43 (431), then Lee Coleman took over until the last issue of NAAFI News was produced for August 2011 issue 52 but little did they know that this was issue 440 due to some misprints and miscalculations over the years 66 years, that it had been in production, and the 83 years that an in-house publication had been produced.

Ship staff swap ideas ashore 1995

In August 1995 over 30 NAAFI canteen managers from Her Majesty's ships and Royal Fleet Auxiliary, based in Portsmouth and Plymouth, had the rare chance to compare notes when they attended a meeting at HMS Drake.

The managers took advantage of their August block leave period to hold a meeting, which was attended by Brian Levy, manager PFM shipments, Andrew Cowan, district manager Portsmouth ships, and Pat Corlett, regional manager Southern. Then followed a social evening in the 'Drum Beat Club', Plymouth which was followed by a sales and development meeting the next day, where staff discussed new innovations and ideas, such as the implementation of microwave ovens and extra refrigeration for NAAFI canteens.

This was the first time so many ships' managers had been able to get together in this way; it was good for morale and helped strengthen team spirit. It was hoped that another meeting sometime in the future would happen on the same scale. One of the highlights of the meetings was a presentation by Mr Corlett, of the United Nations medal to RFA food supply officer, Brian Whitaker, as a reward for his work aboard RFAs Fort Austin and Resource, serving in the Adriatic off the former Yugoslavia.

Mr Whittaker was just about to deploy again as a food supply officer on RFA Fort Grange, with assistants David Kirman and Jake Johnson.

More EFI sent to Former Yugoslavia 1995

A complement of EFI staff serving in Bosnia had been increased from 7 to 10 members. The escalation of hostilities in the former Yugoslavia, coupled with the reinforcement of British troops in the warzone, had prompted the increase.

Cpl Gary Britt, Cpl Craig Johns, Cpl Lloyd Byfield, joined with seven other EFI members to run the Dalma bulk issue store, near Split in Croatia. They served with the British logistic battalion (BRIT LOGBAT), for the duration of the six-month tour. Lt Col Smith, CO EFI, said that the new members were settling in fine, they were working 16 to 18-hour days in cramped conditions, but they were all coping well. Alongside their work at Dalma, the EFI team also opened a temporary shop, 2½ hours north of Dubrovnik.

EFI member Sgt Nigel Hall said that the shop was open two days a week, and it served 4500 troops of the 24 Air Mobile brigade. The sales figures were good, and this increased the sales from the bulk issue store at Dalma. With the recent escalation of the hostilities in the former Yugoslavia, NAAFI was doing its best to make life more bearable for the British troops based in the warzone. With the recent membership to NISA todays, a L/Cpl had written to them asking for specific brand of Jaffa cake. In response to this they asked NAAFI to range for a complimentary case of the product, along with a NISA tee shirt to be delivered by the EFI bulk issue store at Dalma.

The request was dealt with immediately, and this resulted in the L/Cpl now enjoying his favourite food in the middle of a warzone. This just showed that even if EFI received a request or comment from troops serving overseas they would go out of their way to meet their needs.

Remember them 1995

In November 1995, as they did every year, NAAFI staff paid their respects on Remembrance Sunday during a wreath laying ceremony at the War Memorial plaque, in the HQ block at Amesbury headquarters. Colin Cullimore, chairman, made a short speech before placing a NAAFI wreath at the foot of the War Memorial. Maj Tommy Booth and Maj Ben White, members of the EFI, OCA, also laid a wreath while the current members of EFI paid their tributes.

Following the ceremony, staff had the opportunity to pay individual respects at the memorial and book of Remembrance. John Busby, MD, attended the ceremony, along with Lt Col Murray Smith, CO EFI RLC, senior management representatives and present NAAFI staff. The ceremony followed the Remembrance service at St George's church, Bulford, where Maj Booth took the reading, representing EFI.

Earlier in the week members of the EFI had laid crosses in the garden of Remembrance at Westminster Abbey, to commemorate every Theatre of war in which the NCS and EFI had served since inception.

1996

First NCS ladies onboard ship 1996

For the first time in their 75-year history, NAAFI girls are going to sea. Allison Sehar and Charlotte Stansfield have joined the NAAFI canteen on board aircraft carrier HMS Illustrious, which was serving in the Adriatic. They will serve the ship's crew in the canteen, gift shop, and vending area. They lived and worked alongside the Wren and got on with them very well. The Wren

said that it was about time that female NAAFI staff serve them. Allison previously worked at RAF Halton, and Charlotte at Brighouse in Yorkshire, had worked for NAAFI for seven years, most recently in Northern Ireland. They volunteered to go to sea because it was going to be a great challenge to them, and they'll get a chance to see the world.

The girls underwent a week sea survival training at HMS Excellent in Portsmouth before they joined the ship. The training, which included firefighting and nuclear, biological, and chemical warfare, is extremely tough, to give the recruits a taste of what life could be like at sea. Whilst onboard Illustrious, NAAFI staff were part of the ship's crew, bound by military law and answerable to the ship's captain. In an emergency they abandoned their duties as canteen assistants and became message runners.

Increased EFI service 1996

NAAFI ensured that Christmas 1995 remained on the menu for troops serving in Bosnia and Croatia over the festive season. The food supply contract distributed hundreds of Christmas cakes, puddings and mince pies following a huge surge in orders to Amesbury distribution centre.

One delivery alone contained 800 turkey breasts, 10,000 chickens, 576 Christmas puddings and 900 boxes of mince pies, the NAAFI supplied 525 pallets of food in the two weeks before Christmas.

In December, NATO's IFOR arrived in the former Yugoslavia in large numbers and the EFI RLC was stretched to the limit to cope with the influx of personnel. Despite the pressure sales records were quickly broken, earning the EFI praise from all involved. The upturn in business continued and, apart from major efforts in Split, further EFI detachments had to be established, in Sarajevo, with a return to Zagreb also possible.

Capt Tim Bennett, detachment commander, said: 'It is a very difficult and demanding time for the team, but everyone's risen to the challenge. We've worked long hours to make sure the supplies get through. Warehouse and transport staff kept the food coming and we are very grateful for their efforts.'

The number of EFI personnel serving in Theatre had increased from 10 to 15. Serving at RAF at Gioia del Colle, Italy, over Christmas, was S/Sgt Nigel Hall; he said it was far from a normal Christmas, but they made the most of it. Christmas dinner took place on Christmas Eve, and along with the decorations and Santa hats that they sold, there were plenty of homely touches, with 400 service personnel at the detachment.

Meanwhile 18 EFI staff travelled to Norway, to supply troops taking part in the annual allied mobile forces (land) winter deployment. Among them, Sgt Martin Parker travelled to Norway for the first time, with Capt Mark Parry. The EFI members were running a bulk issue store and shops in the Voss, Gol, Ringebu, Bardufoss, and Andalsnes area. Alongside the essentials, they were stocking special items such as Norwegian trolls and locally made pewter gifts.

In Germany, the three base ammunition depot training wing had witnessed its last passing out parade for EFI. The final NAAFI recruits under 21-week intensive training programme which involved teaching in map reading, first aid, basic fieldcraft, and live firing exercises. This culminated with a parade in front of Lt Col Murray Smith, CO EFI RLC. All future training for EFI recruits would now take place at 5 Territorial Army training regiment, Royal Logistic Corps, in Grantham, Lincolnshire.

Changes in store, review is published 1996

The independent review of NAAFI, commissioned by the Ministry of Defence, was made public in the House of Commons in February 1996. The review was carried out over a three-month period by Jeffrey Dart, divisional director of Marks and Spencer's with responsibility for financial control. The aim of the review was to identify:

- The services and trading activities provided by NAAFI and access to those essential for the continued comfort and wellbeing of Her Majesty's armed forces and their families
- Whether such essential services could or should be provided by alternative means to a Crown owned body
- The most cost-effective means of delivering such essential services and activities, whether by NAAFI, a third party, or the armed forces themselves, and how this should be financed
- The role of other services provided by NAAFI to the armed forces whether these should, or could be provided by alternative means
- The justification on scope for the rebate currently provided by NAAFI to support Armed Forces Services Institute funds.

Within these areas, the review also had to take into account such things as levels of military commitments and employment patterns, the environment in which the service personnel and their families live, and social, economic, and regulatory changes. Mr Dart followed guidelines laid down by the Cabinetsx and the Treasury. Under these he gave a welfare rating to NAAFI services and Trading functions. These were based on:

- Assessing whether a similar facility provided by the taxpayer to the community as a whole and, if not, whether there were special circumstances which justified its continuation for the services

- The profit and loss incurred by each activity and whether subsidy represented value to the end customer
- Alternative sources of the service or activity, and whether these were used extensively by the junior service personnel.

Mr Dart also studied financial information about NAAFI, to the results of an independent market research survey into the customer attitudes, and database showing alternative shopping locations to NAAFI family shops in the UK. Additionally, he visited various units of all three services in the UK, Northern Ireland, Germany, and the former Yugoslavia. Groups of service personnel, the wives, and NAAFI representatives' committees were also consulted. Decisions were held with civil servants at MoD, HM Treasury, and the National Audit Office. The review itself ran to nearly 100 pages. Listed here are its main points and recommendations.

UK family shops

The growth of large supermarkets in recent years and the attractiveness of other ranges and prices, led to the vast majority of the service personnel to use these facilities rather than NAAFI family shops for the bulk of their shopping needs. The losses caused by this are not justified by the welfare service family shops offer. All but the most geographically isolated and those in Northern Ireland should close unless NAAFI can appropriate them on a commercial and profitable basis.

UK services shops

Services shops are essentially in isolated areas, in Northern Ireland, and in training establishments. They also have a significant role in meeting the day-to-day needs of the single service personnel whose ability to shop outside the base is limited by their duties. The current number of competing retail facilities operated by NAAFI within a location, both family shops and service shops, is often not justified by the customer base or turnover. These facilities should be rationalised.

Junior ranks clubs in the UK

There is a requirement for a relaxation and recreational area on the service bases for living in junior service personnel. Current provisions need to be reviewed to provide a more appropriate and acceptable format and, in a number of cases, clubs are excessive both in number and size.

NAAFI in Germany

The greater use of NAAFI facilities in Germany and the relative lack of local alternatives makes these facilities necessary or, in the case of the family shop, highly desirable. They also produce significant profits to fund other business segments of NAAFI, particularly losses in the UK.

EFI RLC and NCS

The Expeditionary Force Institutes' members provide an essential welfare service to the armed forces and, in many ways, optimize the original functions and spirit of NAAFI when it was created in 1921. The hazardous and arduous nature of such provision is outside normal retail competence or experience. Activities in HM ships are similarly regarded.

Public Funded Messing

PFM has no welfare function but exploits the obvious synergy between the services NAAFI already delivers. The loss of this contract in 1997 would fundamentally affect the viability of NAAFI in its current form.

Financial services

Financial services, while a significant contributor of gross revenue, has only a minor welfare role and commercial alternatives are available, although less so in Germany.

Other recommendations included further reductions in central support costs, and investigation into partnerships with other companies and suppliers in provision of NAAFI services.

The review also concluded that privatisation of NAAFI at present was not a reasonable option. To drive through the recommendations of the review, the Ministry of Defence has agreed to the secondment of Jeffrey Dart as chief executive with effect from the 29th of April 1996.

Colin Cullimore, NAAFI chairman, gave us reaction to Mr Dart's findings: 'The review underlined virtually all of the points that NAAFI main board has been making for some time. We cannot continue to run an operation designed to serve half a million customers when that number is now down to 220,000. NAAFI must become more flexible. To help this, the joint service publications by which trading activities are governed will be replaced by a charter which will recognise our new situation.

'A key finding of the review is the responsibility for overall performance must switch from the NAAFI council to the main board. This will allow the board to act in a more commercial manner and react promptly to the needs of the business. NAAFI's prime aim is still to provide a welfare service where it is needed. We must ensure that the best commercial practices are adopted to meet the needs of customers.

'The service representatives will have a key role in cooperating with the main board and unit commanders in the formulation of local business plans which assess these needs and the best ways to meet them.'

The review highlighted the need for responsibility and ownership of jobs within NAAFI. This will start at the top, as Mr Cullimore explained: 'We need to restructure the main board to include more executive directors who will have a specific responsibility for their profit centres. We need to encourage senior and middle executives as part of NAAFI management team to take a greater responsibility to employ entrepreneurial skills in the development of their own profit centres. Unfortunately, the board still faces a challenging timescale to submit its food supply tender and write the 1996/97 business plan. Because of this we cannot make a financial announcement about the full implications of the review yet. We will, however, make sure that the staff are kept fully up to date through the pages of NAAFI News, and any special announcements where necessary.

The NAAFI council met on 15th of March for the first time since the review was published. At this meeting they endorsed the major items in principle and the review including the payment of rebate on profit and the management of reimbursement of gaming and amusement machines income. Details of this will not be agreed until the service personnel board meeting on the 17th of April. A further announcement will be made around this time.'

The priorities for NAAFI, according to the chairman, are clear: the future structure and turnover NAAFI depends to a large extent on our being awarded the food supply contract for another term. We must work hard to ensure this happens. Additionally, a number of unprofitable retail establishments in the UK will close, alongside a rationalisation of facilities on all bases, centred on the junior rank's clubs.

Nevertheless, the council, supported by the main board, recommends that in addition to facilities staying open for welfare needs, no establishment will be closed until a local business plan had demonstrated it could not be turned into profit within the next two years. In addition, there had been success over the past 18 months in reducing central support costs and a business plan to reduce costs further would be submitted to the council by the 10th of July.

There will be a reduction in the number of field supervisors, and it is hoped that this can be achieved by voluntary redundancy.

One of the key areas of the review focused on the way NAAFI paid rebate. The recommendations made on this are still under discussion. The chairman, however, said although the review says rebate should only be paid on profit to meet the welfare needs of the units, rebate will be distributed in relation to sales for the time being until long term arrangements can be finalised. Rebate, however, will be decided by the level of profit but distributed in relation to the turnover.

John Busby, managing director, said: 'Another requirement for successful implementation of the review recommendations is a culture change from the armed forces in their attitude to NAAFI in order to get the best service for our establishments.

'We must also be aware of our own needs to embrace change in the way we operate. However, everybody throughout NAAFI can take pride in the fact that Mr Dart made a specific point of highlighting the commitment and dedication of staff. I also believe that the conclusion to the foreword of the report says much about NAAFI's future.'

Mr Dart said: 'My objective is to provide the armed forces and their families with a world class service, which I am confident NAAFI has the potential to deliver.'

New shops open to meet need in Bosnia 1996

Following the increase in troops in Bosnia, EFI has responded to appeals for shops and BIS in Sipovo and Sarajevo. Six members of the EFI were living in field conditions to ensure that IFOR troops, the force responsible for implementing the Dayton peace agreement in Bosnia, get a few of life's little luxuries.

Warrant Officer Dave Forster and Cpls Sean Wroe and Heather Spears are based in Sipovo, where they run a bulk issue store, a shop from an old sawmill and disused storage and transport containers. Sgt Gary Fletcher and Cpls Nicky Bell and Derek Pemberton have established their BIS and shop in a small kiosk in a Sarajevo hotel.

Lt Col Murray Smith OC EFI RLC said that these outlets offered a full range of goods you can get at any NAAFI shop. It made life for the troops a little more bearable. EFI had served in the Balkans since 1992, when they went to Zagreb with the British medical battalion.

Directors job swap 1996

Eddie Wright had returned to the European service as new director of operations, Germany. He swapped jobs with Tim Elliott, who replaced him as director of operations UK. Mr Wright said: 'The operation in Germany remains the most important contributor to performance of NAAFI as a whole. Because of this, I look forward to guiding it through the challenging times ahead. I don't think that there was anyone in NAAFI who does not appreciate the hard tasks that face us. However, by remaining dedicated to providing the highest quality service, with high standards of merchandising, I am sure we will be successful. I will be particularly looking at areas such as customer care and staff training to make sure we provide a professional, sensitive, and competitive service to our customers.'

Mr Wright started his career with NAAFI in 1967 as a storeman in Germany. From there he went into shop and then district, regional, and departmental management. His many postings included Ascension Island, Hong Kong, and Singapore.

Mr Elliott's return to UK followed 3.5 years as a manager of European Service. It was a difficult time in many ways with the full impact of operations for change resulting in the closure of more than 110 establishments and a reduction in staff of 2200.

He was looking forward to working in the UK again as it would give him the opportunity to meet staff he had worked with in previous appointments. He had worked for NAAFI since 1964. In that time, he had worked in Malaysia, Singapore, the Maldives, Gibraltar, the Falkland Islands and Germany. There is no doubt that NAAFI faced a challenging time, but he was positive that the determination, commitment, and loyalty of all staff would be the basis of the success in meeting those challenges.

Revised charter opens Door to new era 1996

There had been a significant change in NAAFI's relationship with the armed forces following the publication of the new charter between the Ministry of Defence and NAAFI. The new charter replaced the joint services publication 393 on the rules for NAAFI services, used by many as a rule book from which there could be no deviation.

This generally led to no one accepting responsibility for their actions as far as relationships with the company were concerned. The new charter is a more flexible document which gives the company a greater commercial freedom, providing the company can conduct business competitively. It also allowed NAAFI to tailor services on a local basis, giving a more effective response to the needs of the armed forces. This meant, however, that NAAFI must continue to provide high standards of service efficiently and effectively, a task which Air Commodore Alan Vaughan, retail, and recreational services director, believe staff in shops and clubs would achieve. He had every confidence that the staff would continue to meet the challenges the company faced, in a professional and competent way. While the comfort blanket of the JSP had been removed, the benefit to NAAFI was that it can operate in a more commercial manner and actively seek additional businesses.

The charter also detailed changes in the way the rebate would be paid in the future; currently rebate to units was based on the turnover in clubs and services' shops. In future, a dividend will only be paid if the company made a profit in that area. Some of the profits were likely to be retained by the principal personnel office. This money would be used to assist units where NAAFI provided an essential welfare service but could not do so profitably.

Air Commodore Vaughan stressed that ideas were in the early stages and as yet no firm policy had been agreed by the services. The new charter, published as a defence counsel instruction, was recommended in the independent review of NAAFI. It also allowed civilians and civil servants working on military bases to use the company's facilities and gives the veterans the opportunity to enjoy the services too. But for some time the armed forces have been examining ways to make veterans feel part of their local service community.

The opportunity to use the facilities was welcome as a step in the right direction by veterans that had been spoken to. They just needed to ensure that they could deliver on that service. Unlike the JSP, the charter would be reviewed and agreed between the services and NAAFI on an annual basis. They also welcomed any staff to put forward any ideas they had for changes in the future.

Sales rocket as shop trials are launched 1996

Londis, Costcutter, Spar, High Street names that everybody had heard of. They were market leaders in the convenience retailing and now, they are the companies recruited by NAAFI to help turn the UK shops into a profit-making operation.

NAAFI had reopened twelve of its shops large and small, families and services shops in trial partnership with Londis, Costcutter and Spar. There were early indications that the trial sites were excellent. For example, the NAAFI /Londis family shop at Brize Norton was an average of 45% ahead of previous turnover and the family shop in Bicester improved turnover by 106% in the week after it reopened in conjunction with Londis. The NAAFI /Costcutter shop at Shute Road, Catterick, added a 33% increase compared with the average before.

The trials would pass for new formula UK shops project, sponsored by Allen Born, retail and recreational services director, led by Richard Burton, former regional manager, and now special projects manager. The UK shops were overall a lossmaking operation, and this could not continue. If it did, then only a small proportion of shops would remain open; those were the welfare requirement, and a few that are economically viable.

For example, Brize Norton family shop was one of NAAFI top six shops in terms of turnover, yet in 1995/96 it was at a loss. This being the case, NAAFI had to look at ways of improving performance with the aim of keeping as many shops as possible open. There was also the perception among NAAFI customers that we were not running a modern Convenience store operation, and if they did not meet customers' expectations in pricing and convenience, then they were on a downward slope.

Customer surveys carried out by the partners and independent market research agency also came up with two positive trends in NAAFI stores: friendly staff, and convenience in terms of location. They were in the right place with the right staff which gave them something to build on and the rest could change. Choosing partners was the right way to change it. They wanted to take the best practice available in the commercial world to see if it could be applied to NAAFI business. It seems that there is no difference between the customer's expectation and those of its civilian customer, so they looked at proven retailing groups that had a format that suited NAAFI and were at the cutting edge of the sector.

The partners' efforts would be compared to what they could achieve inhouse, and early indications said that they did bring added value to the business. The partners had to bring about 3 basic improvements to the NAAFI shop operations in the UK if they were going to be a success. They needed to be better, cheaper, and quicker. This with the stark reality that NAAFI shops in the UK were losing money and this could not continue.

A prime example of this was NAAFI had spent three years trying to develop an EPOS system for shops; in contrast, they started talking to the partners in July 1996 and they had their systems in place by October. All three of the groups were given a clean slate at each location and they were contributing all services, while NAAFI provided financial investment. All of these services were basically incorporated into the wholesale price of the goods from the partners.

NAAFI would produce profits from the goods when they were sold to the customer for reinvestment in the business and rebate payments to the forces. It was as much in the partners' interest as NAAFI to develop the business. The more they sold the more they had to supply and the more profit they made. For the purpose of the trials the company did not constrain the partners in any way. They had to be given the freedom to show how they could improve the business. They had to be allowed to decide pricing, range, layout of the shop, opening hours and the level of staff needed.

During these trials they would fine tune the formula in consultation with the project team and local management. Then after the trials, when NAAFI decided which partnerships to roll out to other sites, the terms of the partnership agreement would be negotiated and agreed by all parties. Driving these trials fundamentally was NAAFI and not the partners. It had selected them to monitor them to make sure they got the best deal. All three partners saw tremendous opportunity for improving profitability in these shops. None of the three currently had an account as large as NAAFI which put them in a good negotiating position. With partners there in an advisory capacity to help develop the business and NAAFI would take advantage of that. People were concerned that the partners would try and take over staff and ownership of the shops. But this was not the case as it was not their core business. Their interest was providing a full wholesale service to NAAFI stores. All three partners had a vested interest to ensure the trials were a successful shop; if standards did not meet the expectations of the customer the reputation was at stake. This would lead to increased standards and a new established formula for the shops as this was crucial on both sides that they were maintained and increased.

The best thing that could come out of this project was a modern retail operation that reflected the best practice available on the High Street. By attaining that standard, they would be more profitable and therefore more shops would stay open, which meant more security for the staff. The worst consequence of working with partners in that NAAFI was openly saying we will provide support to the shops via partnership and not in-house. That inevitably had one consequence for HQ departments, even with partnership arrangements there were still some shops which were going to be lossmakers. And although improvements could be made to these shops, they could never be significant enough to keep them open.

The most positive message, however, was that by giving the customers a world class value for money service there would be a long-term role for NAAFI in partnership with leading companies. Competition would get harder as the years went on. Petrol stations, newsagents, off licences and, more significantly, major multiples like Tesco, were all turning to the convenience store market.

If they were associated with companies at the cutting edge of retailing, they would move into the future. Without that expertise they would get left behind.

We will remember them 1996

A wreath laying ceremony at NAAFI HQ, Amesbury, followed Remembrance Day services at St George's church, Bulford camp. Geoffrey Dart, chief executive, on behalf of NAAFI at the roll of honour laid a wreath in the management headquarters building. Also paying his respects and laying wreaths on behalf of the OCA was Maj Tommy Booth OBE, chairman of the Association.

Remembrance Sunday also saw wreaths laid at the Naval War Memorial in Great Lanes, Chatham. John Mileham and Bill Claque represented NAAFI and the OCA. A few days earlier the chief executive had laid a wreath at NAAFI plot in the garden of Remembrance at Westminster Abbey, during a service attended by The Queen Mother as well as members of OCA and EFI. At the festival of Remembrance in the Royal Albert Hall, NAAFI and the EFI will represented by Sgt Dawn Hall and Martin Parker.

1997

NAAFI clubs' trial 1997

The traditional image of a NAAFI club conjured up thoughts of a drab surrounding, uncomfortable furniture and above all this was what needed improving. That was to be a thing of the past, thanks to an exciting new concept which would revolutionise the forces' view of NAAFI clubs. The company had called in the professionals to recreate pubs within clubs, as part of the new formula UK pubs project. The much-needed facelift would raise the profiles and produce quality facilities. Bass, Scottish courage and Whitbread are currently involved in trials of three clubs with a budget that was approved by Jeffrey Dart, chief executive, for the update of each. The three trial sites were RAF Leeming, Whitbread; Navy Faslane, Bass; Army, Arborfield, Scottish courage.

The trial pubs at Leeming and Faslane, were launched in mid-November 1996, with Arborfield getting underway on the 11th of December. Looking at sales NAAFI was onto a winner from the very start, at Leeming the takings on the first week were up three times on the same the previous year. Faslane was 13% ahead of the first week's trade although this figure was bound to fluctuate depending on which ships were in dock. And in the first few days the Arborfield site took nearly nine times the takings than the same time in the previous year. The style of each pub had been tailored to give the customers exactly what they wanted. Each trial would be evaluated in the spring with the aim of rolling out across the other sites. The pubs in the roll out programme would have their own individual style.

Gary De Buse, Project team leader, said that the aim was to update the image, secure the customers and manage the facility in a more pub like professional manner. NAAFI got a more professional image, more customers, and more profit. While the Brewers, if they were successful, would sell more beer and the armed forces will have a better and more enjoyable club. Bass, Scottish Courage and Whitbread had all been chosen because they were a national company and already delivered to NAAFI establishments. Each Brewer employed designers in their trial site with the remit to provide a High Street style pub for the 18 to 30 age bracket that was also welcoming enough to attract young married couples. The Brewers had been given a checklist of what NAAFI was looking for.

This is what they were providing:

- A new look and welcoming atmosphere
- professional training, particularly in range, merchandising and service
- an appropriate promotional package, including entertainment.

The trials would also be assessed on:

- Sales and customer reaction (Measured by customer surveys)
- Long term commitment and support services.

There were no hard and fast rules about how many Brewers may be chosen for the roll out scheme. It would be all three, in fact they didn't think that it would be only one because NAAFI didn't want to put all of its eggs in one basket. The main thing to come out of these trials was that they would get top notch training designed and tailored to them by instilling a confidence that they didn't have before. Previously training to make a Club assistant meant you were a jack of all trades. Now they would specialise and work only on one bar. Being part of something new would boost morale as they would be lots of praise from customers and eventually there would be a financial reward, subject to the success of the establishment. For those who were not involved in the trials they were invited along to go and look at what had been done. Field management were encouraged to hold meetings at these pubs, so people could see for themselves what had been achieved.

Based on the sales in the trial clubs it meant that there would be finance available to convert the rest of the clubs in the UK in the next two to three years. However, a lot of the clubs were not big enough to convert to the standard of trial sites so there would be different packages available for different places. It was also stressed that staff working in all clubs would remain employees of NAAFI.

Operation Ocean Wave 1997

Months of planning finally paid off in January 1997 when the biggest Royal Navy exercise in years left the UK shores. The aim of the operation Ocean Wave, which involved 7500 personnel, are threefold, involving defence sales, exercises with and without foreign forces and coordinating British withdrawal from Hong Kong. To ensure proper support from NAAFI food services, a planning committee included high ranking service personnel, ships and managers, district managers and NAAFI HQ personnel, working tirelessly in the months beforehand.

Six RFAs were taking part in the exercise and would not return until the middle of August 97. They were visiting a wide variety of ports but the major opportunity for resupplying stocks would be in Singapore, which all ships would visit for maintenance sometime between the 10th of March and the 9th of July. Stores support during the operation was being provided by RFA Fort Austin and Fort George. Added to these would be additional canteen items and mess orders and selected frozen messing items.

NAAFI managers on RFAs were replenished at Jebel Ali, Manila, and Singapore, sending orders via NAAFI HQ to Hutton's of Hull who would arrange supply through a local chandler. The cost of the goods was based on local prices.

NAAFI was also involved in providing thousands of pounds worth of 'gizzits' (gift items) for ships to give to visitors. Other areas of involvement included organising greeting cards, crested wines, vending spares and beer and mineral orders for ships' Messes.

Farewell to Hong Kong 1997

The lead up to the handover of Hong Kong to China saw the services shop at Prince of Wales barracks in Hong Kong attract some new trade. They were members of the Chinese People's Liberation Army and keen buyers of minerals and cordials. The troops were among three advanced parties in Hong Kong to prepare for the defence duties after the handover. They helped make arrangements for when the bulk of the special Administration region troops arrived after the 1st of July. This included liaising with the British forces in the Hong Kong government and coordinating communications support and movement of supplies. In all, the pre handover presence in the territory was 196 troops and most were housed in military bases still used by the British; 723 troops were based at Prince of Wales barracks, another 34 at Sek Kong Camp, 24 at Stonecutters Island and 25 at Gun Club Hill barracks.

Other bases used were Cassino Lines, Gallipoli Lines, Stanley Fort and Osborn barracks, Bonham Towers.

This all culminated in the end of an era for everyone in Hong Kong not least NAAFI, which had provided a service there since before the war. Despite all that was going on around them staff maintained a service to troops right up until the last few hours of British sovereignty.

In the final few days John Williams, regional manager, paid tribute to the hard work of his staff. Of course, there was 300 there three years previously and 22 remained to the end. 'There had been tremendous loyalty. I was able to do my job because I could still rely on them when all the time, they knew there was no future for them with NAAFI.' Of the original 20 clubs, Services and family shop which closed in the last three years, those which remained open were the services shops and clubs at Stonecutters Island and Prince of Wales barracks. 'It had been tremendously exciting for everybody here and with 550 bandsman flown in for the last day's presentation we were busy right up until the end,' said John. 'We were under fantastic pressure, but it was very satisfying.'

Service was provided right up until 1500 hours on the last afternoon and then work began behind the scenes so that the building was ready for the midnight deadline. This included the stocking, finalising accounts and paying off staff. Even then the work wasn't over for the two UK officials, John and his colleague Ken Rockett, Regional auditor. With his own departure from the former colony planned for the 12th of July, paying off merchants, sending back residual stock, as well as phones and faxes, more work on the accounts, and administration all had to be dealt with. John was now to move to Germany to take up the post as retail projects manager.

Portsmouth dockyard HMS Nelson 1997

NAAFI retail and leisure division had joined forces to provide a transform services shop, revamped vending, a Twilight zone, and an American diner, called Scoobys. A Burger King takeaway was also planned. Alongside this the Tavern bar had been refurbished thanks to the unit and NAAFI funding and now it looks like a civilian pub.

The entire scheme is one of the first local business plans to come to fruition and the first in the Spar roll out programme. Retail partner Spar provided the fixtures and fittings to refurbish the services shop, which closed for just a weekend while work was being carried out. Previously this was a dull and dark shop, but the layout had been changed along with the flooring, ceiling, and lighting. It was now a lot brighter and looked a lot bigger. Customers had shown their approval for the new look shop and this meant that the troops would use it a lot more.

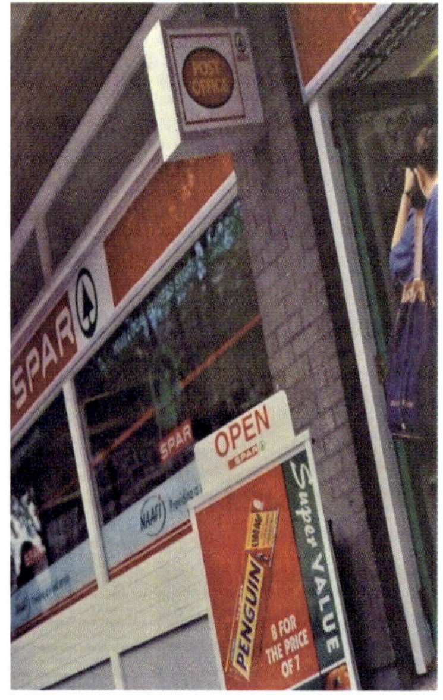

The new offerings included fresh bread, a hot pie counter and video hire. Opening hours had been extended to catch early morning and late evening trade. To help the staff enable smoother running an EPOS system had also been installed. The American diner offered a range of branded foods through NAAFI partner Eurest.

Ritazza coffee, Not just Donuts, Mamma Luigi's pizza and Upper Crust baguettes were big names to tempt and NAAFI was also providing jacket potatoes. Eurest had proved its flexibility by developing a range of pizza toppings for the takeaway service so customers could create their own 9-inch pizzas. Large 14-inch pizzas were also available along with the delivery service to the ships in the dock.

Nelson was so different from any other of the schemes that had gone before as a whole new diner was built for them. Although there are fewer vending machines than before there was now more choice. The four brand new machines sell everything from cold drinks, sweets, pies, burgers and cartons of milk, 24 hours a day. Also open 24 hours a day was the new Twilight zone with its state-of-the-art amusements. This proved a big hit with all the service personnel on site and was long overdue.

'The unit has not been running at its full potential for a long time and now it was a case of waiting for all of the ships to come back at the end of August to see what they thought of it,' explained Wendy Davis, leisure manager. Dean Jackson, Scoobys staff member, said: 'Pizza deliveries to the ships' dock had taken off well. Once they're all in dock I don't know how we're going to keep up with demand.'

Wilson's welcomes all ages 1997

The new look in a brand-new name was what used to be The Pack Horse has now gone down well with customers of all ages, says Heidi Beth Hudson, project coordinator, leisure division. Because the pub was outside the wire, it aimed to appeal to families and young service personnel.

The response had been very positive and the support by the unit and Ministry of Defence police during the project had been helpful. Wilson's was now a warm comfortable atmosphere for families during the day and the advantage of a children's menu and baby changing facilities

with more family orientated events planned for the future. In the evening it provided an ideal spot for young singles out for a good time.

To underline this Eurest went with the big food offering and the emphasis on Mexican spicy flavours, including platters of finger food, ideal for large parties. They could enjoy drinks provided through Scottish Courage. There was also pool, Sky TV, and a jukebox. Wilson's success could be measured by the effect it had on pubs in nearby Amesbury, said Jon Norie, pub manager. The taxis used to come up to the Pack Horse to take customers to Amesbury, but now it was happening the other way around and the local pubs were suffering.

They hadn't had to try before but now they're putting on entertainment and with the new look they were winning hands down. Even the families that had been there for a few years had said that it is a shame it was not done earlier. Before it was a dismal place, but now there was more room and it was much livelier and more modern.

Where the troops go EFI follows 1997

Even though the guns had stopped firing, life was still precarious, with ethnic rivalries at the forefront many still could not return to their homes and those who could find devastated villages with no savings to rebuild their houses and livelihoods. More than two million mines were laid during the war and with over 800,000 unmapped, many villages remained out of bounds. It had been estimated that it would take over 20 years to clear but it was accepted that many would never be found.

As the peace continued to hold, the number of troops was slowly diminishing. However, EFI at work, providing the home comforts for the troops on operational deployment and an exercise, far from winding down, is in fact increasing. Self-service shops as previously all shops were kiosks, beer bars as well as EFI's first ever restaurant, offered leading Eurest branded foods, were all new dimensions in NAAFI frontline operation, demonstrating the company's commitment to the troops.

Life with EFI was not glamorous nor was it an easy option. Battling against the intense heat of the summer and the extremities of winter, working long hours, with only one day off a week as well as the practical problems of transport, they could expect that morale and commitment could be low. Nothing could be further from the truth. One of the most striking features of the trip that was taken by management was the positive attitude of all of those they met. Their enjoyment of the challenges they faced, their dedication to provide the best service possible shone through. It was the desire to give that little bit extra, the wearing of the uniform and following the same discipline of the serving soldier which endears EFI to the forces and made them part of a larger organisation of the British army.

At Sarajevo airport the effects of the war were only too clear to see. Shelled and bombed outbuildings surrounded the airport, while tape marks the area where land mines were known. Butmiu Camp was a construction site at the time, it would be a base for troops as they were being moved from Zetra stadium. Escorted by Maj Tom Lafferty and WO2 Nigel Hall, as they explained the plan to build a new self-service shop. All troops had their own EFI of which the American PX was the most famous and with a policy that any nationality could buy from anyone, competition was fierce. However, EFI prices were favourable and as a result they gained customers from many different nationalities.

Zetra Stadium, where Torvill and Dean won the gold medal at the 1984 Winter Olympics, was now a shelled building. The scoreboard from the Olympics hung from the roof, reminding all to see of its past glory. It was now a logistics base but for a large part of the war it served as a morgue. The hillsides surrounding the stadium were now enormous graveyards, where people dragged the dead for burial, while avoiding the hail of bullets.

It was a multinational base at Illisza where they found the first EFI organisation. Some 900 troops were now based in what was once a beautiful hotel complex, where people used to sample the Spa waters. On the 19th of May 1997 NAAFI opened its first self-service shop, selling some of the home comforts which would be taken for granted. Electrical goods, clothing, toiletries, perfumes, and cigarettes and food served as a reminder off home life. The self-service concept benefited from allowing people to browse and look at goods rather than relying on a kiosk system. With clothing and electrical goods being the most popular items, the benefits of this was self-evident.

The long drive northwards from Sarajevo through green countryside, which in places looked untouched by the war, took our party to the main British base at divisional headquarters Banja Luka, situated in an old metal factory; it was clearly evident that life in Bosnia was not easier. Accommodation was basic rows of metal dormitories providing cramped and airless living – well, troops are not allowed to leave the base. EFI staff are not separated from the troops, enjoying the same living conditions.

Two bright lights, a bar and a cafe, now provided a sense of normal activity. The swamp, a long green bubble tent, gave the service personnel the chance to relax and unwind in a natural atmosphere. There are no formalities, the tables and surroundings are basic, but its constant popularity emphasises that EFI is providing the desired service.

On the 28th of June 1997 the youngest serving signaller opened the first ever NAAFI / Eurest restaurant. It was run by Patrick McClanney from Eurest, the wooden building provided a number of branded goods including Mama Luigi pizzas, Not just Donuts, Upper Crust baguettes, and fish and chips. It was open till 2300hrs daily, it provided a place where service personnel could go for a break, to watch television, read newspapers and to relax. Its success was instant. Supplies which were originally ordered to last for three months lasted a mere two weeks.

As with all the projects EFI always used its initiative. When the idea of providing a restaurant facility was agreed the problem of finding a suitable building arose. A 300 square metre building and 240-foot refrigeration containers were purchased in Holland. They were transported by Kempen drivers to Banja Luka, and assembled in nine days by Dutch engineers. Cooking equipment, furnishings and opening stocks were transported from England. The Royal Engineers provided power and water and installed the equipment to enable the opening to take place in only nine weeks after the financial approval was given.

A Dutch library was dismantled, taken to Kempen, transported to Bosnia and erected as EFI's new restaurant. Cooperation was essential and EFI's good relationship with the Royal Logistic Corps was crucial as it was their troops who helped to erect the building.

NAAFI also promoted local employment in its restaurant of 11 staff, all of whom lived locally. They were attracted to the work, mainly because of the wages but also for the assured training. Alongside the restaurant was another one of EFI's self-service shops. Cpl Heather Speirs was on her third EFI tour and about to take up the post in Split; for her it was all about job satisfaction working for EFI. The work could be hard; in particular she remembered when EFI set up at Sipavo, when she shared a tent in the mud. But now it was wonderful to see the progress that had been achieved.

20 years and still going strong, Memories by Sgt Brian McCourt to Mr and Mrs McCourt 1997

The year was 1997 and I was serving as detachment commander in Banja Luka. I received a call from HQ Split asking me to be prepared to go to Sarajevo, I was excited by this as I had a previous deployment within this area of Bosnia. Within a few days I found myself packing up my room and heading to Banja Luka airport to make the flight across to Sarajevo. It was a Sunday and I always recall this as the flight crew stating "Not sure what's going on as we don't fly Sundays, and it's been authorized from a high level within HQ Bosnia, this needs to happen". For that short moment I did feel special!!

Arriving at Sarajevo, later that day and begun to take over from the outgoing Detachment commander and settle into the role. Within Sarajevo, there was another EFI shop in Iledia camp, this was located at the other side of the international airport. Travel between sites was restricted and we were always escorted by armed guards. After all it was a war zone going through a transition towards peace.

One day I was reading an SFOR magazine and came across an article about Cpl Hannah Derry who was located at the Iledia detachment, she was also a serving member of the EFI. I did not know Hannah then. One day I was over in the other EFI shop and recognized Hannah from the picture within the magazine. I introduced myself and her first words were, "I know who you are, stay away from me, I'm not interested". I was taken back as I was only saying hello. Having said that and at the time I was a single with a reputation with my female colleagues.

Over the coming weeks and many a party, I got to know Hannah and started spending a little more time together. One night, I asked her out for a beer and pizza, she said yes ok . . . By this stage, I really liked Hannah and was hoping to take things to another level. It was clear Hannah was not looking for a relationship and was going through a divorce and started seeing another guy, who was based in Split. One night Hannah gave me a letter starting she really liked me as a friend and that's all it could be. I was saddened but accepted her decision.

People will say within EFI, you work hard and play hard, that we did and over the coming weeks, and fast approaching Christmas which saw the relationship taking shape and, in the direction, I was hoping for. The icing on the cake was when we both got a 4-day R&R break to Naples in Italy. Being separated away from the military life for a few days was going to be a test and other than being ripped off in Italy (train, taxi and camera stolen), we came through good. As we came to the end of our tour and headed back to the UK for a well-earned break, Hannah and I found ourselves in Mauritius for three weeks which was amazing and was the place we got engaged.

Holiday over, heading back to Sarajevo via Split. On arrival back at Butmir, I was met by Captain Ian Goodwin, who then told me there was some operational changes required and I would need to go back to Banja Luke. This was without Hannah and the following morning. Looking back at my reaction (Sorry Ian), I never handled it very well. Before I packed my room up, I decided to call Lt Col Smith back in the UK to see what he could do to support me staying in Sarajevo and with Hannah. I suppose as a member of the EFI Cadre team, I was trying to use my permanent status to get what I wanted. I asked if Hannah could come with me to Banja Luke, which was turned down, but did say it would be considered. It never worked, packed up my room and it would be fair to say, there was a few tears between Hannah and myself. The following morning, I began the long drive over Bosnia to Banja Luka. One-month later Hannah and I were reunited, permanently in Banja Luka.

During our time together, we reflected on what we both wanted, and I was prepared to give up my role within EFI of a decade and leave for a settled life in the UK. The boss, Lt Col Smith MBE, tried to talk me out of leaving and offered me a role as Country Manager as a WO2 in either, Kenya, Brunei or Belize. Whilst this was a great opportunity the snag was it was unaccompanied and I would need to leave Hannah behind. It was clear I would leave EFI and settle back into civvy street with Hannah. So, Hannah and I settled in her hometown of Leicester and have two children named Connor and Kiera and whilst I missed the EFI lifestyle, I found a gem of a girl!! Hannah and I will be 20 years married in 2020 and believe this to be the longest EFI relationship.

1998

New image for 3 of the Sennelager stores 1998

Seven shops in the Sennelager area, with the first one joining the range of goods being supplied directly through one of Spar's UK wholesaler and distributor James Hall and Co. This had been followed up with internal refits to support the new product lines at Normandy barracks and Barker barracks, the two service shops and the Uhland Strasse 'B' shop. This was a case of a total image change without having to spend too much or indeed causing too much disruption for the customers. The shops looked very different and this would improve the performance as a result. Spar had three very distinct offers. An express store, which went well within our services shops, a neighbourhood store, and a supermarket. The difference was the product lines.

In all the stores the sales are up by over 10% and the customers' reaction had been largely positive. Shops in the Fallingbostel / Hohne area also opened with a new range by the end of February 1998 and by the end of April they would be up and running in all areas. Mike Pugh, retail development manager was leading the conversion programme. He said that first and foremost they would establish what the customers wanted from the company and the marketplace in Germany was very different to the UK. In the UK the convenience store format with extended opening hours was the formula that had really worked well. But they would be testing what was right for all the customers there and they would do that quite simply by talking to them.

Tidworth the 100th store to have the Spar conversion 1998

The NAAFI council, Garrison commander, the chairman and members of the NAAFI board all joined shoppers at Tidworth to see the opening of the most expensive conversion of a neighbourhood store yet. The brand-new NAAFI Spar store was 5000 square feet of space, but Dougie Ross, manager, could say it was worth it. They didn't want to be called the flagship and then just be a carbon copy of other shops; they wanted their customers to have more.

Some of the features of the new shop were: 24 hour opening seven days a week, a new concept of food to go, 8 essential items at lower prices more competitive than before, video hire, the delicatessen, a photocopying service, a free phone point for the NAAFI Select catalogue, and the financial services centre.

The Tidworth store would be open 24 hours a day every day of the week for a trial period. The only way to find out when the best trading times were, was to open all the time. It was the way the convenience sector was moving and would soon be the industry standard. The manager had recruited an extra 12 members of staff to cope with the longer opening hours which took the total members of staff to 46.

The retail division was now trialling a new takeaway food counter in the Tidworth store. The food to go counter would stay open from 0800 – 2300hrs selling a full range of takeaway dishes; this included country fried chicken, pizzas, cuisine de France products including a wide range of selection of breads, pies, cakes and pastries to take away, and in the weeks following the opening the introduction of ethnic foods such as Indian and Chinese.

Auf Wiedersehen Kempen 1998

In 1989 the distribution centre at Kempen replaced separate facilities in and around Krefeld. Over the years it had supplied around 200 clubs and shops in locations as far afield as Kiel in northern Germany, Berlin, Sardinia, and Bosnia. The complex was purpose built to include a main warehouse the size of three football pitches, an administration block for support services and transport workshop. It became the heart of NAAFI's distribution network in Europe.

There's been a sense of pride for all working for NAAFI in Germany in Kempen, they had a fantastic mix of staff from all different nationalities, said Steve Smith, administration manager, distribution. 'But I think you can say that it really was a warehouse too far. It all came together at the wrong time because of the German reunification, the end of the Cold War, and the UK government's desire to reduce the forces. No one is unhappy about going. We think drawing the line is the right thing as we cannot maintain such a huge site.'

Most of the staff agreed that one of Kempen's proudest achievements was continuing to make deliveries using their standalone system when the food supply computer system suffered problems.

Although NAAFI had a good redundancy package, they also had access to jobs through the Internet in both Germany and the UK by the end of April 1998 and they also hope to have placed 40 people within the business. Those staying in Germany were also attending special courses on German interview techniques.

They continued to deliver the goods in some difficult and dangerous situations. They had to tackle problems ranging from hostile border guards to hazardous terrain. But despite it all, Jim said: 'I've enjoyed my time with NAAFI. It's been hard work from one tour to another, but I've been happy and there have been good rewards as well.'

Ted Timmins, transport manager, added: 'Bosnia was a permanent problem. It had been the drivers who had made the operation work there.' In a tribute to the hard work of the staff in the workshops he added: 'They had to be flexible. Sometimes they'd make plans, then something would go wrong, and the vehicle would have to go into workshops, but it would still be needed for the following day.'

Even the transport clerk said the company had been fair to us all and we would continue to work to the end to support our manager. On the whole it has been a very tolerant firm and a very generous one.

Cold comforts courtesy of EFI 1998

The annual exercise to Norway where EFI support the services for three months during Arctic training. This involved 5000 Royal Marines and troops of the allied mobile force (land). This year there were 5 EFI detachments serving in Norway, from Voss in the South to Tromso in the North.

Lt Col Murray Smith, CO EFI RLC, during a visit to one of the smallest and largest detachment's staff from 2 to 6 personnel. At Setnesmoen barracks and Norwegian Army base at Andalsnes, a building was provided for detachment commander Sgt Martin Barker, Cpl Anne flood and Cpl John Evans to set up a shop in Boca shoe store. The store was also doubled up as Martin's office and sleeping quarters for the women. There was also a tiny box room for Martin to sleep in and a small kitchen and toilet. It wasn't exactly home from home but EFI staff enjoyed that way of life. 'The first time I went out to Bosnia I had to share a room with twenty others. I've never had to do that before. But we're all in the same boat and life is what you make it,' said Jan.

The shop provided a service to more than 200 troops, but this could drop to as little as 30 when the exercise was on. All the necessary items from toiletries to writing paper and suites are provided plus items like cameras, cassette recorders and last-minute presents, and as it was Norway there was plenty of strange trolls to choose from. During this exercise Jan gained her snow and ice driver training permit to drive a military vehicle. This is something you had to do before you could drive on the roads and it meant that she could drive once a week to meet up with colleagues at Trondheim to collect their takings so they could be banked, which was a 2 hour trip.

As detachment commander of both groups, Martin was in charge of the paperwork, stores and arranging transport out to exercises. Although serving only a small number of personnel, Martin pointed out that the amount of takings may be small compared to somewhere like Sarajevo, but the aim is still the same, keeping the troops happy.

Over at Bomoen camp at Voss, detachment commander captain Alan Robertson, one of the 6 EFI staff serving 1500 troops. Unlike Andalsnes, they were required to run a canteen as well as the Mobile Shop. The large purpose-built shop sold the same range of goods as Andalsnes but in larger quantities. There was also a kitchen, canteen area and seating, games machines, pool, and Sky TV. Trading hours were longer than the other sites 0930 to 2230hrs with a 5-hour break in between for restocking.

Bread rolls made up by staff every day, were sold in both the shop and from Land Rovers which doubled as Mobile Shops. Hot food from the canteen ranged from hot dogs to bacon rolls. Two days a week the mobile went out to troops on exercise. And whereas the girls in Andalsnes didn't have much in the way of entertainment in the evening, staff at Voss did have the facilities of a nearby town to enjoy and also separate sleeping accommodation from work.

More than just NAAFI in uniform 1998

Since the times of the EFC, the EFI had served in every Theatre of war. EFI existed to provide a service to the services, wherever they may be normally where there are no civilian NAAFI civilian establishments. Now the headquarters for EFI RLC was at Bulford, Lt Col Smith had 21 officers and 162 staff to call upon at any one time. Aged between 18 to 45, and were usually drawn from NAAFI and on occasions from the regular army. It was not for the faint hearted as training was provided on a two-week Territorial Army course and passed out the same as any other TA/Reservist soldier. This also included passing a service medical and rank was dependent on what job they did whilst working for NAAFI, but there was plenty of room for promotion.

Tours of duty could last anything from 6-7 months, and when on active service EFI staff are enlisted into the regular army with the same obligations to duty. Once out in the field they learned about all aspects of the wholesale, retail, and leisure trade. With their military trade being listed as 'Supply Specialists'. Generally, all members of staff would become Jack of all trades and master of all trades whilst serving.

Handover in Brunei 1998

The handover of the final Royal Brunei armed forces NAAFI shop at Berakas barracks in Brunei to the Brunei armed forces had now taken place. Seven RBAF shops had been handed over leaving only the British base in Seria, which was a combined shop and club operation. Graham Taylor, business administration manager, would be transferring in November to work in Belize, leaving Clive Hayhoe, business manager and Mariah Binti Kilat, senior office clerk, to move to the district office at Seria where there will be a total of 12 staff.

Pictured outside the NAAFI district office on Berakas camp are: Graham Taylor, business administration manager, Tony Yang Ah Bon, shop manager, Hjh Ida Maria, personnel and administration manager, Wong Chak Ming, officer in charge of supplies, Mariah Binti Lilat, senior office clerk, Patrick Chan Kok Wah, senior shop assistant, and Clive Hayhoe, business manager. Altogether they had a combined total of 200 years' service.

Troops tuck in and HRH Princess Anne has tea 1998

When HRH the Princess Royal visited the reserve officers' conference, to present prizes for military competitions sponsored by NAAFI, she was also on the receiving end of a presentation herself. The opportunity was taken to present her with a NAAFI tea caddy, said Col David Shepherd, NAAFI special projects team, who was helping to run the NAAFI stand at the Brighton conference centre.

The five day event involved reserve forces from 3 services in NATO and was divided between the Brighton conference centre and where there were VIP speakers, and the Minley Manor, near Camberley where the military competitions and demonstrations were held and EFI had four Tommy Tucker mobiles.

It was the largest demonstration of the UK's reserve forces ever undertaken involving more than 1400 reservists from 74 units of 400 vehicles and specialist equipment. Tommy Tucker pizzas, burgers and chips were in demand throughout. They were invited to take part and it was important that they were to be seen to be supporting such events.

Tommy Tucker on the way to Bosnia 1998

The third Tommy Tucker mobile was up and running in Bosnia, thanks to the hard work of the teams from the EFI. The latest one opened up at North Port, Split, offering everything from bacon baguettes to chips and pizzas. In its first week it sold what was estimated to be the first month's sales. The first open was at Dalma, followed by Sipovo and Gornji Vakuf. It was planned for another two to join them according to where the military needed them.

OCA AGM 1998

It was a race to the finish, at the NCS EFI OCA reunion and their AGM. Horse racing and raffle proved to be ideal entertainment following a meeting and a buffet lunch at new Normandy barracks. Some 90 members and their families attended and were addressed by their president, David Roberts MC. David thanked retiring chairman Tommy Booth and two of his long service committee members Jimmy Howard and Ben White, who had notched up between them a combined service of 45 years on the committee. The event was attended by over 50 members who enjoyed the reunion every year.

1999

Retail begins to change in Germany 1999

The way forward for retail in Germany was now clear. Changes in both store and staff structures were being made in response to a number of different pressures. The most significant being the declining customer base. In 1995 there were nearly 60,000 troops in Germany, last year that figure had gone down to 30,000 and at the start of the new Millennium it would be down to well under 20,000 due to the withdrawal of the RAF from Laarbruch and Bruggen and the redeployment of 2500 personnel announced in The strategic defence review.

The decline had, inevitably, affected NAAFI's total sales in Germany from the record highs in 1993/94 then to 2/3 of that in 1997/98. Change was therefore necessary, NAAFI simply could not afford to offer the same extent of range of goods to customers in all locations. The new retail structure would see the current 8 'A' stores reduced to four regional shopping centres at Fallingbostel, Sennelager, Osnabruck and JHQ.

It was still intended that these would become centres of excellence, the sort of shops that people would be willing to travel to. They would continue to offer Home and leisure goods, clothing and extensive food offer. The former 'B' stores would be renamed as neighbourhood stores and would offer fragrances, basic clothing and a convenience food offer aimed at the family. Services shops would become express stores, small, modern convenience stores targeted at single service personnel.

First British pub in Bosnia 1999

EFI had opened the first NAAFI pub in Bosnia and it was attracting customers from the many different nations serving there. The Cafe Royal on Butmir camp in Sarajevo had been completely refurbished to bring it up to date. It then offered a relaxed an inviting atmosphere for customers from 0700 to 2300hrs, it served up food, refreshments, and entertainment.

'The pub was popular before it was taken over but afterwards it became a lot busier. Before it was very bland in the bar but once it was refurbished it was warmer and it changed the atmosphere,' said Sue Murdoch who became the manager of the Cafe Royal. They served food and soft drinks from 0700 to 1900 hours and then the customers could buy beer, wine and cider until 2230 hours, Spirits were not allowed.

The menu was varied as they wanted to cater for all nationalities on the camp. Continental foods like croissants, toasties as well as muffins, doughnuts, and hot dogs to cater for the Americans. They could also serve up homemade soup, which was made by the staff. they also managed to find entertainment for the customers. With live music like a TexMex band, a country and western singer, karaoke, and an American army band. The grand opening of the Cafe Royal was during a visit to Bosnia by Allan Vaughn, director, international and corporate development.

A trip too far! Macedonia/Kosovo (Op Agricola/KFOR) Memories by Ewan Fyfe 1999

I can remember it as if it were yesterday. The year was 1999. I was fresh from basic training, still naive and wet behind the ears.

We landed in Macedonia in the afternoon. You could feel the heat as soon as the plane doors opened. I stepped out into the baking sun and squinted my eyes. A sea of activity, a hustle and bustle that you would expect from a busy airport. Except there were no holiday makers, no screaming kids, no businessmen on their laptops. Military. As far as the eye could see!

We eventually got our baggage and were met by our CO, Tom Lafferty. "Welcome to the war zone!" was his opening line. It had now sunk in. What the hell was I doing here! I was a lowly shop assistant from Falkirk, not "Rambo"! A few weeks passed and I had settled right in. I was having the time of my life!

We had been tasked to take one of the infamous "Tommy Tucker" Trailers to a small encampment near the border. There the Paras were camped, awaiting instructions. The place was mobbed! Maroon berets as far as the eye could see. We sold out of everything in no time at all. It was nonstop! All of a sudden, the words "Bugging out" were echoing through the camp. What was going on? I was in a bit of a panic! Paras were scrambling everywhere, the sound of chinooks coming in filled the air. I could see in a field next to the camp chinooks swooping in to land, Paras jumping in, then swooping off again. Within ten minutes the camp was deserted. I had never seen anything like that in all my life.

When we returned to camp, I was taken to one side. "We have been tasked to go in with a convoy and set up a small shop in Lipljan," said Colonel Lafferty. "Are you up for it?" – "Hell yeah!" was my reply. Will Nurse and I got our kit together, filled a trailer full of stock and set off to join the convoy.

We reached Lipljan and set up our own wee camp. Our shop was an ISO container. We worked hard and helped provide some much-needed home comforts to the lads. After a few days we were approached by the CO of 2 Para (I think!). He wanted us to go out with a trailer full of stock and visit some encampments in the surrounding area. This wouldn't be a problem.

On the day of our first "Trip Out" we got everything ready. Then, armed with our SA80s and map we set off to find the encampments. The first 2 we found with no difficulties. The 3rd was a school which, according to the map, was in the middle of nowhere! On the journey we both remarked on the number of craters in the countryside and also near the sides of the road. We arrived at the school and was greeted by a young Captain. "Great to see you guys! We have been expecting you."

Once we had finished serving the personnel, we were packing up when the young Captain came over to us. "How did you get here?" he asked. Will showed him the route on our map. The colour drained from his face. "Holy shit!" he exclaimed. "That road has not been cleared!" We had just drove approx 20 miles through a heavily mined area! The Captain showed us the "Safe" route. "Lucky Bastards" was his final words to us before we left! Will and I were probably inches away from never returning home . . .

XL Leisure 1999

This was the start of the Millennium celebrations where planning was 12 months in advance and everybody was talking about it. The plans for the launch of the celebrations for the dawn of the 21st century. Most of NAAFI's customers would not be celebrating the 31st of December 1999 on camp so XL had come up with a fantastic loyalty scheme that lasted from spring 1999 to February 2000.

In association with some of the partners, they would be offering customers the chance to win a fantastic prize every month. Trips to New York, Orlando and European cities to name just a few. Each month the first 100 customers through the doors of each club would receive a calendar and a Millennium passport. This passport would be stamped when they bought a drink or products from the XL and when it was full the customers would be given a gift voucher and entered into that month's prize draw. The first available prize was for the March draw of a trip for two to New York, plus $500 spending money.

How I became a dual citizen, Memories by Allison Roles 1999

While serving on the HMS Illustrious in 1999 as a trainee canteen manager, the Captain asked me why I had never joined the Navy, he said I was more Jack than most of the Wrens!

I explained that I was born in America and that I had never obtained British Citizenship. This was because when my family had moved to Scotland in 1979, it was not possible to get dual citizenship. If I had wanted British Citizenship at that time, I would have had to give up my American citizenship and I hadn't wanted to do that.

He said he was not having a Yank on his ship (he was obviously only joking but said leave it with him).

Following this conversation, I had a few meetings with the Captain's secretary about dates of immigration etc.

Next thing I know on the 10th November 1999, the Captain had asked Steve Cooper (The Canteen Manager) if I could have the next day off as we were alongside in Barcelona. He had arranged for me to go to the Embassy and pledge my oath of allegiance to become a British citizen. He also arranged for PO Free to come with me and for us to have a celebration brunch.

So, this is how on the 11th of November 1999 I became a dual citizen thanks to the RN.

EFI update 1999

EFI was deployed all over the world and 1999 was no different. Arctic training had come in handy for Sgt Glenys Jones, Cpl Ronald Moules-Burton when they were deployed to Macedonia in support of operation Upminster in December 1998. They arrived in temperatures of minus 32C and most of their stock had to be transferred into the unit's temperature-controlled reefers before cans and bottles started popping. They were now running a shop and a bulk issue store in the basement of a Hotel Panorama in Skopje and would be deployed there for at least six months.

The annual trip to Norway also got underway, and this year this deployment was smaller than usual due to the operational commitments of the regular army; Sgt Heather Stevens and her team would be supporting AMF (L) in southern Norway at Voss, with just two Cpls and L/Cpl Sue Lowe to assist.

Supporting the Royal Marines in northern Norway would be WO2 Nigel Hall and his team at Grotsund Fort, a Norwegian naval base. They would be assisted by Cpl Taffy Reese at his sub location at Brennfjell.

Further in land at Bardufoss was Sgt Chris Blyth who, having come from the Falklands, would be comparing the islands to the frozen wastelands of Norway.

Just seven months after closing the detachment in Gioia Del Colle in southern Italy, EFI was asked to return to support RAF once more. Sgt Heather Stevens, who closed the shop in March, was diverted from the end of her tour in Bosnia to reopen the shop along with Cpl Sean Jones. This meant that EFI could respond very quickly to the RAF initial order request with the help of the team at Dalma warehouse. It also allowed time to call Sgt Michelle Lang and allow Heather home for a well-deserved Christmas break before her trip to Norway.

Ex Snow Hole 1999, memories by Sue A Lowe

In 1999 October I was posted to Norway. There were 4 of us going to Voss. Once we had landed in the Hercules, the others told me it had slid across the runway and it was bumpy landing – I had actually slept through everything and they had to wake me up. As we got off the flight out of the tail of the aircraft, it was biting cold. I remember quite clearly, as we got on the bus I put my headphones in 'The Corrs' was on My Walkman, somehow it fitted, as I watched out the window and saw the mountains and trees covered in snow. It was calm and quiet. It was quite dark and most of the others had fallen asleep and some of us sat staring out of the window. The journey took us a few hours, when we got there, we had to find our kit and pulled it off the coaches into the snow. Then we had to find our accommodation. The two Cpls knew exactly where we were going as they been here before.

The next day we went to find the EFI, where we were going to set everything up. The Containers had arrived the day before. We had to unload the containers, organise into the bulk issue store. The Sgt knew exactly where everything was supposed to go, she was extremely organized.

Setting up the shop was easy, the refrigerators had arrived and now it was our task to fill them, the Sgt was quite specific – every single can had to be front facing. I felt that even if one was out of alignment she would know even if she couldn't see it. The 2 Cpls were busy merchandising the 'stickies' and some of the other items, we had plenty of twisters and more boot polish than a parade at Horse Guards would need.

Later, in the afternoon the Sgt came back with a strange looking grill and a large bag full of Norwegian bacon and fresh bread, so when it got to NAAFI break guys could have bacon butties and a brew. It became quite a routine every single morning, bacon butties and more brews in polystyrene cups than anybody would need but the smell of that bacon was amazing even with a hangover. The damage a night on local Norwegian pilsner could do was untold.

The EFI was the main hub and everyday whether it was 10 o'clock NAAFI Break, lunchtime, or afternoon break or after the guys had been on duty, the place was full. In the main area were 2 pool tables, 2 gaming machines and a dart board, it was one telly and no extra speakers. We had Paras and AMF with us. Of an evening they would make up games and rituals, traditions, pretty much anything for a laugh, some downright dangerous like the dance of the flaming arseholes and some if you caught sight of them would even make your eyes water. The guys would make this good-hearted fun and they seemed to enjoy themselves.

In between all of this it was just 3 of us making sure the guys' downtime was enjoyable. There were a couple of guys that were having problems at home and issues with relationships and family and they would just pour their heart out and they were thankful for the ear, just listening was enough. It was quite sad when one of the guys brought a Dear John letter in, there was not much you could do when you are stuck on exercise in the middle of the mountains in Norway, you got on with the job and everything else has to wait until you got home.

The Sgt had rented a sunbed and for those that got to use it, went home with a tan, in consideration we were in the middle of the mountains and the only sun, was what was bouncing off the snow in the below freezing temperatures. We were quite lucky our accommodation was in the same block as the ski team; they were a good bunch of lads, many a night sat in the stairwell, with a case of beer and then somebody would get speakers on a Walkman and then it would turn into a party, until the beer was gone. For those that smoked, if you went outside for a cigarette break it pretty much took half an hour because it was that cold lighting it took even longer.

The privileges of having a good laugh with the ski team, meant they managed to save the only pair of size 5 boots for me and I learnt to ski. The other girls had no issue, there are plenty of 6 and 7s size boots. One of the girls actually managed to go off and landed on a frozen river face down, skis stuck up in the air. Did not think I would learn how to rescue someone, from a frozen river. We got back on to the ski run as safely as possible, but I do have to say it was really quite funny.

Later on, in the exercise, we had a couple of skidoos and they let me have a go, which was fun. The idea was to slowly weave between iron bollards on the old runway, learning how to ride the skidoo. I did go slowly the first few times and then the Sgt told me to go faster, he was sat on the back. I got more confident then I has a sneaky feeling I was on my own, that he wasn't on the back anymore, he'd fallen off about 100 yards back and caught his boot in the back of the skidoo – I was dragging him over the iced up airfield. I never lived it down the rest of the time I was there, the guy was a 'tough para' a big article too! He was quite red faced about it.

We were allowed to go into the main town, Voss. There was a couple of gift shops you could buy husky teddy bears, trolls and more trolls – apparently, they brought luck, so I bought a few for the relatives. Now the other thing about the town, was the price of food and drink. We went to the railway cafe a couple of times, and we only had 2 nights out the whole time we were there. We would bundle into the back of a BV and be taken to town, only to find out that a half a litre of lager in 1999, was a fiver! Super expensive but the music was good, and the guys were a good laugh. I still have the ticket to get into Jarls nightclub.

No matter how much fun we were having or how hard we worked, the Sgt back at camp would want everything to be absolutely spot on before we went anywhere, every single can faced up, every sticky bar in the correct date order. Always making sure that we were ready to open up on the next shift.

Old comrades seek young members 1999

The EFI /NCS OCA had been in existence for many years. The future, however, was in danger of dying out because of the lack of interest from the young prospective members. Largely as a result of the name, OCA had always been considered a pensioner's organisation but as Lt Col Murray Smith, its general secretary, explained that this was not the case.

The main aim was to encourage the younger generation who had left NCS or EFI, but still worked for NAAFI, to join. This also meant those who had left the organisation altogether but still wanted to keep in touch with old comrades. The Association was not only a way of keeping in touch with old friends but also with Ex EFI or NCS members who had fallen on hard times which we might not otherwise have heard about. It provided a network of support. The Association has its own fund, which was mainly used for charitable work. It could also call in the Navy and army benevolent funds for financial assistance for members.

Although, in general, it's not until later in life that members need to call on the OCA for help, you never know when it's going to happen in the future and we would like to see the younger elements joining and supporting the organisation so that it did not die off. There were no current serving members of NCS in the OCA although the EFI is represented very well. Once a serving member leaves EFI they are asked to fill out a membership form. The committee is headed by Maj Tim Elliott, Bob Lewis is vice president, Ray Yeomans archivist and research, WO2 Nigel Hall and Lt Col Murray Smith, general secretary.

Membership at the time was only open to all ranks commissioned, enrolled or attested, who had served or were serving in the NCS, RAOC/EFI, RASC/EFI, RLC/EFI, and ATS/EFI. Membership in 1999 stood at 650 and instead of two separate functions of an AGM and reunion they were both joined together.

Exercise Brightstar 1999 Memories by Sue A Lowe

In 1999 I was told that I would be going on the 10th Brightstar exercise in Egypt. The history of this exercise can be traced back to 1979, the Camp David peace accord, when members of the United States armed forces began training side by side with their Egyptian military counterparts in the Egyptian desert. This evolved into an annual exercise known as Brightstar, which was first conducted in the summer of 1980, as a single service bilateral ground manoeuvre, then again in 1981 a similar event also occurred.

Due to the logistics involved it quickly became a larger exercise and was decided Brightstar would become a biannual event starting in 1983. The limitation of the ground forces was changed in 1985 when the air forces, both the US and the Egyptian military, added to the exercise. This marked the joint endeavour meaning that more than one United States service was involved. Special naval forces in 1987 joined the exercise. Then at Brightstar 1989 the exercise would be held during the autumn months instead of the summer. In 1991 the US forces committed to the Arabian Gulf region following the Gulf war, and Brightstar 1992 was cancelled. It then resumed in 1994 and was bigger and better than before.

Brightstar 96 then marked the beginning of countries other than the United States and Egypt participating in the exercise, NATO nations including France, United Kingdom, and Germany and the UAE from the Gulf. In 1998 these included the same countries but added Kuwait as the 7th participating nation, meaning that from a small unit training event it became the largest exercise involving the United States troops anywhere in the world.

Brightstar 1999/00 became its 10th event and was the most significant as this would give the baseline for more ambitious coalition in the future. So, this increased with the addition of the Netherlands, Italy, Greece and Jordan. Brightstar involved the forces of 11 nations over 70,000 troops.

The aim in all of this was bringing together a coalition of military forces to build friendship, cooperation and a better understanding in the professional military environments of each of the countries. It also gave an increased awareness and appreciation for the cultures and customs of other nations.

So there it was Egypt, France, Germany, Greece, Italy, Jordan, Kuwait, the Netherlands, UAE, United Kingdom and the United States, all on one major exercise together.

We arrived approximately 20 of us. We got off the flight and watched our bags thrown onto the back of an Egyptian lorry with a few hundred other service personnel as they threw nets over and they bobbed along roads which had seen better days. A few hours later somewhere South of Alexandria and West of Cairo in the middle of the desert we got off the back of the trucks, found our kit and went for a hunt to find our ISO containers. But they had not arrived yet and the rumour had already started to go round that the EFI had arrived. A large proportion of the lads had run out of cigarettes within a few days and they were all desperate for a can of Coke and not the questionable squash in the cook house tent.

So in true style of being able to source products, we managed to get some of the local Egyptian Team to go into town and get some cigarettes and pop; within a few hours they came back with Egyptian Cola in glass bottles and numerous packets of local cigarettes. The lads were overjoyed until they lit them up – they even smelt like camel dung.

That evening the sight of ISO containers rumbling down the battered roads towards us was a welcome sight and we could only hope that they were ours. That day we had been told how we were being split up and where we would be going. I was off to a camp with one of my colleagues Steve who was fairly old hat at the job; we jumped into the front of the lorry with our ISO container on the back stacked with stock. When we got there Steve was overjoyed that the French had already arrived and the Americans were already settled in. Why the French? Well it was going to take a couple of weeks but I would realise Steve's excitement that they had the closest thing to proper showers than any of the other nations, it made our mobile bathroom laundry unit showers (MBLU) look like a broken pipe and lukewarm at that. The Americans, yes they brought KFC with them, Pizza Hut and the PX.

One of the pioneer Sgts pointed us towards a patch of sand next to the Mess hall and the cook house and congratulated us on our new home. Our container dropped into position and we got to work. As we opened up the doors we expected to see our tentage waiting for us but unfortunately all we had was our stock stacked front to back, top to bottom. So, off I went with a couple of packets of cigarettes and pockets full of lukewarm pop, and came back with the Land Rover and two 9 by 9 tents in the back and a big roll of paracord. Then we got to work, we had to erect both tents and lace them together because our allocated tent had already been taken, as we had been delayed when the ISO containers hadn't arrived on time.

The next task was to set up shop and off I went again to the cook house. I needed six benches and at least four tables to build a shop while Steve guarded our ISO container as we were still waiting for our padlocks. It wasn't long before the Sgt in the cook house arrived with two lads and a fridge freezer, in the realisation that if we didn't have a tent or anything to stick the stock on we wouldn't have had that either. A few hours later a couple of the guys tipped up and sorted our electrics out for us with three lights and half a dozen plug sockets.

By that evening we had a shop, I had a bed space and we were almost settled in for the night but we opened up for a few hours, and then roughed out opening hours so the guys and girls roughly knew when we were going to be open. Steve sent a signal requesting more stock within a few days.

A week or two into the exercise we got news that we'd be getting another fridge and this was because the next week, they were going to be allowed two bottles of beer each, which brought excitement.

We didn't mind the other nationalities using the shop or the Egyptian locals from the Bazaar, but what we didn't realise was that the frequent visits from some of the locals, and the fact we were there, made us a target. Late one evening, as I was just settling down, I heard the little mouse taking my crisp packet and I fell asleep. I was woken by the two benches I'd had stacked at the front of the tent, fallen to the floor, they had been knocked over by somebody trying to get in, but what I hadn't realised is they were already in. I was on my own in the shop with one of the local Egyptians trying to steal stock. As I shouted out, I also heard some of the 'Pet Ops' who would become friends, shouting as they had seen them trying to get in. What they didn't know was they had, and I was still in the tent, in the pitch dark, with an Egyptian

man shouting at me. Seconds later the lads had got in and the Egyptian guy ran out. A bit shaken, they helped secure the tent, the lads pulled up their sleeping bags and we settled down for the night. The next day Steve moved all his kit into the front of the shop and took up guard at the front, I took up guard at the back for the rest of the exercise.

One of the RLC captains visited the next day and shook my hand, he had heard all about what had happened, and he handed me a pickaxe handle to go under my camp cot to protect myself just in case it happened again. He also promised to up patrols to make sure they knew they were being watched. It was quite funny, even some of the American lads, who used to shop twice daily had heard all about the events of the night before.

We had some amazing news that two-day trips were going to be laid on, both Steve and I were invited on either of them, so I went first and we went into Cairo to see the pyramids. It was quite bizarre as the driver of our minibus, one of the local Egyptians, made an unscheduled stop for fuel and the lads that were going with me, jumped out to go into the local shop and I was told I had to stay in the vehicle. It was only then two Egyptian men came round the side and wanted to see my feet, and once our driver had spotted them, shouted at the rest of the lads to get back in the vehicle and we drove off. It was quite an amazing day; we had camel/horse rides around the pyramids and we went into some of the local shops to buy gifts which in all fairness were pretty much the same as the bazaars that had set up around us.

Then the drawdown, slowly but surely, we started to run out of stock and then all we had, was enough left to set up a small shop in the ISO container to sell what we had left. The exercise itself was absolutely fantastic. I even got to use the French showers a few times which meant I actually got a proper wash.

2000–2009

2000

Front line force 2000

Both NCS and EFI staff were currently serving on the frontline with troops in the well-publicised trouble spot of Sierra Leone, Africa. The EFI were carrying out three detachments across Europe, when two were redirected for the emergency evacuation in Sierra Leone.

While landing, ship logistics (LSL) Sir Tristram crew, including EFI staff, managed to complete a two week land based exercise in France before it, along with another fleet ship, LSL Sir Bedivere, received immediate instructions to redirect to Sierra Leone on the 7th of May 2000. The Royal Navy had been supporting land-based troops there, evacuating people back from the dangerous civil war.

Just after the troops left for Sierra Leone, Lt Col Smith said, 'The situation is volatile and the commitment of HM Forces to assist with the evacuation only, at this stage. However, EFI and the NCS had the ability to sustain a longer deployment if they were needed.'

The reason that EFI staff, rather than the NCS were onboard LSL Sir Tristram and Sir Bedivere is that the ships were carrying troops, cargo, and vehicles for a land-based exercise in the Mediterranean. Therefore, before the ships were redirected to Sierra Leone, the EFI teams would have been required to disembark with the troops and continue to support them ashore.

The NCS, however, weren't far behind on-board HMS Ocean and HMS Illustrious, HMS Argyll and HMS Chatham also being deployed off Sierra Leone. Sixteen NCS members were on board, serving troops, a commando unit, and a helicopter squadron. RFA Fort George, supplies ship, also went along to replenish the ships.

The ship's business manager, Dave Frampton, said: 'At the moment, we don't know when the ships will return. HMS Illustrious should have come home in May, so the NCS staff are going to be very busy serving troops and providing a valuable service to the Navy.'

In another EFI detachment, 4 staff left the UK on the 25th of April for a three-week deployment to Hungary. The group set up a shop and BIS in tented field accommodation, the troops taking part in a live fire artillery exercise.

Norway and back again, Memories by Heather Young 1996 – 2000

I started off working for NAAFI, on a TACM course but didn't make the grade so went to Weeton Barracks in Preston. Was then sent on EFI training in Bracht with Roger Meadows, and a few others. Not getting any postings as soon as I thought with EFI, I took a posting to Northern Ireland. It was 3 years before Col Smith managed to get me out, and off I went to Split. We were living basically inside a factory with rooms made of cardboard boxes, the boys all stayed downstairs in the warehouse. Split was great fun, loved it when we managed to outsell JHQ Germany, it was a fantastic achievement and the bonus was great guys to work with too.

Then I managed to rupture my ankle whilst up on top of a stack of 4/5 pallets of cigarettes, carted out to first aid, but us Brits could not compete with the German medics, all white air conned tents, so they gave me treatment. I was sent to Sarajevo to cover while Nicki Bell went on leave, the shop was a concierge desk in the hotel, and Sipovo, the locals sold lots of cheap counterfeit CDs.

I was sent out to Norway Nov 1996, coming back in Dec, then in January till March, where I met my husband – he met me looking very undesirable, we were doing an exercise, so that we could travel north with the unit (AMFL) but as we didn't have the proper kit I had the saucepan dangling from my Bergen, which clanged every move I made. They didn't expect me to be a female as previous years there weren't any, so they put me into the officers' house. We had to do Arctic training survival. The good thing about meeting my soon to be husband when we set up a bacon butty run, as he was REME (hubby was WO2) they looked after our vehicle, swapping the rubbish one we got in Bergen to the best heated one in camp, we made sure they got butties first.

As I was EFI and he was REME it was a perfect story, EFI had a brilliant Land Rover heating that worked, whilst REME had a bar that never ran out. Returning to Bulford I thought our little affair would fizzle out, but 20 years together, 6 of them married, I have a lot to thank Col Murray Smith for. My husband had served his time, and this was his last tour.

I went out on exercise to Turkey, leaving him in the UK, he proceeded to book us a holiday for my return, when I got back I'd built up quite a rapport with a few people of AMF(L), so much so we managed to get a mock signal made up, supposedly sending him to Rwanda for 2 months (encompassing our booked and paid for holiday to St Lucia). We sent the fax from the EFI office to his commanding officer (who was also in on it) for a Friday afternoon so he couldn't react, meanwhile I sauntered over to see him as normal . . . what a state, how to explain to me that our holiday was having to be cancelled, I couldn't keep a straight face, he thought I thought it was a joke, whilst he was trying to convince me it was the real thing and he'd do his best on Monday to change things. When he found out, the signal was produced on his leaving do. The Colonel thought it was funny but naughty.

One night Lee Gibbons called me to the bar, so much noise so went in through the door to find all the Paras naked with a wall of cans, when they saw me I ran, the guys laughing but it was a tad scary so many drunk paras, they were throwing each other in the snow (–20c), they then went down the town wearing the duvet covers.

We were moved up to Bardufoss in the January, I went out with Heather Spiers on deliveries to the outlaying dets, the Paras offered us a ride round their moon base as they called it on a souped up skidoo . . . I went first, it was pretty scary with these mad men, Heather Spiers chickened out when she saw how mad they were (I loved it).

After many tours in between and some seeing the most amazing places, I was back off to Norway for the final time.

Then in 1999 off to Norway my last Tour, Voss, where we ended up being lent a sunbed, and the ski team wanted to use it, there was almost a rota. AMF(L), but we did get frequent visits from SBS who flew their helicopter in to collect stock.

Moving up North we ended up sleeping in a laundry, on sleeping bags the whole unit not just EFI. On our way to Northern Norway think it was Skibotn, the furthest north EFI had ever been, our shop was in a disused office, the stock room and old Abattoir which I ended up in as the others didn't like going in there. This was my last tour 2000.

Keeping in touch 2000

Phoning home was an important part of life for service personnel, whether or not they were posted to counties or continents away from their families and friends. Now, thanks to an arrangement with a telecommunications company, NAAFI made keeping in touch (KIT) much cheaper. KIT cards, a product design specifically for the armed forces by Servi-Tel, were only available from NAAFI stores. They were phone cards that could be bought in denominations of £5 and £10 and used from any touch tone phone. Customers simply dialled in an 0800 number which asked them to enter a pin number on the card. Then, they heard a dialling tone and could put in the phone number they required. The cards themselves were much cheaper than BT calls and customers could recharge the card using a credit or debit card.

Alternatively, NAAFI customers who had access to their own phone could use a prefix dialling service. They just put a four-digit code in front of the number they were dialling to receive up to 75% discount on all calls. Although both of these offers had only been launched in NAAFI stores in the UK, the beauty of them was that they travel; this meant that the customers could still take advantage of the cost savings, no matter where they were in the world. It wouldn't be long before they launched the products in international stores.

In addition to this new service they had already started to negotiate a contract to supply NAAFI staff and their families and friends. Partnership was now looking at a further development in the relationship with Servi-Tel to consider a joint venture to supply worldwide telecommunications solutions to the military.

Dining out on our expertise 2000

Pay as you dine (PAYD) was a major project for members of NAAFI partnerships team and it had implications and opportunities for many areas of the business.

PAYD initially was to be rolled out in the summer of 2000 where the tender process was where contract caterers would bid for the opportunity to provide food service in junior ranks messes. The idea was that the service personnel would only pay for food they consume. In addition, the Ministry of Defence hope that contractors would modernise, and upgrade duty ranks messes/cook house.

The thought was that one company would win the contract to provide the computer technology whereby all junior ranks would carry out a special swipe card that they would use to pay for their food. It was unlikely, however, that the MoD would award the catering contract to just one provider across the country. It would probably be divided into geographical locations which would be serviced by different companies. NAAFI would not be part of the contract catering bidding.

They would, however, be working on a framework for standard relationship, which allowed NAAFI to work with whoever was operating the PAYD in any given location. The MoD asked that NAAFI and these catering companies got together to make sure each one was prepared to accommodate the other and where possible avoid competition. The company would run its standalone shops and clubs but there was bound to be areas of crossover between the establishments and messes. For example, some contract caterers would provide vending services, certain retail elements and a bar in the mess. This could have a big impact on the business. Therefore, they would be involved in the early process to find out what the bidders' ideas were and how to ensure that they were clear on the areas in which NAAFI would operate.

PAYD could be very good news. But this was only on the proviso that positive relationships could be built with these companies then there may be some profitable new business opportunities for NAAFI Partnerships. In overseas areas particularly, the PAYD operators would need the NAAFI experience and their tax-free status.

Duo take up the reins 2000

Richard Burton, director UK, would provide the best support possible for the teams working in the NAAFI stores and clubs. To achieve this, he had appointed a head office team that combined expertise in both retail and leisure fields. The two key members of his team were David Mackenzie, operations controller (leisure), and Julie McAulay, operations controller (retail). They were already in place, the jobs involved developing the NAAFI XL and NAAFI Spar brands respectively, and they also each have the responsibility for the operations of six regions, combining both stores and clubs.

David's role started a year before, in XL leisure, although he now had operational responsibility for the stores as well as clubs. His new role was to develop the leisure brand within the UK division, building on the work of the last three years and continuing to offer High Street products and standards to the customers. One of the biggest challenges ahead of him was now he had retail and leisure operations managers reporting into him. An important part of his role was to be able to identify the opportunities that were available in both retail and leisure operations to make them most efficient and therefore most profitable.

Julie, however, started her NAAFI career as a retail operations manager. As operations controller (retail), Julie had responsibility for developing the retail brand and the business to boost profitability and store development. She also led NAAFI partnership relationship with SPAR. One of the key objectives was to make sure that there was a successful integration of the retail and leisure businesses at operational managers level. One of her main aims was to understand what made the club businesses tick and she looked forward to working with the operation managers who had a leisure background, as she could draw from their experience.

We're getting there 2000

It was easy to take for granted that NAAFI ran the shops and clubs all over the world. But, whether on an island in the Mediterranean, or posted to the war-torn Balkans or South American jungle, the British troops still relied on NAAFI for their home comforts.

Making sure that those home comforts arrived in the far-flung locations, was the international division exporter logistic team, based in Amesbury and managed by Taffy Davies MBE.

Export logistics was a good example of how far NAAFI had come in developing mutually beneficial partnerships to improve the service and products offered to service personnel wherever they were. NAAFI international may work with more than one partner in any single location, to ensure the right goods arrived on time, making for a real team effort. The EFI establishments in the Balkans for example, NAAFI's partnership with SPAR provided the groceries but two different transport company delivered them. Hogg Robinson took goods to Split in the former Yugoslavia, while Eddie Stobart delivered to Skopje in Macedonia where EFI stocks establishments in Kosovo.

Duty free beer, wines, spirits, and tobacco for troops in the Balkans were supplied through Chacalli-de-Decker in Antwerp. It also brought together other products like electrical goods and clothing, which were brought direct from the supplier. These are then transported by K. Ijzerman or Matra transport. Arrangements were different again for NAAFI shops in the Falkland Islands, Ascension Island and Cyprus in Kenya, whose food was supplied by Tesco export. Hutton's international purchases most other products for these locations, as well as supplying the needs of troops in Brunei, Belize and Arctic training exercises in Norway.

Macintyre Scott supplies the duty-free goods for HM ships, while SPAR provided the confectionery, toiletries, and other goods. Taffy said: 'For all the locations worldwide, including Saudi Arabia, Kuwait, and exercises in Hungary and the Mediterranean, we arrange supplies through Hutton's but use whatever transport was best suited to the job. This could be the RAF or civilian airlines, rail, or shipping. In fact, recently we used the Russian airline, Aeroflot, to transport goods from Hamburg to Cyprus! Quality of service and cost are always our chief considerations.'

Troops get new home from home in TFA 2000

EFI in Kosovo could now save customers in comfort thanks to the completion of nine brand new temporary field accommodation units (TFA Mike Sheriff, director international, was one of the first people to take a look at them when they flew out to Kosovo at the end of May 2000).

The TFA, also called Expeditionary campaign infrastructure units by the army, were having their finishing touches added while Mike was there. He was extremely impressed and the contractors, JFD India, had done an excellent job. The units were some of the best he'd seen, and he believed they would be the single biggest improvement to date to enhance the service they provided an active duty locations.

Six clubs and three shops were now up and running and two smaller shops would be finished by September.

The new TFA meant that rather than ducking into a freezing tent to buy a drink or a bar of chocolate, customers could enjoy warmer, more inviting, surroundings. In addition, staff could offer the same promotions as other NAAFI locations around the world. For example, during June, they gave away Euro 2000 football merchandise.

As well as more promotions locally employed civilian (LEC) Staff would also be wearing that NAAFI logo on their chests when the new uniforms were introduced later in 2000. The staff morale in Kosovo was high and the only concerns were the communication between establishments for the LEC – most of them relied on text messages via their own mobile phones. They still had some more work to do improving matters like that but thanks to the TFA, things were definitely changing for the better.

Operations get wrapped up at Dalma 2000

Dalma warehouse, the EFI main Depot in Bosnia, had finally closed its doors to make way for a new delivery system. Cpt Nigel Edwards, CO EFI RLC Bosnia, said that they had introduced a direct supply system to reduce stockholding and costs, as well as making deliveries faster and easier. NAAFI had teamed up with Antwerp based Chacalli de Decker, which was acting as a supply and consolidation company. The staff collect orders from various supplies throughout Europe, then the goods were delivered by road, doing multi drop deliveries to the stores. After six years it was sad to see the warehouse go but times moved on and the staff had done an amazing job and kept it running efficiently. The six uniform staff who worked in the warehouse had all moved to other posts within EFI.

Making a difference where it matters 2000

When NAAFI restructure took place, in May 2000 it was announced that the organisation was to operate by three geographical areas, UK, Germany and International rather than by retail and leisure divisions. Much greater emphasis was placed on overseas operations, including NCS and EFI RLC, some of which had lacked investment in recent years.

As the international division embarked on a 2-year programme of investments to bring the establishments up to scratch with the company's new modern image, NAAFI international employed around 500 staff and operated 100 establishments in more than 12 different countries. While every outlet, regardless of its size, was important to its customers, the five areas of the business with the highest turnover was the Falklands, Cyprus, the Balkans (Bosnia and Kosovo, EFI and NCS).

Progress has been made and had been achieved since the restructure, and Mike Sheriff the director wanted to lay out the agenda for the next move. He recognised that some areas needed significant change. Cyprus, which was one of the largest operations, achieved 30% of the overall sales at the end of the last financial year, but it was only equated to 12% of the profit. Now, thanks to the team of dedicated staff led by Andy Leonard, the international manager, a lot of hard work would be going in to improve the facilities, more customers coming through the doors.

Witnessing the progress of projects and meeting staff are two roles that Mike Sheriff considered very important but flying all over the world did have its disadvantages and people thought that jet setting around the globe was glamorous but in the NAAFI locations this was not so. He had seen first-hand the work that had gone into making the establishments the places in which NAAFI staff were proud to work. The investment programme had not finished yet and there were more exciting projects on the horizon. For example, the next year would see the international sector have a renewed focus on EFI and NCS Royal Navy ships are serviced every few years and discussions were underway with the Navy to develop a refurbishment plan for 36 ships that had canteens on board.

Mike and Peter had already had their programme or visits planned for 2001, taking them individually around 13 countries including Bosnia, Kosovo, Cyprus, Brunei, Kenya, the Falklands, Gibraltar, and Saudi Arabia.

2001

New products fill a gap in NAAFI stores

Already a supplier in Cyprus and Falkland Islands, this was the first time that the supermarket giant Tesco had agreed to put its products on the shelves of large in-NAAFI stores in Germany. Some stores will carry a limited range of Tesco food products; this would be to fill the gaps of the current SPAR range. The Tesco own label range meant a larger range and pack sizes, healthy eating products and a wide range of toiletries. The next step, as far as foods were concerned was to introduce the chilled and frozen products. However, this would not be until restrictions on BSE and Foot and mouth disease had been lifted. Just nine stores would have the products and Tesco clothing was introduced to JHQ, Sennelager and Fallingbostel. This was set alongside the sportswear selection that NAAFI selected elsewhere. John Addison, Europe's head of purchasing, stressed the importance of increasing lines and also filling gaps in the SPAR range and the agreement with Tesco's allowed them to do that. Kitchen utensils, toys and confectionery from Tesco were also part of the new products. The move proved to be successful.

EFI need more staff for the Middle East 2001

At the beginning of 2001 the EFI was gearing up to support a major deployment of troops to the Middle East at the end of the summer. Thousands of soldiers would be making their way to the desert for an 8-week exercise, which would involve the biggest deployment of British troops since the Gulf War 10 years previously. Of course, EFI will be right behind them to provide home comforts. An exercise of this size does, however, need to be staffed so an EFI recruitment drive was currently underway. Robin Barrass, international division's HR advisor, said: 'We are looking for experienced NAAFI shop and club staff to join EFI. They would be given full training and development programme in order to meet the challenge of the career in NAAFI's uniform branch. Whether they end up serving in the Middle East, Bosnia, Kosovo, Norway, or Belize, they will enjoy the experience of being at the heart of the welfare of NAAFI provides for HM Forces.'

Ex Saif Sareea II/ Op Veritas 2001 with memories by Sue A Lowe

Thirty-four members of EFI and 26 NCS staff were deployed to Oman to support the tri services training exercise Saif Sareea II. This was the largest deployment of British troops since the Gulf War, 8500 Navy personnel, 12,000 soldiers and 2500 members of the RAF had been living and working in the desert. They had been supported in increasingly difficult conditions, by 11 EFI detachments based across Oman. At sea, NCS staff onboard 8 ships doing what they did best.

Despite the arduous conditions working in the desert, the exercise was meant to be a routine, unusually large, training exercise. On the 11th of September, however, the terrorist attacks on America and ensuing global war on terrorism meant that this Tri service exercise took on a much greater significance.

Oman is situated in the Middle East neighbouring Saudi Arabia, United Arab Emirates and Yemen. Across the Gulf of Oman, the Indian Ocean, lay Pakistan, Iran and beyond that Afghanistan. Despite the uncertain world situation, and soaring temperatures, EFI and NCS staff had continued to serve the services when they need it most, they had earned themselves a great deal of praise into the bargain.

Shortly after the terror attack on the Twin Towers Op Veritas began and the British support of America's attack on the Taliban in Afghanistan had started. In camp South L/Cpl Sue Lowe recalled how the news was broken: I was working in the BIS Camp South just a short drive outside Thumraite. Before I walked the quarter of a mile across the desert to go back to work, I would stop off and grab a cold drink from the EFI tented shop which was next to the cook house. Whilst sat outside minding my own business, two officers came over and started asking who was very good at using the Internet in the Paradigm huts. The Corporal behind the counter pointed me out, so I went with the officers and brought up the BBC News. As the video feed started I actually thought it was some sort of a CGI Film but the officers behind me reassured me that this was happening and it was very real. As I turned my face back to the screen the second plane hit and the officer said, 'It looks like we're going to war.' Everybody that was in the paradigm hut was asked to leave and I left the two officers with the computer and a few brief instructions.

Walking back to the EFI shop in a bit of a daze wondering what to make of what I just seen, then telling my colleagues behind the counter, things were going to get a bit messy. The next day we were all briefed that no one would be going anywhere, and any movements had to be authorised well in advance. It was not long before we had the heads up that the Americans were at the port and we needed to supply stock from the BIS to support them. The trip to the port was a break from being at the BIS and we offloaded the stock into their ISO containers.

Things started to change and issuing stock from the BIS increased and we had to be replenished with cans of pop from a local supplier. The sandy roads were very well worn and often dangerous if you followed exactly the tracks from the vehicles before you. As its heavily laden lorry started to edge slowly closer to the BIS to be unloaded, it stopped just on the other side of a bank of ISO containers and the whole lorry started to slide, dumping hundreds of cans into the sand. Although most of the load stayed on, it still left us an awful mess to clean up before we could unload. But we did it with a bit of help from some of the lads with a couple of cold cans as their reward. Several ISO containers were filled and we spent a number of spare hours in between issuing stock cleaning off the cans, so not all of the spoiled stock was wasted.

It was not long before we were told that our part in the exercise had turned into Op

Veritas, the name 'Veritas' which was on the side of our ISO containers, so we knew where they got the name from – after all we had been surrounded by more than 20 of them since we had been there. From this we knew we would be there a little bit longer than planned but this was part of our job in serving the services.

Op Veritas, When the going gets tough 2001

Heat, sand, and sanitation were problems that had been accounted for before EFI and NCS were deployed. What nobody could have anticipated in the years spent planning the exercise, that war would be waged against terrorism during this time.

The air strikes in Afghanistan started while Mike Sheriff and Lt Col Murray Smith, commanding officer, EFI RLC were in Oman. Mike said: 'On the Tuesday I was there, the

Americans started their operation against the Taliban in Afghanistan and, for the RAF the exercise became a deployment for war. HQ land informed us of Op Veritas, and they asked us to leave three detachments behind, long after the exercise was over at the end of November. In true style EFI staff had already volunteered to switch to the Op and stay to ensure the troops continued to get the support they needed.'

EFI was not only part of the NAAFI contingent in Oman but NCS staff on board HMS Illustrious, Ocean, Fearless, Monmouth, Southampton, Nottingham, Marlborough, and Cornwall were also playing their part. Charles Hill, operations manager, HM ships based in Portsmouth said did he have to communicate with teams on an ad hoc basis, but he got weekly emails from them to report sales figures. With the updates being very detailed.

My time as NAAFI Chairman 2001-2008 Memories by Tony Hales CBE, President of the NEA

I joined NAAFI in September 2001, the week of the 9/11 terror attacks on the Twin Towers in New York, and a week that changed the world and acted as the precursor for the wars in Iraq and Afghanistan, and a week that took our troops, NAAFI, and myself to these hostile places. Actually it was at the second time of application that I was offered the job. On the first application, I had been the runner up so persistence paid off. Having been a Company Sergeant Major in the CCF at school, I had nearly followed on to become a regular officer but in the end chose a commercial career mainly in the alcohol industry. Some people have all the luck! Actually we had a number of links with the military – Lambs Navy Rum with the Royal Navy, Baskin Robbins ice cream in partnership with the Chinese Army, and a winery with the former Viet Cong in Vietnam. In the first Gulf War our Baskin Robbins unit entered Kuwait between two tanks, ahead of the American PX! I was very proud that we were there to support the troops, who had fought their way through the desert but this photograph from Kuwait was met with uninterested disdain by the young financial analysts in London – perhaps that said much for their values.

NAAFI was set up to 'Serve the Services'. It was not set up to make a profit but unless it generates a modest profit it will not generate the money to invest in modern facilities. This is the balance that always presents one of the key challenges for NAAFI.

The Challenge

In 1996 the balance sheet for NAAFI showed net assets of over £100 million, which on my arrival in 2001 had shrunk, due to losses and write-offs to just £13 million

The corporation was continuing to lose money and cash was only available to fund, at its low point, just four more months of trading. There was a serious danger of insolvency and an insolvent NAAFI could not carry out its mission to 'serve the services'. In addition, the accounting centre in Nottingham, where the systems were old but managed by experienced staff, had been closed and the work outsourced to Capita in Darlington, using their people who had previously run the Teachers' Pension Fund. These people had no understanding of a retail operation. The move was a disaster and most of the basic accounting systems and checks had failed, resulting in heavily qualified accounts for 3 years and substantial bills from the auditors and consultants to try to rectify the problem. The image at the Darlington Capita office was one of chaos with a large open plan office stacked with boxes of paper that no one had time to open.

The business operated on the goodwill and honesty of suppliers, who helped themselves via direct debit. It was a wonder the National Audit Office had not held a major investigation.

From a management accounting point of view, we did not know where we had been, or where we were, and therefore planning was not easy!

Other issues included escalating claims for mis-selling insurance policies in the nineties, an onerous property lease in Germany, and an imminent tax inspection covering part-time employees and previous cash payments to suppliers. A pension fund 20 times the size of the corporation demanded careful attention.

On the positive side two good executives had just arrived – a new Chief Executive, Neil McCausland, and a new Finance Director, Chris Reilly, and they were taking steps to grip the situation. The Chief Executive was strongly advocating a strategy that MoD could not accept, involving transfer of public value through MoD granting long leases to NAAFI and then the sale of NAAFI GB with those leases to contractors. Three months after my arrival, the Chief Executive tendered his resignation, after some strong words with the then Deputy Chief of Defence Staff [Personnel] Air Marshal Sir Malcolm Pledger.

The agenda was obvious and dictated by events:

1. Stop the cash out flow to avoid insolvency or administration
2. Restore proper financial control with meaningful accounts
3. Stabilise senior management
4. Agree a strategy to stop losses and give the corporation a sustainable base for the future.

Initial Steps

Taking harsh but simple measures quickly stemmed the cash flow. Dividends, trading stamps in Germany, and capital expenditure were all stopped. Old and excess stock was sold off at reduced prices and new terms were agreed with suppliers. Overheads were cut. Reputational damage to the NAAFI name was considerable and despite much communication by those of us just arrived, we could only marginally mitigate the impact of these painful real cuts. NAAFI – "No ambition and f*** all interest" became an unpleasant, sardonic but understandable explanation of what NAAFI stood for and many an officer drew my attention to this with a cynical smile. They thought I might laugh at the joke but I would rather have cried.

The Chief Executive and Finance Director were bonused on cash and restoring the accounts and the Finance Director spent much time at Darlington, recruiting his own team of managers to take control of the Capita staff. The previous Finance Director had stayed away from Darlington and concentrated on attacking Capita rather than taking responsibility for the mess.

At the end of the year the cash outflow had been stopped and indeed reversed, the auditors signed off the balance sheet, and the first basis for normal control was in place.

With the departure of the recently arrived Chief Executive, who himself had moved on several other senior executives, it was essential to retain what talent we had and so the Finance Director Chris Reilly was appointed Chief Executive and the Finance Controller Clive Warner stepped up to become Finance Director and Shaun Stacey moved up to Head of HR. Shortly afterwards a Commercial Director, Christian Rose, was appointed together with a new Operations Director Milton Guffogg from Woolworths, and new but highly experienced Company Secretary David Mitchell from Allied Domecq, where we had previously worked well together. We had the nucleus of a team.

An initial strategy for survival was not difficult. The business made significant losses in mainland Britain, which overwhelmed the profits earned overseas.

The NAAFI shops and in particular the clubs (in which previous management had invested heavily at the request of the Chain of Command) were an anachronism in GB. There were ample alternatives off camp, where retail prices were lower in the major supermarkets and where the normal attraction for young people of meeting the opposite sex in a pub was possible.

Increased security as a result of terrorist threats had made it very difficult for civilians to come onto camp for casual social occasions as they had traditionally done in the past. The chain of command – in particular the Army – felt it was their right to maintain these facilities as set out in the NAAFI Charter but they had no responsibility for the financial consequences.

At the same time MoD wanted quite rightly to introduce one contractor into each camp to offer messing, retail and leisure services in a pay as you use regime. The old regime of deducting a monthly amount from service people's pay was becoming more and more anachronistic and attacked by the Pay Review Board and politicians, as the average service person took up only half the number of meals for which they had paid. This left a surplus after allowing sufficient food for those who wanted to eat, for MoD to fund operational feeding and even to feed the horses! This had to change despite huge resistance from parts of the chain of command and had to be addressed as part of a total retail, leisure and catering solution.

It seemed obvious to transfer the NAAFI GB operations to contractors as quickly as possible, meanwhile running them for cash with no investment in the short term.

The Overseas Service was different – it was profitable, it was duty free, giving it a competitive advantage, and service people and their families wanted British brands, when serving away from home. MoD also wanted one principal contractor for each overseas site and it seemed sensible for NAAFI to seek to be that contractor. As a first step NAAFI aimed to acquire the Compass Catering rights in Germany as a prelude to negotiating a full multi-activity contract including "pay as you dine". In addition, NAAFI had the unique uniformed branches of EFI/RLC and NCS. These gave the ultimate flexible and responsive service to meet operational needs in times of conflict, at a fraction of the cost a contractor would demand, albeit a recent report on welfare by the Adjutant General had been critical of EFI in Bosnia.

These then were the basic elements of the strategy:

1. To withdraw from the UK as quickly as possible closing little used outlets immediately and running others for cash until transfer.
2. To expand the Overseas Service incorporating messing and offer relevant services improving the brand range and investing in upgraded facilities and new technology.
3. To reduce costs significantly.

Gaining approval for an essentially no brainer strategy, however, proved a frustrating experience as layers of consultation and indeed objection to any loss of facility had to be handled.

Having submitted the strategy proposals and seen these wallowing in bureaucratic mire I exploded at the NAAFI Council, our governing body. The Council included Deputy Chief of Defence Staff (Personnel) in the chair – Sir Malcolm Pledger, the Second Sea Lord – Sir Peter Spencer (supported by a Commodore – Peter Wilkinson, who in due course became DCDS[Pers] himself), the Adjutant General – Sir Tim Granville Chapman (supported by a Brigadier), the Air Marshal Personnel Sir Christopher Colville (supported by an Air Commodore). In attendance were the NAAFI Service Representatives, a Naval Commander, Army Colonel and RAF Group Captain plus DCDS Pers Aide, an Army Captain. This was a formidable military group, sporting much spaghetti from their shoulders (a group much reduced after changes introduced by Malcolm Pledger's successor). No progress was being made and so I hit the table and remarked I had 'never seen so many important people with such important titles (four Knights of the Realm), spend so much time failing to take any decision at all about a bunch of corner shops'. Unless a decision was made and made soon, the organisation would be bankrupt and 'while my name as a director would be on the list of those responsible so would their names be – as shadow directors'. This obtained attention and apparently caused no offence; in fact, to my relief and surprise this rather petulant outburst had created some respect and was treated positively.

The Defence Management Board duly endorsed the strategy with an exit date from GB of 2005 agreed. We were on our way. The executive team were young, inexperienced but bright, energetic and determined. They were supported by some excellent non-executives – Vic Steele (Deputy Chair), Alan Cole, Terry Morgan and not least the former Quarter Master General and Chief Royal Engineer Lt General Sir Scott Grant – all of whom put in considerable extra time to support the executives including fronting some of the negotiations with suppliers and partners.

Great Britain

I had great respect for David McKenzie, and his team in GB for steadily closing down their part of the business – over £100 million in turnover – while maintaining morale and standards at a very respectable level. The retail outlets all traded under the Spar banner so many people thought NAAFI had already closed down and had handed over to Spar. The Spar concept was sound. It was not a particularly good brand in relation to Tesco or Sainsbury, but it was the best amongst the convenience retailers. Having Spar meant that we needed very little support infrastructure as once the overall contract was agreed then day-to-day buying, ranging, pricing, promotion activity and IT support were all provided by Spar and its wholesale partners. We were the largest franchisee of the Spar brand in the UK, and so important to them, and overall we were given pretty good service, particularly as the business was being run down.

The closedown inevitably took longer than agreed, as MoD Contracts Department could not negotiate all the contracts over the agreed 3-year timescale. Most of the 340 sites, of which the army used 215, were transferred to Compass and Sodexo, with the latter proving much more straightforward to deal with compared to Compass. The larger better sites tended to go first, inevitably leaving a progressively harder tail. Under "pay as you dine" the customers now paid for their meals, these attracted VAT, which removed a significant slice of money previously available for food, with the consequence that customers complained about portion size and the contractors found they could not make the returns they expected. In our view MoD's consultants had failed to adequately identify this problem and the whole programme was slowed down until a fresh injection of more realistic funding was agreed. We insisted all employees were transferred over under TUPE and that we received fair payment for any assets with Shaun Stacey fronting the negotiations for NAAFI. In the end the final sites were transferred to Aramark in 2008 after twice the agreed time. This protracted handover did NAAFI's reputation no good as in the absence of any real capital expenditure in GB, these outlets looked progressively more run down until the date of final handover.

Some investment was made in the main RAF sites, which tended to be away from towns for obvious reasons and where the number of service people on camp was higher, making them more attractive for NAAFI compared to, for example, small army sites near towns. Brize Norton as the gateway for troops going on operation was significantly improved particularly in the air terminal itself. In the long term we wanted a new "deal" with the RAF sites in GB – the old model was broken but a wider MAC contact was our aim. MoD contracts department were always against with one reason regularly quoted that we would fall foul of EU laws preventing state aid, being used to support state companies in competition with the private sector. We continued to retain a useful part of the 1500 amusement machines business to retain sufficient buying power worldwide and to help the military control the contractors.

The one area where money had to be spent widely was Health & Safety. On one of my first visits with Dave McKenzie, he received a phone call to say one of our staff had received a severe electrical shock at Brize Norton. We went there immediately and found a combination of poor electrics and a leaking roof had proved near fatal. Due to budget pressures the military were reluctant to deal with these issues and their status within the Crown gave them some cover unavailable to non-state organisations. This was unacceptable. We surveyed every outlet and my message was if at all unsafe then close it until they fix it – no compromise – how could it be otherwise? The general standard of army quarters was bad as we heard in graphic detail at the Army Family Federation conferences, when the wives did not mince their words. It has improved steadily over my time at NAAFI with large MoD investment.

In terms of experiences, the visits to RAF Cranwell and RAF Valley on Anglesey were undoubted highlights. Cranwell was the RAF Officer Training School and an opportunity to have a first flying lesson in a trainer on a slightly overcast autumn day.

Anglesey was very different as we were taken up on a Hawk Jet training flight. It was May with a clear blue sky and while the sun was very hot, the sea was cold. We therefore had to wear 7 layers of clothing in case we ditched in the sea. It was boiling inside those clothes, and the heat together with the G force made me feel very queasy as we twisted and turned, contouring at low level through the Welsh valleys. As the G force forced the blood away from the head, my vision narrowed and turned grey until the effects of the G suit kicked in and countered the G force, pushing the blood up from abdomen to head again. The rules were simple – if you were going to be sick, take off the mask, use the bag and then put the mask back on. The previous NAAFI visitor had disgraced himself and us by failing to remove his mask in time with very unpleasant consequences for himself and the cabin, as he had to continue breathing through the mask until he landed! When we landed the feeling was a mixture of exhilaration and pride as I walked feeling like Tom Cruise in Top Gun next to my very attractive female pilot, and at the same time aware of the need to make the men's room quickly but looking casual!

One of the main armed forces charities in the UK was SSAFA and we gave what support we could mainly through the annual carol service in the Guards Chapel at Wellington Barracks. This was a great occasion and a real start to the Christmas season. It was organised by the most senior officers' wives and a real credit to them all, not least the long serving senior wife Lady Mary Stirrup, always a very gracious host. It was just one example of the tremendous amount of voluntary work, army wives put in to support the armed forces, and in this case particularly to provide some support to the many service people and their families who suffer from injury or, as too many do, find it difficult to adjust to civilian life and end up living rough on the streets.

Germany

In Germany the business progressed with the support of each of the three General Officers in Command over the seven years, Generals Moore-Bick, Bill, and Melville. The NAAFI business was always profitable and we were aligned with the Generals in wanting to see BFG (British Forces Germany) benefit from the support that they gave NAAFI. Whether it was dividend or the gain share generated from catering, there was always pressure from their masters in GB to return a good portion for use elsewhere, where it had no value to the NAAFI reputation. Gain share payments from the contractors in GB were minimal, and in a way we were subsidising that failure.

Buying out the Compass interest in the catering in 2003 was an early target and proved relatively easy, with Sir Scott and Chris Reilly strong negotiators for NAAFI.

The command supported this move to give NAAFI full control over the catering as it eased communication, removed a possible SOFA anomaly and standards of service were raised. The contract with British Forces Germany was now operated with reasonable give and take to benefit both parties rather than a basis for a minimum standard to which every variation was of benefit to the supplier.

Long and detailed negotiations ensued in 2004 to agree the multi-activity contract incorporating 'Pay as you Dine' at Elmpt station. NAAFI conducted substantive market research with different customer groups to develop a model that fitted the customer as opposed to the consultant's 'production led' model developed in the UK for worldwide implementation. Elmpt was the most successful trial both in terms of customer satisfaction and financial viability, as confirmed by the MoD Project Head Brigadier Andy Mantell. The Elmpt format, contract and process provided the model for roll out for PAYD across Germany to Fallingbostel, Hohne, Paderborn, Munster, Gütersloh and Rhine. Each time careful research was carried out to ascertain the needs of our customers. The army chefs were also key, particularly the staff sergeants who had to change from delivering food in an efficient way to their juniors – with all that that meant – to treating their customers as just that – paying customers expecting choice and service – and to take responsibility for the profit or loss of their site. They quickly grasped the opportunity presented and realised that the extra training and experience they were receiving would enhance their value in Civvy Street. I really think the relationship that NAAFI had with the armed services made this new relationship more successful than with any other contractor.

At each new PAYD location the issue of squadron bars and local Christian-related shops proved a sensitive issue. To justify the investment in new facilities NAAFI started to sell newspapers, previously the sole prerogative of the CVWW (Christian/ pastoral care) organisation's shops and NAAFI insisted on some limitation to the sales by squadron bars. This issue of squadron bars is a perpetual thorny issue as squadron bar profits, reliant on free junior rank labour, go directly to the unit and are therefore encouraged by unit commanders at the expense of the NAAFI offer, where any profits go up the chain. The loss of newspapers and the associated sales was a hammer blow to part of the CVWW operation, resulting in shop closures in Germany, and ensured their strong opposition to NAAFI for some time.

An unseen part of the catering operation was the schools. NAAFI provided seven thousand meals per day in the schools delivering high nutritional and dietary standards. It was heartening that the uptake of meals in our school catering was significantly higher than in the schools in GB, where the usual list of contractors provided the food.

On the retail side the stores in Germany were functional but dated. Interior fittings were old-fashioned and the exterior signage was a hotchpotch of names, MAX, Local, Family, NAAFI, with a mix of colour designs from NAAFI's history. It symbolised the issue of pride in the name. There was a brief debate as to whether the NAAFI name should be kept not least given its unfortunate interpretations to some. I felt strongly that this was our name, it had been our name for most of a century, it was part of military culture, and it had huge awareness. The challenge was not to find a new name but to make the name NAAFI positive once more with a team proud to work for NAAFI. The red, white and blue logo style was introduced on all paper and promotion material, and on the exterior of our stores. The product range was strengthened with a large Tesco range being added to the Spar range.

Customer reaction was overwhelmingly favourable as Tesco products were seen as the benchmark of the British shopping trolley now brought to Germany by NAAFI. The Commercial Director, now Nigel Samuels, an intelligent strategist and good negotiator, led further changes to the offer.

A real effort was made to introduce a proper range of fresh products – fruit, vegetables, salads and meats. The long supply chain made this much harder than I ever expected. Product was being received in store in Germany from warehouses in the UK with only 2 days of shelf life left on a regular basis.

Write downs and write offs were high. The outbreaks of Foot and Mouth disease were hugely damaging with all meat supplies from Britain stopped for a long period including chilled ready meals and some dairy products. An over enthusiastic Belgian official even consigned a load of 'beef' tomatoes to the skip! The buying team worked hard to slowly improve the range, expanding books, toys, healthcare, children's clothes from Mothercare, Iceland value frozen food packs and continually seeking to add UK High Street brands to create interest and excitement in the stores. With a much smaller catchment population than a normal high street shop, mistakes were punished with significant write offs. Electrical goods were always an important challenge; there were initial interest points but new ranges and lowering prices made range and stock selection critical.

As our ranges and pricing improved so did the standards of the German competitors off base, with UK products and English speaking staff increasingly prevalent. That's life; competition acts to spur change and responsiveness to consumers' needs.

A major programme of store investment was rolled out under the project name 'Store of the Future'. The impact was terrific with new lighting, new fixtures, and new floors bringing standards up to those our customers enjoyed at home. The early stores were over engineered and high cost, but experience led to reduced budgets. Meanwhile operational disciplines led by John Douglass, who succeeded Milton Guffogg, were demonstrably improved with the help of better systems.

In 2002 our staff still had to individually price each item. There were no EPOS systems in our overseas operations. It was incredible to see our staff wasting time on pricing each item, a practice long since gone in normal retailing. The lack of an EPOS system also meant less data, later data, and much greater opportunity for human error with stocks and pricing. A priority project (Project Power) was the introduction of the chosen Navision system, initially tested in Cyprus then rolled out through Germany, with few teething problems.

The frustrating aspect to all this work on delivering a better offer to customers was that this was being done against a backcloth of a declining customer base. Troop numbers permanently based in Germany were declining, with base closures at Osnabruck and JHQ [Rhine] planned. Of those troops based in Germany, more were away on operational tours due to the increased tempo of activity in Iraq and Afghanistan. More families were choosing to stay in the UK rather than face life in Germany with an absent father away on operations. Lifestyles were also changing with health, education and restrictions affecting cigarette and alcohol sales, two of NAAFI's stalwart product areas. Better single soldier accommodation (Project Slam), replacing old dormitory blocks, was being rolled out with internet access in the individual rooms, encouraging more time to be spent in quarters communicating with family and friends on the internet, or downloading a film or entertainment online, while eating a snack from the 24 hour vending machine. The old smoke-filled traditional pub became a memory like a sepia photograph in quick time.

To remain relevant NAAFI has to keep responding to these changed customer needs and work with the chain of command to meet its changing customer needs but in a sustainable financial manner.

Bosnia

In 2001, Bosnia was the main operational theatre for British forces. I travelled with Lt Col Murray Smith, Commanding Officer of EFI or 148 Squadron Royal Logistic Corps. Col Smith was a former paratrooper rising through the ranks; he had served under the future Chief of the General Staff General Sir Mike Jackson, as a Sergeant Major in Northern Ireland and had fought in the Falklands. He left the regular Army as a Major and was appointed Lt Colonel to Head EFI. He was a soldier's soldier and his rank, size, experience and paratrooper wings gave him instant respect and presence wherever he went. He knew little about the detail of retailing but given an obvious problem to fix, staff to deploy or a meeting to arrange, Murray would sort it. He was a popular leader of his little team. Peter Bott supported him commercially. Bott was the antithesis of Murray, a short scruffy man, whose preferred dress was tee shirt and jeans. This unhappy clash of differing styles was a recurring issue in EFI operations as the combination of a commercial retailer and effective military operator was rarely natural in one person.

We moved swiftly through the airport on our identity cards and my 'equivalent rank', stamped by someone on my boarding card as a two-star general, together with Murray's impressive physical presence, made passage very straightforward. Bosnia was in a state of military occupation. Fighting had ceased but the evidence of war was visible everywhere – damaged buildings, bullet marked walls, minefields and giant minefield clearing machines, plus fresh graveyards with rows of little crosses to mark the dead, and roads dominated by military vehicles. Republica Serbska operated as a state within a state at this time and it had its own government, taxes, police force, signs and so on. All the images of Bosnia on the TV were of war and suffering, yet its countryside was beautiful with an Austrian landscape ideal for walking – except walking was impossible beyond the roads due to the extensive minefields sown by every party with few records and no regard for the longer term consequences

The Commanding Officer for EFI in Bosnia was Maj Nigel Edwards, a nice man who lived in a Corimex container with a king size mattress next to his office and shop in the small British base at Sipovo. On weekend leave he retained a flat and boat at the seaside in Croatia, an interesting lifestyle mix. Very sadly he died suddenly running NAAFI in Kenya two years later. His parents were rightly proud of their son and indeed his commission as an officer in EFI.

We also employed a significant number of local Bosnians, many well educated but we had jobs and good pay, two things that were rather absent in their communities. The Sipovo base had 2 regiments who had to have separate bars as a good night together was characterised by a good punch up.

The international headquarters base in Sarajevo was a great mixture of European nationalities, with each nation having its own NAAFI equivalent, on what might be described as a military shopping mall. The NAAFI pub was without doubt the best leisure outlet, popular with all nationalities and pulsated with music, life and humour, a contrast to the atmosphere in the city.

As we headed out of the capital to the British Zone, a building collapsed just yards behind us due to the vibration of a passing lorry. Maj Edwards and the driver were fully armed and always careful to adhere to proscribed routes, without stopping, and ensuring they were timed in and out of camp. The population seemed depressed and down-beaten but not hostile to us and indeed our local Bosnian staff, were invariably over qualified for our shop work having previously worked as teachers or nurses, but now delighted to have a job earning, in local terms, good money. They ran a winning football team, soon to be equipped in Aston Villa colours.

NAAFI ran half a dozen units at the various British camps including the British HQ at Banja Luka, Mckonijgrad, Sipovo and Sarajevo. These were either in Corimex constructions or in factory shells, occupied by our forces. The offer was reasonable in a workman-like way given the surroundings but could be better. There was a fair range, adequate stocks, basic but tidy facilities and a generally enthusiastic team. The main issue was pricing, a regular complaint sometimes fair as we failed to match local competition on key lines like cigarettes or toiletries and sometimes unfair as customers chose to forget the long, expensive and at times hazardous supply chain compared to a high street discount retailer at home.

This was my first experience of seeing British Forces at war first-hand. They had done a remarkable job stopping the fighting and systemised killing of civilians in ethnic cleansing drives by all sides. They had done this based in tented camps in the snow with very poor welfare facilities as the Adjutant General had remarked in his report. We at NAAFI had to be better prepared in future for sudden deployments. Having stopped the war, our forces were now engaged on the longer task of creating peace, re-building communications and ultimately creating a new state. This required great improvisation, diplomacy and leadership – all attributes in which British Forces excel.

Northern Ireland

The transformation of Northern Ireland has been incredible to observe. My first visit was as a 15 year old Corporal in the Army Cadets based out of Ballykinler. We hiked and lived in tents wearing full army uniform across beautiful country that was soon to become no go land as the troubles erupted and escalated. In 2001 the NAAFI at Girdwood Camp between the Shankhill and Falls Road was one of the most physically oppressive and dangerous locations we had. It made Sarajevo look really good and this on our very doorstep, part of the UK. The razor wire, sandbags, metal barriers and shields reaching into the sky at angles, to prevent sniper bullets from the surrounding flats entering its heart, dominated the appearance of the camp. This was the architecture of war – hard, functional, aggressive and vulgar.

It contrasted with the incredible humanity found inside the NAAFI, which was overcrowded, scruffy, vibrant and noisy with the banter of service people.

The heart of the NAAFI was the staff led by two remarkably brave young girls Nicky and Eva – one Protestant, the other Catholic. They came to work through the hospital, entering the front door and then slipping out the back to enter the camp. This charade disguised the true identity of their work from the divided community outside. They left by taxi, normally in a hail of stones. Had they been discovered, their lives were at risk; indeed a disabled boy who worked at the camp as a catering assistant had recently been murdered for working for the British Forces. Their families did not even know the true nature of their work. They loved their work and their customers and ran an excellent operation both functionally and in providing a place where soldiers could relax and enjoy some normality out of hours. Other staff faced regular danger. Michelle was entering Rockwood camp when a bomb at the gates blew her and her NAAFI van into the camp. The auditors travelled by helicopter to access the bases for stock checks. The NAAFI at Omagh became a temporary mortuary after the devastating bomb there. NAAFI operated on all the camps in Northern Ireland through 33 outlets, and with 20,000 troops confined to camp in their leisure hours, these outlets were profitable unlike their counterparts on the mainland.

As the peace process evolved and Northern Ireland returned to normality once more, troop numbers fell to 3,000 and they were no longer confined to camp. Weekends starting at midday on Friday and ending at 1000hrs on Monday, together with cheap Ryanair flights meant many weekends were spent back home with families. NAAFI's sales and profits fell to match those in Great Britain. The wonderful transformation of Northern Ireland meant NAAFI had the same problems as on the mainland, and therefore NAAFI needed to exit or be paid for continuing to operate in the province.

Kosovo

Having learnt the consequences of delay in Bosnia, the international community had moved more quickly in Kosovo to separate the Albanian ethnic Kosovars from the minority Serbs, who controlled this country. Kosovo was effectively under United Nations military rule, with a substantial United Nations civilian aid presence.

The UN Force KFOR was a truly international force. It was astonishing to arrive at Pristina Airport to be met by Nigerian Security Forces on the apron, Bangladeshi soldiers on passport control, and Filipinos guarding the parking area, all supervising a babbling collection of military and aid workers from all over Europe and America as they progressed into the country. We are used to Europeans intervening in Africa or Asia at times of conflict but here in Europe were Africans and Asians helping us sort out our long-standing problems. Here was the third world helping the first – well why not, we can all learn to learn from each other?

Col Murray and I quickly completed the checks and met our Maj Andy Stone, EFI CO in Kosovo. We stayed in the usual Corimex quarters at the main British Camp in Pristina.

Although neighbouring Bosnia, Kosovo was very different physically. It was flat and featureless in terms of geography so man-built structures stood out. These were ugly. The main feature was the power station, restored by the TA after the war, and belching filthy smog into the air from its boilers using coal from the equally ugly open pits nearby. When the wind was right, the city was engulfed in an unpleasant sulphurous smelling cloud. Pristina was a provincial town of Soviet era tower blocks, crumbling and now featuring bullet and mortar scars. It was off limits and had little obvious attraction.

We had operations on 4 sites, all of which were in a reasonable state, mainly operating out of the standard Corimex units. The one extraordinary site was Film City alongside the international force headquarters. Film City was a road of military shops from different nations – British, French, USA, Italian, German, Dutch, Austrian, Canadian and more. Each store had evolved from a general military store to focus on the product lines where it had greatest competitive advantage. The French had the best cigarette offer, the Austrians the best café, and the NAAFI the best electricals. We dominated the electrical sales on the strip with a great range and great prices. Ninety percent of sales plus were to Non-Brits, which gave the local command some concern, but this was a real market, where real trading could yield real profits. Film City was the main recreational place in Pristina available to military personnel and only military personnel and accredited visitors. Every nationality could be seen there – Poles, Finns, Czechs, Italians in designer shades, the Russian comfort platoon in lipstick, Bangladeshis, Filipinos, and Africans as well as all the nationalities represented by the stores. This was the UN shopping and window-shopping.

The peacekeepers were a huge industry in Kosovo, the main industry and the main source of economic activity for a nervous and subdued population, with little other real work. They brought peace but for many of the peacekeepers from Asia and Africa this was also a welcome holiday, a chance to earn real money, and a chance to be properly clothed and equipped at UN expense.

Returning in 2008 with the CO of EFI, Kosovo was transformed. The airport was like any other small international airport. There was no overt military presence on the roads, now bustling with normal traffic. The roadside shops were flourishing with products spilling onto the pavements, including much counterfeit. There was less pollution and the people moved about their daily lives with a vibrancy that did not exist on my last visit. There was only a small contingent of British forces in a part of one camp with one NAAFI shop and two bars. The main concern was that Serbian elections would produce a more hard-line government creating tensions in the border areas. That did not happen and indeed the new Serbian government delivered the former Bosnian Serb leader Radovan Karajzic to The Hague. I returned on a flight sitting next to the new Kosovar Prime Minister, Hashim Thaci, a former warlord now seeming at ease in his new role and looking the total politician in elegant mohair tailored suit. The intervention of the multinational force with its vital British element had stopped the war and was well on the way to delivering peace and normality for the people of Kosovo, a huge success in this tinder bowl of European conflict over the years.

Cyprus

The British Forces had had a long-term presence in Cyprus. At the time of independence in 1960 it was agreed that Britain would retain two sovereign bases on the island governed by the British Forces Commander responsible directly to the Crown. The Akrotiri base included the military airfield, military port, and was an important listening post and staging post for the Middle East. Many of the service people returning from Theatre would spend a few days here on decompression before returning to their families at home.

Britain had a second major base on the east of the island at Dhekelia and some smaller satellites including the mountain training camp on Mt Trudos. There was also a small UN force policing the boundary between the Turkish and Greek sectors.

NAAFI had two big supermarkets amongst its 11 retail outlets and 8 leisure outlets. The operation was second in profitability only to Germany. However, pressures on margins started to build prior to the issuing of a Multi Activity Contract.

Cyprus had clung to the traditional trade structure of sole importer / wholesalers, which perpetuated a form of retail price maintenance. For example, only one wholesaler, who limited price competition by retailers, would import all Cadbury chocolate products, another would have sole rights for Nestle and so on. Retail margins were generally healthy, and the independent trade was protected from the buying power of the multiples, being used to price aggressively to gain consumer market share. These barriers to new market entry and market competition had to be broken as part of the conditions for Cypriot entry to the European Union in 2004. As the barriers broke down the Greek Cypriot supermarkets competed much more aggressively, and international retailers entered the country. Margins reduced but NAAFI could not respond by competing for more volume, as its customer base was strictly limited to the British Service community, which was shrinking both in actual service people and the proportion of dependants. As in Germany families were increasingly reluctant to leave home if the soldier was to be away on regular lengthy operations.

In these more testing market conditions, NAAFI had responded with investment in the stores and in new technology, which had had a positive impact with customers, but the market was driving margins down. Our staff were remarkably loyal. There was a strong core of people, who had worked for forty years for the company – both Greek and Turks united by their work as in Northern Ireland, despite the tensions between the communities. They were slow to change and the union had great power, which supported by government enforced national wage settlements was driving wage inflation ahead of price inflation.

Against this background, MoD issued an invitation to tender for a multi-activity contract for the island. NAAFI had had no prior warning, although this contract had major implications for the pub business, and some implications for the retail business. We were concerned as our business was being cut piece by piece. We asked MoD if we could tender for this MAC but were told only if the MAC could include our retail. This was a difficult call for the Board – did we risk losing a profitable albeit declining retail business to win a larger multi-activity contract against large established international competitors? We believed we had certain tax and cost advantages that would outweigh the better purchasing power of the competition. We believed we understood the market better than the competition. We believed winning would not only secure Cyprus but would establish NAAFI as a credible MAC player elsewhere. On the downside the bid costs would be high, and we had no experience of mounting a competitive bid. The Board decided to bid, recognising the risks.

Our bid was price competitive but was considered technically below Sodexo and Compass. In hindsight our mistakes were in not recognising sufficiently the risks of entering a bid process without experience. There was no doubt we could have presented a better case in the highly prescriptive and structured process with the benefit of this learning. Most people in NAAFI firmly believed that we had put forward a better proposition for the customers on the ground, but the bid had been lost in the process. We may have benefited from more external support but the die was cast. We now had to hand over Cyprus to Sodexo and their retail partner Ermes. Shaun Stacey, our HR Director and now leading Change Management, led the handover with great diplomacy and skill. Service levels were maintained, our employees were treated fairly, and we extracted a good price for our assets. It was a sad day to leave our loyal employees, but it was possible, given the pressures in the market and on NAAFI's cash flow that this was not such a bad out turn economically. In reality the extra capital expenditure and working capital required to implement the contract would have put further pressure on NAAFI's balance sheet at a time when other significant pressures came to bear.

Iraq

It was clear from the reports of our early efforts in the Balkans that NAAFI needed to be more prepared with better equipment for any future major operational deployment. Some early drawings had been made previously of a potential rapid deployment system. I pushed the executive to resurrect these ideas and move forward to a prototype. In 2002, the first prototypes RDS (Rapid Deployment System) 1, 2 and 3 were produced. RDS 1 was essentially a cash box and basic stock to operate from a table in a tent or off a truck, with RDS 3 a container that would fit on a standard container lorry or be moved by helicopter. Its walls dropped down to create a floor, from which a large tent could be pumped up to contain a basic bar and shop fitting. It was a huge step forward, offering a good welfare facility within a few hours of being dropped off. It was tested on exercise in the Balkans and then slightly modified units made for storage and maintained for action.

In March 2003 our armed forces went into action, against the tyrannical regime of Saddam Hussein. Our supply chain team had already done a tremendous job in stocking the fleet at very short notice. Two of those key individuals, Taffy Davies and Charles Hill, were later awarded

MBEs for this and other great work for NAAFI over many years. Our team entered Umm Qasr not far behind the lead troops in Operation Telic.

As the oil wells burned, the shattered hulks of Iraq armour lay in the desert, and the huge guns of the Allied artillery fired, our team, in their tent and truck, were never far from the front, and well ahead of their American equivalents, in dispensing those basic comforts such as cigarettes, shower gel, cold drinks and even condoms to keep the sand out of a rifle or a nether part. These simple basics were important to our soldiers' morale in their mission in hostile conditions of heat and sand. The dangers of chemical weapon attacks were considered very serious and regular drills were carried out wearing the even hotter uncomfortable protective masks and equipment. The EFI team carried full weapons though did not normally fire them operationally, but apart from that they experienced the full rigours of a fighting army in desert warfare.

At home we ensured no wife or dependant of a serving soldier was laid off due to falling sales resulting from customers now transferred to Iraq. We could not add to their worries for their loved ones by taking away their pocket money and social work interaction. This was not a commercial decision, but it was entirely in keeping with the NAAFI mission to serve the services.

The conventional war was quickly over and the initial British presence was welcomed in the Basra region. NAAFI now moved to establish more permanent facilities, to replace our RDS units, which had served their purpose well. The main British camp was being established at Shaibah, an old British Air Force base in WWII, and not far from Basra International Airport. Kelly operated a small NAAFI with great resourcefulness, from tables and primitive racking in one of the old buildings.

However, it was agreed with PJHQ (Permanent Joint Head Quarters) that we would build a large retail shop and a large club facing each other in an area designated for recreation. Two prefabricated buildings were shipped out and a Turkish contractor hired to erect them on footings prepared by the Army Engineers. All was set for a December opening in time for Christmas.

Early in December my wife and I were guests at a dinner held by the Chief of Defence Staff General Sir Mike Walker. I told him we were close to opening and that I wanted to visit Shaibah to review our offering.

The following week I was heading for a lunch in London, when the mobile phone rang. It was Tuesday 16th December and on the phone was an assistant to the CDS. He said there was a plane going to where I wanted to go the following morning, leaving early from Northolt. For security reasons he could give no further detail but did I want a seat and would I arrive at 7am? Yes. I cancelled all engagements for the rest of the week and headed home in the evening for suitable clothes. A sharp start in the morning saw me in the VIP lounge at Northolt.

On arrival I was briefed. This was a Ministerial Visit by the Minister for the Armed Forces, Adam Ingram, his aide plus the Shadow Secretary of State for Defence Nicholas Soames and accompanying press. We would fly out on a BAe 146 aircraft of the Royal Squadron, returning

Friday night with additionally Michael Howard, Leader of the Opposition. We would need two stops each way to refuel, one in Bari, Italy and the other in Cyprus. Adam Ingram had held the post of Armed Forces Minister for several years; he knew the issues, enjoyed the role and had a good rapport with the forces at all levels. He was a very approachable man with no hint of the pomposity of state office. I liked him. Soames was last onto the plane, larger than life in every sense, and clutching 2 large bottles of Premier Cuvee Winston Churchill Champagne, one for each way. Winston Churchill was his grandfather. I had known Nick, as a Junior Minister of Agriculture, in the previous government. Behind his highly entertaining façade was a man who understood the forces having served as a Captain in the Army, and who cared greatly about their welfare. His personality could have upstaged the Minister's more reserved character, but he observed total decorum in never seeking to upstage his host. Despite their different party backgrounds there was clearly a mutual respect between these two politicians. To travel in such luxury was a far cry from previous or future military flights and the company was highly agreeable.

We arrived in Basra in the early evening, after our two scheduled refuelling stops. The aircraft had entered the airport in a steep gradient with all lights out to minimise risk of rocket attack. After we landed, I left the group who were met by the GOC and ambassador and taken for a briefing.

My reception team were nowhere to be seen so I checked into the airport facilities, found a bunk and took a short rest before EFI Detachment Commander Maj Scottie McNair arrived and found me. Scottie was an ex-army regular, he feared nothing, liked driving and a bit of bother, and was good at liaison with the military and fixing but had no interest in retailing or helping in store. We travelled 40 minutes to Shaibah over a mixture of road and track. There were no signs and to become lost was not difficult.

However, moving we required 2 vehicles and 4 armed EFI personnel. We all wore body armour and helmets. All movements required 2 vehicles and each vehicle had to have an armed driver and support person. It was expensive in manpower to move anywhere off base. At Shaibah, a camp housing 3500 personnel, I was shown to my VIP tent, actually the same as everyone else's tent except I had it to myself. The landscape outside was bleak grey / brown flat desert illuminated by the flares from the oil derricks.

We had a team meeting the following morning, we had 45 people in Theatre. I arrived full of enthusiasm but it was obvious at first sight we had a problem. Half the team had been in EFI Bosnia and were hardened to working in tough conditions, the other half were straight from our shops in the UK and had little idea of what to expect. Most of these had never been abroad, let alone lived in tents, with basic latrines, in a desolate, blisteringly hot country. They had not been properly briefed, they did not like what they found, and the gung-ho camaraderie of the veterans was alienating them further. In addition, the buildings were not yet ready, and we had no power, so they were unable to do their job.

I rang Shaun Stacey and asked him to liaise with our country manager, Chris Malcolmson, to offer extra support and a loyalty bonus for our team to give them a lift and then turned to the issue of power. The Army Engineers would not connect the buildings, as the wiring put in by the Turkish contractors did not conform to British standards. Our Property Director, who was on site, had tried a range of persuasion techniques with the Royal Engineers from beer to threats. The Staff Sergeant could/would not move his schedule and his Corporal offered to adjust Phil Howe's face, when threatened by Howe.

This was not going well. I rang Scott Grant and asked for help. A call to the Colonel in charge of the Royal Engineers in Iraq followed. Lt Col Baillis was based at Basra airport. "Lt Gen Sir Scott Grant, the Chief Royal Engineer, and I think your titular boss, said he would be very grateful if you could help NAAFI." The reaction to my reluctant bombastic approach was electric and the engineers worked all day and night to give us power. Regimental funds were given a decent donation and good humour was restored. We now had one day to clean, merchandise, and decorate a supermarket and pub.

With the imminent arrival of power, a special staff bonus agreed with the HR Director in the UK, a deadline to meet and a Chairman working alongside each girl in turn, morale was visibly lifting in the team. Everyone worked flat out. New stock arrived on trucks, the frozen goods had to be moved quickly by hand chain into refrigerated containers given the heat. A consignment of clothes arrived on an open lorry, the tee shirts ruined by rain, the shoes salvageable without boxes. There was no Brasso and I was despatched to borrow vinegar from the cookhouse and finished the day smelling like a chip shop. We knew we had won when Linda Edwards, one of those fantastically cheerful and capable women who present the very best of NAAFI value to the customer, gave me the fairy to put on top of the Christmas tree – a very surreal and funny moment given the location and setting! Outside, the Turkish contractors had also downed tools over a spat with Howe but returned later to finish the pathways just in time. We were exhausted, indeed Linda slept the night in the bar in her working clothes. We hardly looked our parts, when the Senior Colonel arrived the following morning to see all was in order for the Minister's visit. Col Smith, tall, lean, ramrod back and lantern jawed found me sprawled over a table and received a one word reply "f***d", when asked how we were. But both places looked great, we had somewhere for the people on camp to use over Christmas and we were ready for the Minister to formally open the new Oasis Bar and NAAFI Store.

The Oasis Bar had a collection of Premier League Football memorabilia. As a director of Aston Villa, I had asked each club to send us something for Iraq – every club did with some very nice letters.

Adam Ingram opened the NAAFI complex on Friday morning and retail sales in the first 3 hours were £10,000. In addition to Nick Soames, Michael Howard was now in the party and obtaining more media attention than the Minister, to the obvious discomfort of officials. Shortly afterwards we all flew, accompanied by some very heavy duty security men, by Chinook helicopter fast and low from Shaibah to Basra airport to travel back to the UK in the Royal Squadron Jet. Michael Howard was also good company, a keen Liverpool supporter, he knew Doug Ellis of Aston Villa, knew and liked America, and was clearly a man whose real charm is not communicated through TV. Soames of course ate most of the cakes on the plane, hoovering up any left by the rest of us. This was a rather extraordinary but effective 60-hour experience.

As the security situation deteriorated, life became progressively harder for our people in Iraq and personal security issues were a very real threat. A young Bulgarian lorry driver delivering NAAFI supplies had his goods stolen and his throat cut. Children regularly stoned our staff as they travelled between bases and the supply route from Kuwait became progressively more dangerous. The bases were under constant mortar attack, meaning nights regularly interrupted by the need to don protective clothing and take precautionary action. Our staff worked long hours and then had little real sleep. Yet some would return again and again to look after their boys.

Cpl Tracey McKenzie ran the NAAFI store in Basra Palace, the last outpost of British Forces to close beyond Basra Airbase. It was impossible to send stock by road due to the security situation. So she received her stock in the middle of the night by helicopter drop, which she then had to de-palletise and get moved into store. Her stores were blown up by mortar on 3 occasions, fortunately with no one in them at the time. The base received up to 100 mortars in one 24-hour period. Yet in her next posting in Kosovo, she scarcely bothered to mention her experiences. Shop girl, NAAFI girl, and a quiet hero who deserves recognition.

Major Lynn Cassidy was another hero. Lynn was everyone's perfect mum. Her husband was in the army and her two sons were in the army. At one stage they were all in Iraq together and had for those of us who live normal lives, pretty unusual family meetings. Lynn gave a very matter of fact but moving presentation to the board on a day in the life of a NAAFI officer in Iraq. She did tour after tour in Iraq and Afghanistan and was another of our heroes, worthy of recognition.

At the peak NAAFI had nine outlets in Iraq, which by 2008 had reduced to one at Basra Airbase. Adam Ingram asked for and received the opening plaque from Shaibah, when the complex closed in 2007. His genuine commitment stood out amongst the merry go round of ministers at MoD.

Afghanistan

Our flight to Afghanistan in November 2004 was on that old workhorse – a Hercules. My travelling companions were Mike Pemberton, who headed our overseas operations, and Lt Col Richard Horner. Mike was young, enthusiastic, hyperactive, and with an irresistible childish sense of humour, that occasionally wore thin on his more mature colleagues. Richard was the Army Rep to NAAFI, he was employed by the Army but assigned full-time to NAAFI. Richard, a gunner and inevitably suffering some loss of hearing, had risen through the ranks spurred on by marriage. He had been awarded an MBE for his desk job at MoD and enjoyed painting.

We were ushered out of the Brize Norton VIP lounge onto the Herc as the principal passenger arrived – Secretary of State Geoff Hoon. This was entirely coincidental to our visit but had some advantage.

The Secretary of State was the last to board the aircraft; he took one quick look into the body of the plane before heading up to the cockpit and the one comfortable seat. Throughout the flight and the subsequent flights, the following day, he spoke to no one on the plane outside the cockpit. He was always last on, first off – extraordinary. In the body of the plane was an armoured vehicle, being shipped to Kabul, and stacked behind it were pallets and crates of equipment and provisions for our forces. Two portaloos were bolted to the floor at the front of the plane. The motley array of passengers, consisting of regular service people, special forces, drug specialists, diplomatic staff, welfare and aid people were seated on pulled down seats from the sides of the aircraft. The backrest was webbing. There were no windows. This was a fighting aircraft with no luxuries or trappings except the two portaloos. (Normal ablutions were a pull out pipe and quarter screen in the side of the plane at the rear.)

As soon as the aircraft took off, the experienced hands left their seats and spread themselves over the softest parts of the cargo, leaving the rest of us to sleep on the limited metal floor area. Normally the plane would have re-fuelled at Turkey, but because the Secretary of State was on board, the flight was direct to Kabul.

At Kabul airport we were equipped with helmets and body armour and quickly ushered into waiting Saracen armoured troop carriers. Three of these moved in convoy to Camp Souter, the UK forces base in Kabul. Camp Souter was an old fertilizer packing factory with sturdy walls, a good walled perimeter, and with running water, electricity and good showers. We shared a room on the second floor. It wasn't the Holiday Inn, but it felt safe, weather-proof and had plenty of room. The mess served excellent food in terms of choice and quality, and helpings were unlimited. Food quality in forces' messes in Theatre is consistently good.

We had a store and pub "The Toucan", a pun on the two can per night limit normally applied in the army. Our manager was S/Sgt Terina Hart, another stalwart regular of tours in Iraq and Afghanistan. She had three expatriate staff including a girl who worked as a casual exotic dancer in discotheques in Birmingham, when on leave. She was a popular attraction when serving in the bar for the Toucan's customers! Terina's other staff were young Afghan men. The store was small and out of stock of many items.

The dollar was the currency but in the absence of any coinage, Terina had minted her own NAAFI tokens in town to provide change. The supply chain was very unpredictable with product being shipped through Karachi, where bureaucracy and corruption inevitably delayed release, and Kabul commercial airport where Customs Authorities were holding stock.

The bar was basic but well used by all ranks and buzzed at night like the best local pub on a Friday night. A duty corporal checked the two can rule was observed.

The following morning, we returned to the airport the way we had come. The Hercules was taking the Secretary of State to the two other bases and we had the opportunity to hitch a ride. The armoured cars never stopped, the soldiers were vigilant for any attempt to slip a magnetic charge under the vehicle, and the gunner in the roof turret looked very formidable. It was difficult to see much out of the tiny slits.

Our first stop was Mazir-e-Sharif, the second British camp, which was located next to a ramshackle Jordanian field hospital. Mez, as it was affectionately known, was a tented camp seemingly at the back of beyond. The little NAAFI facility was a table and a few shelves in part of a tent, in which our man Cpl Nigel Lobley (Nobby) lived and slept as did the postman – the British Forces Post Office. The shelves were pathetically stocked due to lack of supplies. His stock came either by truck from Camp Souter or by air from Kabul and not much was available. There were no recreational facilities for the men to relax. I was embarrassed and ashamed that we had put Nobby in this position and that our service people were receiving such a lack of service.

We moved onto Kandahar, where the Secretary of State was distressed that the Americans who ran the base would not put a car onto the apron to save him the walk in the heat. The air base at Kandahar had a pretty well developed leisure square with a big PX general store, several fast food outlets – all provided by AAFES (the American version of NAAFI) – various ethnic trinket shops selling mainly Russian goods, and even a Thai massage parlour.

We had no presence there yet but would in due course, so this provided a good intelligence gathering visit.

We returned to Kabul in the Herc, while the Secretary of State headed for home. I was given the opportunity to fly in the cockpit on this leg and saw the incredible scenery of the mountains but Kabul itself was no romantic city from the air or the ground.

Kabul was located in a bowl in the mountains and by 10am an unhealthy smog hung over the city. The smog was a mixture of cheap polluted fuel exhaust, dust from several brick factories, and the dried faeces swept from homes with no sanitation. It was disgusting and led to many foreigners developing the Kabul cough, a dry irritating and tiring cough, or stomach problems – indeed the sick bay had a dozen occupants with just this problem. Fortunately, none of us suffered while we were there, but I had a vicious slimming regime on return! On the ground most of the buildings were either simple one-storey ribbon developments or hideous old Stalin style blocks of flats. These flats were at a premium because they had been built with sanitation.

The following day we had meetings arranged with the Commanding Officer of Camp Souter, the Quartermaster, the Commander of the "Woofers" – the resident battalion, and wanted to visit the International Headquarters for ISAF (International Security and Assistance Force). In between these meetings two incidents occurred happily by chance to help us address the two overwhelming issues of lack of stock, and lack of facilities at Mez. We were walking around the grounds of Camp Souter, when we came across a pair of what might be described as mobile homes, one equipped as a kitchen, the other as a seating area. This was exactly what Mez needed. The Quartermaster confirmed that they did not belong to the army but did belong to the British embassy. An appointment was made to see an embassy representative the following day.

By now a Jingli had arrived full of stock for the shop and bar. The Jinglies were the large colourfully painted trucks that moved goods long distance in this part of the world, so called because of the noise made by the metal chains that hung down to the road from their chassis. Depending on whom you chose to believe these were there to protect the drivers from unwanted animal company when they slept beneath the wagons during the hot months, or to ward off equally unwelcome spirits! Pakistani men, who risked their lives for high pay doing this dangerous job, drove them. The grinning driver opened his sides with a shrug and the stock literally fell off the truck, damaging a proportion and creating a stream of beer in the yard.

The intact pallets were moved by forklift with the remainder hand balled to the store with everyone assisting. An emergency supply was loaded onto one pallet and the flight mover helpfully arranged for it to be on the next regular Hercules flight to Mez. In between meetings everyone set about remerchandising the store and filling the shelves, a laborious job when every item has to be individually priced. Even Lt Col Horner mastered the technique of a price gun, but only when the store was closed and no junior ranks could see such a senior officer engaged in such work! Word soon spread that the NAAFI had new stock and a steady stream of customers came to look and some to buy. Just looking round the NAAFI was an important recreation in a confined place like Camp Souter, with little to do outside the gym.

The following day we went to see the woman from the embassy, who was allegedly responsible for these facilities. The conversation went as follows. Yes, the facilities belonged to the embassy or rather the Foreign Office. No, they were not planning to use them. But they might have some use for them in the future. No, they had no space to use them at the embassy compound now or in the future. So where could they use them? Don't know. Our troops desperately need these facilities with winter coming and the passes soon to be blocked by snow. I can see that. Why can't I have these or borrow these for use by our own servicemen now? I can't give them to you; they are Foreign Office assets. I will buy them from you and here is a personal cheque for £5,000. If it is logically more, we will fund the extra.

This did make the point that we were totally serious and determined and impressed the local command. However, she had no authority to take any decision and nor did anyone at the embassy. We secured the units in the end and moved them to Mez but it took another 8 weeks and a great deal of time and effort through London by Richard Horner. This sort of bureaucracy and inability to take small decisions on an important welfare issue was hugely frustrating for me.

Our visit to Camp Souter coincided with the Remembrance Day Parade and at eleven hundred hours on the 11th November, the Senior Officer led the Service and took the salute. It was particularly moving to experience this parade in this alien place far from home, where many service people had died serving their country and where many were still to do so. It had great meaning. I was also proud that S/Sgt Hart and her little EFI team were there in the column of inevitably nearly all men, marching past as totally integrated members of the force. We then managed a brief visit to the International Headquarters in the heavily guarded green zone, which included the Western embassies. Movement was always in body armour and helmets and in a pair of Saracen armoured vehicles.

The regular Hercules on the shuttle to take us back to the UK had been diverted to Chad. There was no other aircraft spare to take us and much more importantly the servicemen, going home for a short break. We were stuck in the fertilizer factory in Kabul.

Twenty four hours later we were taken by the local milk round British Hercules to Kandahar. From there a packed – literally each row of passengers was interwoven with the facing row – American Hercules took us to the main American base in Qatar in the Gulf.

After an overnight stop, we joined the British troop carrier that flew regularly from Qatar to Brize Norton via Germany. This plane also had a fault and missed the stopover in Germany, going direct to Brize. The German-based soldiers then took a later flight back to Germany – they had lost 3 days of their short 14 days mid-tour "rest and recuperation" leave. This brought home the pressure on our limited air resources, but despite that Brize Norton was very helpful in establishing a regular air bridge for future essentials.

The level of activity in Afghanistan increased substantially over the next two years with troop numbers increasing from several hundred to 5000. The main British Force was in Helmand Province at Camp Bastion, where the initial welfare provision was very limited and was reliant on NAAFI. By 2008 NAAFI had 100 personnel in 11 establishments located in Bastion, Kandahar, Lashkar Gar, Gereshk, and Kabul. Nearly half of these employees were Bosnians, who had transferred initially from their home country as our forces withdrew from there. Our recruitment methods and terms and conditions were not attracting sufficient UK citizens and only they could be enlisted as full members of EFI. Increasing the number of EFI staff became a major priority and required more effort and better wages. Afghanistan, like Iraq before, became largely dry – alcohol banned – overnight due to a policy change by the General in Command. This gave NAAFI particular stock problems with both beer stocks in country and in transit, but one of the advantages of NAAFI over a totally commercial contractor was the flexibility to meet the needs of the command. The beer was sold at discounted prices to other NATO forces!

The eventual facilities at Camp Bastion were good and included the usual store, but also a good Piacetto coffee shop and various franchised stores. Constructing these facilities was never straightforward. The pre-fabricated structures had to wait their turn in an overburdened supply route, where lack of aircraft and breakdown caused regular delays. On the ground, site works were delayed, leaving the containers containing the structures and furniture to be pilfered (with some suspicion that squadron bars were recipients as well as the more obvious local alternatives). The roof of the first store was lost and a second roof had to be prefabricated and sent out. Securing tradespeople to hang around in a very dangerous theatre was also a problem, leading to a limited pool of options – not always the best. We used a mixture of Brits and Germans. The concept of an integrated welfare facility was really starting to gain traction with PJHQ. As the facilities expanded so did the logistical issues. Apart from newspapers, magazines, and emergency provisions, the stock had to come via ship from the UK or Kuwait through Karachi. It was then moved on convoys of Jinglies through the passes of Pakistan and Afghanistan. The threat of mines, roadside bombs and attacks by Taliban or local criminal gangs was constant.

Stock was stolen and 200 Pakistani drivers' lives were lost moving supplies to the force, driving the cost of movement up proportionate to the danger.

Defence Secretary of State Des Browne, who succeeded Hoon, did suggest Tesco might be an alternative to NAAFI in Afghanistan. When I put this to a Tesco director it was met with the derision it deserved. Running a supermarket in a war zone may not be as slick an operation as in Guildford but the bravery, resourcefulness and dedication of the NAAFI and EFI people delivers a remarkable result in very challenging and personally hazardous circumstances. People like Janine Smithies, with 16 operational tours under her belt, including many in Iraq and Afghanistan, provide a service that very few Tesco managers could ever match, if they were prepared to take the risk.

As conditions became more difficult, PJHQ imposed severe restrictions on those travelling to Afghanistan. While understandable in one sense, it meant that people like myself were less likely to travel to see our operations there. On three occasions my visits were cancelled. This was detrimental to our operating standards, innovation and indeed in engaging the support of the wider non-military community in understanding and communicating just what our service people do. General Sir Richard Dannet, Chief of the General Staff, must be applauded for the way he has reengaged the public with the services. Senior visitors also added value to that message.

The Falklands / Ascension Island

David McKenzie and I were extraordinarily lucky in the timing of our flight to the South Atlantic. The regular weekly plane had been an uncomfortable and slow Hercules. By chance we were on the first Tri-Star flight and we had business class seats – fantastic. The staff were a little raw, serving David the meat and myself the vegetables of a VIP meal that was intended to be shared between us – luckily I like potatoes. But having expected the rigour of a Hercules, this was luxury indeed for our 16-hour flight.

The aircraft stopped on Ascension Island for re-fuelling, with passengers disembarked into a cage by name and a cage in practice to stretch their legs. We could not go to see the island's NAAFI facilities on this stop over but arranged for Freddie Crowie, our St Helena manager, to meet us on our way back for a flying visit.

As our aircraft approached the Falklands, two Tornados appeared on the wing tips, a spectacular sight. This was part of the training routine for the pilots, who would intercept regularly the inbound flights to the delight of passengers. We landed at Mount Pleasant Airbase.

Mount Pleasant was an entirely new base built after the Falklands war. It was purpose built, forty minutes from the capital Port Stanley in good weather, and cut off for normal vehicles in bad weather. The giant runway could accommodate any jet and made rapid reinforcement of the islands by air an easy option in any future threat.

The air base had a permanent Tornado squadron with full support team and an infantry company. The living quarters were in a building with a 1km long spine with all sleeping, messing, leisure, faith, sport and shop facilities attached to the spine. It was built for bad weather. NAAFI had some rather tired shops and bars at either end of the spine where refresh investment was already planned plus a bowling alley, and another small facility in Port Stanley. The country manager was Andy Murray, a capable and experienced manager who had the respect of the local command. His staff were mainly St Helenans, who made up the bulk of the basic support staff on the base.

Although the weather was very different to their island, they were comfortable in the small island culture of the Falklands and five years' work would provide the wherewithal to obtain a house back home. The customer base was mainly single service men, with a few families, enough to support a little school. The children had the freedom to roam almost anywhere but carried walkie talkies in case of a sudden snow storm and a day trip was not by coach but by helicopter.

Boredom was the enemy, with no mobile phone reception, poor internet service, and little to do on base after work beyond the gym, the bar and a weekly visit to the bowling alley and the cinema.

There were numerous small issues to discuss and follow up on – range, pricing, staff terms and training. Stock and supply chain is always an issue in these far-flung places. The supply boat from the UK arrived every 6 weeks, making the sale of short shelf life products impossible. Staff had to be very vigilant on date codes of medium shelf life product and indeed in Port Stanley it was evident that the local shops regarded sell by dates as totally irrelevant, as much of the stock by UK terms was out of date and un-saleable. Our stocks could also be heavily affected by the arrival of a passing Royal Navy ship, whose crew would replenish supplies from us. In an ideal world everyone would be warned and plans made well in advance, but practice was rather different, and feast and famine were both too common. Some supplies came from Chile, notably drinks, and the garrison ran a local family shop with some local vegetables and meat – that would not have passed the buyers' standards at home. Andy's experience and common-sense judgement was invaluable as we saw in the adverse results of his less capable successor.

The main issue was the capital investment including ensuring good liaison between the military engineers, who were responsible for the shell and the NAAFI contractors who were responsible for the fit out. As in Iraq, assumptions about wiring were fundamental and given the distance, liaison was not great.

As with the aircraft, I had totally misjudged the accommodation and mess protocol. I had expected to travel on a Hercules, sleep in basic quarters, and wear practical casual clothes. My room was excellent with all facilities en suite and a suit was the dress for dinner. I had to borrow a sports jacket, shirt and tie from Andy and in this ill-fitting and still rather unsuitable combination was clearly under dressed as host at the Officers' Mess Dinner and then the principal guest at the Commander South Atlantic's residence.

Despite my poor form on the sartorial stakes, the community were most welcoming and very keen to have NAAFI support in improving their limited facilities.

We did have time to spare before the weekly flight returned to take us back and were taken on a battlefield tour by a young Captain, who brought the dreadful experience of war into sharp focus. We walked in detail the Battle of Goose Green with its low hump overlooking the gorse strewn gently sloping approach. We stood where Col H Jones was killed and where his adversary fired. We visited the cemeteries for the dead British and dead Argentinean soldiers. Both were immaculately maintained in this remote but beautiful place. On a day when the sun shone, they were all tragically equal. We also saw wonderful wildlife, birds, seals, whales, and penguins experiencing a latitude, the same as London's, though where the wind makes the climate more hostile. Port Stanley was a tiny village akin to a little Scottish village and as far from Argentina as London is from Tangiers. It was no wonder that the population values its protection by the British.

On our return journey we landed on Ascension on a warm balmy evening with a light ocean wind. After the invigorating weather of the Falklands, this was idyllic. Freddie met us at the terminal and whisked us up the volcanic mountain to his shop and bar. The shop was fine as a basic convenience store and the bar was fabulous overlooking the island, and ocean under its coconut roof and a star-spangled sky, serving cold beer from South Africa. I wanted to stay longer with our St Helenan team but one fast beer later and we were back on the plane to Brize Norton.

There were many small things we could do to help Andy to improve our offer in the Falklands, but the Ascension operation was a round peg in a round hole.

Gibraltar

Gibraltar was one of the smallest NAAFI operations. I travelled on my first visit with Commander Malcolm Brown, the Navy Representative to NAAFI, and Mike Pemberton, who continuously sought to irritate Malcolm with his practical jokes. Our operation fluctuated between marginal profit and marginal loss, and despite locations at Europa Point, Devils Tower and the seasonal kiosk at the swimming pool, turnover was very low. Our manager Ron Nichols was nervous. Although his business was very small, it was actually complicated being made up of lots of bitty activities, and it was in poor shape – not his fault.

Europa Point was the location of service family housing and from it you could already see the shore and mountains of Africa. The building leaked due to poor maintenance by the military – lack of budget. It housed a pleasant bar and bowling alley and had plans for a small new shop. Devils Tower had a well located room, overlooking the main square and close to the single women quarters, which was an obvious magnet for the men. This NAAFI shop housed a few tables, some out of date fixtures and a pathetic array of stock. It was awful. The prices were uncompetitive with the local Safeway store, which shipped direct from the UK. We purchased from 23 local suppliers, Gibraltar having the old structure of specialist importer / wholesalers. Ron had too many deliveries, too much paperwork and too many inconsequential suppliers for his turnover.

The local command were unhappy with what they had but were unable to give a clear brief of what they wanted in the medium term due to prospective multi-activity contracts that included "Pay as you Dine", which the island did not want.

There were a number of actions that we could and did take in the short term in terms of range, pricing and suppliers. It took too long but eventually the investment took place at Devils Tower to create an excellent store and Heroes Bar, which I was pleased to show the Governor Lt General Sir Robert Fulton, when he officially opened it in 2008. Ron also had his own small IT system to support Epos and handle suppliers. He was a man reborn with a business that his staff and customers now had pride in ownership and where not surprisingly the sales leapt forward.

While in Gibraltar I did not visit our employee in the Fortress Prison. He had been on the run from the Scottish police for three years; like the French Foreign Legion, NAAFI has in its time provided a useful place to disappear for people seeking to avoid wives, mistresses and various authorities!

Brunei

The flight to Brunei via Dubai was long and uncomfortable on the very back seat of the Air Brunei plane. The country manager Gary Pickett met John Douglass (Operations Director) and myself at the airport and took us straight out to the British Army Base at Seria. The base is home to one of the Ghurkha battalions, the other being based in Chatham, Kent. Supporting Gary were Tony and Wendy Lim, who ran the shop, bar and restaurant on a day-to-day basis. They were Malaysian Chinese and had worked for NAAFI in Malaysia until the withdrawal of British Forces. Deeply religious Buddhists, they had spent their life working for NAAFI. The staff were either local Brunei people or Filipinos.

Brunei is dry and the only official alcohol serving club is the NAAFI, albeit some local restaurants served alcohol from a tea pot to regular customers. NAAFI also supplied on a wholesale basis the messes, the embassy and the small British Military Contingent training the Brunei forces near the capital Darussalam. As a result of its dry status the expatriate population travelled to the nightclubs and bars of neighbouring Sarawak at the weekend, stocking up with duty free from the supermarkets on the border on the return journey.

The issues were the regular issues of stock, supply chain and pricing. Gary would order a container every two months. By the time it arrived he had three weeks of shelf life left on some items such as crisps, and he would then be out of stock until the next container arrived. Our prices had to reflect the local market and not those in Germany. We needed more local supply with Singapore, the obvious place. By the time we left prices were adjusted and the bones of a new sourcing plan in place.

The Ghurkhas are amazing people, whose families cannot join them for five years at least. There were up to 1400 service personnel, support staff and dependants in Brunei if none were away on operation. They did regular tours in Afghanistan, where the terrain and climate naturally suited them. They sign on for 15 years and then return home. The Sultan pays for them to be in Brunei and was building extensive new accommodation during our visit. We attended their birthday parade at 6am, with the whole battalion doing one arm press ups led by the CO to the applause of his men. We had dinner with a number of Ghurkha wives, who seemed incredibly graceful and tolerant by our Western standards.

They mainly shopped at the local indigenous stores, who stocked more familiar products at keen prices. Our shop was geared to Western people, although the bar did a great trade with Ghurkha men, who loved to play the machines. The restaurant was the jewel with great potential and Gary committed to step up the marketing of this facility.

The High Commissioner also arranged a meeting with the Minister of Sport, the Sultan's nephew, who had been my guest in the Aston Villa Boardroom a few years previously. He had matured from the hedonistic young man I had met previously but still loved football and was well informed on the subject.

The High Commissioner's eyes widened when I proposed that the Minister should buy Aston Villa, and we discussed the very outline details of a potential deal. This discussion certainly did NAAFI's credibility no harm, although the eventual purchaser of Aston Villa was the American Randy Lerner supported by General Chuck Krulak, formerly head of the US Marine Corps!

Belize

The visit by Mark Lean (Mike Pemberton's successor as Head of Overseas Operations) and myself was marred by flight delays and cancellations. We had travelled through New York to save on ticket costs, but this was false economy as half our week was spent in America not Belize.

The NAAFI in Belize was quite dreadful. Our first sight was a pile of broken furniture on the balcony of the well situated bar "Raymondo's" above the swimming pool. The main bar the "Sailfish" was a disgrace with electrics hanging difunctionally, insufficient beer coolers to deliver cool beer except to those fortunate or strong enough to be at the front of the queue, and a general air of neglect pervaded the operation. The shop was a mess and staffed by a listless girl out of her depth. The staff had not had a wage review in three years and one was subsequently found to be corrupt. The one positive was the messing contract, which operated smoothly and really supported the other activities. I was ashamed to meet the Commanding Officer of BATSUB, Lt Col Peter Germain. His permanent staff was only about 40 in number, but the camp would take surges of up to 4000 men, in transit to jungle training in the Belize hinterland. This was a dreadful advertisement for the NAAFI brand.

Everything needed addressing – the physical facilities, the range and sourcing, the service and the staff. An experienced new manager was due to arrive shortly – Sammy Morrison – and he started with a long agenda but at least with a strong level of central support.

We agreed to purchase new furniture on the spot and committed to a major refurbishment using the Inter Services Furnishing Scheme budget. To my chagrin the MoD cancelled this budget before we could implement the refurbishment and I sent a grovelling letter of apology to the Commanding Officer. This broken promise to his team made me uncomfortable until the day I left NAAFI. However, Sammy's attention to basic management issues raised standards considerably and his energy and enthusiasm made up for a lack of capital.

The Naval Canteen Service

Another unique institution in its own right, the Naval Canteen Service, or NCS, served around 30 Royal Navy capital ships, and provided wholesale supplies to many more either from our own bases or from a selected list of chandlers in major overseas ports. The largest ships were the

UASC

Aircraft Carriers HMS Ark Royal and HMS Illustrious, plus HMS Ocean, which had mini self-service stores on board. They carry up to 6 Naval Canteen staff and can sell £25,000 per week of goffer (pop), nutty (chocolate), dhobi dust (washing powder) and other daily items from their inboard self-service shops. A fully stocked Ark Royal will carry up to £700,000 worth of stock and at the time of the second Gulf War, she was loaded with this in 4 days. Ships are built to "project force" and the storage space for NAAFI is the last part of the design. It is always in the infill space, which requires hand filling and often access via various bulkheads and staircases from the shop, making shelf filling uniquely arduous. The ships still lack proper retail systems and direct communication would assist stock management and replenishment in ports around the world.

However, security issues were an obstacle with the Royal Navy reluctant, understandably, to have any other computer or communication system on board.

I visited many of these ships in port in Portsmouth but for obvious reasons never saw the real activity with a full crew and on a mission. We did experience an open day at sea to observe various exercises including live firing, which was very impressive and required a variety of protective clothing.

The confined spaces are very small for living and sleeping, and in submarines the crew's bunks – 30 to a mess – are so small a larger man cannot turn over without getting out of the bunk; so sleeping on top of a missile was a more comfortable alternative for some.

The Navy command were very supportive as many senior officers had, during their ship command, first-hand experience of the value of their Canteen Managers on the welfare and morale of men, and increasingly women, at sea.

For example, both the current 2SL Vice Admiral Massey and his predecessor Vice Admiral John had commanded ships in the Iraq war, where they valued their Can Men. On a lighter note we also arranged for the Royal Navy Football coaches in their Association's Centenary year to have some extra training at Villa Park and my old colleague on the Villa board and former England manager, Graham Taylor, was generous with his time and support for our work.

Moving On

In the June 2008 Birthday Honours list, I was appointed a CBE, recognition for the whole team in NAAFI for what everyone had achieved in serving our customers in the armed services, while handling so much change.

NAAFI has continuously adapted to changing military requirements. It has grown and shrunk several times. Its key value is in operational flexibility, but it needs a strong base, from which to feed and support that flexible capability in operations such as the Gulf, the Balkans, Sierra Leone or the regular exercises in Norway, Kenya or Poland. Germany will provide that base until 2015 but beyond then, NAAFI will need some significant position in the UK to compensate for the steady decline in the German military population. These same pressures apply to all military welfare providers and some coalescence of service would be logical. This concept has been recognised by MoD and senior officers, but will require a sensitive approach to progress. Ultimately MoD could have to choose between having one internal consolidated welfare provider or having none, with all aspects contracted out. It will never engender the same commitment from staff or flexibility to serve the services if it lost what it has in NAAFI. I was delighted in my last week to hear that General Sir Richard Dannett had gone out of his way to praise the NAAFI PAYD result in Germany and ask why it was so much better than the contractors at home. The answer is simply it is because our mission is to serve.

I had 4 very different bosses at MoD, Air Marshal Sir Malcolm Pledger, Lt General Anthony Palmer (a wonderful pianist), Air Marshal David Pocock and Vice Admiral Peter Wilkinson (a football fan and Chair of the RN FA) and some 12 different Principal Personnel Officers (2SL, AG, AMP) who represented their service during my time. They were all good men, with huge experience across the service including mainstream operational activity and they gave great support for welfare and for NAAFI sometimes in the face of some hostile internal opposition. I owe my thanks to them all.

My successor is Sir Ian Prosser, a man of great experience and stature in the business world. I knew Ian as a competitor – tough and straight – and was delighted NAAFI had attracted a man of his calibre. General Sir Reddy Watt, former Commander in Chief Land, also joins the Board to add further strength and credibility to a good team of non executives – James Wilde (Deputy Chair), Alison Clifford-King (the diligent Chair of Audit) and helicopter flying Alan Smith.

I will miss NAAFI, particularly the long serving members at its heart; their dedication, cheerfulness and can-do attitude is what NAAFI is all about.

My thanks to Caroline Stokes and to my good friend David Mitchell for assisting with my reflection on 7 great years at NAAFI.

Back to basics 2001

In a quest to bring NAAFI to the forefront of the retail and leisure market, human resources committed to the training and development of its staff. The latest initiative, aimed at new members of staff, cover the basic skills required by the company, and currently being rolled out throughout the organisation.

The new starting out workbook was a combination of leisure, bronze level, key skills used in clubs and previous retail starting out programme, used in stores. It needed to be completed within the 13 weeks of joining the company. After they had finished starting out workbook, staff could then move on to first steps workbook. This combined the skills from the original retail first steps programme and leisure silver level. Starting out of first step workbooks had to be completed before studying for the NVQ qualification.

Several practical courses had also been introduced for new members of staff, and they plan to run pilot courses of NAAFI selling skills programme at JHQ Germany. One day workshops would cover the whole process from selling, from how to approach customers and identifying their needs to match the right product to them and closing the sale. The aim for Garrison managers was to run the course in their own areas when it is rolled out later on in the year. Eventually it was hoped that this course would be made available to EFI staff in international locations. Other workshops on offer were customer care courses. The main aim of these training courses was for all members of staff to understand the importance of excellent customer care and the costs of not providing high levels of service. The courses had already been successfully run in the UK, and 102 members of staff from Cyprus and 65 in Kosovo had already taken part in the locations.

2002

The five-star treatment 2002

Shop and club assistants throughout NAAFI can take control of their own career progression at their own pace, thanks to a new training system that replaced the starting out and first step workbooks only launched a few years previously. The five-star training programme had been devised by Iain Lanng, head of learning and development, following the criticism from staff of the old system. Although there had been many systems in place over the previous 90 years of NAAFI, this was the one that was going to give them the tools that they needed to do the job to not only develop themselves but also helped develop the business.

Staff from all levels of the business had been contributing their thoughts on how this should be progressed, with the operations director NAAFI international Mike Sheriff, and David Mackenzie, director of NAAFI GB, praising their efforts. This was not reinventing the wheel, but it was when a new developed system, devised by learning lessons from the past and using them for the present.

The programme as its name suggested had five stages. Each of which was accompanied by a workbook and a workshop. The workshops would be run by 4 UK and 3 international training advisors. The only compulsory stage was the first, career launch, which new staff would have to complete within 13 weeks of joining the company. After that all the following stages were optional and staff wishing to progress would need to discuss training with their line manager during their personal development plan meeting.

A certificate and badge was awarded after each stage, after career launch would be Star 2, customer service and teamwork, Star 3, achieving profitable sales, Star 4 stock control. At this stage retail staff should have learned enough to gain an NVQ level 2. Staff in other parts of the business may have to complete a further module to pass their relevant NVQ, for example bar and cellar duties for leisure assistants, ration control for staff in Germany and bulk issue for EFI and NCS.

Star 5 was everything that a retail or leisure assistant needed to know to run an establishment in the absence of their manager or supervisor. This was rewarded with a gold badge and certificate.

And an employee must complete Star five before they would be considered for supervisor position. Existing supervisors and managers would be enrolled on Five-star supervisor and management courses within a few years of the launch. This would give them an NVQ Level 3 and Level 4 respectively.

2003

Remembering the fallen 2003

Following the recent war and attacks on troops in Iraq, Remembrance Day seemed to have a fresh poignancy in 2003 as people across Britain and the world stopped to remember. NAAFI was represented at several memorial services.

On the 6th of November, staff from the EFI headquarters in Bulford Wiltshire including Maj Dave Foster and WO Dawn Scott attended the Remembrance service at Westminster Abbey.

9th of November David Mackenzie, director GB, and Maj Tim Elliott laid a wreath on behalf of NAAFI and the OCA respectively at St Georges church, Bulford.

Lt Col Steve Mitchell, CO EFI RLC, represented the organisation at a memorial service in Iraq.

Charles Hill, operations manager, HM ships, and Bill Clague represented NAAFI at Chatham and laid a wreath on behalf of the NCS and the old comrades Association.

2004

My D-Day 60th Anniversary, memories by Sadie Cook, Civilian serving EFI 2004

When I joined NAAFI in 2002 I never expected that I would spend the night sleeping on the solid concrete floor in the middle of a Miela factory. Had the NAAFI made cut backs in relation to staff accommodation, you may well ask; thankfully no; I was in fact in France at the beginning of what was to become an emotional, tiring yet fun few weeks.

After completing my morning shift at Club 47 in Princess Royal Barracks, Gütersloh, Germany, I was thrilled to see a notice on display in the staff quarters requesting volunteers to go and set up and work in a NAAFI post in Arromanches, France. There was initial confusion as to why a NAAFI shop was required in such a place; after all there were no troops there. However, having read down through the description all became clear; the purpose was to support and serve both the present-day troops and those visiting to commemorate the 60th anniversary of the D-Day landings.

Naturally my colleagues and I jumped at the possibility of going to France, knowing that places were minimal and competition was high, I had to think of way in which I could get myself there. If only I could use the excuse that I had once lived in France and could also speak the lingo, oh hang on I could . . . ok fair enough, the second part of that statement was a slight exaggeration, my spoken French was minimal, but I certainly wasn't going to admit that if it prevented me from getting a place.

Upon our arrival in Arromanches we were taken straight to an empty Miela factory, an odd place to take us you may well think, and that was certainly our opinion. There were a few soldiers walking around busying themselves but other than that the place was pretty much empty. It was at this point we were informed that this empty, barren place was to be our home for the next couple of weeks. We all looked somewhat confused and asked the obvious question "where were we supposed to sleep, wash and eat?" – you can only imagine how unimpressed when we were told "here".

As it turned out, we had in fact arrived a little early and before any of the troops who would be providing us with accommodation, so unfortunately (she says with a little grin) we had to find a local hotel for the night. Due to the last minute need for a room, the only place that had availability was a hotel that was also a chateau. Ok so now we were happy, the place albeit bijoux was stunning, with beautiful gardens. After a long journey by road, we quickly checked in and fought between ourselves for the bathroom first, to have a much-needed shower and to dress for dinner in the local town. Prior to heading out, my roommate and I decided to have a 'little drinky poos' as she would put it; and to chill in the garden. Imagine my horror as the bar man poured our two Baileys and then informed us that the price was 32 euros! We very quickly advised him that since they were such large measures we would happily share one; and he could pour the second 16 euro measure of Baileys back into the bottle.

Day two of our little adventure was fun yet hard work, our delivery had arrived and we had to organise it and carry out a full stocktake. The NAAFI was as prepared as ever and had a large stock supply that would cater for almost all needs; in fact it appeared every need! As I was working through the delivery I was both surprised and confused to stumble across a large supply of condoms and hard toffees, an unusual combination taking into consideration who was going to be our main customer demographic . . . still, at least this amused us all.

After a long day building our little NAAFI shop the question was raised again as to where we were sleeping that night. Throughout the day the troops had been busy setting up camp in and around the factory, so we assumed that we would have a little tent set up somewhere for us to set up home for the duration of our stay. How wrong we were. To cut the story short, we woke the following morning on the hard floor of our little NAAFI shop, with soldiers walking past us as we slept in our sleeping bags. At the time we were mortified, but soon found the funny side after the lads had finished mocking us.

As the days passed, the Miela factory became a hub of activity and more and more tents appeared to house the troops. As per norm the NAAFI was a busy focal point, with guys and girls popping in for essentials, snacks and chats. During this time we also went out to set up satellite sites in other areas, so that we were able to serve both troops and visitors in all locations. In the evenings we were permitted to leave the makeshift camp and venture out into town; however we were to adhere to the strict curfew that was in place. Imagine our panic one night when we realised that we had minutes to spare to return to camp as we sat drinking in a local brasserie. Our knight in shining armour appeared as a Sgt major (who shall remain anonymous) who sparked a conversation with us at the bar. We were quick to explain our predicament; however, thankfully he explained that he was exempt from the curfew and that should we return the same time as he, we would not reap any repercussions, phew.

On the day of the anniversary, tensions and excitement were high. The satellite shop that I had been assigned to was super busy with current serving military personnel, visitors and veterans. There was such a good atmosphere and it was an absolute pleasure talking to the veterans and listening to their stories. A highlight was chatting to an ex-NAAFI girl who reminisced, as though her tales were from yesterday. Numerous compliments were received from all in regards to always being able to rely on the NAAFI for a decent brew, so imagine how pleased everybody was when we served up a good old cuppa with traditional NAAFI tea.

A little before the commemorations commenced, we closed up the shop and headed to the beaches of Normandy. Unexpectedly my boss headed towards me in a hurry and announced that he needed me for a little task. Little did I know that he had lined up a radio interview with Yorkshire Radio, and as I was the only 'Yorkshire lass' there I was naturally the most suitable candidate . . . I was not amused, but obviously could not decline the task. My boss was aware of both my nerves and a little excitement so he kindly offered me his mobile so that I could call my grandma to tell her to listen, she was naturally very excited, bless her. The radio interview went well and I kept my nervous stutter to a minimum . . . I hope.

It was a beautiful sunny day in Normandy on the day of the 60th anniversary, and a day that I proudly hold in my heart forever. I will never forget the silence that fell as the service began and the look on the faces of the veterans who reminisced whilst at the same time remembering those who had fallen on the beaches beside them. It was an honour and a privilege to stand side by side with our heroes and equally to serve them in our little NAAFI shop.

EFI from the sweltering desert to the freezing snow 2004

Troops stationed at Shaibah logistics space, Iraq, could now purchase a stereo, enjoy a cold beer, or watch live sport on the big screen in comfortable surroundings, following the opening of NAAFI's new shop and club facilities. This massive NAAFI funded complex, which consisted of an express store and the Oasis club, was officially opened by Adam Ingram MP, minister for the armed forces in December 2003.

But it would not be long before EFI would deploy for the first time in two years to the cold climes of Norway. Eleven members of EFI swapped the extreme heat of the Gulf, where temperatures reached 50C, for the extreme cold of the Arctic where it could drop to –30C. They were supporting 3 Commando Brigade Royal Marines, in what once was an annual training exercise in Norway. The previous two years, troops were taken up in operations in Afghanistan and Iraq, so it could not go ahead.

The team split into five detachments and running a combination of bulk issue stores, mobiles, and retail outlets. Lt Col Steve Mitchell, CO EFI RLC said: 'They are selling a full range of EFI products including locally purchased beer and duty-free goods. There would also be the usual souvenirs that were such a regular staple of the previously annual exercise.'

Pre-deployment training to cope with the freezing conditions included being immersed in an ice hole and kitted out with Arctic clothing and equipment. The OC added: 'Deployment for many of those going, didn't hesitate to volunteer for the 10-week trip. It was very different challenge from Iraq, but they did a sterling job.'

Belize back in business 2004

NAAFI establishments in the region where HM forces conducted jungle warfare training, was like a ghost town for the first five months of 2003/04, as all the exercises were cancelled, due to operations in Iraq. Things had started to return to normality and Kevin Mansfield, country manager, was delighted to announce that his team still had a chance of delivering both budget and sales and profit. At the beginning of the year this did not look possible. The team were totally committed and aware of what was needed to be done to achieve this, they worked tirelessly during the last two exercises to get stock back onto the shelves, as quickly as it was bought, and to make sure that they had enough supplies to satisfy the customers.

Kevin and his staff needed to be flexible and organised in order to provide a high level of service that was expected from NAAFI. There were three locations in Belize, a shop, Raymondo's takeaway and Sailfish club, which were designed to allow the team to be adaptable as possible. Kevin Mansfield the country manager explained: 'The shop stock is an extensive range of goods, while the Sailfish club had two bars, one for permanent junior ranks and another one for exercise troops and a large kitchen to cater for the influx of personnel. We also increased our team from 14 to 21 during busier times to ensure that we were the best prepared to deal with the demands of a bigger customer base.'

For the love of the Job, Memories by Zoe Luxton 2004

I started my journey at age 16 back in 1991 as a summer job following in the footsteps of my mum and my aunty. I aimlessly drifted through college after college course then changed direction, and went to work full-time in Cwrt-y-gollen in Crickhowell, where Mum was the manager. I continued to work there for a number of years and that's where I started the travel bug; I went off to various locations and even did the rounds on the NAAFI van, until eventually we were made redundant, in 1997.

A few years passed and then I re-joined NAAFI in Sennybridge, life was ticking along when the manager announced there were jobs posted for NAAFI staff to volunteer for Iraq as EFI didn't have enough staff to open the dets, that was in 2003 I thought about it more and more and knew this was it, I needed to apply. I wasn't going to join the army and fight a war but I was going to make sure those who did had a taste of home.

I was soon on my way, bags packed then off I went February 2004; my friends gave me a good send off. I had no idea what I was letting myself in for, my stepfather drove me to Bulford one Sunday morning and my journey began. There I met my travel buddy Errol, he made me laugh and kept telling me travel stories and kept me entertained for what seemed like weeks. We arrived at Basra airport. When we stepped through the doors of the airport, I wondered what I had done – there were no cars, no sign of life, it was surreal. We finally arrived at Shaibah on the Tuesday where we met a whole load of fabulous people, most of whom I am still in touch with. I stayed in Iraq for 15months and it became a normal part of life, we had a community and a sense of belonging, like an extended family.

We saw units come and go, took part in camp life, we lived in tents for the first few months until we were upgraded to Corimec, the NAAFI was a real social hub and we spent our down time there as well as working. Work was hard and was always busy; we had good days and bad days but we had each other and we would pick each other up on the homesick days. The place had real camaraderie, we made the best of what we had. Sometimes deliveries wouldn't get through and I was lucky enough to go by Chinook to collect it myself.

We were always invited across camp, where the lads would make their own entertainment – it's surprising what you can make with some black nasty and tin foil. We had a Stars in your eyes night, karaoke and were often in fancy dress. On down days we used to explore our camp and got a few photo opportunities of things we would never have seen. We worked alongside the LECs and it was interesting to learn about their life, and their families, hopes and dreams, and I am still friends with some of them today now I'm home.

I was sad to come home but really proud to be awarded the Iraq medal, that memory lives on when I get to march at the remembrance parade, with some of my other colleagues. I still miss being in Iraq, and the relationships I built with people from all over the world, but I have the fondest memories and have made lifelong friends. I can never say I regretted going – it was one of the best times in my life.

2006

HMS Illustrious in the Indian Ocean 2006

The Royal Navy's HMS Illustrious was leading a task group in the Indian Ocean, supporting maritime security, and demonstrating Britain's ability to deploy, operate and sustain a strike force. HM ship was nicknamed 'Lusty'. NCS took a six-week trip where they stopped off at Tenerife and Crete and then the Arabian Gulf. Wayne Williams, canteen assistant, who had joined HMS Illustrious in September 2005, said: 'We were working in uncomfortably hot temperatures. With three squadrons on board, it was a lot busier than we would be with just the ship's company.' The only thing he found difficult was living in a 33-man mess.

Susan Richardson, canteen assistant, joined HMS Illustrious in July 2004. She explained: 'We were very busy all the time, the shop was constantly full of people, and we were bringing up double the amount of stores than we normally would because the shop and vending machines were virtually emptied every day. We had done two replenishments at sea, getting stores from the RFA ship over to our ship, and down to our stores.' They looked forward to barbecues on deck where they might come back with a little bit of a tan if they were lucky. HMS Illustrious was due then to return to the UK waters mid-July 2006.

EFI recruitment drive 2006

NAAFI HR team and the EFI was celebrating the most successful and challenging EFI recruitment campaign ever. Recruiting people into EFI was vital, with the need to increase troop deployment in Afghanistan, and together with the negative impact of NAAFI GB exit had on the source of internal recruits it became essential to look externally for new people.

The ground-breaking campaign began in January 2006 with the placement of recruitment adverts in newspapers across Glasgow, Newcastle and Leeds. These cities had strong connections with the military. The adverts were eye catching and punchy, attracting over 260 respondents by post, email, phone, online and through a brand-new text messaging service.

The challenge to interview the candidates remained, and this involved Mary Seddon from human resources and her colleague Lisa Kingswell, as well as EFI Stephanie Robinson and Suzy Gunn. Once the applications were sent in, they started to run roadshows where people could drop in for an interview; this was an exhaustive process and a real team effort. They ended up interviewing 75 people in just three days and returned to each city 4 weeks later to interview more. As a result of this hard work an impressive 30 new recruits were going through the final stages of EFI training, prior to deployment in Afghanistan and Iraq.

They were very proud of the campaign success, concluded Mary. The roadshows and adverts not only brought in new recruits for EFI, but 19 new people had joined NAAFI and three were about to board ship with the NCS as well.

Helmand province 2006

Dealing with change is part of the job for every member of EFI but those based in Afghanistan were set to see more than most. On the 1st of May 2006, British forces took over security duties from the southern Afghan province of Helmand from the US. It was a troubled area, with a history of unrest, major Taliban activity and opium production. To cope with this new responsibility the Ministry of Defence deployed 3700 additional UK troops there over the next three years and EFI would be increasing its support to serve them all.

WO2 Terina Hart explained that: 'while we have to close our detachment in Mazar E Sharif, following the camp's handover to foreign Nationals, we were opening 4 new detachments in the South of the country to cope with the influx of additional troops. Bar refurbishment, new cafe area and a bigger shop had also been proposed for Kabul to increase sales and provide a better service for the military.' Terina was based in Camp Souter in Kabul, the country's capital.

'Life for the country's EFI team had been made easier with the opening of a new warehouse to hold stock. They could now order on a weekly basis and not have the problem of delays caused by shipping or customers. This made things better as previously it could take six weeks to receive an order,' Terina went on to say.

The staff are always willing to go the extra mile and the EFI team at the Toucan Bar, Kabul was kept busy. They held bingo nights, quiz nights, karaoke and camel racing nights to keep the troops entertained; the bar was also used for conferences, meetings and other events such as exhibitions, to raise money for local charities.

Operation Telic 2006

Life for EFI teams supporting the troops during Op Telic in Iraq remained a challenging mix of hard work, constant risk, and strong camaraderie. Sgt Michelle Randall, based in Shaibah logistics base: 'The weather was good, though I don't think we've seen the last of the rain. The mornings are getting lighter, so much so that running a more pleasant operation for kickstarting the day. Road and helicopter moves are more difficult than they were last year. Greater forward planning and coordination is needed to ensure that we get where we need to go and there's always the possibility of getting stuck somewhere. So far I've been lucky but there are five more months of moves to go!'

'With recent events, life has been settled and no camp is being left undisturbed. The logistics base had four rockets launched at it that did not explode on impact, this helped us to tighten up procedures and give instructions to all personnel. Basra Air station is attracting more than its fair share of attacks. Protection measures for all locations were being tightened. Al Almarah is always experiencing one form of attack or another. Our hats go off to Cpl Diane Melvin and her team up there, who have lived in the most difficult forward location where attacks are a way of life.'

'Camp Smitty experienced its first serious attack for a long time recently, but Shatt Al Arab and Basra Palace, for now, are quiet; however, this could change as quickly as the sun goes down in the desert. Friendships are formed while people are on operational tours, we learn more of ourselves and our inner strength. There is a great sense of making the most of the opportunities that lie before us as we strive to offer service to the troops here on Op Telic.'

Iraq, Post New year Blind date, Memories by Chrissy Stewart 2006

I had been home on leave for Christmas 2005 and went back to Iraq just after New Year's Day 2006 and one of the temporary det commanders had met a guy on New Year's Eve and wanted me to meet him. I had only landed in Iraq a few hours before, when she dragged me off to the EFI bar to meet this guy. When he arrived, he had a friend in tow, so as soon as she had introduced me to the guy she'd met and his friend, she made excuses and left me with the friend. His name was David and it was only then, that I had realised that she'd set me up on a blind date. In Iraq of all places. I thank her though as if she had not, I never would've met, and married David and I would never have had my son Charlie. I stayed on with EFI for another year and a half after I had met David before I left.

2007

Gütersloh store launch 2007

2007 was a year of store launches whether it's refurbished or brand new. The new Gütersloh Max Store opened successfully on the 17th of October at 1200hrs after many months of planning and a number of weeks of very hard work. Alison Rogers and Mark Gascoigne, supported by a team from the old Max store and a couple of individuals from Honer and Fallingbostel Garrison, led the merchandising activity. The old Max traded until the night before the new store opened, albeit with reduced range as they were committed to providing an offer to the customers right up until the opening.

At 1030hrs on the 17th of October, 20 representatives of families and single soldiers from across the Garrison were invited to the new store to do a pre-opening shop. After going through the tills, they went into the new cafe for a complimentary drink and completed a questionnaire, giving valuable initial feedback on their shopping experience.

This was a soft opening; the official opening was the 1st of December with NAAFI non-executive chairman Tony Hales and GOC UKSC(G) Major General Mungo Melvin doing the honours of opening the store.

New Kandahar welfare facility (KWF) 2007

December 4th, 2007 represented a new start in Kandahar, with the official opening of the new Kandahar welfare facility or better known as KWF, in Afghanistan. KWF opened its doors to the Armed Services personnel currently on active deployment in the region.

KWF represented a joint venture between NAAFI and the MoD. After completion of the building itself, the entire process, from design to handover of keys and the doors opening for business, took a mere five months to complete. This was down to the fantastic work of the NAAFI team in Afghanistan led by Capt Mike Mould, and the forward locations team based in BFG (British Forces Germany).

The fantastic KWF facility gave deployed troops a comfortable and welcoming place to relax, a real Taste of Home. In their downtime, they could enjoy plasma LCD TVs with BFBS, six PlayStation 3 consoles, pool and football tables, a karaoke machine, as well as Wi-Fi facilities to make it a little easier for them to stay in touch with friends and family at home.

This was a project we're all very proud of, but there was no rest for the wicked as they were already back to work planning a new facility in Camp Bastion which was due to open in 2008.

Romance in the sand, Memories by Stuart Paterson 2007

After joining NAAFI in August 2007 and working in Faslane, JHQ, Harrogate and York I decided to join EFI as a Civilian. After a brief spell at Bulford I was sent to the George hotel to await a flight out to Iraq. The Tristar landed at night in Basra, I remember thinking to myself as I stepped off that flight that "I will never survive the heat". I was then picked up and taken to Shiaba Log Base in a minibus and told to rest and report the next morning for a briefing. I worked in Shiaba for nine months. I liked the lifestyle that much I extended my tour.

I met a lot of EFI uniform staff during that first tour, and subsequently went off to work closely with many of them. During that tour I had noticed a girl called Michelle Petrie; we never spoke much during that first tour. I had decided during that first tour that I would definitely be applying to the uniform side of things, not just for the challenge but the chance to travel further than I would have with the civilian side of NAAFI.

After my leave I was told to report to Bulford once more to start my EFI training. To my surprise Michelle was also there to do the same training. We struck up a friendship as we both had the same sense of humor and we both were determined to be part of the military side of the business. The training was basic back then compared to later on when we went through Chilwell. During this training period I got to know Michelle better, we would go down to the bar on camp and play pool or darts with the other guys.

As the training came to an end, I found out that I was off to Norway whilst Michelle was heading back to Germany. We managed to keep in touch with a few text messages now and then whilst I was in Norway. I didn't admit it then, but I was quite happy that we did.

On returning back from Norway I was again surprised to see Michelle in Bulford, this time she was getting prepared to go through her basic training. We used to meet up for a drink or to go running and got to know each other a lot more. It was at that time we became close and got together.

No sooner had that happened when again we went our separate ways once more, I headed to Afghanistan whilst Michelle headed off to Kosovo. Before we went, we had agreed to meet up on RNR and decided Paris would be nice.

EFI's presence in Afghanistan was pretty small in 2005 so when I landed in Kandahar I had to get myself up to Kabul to meet up the O/C. I was then informed I was heading to Gereshk {FOIB Price} in Helmand Province to establish an EFI within the camp and that my container had left and would be there when I arrived. It took me 6 days to arrive after what felt like travelling the length and breadth of Afghanistan. Price was a small FOB just outside the town of Gereshk, everything was basic, and I had the feeling that this would be a baptism of fire for my first EFI tour.

Once settled the first thing I wanted to do was contact Michelle to let her know I had arrived. We managed to talk quite regularly for the next few months and looked forward to meeting up again. RNR soon came around and we met up at Brize Norton for our break. We headed to Oxford for the night in a place I had booked. It was absolutely awful – which I'm still reminded about to this day. We headed off to Paris and it all fell apart for us, we didn't get along and felt unconfutable, so we parted ways on our return to the UK.

It wasn't until the next tour that we met up again. Michelle was in Kabul whilst I was in Kandahar, we started talking again and with the kindness of Cpt Mac I was allowed to go visit Michelle. We hit it off again and kept in touch and met up when our tours finished, Michelle had bought her house and I would travel down from Scotland and visit then eventually moved in with her. We toured together for a few more tours albeit usually different parts of the same country; we did manage a tour of Iraq together and then Camp Bastion in Afghanistan.

I remember Major Cassidy waking me up one night in KAF to go with her to the airport to pick someone up, I was not a happy bunny and asked why she needed me, I was told just get ready, after waiting a few hours a flight finally arrived and to my surprise Michelle had walked through the gate. Lynn and Michelle had secretly been planning a visit. I was over the moon.

During our tour in Bastion I had decided to ask Michelle to marry me, I had ordered a ring to be sent to my mum's house and then to me in Afghanistan. As always Michelle had found out and pestered the poor 'Posties' continuously about it. They eventually got so annoyed with her asking has it arrived, yet they gave her a Haribo ring to wear until it did. I had planned with the air wing to take Michelle up on a Chinook to propose as she had never flown on one; however an OP was called on that day so I romantically went down on one knee behind a container and proposed. Major Cassidy was there and found the situation hilarious; anyway Michelle said yes. We got married on the 2nd of July 2011 with family and close friends from EFI.

I cannot thank the O/Cs that we served with enough, if it wasn't for them arranging visits, I may not have found my soulmate and love of my life.

Afghanistan goes into Top Gear 2007

Upon landing in KAF the Top Gear trio were whisked across the base to the Piacetto coffee bar. NAAFI proudly hosted Jeremy Clarkson, James May, and Richard Hammond on their first night in Theatre. The trio were on a whirlwind tour of Kandahar and Camp Bastion, starting Friday 14th of December through to Sunday the 16th of December 2007.

Speculation was rife that the Top Gear team was visiting. It was with eager anticipation that the crowds grew both in and outside the cafe. A sneak preview of the team was had, and they made their way under the cover of darkness from the gravel road to their accommodation block.

On entering the cafe James and Richard were met with cheers and applause, while Jeremy Clarkson opted for the cool night air and a cigarette with the lads and lasses outside. Many photographs were posed for while numerous autographs were signed. The trio accompanied by their producer were fed and watered with complimentary non-alcoholic beer and a welcome selection of hot 'bake 'N' bite' pies and pasties.

The team posed and chatted with fans of the show for a good couple of hours despite just stepping off the RAF TriStar moments before. It had been a long journey, but they were all made to feel very welcome and they were most impressed by the facilities that are available for troops in Kandahar. After the first night welcome, the team moved to Bastion where they spent the day being shown around the various military vehicles in use on the ground, a popular vehicle between them was the 'Viking'. During the evening the Top Gear team was hosted by Sgt Michelle Petrie and Sgt Stuart Paterson in the Bastion cafe, where they signed a poster expressing thanks to NAAFI /EFI team working there. The poster then took its pride of place in the cafe.

On returning to Kandahar the stage was set at the new NAAFI Heroes bar, flanked by the newly arrived NAAFI mobile vans, for the Top Gear team to host an uncensored question and answer session for the gathering crowd. All three eagerly answered questions and engaged in banter with the crowd, in a manner not dissimilar to an episode of Top Gear, recounting stories from recent episodes of the show and their trip across the States. As with all good shows, things swiftly ended as Jeremy, James and Richard were ushered away for the waiting TriStar to fly them home.

2008

A fond farewell to NAAFI GB, From Andy Ellis head of operations 2008

A great proportion of the outlets in GB had now been outsourced. Following careful consideration Aramark Limited was selected as the preferred bidder for the contracts. This contract covered 77 outlets, which transferred over to Aramark. The programme of transfers started on the 9th of January 2008 and would continue then until March 2008. The contract with Aramark finally brought a firm timetable for the withdrawal of operations from Great Britain. Nearly six years after the decision was ratified by the defence management board.

Andy Ellis, GB head of operations had a few words to say: 'Well this is our time has finally come to leave and no it's not 2005 but 2008, three years after we should have finished and for most of us it was a day we thought we might never see. But this slow transition has left NAAFI in a position where Great Britain couldn't continue. As a result of this, 2008 saw the establishment leave. NAAFI and everybody should go with their heads held high with what has been achieved in Great Britain.

'Having had the pleasure of working as part of GB team both in field and centrally for the last four years I would like to wish you all the happiness and success in the future. I met plenty of characters who made me laugh and cry but overall, you've all made me extremely proud to lead such a quality team in trying times.

'GB has improved MCS, reduced stock losses and write offs, staff costs remain under budget and spending on other costs had been dropped and the top 10 issues had been relaunched. On top of this morale had not just remained but reached an even higher level.'

Goodbye Bosnia 2008

Not only did NAAFI say goodbye to the GB clubs and shops, they also said goodbye to Bosnia after 15 years' service. EFI had provided an essential service to troops serving on operations in Bosnia. However, with the gradual withdrawal of the United Nations peacekeeping force there, it was time for EFI to wind down and finally close its operations.

The service provided by EFI team over the years had been recognised as being an integral part of the British deployment. Matthew Rycroft, Britain's ambassador in Sarajevo, expressed his thanks to CEO Jim Glover by letter: 'You and your staff have proved a wonderful service to all of us. We have cherished that bit of Britain that you have provided. Can I ask you to pass on our appreciation to all.'

A review of 2008

When the new CEO took command in the middle of 2007, he set a mission to transform NAAFI into a customer-focused sustainable organisation. Ian Clark was the Program Manager put in place to ensure as smooth a transition as possible. To be successful with changes within a business, the transformation needs to be managed with an effective framework, in order to minimise risk through effective mitigation. A clear process was established for the management of the programme, enabling them to be as strategic as possible in the journey. Key milestones were marked out, while the mission was not racing along at speed but with still moving forward.

Jim Glover handed over the navigation to Reg Curtis, and he needed to maintain the momentum of change and continue the successful delivery of the transformation that was mobilised in 2008. Reg Curtis looked forward to working with the change steering group in particular and to ensure he was driving the change programme so that it delivered its strategic objectives that the executives had set out.

These key objectives were based around cultures and behaviours, defined trading territories, driving the profit in core territories, optimising cost base and risk and governance. The key changes that had already happened were some closures within the business: Bosnia, Cyprus, Kenya, Great Britain had closed, completing the programme for those areas; the only one in this area which was still in progress was Osnabrück. Service level agreements were almost complete: Northern Ireland, Gibraltar, NCS, Belize, South Atlantic and Brunei had all been settled, the two outstanding at this stage were EFI and the overarching agreements which needed key documents to replace the original NAAFI charter.

2009

Brand building 2009

From March 2009 the brand building journey gathered pace. Reg Curtis had achieved so much within the plans, in only a few months as they approached August they had already concluded a major refurbishment project in the Falklands, and reduced hundreds of prices of the basic essentials, in Afghanistan and Germany, and they had delivered their very own 'Catering heroes' competition.

They'd achieved all of this and delivered against budget, which any accountant could tell you was simply outstanding. This change with the new value lines and upgraded ranges, had really put in place a solid platform for NAAFI brand to build on. Whilst they could be forgiven for thinking that had turned a corner, they haven't got there just yet. They were only able to introduce these new lines at price cuts because they were saving money elsewhere and the future process team were doing an outstanding job in creating efficiencies within the business.

A lot of this work would go unnoticed but equally it was important for the company. Whilst this was great news, the CEO's job was to ensure that they did not become complacent as a business and they could not afford to take their foot off the pedal.

With any business you are only as good as the reputation you gain along the way, but brand perception can be very difficult to shift, especially if it has been built up and embedded over a long period of time. Changing the perception of a brand is not easy but the company was well on their way and heading in the right direction.

Sandstorms and vanilla milkshakes. Memories by Sadie Cook 2009

If you had told me a year before that I would have been packing my bags and heading to a military camp in the middle of the Helmand Province, I would have laughed in your face. But yes, perhaps in a moment of madness that is what I had decided to do, so in April 2009 my journey began and little did I know what was awaiting me.

After completing our pre-tour training there was a buzz of both excitement and nerves as we boarded our flight to Kandahar, Afghanistan. The journey was surprisingly comfortable and it helped sitting next to Matt, who kept me entertained when I wasn't reading the general inflight booklets and learning that the C-17 engines were made by Rolls Royce . . . (the little things you remember!), oh and I mustn't forget the endless munching on compulsory flight snacks.

The landing was swift and in darkness which wasn't ideal for somebody who isn't overly comfortable with the dark, but at least I had a hand to hold. The first thing I recall is the huge flies and moths, a mass of them swarming around the lights. Secondly the sweet, stale, dry heat that hit you as we exited the plane. The whole experience was overwhelming, the unknown of what we were entering combined with the fatigue of the long journey.

Checking in was well managed with swift systems in place and as soon as we had collected our belongings we were taken to a huge hangar. Upon our arrival we were advised that we would have to locate a bed or floor space to sleep on to bed down for the night. Because we were late no beds were available and the hangar was filled with sleeping bodies, of which some were accidentally stepped on during our search for a place to rest our weary heads. After a while we settled for a bit of floor space in desperate need for sleep; little did I know after being hit with a wall of heat upon exiting the plane the temperature would drop so much in the night. What had started off with me stripping down to some shorts and a t-shirt, ended with me scrambling to put on layers quietly along with my chunky desert boots.

I will always remember the flight to Bastion, the moment we were instructed to queue up at the back of the Hercules, to then run up the ramp to the rear whilst wearing our body armour. Imagine my panic as everybody seated quickly and strapped themselves in with ease. Having never being on such a fight I awkwardly fumbled with my safety belt whilst naively looking at a gentleman wearing traditional Afghan dress, wondering why the general public was flying on a military flight. Thankfully as the engines rumbled I was assisted with my belt and we took off to endure a noisy, dark flight. I copied the others and utilised my helmet to rest on the body armour to get comfortable and prayed that I would make it to Bastion safe and ultimately that I would not need to wee behind the toilet curtain.

The morning of our arrival in Bastion we woke again in a huge hangar in the stifling morning heat, hot, sweaty and in much need of a shower. We were met by a fellow NAAFI girl and taken to meet our team and to be shown to our accommodation for the next six months. Imagine my joy as we were taken to our accommodation which was not a tent. Having met Lorraine during training we had established a bond and were thrilled to be sharing a room, which we quickly took to cleaning with my ever essential Dettol wipes. The accommodation blocks consisted of two storeys each with a corridor with rooms on either side; each corridor was equipped with bathrooms and toilets, or should I say ablutions. Imagine my embarrassment upon arrival when I was tired and in much need of the loo, walking up and down the corridor looking for a toilet, to embarrassingly ask a squaddie where the toilet was to be told it was directly behind me. Yes, I had never even heard of that name for a bathroom before, but certainly will not forget it.

Once settled we went for a wander and found the NAAFI again and the local market stalls, which little did I know then that I would spend a lot of time there supping Afghan çay (tea) and chatting with a store holder named Smiley. We were pleasantly surprised to see a fully stocked NAAFI shop and an iso container converted into a Pizza Hut, so we were confident that we wouldn't run out of our essentials.

My time in Bastion 1 was spent as the supervisor of the café bar, a wooden structure a little like a big shed, with the most appalling excuse for air conditioning, but I grew to love it. I took great pride, much to the annoyance of the team, in cleaning it daily to rid it of dust and sand. However, you could almost guarantee that upon the completion of a full wall clean, a sandstorm would arrive. My first experience of a sandstorm was whilst I was talking to the head chef, only a few days after my arrival. Mid conversation at the back of the NAAFI he ran off, very rude I thought, little did I know that there was a sandstorm approaching me from behind and he had quickly ran for shelter without telling me, much to his amusement. Within seconds I was covered head to toe in an orange dusty sand, it managed to get everywhere and whilst quickly covering my mouth and nose I rushed to find a place of sanctuary, which was unfortunately in between the industrial bins, which you can imagine smelt lovely in that heat.

Deliveries arrived by a convoy of colourfully decorated wagons, driven by local Afghanis. Receiving the deliveries was always a challenge, in the airless plus 40C heat us girls would dress in tiny shorts and boob tubes for optimal sunbathing coverage, much to the shock of the delivery drivers who had to sit and wait, sometimes hours, whilst we unloaded each wagon by hand. I always felt a little sorry for the bored looking drivers, being away from their families whilst risking their lives to deliver Coke, Mars bars and food rations to us. I often raided the packed lunch supplies of fruit to take to them and in addition to the shock on their faces seeing a girl wearing so little, they always managed a smile, probably out of politeness from me trying to speak their language. They must have thought we were all crazy.

Unfortunately, as a result of our location, deliveries didn't always make it. Knowing that a driver had potentially lost their life filled me with sadness, and sometimes anger when a customer would have a good old moan because we had ran out of their favourite Rani juice. As a result of occasional low stock levels we had to be resourceful and I often found myself being very inventive. One particular time our fridges were empty and a delivery was overdue. Having checked what we had left it was noted that we for some reason had a mass of vanilla milkshakes going out of date, so I did some experimenting and realised that if you put it through a slush machine with some fresh coffee, you could make amazing iced coffees which went down a treat. Iced tea also sold well, after making it in huge trays in the oven and sweet talking the chefs from the cook house for lemons.

In addition to our makeshift drinks we also had the task of entertaining our customers. Quiz nights were always popular and it was great fun to sit on the bar shouting out the questions and answers, whilst telling the loud ones to pipe down. The NAAFI staff certainly owned the café bar and what we said went. In addition to this I also managed to arrange a salsa night with the Americans which was hilarious.

Being confined to a camp 24/7 was hard at times, in particular during an Op lockdown when there was no access to the internet or phones, resulting in you being unable to contact friends and family back home. For this reason it was so important that friendships were formed and that we were able to entertain ourselves. During my second tour, myself and the girls spent our evenings sat with the RAF firefighters who lived downstairs, playing poker, drinking tea and chatting; it certainly helped pass the time. Working in the NAAFI we also got the opportunity to meet other civilian teams such as the KBR gang, which was perfect if you needed some time away or a change of scenery.

It was down to these guys that I had shall we say a memorable 30th birthday at Bastion. My day began with Lorraine and myself being taken to look at some Black Hawks by my American Air Force friend Mico, which was an amazing experience. Later that day, knowing that I loved Indian cuisine, the KBR guys had arranged for one of their Sri Lankan colleagues to cook me some amazing food for my birthday celebrations. We all thoroughly enjoyed this, but literally as soon as we finished eating, a blasted sandstorm hit. We all ran into one of the rooms to hide, until the storm passed, but this one took forever. Naturally the time came when I needed the loo which was outside in another block, the sandstorm was so fierce that I had to completely cover my face and feel my way to the ablutions, which not only seemed to take forever, but was also painful as the sand whipped my bare arms. Of course the guys found it hilarious when I returned looking like an Oompa Loompa. It certainly was a 30th to remember.

One of the highlights of having downtime was if the wagon was available, as everybody knew that one of those permitted to drive it would be making a trip to the American PX to get a supply of cheap treats. You would be given a list of things to buy and bring back, including Aussie shampoo, crisps, American pop and peanut sweets; there was no wonder that I had an ever-extended waistline during my time there.

Afghanistan was, however, not always a place of sunshine and fun even for us NAAFI staff who remained behind the boundaries of the camp. The location of Bastion 1 NAAFI was directly behind the helipads, just to the side of the field hospital. The arrival of medivac Black Hawks and Chinooks is something that I will never forget, seeing the injured and deceased being carefully but quickly transported to the hospital a few metres away by ambulance, or by hand carried stretchers during periods when there physically wasn't enough ambulances. It was these moments that made you realise where you were and the true sadness and horrors of combat.

During one tour we learnt that there was a lot of civilian casualties being treated in the hospital, in particular children, so we all put together children's books and treats that we had posted from home and took them along to the hospital. It was heart breaking to see their scared faces, their injuries and worried family members. Even the offering of a gift, albeit small didn't manage to bring a smile to their faces, which truly demonstrated how the presence of war can impact the innocent.

Working for the NAAFI you need to be robust, adaptable whilst providing good service, humour and banter. But working in a tour based NAAFI is not just that, yes the above is a sign of a good customer care, but being a NAAFI member is about recognising those who are really suffering, those in need of a moment of your time, a shoulder to cry on, or just some support . . . along with a good old NAAFI brew.

I will never forget my two tours in Bastion. Not only have I have made friends, but my time there has made me appreciate life, freedom and the importance of a world without hate and war.

Operational service medals for EFI RLC and EFI civilian personnel 2009

When the going gets tough, NAAFI can be relied upon to stand up and be counted. Nowhere is this scene more plain than in Theatre. The operational service medal is awarded to soldiers and civilian personnel who complete a minimum of 30 consecutive days in Theatre. Reg Curtis took great pleasure in recognising the efforts and achievements of 10 Iraq, 28 Afghanistan and one non-Article 5 ISAF medal to members of staff who continue to make a difference overseas. These were awarded to uniformed EFI RLC and EFI civilian staff worked alongside each other. The first Civilian EFI staff to be deployed were posted to Iraq in late 2004 with more following them in early 2005.

NAAFI break 2009

For many years the NAAFI Break has been a mainstay for the British armed forces. Wherever you are in the world, whether it be onboard ship or out in Theatre or Germany or even the Falklands, NAAFI Break is as natural as having a cup of tea itself. NAAFI tea has been made by the company since the 1920s; it can even be traced back further. In its early days it was called a nice Cup of char, which a 'wad' would be the normal thing to have with it. NAAFI relaunched the NAAFI tea as 'NAAFI Break', With the intention that with every cup would help support military causes as NAAFI donated 50p for every box of tea sold. This was more than just packaging, this was a full rebranding and the NAAFI Break logo and the new packaging had been designed to reflect the heritage and the military connection in a fresh and modern way. Items like mugs, plates, key rings and even a teapot, were available to purchase alongside the brand-new branded tea and became collectors' items for the future.

Exercise at Sennelager 2009

In early September HQ 6th (UK) division held a command exercise at Sennelager to prepare for the next important operation, taking over command of Kandahar in Afghanistan. NAAFI were asked to supply an operational feeding over 24 hours a day, with facilities support. This would mean marquees, power, portacabins and all the trimmings with the management to go with it, as well as being asked to provide a full catering service for 700 multinational troops. This was the first major exercise support on this scale for quite some years! Following the last-minute change of location, the team had a mere six weeks to agree the services, right the statement of requirement and order the equipment; this left a mad dash to ensure everything was taken care of on the day.

Brian Williams who is in charge of the project management, said that the OPS team had been the backbone of the exercise. The exercise had enabled them to be seen as the multifaced company who are willing to go the extra mile when required. Looking back at the days of summer camps and tented canteens, the old school NAAFI would have been very proud of their efforts. The processes and plans had been put in place and the commercial team in HQ 1Div praised the professionalism and methodical approach to what they deemed a very tall order in the tight time constraints.

Remembrance Day 2009

On the 5th of November the chairman Sir Ian Prosser was joined by non-executive director, Alan Smith to lay crosses in the garden of Remembrance at Westminster Abbey. This was followed by a special festival of Remembrance service at the Royal Albert Hall on the 7th of November attended by Maj Lynn Cassidy and Cpl Nigel Lobley of EFI.

On Remembrance Sunday, Sir Ian and our chief executive, Reg Curtis, laid wreaths at the cenotaph in Whitehall on behalf of the board of management and EFI, where NAAFI was also proudly represented by Garreth Western, Andrew Murray, Marie Patten, and Mike Koziol from the overseas service, Riz Sizzon and Claire Duffield from CSO, Maj Lynn Cassidy and Sergeant Mike Corker of EFI and non-executive director, Allison Clifford-King, who gathered to pay their respects on what was a very moving occasion.

At the same time a service was held at St Georges church in Bulford where the NAAFI War Memorial is laid. In attendance with CO EFI Kevin Pembroke, Tim Elliott, chairman of the NCS EFI OCA, Sean Stacey, Cpl Marcus Waters and Cpl Nigel Lobley and Alice Membury.

A special Naval Service was also held on Sunday at Chatham, Gillingham, where Theresa Cooper, John Hughes, and Bill Clauge laid a wreath on behalf of NCS in memory of those who had lost their lives at sea. As many had been lost over the years with the biggest loss during World War II, NAAFI are very proud of those who went before them and gave their lives so bravely.

OCA to NEA 2009

Lt Col Pullen proposed a change to the name of the OCA. He said he was aware that the committee had for some time been considering ways of attracting younger EFI personnel to join the OCA. He felt that the words "old comrades" had connotations of previous generations and, in particular, WW2. The fact that personnel no longer worked for NAAFI or the EFI for a lifetime had caused a major change in attitude and the retention of the words "old comrades" in the OCA name was a hindrance to encouraging younger members. He therefore proposed that the name of the association be changed to the **NCS EFI Association**. This was a welcome change and a new crest was designed to reflect the changes.

2010–2020

2010

Five-star programme Project 148 by Mary Pittuck HR Business Partner 2010

Whilst out delivering the people's toolkit sessions in Germany, I had the pleasure of meeting one of our employees, Debbie Sibley who was nearing the final stages of completing a Five-star supervisors' programme.

As the name suggested, the supervisors' programme was made up of five stars, with modules completed in establishments before a final review took place. The whole programme resulted in a business plan, which in the past have not always been implemented, meaning there was no objective framework for the station business manager or country manager to sign off against. Consequently, employees could potentially finish the programme having completed none of the activities, with the skill levels of supervisors varying considerably.

A programme review highlighted that essentially the programmes themselves were comprehensive and benchmarked quite well against the other organisations, they just liked the framework that could drive consistent standards and evaluate where NAAFI benefited from the investment in development. To address this, the transformation project developed a framework that focused on our people, their behaviours, and their values, while at the same time providing the tools and practices needed to succeed in their roles. This included learning and development programmes which the pilot programme was put out before implementing across the whole business.

Having met Debbie at the October roadshow in 2009, she was keen to know how these changes would affect her and it was at this point that I knew she was the right person to pilot the new sign off, and provide constructive feedback, whether good or bad! Debbie was a truly forward-thinking individual and had a keen interest in learning and development, as I do! However, this wasn't what made Debbie inspirational. The truly amazing thing about Debbie was that you would never guess from meeting her that she was registered blind.

Despite this she managed to maintain almost impossible high standards at work, taking real pride in everything she achieved and did activities in her personal life that would scare most adventurous adrenaline junkies. The fact that she applied to go out and work for EFI only added to her character, and as the soon to be EFI business partner we were glad to have her. She didn't moan about her lot in life as she was one of the most positive employees that we'd met and Liz Walker and I both left inspired after our meeting; she could make a fortune telling her story all through motivational speaking! With continued support from Liz and me, the new sign off would be the ideal thing for her. Debbie had extracted every last ounce of development she could from the current programme, under Trish Prothero's guidance and supported by HR, and her development was continually monitored until her full sign off was completed.

Sandstorm and Fire, Op Herrick 12, Camp Bastion & Camp Leatherneck, Afghanistan, Memories by Charlene Watkinson May 2010

The sandstorm that happened on the night of the fire was one of the most spine-chilling occasions of my life. Suddenly out of nowhere I lost my vision, completely blinded by sand and dust I had no idea where I was or what I could do. Sitting in a 4 × 4 is normally quite comfortable, plenty of leg room and as an automatic vehicle there is never the worry of stalling the car or whether it's in gear. Tonight, was different, the whole car shook violently from side to side and I couldn't even see the front of the bonnet. I was on the main sand track road heading from Bastion 1 towards the flight line ready for the turn off to the right to head for Bastion 2.

We didn't make it that far. The traffic came to a standstill and Lorraine and I made a split-second decision to go with the flow, which was all we could do to be fair. There was a truck approaching from behind, I panicked that it wouldn't see us, we were encased in the middle of a sandstorm, everyone loses all visibility never mind those driving trucks higher up than us in our small by comparison 4 × 4. There was no turning in sight and before we knew it we had come to the T junction on the flight line, if I hadn't have realised where we were we could have ended up in one of two locations, first being down a ditch and the second being in the middle of the runway at Camp Bastion airfield, which was then busier than some of the UK airports by far.

After heading right, we ended up in the Supreme DFAC (dining facility) car park where I stopped the vehicle with a major sense of relief as I was no longer being pushed along by a row of traffic. I turned off the engine and sat back in a total blur, I couldn't believe we had actually made it as far as we did. I took one look at the Pizza Hut box on the back seat of the car and dived straight in as if this could be my last meal: so melodramatic! When the air started to clear we decided to try head back to Bastion 2 as we had Pizza Hut to deliver to some of the staff down there. When we did get there I actually couldn't believe my eyes, the sand and dust in the shop and the Piacetto Cafe was at least two inches thick, staff were desperately trying to sweep and wipe away as much as they could but it was pointless – once they had swept, by the time they got to sweep the dust out of the door the building would be covered again.

We headed back to Bastion 1 and quickly handed back the keys to the car, never again, no thank you, next time I think I will stick to ordering my own pizza, got to look after number one or no one else will as I was taught much earlier in life. At this point the fire at Leatherneck was still raging, taking up in flames anything and everything that stood in its way including ISO containers and even two American fire trucks. How ironic is it that a fire truck attempting to tackle the blaze was itself engulfed in flames and destroyed?

Camp Leatherneck was a 1600 acre American and Afghan forces base attached to Camp Bastion in Helmand province. On this night the Supply Management Unit lot had a fire that burned for approximately 8 hours. This fire caused so much damage and was fought by both American and British military fire crews on camp. Fire is by far one of the most terrifying occurrences to happen not only on a military camp but anywhere. Fire is unpredictable, life taking, and its destruction is clearly visible, even from space. Fire can take lives yet luckily not

Copyright Charlene Watkinson

one single person lost their life that night due to the planning and tackling of the fire from the RAF Fire Section at Camp Bastion. The RAF 90EW Regiment were thanked personally by a US General and hell they deserved it. The damage from the fire was hundreds of square feet in area, and the blackness of the scene totally reflects the damage and destruction caused that night.

I won't ever forget climbing onto the roof of an ISO container out the back of the NAAFI in Bastion 1 to watch on in horror as the flames spread. It was so bright; I've never seen a fire that big and it is something I wouldn't want to experience. The way we stood and watched the fire grow and spread was like a scene from a film; it's like it wasn't real. But it certainly was real and the effect it had on everyone in camp was not surprising. Everyone hugged each other a little tighter after that night and everyone came to appreciate life a little bit more because the outcome could have been so different if the fire had reached accommodation blocks or ammunition stores. Thank goodness for the Fire Services and service men and women from all over the world, for working together so well to contain the mass fire so it could burn itself out in a controlled and managed way.

EFI news from the frontline 2010

The EFI world continued to be a fluid and changing environment, and it remained challenging. The remains of project 148 were being implemented and of course the military component was being refocused in operational terms, so it was more aligned to the rest of the deployment force and able to move forward to the hostile areas.

This meant higher military standards to be reached at RTMC Chilwell in order to mobilise but that meant that they could justify their place in Afghanistan. The deployment into FOB Jackson had been highly successful, both in terms of the service provided and how well it had been received, but also in financial terms.

Our military recruiting continued to gear up and we were about to reach out to the regular reserve to see if we could tempt them to join us. The Royal Marines were also keen to pass our details on to those who chose to leave their recruit training programmes for personal reasons and also wish to do something different before going back again. However, they would always need NAAFI and EFI staff to continue applying for military training.

Dinner with David Beckham OBE memories by Charlene Watkinson, Op Herrick 12, Camp Bastion, Afghanistan 22nd May 2010

David Beckham is an idol to hundreds of thousands of people globally; he has proven to be a dab hand at controlling a football and scoring umpteen goals for football clubs worldwide and also for his country. Yet away from football he is also a genuinely nice man, a morale boost to Britain's troops and also quite a funny guy.

David Beckham had wanted to visit Afghanistan for a while but with football commitments and a family to think of it had, until now, never been possible. I may have been living in a hostile, war torn country, but David Beckham had wanted to lift morale, so he came and visited Camp Bastion. Rumours were always rife in camp and I had learnt the hard way to never to believe anything until I had seen it with my own eyes or heard it with my own ears. The rumour was that the one and only David Beckham was due to visit on a whistle stop tour, in and out of Afghanistan in a weekend.

However, this wasn't a rumour, this was gospel truth. I remember popping into the MT tent as I did on so many occasions except this time was different. Everyone was excited and upbeat, not the usual MT Squadron that I normally visited with goods to boost their morale. Someone was normally moaning about something or someone but not this time. "I'm driving a VIP tomorrow," said one lad; "Yeah, well I'm having tea with him," said another. I remember thinking hang on a minute; are you lot winding me up? But no, they weren't, not in the slightest, David Beckham was finally up in the air on an RAF flight from Brize Norton to Bastion!

Me being me wanted to get in on this little piece of history, well he was the first international football star to visit us aside from Gary Lineker, but he doesn't really count! So, two packs of Hamlet cigars used as bribery along with a big huge smile and there I was, in line, stood outside the cookhouse tent, waiting to enter to have tea with David Beckham himself! There were a few other people there too, like the MT section and a few Quarter Masters but in my head, there was just David and me. After the meal David visited every single table, shook hands with everyone, signed autographs, asked about people's experiences and families back home and posed for umpteen photographs.

What a lovely guy, genuinely happy to be a source of morale amongst troops at war and us civilians working alongside them. It was clear to me that visiting us and the camp really wasn't a publicity stunt or something he had been made to do by his PR team or management. David

Beckham indisputably wanted to do this for us, and it had worked. After spending time in the cookhouse David also held a talk including a question and answer session for everyone on Camp which was really interesting; it was nice to hear from him how much he admired the British Army and everyone else working to keep the camp running.

Amesbury becomes a much-loved part of history 2010

The closing of the NAAFI site at Amesbury signalled the end of one of the most historic sites in our long and distinguished history. Like our home at Imperial Court in Kennington Lane, there were a few places that had such an impact on the organisation than our former head office at Amesbury. Since the company established in 1920, Kennings Way in London was previously NAAFI's only general warehouse in the UK. The outbreak of the Second World War, however, changed all that and in 1939 the Amesbury site was acquired after it was agreed that the messing stores on the Salisbury Plain were not large enough to hold all the stock required.

At the time there was just a few Nissen huts on the site, but soon a makeshift warehouse was built to accommodate the growing demand for space. The situation was ideal due to the railway running alongside with the facilities lasting throughout the war. In 1969 the first modern warehouse block was built on the Amesbury site with much of the stock transferred from Kennings Way. When Kennings Way closed in October 1971, Amesbury became the distribution centre for the whole of the southern half of England. Over the years more warehouses and office blocks were added, and the famous NAAFI tea factory moved onto the Amesbury site next door.

Following the closure of Imperial Court offices in 1991, the majority of staff were transferred to Amesbury and at its peak between 1994 and 97 there were 629 staff working at the site. In October 1997, NAAFI's contract for supplying goods was won by Booker and subsequently the NAAFI distribution centre was closed. This resulted in a loss of many jobs from the warehouses and support services. Support staff levels decreased year on year, before the doors finally closed with only 12 staff occupying a single office room in Amesbury in 2010.

For its final two years Amesbury's office had been the hub of support to the overseas service areas but following the restructure this support moved to the central support office in Darlington and the EFI offices in Grantham. The closing of the office signalled the end of an era for residents of Amesbury and the surrounding area. Most people who lived in Amesbury had worked or known someone who had worked with NAAFI at some time or another. The bus stop outside was named the NAAFI bus stop!

Rhine Garrison changes 2010

Since 2008 project BORONA was the MoD project to reduce the number of serving military personnel in Germany over a five-year plan that started in the summer of 2010 with the move of NATO ARRC (allied rapid reaction Corps), from JHQ to the UK. The move reduced the population of JHQ by around half and the consequence of this move would see facilities and services that supported the larger population close in the summer of 2010. The next stage of the programme BORONA would not impact until 2013.

For NAAFI this meant they had to plan for the impact to start to develop the best offer for our customers who still remained in JHQ for the foreseeable future. Late in 2009 the first stage of this action plan took place with the refurbishment and the reduction in size of the Max store on JHQ. The significant investment had enabled them to keep a modern and extensive retail offer in the community with no loss of range.

The next stage had a much bigger impact on NAAFI. During the first week of August 2010 the 'Big house shop' closed, and the cafe provided a small retail offer. The closure of the Buschof local, Express shop, the junior ranks' club and the fish and chip shop followed, with all facilities closing their doors for the last time. However, the Max store opening hours increased to allow customers the convenience of shopping until 2200hrs.

In the nearby JB's they invested in creating a catering, retail, and leisure under one roof. This development would deliver a new bottle bar for junior ranks, a new gaming and vending zone, a small retail area and a fish and chip offer alongside the successful JB's restaurant. While completing this, David Jones and Linda Edwards and their team had moved people around the business to alternative sites and also worked closely with the local command to ensure that all customer requests were met as close as possible.

September 2010 brought about a new era to the Rhine Garrison and many offers such as the American PX colour Dutch PMC, a civilian mess, had gone. However, NAAFI would remain serving the services into the future.

NAAFI Uncovered silencing the myths 2010

In 2009 November NAAFI had been asking customers questions about the business, including what it stood for, where the profits went to and who actually owned the company. Some of the answers were shocking and just showed that some of the rumours were so far off the mark.

The NAAFI Uncovered campaign was the result of the consumer research carried out which pointed to the fact that many of the customers didn't know what NAAFI stood for, what the role was in the armed forces and how we are here for the benefit of the forces community. Contrary to popular belief amongst some customers, we weren't part of the SPAR group or even owned by them, and they weren't even headed up by a retired Brigadier or any other company for that matter.

The simple truth of the matter is that NAAFI was a non-profit organisation with no shareholders to reward and any financial surpluses were reinvested back into the community for the benefit of service personnel and their families. It was that simple and it had been that simple since the day of its conception and even before when Fortescue laid the groundwork for the now legendary NAAFI and all it stood for.

Remembrance Day 2010 by Tim Elliot

On the 11th of November, finance director Sally Ann Dixon was joined by deputy chairman James Wild, non-executive director, Alan Smith, CO EFI RLC, Lt Col Kevin Pembroke and Tim Elliott, chairman of the NEA to lay crosses in the garden of Remembrance at Westminster Abbey. An occasion that was attended by HRH the Duke of Edinburgh. The field which was established for the first time in 1928, paid tribute to all service and civilian serving personnel who have served since WWI.

This occasion was followed by a number of Remembrance Day services on Sunday the 14th of November. In Bulford director of risk management Martin Percy was joined by Alan Smith and NEA members, Tim Elliott, and Bob Lewis, to lay wreaths during the memorial service at St George's church where the NAAFI War Memorial resides. A special Naval Service was also held at Great Lines Naval War Memorial, Gillingham, where chief executive Reg Curtis was joined by James Wild buying director, Chris Emmel, Roger Bentley of NCS and Ray Yeomans of the NEA in laying a wreath in memory of those who lost their lives at sea. Following the EFI team's recent move to Grantham, they were also proud to attend a local services and St Wulframs church, which was attended by the head office of overseas, Garreth Weston, and RSM Felix Ralph.

At Whitehall director of marketing Andrew Smart and Lt Col Kevin Pembroke laid wreaths at the cenotaph on behalf of the board of management and EFI. NAAFI was represented in the Remembrance Sunday parade by non-executive director General Sir Reddy Watt, and other members of staff. They were proud to have John Fieldman the NAAFI trustee committee and Norman Brown, brother of the late WWII hero Tommy Brown, GM, along with them, who both braved the elements to pay their respects on what was a very moving occasion.

For the first time a live interview with Lt Col Kevin Pembroke on Sky News happened shortly after the parade, paying tribute to the 550 NAAFI employees who lost their lives in WWII.

2011

BSN expansion project 2011

As part of the commitment to the Serving the Services and providing that little Taste of Home out in the operational zones, NAAFI had opened a brand-new cafe bar and shop in Camp Bastion, Afghanistan. The New Piacetto cafe in Bastion 1 provided serving personnel with an offer they had come to expect at Bastion 2 and Kandahar, with coffee, pastries and television screens providing that Taste of Home and a welcome place to relax.

Thirteen German contractors arrived in Camp Bastion on the 1st of October 2010, with work commencing two days later on Sunday the 3rd of October. The original completion date for Bastion 1 new build and fit out was the 4th of November 2010 but thanks to the efficient planning and a lot of hard work, the outlet opened for business on the 25th October, 9 days ahead of schedule! This created its own set of problems, as the new EFI team who were due to work in the facility was still in flight. Thankfully the EFI staff on site did a fantastic job of holding the Fort until they arrived, ensuring a smooth transition and a great service to the customers.

As soon as the first new build had been completed, the next part of the project was to refurbish the existing shop next door and turn the facility into a 'Heroes bar'. The refurbishment was designed to be more relaxed than other outlets with numerous free to play games consoles, fruit machines and even pool tables, giving the customers a place where they could escape from the pressures of their day-to-day work in an operational area.

Lt Col Kevin Pembroke CO EFI RLC said: 'Both of these facilities were absolutely vital. For these men and women, it provided that ability to do something normal, even if it was just to queue up for a coffee, pay for it and then spend time chatting with their mates in a completely relaxed environment. I think in these facilities people can easily forget about what's happening immediately outside and beyond the wire, so in that respect they are absolutely vital.'

News from Brunei 2011

On the 18th of May 2011 Reg Curtis, Steve Marshall and David Jones paid their annual visit to Brunei to see the current offer and make sure that it was in line with the global NAAFI strategy. As well as checking on current progress, the annual visit also gave Reg the chance to see the development of the new swimming pool kiosk and the Chautari Club refurbishment, with all parties keen to get this completed before the battalion returns from their six month tour of Afghanistan. Whilst the main purpose of the trip was to view and review the current progress and assess what can be done to further improve the overall offer, it also gave him the chance to maintain the relationship with the local senior Garrison personalities.

This was further reinforced when Reg was invited by the deputy chief of staff and acting Garrison commander Maj Vince Young to come back to Brunei and carry out the official opening of the Chautari club and Garrison swimming pool once completed.

Whilst on a visit David Jones was also able to present some welfare cheques to four different sections of the community, as well as present some long service and employee of the month awards to members of staff. Awards for five years' service were presented to Erland Felizar, second cook, Kennedy Pasan, CSA, Michelle Sue Lee, CSA, and me, Gary Pickett, country manager, Brunei. Whilst the gold employee of the month was awarded to Badeth Garavillas, who was also part of the team that won the silver team of the month award.

2012

Chief Executive, NAAFI 2012

In 2012, Mr Curtis gave an address to the NEA/OCA on NAAFI's trading position as at the end of April, and the progress that the business had made, and was making, on several fronts. 2011 had marked the successful end of NAAFI's 5-year recovery plan, and because of this, the 2012/13 financial year started with a sustainable business, and the strongest set of results for NAAFI since 1993.

As part of the government's Strategic Defence and Security Review (SDSR) was turning into the reality of a plan, which would mean that all British troops based in Germany would be re-based back to the UK. This implied that NAAFI's business would half by 2016, and eventually cease to exist in its present form by 2020. MOD was sensitive to this and had effectively guaranteed NAAFI's business until 2020.

Nevertheless, 2020 was still a long way off and, in the meantime, the aim remained to provide a great business for NAAFI's customers for some time yet! NAAFI's strategy to 2020 had been developed with the aim of providing a sustainable business until then, preserving the "Service to the Services" ethos.

In 2011, Costa Coffee branding had been brought to cafes in Germany and Northern Ireland, facilities in Brunei and the Falkland Islands had been upgraded, and all sites in Northern Ireland and Gibraltar had been re-fitted. All sites worldwide (barring NCS ships) were now managed by an EPOS system, and Afghanistan continued to trade well with new facilities opened in Bastion.

Lt Colonel Kevin Pembroke, Commanding Officer EFI and NCS 2012

NCS service was now being provided on 19 operational vessels (with a further 3 in re-fit), by 27 ocean-going staff with 4 shore-based support staff. NCS staff had deployed on two RFAs and other vessels to Libya as part of Operation COUGAR the previous year. NCS staff would also be providing a 24-hour service on board HMS Ocean, which was to serve as accommodation for troops providing security in London during the Olympics.

EFI staff were now working more closely with deploying troops to Afghanistan, commencing with three months of training and preparation, which was aiding integration. In addition to existing locations, EFI staff were also now deployed in three forward operating bases. The border closures between Pakistan and Afghanistan concentrated sales on core and essential ranges while alternative supply routes were being utilised.

Customer feedback graded the EFI experience overall as excellent/good and the Commander Task Force Helmand had recently endorsed EFI's 3 Rapidly Deployable Shops in patrol bases as 'a highly valued but limited resource that are vital to the moral component'. Recruitment continued to develop and evolve, and work was underway to define a peace-time structure for the military EFI role.

2013

10th Anniversary of the commencement 2013

As 2013 was the 10th anniversary of the commencement of what became a 5-year long commitment for EFI – Op TELIC – the chairman said that it was a particular pleasure for him to see 'veterans' of that Operation at the meeting. They had all done NAAFI proud but none more so, than those who were there at the very beginning, when they came under missile fire and lived with the daily fear of a chemical or biological attack. He said that he could still hear EFI's Operational Commander, then Lt Col (subsequently Brigadier) Rory Maxwell telling a visiting General that it took the US welfare organisation AAFES 3 months to provide retail facilities at the joint logistical support base. In the Kuwait desert a detachment led by Sgt Debbie Loftus, had opened an EFI shop within a matter of days of arriving. Cpl Mike Corker had done the same subsequently when the Force moved north to Camp Smitty, near al Samawah in Iraq, within just 24 hours of the EFI staff, stock and 'flat-packed' accommodation arrived on site.

There were many more stories of heroic examples of commitment above and beyond the call of duty that followed. While the conflict was relatively swift, the subsequent insurgency meant that playing their part in keeping the peace in Iraq during the following 4 and a half years, often placed EFI staff in situations of life-threatening danger.

The chairman of the NEA said that, time and time again, he had found himself humbled by their bravery and determination to serve the 'lads' as they referred to their customers. But perhaps none more so than Cpl Tracey Mackenzie, who had to be ordered to leave the Shatt-al-Arab location in Basrah, after it came under an average of over 100 indirect fire attacks every 24 hours, over a three-day period. One mortar had actually landed in the ISO container that had been used to store stock. By some strange act of providence, Tracey had seen the need to transfer most of her remaining stock into the shop just the previous day.

Having been the first member of EFI to arrive in Kuwait as the coalition forces prepared for the conflict in 2003 and being the last to leave Iraq in 2008 when EFI's work was done, he had witnessed many such acts of selflessness, during the 5 years.

Reg Curtis, Chief Executive, NAAFI 2013

Mr Curtis said that the past year had been a difficult one for the organisation and the toughest that he had experienced during his tenure as chief executive.

Although the reduction in the military population in Germany had caused a decline in sales, NAAFI had been successful in maintaining the previous year's momentum and had achieved both trading surplus and cash targets; a reflection of how hard everyone was working to minimise costs and improve service. Nearly £1.8m in welfare returns had been given to garrisons worldwide in the previous year. The growth in online shopping had also affected NAAFI and, going forward, concentration would be on maintaining ranges which customers wanted to continue buying from NAAFI with the less popular categories being dropped.

IT support had been consolidated into one global infrastructure to provide a consistent offer and better efficiencies and the customer service strategy continued to go from strength to strength. Customer-facing projects had delivered refits in Brunei and the Falklands. Older canteens on-board HM ships had been re-fitted as had 5 more stores in Germany, and NAAFI were in the process of relocating its support office from JHQ to Bielefeld.

NAAFI's people continued to be its bedrock and a number of initiatives had been introduced to support and encourage them including a 'People First' Award Scheme to recognise those staff that truly put the customer first. The results were appreciated by customers and NAAFI was excelling at serving the Services with one of the results being that SLAs were being extended, including in Northern Ireland.

Turning to EFI, Mr Curtis said that an outstanding service continued to be offered to troops in-Theatre, a fact that was recognised by individual customers and the Chain of Command alike. EFI personnel continued to remain in the firing line and, in one particular instance, being directly involved in insurgency action. They could justifiably claim to be soldiers first and shopkeepers second.

From Court Security to the Desert, Memories by Matt Warner 2013

Friday January 4th 2013: As I conducted my last patrol of the Court building I contemplated what I was about to embark on in the next couple of days, I thought about the last 4 years as a Court Security Officer and all of the experiences I've had until this point.

As I walked the halls of the Court for the final time I thought about all of the people I'd met and all of the incidents and situations I'd found myself in and wondered how I'd managed to come out the other side. I finalised my patrol, called in my final end of duty patrol, set the intruder alarm and made my final exit. As I locked the door for the last time, I realised that it was raining heavily, "Bloody hell, typical!" I said to myself. I set off home, stopped a little way and looked back at the building and institution I'd spent 4 years of my life and career protecting and realised that this was it.

Sunday January 6th, 2013: Having spent the weekend with family and getting all of my kit ready in my gorilla box and bag I set out with my dad and his then fiancée. I spent much of the car journey to Grantham in silence, watching the world go by and thinking about what was coming and not knowing what to expect. All I could think about is how I had gone from a job I loved to something completely different and unknown. We arrived at Prince William of Gloucester Barracks, Grantham, sometime in the early afternoon. As we approached the gate house, I could feel my pulse racing, I was sweating and terrified at what I'd gotten myself into.

We entered the gate house and got issued our passes to go into the Camp, we found the building in which I'd spend the next few days. A senior member of the EFI staff met us, she introduced herself and we all got chatting; she showed me to the correct building and room that I'd be staying in for the week. The room was a sergeant's dorm room, all the beds were neatly made but looked as if they had been made back in the 1950s; upon closer inspection most of the rubberised mattresses dated back to the early 90s.

Monday 7th January to Friday 11th January 2013: During the week we learned things about the NAAFI along with our branch, the EFI. We learned some basic battlefield first aid, did marches in full kit which included body armour and combat helmet and eventually we went to another camp to collect our MOD issue Body Armour and Combat Helmets along with ballistic goggles and other essential deployment gear.

By Friday the 11th January myself and colleagues were ready to deploy, our other colleagues had some finalisations to their checks to be completed and would join us shortly after our deployment. With that in mind we said our goodbyes and headed over to the EFI HQ building, by the parade square in the Prince William of Gloucester Barracks, to do some final administration and to mount up onto the minibus; we were to go to RAF Brize Norton and from there we'd fly to various locations before finally arriving at Camp Bastion Airfield to begin our first tour. We arrived at RAF Brize Norton and met up with a larger group of EFI Colleagues who were all headed out to Afghanistan the next morning with us.

Eventually we ended up in a bar where I met Steven, I got chatting to him and admitted that sometimes I would feel depressed and had suffered from nightmares due to some of the situations I'd been involved with whilst serving as a Court Security Officer; he understood how I felt and told me to come and talk to him whenever I felt I needed to. Later on, in the evening we went to collect our things and headed to the terminal, this was it! Once past the entry point there was no going back, I would be committed. I took some hours to finally board the plane and it was quite early in the morning by the time we started to taxi onto the runway, none of us has slept yet and it showed. As the plane readied for take-off I gripped the chair arm tightly, we started to take off, we hurtled down the runway at speed and took off into the morning sky, the adventure had just begun and I had no idea what to expect.

Between the 12th January and 14th January 2013 (Travelling): I spent a great deal of the journey asleep, the drone of the engines would knock me out, eventually I was awoken by the smell of food, I was starving. A member of the air crew came by with hot food and drink. I fell back to sleep almost as soon as I was done eating.

Arriving at Camp Bastion: The lights dimmed and then turned off, we sat there in pitch blackness as the plane started to bank and turn for its final approach to land in Camp Bastion. I took a deep breath and thought 'this is it, here we go'.

The landing took some time but eventually we had hit the runway and it was time to get off. We were told to put on our armour and have our helmets ready and to make our way across the airfield to the safety of the blast walls and terminal as quickly and safely as possible, I was terrified; I knew that the Camp airfield had been attacked in 2012 as my father had been working in Camp Bastion that year and was present during the attack, my heart raced and I struggled to keep up with the rest of my colleagues.

I reached the terminal and blast walls and felt a little bit safer; upon arrival we were sorted into various groups and given an introduction to the Camp, told what was expected of us and given a demonstration of what sirens to listen out for and what to do if we heard the sirens sounding if they were not preceded with a warning letting us know it was a test. We signed our paperwork, collected all of our things and met up with our drivers who would take us to the small camp site I would call home for the next 14 months.

Arrival at Camp 601 Royal Logistics Corps and EFI, Camp Bastion 2: I was struck by how dark the camp was, despite all of the floodlighting inside the various compounds we passed, the road was dark, unpaved and not quite as bumpy as I had expected.

We were taken to the EFI accommodation which consisted of a large tent hallway with multiple tents attached, it sort of reminded me of the layout of a space station; one central compartment with lots of other habitats docked to it. The floor was made up of interlocking plastic tiles with no support structure below them, they were often wonky and easy to trip over if you were not paying attention.

Once we had found a bed space we headed out with more senior members of the EFI to find some food, the cook house had closed several hours before we landed so we were taken to the EFI shop, coffee shop and the Kentucky Fried Chicken, to get some drinks and food.

Camp 601, Camp Bastion 2, Day Zero (Rest Day): I woke up early, I sat up in my bed listening to the noises coming from outside. The tent was totally dark except for spots of light coming in through gaps in the tent door. I looked for my gorilla box and dug out my towel and other toiletries. After my shower I went back to my bed space, I had been told the night before to dress in my EFI uniform as I would be getting my Camp Bastion ID card today and would be travelling to my work location in Bastion 2 to meet my new colleagues.

We all set off in the car to go to "The badging office" which was located on a long-tarmacked road separating Camp Bastion and the American Camp Leatherneck. Whilst we drove to the badging office I was surprised at just how large and vast the Camp was, the roads were enormous and there was the bustle of activity which reminded me of a normal working day in Bristol.

Once we had our badges we got back into the car and headed back to Camp 601 in Bastion 2, stopping off at Bastion 1 Heroes first, we were taken to our respective places of work and introduced to our new colleagues. This is where I met Chris, he was one of the senior members of staff and he gave us an introduction into both locations and explained the different jobs we'd be doing whilst working there, I was to be placed in the EFI Shop next door to the EFI Coffee Shop in Bastion 2.

Day 1, Camp 601, Camp Bastion 2 & RSOI: We headed for the RSOI tent in Bastion 3 – RSOI stands for Reception, Staging, Onward movement and Integration – we were to complete one day of this week-long introduction to Afghanistan as we were not due to go outside of Camp Bastion.

RSOI took the majority of the day and consisted of drinking copious amounts of tea and coffee to stay awake as we were all quite jetlagged and really feeling it by that time; we experienced what was jokingly called "Death by power point" which showed us everything from how to use the dining facilities to what the Afghan national police and army uniforms looked like. By the end of the day we were all exhausted and headed back to Camp 601. Our training was complete, our integration into the EFI finalised and we were ready to start work the very next day.

First Tour and as much as I can remember from beginning to end: The first few weeks of my first 6-month tour were spent getting used to my new job, meeting new people and exploring both Camp Bastion and Camp Leatherneck.

I was introduced to the Danish Contingent march by Mehdi. The first march was held on the 4th May 2013 and it absolutely destroyed me for a good two weeks, but I did complete it within the 6-hour time limit, barely. The march was held on the 1st June 2013 which I successfully completed with a bit of difficulty but did much better and the final march I participated in was held on the 6th July 2013 where I did my best performance and even helped to spur along a newly arrived female soldier of the RLC who was, in my opinion, insane enough to participate so early into her tour; each march was two laps around Camp Bastion totalling 25 km.

I fell in love with long distance walking and the time it gave me to both exercise but also have time to myself, the ability to just pop in headphones and walk around by myself was something I loved. The march route became my normal walking route every single morning before work with the exception of my day off and I would walk it with my backpack and just over 10 Kilograms of weight.

My first 6 months felt quite turbulent, I was suffering severe depression for a number of years before my arrival to Afghanistan and during my first 2 months on Camp; at this time my depression had never been diagnosed and I didn't realise that I had a problem. Being at Camp Bastion almost certainly saved my life as I had contemplated suicide on quite a few occasions, including when I first got to the Camp. With my weight loss and newfound healthy diet and exercise I started to feel much better about myself both physically and mentally; for this, my time with the EFI and in Camp Bastion will hold a very special place in my heart. I arrived in Camp Bastion 28 Stone, bordering 29 Stone, and finished my first tour at 16.5 stone; it was a painful transition from being morbidly obese to a more healthy weight with things such as mouth ulcers making my daily life a nightmare but well worth it in the end. Despite doing so well I would still slip, frequently, into bouts of depression and this would continue until I finally had an official diagnosis of severe depression and anxiety at crisis stage in 2017.

The end of my first tour July 2013: So the day to leave Camp Bastion came, we were given our leaving date details and papers and prepared ourselves for our end of Tour only to be told that the Aircraft had "broken down" and that we would have to wait until the next day before we could head home. With that I decided to go to the Danish Camp Viking to watch an Elvis impersonation act, we got set up and I had my camera ready to film the act when one of our colleagues came screeching into the car parking area in a plume of dust and called us to the car shouting that we were due to fly out within half an hour and we were to get to Bastion airfield as quickly as possible with our things. We ran to the car, went back to Camp 601 to collect our gear and made way to the Airfield; we booked in with the airfield staff.

We spent some hours stuck inside the terminal waiting to board an aircraft, this is where we were informed that we would be flying home on a C-17 cargo plane filled with heavy cargo like equipment and vehicles, they were not lying; I spent the flight sleeping next to a large fuel truck. After a long, cold flight we made it to RAF Brize Norton, despite it being the middle of summer in the UK I felt cold and kept my body armour on for warmth. Eventually my father got to the airport and I went to meet him; he was shocked at how much weight I had lost and how different I looked. That began my 6 weeks' leave before I redeployed for my second tour.

Six weeks later, redeployment, second tour 2013: Having completed the now familiar journey back to Camp Bastion I was back waiting in the terminal waiting for a pickup to go back to Camp 601 and to be told where I would be based this tour. I was quite nervous because I was no good at making coffees or food, so the Coffee shop or Heroes bar were a terrifying prospect to me.

The next day I went to work at the Heroes bar. For the first couple of weeks I had difficulty keeping up with the fast pace of the establishment and my mental health took quite a hit. I spoke to the person in charge about it and she agreed to have me sent back to the store I had spent my first tour in, but warned that it might not be for very long. Sure enough, after a few weeks in the store I was back at Heroes; I was still nervous but willing to try my best to keep up with everyone else. After a few weeks I got the hang of the different processes and managed to find a shift I was best at, the late shift. The second tour was largely uneventful, aside from a few incidents which I was not involved with as they were military level incidents which I was not trained nor equipped to deal with.

I forget when but there was also a day that I went with colleagues to see the Apache attack helicopters and their compound, I had a great time visiting that compound and even got to see two helicopters making a landing having just returned from a mission. With the introduction of a curfew, due to dwindling numbers of armed personnel on the camp, I was restricted on when I could go out to different places – where I had previously been able to go to 'Green Beans Coffee' in Camp Leatherneck in the middle of the night, I could no longer do this, this solidified my desire to conduct physical training in the mornings and work in the afternoons and night.

Towards the end of my second tour, the Camp experienced extremely cold weather with a huge deposit of snow. One thing that irritated me about this was that the quality of the snow was so much better than what we get in the UK.

Not long after that, a few days, I was boarding the aircraft to go back to the UK; I was excited to get home but at the same time I was sad to be leaving Camp Bastion. I spent time reflecting on my complete shift from being absolutely terrified of the place to wanting to go back and spend more time there. I returned to the UK in February 2014.

2014

NEA prepare to stand alone 2014

2014 had been an important year for the Association as they prepared to 'stand alone' and be less reliant on NAAFI, considering the downsizing process that the organisation was going through. They had taken over responsibility for providing Remembrance wreaths and crosses which were laid in memory of fallen NAAFI colleagues and various other activities which would mean the need for greater use on the funds. At the AGM when the subject of finances came up, there was a strong representation from members to reinstate the annual subscription charge. It was decided that, for the time being at least, we would refrain from the reintroduction of a subscription fee.

Since conception in 1946 the members had been those who had been EFI enlisted, NCS attested and NCS only members. It was decided to introduce a new membership category – that of Associate Member – which will be open to UK-based civilian NAAFI personnel who had supported EFI in operational theatres. This was in recognition of the remarkable contribution made by civilian staff towards EFI's presence in both Iraq and, more recently, Afghanistan. They would not be able to vote or draw on the benevolence fund or be entitled to assistance from the Military charities due to not being enlisted like their uniformed colleagues, but would benefit form the core values from the NEA of comradeship and be able to attend remembrance events as an Associate member.

The saddest moment of the NEA was that 2014 marked 148 Sqn EFI RLC's closure as a military unit, with the withdrawal of British troops from Afghanistan, it had been disbanded. Those who served in EFI over the years could look back with pride, on the part that they played in providing a service to the Services, often in very difficult and unpleasant circumstances. There was no doubt that all personnel helped to make the life of servicemen and women on operational tours much more bearable.

Chief Executive, NAAFI 2014

Mr Curtis provided members with a full resume of NAAFI's situation and started by announcing that, since the previous AGM, the central support headcount had reduced by a targeted 45% with the attendant costs having reduced by 77% over the past 6 years. One of the key factors in achieving this had been the on-time, on-budget, introduction of a new IT system which enabled all of NAAFI worldwide to operate on one simplified system.

He predicted that the 2014/15 financial year would see a continuation of the cost reduction plan although the focus would be on retaining key people, helping them to build their CVs and to prepare them for life after NAAFI.

However, as the re-basing of troops from Germany and Afghanistan gathered pace, sales were expected to decline further. Nevertheless, Mr Curtis said that he expected that NAAFI would maintain its cash generative capacity, by keeping cost ratios in line with reduced sales.

Brunei continued to be a success story with improved year-on-year sales, Gibraltar continued to struggle due to a reduction in the military population on the Rock. Trade remained steady in NCS with a further three ship's canteen upgrades programmed for the year. Trade in the Falklands and on Ascension Island was showing positive growth following the completion of major re-fits in both areas, in June 2014. Trade in Northern Ireland remained challenging as the military population there continued to dwindle.

In the shops, in Germany, NAAFI had ceased to stock a non-food range with the shop floor space freed up, being filled by, installing community centres and SSVC electrical stores in Gütersloh, Sennelager, and Bielefeld. NAAFI would continue to support the British Forces in Germany until they finally depart in 2018/19 but recognised that the cost of doing so might outweigh the need and that a balance might have to be struck.

In Afghanistan the military exit was well under way, with all Forward Operating Bases now closed. Bastion facilities would have a phased close down that was expected to be completed in December 2014, with Kandahar having closed in late autumn 2014, although there was a possibility of a future into 2015 for NAAFI in Kabul under a planned Operation named Op TORAL.

All uniformed EFI staff had returned from operations and a redundancy programme was reaching its final stages. NAAFI no longer had any deployable uniformed EFI personnel for the first time since it was established, truly the end of an era. He confidently predicted that NAAFI would endure beyond its Centenary in 2020.

2015

NEA and Remembrance 2015

Field of Remembrance Service took place outside St Margaret's Church, opposite the Houses of Parliament. Ex-WOII Terina Hounsell would be fronting the plot once again. Tim Elliott and other members of the committee in attendance.

Chatham Naval Dockyard, Ray Yeomans and new member Ray Barnett laid wreaths at the Chatham Dockyard Service on behalf of NAAFI as well as the Association.

St George's Church, Bulford was the location of NAAFI's memorial to those who made the ultimate sacrifice.

National Memorial Arboretum, near Lichfield, Richard Gaymer attended the service and would welcome other members of the Association to join him. Richard would particularly like a volunteer to lay a wreath on behalf of NAAFI whilst he does the same on behalf of the Association. The Iraq memorial, which was at the COB, Basra Airport, had been re-constructed along with the Bastion memorial to those who fell in Afghanistan at the NMA.

The Cenotaph, Whitehall. The Association had been given the opportunity, for the first time, to represent 148 Sqn EFI and NCS at the Cenotaph march-past. Twelve ex-members of EFI and NCS were permitted to attend. This was a key turning point in the recognition of service of the military side of NAAFI.

St Nazaire, France, Taffy Davies, attended the Service to commemorate the 75th anniversary of the sinking of the Lancastria, and to attend a civic reception afterwards which was hosted by the mayor of St Nazaire.

Chief Executive, NAAFI 2015

Mr Curtis provided members with a detailed account of NAAFI's activities since the previous AGM which had delivered very strong financial results. In recognition of the performance and increasing standards, the MoD had agreed that the Service Level Agreements (SLA) for Brunei, the South Atlantic, and Northern Ireland would be extended to 2018, in line with the SLAs for Germany and the Royal Navy.

A cost reduction plan had enabled NAAFI to remain cash generative and, despite sales in Germany being 16% lower than a year previous, the amount of welfare returns delivered to the Forces in Germany had increased. Retail sales in Germany were reducing, as to be expected with the drawdown, and stockholdings as well as staff hours had reduced accordingly, with retail and leisure services being consolidated wherever possible. NAAFI's catering service continued to receive excellent feedback from both customers and the Authority with the SLA target being exceeded.

The last remaining outlet in Afghanistan had closed in December 2014 and EFI HQ in Grantham was then closed. Although 148 Sqn EFI RLC had disbanded, NAAFI maintained the ability within Germany to provide expeditionary services immediately on request with non-uniformed staff, and within 6 to 9 weeks for uniformed support, should it be requested by PJHQ.

Northern Ireland, the Falkland Islands, and Brunei continued to trade well. NCS sales had been a challenge over the previous year with so many ships either alongside, or under-going refits, but NCS remained a core part of NAAFI with an SLA to 2018.

Memories of Lt. Col M.L Smith MBE by Capt. N.S Hall, 148 Squadron EFI RLC 2015

Having joined NAAFI in 1984, a twist of fate saw me move straight to EFI and 4 consecutive tours in the Falklands. After the first tour, I was hooked, and it was all I wanted to do. Major Randerson fended off my repeated requests to join the "cadre" at Wingham but promised me a spot if I could make a go of it as a Club Manager first.

Three years in Northern Ireland with a few exercises in between saw me called to my dream job at HQ EFI in the summer of 1991. Major Bob had come good as always, but I was due at Wingham following his retirement.

His replacement was Major Smith, ex-Paras and I had little or no idea of what kind of man he was.

Settling into a new team is always a little bit nerve racking but little did I know that a bounced cheque had followed me from Northern Ireland and "The Boss" was not happy!

So, my first meeting with Major Smith (as he was then) saw me marched into his office by Sgt Maj Dungay and I got one of the biggest rollickings of my life. Not the best start!

In fairness to the Boss, he didn't mark my card too badly and I soon settled into full-time EFI life. The Boss didn't suffer fools gladly and pity the poor sod that tried to get one over on him. As an ex-Para who had worked his way through the ranks, there was no trick in the book that he hadn't either done or tried himself!

The Scots (unfairly in my experience) have a reputation for being tight with money which, to a degree, he perpetuated the myth. But then again, why employ window cleaners when you have 8 squaddies to do it for nothing?!

When we were away on OPs or exercises, we were always under his orders to get a phone line set up. Not so that we could call out, it was so he could call us.

There must have been thousands of times I'd answer the phone and hear his dulcet Scottish voice saying, "ring me back!" before hanging up to save his phone bill!

Washing the van, unblocking the drain in the car park, burning documents, repairing Wingham's old wooden benches . . . you name it, the Cadre team did it! And above all else, our main role was to keep him supplied with cups of tea. I've never known anyone drink so much tea in my life. If he cut himself, I'm sure he would have bled the stuff!

His favourite china mug with the (I think) Joint Forces logo on was constantly filled, emptied, cleaned and filled again. The 2 most important items in the top drawer of his desk were his NAAFI silver teaspoon and a box of Hermesetas.

The Boss was a hard taskmaster but fiercely loyal to his troops. He was never one to openly lavish praise on people, but he often did so in his own way. He always did his best to look out for his team and was often generous with time and, occasionally, the odd favour or two.

I worked with him for 9 years and we spent many hours working and travelling together. On the odd occasion, a road trip to Bracht in Germany comes to mind. Mrs Smith joined us which was always good for a laugh because she hated his driving and wasn't afraid to tell him, regardless of the company!

When my time to leave EFI arrived, we didn't part on the best of terms which has always been a lasting regret to me. In hindsight, neither of us were to blame for that but that's sometimes just how life goes.

The man was a legend to those of us in EFI and I am fiercely proud to have served under his command. He is missed by all those who knew him, but he will always live on in our memories.

Sadly, Lt Col Murray Smith MBE passed in December 2015, a true legend to all that served under his command.

2016

NEA 2016

2016 was tinged with the sad news that Lt Col (retired) Murray Smith, CO of 148 Sqn EFI RLC and also a former Chairman of the NEA, had passed away. Murray came to EFI after a long and distinguished service with the Paras. He brought with him a unique blend of leadership, knowledge, organisation, drive and determination. With his sense of purpose, he quickly set about building on the firm foundation that he had inherited from his predecessor, Maj Bob Randerson, to develop 148 Squadron into an integral 'go to' service-provider which the military always wanted to have with them on overseas exercises and operations, as the mainstay of its morale component. He was highly respected by its management, his peers, and all those who served under him.

Mr Brian Whitaker CBE had also passed away in 2015. Brian had a long and successful career with NAAFI and was managing director of the company, from 1978 to 1986. Brian was an incisive, yet compassionate, man who possessed determination and, like all who worked for him, I had the utmost respect for him and held him in the highest regard. He visited the EFI troops serving in locations on the Falkland Islands in 1984/5.

The chairman of the NEA welcomed Steve Marshall, NAAFI's new managing director. Reg Curtis had stood down as NAAFI's CEO and had taken up a non-executive director's role with the organisation.

Around 80 ex-UK based Civilian staff, who had served alongside their uniformed counterparts on operational deployments, were welcomed as new Associate Membership, while Full Membership numbers remained in excess of 120 and, at a time when other similar organisations were seeing their numbers decline, it was encouraging that the Association continued to provide a focal point for those who had served the Services with both EFI and NCS under operational conditions.

Steve Marshall, Managing Director, NAAFI 2016

Steve Marshall had been with the organisation for 10 years, 5 of which were as a member of its board of management. He had also undertaken the duties of company secretary, and although he was the only executive director serving on NAAFI's board, he enjoyed the support of a strong management team, including Garreth Weston, the head of operations.

MOD had extended all NAAFI Service Level Agreements (with the exception of Northern Ireland where special contractual arrangements were being drawn up) to April 2020. NAAFI was seen as the best provider of catering in the British Army, something which had further enhanced the reputation which had grown out of the operational support provided by EFI in Iraq and Afghanistan prior to its disbandment.

In line with the shrinking customer base, NAAFI had reduced its support overheads and was operating with a central support team of just 28 full-time employees. It was expected that NAAFI would continue to have a presence in Germany until Summer 2019 although there remained flexibility in this forecast. As well as Germany, NAAFI continued to have a presence in Brunei, the South Atlantic, Gibraltar, and to provide a service, through NCS, to the Royal Navy.

2017

NEA 2017

Field of Remembrance, St Margaret's, Westminster, ex-WOII Terina Hounsell fronted our plot once again and Tim Elliott was also present, representing the Committee.

Chatham Naval Dockyard was attended by Ray Barnett, and joined by Ray Yeomans, who both laid a wreath.

St George's Church, Bulford, Tim Elliott and Martyn Willey represented NAAFI and the NEA.

National Memorial Arboretum, near Lichfield, Richard Gaymer again represented the NEA.

The Cenotaph, Whitehall, the NEA were invited to march for the 3rd time. The Association has been given the opportunity to represent 148 Sqn EFI and the NCS at the Cenotaph march-past. Increased security conditions meant that the names of participants had to be submitted well in advance.

Association membership had increased with the introduction of a social media group, revealed that there were a total of 424 people who had been admitted as members of the group having served with NCS or EFI either in uniform or as UK-based civilians.

Steve Marshall, NAAFI's Managing Director 2017

Steve Marshall, NAAFI's Managing Director, updated the NEA on NAAFI. The next closure was the Darlington central support office, which now left just 20 full-time support employees based in a single head office in Bielefeld, Germany.

The future meant that all SLAs had been extended to April 2020, with the exception of Northern Ireland, which was handed to a new contractor in late 2017. Although current planning was based on NAAFI ceasing to trade after 2020, MoD had indicated that there remained a possibility that NAAFI could continue to exist beyond this date as the organisation had a unique status in some territories which enabled it, for instance, to trade free of tax and duty in Germany and, even though NAAFI was presently not operating there, Cyprus. This unique position also allowed NAAFI to import otherwise restricted goods to Brunei.

NAAFI had always excelled in providing services in locations which would be either too small or too difficult for other organisations to take on, such as Gibraltar, NCS, and the South Atlantic, as well as on military deployments and that, because of this, it was entirely feasible that there might be a future for the business beyond 2020.

2018

NEA 2018

2018 was the 71st Annual General Meeting, which would be his last meeting as the Association's chairman, Lt Col (Ret) D Pullen. In the process of stepping down as chairman, Dougie then said that he had one final request which he had to all members of the Association. He asked that every November, when as a nation Remembrance Day is commemorated, each member should take a few moments not only to remind themselves of the sacrifice that others had made, but to also look back with pride on the great work that they had done, wherever they had served in NCS or EFI.

He said would never forget the part that they had played in supporting the Services, and he thanked every member of the Association for all the support that he had received during the time that he had served in EFI.

Tim Elliott would be stepping down as a member of the committee. Tim has served on the Committee not just as a member but also as a chairman of the Association. Many members would be unaware that the NEA/OCA was still in existence was down to Tim because, at a time in NAAFI's history when it had gone through a re-structuring process, it was only through his determination that the OCA/NEA, had survived.

Tim reminded members that the NEA was an opportunity of comradeship, the Association primarily served to provide benevolent support to its full members in times of hardship. Just one case had been brought to the committee's attention in the past year.

During Remembrance week, Tim and Dougie had attended the Field of Remembrance service at Westminster where Terina Hounsell had fronted the NAAFI plot. On Remembrance Sunday, Richard Gaymer had laid wreaths on behalf of both NAAFI and the Association at the National Memorial Arboretum while Tim, together with Association member Martyn Willey, had done the same at St. George's church in Bulford. Association member Ray Barnett had laid two wreaths on behalf of NAAFI and the Association at the Naval service held at Chatham, in Kent and. In London, Stephanie Abel had led the NAAFI contingent which marched past the Cenotaph for their 4th year in November.

The Association rules required that two members of the Committee should retire in rotation at each AGM and indicate whether they were prepared to stand for re-election. As well as D Pullen, Taffy Davies was due to retire from the Committee in 2018. In addition, Tim confirmed that he too would be standing down. Referring to the fact that while the Association originally had just 120 members on its mailing list in 2010, since Stephanie had subsequently created the NEA social media presence, membership had swelled to nearly 450, he said that it was clear to him that the work of the Association could only continue to grow and expand if those who were 'au fait' with modern social media were given the opportunity to have a greater influence on its direction.

Reflecting on his career when as a Regional Manager, Tim remembered that until he served as the OC EFI on the Falkland Islands, he had always felt that the call for staff to be released for EFI duties to be an inconvenience. His perception then changed, and he became a strong supporter of EFI and had taken great pride in the work of EFI personnel on the Falklands while he was there. He said that between his father and himself, they had served NAAFI for 66 years and that he had regarded his subsequent work for the Association as a privilege but that it was now time to step aside and allow a younger generation to have its opportunity to serve the Association and its members.

Taffy endorsed Tim's sentiments and said that, as much as he had enjoyed the duties of being a committee member, he too felt that it would be an appropriate time to stand down for similar reasons.

In all, this created three vacancies on the committee and, in response to a recent invitation to members to put themselves forward to stand for election there had, conveniently, been three applications, from Sue A Lowe, Terina Hounsell, and Kevin Storey, to fill the vacancies. He therefore proposed that all three should serve on the Committee and this proposal was unanimously agreed by all present.

Tim advised that, at its most recent meeting, the committee had agreed that Stephanie Abel should be proposed to become the Association's new chairperson. Stephanie was well known to the majority of Association members and had served on EFI tours of operational duty as well as working in EFI HQ.

To complete the change in the stewardship of the Association, its President, Sir Ian Prosser, had informed NAAFI that he too wished to stand down, as he was in the process of reducing his many commitments. The committee had unanimously agreed that the vacancy that this created should be offered to Tony Hales. Tony had been Chairman of the NAAFI Board and was presently the Chairman of the Board of NAAFI Pension Fund Trustees. He had always shown a keen interest in the work of both NCS and EFI, and the welfare of their personnel. Tony had accepted the appointment as its President.

In accepting her nomination as the incoming Chair of the Association, Stephanie Abel thanked everyone for their confidence in her and said that she was proud to become the new Chairperson. She wished to acknowledge the considerable contributions made by Taffy, Tim, and Dougie and that she was excited to take over the reins of the Association and start a new era. Her main priority was to raise awareness of the NEA among those who had served in NCS and EFI but were not yet Association members, and to encourage greater attendance at this annual reunion and general meeting each year. A replica cap badge was given to each of them as a token of thanks for all their work.

From the extensive research I had been doing for this book, Stephanie became the 13th Chairperson and the first woman. Although some dates are unclear (?) the Chairmen are in order.

1946 – 1954	Lt Col R Merry
1955 – 1961	TE Pegg, Esq, OBE
1962 – 1963	CA Layard
1964 – 1965	Col HG Swithenbank
1966 – 1970?	Sir William Beale
1971? – 1976?	Maj Ben White
1977? – 1982	Maj Dickie Bullen
1983 – 1992	Maj Tommy Booth
1993 – 1995	Lt Col Murray Smith MBE
1996 – 1998	Maj Tommy Booth OBE
1998 – 2009	Maj Tim Elliott
2010 – 2018	Lt Col D Pullen
2019 – present	Sgt Stephanie Abel

Replica NAAFI Cap Badges 2018

Sue A Lowe had successfully arranged for limited-edition replicas of the original NAAFI cap badge to be manufactured and that subsequent sales to members had resulted in the profit being donated to the NEA. This was my first idea generated while stood on Whitehall waiting to march past the cenotaph in 2017. The project was Ok'ed by the committee.

All of the Profit would go directly to the Association, every few months, depending on the levels of sales; a total of 250 badges were made overall, some of them had lug and pin fixings to the back and others had a brooch back – this would enable the wearer to have them proudly displayed on their lapel during Remembrance parades. They were presented in a box with a small piece of history on the inside. On the back they would all be individually numbered, which was in keeping with the originals as they were issued. It was only the voided type that had been remade, the non-voided and collar badges had not been.

The badges would also appear on the ENSA girls' head dress and uniform in the BBC's 'World on Fire' 2019. A number of them were bought to ensure that the uniforms were historically correct for that time in the war prior to the ENSA badges being made.

Later the first badge of its number, 2018001 was sent to HM the Queen and a letter of warmest good wishes was received by the NEA.

NAAFI Update 2018

It had been a particularly strong year for sales being achieved in Germany where stability had been achieved in advance of the anticipated drawdown scheduled for late 2019. Thereafter, a training estate in the Paderborn area would continue which NAAFI would support, along with other elements of the military European Support Group in places like Ramstein and Naples.

After half a century of excellent service to troops in Northern Ireland, NAAFI's presence there had been closed down but a healthy business presence continued in Brunei and Gibraltar while, in the South Atlantic, NAAFI was looking to continue the scale and stability of its presence, that was so crucial to the underpinning of efforts to broaden the NAAFI footprint into new locations, by consolidating and enhancing a myriad of welfare services into the Gull and Penguin facility at Mount Pleasant. Support to NATO ARRC continued and NAAFI was looking to extend that support to the Corps' major exercises in southern Germany and, where possible, elsewhere.

The commissioning of the aircraft carrier HMS Queen Elizabeth, had been accomplished with enhanced NCS facilities being provided on board, thus providing a rise in overall turnover for the NCS element of the business which, in turn, provided confidence that its business model would be robust enough to be sustainable into the foreseeable future without any need for financial support from MoD. However, he cautioned, there was no room for complacency and NAAFI would continue to look for opportunities to enhance its support to the Navy both at sea and on land. NAAFI, he concluded, was grateful to all staff, and those serving NCS in particular who continued to provide a flexible, dedicated and adaptable service to the Royal Navy which had allowed it to suit the tempo and changing size of the Royal Navy, which was so highly valued by the senior Service.

2019

NEA 72nd AGM at the Union Jack Club 2019

It was Stephanie Abel's first year as Chair of the committee, she changed the format slightly and had invited speakers to the AGM to highlight important issues, such as PTSD, hosting Combat stress as the first speakers at the meeting. The Association had lost 4 members in a year to PTSD and highlighting to service/full members where help and assistance could be obtained. Other ways of helping Associate members would be highlighted at a later date.

For the remembrance events, the RBL asked for all units to resubmit an application for inclusion in the parade at the Cenotaph which she had done and had been accepted. This time instead of forming up on Whitehall NCS/EFI Association would form up on Horse guards for the first time.

At the field of remembrance, Alison had fronted the plot and shook the hand of HRH Prince Harry. The Association was also represented at the NMA, Chatham Memorial and Bulford.

NAAFI update 2019

NAAFI were now formally known as the MOD's in-house provider. In the meantime, the world of Defence budgets and spending has continued to evolve, and the current challenge was to prove to the MOD and the TLBs that we represent good value for money in each of the locations where they operate. In September 2019 the long awaited 10-year overarching agreement was signed, and NAAFI would be here into the future. They had successfully agreed the 10 year SLAs for all of the locations and as a result not only see NAAFI easily break through its 100 year anniversary but also once they had all of the current territories secured, work with the MOD to identify opportunities elsewhere.

NAAFI as the MOD's in-house provider would not tender 'commercial bids' for existing contracts such as Hestia and Cyprus and would only enter territories that have not been the subject of previous bids or where is there was no alternative.

All of the above meant that they need to be very lean to ensure value for money, yet agile enough to respond to opportunities as they arise – an interesting challenge but infinitely more positive than the march towards closure that has been muted over recent years. Pictured are Sir Ian Prosser, Chairman of the NAAFI Board, and Lt General Richard Nugee, Chief of Defence People, following the signing which took place in Whitehall. This arrangement offers both significant stability and a bright new future for NAAFI. The meant that they would celebrate their 100th Anniversary and beyond.

NAAFI Drawdown Germany 2019

The Diary of closures, refurbishments and Service as usual 2019

As the drawdown of Germany was fully under way and many Barracks were closed down.

May 2019

The closure of Mansergh Barracks in Gütersloh on the 11th May 2019, saw the closure of all facilities on site. 26th Regiment Royal Artillery had been there for over the 30 years, with NAAFI right by their side for the duration.

June 2019

5th June 2019 to 7th June 2019; NAAFI supported the service personnel attending D-Day commemorations in Normandy. Just like they did 75 years ago. 'Serving the Services' during the D-Day commemorations was a great day and although the tools of the trade had changed, the tea and service brought back fond memories.

July 2019

20th July 2019; in line with the drawdown of BFG, Athlone Express Shop, Athlone JB's, Athlone Coffee Forum and Mansergh JB's closed its doors for the last time.

16th July 2019; they proudly presented the annual BFG Welfare payment cheque for €243,997! This took the total over a whopping €9m paid back to BFG in the last 15 years!

August 2019

9 more BFG establishments closed.

13th August 2019; Paderborn Families Shop, BFG closed, with many fond memories from all the staff and service personnel and families. The facilities had gone through royal visits and refurbishments over the years and now it was a silent hall and a shadow of its former years.

1st August 2019; Dempsey Express Shop, Dempsey JB's, The Harden Arms Pub and Rochdale JB's all closed their doors.

31st August 2019; Barker Express Shop, Barker Coffee Forum, Barker JB's and Montgomery's Pub, were 4 more to follow the closures.

September 2019

1st September 2019; Catterick Barracks JB's and Mansergh Families Shop, BFG closed.

4th September 2019; with the drawdown of British Forces Germany almost complete, the good news was the establishment staying open.

Outside Normandy Barracks: Sennelager Families Shop.
Normandy Barracks: Express Shop, Coffee Forum, JB's.
Ayrshire Barracks: Express Shop.

October 2019

31st October 2019; Bielefeld Families Shop closed its doors.

November

29th November 2019; the last closure of the year in BFG was Catterick Bks Express shop.

It was sad to see all of these establishments go but without its customers, they were no longer needed, as they moved back to the UK in line with the British forces' plans.

2020

Germany

In 2020 several refurbishments took place. The Normandy express shop underwent a complete refurbishment. The Normandy arms pub was refreshed with a full redecoration, to give it a fresh and modern look. The Minden rooms introduced a new lounge concept appealing to the comfort of the service personnel. Normandy JB's had a refresh with a brand-new menu to serve. Along with these, the refurbishment of Sennelager family's shop, and a new 24-hour vending area. A shop and coffee offer in Athlone barracks was installed.

The grand openings took place on the 14th February 2020, when the Normandy Express Shop opened its doors. It introduced a brand new 'Food to Go' concept, including freshly pressed orange juice, doughnuts, pizza plus the other popular hot food & drinks. On the 21st February 2020 the Sennelager Pub on Normandy Barracks, offering a selection of draught beers, British ales and a bar food menu.

NAAFI also took on a new role in regard to facilities management and began providing cleaning services from the new 'Cleaning Hub' in Normandy Bks.

These establishments In Germany would take them forward with the new overarching agreement, through their centenary year and beyond.

Falkland Islands

The Falkland island benefits from 3 shops, two pubs, a coffee forum, A bulk issue store, 24 hour vending and an air terminal kiosk. Alongside this runs a NAAFI waggon mobile offer which carries a small range of products directly to the service personnel.

In 2021 the island will see a full refurbishment of the Gull and Penguin facilities. The lounge bar will become an all-day concept featuring premium coffee a UK pub and Asian food menus with a full bar offering, the shop will introduce a new food to go zone featuring Donuts, freshly squeezed orange juice and pizzas. The sports bar will benefit from a new bar as well as further enhancements, including a brand-new big screen TV with UK sport, a new pool table jukebox and amusement machines, plus a new bar. The Cinema and bowling re-fit will include a new 'all in one' service counter where you can purchase your cinema ticket, buy your popcorn and soft drinks and book a bowling lane. The air terminal will have a brand-new shop with premium coffee and updated duty free products, soft drinks, snacks and travel accessories.

Finally, the Dolphin pub and diner will be refreshed with new furniture and decoration.

NAAFI also runs a bulk issue store on the island as well as catering for special events, birthday parties to a barbecue where they cover the catering, bar services and entertainment to make each event perfect!

It just goes to show that no matter where NAAFI is in the world we are always seeking to provide the best facilities to continue in our mission. To 'serve the services'.

Ascension Island

NAAFI Georgetown and Saint Helena

30th June 2020; The brand-new NAAFI Wagon had officially began its journey from Marchwood to Ascension Island. It finally arrived a few weeks later and made its first outing to much excitement within a week. The Wagon provides customers at their workplaces with a range of hot and cold foods, snacks and drinks. This adds to the existing offers on Travellers Hill of a retail shop, Bar and Food Bar as well as the retail offer in the Air Terminal. It had been well received as a valuable addition to the overall offer.

Travellers Hill and the Air Terminal will also benefit from a re-fit as part of our rolling improvement programme.

Brunei

NAAFI occupies three buildings in Brunei: Chautari is a bar/restaurant open to entitled Garrison personnel only and offers a selection of alcoholic and non-alcoholic beverages, as well as an Asian style hot food menu which can be eaten in, takeaway or delivered.

NAAFI Families Shop is open to both entitled Garrison personnel and local Bruneians and sells a range of popular British groceries plus a selection of hot and cold food for immediate consumption and premium Lavazza Coffee.

The Bulk Issue Store is located to the rear of the Families Shop and is for the sole use of entitled personnel for the purchase of Beers, Wines, Spirits and Tobacco. It also acts as the Wholesale hub for supply to Messes and other unit facilities.

NAAFI also has a mobile retail wagon which operates six days per week and visits both Tuker Lines and Medicina Lines and the SFA areas daily. It can also be utilised to support BFB events whenever required.

NAAFI has a workforce of 25 personnel, consisting of 2× UKBC, 5× foreign workers and 18× LECs.

Brunei will also benefit from a re-fit as part of the NAAFI 5-year Strategic Plan.

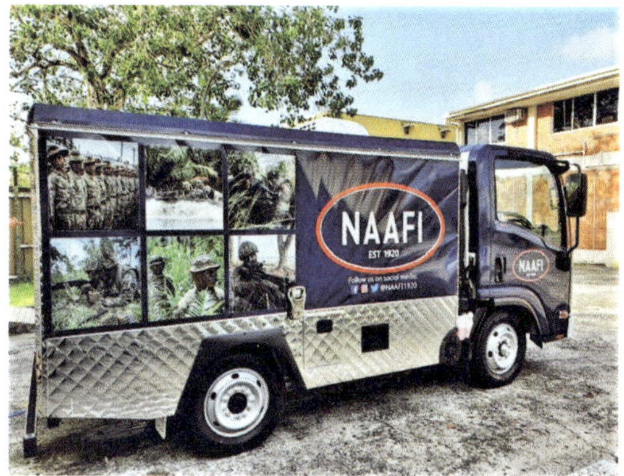

Gibraltar

The New NAAFI waggon was on its way to Gibraltar and at the same time they were taking a break I was leaving the supermarket in Portsmouth. Coincidence meant for the first time in years I saw the NAAFI logo on the side of a waggon and could not help but go and say hello.

The NAAFI offer in Gibraltar consists of a retail offer and Boyds bar on Devils Tower Camp and a Coffee Forum with a small retail offer at the new swimming pool. The shop and Boyds bar will soon benefit from a re-fit as part of our rolling improvement programme.

NCS

NCS operates from three sites, Faslane in Scotland, Devonport in Plymouth and HMNB Portsmouth. From these hubs NAAFI delivers the retail and wholesale offers. 29th feb 2020; The amazing opportunity to be a part of the 'open day' on board HMS Prince of Wales in Liverpool gave the NCS team a boost. They were very proud to be on board and part of the open day. The Naval Canteen Service and the taste of home it delivers to Royal Navy personnel around the world was on show and showed it continues support of the Royal Navy wherever they are in the world.

NMA Memorial Replacement Subcommittee led by Tim Elliott 2020

"Arising from a decision taken by the committee of the NEA in 2017, and subsequently endorsed by the AGM, it was agreed that the existing NAAFI plot at the National Memorial Arboretum, established in the early 2000's needed to be upgraded. Whilst we were one of the early occupants of a plot, time and popularity had overtaken our site so that we are now difficult to find and hedged in with later sites. Following initial discussions with the NMA authorities in early 2020, they indicated that a new memorial for NAAFI would be a good idea and

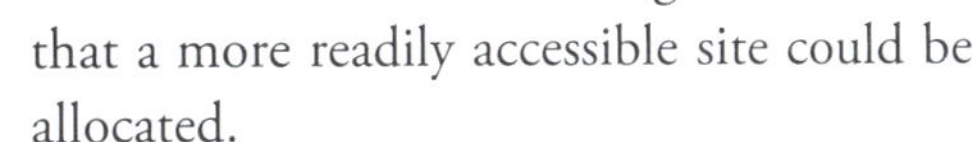

that a more readily accessible site could be allocated.

We have subsequently worked with a stone mason who has masterminded several sites at the NMA and he suggested a simple sandstone memorial with an insert featuring the NAAFI crest laminated in glass, with suitable wording on the front. We have incorporated the wording from our original plaque at NMA but also added reference to the more than 550 NAAFI staff who lost their lives in WW2, as recorded on NAAFI's official War Memorial.

Myself, Mary Pittuck, Greame Mitcheson, the sculptor met with Andy Ansel from the NMA in September to review proposed new sites for the memorial and unanimously agreed on the new site. Once approved, work will commence in the Spring when ground conditions allow with dedication anticipated in May, 2021.

In the planning stages, obviously finance was a major consideration, but I am delighted to say that as part of the centenary celebrations the NAAFI Board have very kindly agreed to fund the project in full. For that, we are very grateful."

NAAFI 2020 and beyond

NAAFI has had an incredibly busy 12 months and yet despite this, we have once again delivered an excellent set of financial results at the end of April 2020. This was delivered, as always, by the hard work and dedication of our employees.

This year we gave back over £450,000 to the MOD as a Welfare payment, our best return in a number of years, which was very welcome in the face of challenging Defence budgets.

We signed a new Overarching Service Arrangement (OSA) and subsequently agreed and signed new individual 10-year Service Levels Agreements (SLAs) with each trading location to set out what our future offer looks like, including significant investment in our NAAFI facilities. Our new OSA directs 70% of our surpluses back to the MOD (split approximately 50% remaining with the Service HQ and 20% remaining as local welfare funds) and NAAFI then retains 30% as working capital and for future investments.

As recognition of our long-term secured future, we committed to a one-off welfare payment to the MOD of £7.5m. It has been decided to pay this across in 10 equal instalments through the life of the current OSA. The Armed Forces Covenant Fund Trust (AFCFT) was the MOD's chosen administrator of the grant and we recently made the first £750k donation to the AFCFT, who will manage the 'NAAFI Fund' on behalf of both NAAFI and the MOD. They have established a Trustee Board and the monies in the Trust will be used for unfunded welfare projects for serving Armed Forces personnel and their families across all MOD locations.

We are continually exploring future opportunities for NAAFI both in areas where we already operate, those we have operated in in the past and in new territories. A recent example of this is the new cleaning contract as the in-house provider in Germany. We had to react very swiftly to this, as we were given the go ahead in November and we had a new team ready to work in January. This was a real refreshing change to be recruiting after going in the opposite direction for many previous years!

These new employees are proving a great addition to the team and all of them are quickly demonstrating the NAAFI ethos of 'serving the services'. This is evident from the excellent feedback we have received in the early part of this service and we are hopeful that more opportunities like this will follow.

Our HQ has moved once again due to Germany drawdown and is now located within our retail store in Sennelager. The HQ team has settled into its new surroundings and continue to enjoy and benefit from the ability to see first-hand the operation and participate as much as possible.

The timing of this book requires a reflection on the significant impact of COVID-19 on our business and our people. We have had three main priorities during this time with people the number one priority. We also focused on our supply chain and finally our financial impacts.

We reacted quickly to ensure the safety of our employees in adapting the workplace and introducing safety measures in our outlets earlier than both UK and Germany. This included hand sanitiser, screens in outlets, one-way systems and social distancing measures. It is of the utmost importance to us that we protect the welfare of our employees and in doing so, the wider community. To do this we have:

- Increased our services in the community which also helps to vary our employee work;
- Kept our employees informed and involved, including communicating ways to maintain their mental health and wellbeing in partnership with our occupational health providers, BUPA;
- Enabled employees that can, to work from home;
- Ensured that any employees unable to work as a direct consequence of COVID-19 due to shielding or childcare issues, have remained on full pay.

We continue to work closely with the MOD in each location to ensure that we are complying with their local rules as well as those imposed by the host Country and the UK standards that the MOD generally follow. As I am sure you can all appreciate, this is quite a complex operation!

Our second priority was supply chain. Whilst we have seen some difficulties in this area, they have been minor, and we have not suffered shortages or panic buying in the same way as UK high streets. In the Falkland Islands, we were able to send an 18-month supply of toilet paper for example!

Finally, we must minimise the financial impact of COVID-19 as best we can so that we can exit out of the crisis well – if it ever ends! Most of our outlets were closed during the early part of the crisis and re-opened as restrictions eased so we could deliver a limited service throughout the summer and into the autumn. At the time of writing, however, we have now again had to close some offers, restrict others to take way and introduce new retail limitations.

A key impact of COVID -19 so far has been the cancellation of training and visiting troops, causing a significant downturn, albeit, so far better than first anticipated. We put this down to the excellent endeavours of our team to find new and innovative ways to keep trade moving.

We are now in the planning stage of our 100th birthday celebrations that will begin in December. Although we plan on low-key events, due to the un-knowns brought about by COVID 19, we are still excited particularly given that for many years we did not think we would reach this milestone.

So what next?

2020/2021 has been very challenging for NAAFI, as it has for many other organization/ employers due to CV-19. It is also an exciting time for us with so many possibilities? Is there a route back to places we've been before? Are the new opportunities to provide services in new locations or to offer new services? Whilst the guys on the ground do the utmost to deliver the very best NAAFI experience, be that retail, leisure cleaning catering, the Senior Management team are also working hard to pursue all opportunities that we can find.

Here at NAAFI, we remain truly honoured to be part of the continuing story of this wonderful organisation and are thankful to all our NAAFI predecessors for laying the foundations for us to continue to build on.

If you are interested in what NAAFI is currently up to, you are invited you to follow us on social media to keep up to date with our activities:

www.facebook.com/NAAFI1920
www.twitter.com/NAAFI1920
www.instagram.com/naafi1920

NEA 2020

It was scheduled to have the AGM in May as usual, but due to COVID-19 unfortunately this had to be cancelled. As the country went into lockdown just like everybody else, our lives changed.

Plans have already started to come together for the 75th anniversary of the NCS EFI Association, and the belated centenary anniversary of NAAFI.

This is where the NAAFI story comes to a pause, all be it in the grip of a pandemic but in the knowledge of the years ahead seeing us through our centenary year.

I do hope that you have enjoyed over 100 years of history and an insight into the lives and workings of NAAFI, NCS and EFI. I wish NAAFI and NCS EFI Association a long and happy future 'serving the services'.

Original Badges

In the 1920s NAAFI used 3 badges on simple uniforms. The crest would be the first symbol of NAAFI and evolve to the crest used today.

Then and Now WWII to 2019

NAAFI through the ages

NAAFI is registered as an Association not for profit, has no shareholders and is strictly limited to dealing with members of the Armed Forces, their families and the communities that supports them. Today, 70 % of all our profit is returned to the Armed Forces, only 30 % is retained to invest in improving the facilities and services we provide.

Since we began trading in January 1921, NAAFI has relied on its ability to adapt and change to suit the times. Our services have followed the needs of our customers who we continue to support wherever they go. Over the past 100 years our branding has also moved with the times. The following brand logos demonstrate our journey through the years.

Today, as always, we remain dedicated in our mission to 'Serve the Services' whenever and wherever we are needed.

1920 – 1939

The Navy, Army & Air Force Institutes (NAAFI) was originally created in 1920 by Winston Churchill to conduct the 'Canteen and Institute' Service for His Majesty's Forces, and began trading in 1921.

1940 - 1952

NAAFI has enjoyed a long history of Royal association, with King George VI not only granting his patronage to the organisation in 1946, but also employing NAAFI to cater for the staff at Buckingham Palace, Windsor Castle, Sandringham, Balmoral and Holyrood House.

1953 - 1960

On Queen Elizabeth II's accession to the throne in 1953, the NAAFI crest was updated to include the new royal crown, and this Royal patronage has been retained to this day, as has the fouled anchor and wings with the motto 'Servitor Servientium'.

1920-1960

Whilst the crest was retained for official use, a more practical version of the logo was required. As NAAFI became more commercially focused, this simpler way of presenting the brand to customers was used on stores, adverts and much more.

1960 - 1989

This simple shape with clean lines was created as part of a logo competition. Designed to modernise NAAFI, the logo was instantly recognisable from a distance and would be a reminder of the triple loyalties and unbreakable links between all three services.

1989 - 1997

As competition started to increase, NAAFI revised its logo to present the company name more clearly and simply. Use of lower case lettering added friendliness and the orange colour with a green border was bang on the 80s trend.

1997 - 1998

In the late 90s the logo was developed to incorporate a nod to the past. The italic, retro typeface suggested responsiveness and tradition, whilst the zoom device around the red dot on the i highlighted NAAFI's focus on the individuals it served.

1998 - 2010

The logo was soon updated further to create greater impact and a more of a unified look. Now featuring British red, white and blue, the new lozenge shape was introduced, and quickly became associated with NAAFI's retail offer in particular.

2010 - present

NAAFI is extremely proud of its heritage as well as recognising the need for a modern, forward-thinking approach. The latest logo therefore retains a nod to all that has gone before, with the use of a retro font and the tag 'est 1920', whilst using modern design language.

With thanks for their help and support:

Navy Army Air Force Institutes (NAAFI), Imperial War Museum (IWM) and National Army Museum (NAM) research rooms, Commonwealth War Graves Commission (CWGC), Royal Hospital Chelsea (RHC), RLC Museum and Mals Tokens, without their dedication to the preservation of history most of this information would be lost.

All of those who contributed their stories and pictures and numerous former staff who sent copies of the publications, badges, pictures and parts of their own NAAFI, NCS and EFI collections.

Special thanks to:

Tony Hales CBE, Mary Pittuck, HR & Risk manager NAAFI HQ, John and Penny Perry, Tim Elliott, Taffy Davies MBE, Ellsa and Steve Mealing for their support and knowledge in their individual way.

The NEA committee: Stephanie Abel (Chairperson), Kevin Storey (Treasurer), David Atkinson (NCS), Terina Hounsell and Stuart Paterson and the members for the support in this endeavour, I hope that the funds raised from the sale of this book, will go a long way to helping those who need assistance for many years to come. With the 75th anniversary in 2021, I wish the NCS EFI Association a long and successful future, fostering comradeship and supporting those who served our services with NCS and EFI.

Research materials:

Imperial Club Magazine, NAAFI News, NAAFI Review, EFI SEArchlight and other NAAFI in-house Publications.

West and East with the EFC by Capt. E Vrendenburg (Late 10th London Regt), Published by Raphael Tuck and Sons Ltd in 1919.

Sections of the pre 1920s chapters were "Reproduced, with permission, from John Fortescue, A Short Account of Canteens in the British Army, originally published 1928, reissued 2015, Cambridge University Press" (originally commissioned by Sir Frank Benson, CVO, CBE, then published).

Most of the items collected have been donated by me to the archive at NAAFI HQ and will be added to the rest of the collection in London to be preserved for years to come.